Acclaim for Jimmy McDonough's

SHAKEY

"A mammoth portrait of the artist an history. . . . [McDonough] traces a rich
 —New York Times

"Imaginatively written . . . not only is *Shakey* an extraordinary literary feat
of research and affection and endurance, it's an insight into the art of biography itself."　　　　　　　　　　　　　　　*—Fort Worth Star-Telegram*

"This book is a necessity for the rabid Neil Young fan."
　　　　　　　　　　　　　　　　　　　　　　—The Calgary Herald

"The Neil Young in *Shakey*. . . .[is] impossible to predict, impossible to cat-
egorize, impossible to unreservedly love, perhaps, but just as impossible
to really hate."　　　　　　　　　　　　　　　　*—The Globe and Mail*

"Exhaustively researched, impressively detailed. . . . The long passages in
which McDonough steps aside to let Young talk are the most revealing.
'One day I'm a jerk,' Young says, 'the next day I'm a genius.' This book
argues artfully for the latter."　　　　　　　　　　　　　　*—People*

"Like meeting Brando's Kurtz in a cave at the end of *Apocalypse Now*. . . .
Young comes across as a Jekyll-and-Hyde loner whose life has unfolded
like a reckless chemistry experiment—a control freak on an endless quest
for the uncontrolled moment."　　　　　　　　　　　　　*—Macleans*

"McDonough is an avid fan, music critic and impartial journalist all in
one. . . . [He] deftly weaves Young's life, actions and art together. . . . What
was known of Young's life before was akin to a series of rough demos. In
Shakey, McDonough delivers a full double-album."
　　　　　　　　　　　　　　　　　　　　—Rocky Mountain News

"Does what most rock bios don't: It fails to fawn, it delivers the juice, it subjects the hero to the scrutiny and disappointment of a fan. . . . A page-turning good read." —*Houston Chronicle*

"[*Shakey*'s] unprecedented access makes for an entertaining read: McDonough, more than any music journalist since Peter Guralnick in his authoritative *Careless Love: The Unmaking of Elvis Presley*, has succeeded in stripping a star of his iconography." —*The Observer* (London)

"Crammed with razor-sharp insights and mind-boggling detail, *Shakey* is a rock-solid literary triumph, as inspired and inspiring as the eccentric figure it evokes with such frustrated devotion."
—*The Guardian* (London)

"McDonough . . . pores through Young's life with vivid prose and blunt detail, and he is unashamed to insert some stinging opinions. In his probing conversations with Young . . . he challenges the formidable artist in ways that few others would dare." —*Pittsburgh Post-Gazette*

"It's hard to imagine anyone trying to better this book. . . It has what Young values above all else. . . passion." —*Evening Standard* (London)

JIMMY MCDONOUGH

SHAKEY

Jimmy McDonough is a journalist who has contributed to such publications as *Variety, Film Comment, Mojo, Spin,* and *Juggs.* But he is perhaps best known for his intense, definitive *Village Voice* profiles of such artists as Jimmy Scott, Neil Young, and Hubert Selby, Jr. Jimmy is also the author of *The Ghastly One: The Sex-Gore Netherworld of Filmmaker Andy Milligan.* He lives in the Pacific Northwest.

Vintage Canada

SHAKEY

Neil Young's Biography

JIMMY McDONOUGH

VINTAGE CANADA EDITION, 2003

www.randomhouse.ca

National Library of Canada Cataloguing in Publication

McDonough, Jimmy
        Shakey : Neil Young's biography / Jimmy McDonough.

Includes index.
ISBN 0-679-31193-9

        1. Young, Neil, 1945–   2. Rock musicians—Canada—Biography.
I. Title.

ML420.Y75M136 2003   782.42166'092   C2002-904400-6

Author photograph © Natalia Wisdom
Book design by Mercedes Everett

Printed in the United States of America

10   9   8   7   6   5   4   3   2   1

for George "The Johnson" Hedges

for Carole Nicksin and her Razor Love

Just think of me as one you never figured.

—Neil Young, "Powderfinger"

acknowledgments

Without friend, lawyer, musician and soon-to-be author George Hedges, this book would not exist. Thanks to Christy Hedges, too.

One very big reason this book made it to print is John Kopf. John, I was an absentee friend for many years and yet you still stood by me at a particularly critical juncture. I thank you for your many ideas, not to mention your finesse at delivering a summons. Thanks as well to Joni and Loretta Alice Kopf.

Charlie Beesley has been a selfless force in many people's lives—particularly my own. He went over the manuscript thousands of times, making countless improvements and bringing out the best of me in the process. I consider this his book as much as mine. By the way, Charlie—the monkey's gone, but Darin stayed in.

Editor Bruce Tracy entered the picture at the eleventh hour (well, the first eleventh hour), and saved this project from doom, making sense of a thousand-page-plus manuscript without diluting any of its many peculiarities. Bruce stuck by *Shakey*—for years. Ann Godoff, thanks for publishing this book. Diana Frost: a very heartfelt (but bland) thank you. Private joke.

Bill Bentley, senior vice president/Media Relations at Warner Bros./Reprise Records, got me to Neil Young in the first place, and he believed in this project when everybody else laughed in my face. He is a rare entity at a record company: He loves music and the people who make it. I owe it all to you, Bill.

I would particularly like to thank three of the greatest guys in the world: the late David Briggs, the late Jack Nitzsche and Frank "Poncho" Sampedro.

Joel Bernstein went to absurd lengths to help this project, while at the same time remaining loyal and protective of his boss (not to mention his archives). It is regrettable that he was unable to go over the manuscript for errors before publication, but as Joe Simon once sang, "It be's that way sometimes." Hopefully Joel's eight-CD edit of the Neil Young Archives will someday see light of day. David Briggs certainly approved of the idea.

Bruce Van Dalsem worked through the many, many complexities of publication with the finesse of a master jeweler. I still don't know how he did it.

Thanks to the mighty Henry Gradstein and also Greg Bodell.

Agent Jeff Posternak stayed the fraught-with-obstacles course while policing every detail. Andrew Wylie guided with an iron hand. Special thanks to the extremely patient Bridget Love (wherever you are).

A long time ago I wrote a story about Gary Stewart. It evolved into an epic longer than the Bible. Kit Rachlis recognized my abilities when no one else cared and taught me plenty about how to tell a story. A writer couldn't have a better mentor.

Yuval Taylor is a great editor who initially unlocked the ideas I had within. His help came at a crucial time.

It has been my good fortune to have a once-a-week lunch with Richard Meltzer for the past few years. We were in some awful hamburger joint one smoky afternoon when Richard pointed to one of my interview transcripts and suggested an idea that completely changed the direction of my last two books. Idiots who don't know any better label Meltzer a music writer. Richard's talents are way beyond that. He doesn't compromise, and he stands taller than any of his peers. One day the world will recognize him for what he is: a complete original.

My deepest thanks to Allison Brown—wherever you are—for playing me "A Man Needs a Maid" many years ago.

So many people around Neil Young helped me and asked nothing in return. Some remain off the record; others spoke freely. Interviewees are listed in the Source Notes. In particular I would like to thank Zeke Young, Sandy Mazzeo, Ralph Molina, Billy Talbot, Ken Viola, Brian Stone and Charlie Greene. Personal to Dave McFarlin: It's all your fault. Special thanks to Leo Trombetta for all his ideas, and for keeping me laughing.

My thanks to the archivists: Pete Long was helpful with many a panicked last-minute query. His book *Ghosts on the Road: Neil Young in Concert* remains definitive. Also thanks to Scott Oxman, Jef Michael Piehler,

Bill Wilner, Neil Skok, David Koepp, Steve Espinola, Mike Thomas, Nathan Wirth, Steve Virone, Kristopher J. Sproul and Frank Zychowitz. A particular thanks to Dave Zimmer and video archivist extraordinaire David Peck at Reelin' in the Years Productions. Colleen Jean Matan for her friendship and support. NPFHs do amount to something, Colleen.

Janet Wygal (aka the "Wygalator") and her copyediting crew did a superb job fine-tuning a total mess of a manuscript (special thanks to Beth "Mouth Like a Sailor" Thomas). My thanks as well to Daniel Rembert for the stunning cover design, and Katie Zug, who was exceptional at handling production details and ferreting out photo rights.

My brother, John McDonough, was a great help when I needed it most. My gratitude goes out to Janet, Nancy, Megan and Kate McDonough; Mary Jo, Robert, Andy, Emilee and (the future) Lee Berner; Chris and Kelly Richards. I believe I got a lot of my moxie from my father, Joe McDonough. Too bad you're not around to see this, Dad.

Thanks to those who have always been there one way or another: Elizabeth Main, Bruce Kitzmeyer, Eliza Paley, Craig Leibner, Krissy Boden, Leo Trombetta, Dale Lawrence, Sally Mayrose, Sarah Heldman, Kat Heldman, Joy Heldman, Nicki Laurin, and in particular my guardian angel, Neva Friedenn. A very special thanks to Bettina Briggs. And, as always, the incomparable Lux and Ivy.

Also thanks to: Wendy Swanson, Rudolph Grey, Kathy Kerr, Arvella Kinkaid, Dave Dunton, Jaan Uhelszki, Jonny Whiteside, Karen Schneider, Bill Rhodes, Jerry Morris, Kim Morgan, Amy Salit, Gregg Turkington, Link and Olive Wray, Jimmy Vapor, Maria Wirtanen, Gary Kincade, Barb Dehgan, Anna Hinterkopf, Isaac the waiter, Isaako Si'uleo, Jill Nees, Mark Linn and Christy Canyon. In Australia: Kate, Carl, Sean and Debbie Wisdom; Bill, Eleanor and Graham Bowen; Kerry and Rita Wisdom; and movie expert supreme Sam McBride. Thanks to the Waser and Roberts families, particularly Lorraine and Ray Waser—a great logger, farmer and good friend. Thanks to Stan Pachter for just about everything. Hair by Jerry Ripley, Tonsorial Parlor. Eliza Wimberly, period. In dreams.

In the early years of this project, Kent and Nancy Beyda not only put up with me but kept a roof over my head and food in mouth. I turned their lives upside down in the process, and I don't know why they put up with it, but they never gave less than everything. Their daughter, Emily, always brought a smile to my lips, even in the darker moments. Emily, your parents are true patrons of the arts.

A very special thank you to the Fabulous Lucy Fur and her favorite Shakey fan, Mike "Mad Dog" Merrigan.

Natalia Wisdom endured many a hippie nightmare in the past decade plus. Against all odds, she kept me—and my crazy dreams—alive. Natalia, I know the many sacrifices you made so I could finally accomplish what I set out to do. Now let's make a few of your dreams come true.

—Jimmy McDonough

SHAKEY

innaresting characters

—Who gave you the Nixon mask?

I can't recall, as John Dean would say. I'll always tell ya if I remember,
Jimmy. You talk about things and it comes back.

—Every question seems to stir up something in you.

Not the answers you were looking for . . . but they're answers, heh heh.
Hard to remember things. It's all there, though. Maybe we oughta go
into hypnotherapy, fuckin' go right back. Take like, six months to get
zoned in on the Tonight's the Night *sessions—exactly what was happen-*
ing? "Okay, we're gonna go back a little further today, Neil. . . ."

—I'm frustrated.

Hey, well, you've been frustrated since the beginning, heh heh. You're not
frustrated because of this—we're doing *it. You're asking questions and I'm*
answering them. What could be less frustrating than THAT?

—Maybe I should tell people in the intro you don't wanna do the book.

You can tell 'em if you want. The bottom line is if it went against the
grain so hard, I wouldn't be doin' it. The thing is, it's not necessarily my
first love. I think that's a subtle *way of puttin' it. Heh heh.*

The first time Jon McKeig really encountered Shakey he was under a car.
Shakey's a nickname—from alter ego Bernard Shakey, sometime movie-
maker. It's just one of many aliases: Joe Yankee, overdubber; Shakey Deal,
blues singer; Phil Perspective, producer. The world knows him as Neil
Young.

McKeig had been toiling away on Nanoo, a blue and white '59 Cadillac
Eldorado Biarritz convertible of Young's, for months without actually see-
ing him. The car was a mess, but McKeig would soon realize that this was
Shakey's M.O., buying beyond-dead wrecks for peanuts, then sparing no

expense to bring them back to life. "I can name five automobiles he has that the parts cars were in better shape than the cars that were *restored*." McKeig shook his head. "That's extreme. I don't believe anybody *any-where* goes to that length. If the car smells wrong, you're screwed; if it squeaks, it's not cool . . . he's fanatical."

One day Neil happened in for a personal inspection. "Neil came right over to the car, looked at it and—I'll be damned—all of a sudden he went down to the concrete and slid right underneath. All you could see was his tennis shoes."

McKeig asked Young how far he wanted to go with the thrashed Cadillac. "Neil looked me straight in the eye and said calmly, 'As long as it's museum quality.' " McKeig shuddered. "I never heard it said like that—'museum quality.' Then he left. That's all that was said. I never saw him—for years after." Decades later, Nanoo still isn't finished.

Cars are a major part of Shakey's world. He's written countless songs in them and they figure into more than a few of his lyrics: "Trans Am," "Long May You Run," "Motor City," "Like an Inca (Hitchhiker)," "Drifter," "Roll Another Number (For the Road)," "Sedan Delivery," "Get Gone"; the list goes on.

Young would even advise me on touch-up paint and carburetor problems—until I flipped my '66 Falcon Futura twice off the side of a two-lane, nearly killing myself. Out on the road in his bus, Young called me a few days after. "See, Neil?" I said. "You tried to bump me off, but I'm still here. Now I *gotta* finish the book." Unnerved, he immediately called back after we hung up. "Jimmy," he said, his voice awash in cellular static, "just want ya to know I'm *glad* ya didn't *die* in the wreck." Shakey and I had a colorful relationship. But that was all in the future.

Right now it was April 1991, and I was in Los Angeles, watching McKeig—now Young's live-in auto restorer and maintenance man—pilot members of Neil's family through the service areas of the L.A. Sports Arena in a sleek black '54 Caddy that Young called Pearl: He nicknames everything. It was a stunning vehicle. He had paid $400 for the car in 1974 and spent years and a fortune restoring it. Legend has it that some rich Arab saw Young tooling Pearl through Hollywood and offered him a pile of loot on the spot.

Out of the Caddy's backseat emerged Neil's wife, Pegi, a striking blonde and a powerful force in her own right. She and Neil have two children, Ben and Amber. Family is a priority to both of them. Ben, born spastic, nonoral and quadriplegic, went everywhere with his mom and pop. It wasn't unusual to see him at the side of the stage in his wheelchair, watching his father work.

"Spud," Ben's nickname, graced the door of Pocahontas, which was parked not far from Pearl. A huge, Belgian-made '70 Silver Eagle, forty feet long and sporting a souped-up mill, the bus had been Young's home on the road since 1976. Young had gone to outlandish lengths in customizing it. Down one side was an extravagant stained-glass comet circling the earth; the roof was domed with vintage Hudson Hornet/Studebaker Starlight Coupe cartops that acted as skylights. The interior of the bus—designed under Young's supervision to resemble the skeletal structure of a giant bird—was lavish with hand-carved wood, down to the door handle of the microwave. Above the big front windows hung a large brass eagle's eye. "This bus is so fucked up and over the top," Young would tell me with a grin. "Which is just how I was back in the mid-seventies when I built it."

Bus driver Joe McKenna was making sure Pocahontas was shipshape for Neil's arrival. An Irishman with a low-slung belly, a silver pompadour and a voice lower than a frog's, Joe loved the golf course and let little faze him. He seemed to have a calming effect on Young, who once dubbed him "The Lucky Leprechaun." McKenna would beat cancer after Young helped him get alternative medical help. "Neil Young saved my life," he told me. "Put that in your book."

Next to the steering wheel hung a sign that read in bold block letters, DON'T SPILL THE SOUP. I wouldn't have driven that bus for love, money or drugs. When it came to Pocahontas, Shakey was like a hawk. He knew every ding and dimple and wanted the ones he didn't know explained immediately.

An intense relationship with his bus drivers, I mused, but tour manager Bob Sterne set me straight. "In all honesty, I think the intense relationship is with the bus," said Sterne, a big, bearded, no-nonsense monolith with a constantly peeling nose and sporting a Cruex jock itch ointment T-shirt. Sterne and Joe McKenna weren't exactly the best of pals. Sterne was forever seeking info on Young's elusive doings and one of McKenna's jobs was to keep the world away.

Bob was no stranger to that task—his makeshift office inside the sports arena was plastered with signs like IF YOU WANT A BACKSTAGE PASS, GET LOST. Sterne was hard-core. It came with the territory. "Neil's not gonna do what you think he's gonna do or what he said last week—it's not a good place for the average person to be. The people who are looking for a paycheck don't last long."

Young likes to keep everyone on their toes. "Neil's come to me and said, 'Go get all the set lists and throw 'em in the trash can'—and he said this to me fifteen minutes before the show," said Sterne. "He's not just talking about the band's set list, he's talking about the lighting guys, the sound guys—every single set list *in the building*."

Sitting in the office not far from Sterne was Tim Foster, Young's stage manager and primary roadie. Foster had worked for Young off and on—mostly on—since 1973. With a Dick Tracy chin, a mustache and a baseball cap pulled down to his eyes, Foster saw everything and said little. "Tim never gets flustered," said Sterne. "He understands Neil has no schedule."

Making his way through the backstage maze out to the arena's mixing station was Tim Mulligan, his long hair, mustache and shades making him look like the world's most sullen Doobie Brother. Nothing impresses Mulligan. He's been working on Young's albums and mixing his live sound for decades. "Producers, engineers come and go," said Sterne. "Mulligan hangs in there. He doesn't have an opinion." Tim lives alone on Young's ranch, without a phone. "Mulligan has this incredible allegiance," said longtime Young associate "Ranger Dave" Cline. "He lives and breathes Neil. It's his whole life."

It took years for Mulligan to warm to me, and even then he wouldn't give me an interview, just tersely answered a few questions. Getting any one of Young's crew to talk was like breaking into the Mafia. They were fiercely devoted, and although they'd all been subject to the ferocious twists and turns of Neil's psyche, most had been around for decades. And every one of them was an individual. "Innaresting characters," as Young would put it. "They're all Neil," said Graham Nash. "They all represent a slice of Neil's personality."

"Neil likes quirky people around him," said Elliot Roberts, Young's manager since the late sixties. "I think having quirky people around him lessens—in his mind—his own quirkiness. 'Yes, I am standing on my head, but look at these two other guys *nude* standing on their head.' "

His mane of gray hair flying, Roberts was on his ninety-sixth phone call of the day, either chewing out some record-company underling or closing a million-dollar deal. Not far away, a bearded, sunglassed David Briggs— Young's producer—prowled the stage, palming a cigarette J.D.-style and looking like the devil himself. Briggs and Roberts were the twin engines that powered the Neil Young hot rod. Feared, at times hated, both men possessed killer instincts and had been with Neil almost from the beginning. Roberts was a genius at pushing Young's career, Briggs at pushing his art. It's an understatement to say the two didn't always see eye to eye.

Roberts and Briggs were two of the quirkiest characters around— difficult, complicated men—but then so was just about everybody and everything in Young's world. "Let's look at Neil's whole trip—the ranch, the people he plays with," said computer wizard Bryan Bell, who worked extensively with Young in the late eighties. " 'Easy' isn't in the vocabulary."

"Neil is wonderful to work for in many ways and very difficult to work with in many ways," said Roger Katz, former captain of Young's boat. "He's able to control most everything." As David Briggs put it, "It's not fun at all working with Neil—fun's not part of the deal—but it's very fulfilling."

I asked Young's guitar tech Larry Cragg what the hardest tour had been. "*All* of 'em," he said. "They've all been rough—every one of 'em made workin' for anybody else real easy. The tours are out of the ordinary, the music, the movies—everything's out of the ordinary. We do things differently around here. That's just the way it is."

Cragg was tinkering with Young's guitar rig, which sat in a little area to the rear of the stage. A gaggle of amps—a Magnatone, a huge transistorized Baldwin Exterminator, a Fender Reverb unit and the heart of it all: a small, weather-beaten box covered in worn-out tweed, 1959 vintage. "The Deluxe," muttered amp tech Sal Trentino with awe. "Neil's got four hundred and fifty-six identical Deluxes. They sound *nothing* like this one." Young runs the amp with oversized tubes, and Cragg has to keep portable fans trained on the back so it doesn't melt down. "It really is ready to just go up in smoke, and it sounds that way—flat-out, overdriven, ready to self-destruct."

Young has a personal relationship with electricity. In Europe, where the electrical current is sixty cycles, not fifty, he can pinpoint the fluctuation—by degrees. It dumbfounded Cragg. "He'll say, 'Larry, there's a hundred and seventeen volts coming out of the wall, isn't there?' I'll go measure it, and yeah, sure—he can hear the difference."

Shakey's innovations are everywhere. Intent on controlling amp volume from his guitar instead of the amp, Young had a remote device designed called the Whizzer. Guitarists marvel at the stomp box that lies onstage at Young's feet: a byzantine gang of effects that can be utilized without any degradation to the original signal. Just constructing the box's angular red wooden housing to Young's extreme specifications had craftsmen pulling their hair out.

Cradled in a stand in front of the amps is the fuse for the dynamite, Young's trademark ax—Old Black, a '53 Gold Top Les Paul some knot-head daubed with black paint eons ago. Old Black's features include a Bigsby wang bar, which pulls strings and bends notes, and a Firebird pickup so sensitive you can talk through it. It's a demonic instrument. "Old Black doesn't sound like any other guitar," said Cragg, shaking his head.

For Cragg, Old Black is a nightmare. Young won't permit the ancient frets to be changed, likes his strings old and used, and the Bigsby causes the guitar to go out of tune constantly. "At sound check, everything will work great. Neil picks up the guitar, and for some reason that's when things go wrong."

•   •   •

Meanwhile, things were starting to pick up backstage. The usual music-biz ninnies and nincompoops were filtering in—a record exec here, a rock critic there—along with the requisite local celebrities, among them such actual friends of Young's as actors Russ Tamblyn and Dennis Hopper. After the show, most would've given up waiting by the time Young would finally emerge from the dressing room.

Show time was fast approaching. I saw no sign of Shakey, but every-body seemed to be walking a bit straighter backstage. I figured he must be holed up in his bus. Zeke Young, the product of Neil's troubled, long-ago liaison with actress Carrie Snodgress, confirmed it. Zeke's furrowed brow, crooked grin and lonesome, lost-in-a-dream look made him a dirty-blond ringer for his father circa 1971. Looking toward Pocahontas, Zeke clued me in to the meaning of the California state flag draped inside the big front window: "The flag with the bear means chill. Nobody goes on the bus."

Which meant Shakey would come out when he felt like it. Out in the house, Joel Bernstein—a baby-faced longhair who made the leap from fan to Young's primary archivist—put it succinctly: "Neil does what he wants to do when he wants to do it and doesn't do what he doesn't want to do when he doesn't want to do it."

Here in the summer of 1991, Bernstein was deep into a career retrospective of Young's work, and he was excited. Little did Bernstein know that it still wouldn't be finished ten years later and he'd have a few new gray hairs to show for his trouble.

The Neil Young Archives, a projected multi-CD set of Young's entire recorded output—released and unreleased—is emblematic of his tenaciousness and perversity. Numerous tentative release dates have come and gone since the project began in 1989. Exhaustively seeking CD technology refinements, Young has transferred his mammoth analog tape vault to digital not once but three times—so far. He's blocked any attempts to corral Archives into a practical size and driven everybody crazy by repeatedly abandoning the project to create new music. A booklet mock-up was designed only to be immediately rejected; Young wanted a four-hundred-page book. His vision encompasses every aspect of the project down to the box cover, and rest assured, one way or another it will be carried out. Like everything else, it'll be the way Neil Young wants it, or it won't be done at all.

Everybody keeps putting their own concept on this Archives thing— what songs should be in it, shortening it, doing all this shit that has nothing to do with what I'm going to do, y'know? So what I've done is, I've just stopped all that from happening—no one can complete anything.
—*They, uh, noticed, Neil.*
They did?

—Oh, yeah. They noticed big-time.

It was a helluva try. Real good. But it's not what I want. I don't mind the suggestions about what are good songs . . . But the pieces of shit should be there, too.

—Why?

So you know the difference. Some of it is good, some of it *is* crap that wasn't released—there's a reason. Take a look, see what it is. That's what a fuckin' archive is about, not "Here's Neil Young in all his wonderfulness—the great, phenomenal fucking wonderfulness." That's not what I want.

I want people to know how fuckin' terrible I was. *How scared I was* and how great I was. The real picture—that's what I'm looking for. Not a product. And I think that's what the die-hard fans want—the whole fuckin' thing.

And when I've done the Archives, selected everything and it's all finished, I'm gonna destroy everything else.

—Really?

I'm gonna bury it.

—You're not being glib? This is a decision you've made?

Definitely. I'm gonna dig a big fuckin' hole, dump it all in there, cover it all up. And it's gonna go away.

—But people have shovels. People close to you.

People close to me have shovels?!

—Are you the right guy to put the Archives together?

Hey—it's already together. All you have to do is make sure it's in chronological order, pick the art that goes with it, pick the packaging, put it out.

Y'know, I don't give a shit whether anybody BUYS it or not. I just wanna do it. And there may only be two hundred copies, signed by me. But it's gonna fuckin' exist. When it's done, people can do whatever the fuck they want, make any fuckin' order they want out of it. But they're gonna have the whole fuckin' thing to choose from. They're not gonna get part of it. Everything—the good, the bad, the ugly.

—Should I approach the book the same way?

No—music's different. If you put everything in the fuckin' book . . . First of all, the book would be fuckin' twenty volumes long and you'd never *finish it. Second of all, it'd have all kinds of shit in it that might hurt people.*

At the same time, it shouldn't be a book that makes me look like I'm great and that everything I did is perfect and that the whole book is contrived and put together to justify every fuckin' thing I ever did.
—YEAH, RIGHT.
So obviously it's not gonna be that kinda book. But that's the one thing—I really don't want to hurt people. There are ways to say things where the reader can put things together. Draw their own conclusions.

The weakness of an autobiography is the lack of perspective of the person who's writing it. So, for that reason, I'll never write an autobiography. Never. I told Pegi, "Never let me do it." There's no reason.

People keep telling me that my music has helped them through periods of their life, and I've never understood how that happens, but it must happen because of the way I do it. The way I do things is I give enough facts to make people get a feeling—and then they can associate their own lives with these images that make it seem to apply directly to them. Like the song was written for them. They can't believe it's so directly and obviously about their life. That's because it's not so specific that it eliminates them.

To write an autobiography would go against the grain of all that. Plus it would be too hard. I'd rather make records. That's where my thing is. Now you say something.
—I'm gonna be institutionalized.
Fuck, we can make a lifetime outta this. This could be worse than the Archives, heh heh. We'll make an art project out of it if it fuckin' kills us. It's a book. As far as what's in it—that's up to you. I'm not gonna read it.

The show at the L.A. Sports Arena opened just like the other fifty-two on the tour—with the gut-crunching chords of "Hey Hey, My My (Into the Black)." A lean look at the demon that sometimes is rock and roll, it sports that infamous line "It's better to burn out than to fade away." Some take it as an anthem, while others are outraged. I thought it was funny, beyond cliché. Like many Young songs, it means different things to different people.

The number had the crowd bouncing off the walls. And Shakey wasn't

just preaching to the choir. There were kids, lots of them—mere babies
when the song was first released—all totally lost in the moment. Young's
surname is to the point: Neil Young, perhaps more than any of his peers,
understands what rock is. "Rock and roll is just a name for the music of the
young spirit—of what is happening right in front of us," he said. "Something you can't plan for. Something that you didn't expect."

Tonight Young was onstage with his greatest rock band, Crazy Horse:
Frank "Poncho" Sampedro, Ralph Molina, Billy Talbot. Three musical
misfits, and a band only Young could love. At any given moment, they're
capable of flubbing notes, speeding up, slowing down and generally stumbling through songs they've been playing for twenty years. The Horse are
far from virtuosos, and so-called professional musicians have snickered at
them for years. But I'd take ten hours of Crazy Horse at their absolute
worst over the complete solo works of Clapton or Sting—at least it's rarely
dull. Will the song take off like a rocket or collapse before it starts? Anything's possible with the Horse. That's the thrill.

In the nineties, touring behind a critically acclaimed "comeback"
record—*Ragged Glory*—Crazy Horse suddenly found themselves the
most unlikely institution in rock. Not that it's been a big picnic. Young has
kept the Horse alive the only way he knows how: by leaving to play with
other musicians, then returning when things are fresh and the urge hits. It
keeps the band relevant, keeps the edge. But the toll on the Horse has been
heavy. Married, then divorced, then married again.

The 1991 tour was particularly grueling, with everybody at one another's throats by the end. But tonight Shakey was giving his all, blasting
notes from Old Black that hurt—some of the best, most extreme music of
his life. Not bad for a forty-five-year-old. "You can feel he surrenders,"
said James Taylor. "Neil surrenders."

Being real: This is what Young constantly strives for. Few other musicians of his stature have gone to such lengths to keep things real. He's
never put out a greatest-hits package, unless you count 1977's *Decade,* an
eccentric three-record career retrospective that didn't even have his picture
on the front cover. Young has abandoned entire albums, dumped bands and
tours in a heartbeat, walked away from massive success to release drunk,
out-of-tune albums guaranteed to sell three copies, all to follow his muse.
You know those one-hit wonders from days yonder, cherished because

their thrown-together cacophanies somehow capture a moment in time? Nearly *all* of Young's work contains that crazy spark. And as rock has gotten bigger and slicker to the point of absurdity, Young's tried to remain as defiantly raw as ever.

"Neil's run by his art," said Elliot Roberts. "If Neil perceives he's being jive, he can't do it."

> *You have to be ready to give everything you have, and you have to make sure you've really got a lot to give. Because if you go out there and you're not ready to give everything you have— and you're not strong enough to give as much as you possibly can—to go right to the end of the candle, to right where it's gonna melt and be gone, then you're* nothin'. *You shouldn't even be* there. *You're just markin' time. . . .*
> —Interview with Laura Gross, 1988

Ten months later, Young was out on the road again, playing a six-day solo stand at the Beacon Theatre in New York City. Watching him alone on the stage, encircled by acoustic instruments, I found it hard to believe that this was the same guy who'd been thrashing bent notes and noise out of Old Black. "Neil likes playing in groups, but basically he's a solo artist," the late Horse guitarist, Danny Whitten, had said. "Deep down he knows he has to do the gig by himself."

The Beacon shows were as tranquil as the Horse shows were deafening, a completely different animal. "I get into each thing I do—to the point where nothing else matters. I guess I'm an extremist," said Young in 1989.

A chameleon, Young has thrown himself whole hog into everything he's done, from fifties rock and country to R&B and techno pop, but it all spirals out of two extremes: raw, rampaging four-piece rock and roll or lonesome, naked solo acoustic. "Neil can captivate an audience and hold 'em there for two hours—just him and his guitar," said Willie Nelson.

But here he faced your typical New York City crowd—hungry for blood. They wanted the hits, they wanted Old Black and they wanted anything but what Young was giving them—a bunch of tender new songs they'd never heard before. He sparred with the audience, yelled at them, cajoled them, but most of all he kept right on playing. "What a fuckin' horror show," Young said later. "They sure didn't wanna hear any of those songs—but they did anyway, didn't they?" Young would have the last laugh, as usual. *Harvest Moon,* consisting of the songs the audience had been so impatient with, would be one of the biggest hits of his career.

Compared to the *Ragged Glory* extravaganza, the *Harvest Moon* tour was bare bones—a handful of crew guys, Shakey and his bus. Golfing would take the place of rehearsals, and Young seemed to revel in the unpredictability of the shows. I went skulking around backstage, hoping to nab an interview. Little did I know I'd have to chase Young for another year and a half. The usual celebrity flotsam milled about—tired hipster comedians and the latest rock nonentities, all groveling. But one guest was being mentioned only in reverential whispers: Bob Dylan.

Dylan attended all six of the Beacon shows, hanging out in Young's tour bus between performances. Two of rock's greatest iconoclasts sitting around shooting the shit. They've been friends for decades and, since the mid-seventies, have played the occasional benefit together, with Young also showing up at a few Dylan shows, guitar in hand. Young has covered Dylan songs, most notably "All Along the Watchtower"; Dylan, to my knowledge, has never returned the favor (outside of singing along on a ragged "Helpless" during a 1974 benefit). Four years older than Young, Dylan had done it all first and best, and without him you'd have no Neil, who has no illusions of where he stands in comparison. "I'm, like, a B student of this fuckin' guy—he's the real thing." But these days, who was there after Dylan?

Elliot Roberts has managed both Dylan and Young. "They're both very flighty. They have the exact same road habits, they prep the same way. They're very, very similar in what satisfies them—good shows, bad shows. There's some huge dissimilarities. Bob likes to have his families in place and go to them. He's on the move, doesn't like to stay in one place long. Neil will stay in one place forever, given the opportunity."

"Neil's eccentric with a purpose—Bob's eccentric with a purpose, but I'm not quite sure what that purpose is, and the only person who knows what that purpose is may be Bob," said tour manager Richard Fernandez, who's worked for both of them. "Everybody else is speculating."

The difference in their art? Neil's longtime friend Sandy Mazzeo saw it this way: "Dylan's songs are what's happening all around him. Neil writes about inside."

The quintessential Dylan/Young interaction occurred in June 1988. Dylan was on tour in California when Neil decided to sit in for a couple of shows. "Neil drove up in his Cadillac convertible, his Silvertone amp in the back," recalls Fernandez. Was Young ever intimidated to be joining one of his heroes onstage? "I've never seen him be intimidated by *anyone* musically," said David Briggs. "If Willie is playin' with Neil, Willie follows Neil. If Neil is playin' with Waylon, Waylon follows Neil. When he's got his ax in hand, his aura becomes solid. He's the gun."

Even with Dylan, Young was the gun, and as much as Bob loves Neil, he quickly found himself in the line of fire. "Neil took over the whole show," said Elliot Roberts, who was listening to Dylan's postshow apprehension over Young playing the next night when Neil bounded over. "Great show! See ya tomorrow night, Bob?" "Yeah, Neil," said Bob wearily. Even Dylan can't say no.

At the Beacon, an extra guitar was set up at the end of the final show, and the buzz was that Dylan was going to step out for a number or two. He never showed.

•   •   •

"The other day I was thinking about Neil Young's voice," Rickie Lee Jones writes. "Hesitant, whiny, masculine and feminine. . . . all the sadness and the unresolved [in his voice conveys] what it's like to be a teenager. You are saying goodbye to childhood in those years." For Jones, Young is the sound of that goodbye, a voice that speaks freely and immediately, unhampered by "adult" restraints. The impromptu, unedited nature of Young's art only adds to the reality, and what's left off the canvas is just as important as the paint sloshed on.

"His songs were never finished pictures. He'd look at this, he'd say this, he'd feel this. But things usually didn't have a clear moral meaning at the end, there was no punch line, no reason for the lyrical journey. . . ." In these unfanciful sentences Jones conjures up much of what's special about this guy. For her, as for so many others, Neil Young possesses an "unquestioned integrity."

Although it's mellowed into melancholy over the years, Young's voice is one of pain. A Canadian, he's written a cockeyed history of America as evocative and spare as any Walker Evans photograph. His songs don't provide any answers, they just underline the questions.

Young's output is overwhelming. From 1967 to 2001, forty-six albums, seven certified platinum, nine gold (as of 1997). Over four hundred songs. First-person confessional songs, time-travel songs, character songs, hallucinatory songs, one-joke songs—*every* kind of song, yet all instantly identifiable as Neil Young. "Expecting to Fly," "Mr. Soul," "Cowgirl in the Sand," "Helpless," "I Believe in You," "Harvest," "Tired Eyes," "On the Beach," "Star of Bethlehem," "Will to Love," "Like a Hurricane," "Danger Bird," "Powderfinger," "Transformer Man," "Depression Blues," "Rockin' in the Free World," "Fuckin' Up," "Unknown Legend," "My Heart," "I'm the Ocean."

And that's just a few highlights from released material. In the Archives lurk songs and performances that stand among his absolute greatest, yet have never been heard. Entire albums that were hidden away because Neil changed his mind. Add to that three feature-length films, two soundtracks, scores of video projects and countless tours. Everything Young touches bears his unmistakable stamp, whether it's a song, an album cover, car or guitar. Neil Young is a visionary, and for many he's one of the few reminders outside of Dylan that anything happened at all in the sixties.

RANDY NEWMAN: Most people did their best work when they were younger. Neil Young is as good as he ever was, which is quite an accomplishment. . . . It seems like there's no tricks to him. I don't know if you could name anybody better who came out of rock and roll.

LINK WRAY: Neil's a superstar, but he don't let it get in the way. If he wanted to be a phony, he could. Not this guy. He chooses not to. Neil's always been real.

LINDA RONSTADT: Most of us only get a year to top the charts, then you're out of style. Neil has had an *astounding* career.

ELTON JOHN: Neil has remained on top of his game on all counts— there's not many people you can say that about. He can move me whether he's playing loud music, soft music or country music. There's so many different facets to Neil, and I think that's why he has so much respect from everybody, whether they're older musicians like myself or the younger generation like the Pearl Jams. He just goes out there and gives it his all.

JAMES TAYLOR: I love his attitude. It's meant a lot to me. His clear stand on things like sponsorship and the sort of corporate takeover of music . . . Neil's always resisted that. It's good to have someone like him out there talk the way he talks—and walk the walk, too.

DAVID BOWIE: I have an incredible admiration for Neil. There's a youthful redemption in everything he does, a joyfulness about being an independent thinker in America.

WILLIE NELSON: What can you say? The guy knows how to write a song. He's more than a writer, more than a singer, he's an entertainer. To be a triple threat like that is very rare.

BRYAN FERRY: I like Neil Young. Very much.

J. J. CALE: There's nobody that sounds like Neil Young. A very, very original sound. If he has influences, they don't show.

DEAN STOCKWELL: I can't think of anyone I respect more than Neil Young. I think he's one of the greatest—if not the greatest—living artists.

PETER BUCK: I'm always inspired when I look at Neil Young and realize he's doing whatever the fuck he wants. Some of his messages are positive, some are negative, some don't make any sense at all.

EDDIE VEDDER: I don't know if there's been another artist inducted into the Rock and Roll Hall of Fame that is still as vital as he is today. Some of his best songs were on his last record.

EMMYLOU HARRIS: He's timeless, his music is almost mystical. Neil makes brilliant records and they're easily identifiable. You don't have to be told who it is. He's an original. I can't think of anybody who's even close to him.

THURSTON MOORE: Neil's the real thing. He's Hank Williams.

TOWNES VAN ZANDT: I can read auras—pale green is trouble, boy. I know a lotta cats with green ones—most of them are dead. And there's one that's more golden, glowing, approaching fulfilled—that has fulfilled other people. Neil has that. Neil's is gold. Gold.

Despite the platitudes, Neil Young remains a lonesome figure. He is reclusive and mysterious even to those closest to him. His friendships are all based on his work, which never seems to end. And while Young has played with many bands—Buffalo Springfield; Crosby, Stills, Nash and Young; Crazy Horse; the Stray Gators; Booker T. and the MGs; Pearl Jam—he would tell the audience at the Rock and Roll Hall of Fame in 1995, "It's a solo trip."

And, though he'd never admit it, it's not an easy journey. From the beginning, Young faced ridiculous odds. He was told he couldn't sing, couldn't play guitar, couldn't write. But he's let nothing stop him. Young has not only succeeded, he's prevailed.

He's a model-train mogul, actor, rancher and, although he'd probably be loath to admit it, a humanitarian. He's raised millions for the American farmer as a founding member of Farm Aid and, with Pegi, done the same for children through the Bridge School. Young shoots from the hip. He's been a cantankerous critic of the music business, particularly when it comes to digital recording and corporate sponsorship. He's been critical of the government on environmental issues. In the eighties, he was an outspoken supporter of Ronald Reagan. One thing he is not is predictable. For better or worse, Neil Young has done it his way.

His single-mindedness is inspirational. It can also be exhausting. Even frightening. There is a dark side to Neil Young. By his own admission, he's left behind "a lotta destruction . . . a big wake."

One day, while I was talking to Gary Burden—art director for Young's greatest album covers and a longtime friend of his—the subject of Neil's will came up. It didn't seem to matter who it was, I mused, they all deferred to Shakey. Burden laughed. "Oh, yeah. So did I. So do *you*. Neil's a real artist, but he's also a ruthless motherfucker. He's on his trip all the time. The wheels are always turning."

—*Have you ever looked the Devil in the eye?*
No. *Don't do that.*
—*This is a phrase you use a lot in interviews.*
Yeah . . . *[looks in the author's eyes] Jimmy, level with me—heh heh. I gotta ask you—you're not him, are ya?*
    Boy, I'd hate to write an autobiography, the more I think about it.
—*Maybe we should just give the fuckin' money back.*
Heh heh. *Why don't you just get as much money as you can, then bury the fuckin' thing? You can run to Panama. I'll cover ya—heh heh. And then when I die, everybody can read it. Waddya think? It's a good idea, but it involves me dying too fast.*
—*Or* me.
Or you.

Neil Young's music changed my life when I was a kid. Through a lucky break, I was dropped into his world. He was someone I admired and I wanted to find out what made him tick. I wanted to take a can opener to his brain, get some sense of what coursed through there that could stir the emotions and affect the spirits of half the planet.

It was a long journey. There were times when I thought I would end before it did. During the decade-plus process, ten people I had interviewed died. Marriages collapsed, families drifted apart. Musicians came and went. And Young kept moving, searching, creating. It was maddening to keep up with. Our interviews sprawled the continent and always took place on the run—in planes, cars, even boats. It must be said that I still have enough unanswered questions to last another decade. This work is not an obituary but an action painting. Still in progress.

Young wasn't entirely thrilled with the prospect of losing what privacy he'd managed to retain over the years to a hundred million microscopes. Would you be? Early on he said to one associate, "I told Jimmy he'd face a lotta resistance on this project. I didn't tell him where it would come from." I should've known better. Neil is no publicity junkie—on the subject of interviews, he once told *Newsweek* magazine, "It's not really advantageous for me to do them. I don't want to be there. I'd rather be noted for my absence."

So in part this book is a mystery. A psychedelic detective story. In a quote from an old yellowed clipping, Young offered one lead: "Some people around me think I'm the phenomenon, but it's all these people around me who are the real phenomenon." I took the hint, interviewing hundreds of people who'd played some part in Young's life, many speaking for the first time. They were the witnesses and they were my guides. I went on my own journey through the past, following his trail from Canada to Los Angeles and out into the world. Curiously, when I finally got to him, Young was more than a little interested in what I'd brought back. "I can't go," he said wistfully. "But you can."

Interspersed with the biographical text is one endless, ongoing interview with Young, floating through his own life like a ghost. Imagine *Citizen Kane* with Charles Foster Kane still alive and well in Xanadu, not only willing to talk—however begrudgingly—but, in the end, taking me into the very heart of his creative process, revealing what it takes to keep the flame alive.

Of course this is also a story about rock and roll, what it means to Young and what his has meant to me. Is it strange to change or just the only way to survive? And is it better to burn out than to fade away?

—*What do you think your faults are?*
Fuck, how much time do you have?
—*Plenty.*
Yeah, well, I don't have that kind of time. Just go over your other tapes. People will fill you in on all the faults, and they're all right. All of them.
—*That was easy. My fact checking is done.*
Heh heh.
—*Are you a guarded person?*
No, no, no. You think so?
—*Oh, fuckin' A.*
Guarded. Waddya mean? In what way? Well, shit, you ask questions, it's my whole fuckin' life! When you look at me, I'm goin', "Fuck, this guy's talked to, like, every fuckin' person I know. People I've forgotten about."

I keep turning you on to these people. I've given you all my friends. I'm responsible now. You better do a good fucking book or I'm really an ass-hole. Whew, Jimmy—I'd hate to be in your shoes.
—Aaaaah, we're getting near the end. You can't bullshit me now.
I liked that remark. That *was encouraging . . . I tried to cooperate in a way that I can cooperate. I'm gleeful now that it's almost over. I'm reaching nirvana just anticipating it, but I'm dedicated to completing the task as far as it can go—up to this point. After that . . .*

It's hard to write a story about me, because this is only part one.
—I want the book to say that. On the cover.
Part one? It's up to you, man. It's your book.
—What?
It's your book—now waddya gonna do with it, heh heh heh.

mr. blue & mr. red

"C'mon in. The door's open." I was standing at the screen, hand poised and ready to knock, when the disembodied voice emanating from somewhere inside gruffly offered the invitation. The Florida heat was stifling.

Once inside, I came face-to-face with Rassy Young, a compact, intense woman wearing an ill-fitting polyester ensemble, soft drink in one hand, remote in the other, eyes riveted to a tennis tournament on the screen before her. Since her back was to the door and the TV was blaring, I wondered aloud as to how she knew I was out there. Without shifting her gaze from the match, Rassy jerked a thumb in the direction of her little security system on the mantel: a framed portrait of Neil's family positioned at just the right angle so she could see the reflection of any interloper invading her driveway.

"Pretty tricky, eh?" said Rassy, emphasizing the "eh" like a true Canadian. I'd think of Rassy when Neil remarked on encountering strangers at sea from the safety of his boat. "You can see them before they see *you*— and in every direction," he enthused.

Rassy lived alone. A tempestuous nineteen-year union to Scott Young, Neil's father, ended in 1959, and she never remarried. "I have no interest in marriage. Too damn much trouble. I run my life my own way." Rassy was a proud woman, and although the split had taken place over thirty years before, the indignity was still fresh in her mind. It was a betrayal Rassy could never forgive—right up to her dying breath.

The last few years had not been kind to Rassy. A stubbornly independent woman, she had been an avid golfer and hunter, but now cancer confined her to a living room chair. She watched as her garden slowly died and the birds she loved feeding no longer came to roost. "I don't do a damn thing," she said, sighing. "Every once in a while I'll start to do somethin'—

I get half done and I can't finish it. I'll get so I can't stand it." Rassy claimed she was not afraid of death. "I'm gonna be cremated and flung in the trash. I already paid for it," she said, chuckling. "Four hundred and eighty-five dollars—the high price of dying."

Rassy had left Winnipeg decades ago for this modest bungalow in New Smyrna Beach, Florida. Like Rassy, it was nothing fancy—spartan furniture and a few dusty knickknacks. Neil had bought his mother the house and picked up the tab for her life, and you didn't have to look far to find his presence. The living room wall was heavy with his gold records; on a table next to her easy chair were dusty cassettes that archivist Joel Bernstein had made for her years earlier, featuring Rassy's eclectic favorites from her son's work—like "Sedan Delivery," a maniacal rocker she liked to blast while washing her car, much to the chagrin of her elderly neighbors.

Rassy's sentences were punctuated with a litany of exclamations such as "Holy smut!" or "What in Sam Hill?" and peppered with a lexicon of poetically mangled words—"basedump" for basement, "snthudderstorms" for thunderstorms. Country/western was "cow music." Rassy could cuss like a sailor and drink like one to boot. Since she gave up her beloved Black Cat Plain cigarettes—a particularly nicotine-potent Canadian brand—Rassy retained only liquid vices. "What would I do without Coke?" she'd ponder, snapping open can after can. Coke would invariably turn to rye and water at some point early in the afternoon. "Well, I'm gonna have a drink or drop dead!" she'd bark as she shuffled off to the kitchen, my abstention only increasing her suspicion.

"Make way for the star's mother," she'd announce imperiously at her son's shows, pouncing on the first backstage lackey who didn't fetch her a beer. No one escaped the wrath of Rassy. Certain waitresses in New Smyrna Beach still tremble at the memory of serving Rassy a steak. She kept close tabs on all her neighbors, each of whom seemed to annoy her in one way or another.

Today she was planning to turn in one fellow senior for watering his lawn during rationing season and was threatening another poor old soul for not tending to an unwieldy woodpile. "The ninny next door and her stick farm," said Rassy with a harrumph as she eyed the inconsequential pile out the back window. "She drives me into the middle of next week."

A tough old dame, yet beneath the bulldog exterior lurked a sensitive soul. "Rassy was a lady," said close friend Nola Halter. "Her manners were impeccable—after every gathering was a phone call or a note or a gift. Rassy didn't forget people. Y'know, some people can swear and still be a lady. I loved her. I understood her. Many people didn't, but Rassy didn't give a damn."

Rassy didn't give a damn for her son's biographer, either, as she made abundantly clear to anyone within earshot the moment I left New Smyrna Beach. Due to her precarious health, I had rushed off to talk to her immediately upon starting this project. My only previous background on Neil's childhood had come from his father's 1984 book, *Neil and Me*. Rassy brought up the book almost upon my arrival, complaining angrily and endlessly about its lack of veracity. "It's *all* wrong. I made Scott take a lotta the stuff out—'Take it out or I'll sue.' " When I inquired about specific passages in an attempt to set the record straight, she threatened to sue *me*. "I'm not going to discuss that book any further," she'd say, then ten minutes later she'd begin ranting all over again.*

Nor were Neil's highfalutin showbiz friends exempt from the hot seat. "David got mad at me once. He said, 'I'm *sick* of people sayin', "Are you *David Crosby*?" ' I said, 'Tell 'em you're Eric Clapton.' God, did he get mad. I can still see his face. Ask a stupid question . . ." She rolled her eyes. Even the famous son suffered Rassy's caustic comments, as witnessed by her review of "Mother Earth," a solo electric song Neil had recently performed at "Farm Aid, Band Aid—whatever the hell it is. Neil sang that song for me. I was *horrified*. The guitar sounded like Jimi Hendrix playing 'The Star-Spangled Banner.' " Rassy made a face like a constipated bulldog.

"I *told* Neil the thing was garbled. I knew *damn well* he'd done it on purpose. There's no point in writing a song with a message if you're gonna distract everybody with the racket the music makes. That isn't music. Well, it *isn't*."

---

*Scott had a different version of events surrounding *Neil and Me*. When the manuscript was in galleys, Rassy called up, threatened all sorts of legal action and claimed Neil—conveniently on a boat trip at the time—had given her permission to edit the book. Scott gave her five days to peruse the manuscript and make any factual corrections. A few days later she called back with a very minor correction. She then offered her congratulations on the book, telling Scott how much she had enjoyed it. Scott later repeated Rassy's flattering review to Neil. "Well, Dad, you're the only person she said that to," he quipped.

While I was there, Neil called and said, just before he hung up, "Tell my mother I love her." Which I dutifully repeated, although if it registered Rassy didn't let on. She seemed hungry for any scrap of information I could offer on her son and tried to laugh off his mystery. "Neil can disappear while you're blinkin' your eye," she told me. "And half the time he looks like so many other damn people it slays me. I got a picture around here where you'd swear he was John Davidson."

Neil was as elusive to his mother as to anyone else, but when I looked into Rassy's eyes I saw him. Both mother and son possessed the same fierce, thousand-yard stare that when it locked on your eyes seemed to conduct a brief autopsy on your soul. Neil had no greater supporter in life than his mother and he was a devoted and dutiful son. But she could drain you. As Scott put it with some affectionate humor, "It was not a mistake Rassy lived in Florida and Neil lives in California."

• • •

Born October 16, 1918, Edna Blow Ragland was the youngest of three very spunky and independent sisters—Virginia, Lavinia and Edna— nicknamed by their father Snooky, Toots and Rassy. "I was a spoiled brat," recalled Rassy. "I played golf and tennis and swam and drove around in my car and charged the gas to Daddy."

"Daddy" was Bill Ragland, fondly remembered by scores of Canadians who made his acquaintance. "Half of Winnipeg called him Daddy," said Rassy proudly. Raised on a plantation near Petersburg, Virginia, Bill Ragland was the son of a banker whose roots stretched back to the first British settlers in the state. He would proudly recall that his grandfather had freed the slaves on the plantation, but this didn't prevent Bill from nicknaming a family cat "Nigger" or demanding that a black man ride in the back of a train. "Daddy wasn't exactly racist, but he was southern," said Virginia "Snooky" Ridgeway.

The Raglands were a prominent family and lived well. They had the first radio and first gramophone in Winnipeg, and even during the Depression the family had a maid. As Rassy stated, "We never went without a damn thing ever." Mother Pearl was an expert seamstress who kept her three girls among the best dressed in Manitoba.

Bill and Pearl married in 1911. Both had emigrated to Winnipeg from the United States, neither of them taking Canadian citizenship. "Daddy was American from day one—he voted in the States," said Snooky. "Just the fact that he ran Winnipeg politics didn't mean he had to vote there." Toots recalled her father's fury over an anti-American poem that had been introduced into her school curriculum. "He went steaming over to the school and raised hell. I was very startled, because it was the only time I can remember him intervening."

For the most part, the Ragland family lived just across the Red River from Winnipeg in the Norwood district. One-forty-five Monck Avenue was a sprawling house and as close to a southern mansion as Bill Ragland could find. As western district manager for the Barrett Roofing Company, Bill Ragland was a man of few words and great influence. "An expert manipulator," said Snooky, who maintained that her father "looked after his girls in a very silent way."

Bill worked, hunted and played cards at Winnipeg's Carleton Club. "He spent as little time at home as he could manage," said Toots. "I have the utmost respect for Daddy as a businessman, as a father and as a hunter; I don't hold him in high esteem as a husband," said Snooky. "I think the marriage fell apart early on, but they raised the children with every effort to keep us from knowing."

Bill Ragland was a duck hunter extraordinaire. The trunk of his company Ford was packed full of shells, and it is said that he never missed a shot. His understanding of waterfowl bordered on the mystical. "He could walk right into the middle of a flock of wild geese and they wouldn't turn a hair," said Rassy. "Daddy could outwit any bird in the world."

After the hunt came breakfast: apple pie and a Coke stoked with rye, with a Bromo-Seltzer chaser. More often than not, his cohort on these early morning duck hunts was Rassy—swilling whiskey and toting a gun just like her old man. "She was a great deal like Bill. The same kind of opinions," recalls Nola Halter. "Bill was gonna shoot somebody all the time, and usually it was an American politician." Rassy was "the closest thing to the son my father always wanted," said daughter Toots.

As far as rearing the children, "Daddy left all that to Mother," Toots continues. But while Pearl might've been proud of the Ragland family roots, she revealed little concerning her own. "Mother was very socially conscious and I think she felt the less she said about her background, the better." Pearl's mother was a French immigrant, her father an Irishman who had raised horses in Kentucky. "French and Irish. An absolutely God-awful combination. That's where all the temperament comes from. Lots of rows and tantrums. Mother and Rassy were particularly dramatic. They were birds of a feather. Spoilers."

What were the musical roots in the Ragland family? "None," said Toots. "We never even sang." Snooky disagreed. "My mother was extremely musical. She sang beautifully." In fact, Pearl's mother had dragged her out to sing and play piano in public.

"Mother was so absolutely determined that no child of hers would have to go through all that, that she would not have a piano in the house," said Snooky, adding "Rassy was like Neil—she could sit at the piano and play." Snooky recalls Rassy telling their mother she was playing with her friend Ruth when she was actually sneaking off to the home of a widow down the street, Mrs. Robinson, to play piano. "Rassy didn't dare tell mother she was playing piano. Mother was dead set against it. Dead set."

As adults, both of Rassy's sisters would enjoy successful careers in addition to raising families—Snooky running a public relations firm in Texas, and Toots a popular columnist and radio personality in Winnipeg. If Rassy had such desires, no one knew it. A vivacious, vivid young woman—her nickname was short for Rastus, bestowed upon her for the dark hair and eyes she'd inherited from Pearl—Rassy was popular with the boys "in a sort of arm-wrestling kind of way," said Toots. Rassy was a born athlete. She told me of watching her sister Snooky play tennis: "I said, 'This isn't so hard,' and I immediately beat her. I played golf and skied and whatever the hell else was goin' on. I wasn't that good. All I wanted to do was win."

Most of the playing took place at the Winnipeg Canoe Club, where Rassy and her sisters apparently wreaked havoc with the opposite sex. "Boys didn't dump the Raglands," said Snooky. "The Ragland girls just moved on—to another boy."

It was at the Canoe Club in the summer of 1938 that a struggling young sportswriter from the wrong side of the tracks, enjoying a free membership provided by the club to ensure newspaper coverage of their sporting events, first encountered Rassy Ragland. Watching her yell endearments across the water to boyfriend Jack McDowell as if calling a dog for supper, Scott

Young was intrigued, while women nearby cursed out loud because Rassy had stolen a boyfriend or two from all of them.

"Rassy was very quick and very witty—you didn't have to explain things to her twice," said Scott. "In some cases you didn't have to explain them at all."

My mother, Rassy, and her two sisters—Toots and Snooky. The Ragland girls. My grandpa was American, from Virginia—he was livin' in our house for quite a while when I was a teenager. Pretty low-key, though— he just went to the club and back, sat and drank rye with his friends. I didn't know him that well. He was probably on much better behavior when he was around me—his grandchildren, he's gotta act cool. What he did at the club, I have no fuckin' idea on earth, okay? Apparently he played a lotta cards. But they used to kinda hide me from everything. My mother . . . I dunno.

Pearl was very old. They lived in an apartment, and we went there and saw them a couple of times with my dad and my brother. We'd all get dressed up. That's one thing I remember. "What the hell am I having to get dressed up *so* nice *. . . " What a head space. It's not like, "Wow, we're gonna go over and see Grandma and Grandpa and hang out." No—we're gonna get* dressed up. *I don't know why my mother had to do that. I'm sure my father was much looser in the dress code.*

"Look at Scott now. Seventy-seven years old, for God's sake and he switched to writing *fiction,*" mutters his longtime friend and rival Trent Frayne with begrudging admiration. "At seventy-seven, he oughtta siddown and put his feet up!"

When I headed for Ontario to visit Scott Young in April 1995, I got the distinct impression that while he might not be putting his feet up, the intense drive of his younger days had relaxed into a much more manageable force. These days, he lives on a farm not far from Omemee, the small town where Neil spent some of the happiest days of his childhood and where, the year before, a school had been dedicated in Scott Young's honor. Mildly annoyed that he hadn't finished his day's work, Young turned from his ancient computer and left his office, moving in a slow, deliberate shuffle but with a fire in his eyes that belied his age. In recalling some lost love, he cracked an expansive, lipless smile and muttered, "She was bee—*yoo*—tee—ful." There was a dreamy look on his face, like a kid's at a candy-store window. "My dad's the coolest. He's my hero till the end," said Neil's half sister, Astrid. "As old as he is, he's the youngest guy in the world."

Even with the advancing years, Young remains a charismatic, handsome man. Scott's is a craggy, authoritative face, framed by wispy gray hair and owlish eyebrows; I could imagine him as a black-robed judge deciding the fate of some reprobate and doing an eminently fair job of it, too. Scott can be prickly when it comes to ideals—he quit the Toronto *Globe and Mail* twice over matters of principle—but these days he seems very laid-back. "My dad's changed a whole lot," said Astrid. "When I grew up, he was pretty conservative."

Scott Young speaks slowly and deliberately. Questions are carefully considered and, as with Neil, you often have to read between the lines. Compared to Rassy, who wore her heart on her sleeve, there is a lot of restraint. I couldn't imagine the pair in the same room together, let alone married.

"Scott's a very warm man," said Canadian author and television personality Pierre Berton, one of many people Scott helped get started in a career. "I like Scott—*everybody* likes him, y'know. I don't think he has any enemies."

Most Canadians I talked to got revved up at the mere mention of Scott's name. Folksinger Murray McLauchlan was far more excited to talk about Scott Young than Neil. "Scott is a literary cultural icon. In this country, Scott Young is every bit as famous as his kid." McLauchlan went on to enthuse over Young's 1952 schoolboy favorite, *Scrubs on Skates:* "It's the two little savages of hockey. The archetypal work of dreams—if you're a little kid in Shawinigan Falls dreaming of the NHL, that's your book." Forty years later, McLauchlan could quote word for word the book's dedication: "To Neil and Bob, whose greatest games are still ahead of them."

Father and son are prolific—Neil has put out over forty albums, Scott over thirty books, including biographies, mysteries, children's fiction and short stories. He's worked as a television commentator and newspaper columnist, initially making a name for himself as a sportswriter covering hockey. Lately he's been writing mysteries featuring an Inuit inspector, Matteesie Kitologitak.

While Rassy never remarried, Scott has twice, and friends feel his marriage to writer Margaret Hogan—his constant companion since the late seventies—has settled him. During the few days I stayed with Scott, he seemed continually curious as to what his partner, off working at the time, was up to. It reminded me of Neil's devotion to Pegi; both men had finally found mates that captivated them completely.

Scott Young has his critics. Supporters of Rassy view his book about the family he left behind as tantamount to treason. Some see Scott as the square, uptight authority figure that Neil had to rebel against in order to survive. "Mild-mannered, never rash, a voice of reason in the quagmire of changing times . . . his tie is never unknotted," wrote Juan Rodriguez in a 1972 article entitled "Neil Young's Father." "His feet are planted firmly on the ground. His opinions are Moderate and Sensible. He is Decent. He is a true Canadian." The like-minded usually depict Rassy as the selfless savior who, against all odds, gave Neil the freedom to make his dreams come true. The actual story is a little more complicated than that.

While there is no question that the collapse of his marriage to Rassy wreaked havoc in his son's life, Scott has been a figure of inspiration to Neil. "As a writer, the one thing you have to do is lay yourself bare," Neil recalls Scott telling him. A hell of a lesson to learn from your own father. And although its intensity has ebbed and flowed over time, the bond between father and son—much of it unspoken—remains a deep one.

"Very similar in a lot of their outlooks" is how Astrid puts it. "My dad tends to be a little bit less serious than Neil is. He can see the humor in everything . . . Neil's a little more intense." She said both men have slow fuses that, when detonated, explode big. "My dad's the kind of person who will let things go and let things go—he'll kind of absorb it all in. And all of a sudden one little thing will happen, like you left the screen door open—and *boom!* It blows up."

I noticed one striking similarity between the two men. After hammering Scott with days of questions—all of which he answered without complaint— I still felt plenty lurked beneath the surface. I liked the guy, but did I get to know him? Can't say. Scott Young seemed just as elusive as his son.

Scott Young was born in Manitoba on April 14, 1918. His father, Percy, was a handsome, soft-spoken druggist and the son of a Methodist pioneer farmer. Mother Jean was the daughter of a Presbyterian minister who demolished his church career in the twenties when he took off for the States after a comely faith healer. Percy and Jean were another volatile couple. "He and my grandmother would get together, she would get pregnant, they would yell and scream and rant and rave and they would get separated," said granddaughter Marny Smith. Their unions resulted in three children— Scott, Bob and Dorothy—and each would have radically different childhoods as their father went broke in 1926 and then (although the couple never divorced) the marriage collapsed in the midst of the Depression in 1931. Dorothy remained home with her mother; Bob went to live with missionary grandparents on an Indian reservation; Scott was farmed out to relatives in Prince Albert.

A year later, living on relief and sharing lodging with three bachelor bank clerks, Jean reunited her children in Winnipeg. In his autobiography, Scott speaks of his mother's relationships with her boarders and assorted others, remembering her as "very sexual and attractive to guys." Relatives disturbed by the characterization argue that Jean did whatever was necessary to keep her children together through the Depression.

Another of the strong women who populate both sides of Neil's lineage, Jean Young was "a feisty old broad," said Marny Smith. "If she wanted to come in your house and sit up on your counter and put three beers down the row, by God, that's what she did."

In the late thirties, Jean would find a real home in Flin Flon, Manitoba, writing for various local papers, working as a church organist and founding a renowned music festival as well as creating Flin Flon's first library. "She was the matriarch of the entire town," said son Bob. Scott was the light of his mother's life. Trent Frayne remembers visiting Jean when "all she said was, 'Ohhh, isn't he wonderful? Have you ever met a man who's so wonderful?' And I would sit there thinking, 'Jesus Christ, he's not *that* wonderful.' "

•   •   •

Even as a child, Scott charmed those around him. He had a reputation as an industrious, enterprising child, earning pocket money by catching gophers and selling the tails for two cents apiece. As brother, Bob, recalls, "Scott was a miracle worker with a gopher trap."

Sports made an indelible impression on Scott, stirring deep emotions in him even as a youth. He can still recall listening to the 1926 Gene Tunney/Jack Dempsey fight for the heavyweight championship of the world. When Dempsey lost the dramatic battle, Scott, all of eight years old, went to bed weeping uncontrollably. As he wrote in his autobiography, "It was something about defeat, any defeat, that got to me."

The impetus to write came by way of Scott's high-living uncle Jack Paterson, a dashing figure who traversed the rowdy logging camps of British Columbia in search of material for his lusty short stories and magazine articles. "Uncle Jack's freedom inspired me. He'd fall out of the sky with his beautiful blond wife and eat, drink and tell stories. You'd walk into a room and he'd have a drink in one hand, his elbow on the fireplace mantel, and everybody would be spellbound by the stories of the North."

Buying a $48 Remington typewriter on credit in 1936, Scott began to submit work for publication, earning his first byline (and $3) from the *Winnipeg Free Press* for a short article on an old black shoeshine man. This led to a job as copyboy for the paper, and by the end of the year he had fallen into the sports department, covering local hockey.

Scott was—just as Neil would be—lucky, adventurous and driven to the point of mania. On an early live assignment covering the escape of German prisoners from a POW camp, Young sneaked into the encampment by railway handcar, eavesdropped on soldiers through a heating grille in his hotel-room floor, found booze in the middle of the wilderness to loosen officers' tongues and was even threatened with arrest by gun-toting officers of the Royal Canadian Mounted Police. All this in search of "news that other people didn't have," as he puts it in his autobiography. "I certainly admire Scott's tenacity," said Trent Frayne. "He used to say, 'Just open up a vein and let a little blood come out.'"

Another product of the Depression, Frayne lived with Young and a gaggle of other struggling writers at 55 Donnell Street in what Trent's wife, author June Callwood, calls "a magnificently awful boardinghouse." Some of the writers Young met there would remain lifelong friends, and the group would eventually expand to include such notable Canadians as Farley Mowat, Robertson Davies and Pierre Berton. Most were discovered and brought into the group by Young. As Callwood said, "Scott moves effortlessly into other milieus. He is such a charming, ingratiating man. A lot of doors open for Scott."

With his wavy hair and wide, warm smile, Scott was a lady-killer. Birdeen Laurence, a young raven-haired knockout, was torn between Scott and another writer in the boardinghouse gang, Ralph Allen. Allen was nowhere near as dashing as Young, but his career was happening faster, and when Birdeen sought Scott's advice on the situation, he told her to go with the sure thing. Birdeen slid a heartbreaking farewell note under Scott's door, declaring him "noble," but friends saw it as a tragedy. "Her heart was with Scott," said June Callwood. "But he didn't put in a strong enough bid. I think they both regretted it all their lives. I think Birdeen Allen was the love of Scott's life, and both Ralph and Rassy were always conscious of that. It drove Rassy up the walls."

So did Merle Davies. Davies was another beauty who haunted the Canoe Club. Because she was from Montreal, and because of her interest in Scott, Rassy called her "that damned foreigner"—even, ironically enough, after she married Scott's brother, Bob. At times, Rassy must've felt surrounded. Scott seemed to fall for women frequently and passionately, causing complications throughout his life. In his autobiography, Young relates how he once overheard a woman friend telling Birdeen Allen how Scott had asked her to marry him. "So what?" quipped Allen. "He asks *everybody* to marry him."

When I asked Scott if he saw any of himself in Neil, the subject of women came up first. "I've got an idea that Neil has some of my attitudes about women. As far as I know, neither one of us is bucking for the job of patron saint. I used to ask everyone I ran into to marry me. A fella told me once that I was a 'marryallator'—meaning that I worship women and don't exercise any kind of proper judgment when I'm faced with somebody I really like. But I've given that up."

As his brother, Bob, quipped, "Scott's attitude was 'love 'em and leave 'em,' but Scott never left 'em and he kept on lovin' 'em. Scott left a trail. He had a lot of my father in him in terms of being attractive to girls. They thought he was the real thing, y'know?"

Apparently Rassy Ragland thought so, too. Over the protests of her friends, she broke off a previous wedding engagement to marry Scott on June 18, 1940.* They were both twenty-two years old. "We were children," said Scott, recounting his proposal during a passionate visit at the boardinghouse. "In the heat of the moment, I said, 'Maybe we should get married.' Rassy immediately bolted upright and said, 'When?' It was characteristic of both of us that Rassy had decided she was gonna marry me and I was not gonna fight it."

Rassy and Scott were a lively match, both possessing sharp minds and strong wills. "Rassy was quite different from Scott," said Pierre Berton. "Scott was very easygoing, never got very upset—Rassy could hit the roof easily and come right down again." Rassy saw Scott's manner as a little restrained for the hot-blooded Raglands. "Mother hated Scott," she said. "Thought he was too English."

Rassy would stop at nothing to get her way. Scott tells how he got into an argument with her over inviting one of his old flames to the wedding. After a long battle, Rassy finally acquiesced, but months later Scott found the woman's unsent invitation hidden under some catalogs. "There's more than one way to win an argument," he said, chuckling. "Rassy brooked little interference, and if you opposed her, it was a real federal offense."

"Rassy would not be intimidated by anybody," said Neil's brother, Bob. "She treated authority with disdain—*her* authority was the only authority that mattered. My father, on the other hand, came from abject poverty and sort of climbed his way out, and was never comfortable confronting authority."

Still, Scott continually stood up for Rassy, even under the most difficult circumstances. Rassy had a reputation as a gossip and once spread some information that was particularly damaging to one of the couple's female friends, much to the dismay of the other women in their circle. "Birdeen and June, I don't know who else, ganged up on Rassy," Scott recalls. "They

---

*Rassy's wedding was a pretty dramatic affair, according to her sister Snooky. Rassy was set to marry star athlete and Canoe Club favorite Jack McDowell, and invitations had long since been sent out when, one week before the wedding, Rassy changed her mind. "Instead of marrying Jack McDowell, who was the gentleman on the invitation, Rassy informed Mother she was marrying Scott," said Snooky, who recalls the Raglands returning a mountain of wedding gifts with "a little announcement that the wedding was still on—but the bridegroom had changed."

wanted her to come to a *meeting,* if you can imagine that. I wrote a note—carbon copies to every woman involved—and I told them to fuck off."

Thirty years later, when writing about his family in *Neil and Me,* Scott remained respectful. There was no discussion of Rassy's shortcomings, and Scott disparaged only himself in frankly revealing his numerous affairs—which perhaps has helped to further damn him as the father who left. Even Rassy's friends thought he was a little too easy on her in the book, but it didn't surprise them. "Scott's gallant with women," said June Callwood. "He doesn't speak of their failings."

· · ·

Unlike her two sisters, Rassy would have no career other than that of being a wife, and domesticity was a duty she didn't take lightly. "She was passionate about Scott, so she put everything into being the most wonderful wife and support," said June Callwood. "Rassy put all her creative energy into being the world's best cook—nobody will ever forget her duck, and the kids used to say about her cakes, 'Hold it down or it'll float away.' She made her own drapes and slipcovers to save money . . . everything was perfect. She organized her home to create shame in every woman in the country. It was all to hold Scott, as I saw it. Because Scott had a roving eye all his life."

This couldn't have been easy for Rassy; nor was Scott's reserved manner. While she was blunt about speaking her mind, her husband wasn't always the easiest individual to read. "I always think of Scott as somebody who avoids confrontation at all costs," said his niece Stephanie Fillingham. "So when things got tough, he just kind of backed away—and his women spent their whole lives trying to catch him." As Rassy put it, "How can you fight with somebody who won't talk?"

Scott Young was, in his own subtle way, as intricate an individual as Rassy, and freelance career struggles only exacerbated his idiosyncrasies. "As I was often told, in times of financial stress I was not easy to live with," Scott writes in his autobiography. He worked at home, and his insistence on absolute quiet was extreme even to other writers. "Scott was hysterical about noise," said June Callwood. "Rassy used to say, 'I can't run a vacuum cleaner, I can't wash dishes.' It had to be total silence in the house."

Yeah, it was quiet around the house when Daddy was up there writing—until a certain time and then you could be noisy. He's a real writer. That's what he does. He'd force himself to do five pages—some days they came real easy and some days it was like pullin' teeth. That's what he told me.

I can still remember goin' up the steps, up into the attic. He'd be on the typewriter and I'd just walk right up and stand there looking at him—my head was just a little bit higher than his desk. He never, never got mad at me. It was always "Nice to see you."
—Your brother, Bob, might've gotten a different reaction.
Maybe, yeah. He was a pretty mellow guy—with me. I think somethin' about me made it a lot easier to get along. . . .

Whatever people's criticisms of Scott, in the early days of their relationship, Rassy wouldn't hear them. "She was loyal to a fault," said June Callwood. She typed all of Scott's stories ("Everything had to be in triplicate," muttered Rassy, rolling her eyes), kept away anyone who disturbed Scott's concentration at the typewriter and generally battled the world on his behalf. As Scott writes in *Neil and Me,* Rassy was "with me all the way, never complaining about my quitting a job, selling house after house, moving from places she had decorated (and, boy, could she paint, as she herself used to say)."

For their first Christmas together—which Scott would immortalize in a short story entitled "Once upon a Time in Toronto"—Rassy decorated the tree with red paper roses and a note to her new husband: "This is our first Christmas. We don't have much except each other, but I have cut up little bits of my heart for you, to put on our first tree." This was Rassy. When it came to her husband, it was till death do us part.

And Scott obviously loved Rassy, although those close to him felt he was driven by forces beyond his control. "Scott had ambition," said his brother, Bob. "He had a pretty clear view of what he was gonna be, what he was gonna do, and he was bloody well gonna do it—and Rassy helped, but win, lose or draw, with Rassy there or *not* there, it wasn't gonna stop him."

·   ·   ·

"Christ, we lived all over hell's half-acre," said Rassy. "I moved sixty-seven times during my married life." An exaggeration, but Scott's career machinations did have them relocating often. After their marriage, the couple remained briefly in Winnipeg, then moved to Toronto in November 1940 when Scott got a job with the Canadian Press. On April 27, 1942, a son, Robert Ragland Young, was born, and the couple spent much of the next three years apart, as Scott was sent to London to cover the war, then enlisted in the navy: "I no longer wanted to be in the war as a bystander." Rassy and Bob lived with Scott's relatives in Flin Flon until Scott returned home for good in 1945.

"I know the exact time when Neil was conceived," Scott writes, describing a romantic snowbound night at a friend's Toronto apartment during one of his infrequent leaves from navy duty. Needless to say, Rassy contested this as she did just about everything her ex-husband remembers. At any rate, Neil Percival Young was born at Toronto General Hospital at 6:45 A.M. on November 12, 1945.*

•   •   •

"Very open, very honest, very naïve" is how Elliot Roberts defines Canadians: they don't seem to burn out, just get more eccentric. They are the oddest breed I've ever run into, but I'll let Neil Young exemplify that. He's never renounced his Canadian citizenship.

Canadians? They're very resolute about some things. They're conservative, they're liberal. People speak out, say what they think to a great degree. They don't seem to be quite as worried about how they look or what people think about them.

It's my roots. I really don't have a yearning to return to Canada— although I might someday. To me, Canada is my family, where I grew up, memories of bein' young and bein' open to ideas. And then tryin' to get outta *Canada because it was limiting. At sixteen, I was already goin' down visiting the consulates, finding out what you had to do to go down to the States, to legally go down there. Once you get there, you find out*

*There is some controversy about Young's middle name(s)—which he wouldn't confirm for me—but both his father and a musician who's seen his passport say "Percival." Young is allegedly a triple Scorpio.

how beautiful Canada is and what it has to offer—natural resources that are awe-inspiring. So I'm proud to be a Canadian—but I don't let it hold me back. Part of the planet, not part of the nation.

I wonder if some Canadians resent the fact that I left Canada. They probably do.
—*Filmmaker, and Canadian, David Cronenberg feels there is a tendency to consider all sides of the story to the point of paralysis: "It's a Canadian thing, this balance. Up to a point it's virtue, beyond that it's neurotic."*
I agree with that. There's something in Canada that teaches you that you always gotta look at both sides. See how other people could figure out why what you're saying is wrong before you're so sure you're right.
—*Songs like "Rockin' in the Free World" or "Change Your Mind"—you think there might be something Canadian in the ambiguity of those songs?*
Yeah. That's all it is, heh heh.

I don't really have the confidence to stand behind things that I say— because I really don't think I know that much. I'm not confident that I know what I'm talking about. That's better than somebody who's confident that they know what they're talking about and they're sure— because that leads them down a path. I never believe what I know is good or not, so I'm always scanning. Even the things I believe in the most, I doubt. And so when I see something that I've said, or hear it—it makes sense to me that I might not feel the same way the next time. Because that's the way I am.

"Neil was funny as hell," said Rassy. "Great big eyes, yards of black hair and fat—my God, you could not fill him up. He ate and ate and ate. Wide as he was high." While still in diapers, Neil—or Neiler, as he was to be known—exhibited a musical bent any time his mother played an old 78 of Pinetop Smith's "Boogie-Woogie." "God, he loved that record! Just leap up in his playpen, hold on to the railing and jig away."

The family moved into a three-bedroom bungalow at 335 Brooke Avenue in Toronto, Bob and Neil sharing a room so that Scott could have an office. He worked as an assistant editor for *Maclean's* magazine, supplementing his $4,000-a-year salary by selling short stories to magazines throughout Canada and the United States. By 1947 the family was solvent enough to buy their first car, a feisty '31 Willys-Knight that Rassy drove, as Scott had no license. The Youngs continued to relocate, living in rural areas outside Toronto, first at the Lake of Bays, then Jackson's Point.

Raising children was an area where the couple clashed, according to Scott. "I used to infuriate Rassy when she and the two boys would be arguing—I would say, 'Now children, now . . .' " Looking back, Scott said, "I think there were more battles between Rassy and the kids than between the two of us." Bob Young described his mother as "aristocratic. When I look back at it now, she was obviously caring, concerned, put a lot of effort into it. She had the presence of mind to make sure we were introduced to books and music at a very early age."

June Callwood, who visited the family in Jackson's Point, saw Scott and Rassy as too absorbed with themselves—and their tangled relationship— to concentrate fully on their two very different children: outgoing Bob, nervy and full of bluster; Neil, withdrawn and solemn. "Neil was a sullen, fat, dark-eyed little baby. Not a happy baby, not a smiler, not a joiner. Not getting much. Neil got good primary care, but he didn't get affection, hugs, from either of his parents. So he became a little watcher."

· · ·

The cover story of the *Toronto Telegram* for September 9, 1950, concerns a small country village called Omemee, and not far from the headline OMEMEE KIDS LIKE SCHOOL is a large photograph of a jolly-looking four-year-old with spiky black hair holding a whopper of a fish and smiling for the camera. The picture was faked; the fish was frozen and procured for the picture. Somehow it seems appropriate that an artist as media-savvy as Neil Young would make his earliest known public appearance learning the con. Still, it's an appropriate image—most people's earliest memories of Neil involve him either carrying a fish nearly as big as himself over his shoulder or dragging an oversized snapping turtle through town in his wagon, blissfully unaware of the small army of hungry cats and dogs following close behind.

Omemee is a town conjured up in the first line of one of Young's most indelible songs, "Helpless," and as his brother, Bob, states, "I think Neil would probably agree if there's anywhere either of us would point to as home, it would be Omemee." In the summer of 1949, Scott Young bought a three-story turn-of-the-century house on five acres right in the center of town for $5,400, and for the next few years, Neil would lead a Huck Finn existence there.

Young urged me to visit Omemee. As he put it, "They remember me like I don't."

·   ·   ·

"Dummy died," said Jay Hayes, a Gaelic lilt to his voice and a twinkle in his sad Irish eyes. "His brother came down to see Lester Markham—that's the undertaker—and he says, 'Les, I want you to come and get my brother and bury him, he's dead.' Markham says, 'I can't go and get him. You hafta go and get a *doctor*.' The brother says, 'Jesus, I don't need a doctor, the guy's dead—he hasn't moved in three days!' " The barest hint of a smile crept across Jay's friendly face. "Typical," he muttered. Scott Young and I, sitting across from Hayes in the kitchen of his comfortable old house, chuckled appreciatively as he recounted tales of some of Omemee's more memorable characters.

Over forty years before, it had been at this house, across the road from the old mill bridge, that a chubby Neil Young—dressed, no doubt, in the ragtag corduroy overalls he refused to let Rassy mend—marched up to the door and calmly requested that Jay's father, Austin, remove the fishhook embedded in his stomach. Apparently Neil accepted this as an occupational hazard in the life of a fisherman. "God, Neiler had little pinprick scars all over his stomach for years," said Rassy.

The old mill is gone, as is the tannery, and the train no longer stops in town, but Omemee, said Jay Hayes, "hasn't changed that much since I was a kid, really." People still get their eggs from a farmer on the outskirts of town, taking what they need and leaving their money on the kitchen table. Scott Young recalls Omemee's crime waves—the stickup man who, after robbing the gas station, found his getaway car had left without him and sheepishly went back in to return the money; and the time the bank manager's wife was taken hostage and plied her captor with cigarettes and booze until the police arrived. Hayes remembers when stealing an apple earned you "a kick right in the backside. Certainly was different, I'll tell ya, than it is today—and I don't see that much wrong with what happened then."

Founded in 1820, Omemee went through several name changes before settling on an Iroquois word meaning "wild pigeons." Although just eighty-seven miles from Toronto, the village of 750 could've been from another century, even when the Youngs lived here in the early fifties. Some residents were still without electricity. For refrigeration, Jay Hayes remembers, "a wagon came around with a block of ice." Most folks farmed or worked at the tannery, North American Leather. Doctor bills were sometimes paid "in potatoes and carrots," said Hayes. "Nobody had any money, eh."

Somehow, authors fit in. The Young household was often visited by Scott's fellow scribes. As Jay Hayes put it, "Writers? We were overrun by 'em." And not ashamed of it, as Scott Young would find out when he contributed a daily column on the 1950 Winnipeg flood to the Toronto *Globe and Mail*. "I saw myself as a real national hotshot, printed in Montreal, Toronto, across the country," said Young. Back home at the post office, he encountered a local who had taken turns with his sister reading the column aloud. "Nobody in Omemee coulda did better," the local told the writer proudly. *"Nobody."*

It was an idyllic time. Scott was able to focus primarily on fiction for the first time, writing short stories and novels. In his spare time, he took his sons for long rides in the family jalopy, entertaining them with old songs like "Bury Me Not on the Lone Prairie." Their dog, Skippy, rode along in the trunk when not watching over Neil. "Nobody got within half a mile of Neil without Skippy being there," said Rassy, who often went hunting with her father, returning home to whip up a roast duck stuffed with wild rice that people remember to this day. Unlike Bob, Neil would have nothing to do with hunting. "If they came back with no ducks, he'd laugh. He'd figure it was a victory," said Bob. "But Neil did eat the duck."

If it wasn't fishing, it was turtles. Rassy recalls trying to make soup out of a gigantic snapper "that went bad in the heat. I'm staggering around with this stinkin' turtle, and Neil decided this was funny. He was leaning on the barn killing himself laughing. Neil could never stop laughing when he started guffawing about something." Turtles could serve a multitude of purposes—as his friend Garfield "Goof" Whitney III recalls, "Neil used to scare the girls with 'em."

When asked what kind of child Neil was, Scott replied with a description that a relative had given him: "A droll little boy." Already he was earning a reputation as an upstart in school. By 1953, the Omemee principal was routinely sending home missives such as the one beginning, "Dear Mrs. Young, this small person has been causing Miss Jones a great deal of trouble over a long period. . . ." As Scott writes, Neil "had a zany kind of a wit that gave his report cards for years one constant: his teachers always wanted an improvement in his conduct."

"Neil was a great little kid," said his cousin Marny Smith. "Life was always a little more cheerful with Neil around. He never let anything stop him." Others remember him for the things he didn't do. "When we'd have summer holidays, main thing would be playin' ball or somethin'," said Goof Whitney. "Neil was more of a loner—all he wanted to do was fish."

"I was always shy," Young told Dave Zimmer in 1988. "I never took part in anything. If there was some sort of group thing, I always just sort of stood and watched." Whitney, a bit older, subjected Neil to endless tortures. "There used to be a woman who lived next door to Neil, Olive Lloyd—we used to tease her to get her goat. She was a real outlaw, this woman—she'd chase you with a butcher knife. I said to Neil, 'Call her Mrs. Peeniehammer and she'll give ya candy.' And he yelled it out, and Holy Jesus, she come right out chasin' Neil. Every time he walked to school he'd have to cross the street. He was scared to walk by the place."

Yeah, the—Peeniehammers. *That probably wasn't their name. I thought it was, because of my friend Goof. I was so fuckin' naïve. When you're a little kid and you're real gullible and you go for anything anybody said, people* remember *that. Next time you come by, they've got a new idea for ya.*

I had several pet turtles. I guess the one that comes to mind is the one that got stepped on at one of my father's parties. It was just a little guy— some of the kids were playin' with it and they took him out and put him on the floor and phhhhhhht! *A sad case. But before that, I had a sandbox and it was all full of turtles. Then I'd let 'em out or forget about 'em—which has sometimes been my history with pets.*

Omemee's a nice little town. Sleepy little place. I remember this one guy, Reel. Skinny Reel used to have this great little shop—it's still there—and there used to be all these pansies out in these wooden boxes. The sidewalk was pretty wide and you'd go walkin' along and there'd be all these boxes of pansies, the colors were so great . . . walkin' through, y'know, and it's all happening. Life was real basic and simple in that town. Walk to school, walk back. Everybody knew who you were. Everybody knew everybody.

We had a TV in Omemee. Saturday mornings—Lone Ranger—that made an impression. Hopalong Cassidy. That and toy trains . . . that was kind of my world at that time. The Tommy and Jimmy Dorsey show. The Honeymooners. Dragnet. The $64,000 Question. This Is Your Life. Jack Benny. The Perry Como Show—I remember that my mom—our family—used to watch Perry Como all the time. I couldn't fuckin' figure out what the hell that was about. Y'know . . . I just don't understand the cardigan. The stool. I mean, when I look at it now, it's pretty cool—the guy's just tryin' to be laid-back and do a really mellow show. . . . Who knows?

Out behind our house in Omemee the railroad tracks went by. Maybe a thousand yards back from the house, maybe less. I used to put a penny or a nickle down on the track so I could get it flat when the train came around. The steam engines would come through with passenger trains, every once in a while a freight train would come through. With a lot of passengers—it was the mode of transportation in the early fifties. So I was familiar with the big steam engines. I can still remember seeing them standing there . . . I liked the smell of the track, I liked the railroad bridge—which is still there. Took out the tracks, though. I've got a couple of the nails.

First train my dad got me—my dad and mom—was when I was livin' in Omemee. Marx. Got it through the Eaton's catalog. Five years old or somethin'. My dad built the table and we put the thing together. Just before I went to sleep at night I'd turn the train on. It was all dark in the room and it was right there by my bed. I'd turn it on and just watch it go around in the dark, and pretty soon that old AC motor inside would start smelling that ozone smell. I don't know if you know that Lionel smell, but now when I smell that, I remember that feeling. Trains. I find their sounds inspirational. So fuckin' big—wide—vibrating. Awesome.

I enjoyed the dedication of the school in Omemee to my dad a lot. It was *great seein' my dad and all the old-timers. . . . Principal got up and talked. At one point, the choir walked in and they were about to sing and they started talking and they were saying the words to "Helpless"—"There is a town . . ." One kid would say it, and way over on the other side in another row, the other kid would say the next line, and they just dotted around through the whole choir like that and repeated the lyrics to the first verse. That was just really moving. I was just sitting there, y'know . . . it was an emotional night.*

In some fantasy *world, I think, "Okay, I can go back there." But I really couldn't. It's not possible. At least not for the next several years. But to be able to come and go—just drop in and pull out—that's gonna work. It's funny, maybe because I'm getting older, I feel a kind of pulling from the area where I remember things as a kid. It's an innaresting sensation.*

"Neil got polio and lost all his girlish curves," said Rassy, shuddering at the memory. "Damn near died. Gawd, that was awful." Nineteen fifty-one was the year of the last major outbreak of poliomyelitis in Ontario. The virus preyed mostly upon young children, and nearly half those afflicted suffered some form of paralysis or muscle loss. There would be 1,701 cases of polio in Ontario alone during 1951, and in Peterborough, Omemee's county, seven people would die, including one child from the village.

"Polio always struck everybody to the marrow of their bones," recalled Rassy. "The worst thing was, the doctors would say, 'Well, good luck.' 'Cause nobody knew what to do." The Salk vaccine was still a few years away, so when late-summer "polio season" came, people were afraid. "In the cities the ultra-cautious walked instead of taking streetcars, and kept their distance from everyone else," writes Scott. "City or country, the fearful woke in the night wondering if that back pain was polio back pain, or that sore throat was the polio sore throat."

In the wee hours of the morning on August 31, 1951, Neil Young, nearly six at the time, awoke suddenly. The previous day, he'd gone swimming with his dad in the Pigeon River, and now, at one in the morning, his moans attracted the attention of his father, reading in bed. Neil had a sharp pain in his right shoulder blade and felt feverish. By noon the next day when Dr.

Bill came to examine him, he couldn't touch his chin to his chest and yelped in pain when his knees were bent up against his stomach. A few hours later, Neil was so stiff, Scott writes, that he moved like "a mechanical man."

Dr. Bill suspected polio and suggested that the boy be taken to the Hospital for Sick Children in Toronto. Neil, wearing a surgical mask and clutching a toy train his father bought him that morning, rode stretched out in the back of the family car. Up in the front seat were Scott, Bob and Rassy, who, despite being bedridden from a minor surgery, insisted on coming along. "Rassy never came up empty when there was a challenge," said Scott. A storm raged as Scott battled Labor Day traffic to make the ninety-mile journey.

When they arrived at the emergency room, Scott listed his son's symptoms and the nurses recoiled. "It was like a scene from the Middle Ages when a man spoke of having the plague," he writes. Neil was whisked off for tests, and Rassy, unable to bear Neil's yowls of pain as they extracted a sample of his spinal fluid, had to leave twice. "Neil refused to have an anesthetic," she recalled. "I was scared stiff."

A little while later, a doctor informed the Youngs that their son was indeed suffering from polio, and a masked nurse wheeled him away to isolation. The others returned to Omemee, where a white quarantine sign was soon placed in front of their house. Only Scott was allowed out to purchase supplies, while the family waited by the phone for word of Neil's condition. "We spent a lot of time clinging to each other in the middle of the night," said Scott.

Six agonizing days later came word from Toronto that the Youngs could take their son home. When they got to the hospital, Neil was fresh from a disinfectant bath, his black hair in spikes. "I didn't die, did I?" were the first words out of his mouth. "He was so glad to see everybody," said Rassy. "The nurses sang 'Beautiful, Beautiful Brown Eyes,' Neil crying away. Christ, he looked like hell on the highway. Skin and bones. He never got fat again."

Neil spent that fall convalescing at home. "We knew he wasn't gonna be dead, but that's about all we knew," said Rassy. "We didn't even know if he'd ever walk. His left leg wouldn't go where it was supposed to." Rassy's sister Toots came to help care for him, and the sickly boy amused himself by drawing pictures of trains. "Neil was ambidextrous," Rassy recalled. "You couldn't tell where one hand left off and the other began. I used to say, 'You'll either be a musician or an architect.' "

"When it finally got to where he could walk, he'd walk very slowly," said Rassy. "He'd walk to Dr. Bill's, two or three houses away. I said, 'That's kind of far, isn't it?' He said, 'Well, I can sit on the sidewalk and talk to Mrs. Hoosit.' He didn't want me to go, 'cause then he figured he wasn't doin' it by himself. And he fell—I knew goddamn well he was going to fall—and everybody went shootin' out of their houses to collect Neil so he didn't get hurt. He continued—went to see Dr. Bill. When Neil makes up his mind he's gonna do somethin', he does, y'know—and nothing could stop him."

When winter clothes proved too heavy for Neil's frail body, the Youngs rented a $100-a-month cottage in New Smyrna Beach, Florida. They left Canada by car on December 26, arriving in Florida on New Year's Day, 1952. They would remain there until May, allowing Neil to gather strength in the hot sun as well as his very first impressions of the United States.

Scary. Couldn't move very well. Had to lay still for a long, long time. Propped up on pillows in the bed. Then I'd fall asleep, and when I'd fall over it would hurt. I was real young and I had no idea what the fuck was goin' on. I just remember lying there, partially paralyzed. The doctor came in that morning. Later that day, we got into the car. I was lyin' down in the backseat. Sleepin'. Drove all the way to Toronto—my dad drivin', my mum in the front seat. A rainy, stormy night. Checked me in to the hospital. Got in the waiting room—the white outfits and everything— they took me in right away, put me on a table. They did a lumbar puncture, where they go into your spine and extract spinal fluid. They did that right away. That was the most painful thing they did . . . I probably didn't want the needle.

Polio fucked up my body a little bit. The left-hand side got a little screwed. Feels different from the right. If I close my eyes, my left side, I really don't know where it is—but over the years I've discovered that almost one hundred percent for sure it's gonna be very close to my right side . . . probably to the left.

That's why I started appearing to be ambidextrous, I think. Because polio affected my left side, and I think I was left-handed when I was born. What I have done is use the weak side as the dominant one because the strong side was injured.

I never gave it a lot of thought growin' up, but I think if I'd had the dedication, architecture would've been like fallin' off a fuckin' log for me. The only thing I can't do is draw. I can sketch, but my sketches are so rough, I obliterate out all detail. I used to draw this same boat. Had this big front end, came back to this little thing with a motor on it. It was like a wedge. Made it so it lifted out of the water . . . most of the front end sort of flying along, only this little part in the back where it was real skinny still in the water. I failed to take things like windage into account, heh heh. Critical flaws in the plan. I just drew pictures of things I wanted built. Plans for sailboats, plans for speedboats. . . .

I always liked building things. I like having crews working, stuff going on. Creativity. People working and getting paid and creating something—feeling good about what they're doing.

I like Frank Lloyd Wright and Gaudí . . . ancient things in architecture— like Aztec architecture. The Indians and the architecture of the tepee— basic architecture. Basic. *Think of how incredible it would be to come up with a form that could be used in the way that the Indians used the tepee? Imagine what it would be like to think of* that. *Architecture is a reflection not of the one person, but of a time and place where civilization is at. The architecture is more important than the artist, where a lot of other art, the line's kinda blurred—like, fer instance, rock and roll, okay?*

I remember drivin' down to Florida. Seein' all the new cars. Going down in the winter of '52, seein' a new '53 Pontiac. Wow. Fuck, man. With two bars goin' down the side. Unbelievable. Canadian cars were like American cars, but you never saw so many new *ones. And in Canada you tend to get the bottom of the line—people couldn't afford them because they were so expensive. I can remember seein' these new cars I'd only seen pictures of and they were all* over *the place—the cool ones. "Wow! Look at that!" I could name any car, who made it, what year it was, what model, if it was the big one or not. I knew every car on the fuckin' road.*

I love old cars. Forties, fifties. Big cars. Heavy metal. I even love new

*cars. 'Cause they get me where I wanna go. I love travel. I got hooked
on those trips when I was five, six years old. I think it was my dad. The
highway bug. I've always loved it.*
—What did the cars here tell you about the States?
Well, dreams come true, heh heh. What can you say?

"We were not a close family," said Scott Young. "There were far too many
thistles in the salad." Both sides of Neil's family were populated with outspoken, independent individuals who didn't necessarily get along, particularly the women. The rivalry between Rassy and Bob's wife, Merle,
continued unabated. To Rassy, Merle was still the goddamn foreigner
who'd once had designs on her husband. Get-togethers between Scott's and
Bob's families were intense. "When Rassy was around, everything was so
stressful," said Neil's cousin Stephanie Fillingham. "The kids would all
kind of hide."

On one visit, Bob Sr. entered his brother's kitchen expecting to engage
in innocuous conversational niceties with Rassy. "I said, 'Morning, Rassy.
How are you?' She answered, 'What the *hell* kind of a *crack* is that?' "

Then it was Merle's turn when one of the kids started crying. "Rassy
was furious—'Get that kid to shut up. It'll disturb Scott.' Jesus Murphy,
Rassy gave us a bad time. And Merle wouldn't take it, so we packed up the
kids. Scott stood on the porch crying. He said the two people he loved most
were fighting—Rassy and Merle. He begged us to stay."

Scenes like this took a toll on the marriage. At one point, Scott took
refuge with Bob's family. Bob's daughter Penny Lowe remembers her
uncle staying in the next room, weeping. "I'd get furious," said Scott. "Or
I'd get attracted to somebody who didn't give me all the hassle I was getting at home."

In 1954, while on assignment for *Sports Illustrated,* Young became involved with another woman, and on a subsequent trip away from home,
after commiserating with a photographer going through a similar situation,
he sent home a long letter requesting a divorce. His son Bob recalls being
in the car when Rassy drove to the airport to pick up his father and saw the
other woman. "We gave her a ride back to Toronto," said Bob.

Somehow Rassy and Scott managed to patch things together, relocating to a duplex on Rose Park Drive. Scott spent much of his time cooped up in a cheap boardinghouse writing his first adult novel, *The Flood*. The idyllic days in Omemee were over. "It was a terrible time," writes Scott. "The year was full of tears and recriminations and reunions and separations again."

This bleak mood would permeate much of *The Flood*. Reading the book today, one can recognize certain similarities between Scott's prose and Neil's songwriting: the restrained but intense tone; long interior monologues; detailed, dramatic descriptions of weather; even the use of a bombastic preacher who condemns all in the name of God.

Set against the backdrop of an actual disaster—the 1950 Winnipeg flood—it is the story of the recently widowed Martin Stewart, a public relations man with two young sons, Don and Mac. Martin finds himself torn between his now married first love, Martha, and a young teacher named Elaine. The book's unsettling climax comes when Don sees Elaine and his father making love and, because the boy is still attached to his dead mother, he runs away in horror and anger. Don is found, father and son reconcile, Martin finds love with Elaine, but the happy ending is tainted. Don makes his father promise they will never reveal to Mac what has happened, and the final sentences of the story find Martin worrying over what effect his actions have had on Don.

Scott admitted that the characters of Don and Mac were based on his own sons. The ebullient Mac—inspired by Neil—Martin loves "deeply and without reservation. Sometimes he thought it a little silly for a man to feel that he could tell everything to a nine-year-old and it would be understood, or that it would be understood without telling, but that was how he felt about Mac."

Published in 1956, *The Flood* was dedicated to Rassy. "She had to suffer through the writing of it," said Scott. "I had, one way or another, caused her quite a bit of hurt, and I sure as hell wasn't going to dedicate it to anybody else." Unfortunately, the gesture was lost on Rassy, who recognized herself as Martin's wife, Fay, dead from a car crash. The incident *was* based on a real-life brush with death that Rassy had while the Youngs were in Florida. "Rassy took that as a wish for her to be out of the way," said Scott. "I certainly didn't wish Rassy dead. This woman in *The Flood* was as far from Rassy as could possibly be—a quiet blonde from Toronto." But as far as Rassy was concerned, Scott had executed her. It didn't bode well for the future.

•   •   •

"We did have a new start," writes Scott about their next move, this time to a clapboard house with two acres on Brock Road in Pickering, just east of Toronto. "I believed it . . . I resolved we would be happy, happier than ever." It seemed possible. In Pickering, Young landed a daily column for the Toronto *Globe and Mail,* which led to a highly successful sports column for the paper. He also began appearing on television, doing intermission commentary for "Canada's most popular show," *Hockey Night in Canada.* Meanwhile, Bob had become one of Ontario's top junior golfers, and Neil, Scott writes, "had two main pursuits—listening to pop music on CHUM on a radio under his pillow and raising chickens to sell the eggs."

"Neil could see a nickle in the bottom of a barrel," said Jay Hayes of Neil's childhood entrepreneurial schemes. In Pickering, he would oversee both a chicken farm and his first paper route. He had a partner: His father would deliver the eggs Neil sold and help him get his papers out. In 1992, Neil would tell a reporter that his happiest memory of his father was coming home to Scott's pancakes after the morning deliveries.

It was the mid-fifties, the dawn of rock and roll, and the sounds wafting over the late-night Toronto airwaves entranced the eleven-year-old. Young fell in love with it all: rock and roll, rockabilly, doo-wop, R&B, country, even the surreal Western pop of Gogi Grant's epic "The Wayward Wind." "I really wanted to be like Elvis Presley when I was a kid," Neil told deejay Tony Pig in 1969.

"When I finish school I plan to go to Ontario Agricultural College and perhaps learn to be a scientific farmer," Neil wrote in a grade-school report, spelling out the arcane specifics of chicken financing and dramatically recounting the massacre that wiped out almost all of his first batch. "Maybe you can imagine the thrill of watching young chicks grow into healthy, husky chickens. They have more body than feathers, more feet than body, and more pep and energy than their odd bodies are capable of. It is very easy to become attached to these abnormal birds. I did."

Petunia—now there *was a chicken. She was one of the original batch. One of the only survivors of the great attack—a fox or a raccoon got in and killed all of 'em. Just took 'em all out. Just when I was gettin' things goin'. I musta had thirty or forty at first—then up to like a hundred or somethin'.*

And I don't know where the fuckin' idea originally came from, but I figured out how to get more chickens by selling golf balls. Go out and find balls in the rough and sell 'em to the golfers. A lotta kids I knew did that to make money. I'd find golf balls, sell 'em, save the money up and go get the chickens.

Things that I wanted, I'd work at them. One thing leads to another if you WANT something. I mean, I can see the other end. I'd be workin' like a motherfucker, seemingly for absolutely nothing, for a long time. And then all of a sudden I'd be in a positon like "How the fuck did I get here?" . . . Know what I mean?

I listened to the transistor radio at night. It was one of the first really small radios that you could put under your pillow. I think it was a little cream-colored one, with a little chrome thing on the front. I saw one sorta like it the other day in a junk store. Transistor radios are fuckin' great. The original boom box. Just the fact that you could have your tunes with *you. That was amazing.*

When I first really started focusing on rock and roll was in Pickering. Brock Road. I remember—I dunno how old I was, maybe ten or somethin'— listenin' to these fuckin' records. When my parents would leave, I'd turn the records up real loud and dance. Go nuts. *Like I was the coolest dancer in the world. I would always have this imaginary dance contest where I won—but I was all by myself, singin' along to records. Kinda made my own videos.*

We were quite up to date on music in Canada. We got Wolfman Jack, we got all the shit. Plus we got the funky Canadian country records, too. Old honky-tonk, raw country stuff. It was just on the radio all the time. Guy Mitchell, early, early, early Johnny Cash, "Singin' the Blues"—"I never felt more like singin' the blues." Great shit. Ferlin Husky, Bobby Comstock—a rockin' version of "Tennessee Waltz"—Marty Robbins, "Don't Worry," with the first FuzzTone guitar . . . See, that's country music—fuckin' feedback *came from country. Who woulda ever thought. But there it was.*

"The Wayward Wind" by Gogi Grant. Way out there. It's just real simple. Straight ahead. I just have this one image that keeps coming to mind with that song—where I used to live in Pickering, there's the Brock Road Public School. Just a two-room school and it's still there. I'd walk there every day from our house, and that song was on the radio at that time. The railroad track used to go right behind the school, and the trains would go by, and there's somethin' about that song—I always think about that one area. There was a little shack back there, a toolshed or something . . . I see it when I hear "The Wayward Wind."

I always remember that same stretch of road, the railroad tracks, the whole thing—every time I hear that song, it comes right back. That feeling when you're young and open, you have all these ideas. Real wide view. I dug the song a lot. You can really get lost in it.

Brock Road. That's when music started getting through to me. Early rock and roll. Real, real early—'55, '56. Elvis, Fats Domino—"Blueberry Hill." All the guys I liked had real good grooves—but I had no idea what "the groove" was, I just knew what I liked. "Maybe" by the Chantels. Raw soul—you cannot miss it. That's the real thing. She was believin' every word she was singin'. It was perfect for the moment.

"Bop-A-lena." Ronnie Self—he was a screamer, wasn't he? The energy was so focused, so real . . . that really appealed to me. "Bop-A-lena" was just hairy. Fuckin' out there. "Scoobedoobee go, gal, go Bop-A-lena"— you just . . . wow! I can't remember anything else about it, except this guy's voice—Ronnie Self, he was fuckin' hammerin' it. I wonder what he looks like today. Find Ronnie Self! Now there's a story worth tellin'.*

One of the first records I ever bought would be "The Book of Love" by the Monotones. And "I Only Have Eyes for You." 'Cause it was so slow—Shoo bop shoo bop, shoo bop shoo bop . . . shoo bop shoo bop.

---

*Wild man Ronnie Self—aka Mr. Frantic—was born in Missouri in 1938. "Bop-A-lena" was a number-sixty-three hit in 1958, and he then wrote both "Sweet Nuthin's" and "I'm Sorry" for Brenda Lee. In and out of jail, married to the same woman three times, Self— according to writer Randy McNutt—"sank into personal troubles and frustration" in Nashville, and at one point "burned his gold records in front of the BMI office." He died in August 1981 at age forty-three.

Another song I used to listen to was "Mr. Blue" by the Fleetwoods. I related to the story. That feeling—if Mr. Blue was more aggressive, he probably wouldn't be Mr. Blue. He probably would've found out either yes or no and would've been able to move on—but he wasn't. He was Mr. Blue. I think I was a little like Mr. Blue. And maybe I hadn't gotten to the point in my life where I realized that Mr. Blue could be squelched at any time by . . . Mr. Red. *Heh heh heh. And that Mr. Blue was just running the show for* entertainment *and Mr. Red was calling the shots . . . y'know?*

Chuck Berry and Little Richard? That's rock and roll. That's the real shit. Never saw them live, only on TV. Little Richard was great on every record back then, but his ballads, like "Send Me Some Lovin' "—I just love the song. "Won't you send me your picture . . ." Great stuff. His emotion was so real, and the feel was so great. I heard "Good Golly Miss Molly" last night—oh, the fuckin' beat's just all over the place and it's so rockin'—boommmboom boom boom boom boom.

No predictable white chops like Jerry Lee. As great as Jerry Lee was, he could never *be Little Richard. How's the Killer doin'? Is he bitter? Always had a chip on his shoulder. Had his feelings hurt at a tender age. Very confused about religion and women. That Baptist upbringing, that overbearing thing, with the spirit of rock and roll—a fuckin' unbelievable combination. He's one of the seminal forces. When you listen to him now and you go back to those days, it's Jerry Lee and Little Richard. That's what it is. Elvis was comin' in a distant third when you get right down to it.*

When I was a little kid, I thought Elvis was pretty hot. On TV. It was a family thing. I just dug it. "All Shook Up" was a really good record. When it came out, it just had this beat that made you feel good. It was like all of a sudden you felt like a human being. Somethin' was movin' ya, y'know? Something that defined *you. Kids get into it and their parents don't understand. That makes it great. Elvis the Pelvis—Rassy was big on that phrase. "One Night," that's probably my favorite Elvis.*
—What do you think happened to Elvis?
It's the American Dream personified. Gary Hart. Remember him? That's the American Dream, too. Another version.
—You're another version.

This is a Canadian dream. It's a Canadian version of an American dream.
—Is rock and roll the devil's music?
Rock and roll is everybody's fuckin' music . . . I would certainly hope that it's the devil's music, but it's not just *the devil's music. I think that's where God and the devil shake hands—right there, heh heh heh.*
—Were you a dreamer as a kid?
Oh yeah . . . everything. You name it, I dreamt about it. Everything. Certainly not just singin' and playin'—that wasn't on my mind that much at that point. You just fixate on things. You want to get some fish and put 'em in the little thing in your room, create this environment—that's where I was at, y'know. Heh heh.
—In your own world?
Absolutely. From the very fucking beginning. I had turtles in the backyard, and that's all I had—and I was groovin' on that. The stuff I did, I'd get so into that I missed a lotta shit. I can see that now. I'd get into things so deep that if I didn't get into it, I didn't even know *about it. And I think that it's still the same way. I don't think that's changed at all . . . and now I have to try to find that joint I left somewhere. Nothing's changed.*

Scott Young's activities as a sports columnist began to heat up, and to minimize his travel time, the family moved to North Toronto, settling in a nice suburban two-story home at 49 Old Orchard Grove. Despite the efforts to be "happier than ever," in the fall of 1959 the Youngs' marriage was once again foundering. "Rassy and I jabbed each other some, maybe even a lot," writes Scott. "We had very different views on many things, from life and love to bringing up children, and sometimes we were rude to each other in public . . . the nineteen years of pinpricks were coming close to adding up to a mortal wound. For myself, I was frankly looking elsewhere, again."

While out covering a Royal tour, Scott Young fell for the woman running the press room. Astrid Meade, writes Scott, "was divorced, had an eight-year-old daughter, drove a blue TR-3, was twenty-nine (to my forty-one), and seemed to like me, too." Scott makes a point of the fact that the relationship wasn't consummated on that first trip, but before returning home he stopped off in Winnipeg to see another old girlfriend. By the time he made it back to Rassy, Scott was feeling more than a little guilty.

"I think Rassy suspected there was more to this tour than the Royal family. I was still determined that everything was gonna work." It was not to be. A short while after his return home, Scott attended a golf tournament Rassy was playing in. "She was shooting terrific golf, but she wound up with sort of a bad score," he recalls. When he asked why, Rassy told him there was another tournament the following week and she didn't want her handicap to be too low.

"I kept saying it was dishonest," said Scott. "I'm not even sure I used the word 'dishonest,' but I implied it. I felt she was cheating and I wasn't gonna sit still for it. I knew she'd done that before, but if you get a name of being a cheat around a club like that . . . I was telling Rassy how to act, and she rejected the whole goddamn thing. She rejected the idea that it was important, and I probably got holier-than-thou."

According to Scott, the argument started at a friend's house and continued at home. By the time it was over, he had packed a bag and left the family for good. "That was it," said Scott. "It seems silly to break up a marriage of quite a few years over something as silly as a golf game—except that we just didn't have the equipment to deal with it." Rassy's brown eyes flared when I asked her how Scott left. "Scott didn't 'left'—I flung him out. There's a difference." She recalled that in the rush to pack his bag, Young spilled a bottle of ink all over the contents of his suitcase. "I thought that was wonderful."

I remember my mother crying at the kitchen table or something. I think she said, "Your father's left and he's not coming back." And I ran upstairs, and as I was goin' upstairs, I said, "I knew it" or "I told you." Yeah—"I knew he would, I knew it, I knew it." 'Cause before then, my dad had taken me out and told me if anything ever happened, that he'd always love me no matter where we were. He just said, "Y'know, there may be a time when your mom and I may not be living together . . . I got things I wanna do with my life, we're not gettin' along too well, it's not working out." It was that kind of a conversation. That it was okay. That it didn't mean he didn't love me. So I wasn't totally unprepared, but still, when it happens, you go, "Holy shit—Dad's gone."

She was very bitter. That really did her in. I think that when my mom and dad broke up, that was it for Rassy.

June Callwood remembers getting a call the day Scott left. "Rassy phoned me in hysterics. I knew what an awful tragedy it was for her. Rassy didn't have a life except for Scott. She had no outlet except for painting chairs."

Callwood was surprised to hear from Rassy at all. Since the fight over Rassy's gossiping, they hadn't exactly been close, but she offered Rassy support. The renewed friendship would last less than twenty-four hours. "The next day Bob called me and said he'd been vomiting all night," said Callwood. "His mother wasn't anywhere around, and Neil—stoic, inward Neil—plodded off to school. Bob couldn't go. He sounded awful."

Rassy's sister Toots soon arrived from Winnipeg to find the household in utter chaos. "I stayed there for three of the worst weeks I've ever lived through. Bob was up all night playing mournful music, and Rassy was having hysterics every ten minutes." For Toots, the only bright spot was Neiler, who'd tromp home from school wearing a hat with a big long feather, intent on cheering everybody up. "Neil tried so hard, the poor kid—trying to act like everything was the way it should be. He'd come in whistling, slam the door and then it went down the drain. But Neil tried every time. I hated to leave him there. I just hated to. But what could I do? I couldn't take over her child."

Snooky came up from Texas to try to help. "Rassy cried all the time. I had never seen her cry. It was absolutely awful. Rassy didn't even hear when I said, 'Don't *cry*. You don't cry over this. That's not the thing to do.' Mother would've gotten angry at Rassy for carrying on like that. She would not approve. 'Course, Rassy was crying so hard she didn't care."

Snooky said she tried to talk to Scott. "His view of Rassy was a one-sentence thing—'She leaves nothing in the bank.' Scott wasn't talking about money, he was talking about relationships—he had to start from square one every day to be accepted as a decent person. I thought it was a dirty remark. I remember the line, because I thought, 'I wonder if he ever knew Rassy.' "

Divorce just wasn't the way things were handled in the Ragland family, where Bill and Pearl had stayed together despite what some say was a passionless marriage. "If my father told you something, it was going to be that way, period," said Snooky. "If it took everything he had in the world, he would deliver on his promise. He raised us the same way—that was pounded into us. We just thought that when we gave our word, that was it. Period. You didn't turn around and change your mind on something important. I know Rassy felt the same way. She was so stunned by Scott.

"Rassy went through life laughing until then. Everything was funny to her . . . after that, it wasn't. She didn't laugh like she used to, and she drank a lot more. I don't know how much she drank, but she drank a lot. Anybody that didn't meet her until after her divorce never really met Rassy. She was never the same. It just broke her heart."

• • •

Within a couple of days of the split, Scott took his two sons out to Ciccione's, an Italian restaurant in Toronto that remains a favorite family haunt, to deliver the bad news. "I tried to explain to them that I loved them but that I didn't want to live with their mother anymore," he writes. "I'm not sure I made much sense . . . I didn't want this thing to end with the boys just going off into the blue, but I didn't know what was going to happen."

After dinner, Bob and Neil walked Scott back to the offices of the *Globe and Mail*. Before they parted, Neil reached out to his father and patted him on the arm, "as if to say he was sorry for me, which perhaps he was." Having been around Neil enough to know he isn't always the most demonstrative person when it comes to his feelings, I wondered what effect this gesture had on Scott. In reply, he launched into a story.

"If Neil was in the room with somebody who was fat or had some disfigurement—somebody who had undergone some loss—and somebody made a reference that could hurt that person, Neil's eyes would fill with tears, and this is when he was five or six years old. He was so sensitive to people's feelings—and I know he's hurt lots of people's feelings one way or another—but when he was a little kid, I noticed this. Neil just had a fantastic sensitivity for the hurts that other people carried with them, and that patting me outside the *Globe and Mail* building? I've never forgotten it."

• • •

As the family disintegrated, Neil's obsession with music intensified. Christmas of 1958 is the first time anyone remembers Neil really playing an instrument: a cheap plastic ukulele. His parents recall getting it for him as a stocking stuffer; Neil said his father had bought it for him a few months earlier in Pickering. Whatever the case, Young started to focus on making music. Scott writes that Neil "would close the door to his room at the top of the stairs and we would hear *plunk,* pause while he moved his fingers to the next chord, *plunk,* pause while he moved again, *plunk. . . .* "

What were the Raglands' musical roots? There is the meager evidence of grandmother Pearl's tormented endeavors on piano and Rassy's love for it. According to Scott, "The only thing that could move her to tears was music—especially operatic music. *The Great Waltz*—Rassy saw that five times. She would go anywhere that was showing. Rassy told me one time that the only thing in life that she would really like to do was have a great voice for singing, so there was that in the mix when Neil started to go."

Scott's side of the family was full of down-home pickers. "If it was raining on the farm, you'd run like hell for the house and get what instrument you could get," recalls Scott's brother, Bob. "Somebody might wind up with a violin, somebody might wind up with a banjo or mandolin or mouth organ. There's sort of a family pride in musicianship."

As a teenager, Neil would find out what formidable musicians the Youngs were when he attended a family funeral in Winnipeg. "When Cousin Alice died, a bunch of us got together at one cousin's house and told Neil to bring his guitar—he was getting to be a hotshot around Winnipeg," recalls Uncle Bob. "Neil walks into this little house, sees all these farmers sitting around—everything but hay stickin' out of their ears—and strikes up. Everybody starts playing, and Jesus, he was really trying to keep up. They were all goin' like hell."

Neil himself doesn't remember this tale, and because his contact with this side of the family was limited, he would retain little awareness of this tradition—although two figures in the family made a big impression: Uncle Bob and Grandma Jean.

Although Bob Young spent most of his life working as a public relations man, his first love was music. "My dad could play any stringed instrument that was put in front of him," said daughter Marny Smith, who, along with her sisters, Stephanie and Penny, performed in a traveling singing group put together by their father. "I remember Neil watching my father wherever we went," she said.

It has been assumed that Scott Young, who knew a few rudimentary chords on the ukulele, was Neil's teacher on the instrument. This claim is hotly contested by Scott's brother, Bob, who, when I first met him, despite being in his eighties and in ill health, whipped out his own Arthur Godfrey uke and tore into "How in the heck can I wash my neck if it ain't gonna rain no more?" Bob is adamant that he gave Neil lessons, although he puts the location at Omemee, which is before Neil had his own instrument. Neil also credits Grandma Jean, matriarch of the Young clan.

Jean was great, just a free-spirited musician. She's got to be the root. It's just . . . the way she was. Everybody liked her. She was outgoing— but there was always something about her that you didn't quite have a grip on. She sang like a bird and played piano. She would gather peo-ple around, sing at the drop of a hat, always putting on shows for the miners and stuff. She was a working musician. I saw her and heard her play the piano, and she was great. I wish I'd known her better, because I really think she was somethin' special.

My uncle Bob, too. He was great. He had his girls—my three cousins. He had 'em trained. I mean, they were like BOOM—"Dah daah dah daaaa!" Three-part harmony, everything perfect, y'know, snappin' along, just groovin' like hell, my uncle playin' ukulele, whatever it was, a big smile on his face and the girls all boogyin'. Then he'd stop. "Well, girls—waddya wanna sing now?" Oh God, they were great.

I started concentrating on the ukulele on Brock Road. Then I picked up on it more when we got to Old Orchard in Toronto. I think the first things were "Billy Boy" and "Rachel and Rachel" and "Bury Me Not on the Lone Prairie." My dad can play, but he doesn't play nearly as well as his brother. We went down and got the ukulele, my dad got me started. And then my uncle came along and showed me. He'd be all over the fuckin' thing—"Uncle Bob, what the hell are you doin'?" Rooop a dooop dooop . . .

I went from a ukulele to a better ukulele to a banjo ukulele to a bari-tone ukulele—everything but a guitar. I was getting into music.

"When I was in school, I always used to change all of a sudden," Young told Dave Zimmer in 1988. "This is when I was just in junior high school, and I'd wear the same kind of clothes and everything for a year and a half. Then one day I'd be wearing all different clothes and I'd never wear those other clothes again. I'd do a whole different thing . . . there's something I didn't like about obviously being who I am. For some reason, I don't feel safe like that."

Neil Young had white bucks on his feet the first time he encountered Comrie Smith, who would be one of the bright points of life on Old Orchard: Neil's first boyhood musical pal. Having met in ninth-grade math at John Wanless High School, they became fast friends over their mutual love for rock and roll. Upon entering high school in the fall of 1959, they'd meet daily in front of the A&P at the corner of Yonge and St. Germain to head off together for Lawrence Park Collegiate.

An adolescent hipster with hair piled high in an attempt at an Elvis pomp, Smith was knocked out by Young's style. "Neil bopped down Yonge Street. Very thin, very tall, with a greased-back D.A. on the sides but a crew cut on top. He had a transistor radio, white bucks, a nice sweater, black pants. Very slick-lookin' guy."

Despite her limited funds as a single parent, Rassy splurged on Neil's wardrobe, buying him sporty sweaters and snazzy corduroy jackets at an upscale shop called Halpern's. Comrie remembers Rassy more as Neil's buddy than his mother. "She was really nice and open with us. She had a kidlike feel to her. I thought it would be so nice to have a mom like Rassy—'Go ahead, do it.' The freedom Neil had was quite admired."

Comrie found a stigma involved in befriending a boy from a broken home. "My parents couldn't really accept Neil, always feeling that it would be better for me to hang out with more balanced people."

Smith remembers Young as very high-strung and deeply affected by his parents' split. "Neil was very twitchy about the breakup. He talked about it a lot. His face would usually be bright red by the time he finished." Accompanying the flushed complexion was a habit Young had "of flicking his fingers forward at such velocity as to cause a loud snapping of the fingernails." Neil somehow managed to turn his nervous tics into classroom shtick. "It was well used," said Smith. "All he'd have to do is walk in, make his face, do a flick and the whole class would break up."

Neil's antics, whether willful or chemical, made him popular with girls. "They all liked him because he was so funny," said Smith, vividly remembering Young bouncing a rubber band off the chest of one female to prove she wore falsies. "See that, Comrie—bounced right off," exclaimed Neil, who, to Smith's amazement, even managed to get his victim laughing. "If I'd done that, *pow!*"

Such behavior earned Neil a fairly permanent seat outside the vice principal's office, although even from there he managed a stunt or two. "I remember the odd firecracker soaring past the classroom window, hurried footsteps, Neil rushing back past the room to his desk in the hall, Miss Smith rocketing out the door to apprehend him en route and the class breaking up."

Then there was an army cadet inspection one very hot day in May. Comrie recalls chewing on a rubber band to keep from passing out in his uniform and black dress oxfords. Young sauntered into line wearing his beloved white bucks. Thrown out of the ceremony, Young was "laughing the whole way," said Smith. "We had to stand there for an hour."

Young felt an empathy for the more misanthropic members of his peer group. No doubt he recognized a little of himself in such misfits. Gary Renzetti was "a streetwise kid with no brains and no money," said Smith. "He looked like he'd been through everybody's garbage cans the night before." One day, Neil decided to help Renzetti through another day of harassment by clobbering one of his tormentors with a math book to the head. The next time a bully started giving Renzetti grief, Neil asked the teacher for a dictionary, and WHAM! Legend has it he knocked the hooligan out cold. "I got expelled for a day and a half, but I let those people know where I was at," Young would tell Cameron Crowe many years later. "That's the way I fight. If you're going to *fight,* you may as well wipe who or whatever it is *out*. Or don't fight at all."

It wasn't like literally "KILL!" But I did hit this person over the head with the dictionary as hard as I could, and it felt great. *I don't advise it, but it sure opens ya up. I could feel good about myself. John Wanless? You had to go at the right time. If I got there a little early, I could get the shit beaten out of me, so I made sure I arrived right on time. And when you got outta that school, you got fuckin' out. Got* away. *People used to be assholes. You know how they pick on you in school.*

There's one guy in every class that nobody fuckin' likes, that is a total weirdo. I just have to have some conversations with this person, y'know? Gary Renzetti. I hardly knew him, except that he was from another fuckin' world, this guy. Everybody picked on him. I don't know—maybe he couldn't speak English very well, that might've been it. He was very big. And the clothes he wore were like from the forties—everything was like, used. I never really got to know him very well, but I liked him. I said, "Renzetti—now this fuckin' guy has got a row to hoe—let's watch and see how he *does." It was innaresting.*

—Some people have said to me, "Look at Neil's childhood—it's a classic case of Revenge of the Nerd."

Revenge of the Nerd? Great.

—Why is that good?

Because to achieve nerd status with only homegrown knowledge of nerddom is a fuckin' great accomplishment—and I'm proud.

I had to wear these fuckin' white bucks. I liked the fact your feet were light and you could move around. I had this Sani-White stuff I used to clean 'em—this white stuff in a bottle with this sponge thing on the end—you paint *them. It's like whitewashing your feet.*

I was always about two or three years behind everybody. There was nothin' new *about white bucks by the time I started wearin' white bucks. They were like,* out. No one *was wearing them. That's when I got mine. They were enough of a statement to piss people off. They set me apart.*

After school, Comrie and Neil would head for Comrie's house at 46 Golfdale and a new Philips hi-fi belonging to his dad. Smith had it all: Jerry Lee Lewis, Elvis 45s and EPs, a 78 of Little Richard screaming "She's Got It," Roy Orbison. Instrumentals by Link Wray and Nashville pianist Floyd Cramer. Hell, Comrie even had a couple of albums: Buddy Holly and the Crickets' *The Chirping Crickets* and *Go Bo Diddley.*

Being true record hounds, Neil and Comrie had very specific tastes. "It was weird sounds we liked," said Smith. "Unusual sounds that hadn't been heard before." Comrie recalls Young going gaga over particular records, usually guitar-based, like the Fendermen's demented bashing of "Muleskinner Blues" or "I Sure Do Love You Baby," a Gene Vincent B-side with a torrid solo that utilized volume control instead of distortion. But it was the attitude of Richie Valens's cover of "Framed" that got to Young: pure J.D. hep talk featuring the immortal couplet "I was walkin' down the street, mindin' my own affair / When along came a cop, grabbed me by my underwear."

"Neil thought that was fabulous," recalls Smith. So fabulous that when the homework assignment in Miss Pat Smith's English class called for copying a poem from memory, Young scrawled down the lyrics to "Framed" and turned them in.

When not obsessing over records, Neil and Comrie attended weekend dances at Saint Leonard's or Saint Timothy's to check out the local groups. "Neil and I would stand by the stage drooling," said Smith, who still recalls the Saturday afternoon they were invited over to an older kid's house to watch the Sultans rehearse.

Inevitably all this led to talk of forming a group, and Smith remembers Neil mulling over the possibilities: Are we gonna play music with lyrics that mean something? Top-forty hits? Instrumentals? Folk music? Rassy's input was considered heavily. "She really wanted him to do more of a lyrical thing like the Kingston Trio," said Smith. "Neil said, 'Well, if we put a group together, think bongos, Comrie, think bongos.' "

At Young's urging, Smith ran out and got a set for twelve bucks. He remembers sitting on the edge of a bed, trying them out while Neil plunked away at his uke, both of them playing along with a 45 of Preston Epps doing "Bongo Rock." "We finally figured out we should have more people in the group."

One Sunday evening when Comrie's parents were away at church, the pair took it to the next level: a quartet. Neil on uke, Comrie on bongos, school chums Bob McConnell and Harold Greer on guitar and bass. "Let's go to the hop, oh baby, let's go to the hop," chirped Danny and the Juniors over and over from the Philips as the group fumbled the chords, eventually braving a run-through on their own. Said Comrie, "Within an hour, we said, 'Wow—we're gonna have to learn more songs!' "

Now they were a band, even though nobody can recall the name of the outfit if indeed it had one. But they did have outfits—gold boat-neck half-sleeve T-shirts with black crisscrosses that Neil had picked out at Halpern's. Young and Smith boldly wore the getups to school, thinking they were two cool cats—until some wisenheimer shouted, "Look! The

Bobbsey Twins!" "Talk about a put-down," muttered Smith some thirty-five years later.

We were pretending we had a band. None of us could play. Without the record going there was nothing happening.

I do remember hearing a lot of Kingston Trio at home. I remember Rassy used to play Lena Horne records, Glenn Miller, those big-band kinda things—she played those quite a bit during that period on Old Orchard Grove.

Comrie really is a cool guy. Still makin' music, has a little band. Sent me a tape—haven't listened to it. I'm so terrible. I never listen to anybody's tape.

People don't realize how little I listen to anything. Anything. *I'm untouched. I really am—compared to the input most people have, their knowledge of music and what's happening . . . I always felt that the less I knew, the better off I was.*

But I did have my own records. I remember bein' fascinated by the fact that the Everly Brothers had done "Lucille." Even though it was the Everly Brothers, I felt there was something missing—it was great, but it's not what the original was. The original—and the copy.

I started buyin' 78s. Larry Williams, "Bony Moronie." Hank Ballard and the Midnighters. "Rawhide" by Link Wray—that's the one that goes, "Dahdahdah dah dardar"? That was his follow-up to "Rumble." Those were both great. Phil Phillips, "Sea of Love." Jack Scott. I liked Sam Cooke, but not quite enough to buy the record. I did like Buddy Holly—but I didn't like that quite enough to buy the record until I bought the album that had all the songs on it. I didn't buy the singles. But with Larry Williams and some of those old records, I bought the 78s as soon as I could. Robinson's was like an appliance store, and there was this nice lady that we used to talk to all the time. I think Comrie and I went in there a lot together. It was just around the corner from his house. You'd go in, it'd be the Hit Parade. *You'd see it all: "Wow, you can buy that* song?" *Take these big things, discs, hide 'em under your arm. "I got a record here. You people have got* shit!"

I used to really love Floyd Cramer, "Last Date." That was really the only one I knew. "Dowdowdowdowwwwdow"—everything's pulled.

Everything. There's always something movin' down there. I liked that sound, so I play the guitar a lot like that . . . pull the notes. I just always have. When I first did it on guitar I thought it was really cool, but it was Randy Bachman who did it first. Randy was the first one I ever heard do things on the guitar that reminded me of Floyd. He'd do these pulls— "darrr darrrr," this two-note thing goin' together—harmony, with one note pulling and the other note stayin' the same. I thought, "I can do that if he can do it. It might take me two years to learn how, and I'll do it at half his speed, but I'll fuckin' get it."

I loved Roy Orbison from the beginning—"Only the Lonely," that was big when we were visiting that lady at the record store. Great singing, great arrangements, great records. Roy was the closest thing to Bob *in rock and roll. He was just so . . . sincere and he just stood so tall. His fuckin' records were brilliant. They were revolutionary records. Hit after hit after hit . . . totally off the wall. Voice like a fucking opera singer—singing these ballads with a Ravel's* Bolero *type of beat. What the fuck? Where did that* come *from, y'know? "Evergreen." "Blue Bayou." I loved that fuckin' record. I played that record* over and over and over. *I just loved the fuckin' track. And the vibe—the way he sings that song. That is a fuckin'* song*. There's a songwriter who sings about tragedy to such a fuckin' degree it's almost impossible to comprehend the depth of that soul. It's so deep and dark it just keeps on goin' down— but it's not* black*. It's blue, deep blue. He's just got it. The drama. There's something sad but proud about Roy's music.*

—What did you like about Del Shannon?

Same thing I liked about Roy Orbison. He used all these weird chords, and there's something about him—such a tragic character.* He struck me as the ultimate dark figure—behind some Bobby Rydell exterior, y'know? "Hats Off to Larry," "Runaway," "Swiss Maid"—very, very inventive. The stuff was weird. Totally unaffected. He was just doin' his thing. How he ever came up with those ideas I don't know.

Bobby Darin. He was pretty funky back then . . . innaresting guy. Actually, his first song came out when I was in Pickering—"Queen of the

---

*Del Shannon ended his life via a self-inflicted .22 bullet to the cranium on February 8, 1990.

Hop." I appreciated what he was doing. It wasn't that I ever got washed away with the message, although "Queen of the Hop" was pretty cool, you could see a picture with that one. "Dream Lover" was good, too. Y'know when he did the Tim Hardin song "If I Were a Carpenter"? Another completely different sound. "Mack the Knife" was cool, too. But it was almost a distraction, 'cause it was such a radical change—you were goin', "Wait a minute. Jesus Christ. This is really good, but who the fuck—is this the same guy? What the hell happened?"

That's the first artist I can remember where you're goin', "Well, shit—he just changed. He's completely different. And he's really into it. Doesn't sound like he's not there." "Dream Lover," "Mack the Knife," "If I Were a Carpenter," "Queen of the Hop," "Splish Splash"—tell me about those records, Mr. Darin. Did you write those all the same day— heh heh heh—or what happened?

He just changed so much. Just kinda went from one place to another. So it's hard to tell who Bobby Darin really was.

Comrie and Neil sometimes headed off to a special secret little neighborhood spot—whipping out a couple of pipes packed with a particularly noxious blend of tobacco called Bond Street—then ruminated over girls, bands, records and other important matters while they puffed away. According to Comrie, the conversations all had a way of creeping back to Neil's home life.

Once Scott and Rassy separated, things went from bad to worse. Scott's new love, Astrid, had been writing to him, sending letters via his brother's address. Bob's wife, Merle, got ahold of one of these letters and, perhaps in retaliation for Rassy's antagonism toward her, forwarded it. "She *knew* Rassy would recognize a woman's handwriting and open it—and read it," said Scott. "This is exactly what happened." In 1960, Rassy filed for divorce. According to Scott, Rassy told him that she'd shown Astrid's letter to their children. For over twenty years Scott believed this to be true, until he was working on *Neil and Me*. Neil told his father he'd never seen the letter. "Why would Rassy say that?" asked Scott. "She was just trying to make you feel good about yourself," quipped Neil.

Scott would be wracked with guilt for years. "First love is very powerful, and you can never be sure of some drastic action you take in relation to a marriage," he said. "I often thought that people who were really sane could handle those things somehow, make it work. There were so many good things in our marriage—our two kids, all the things we did, the career things we fought through together. . . . I think the perfect marriage for Rassy would've been if she and I had worked out and I had become a well-known writer, but without betraying the love we had sworn to one another."

Unfortunately, Scott still suffered from the marryalator blues. His brother, Bob, recalls Scott ranting on about how "he's never gonna get married again, *never,* never, *never,* and we're driving along Yorkville and there was a Northwest breeze, hot day—and an Indian girl wearing a sari walked across the street, the sari plastered to her front in the breeze. She was a beautiful creature. Jesus Murphy, Scott's ears came up. That was five minutes after he told me he was never gonna look at another woman."

• • •

In 1960, divorces were almost impossible to obtain in Canada. "There was only one way to get a divorce, and that was to prove adultery," said Scott. "That was it. And there were these guys and girls who made a living at this. Your handy divorce lawyer would get a girl, she'd sit in her slip or panties on a hotel-room bed, and the guy that was supposed to testify would walk in and see this." Rassy had one special requirement: that Astrid be the corespondent. "She had to be the woman who was found in my room," said Scott, chuckling. "It was tough being in court with Rassy."

Once the marriage was over, it was open warfare for Rassy. She attacked Scott with the same tenacity she had once used to support him. "I seriously disappointed Rassy, and there was no surrender in her makeup," said Scott. "She went all over town saying what a shit I was."

She was still saying it over thirty years later. "Scott was a very odd man—he was never proud of anything anybody ever did. Scott's got no faith in anybody doing anything unless he's running it. He couldn't stand it if somebody admired something I'd done—it really drove him up the wall. A selfish man—he had no idea what other people's needs were. A cold fish is what he is."

Following the breakup, Bob stayed in Toronto with his father, while

Neil returned to Winnipeg with Rassy. "Probably the one mistake I made was not telling them both that they could come and live with me if they felt like it," Scott recalls. "I've always regretted that, because Bob chose to come with me and I couldn't quite face the idea of Rassy being without anybody—'Okay, I'm gone, okay, Bob is gonna go, so . . .' Neil was, in a sense, I wouldn't say the victim . . . I advise people: Don't ever break up with your family without telling them that you love them and you want them if they'll come and live with you."

Bob took the divorce especially hard. "At that time I didn't wanna go anywhere else, I didn't wanna live in a different place, I didn't wanna go somewhere where I didn't know anybody," he said. "I'd had enough of moving all over the place. I played amateur golf—it was like a life-or-death struggle. I figured it was my only way out.

"There was no choice that would ever keep both people happy. From my perspective, it was a no-win situation. It caused me a lot of trouble—I think it caused Neil less trouble because he was still sort of protected in the sense that he was too young to do what I did: work."

Everything would be a battle for Bob; he would quarrel with his family, let his golf career slip away and wander through life in search of a purpose that still seems to elude him. Not long after the family broke up, Bob re-calls tramping around on a wintry Winnipeg day with Neil, each of them promising that whoever made it first would help the other with his dreams. Over forty years later, Neil is still helping his brother pursue his.

Rassy, of course, thought it all would've been different had Bob come to Winnipeg. "Scott didn't like Bob. You can murder somebody with words, just cream 'em right into the garbage by putting them down at every opportunity, and that's what Scott did."

Neil would internalize everything, immersing himself in music. Later in life he'd often find himself the seemingly passive eye in a tornado of quarreling producers, managers and musicians, all clamoring for his attention. Perhaps it is a form of affection Young can understand.

And he'd hold his cards so close to his chest that even those closest to him couldn't be certain of anything. His music might ooze with raw emotion, but as a person, "stoic, inward Neil" was frequently an impassive, impenetrable fortress.

I guess it was kinda early for divorce. My mom and dad were trailblazers, *heh heh.*
—Do you remember a lotta conflict as a kid?
Between my mother and father? Yeah—a fair amount. There was conflict. My mother was very *emotional. Extremely emotional.*
—How would it affect you?
Y'know, I don't remember. I mean, I don't have any vivid remembrance of lying there feeling bad *or anything. It happened—but it didn't happen so much that it was like a big bother. I think when my parents broke up, I realized, "Well, those were real fights." I mean, they were trying to work something out that didn't work out. Somethin' happened. I don't know what.*

My dad kind of got around a little. That's what I think. He was a really friendly guy, heh heh. My dad knew everybody, right?
—And Rassy knew that your dad knew everybody, and she kept tabs on all of 'em!
That must've burned her up, keepin' track of all that shit—and my dad was just havin' a good time. My dad is a cool guy and I could learn a lot from him. Better start pretty soon. . . .

I must've led the most sheltered life in the world—because all the shit that happened, it may have been happenin' right in front of me, but I didn't see any *of it. I didn't. I was just spaced out.*

I still can remember trying to make the best of that situation. 'Cause I thought, "Well, hell—it's not so bad. It's not so bad. *Here we are."*

I don't know. At first I cried, it blew my mind and everything but hey, y'know—on the other hand, I think I knew they weren't happy together. And I was thinkin', "God, maybe my mom will find somebody new. Maybe my dad's gonna be happy." It felt to me like we should try to just keep on goin' and be positive. I mean, I was kind of lookin' forward to the future, y'know.

It hadn't been very happy around the house. The vibes had been pretty heavy. I don't have the best remembrance of that place on Old Orchard. I remember not spending a lotta time there, spending time at other people's houses. So I think that when my dad left, part of me was happy. Now we can have some fun *around here, fer Chrissake! Y'know:*

"Let's go down and buy a new shirt. Look at the fuckin' shirts they got—sparkling shirts. Let's go. Let's get something happening here." Heh heh.
—I asked your dad what he thought you had in common. He said your outlook on women. "I used to ask everyone to marry me," he said. AHAHAHAHAHAhahahaha . . . There you go. Sounds awful familiar to me—I was wonderin' if that was him or me.

It's funny, though—people tell me what a SAD CHILDHOOD I had. What a bummer all this was, how down I seemed to be. And I listen to that and I'm goin', "I don't think it was that bad. *I don't think it was like that." But even today, a lotta people look at my picture and they think that I'm very down and I'm always low. Even my kids. "Dad, lighten up." And I'll be at the movie with Pegi, havin' popcorn—chomp chomp chomp. I'm overamping on something, who knows what it is—Pegi goes, "Come out of it, what's wrong, are you feelin' all right?" Maybe I was obsessing about some fucking detail of something somewhere, about Lionel or how am I gonna tell Billy that certain songs aren't gonna be on the record. . . .*

I work out a lot of shit on my face. I know sometimes I stress, but it seems like I look a lot worse than I am. . . . Apparently I look like I'm a fuckin' maniac half the time. Really heavy. I *think that I'm kinda a fun-loving guy. A fuckin' good-time guy.*

"When I was a young boy / My mama said to me / Your daddy's leavin' home today / I think he's gone to stay / We packed up all our bags / And drove to Winnipeg," Young would write thirteen years later in "Don't Be Denied," as his father puts it, "saying in six lines what took his mother and me a year or more to live, in bitter acrimony."

Bob remembers going to the family house and finding it empty. Rassy and Neil had vanished. "They were gone. I didn't even know they'd left."

Rassy and Neil made their way to Winnipeg, hoping for a new start. The intense focus and support Rassy once had for her husband was now, for better and for worse, concentrated on her son.

He lost himself in music on the trip west. "Neil used to bite his nails, so if he could go an hour without bitin' his nails, I'd let him play the guitar," Rassy recalls. "So that's what we did all the way to Winnipeg—which is a helluva long way."

leaving things behind

"Neil's a guy who likes to collect old things—and I definitely fit that bill," said Harper with a mild laugh.

Jack Harper—or just plain Harper, as Neil calls him—was my guide in Winnipeg. A compact, athletic powerhouse who seemed to have a million projects going at once, Harper is head professor for the faculty of physical education and recreation studies at the University of Manitoba. Married to his high school sweetheart, Pat, Jack was the furthest thing from a rocker I encountered in this project, although he does manage to sneak off and bang drums in Midlife Crisis, a motley band of old-time amateurs that performs, among other Neil Young tunes, "Cinnamon Girl"—and plays it, as Harper puts it, "not very well." They rehearse at the Crescentwood Community Club, an old recreation hall where Neil played with his first real band many decades before.

Neil and Jack met in the fall of 1962 at Kelvin High School. Jack would join Neil's band, and Neil would fire him a month later. "Harper was in track, he was a gym rat, a gregarious, very outgoing guy," said their old phys-ed teacher Mike Katchmar. "I don't think Neil hung out with a heck of a lot of people—he was a very quiet type of individual." The misfit musician and popular jock remain close friends over thirty years later. "Neil and Jack are really an odd couple—one is so outgoing, one is so quiet," said Katchmar. "Different as night and day." Yet when Neil comes to Winnipeg, Harper is the one he looks up. "I don't get the sense that Jack's changed very much from when Neil knew him," said Joel Bernstein, Young's archivist. "I think Neil's comfortable with that."

Long periods will go by without word from Young, or even a return phone call, but Jack understands. "A lot of people lose patience with Neil," said Harper, who chooses his words carefully, not wishing in any way to upset his old friend. "He isn't the greatest corresponder and he isn't the greatest communicator . . . I don't get offended by it. Neil's doin' his thing. I always hear from him when it's important." When Harper lost a parent, Neil wrote him a letter. Young can be a man of painfully few words, and a letter from his own hand is no small matter. Discussing it, Jack was moved to silence.

· · ·

"Biggest small town in North America" is how Harper describes Winnipeg. Topping the news the day I arrived was a story on a local supermarket where the checkout staff hadn't shown up; patrons took the goods they wanted and left their money on the counter.

Bitter cold in winter—as Neil said, when you walk in the snow, you hear your feet squeak—and swarming with mosquitoes in summer; one has to be of hardy stock to survive here. Incorporated in 1873, Winnipeg's location at the crossroads of the Red and Assiniboine rivers made it a center of trade and a gateway to the West, populated by a diverse mix of Ukrainian, Jewish, British, Scottish and native peoples.

"There's something to be said for the geography of the place," said Winnipeg rocker Randy Bachman, who achieved rock stardom through über-Canadian outfits the Guess Who and Bachman Turner Overdrive. "It's very isolated, in the middle of nowhere—it's almost dead center in the middle of North America." Eastern Canadians can be downright snobbish, characterizing the city as a hockey-and-prairie hicksville. "Winnipeg is nowherestown," said writer Juan Rodriguez. "It's not even the windiest city." But when asked to attend Canada's answer to the Grammies, the Juno Awards, Young said he'd attend on one condition: that Winnipeg be allowed to host the show.

"I think Neil's values were shaped by this city, the prairie mentality," said Harper, and as we drove outside the city one day, across the endless prairie, I heard the lonesome clanking of Young's *Harvest* in my head. I felt a lot of Winnipeg in Neil.

· · ·

A big music scene went on in Winnipeg during the early sixties, much of it involving a network of community clubs. These neighborhood halls—

invariably adjacent to the ubiquitous outdoor hockey rink—served families in a multitude of ways. As Randy Bachman recalls, "On Sunday night you'd find a wedding in there, on Tuesday a wedding shower, on Thursday they'd be playing bingo. Somebody said, 'Let's give Friday night to the kids. Let's have dances.' "

For a buck or under you could crowd into a club, see a band, drink a Pepsi and, if you were lucky, dance with a member of the opposite sex. Beat-up phonographs blaring scratchy 45s provided between-set entertainment. Innocence was the name of the game: Parents chaperoned the dances, the drinking age was twenty-one and drugs were still off in the future. "It was a very healthy environment," said Jim Kale. "You didn't have to worry about perverts screwing your children, drive-by shootings—you didn't have to worry about anything. It was all very civilized."

Kale played bass for Allan's Silvertones, aka Chad Allan and the Reflections, aka Chad Allan and the Expressions, eventually and best known as the Guess Who. Chad Allan (aka Allan Kowbel) and the Expressions were the kings of the community-club scene when Neil Young was coming up, and Kale in particular would be a good friend, occasionally thrilling Young by letting him borrow his much coveted Fender Concert amp, a rare piece of equipment in this prairie town. "It was the first big amplifier anybody had in Winnipeg that had the name Fender on it," said Randy Bachman, the band's guitarist and songwriter, whose playing would influence Neil's greatly. "The rest were from Sears."

There were scores of community clubs throughout Winnipeg, and they proved fertile ground for up-and-coming bands seeking to develop their chops and make a few bucks. Deejays were as popular as the bands; you were plugged on the radio and guaranteed a good weekend crowd if you hooked up with a big jock like Bob Bradburn or Irving "Doc" Steen. "Irv Steen was a bloody saint," said Jim Kale, "a big-brother type of character. He'd come out and be the master of ceremonies and take home a tumultuous ten dollars. He helped a lot of kids." CKY and CKRC were the big AM stations, and bands lip-synched on the local music show, *Teen Dance Party.* Off-duty rockers congregated at the Paddlewheel, a restaurant in the Hudson's Bay department store downtown, or downed burgers at the Red Top, where CKRC's Jim Paulsen would interview bands live on the air.

Saturday meant the ritual—take the bus downtown, have fries with gravy at the Paddlewheel, then head to Lowe's Music or Winnipeg Piano to drool over the gear. Before Randy Bachman saved up enough to purchase his beloved Chet Atkins Gretsch, there were countless visitations with Neil Young just to see it hanging in the window. "We'd just stand there and stare, like it was a naked woman or something," he said.

Then there were the nightclubs. Bankrolled by a retired farmer, the Twilight Zone, with its tiny stage, was a big hangout for bands between gigs. The beatnik folkie crowd hung at the Fourth Dimension, a coffeehouse that charged twenty-five cents admission by the hour. There was the swanky Town and Country Supper Club and the notorious Cellar, a smoky basement dive where fists and bottles flew. "The Cellar was a piece of shit," said Jim Kale happily.

Feeding the minds of all these Canadian kids was an amazing confluence of radio waves made possible by a quirk of geography. "The thing about Winnipeg is, it's what they call the top of the great plains—it's *flat,* from Winnipeg almost to Texas," said Randy Bachman. Meaning music-hungry youths could routinely pull in stations as far-flung as Shreveport and New Orleans, which exposed them to all sorts of exotic regional sounds. As Bachman recalls, "I'd say, 'Neil—were you listening to the radio on Wednesday night? Did you hear that song by Slim Harpo? Do ya know how to do the guitar thing?' 'Cause I'd actually have my guitar in the middle of the night right by the radio and hope they'd play the same song night after night. You'd try and figure out the blues chords, you'd try to scribble down some of the lyrics."

"When you move in right up close next to me / That's when I get the shakes all over me," wails Chad Allan on the Guess Who's 1965 hit "Shakin' All Over." Crudely recorded in the middle of the night on one mike at a local TV studio, with the entire band plugged in to Kale's Concert amp and awash in reverb, "Shakin' All Over" is the quintessential document of Winnipeg's early scene: Allan's desperate vocal, Bob Ashley's menacing rhythm piano, and Bachman wrenching violent exclamation points out of his Gretsch.

"Shakin' All Over" had already been a hit in England for Johnny Kidd and the Pirates in 1960. Early on, a friend of Chad Allan's had turned him on to his collection of English imports; this led to Allan's band becoming, in Bachman's words, "the ultimate British copy band." Allan would inadvertently start a trend: Many Canadians had British roots, with relatives who became conduits for overseas records. "They would send us their old 45s," said Bachman. "It was brand-new material for us. It made Winnipeg very different from anyplace else—we had this connection to England. All the top stuff, way before the Beatles or Cliff Richard."

Some of the most influential records from England in the early sixties were made by British pop idol Cliff Richard's backing group, the Shadows, who had a string of instrumental hits on their own. "The Shadows were actually a four-piece band, but they sounded like a symphony," said Bachman. Guitarist Hank B. Marvin augmented his Fender Stratocaster with two key pieces of equipment that would also become integral to Neil Young's guitar sound: a whammy bar—a metal bar attached to the bridge used for bending notes for maximum emotional effect—and an Echoplex, which creates an echo controllable in terms of length and repetition. Marvin played with gizmos like these but kept it clean and simple, the opposite of instrumental trash-rockers like Link Wray. "Hank Marvin was the greatest melodic-guitar player," said Bachman.

A big baby-faced kid with a two-year jump on Young, Randy Bachman could draw blood with a guitar from an early age. He sported a big orange hollow-bodied Chet Atkins Gretsch—the guitar of his mentor, jazz whiz Lenny Breau—that he fed in to a lethal piece of equipment: a German tape recorder that helped him replicate one of the key elements of the Hank B. Marvin sound. Randy Bachman, as Young's soon-to-be bandmate Ken Koblun recalls with awe, "was the only guy in the city with echo."

Bachman stumbled across the setup by accident. "I was desperate. I mean, you couldn't even buy an amp in Winnipeg, let alone an echo machine." Bob Ashley's mother was a schoolteacher and had a Korting tape recorder to help with French lessons—until it was discovered that by slightly repositioning the heads, you could create a gap that induced echo. "Out of the blue, I was able to get a studio type of echo that Elvis had on 'Blue Moon of Kentucky,' " said Bachman. "It blew my mind, because it was the Hank Marvin/Shadows sound, y'see."

Bachman was another fanatic when it came to sound. He'd study the solos on radio and records, then eyeball the guitarists of any bands who came to town. "I used to go see Brenda Lee and the Casuals—'Gee, the guy played the solo on the fifteenth fret'—and I'd write it down." Bachman said this was the only way to learn in Winnipeg. "We didn't know any of the notes on the guitar neck. We were all playing by fake, feel and by ear."

Whatever Bachman picked up was then transferred to a protégé of his own. "Neil would be standing at the foot of the stage, him and Koblun, and they'd be smiling, writing stuff down," Bachman recalls. "I wouldn't show him anything, but he'd see where I played it on the neck. Basically we both wanted to play the same thing—it was James Burton backing Ricky Nelson, Scotty Moore backing Elvis, Hank Marvin backing Cliff Richard."

Randy Bachman was my guitar-playin' hero. He had a big influence on me. The best player in town. Had a lot of style. Very funky. He had some kind of tape recorder that he had rigged up for his echo. It blew my mind.

I knew he'd been listenin' to the same people I'd been listenin' to—Jimmy Reed, the Shadows. Randy was a big Hank B. Marvin fan, too. Marvin had this rich tone, kind of like a brass, ballsy tone. Jet Harris, too—the bass player. They were the hot combo. Had a good groove. Those dance steps were pretty wild. Holy shit. Doin' the little twist and shake—they had to be good to do all that and play. Just playin' *that shit woulda been real hard for me.*

But Randy could really play. I couldn't, but he could—and it's still true to a great degree. I've gotten a little better, and he's still great. He's just funky—a straight-ahead rock and roll guitar player. And in the beginning, he was the happening guy. We'd go stand in the audience and watch. Allan Kowbel, he was great. Bob Ashley, the piano player, he was really cool—big glasses, kinda nerd-lookin'. Cool piano player—timing. Gary Petersen, drums. Jim Kale, the bass player, was really good—Koblun used to go watch Kale, I used to go watch Randy. But I was impressed with the whole fuckin' band. I thought they were all great. There was no weak spot in that band, until a little later. Back in Winnipeg, I listened to some old records that my mom had. They were not hard-core blues, but there was some blue in them. When I really started gettin' into it was hearin' Jimmy Reed. It must've been just around whenever I started learning how to play the guitar. And Sonny Terry and Brownie McGhee came through Winnipeg. I saw that, and I liked what they were doin'.

Listenin' on the radio, I heard "Baby What You Want Me to Do," and oh, fuck. *I just had to have everything he did. First record was* Just Jimmy Reed—*it had "Goin' to New York." Then I got* Rockin' with Reed. *What a wonderful musician. Harmonica—I can't play any of the shit he plays. I still can't. High, screechy notes, and yet they sound really mellow. So soulful and squeaky, this alley-cat sound to it, man. Completely original.* Fuck. *Unconsciously great.*

I think he uses really old harmonicas. That's one thing—with guitar strings, too—a guitar sounds better when it's funky and you're gonna break a string and you're all outta shape. Those old strings sound good. They're mellower.

When I do "Baby, What You Want Me to Do" with the Horse—I mean, I've heard other people do it before, but I've never heard anybody play it like that—other than Jimmy Reed. Because of that laid-back beat, that steady, funky thing. I'm copyin' him, it's fun, and people are groovin' on it. . . . That's the right way to approach a song like that, I think. It's not like I'm ever gonna be doin' a definitive version of that song. There's never *gonna be a definitive version on* any *of his songs—other than his.**

Jimmy Reed proved that it doesn't matter what you play—it's the feeling. *'Cause he played the same thing almost every fuckin' song—the changes were a little different, but* always *that riff—the turnaround riff. "Dededededuhduhduh . . ." Where the fuck did* that *come from? Did he make it up or did he get it from someone else, and why is it that he plays it in* every *song and yet it sounds okay? Seems to be a little different every time he does it . . . Jimmy Reed just had it. There was no bass on those records. No bass. They had a guitar tuned down—listen to any*

---

*A seminal figure of fifties R&B, Jimmy Reed was born on September 6, 1925, in Mississippi. According to his wife, Mary Lee "Mama" Reed, he shot down a chance to record with Chess Records by insisting on playing both guitar and harmonica instead of sharing duties with the far more proficient house band. In 1953, beginning with the atmospheric, melancholy "High and Lonesome," he began a long association with Vee-Jay Records that resulted in eighteen hits on the R&B charts. The second guitar that Young refers to was frequently played by childhood pal Eddie Taylor. Epileptic, alcoholic, Reed was a tragic figure. Mama Reed sometimes had to whisper lyrics in his ear during recording sessions when he was too inebriated to remember them. Jimmy Reed died August 29, 1976, some say of a heart attack; others maintain it was a fatal epileptic fit.

other record, tune in on the bass, then put his records on—you'll just hear low guitars. Pretty amazing. I still can never figure out what it is those people play. It's like watchin' John Lee Hooker. You can't tell what the fuck he's doing. [Stray Gators bassist] Tim Drummond showed me the real notes, but it still *doesn't sound right when I do it.*

Rassy and Neil's first address in Winnipeg was Gray Apartments, number 5, in the working-class neighborhood of Fort Rouge. The location had been picked for Rassy by her mother, Pearl. Sister Toots and her husband, Neil, also lived nearby and were supportive of Rassy until even they could no longer take the bitter person she'd become after the divorce. "She was antagonizing one old friend after another until she had hardly a friend left," said Toots. "Rassy never left anything alone."

Rassy supplemented her alimony by, improbably enough, becoming a panelist on a local TV quiz show. Hosted by crusty Englishman Stewart MacPherson, CJAY's *Twenty Questions* featured panelists Nola Halter, Rassy and a man named Bill Trebilcoe, who would become Rassy's last romantic interest. The object of the program was to guess, in just twenty questions, who or what the mystery guest was. It earned Rassy the grand sum of $70 a week.

It is unfortunate that no copies of the program seem to exist, because it is said that Rassy proved a lively panelist. "I think Stew was fascinated by Rassy because she was pretty convoluted," said Halter. "Rassy would ask the most bizarre questions, oh God! And the rest of us would just slide over and get ready to croak."

Rassy and Neil were quite a pair. "It was like sittin' around with a couple of martians," remembers Neil's future bandmate Allen Bates. "Rassy, this woman, she was from another planet—those black eyes, just like Neil. His eyes cut right through you. If you were tryin' to hide somethin', forget it."

"Neil was a sweetheart of a boy, lovely to his mother," said Halter. "He listened to her." In return, said Snooky, "there was never a moment that Rassy didn't think that Neil hung the moon."

Although there were a few battles on the subject, Rassy would be the first to recognize how serious Neil's obsession with music was, and she encouraged it. "I figured anybody who was practicing like Neil was—at six, eight, hours at a stretch—wasn't just fooling around. Neil was so deter-mined you knew it was a matter of time, and not long, either. That guitar grew right out of the end of his arm. Never left it for five minutes."

While attending Earl Grey School, Young took lessons on guitar from a Mr. Jack Riddell, but only two. Mostly Neil just played by himself in his room, exiting just to torture his mother. "He'd do stuff deliberately to drive me crazy. 'Ghost Riders in the Sky'—he'd play that beautifully, then go flat right at the end—on purpose." Feigning illness, Neil stayed home from school one day, only to declare himself recovered in time for band practice. Realizing she'd been had, Rassy refused to let him go. "Neil went to his bedroom muttering away. Half an hour later he came out and sang this song—it had four million verses—'My Mother Is a Fink.' I nearly died laughing. He never got one of those phony illnesses again."

The lonesome sound of Neil's music got to his mother. "To me his music always had a sort of forlorn and desolate undertone," Rassy would tell her son Bob. "At times I would wonder why his face would light up with a sort of joy when he'd play something that was so sad it brought tears to my eyes."

Neil can't come up with any particular reason why he wanted to make music, although almost every other musician I've talked to cites the same inspiration: "Anyone that tells you they didn't get into rock and roll to get laid," said Graham Nash, "is lying."

I dunno why I played rock and roll. I don't think it was to get laid, be-cause I don't think I got laid for fuckin' years after I got into rock and roll. I think I was in Fort William when I got laid. Me and a nice little In-dian and a deejay. The first time was not really that great . . . at least I didn't get any diseases. So it was good.

A Harmony Monterey. I think I bought it at the little music store in Winnipeg that had Fender equipment and old stuff . . . I might've gotten it in a pawnshop. Thirty bucks. I had two guitar lessons . . . Mr. Riddell taught me everything I know in those two lessons. I would play quite a bit at home in my room on Grosvenor Avenue. I wrote "No" in my bed-room.
—Was "No" a significant first song?
I guess it might. Not a very positive beginning to my songwriting—

"NO!" That was the chorus—"NO, NO, NO!" Maybe that's where I developed my negative attitude, heh heh. That song was my foundation. Something had to be a counterpoint to the positive things I was seeing everywhere else.

I'd work out stuff on my own. Sometimes I'd learn records by listening to 'em—like Shadows records—I'd try to learn 'em, try to figure out what fuckin' chord it was and what they were doing. I mostly learned all that stuff from watching Randy Bachman, though. He knew more about music than I did, so he'd learn it, and I'd learn it by watchin' him.

I tried to make a reverb out of a garden hose. It didn't work too well. You stick a mike in the end of the hose and wrap the hose along the way—about fifty feet of it. You have a small speaker on the other end and you put, like, a funnel on—the sound goes into the garden hose, through a funnel, out the other end into the microphone, back *into the fuckin' amp . . . I could never get it to work. But I saw this diagram of "How to Make Your Own Reverb" . . . I still wanna try and get it working someday, only this time I think I'd use galvanized conduit or something. Get a little more* metallic *sound happening.*

Outlandishly tall with thinning hair, glasses and an inscrutable face, Ken Koblun walked outside to have a smoke after our interview. This led into a mindless discussion of smoking, during which I asked him how he got started. "Neil," he said blandly. "He told me, 'Real men inhale.' "

One of the first of a hundred odd ducks Young would gravitate to, Ken Koblun would be Neil's principal musical cohort for the next few years. Koblun was equally obsessed by music and documented every gig and dollar earned in a meticulous diary Neil called "The Gospel According to Ken." When Neil asked Ken to switch to bass, Ken gave up guitar. When Neil quit school, Ken quit school. Ken would follow Neil to Thunder Bay, Toronto, even New York. As Scott Young put it, "I think maybe Neil led Ken Koblun into areas that he couldn't handle."

"It was a weird relationship," said bandmate Allen Bates. "Almost codependent. I don't know how Ken could live without Neil. He'd light all Neil's cigarettes for him—he was sorta like his right-hand man. But you wondered who was takin' care of who."

Rassy was frequently absent from the Grosvenor apartment, off with her cronies at the Winnipeg Canoe Club; Neil was often alone,"just this kid in an apartment," said Bates. Koblun would come over in the evenings to hang out. "He'd invite me over for supper," said Koblun. "A big loaf of bread, peanut butter and honey. We'd talk about music, play records, maybe watch Rassy on TV." Once Young had gotten Koblun to take the plunge and inhale, the big thrill was stealing a couple of Rassy's Black Cat Plain cigarettes and lighting up. But the main bond between them was music, for Koblun was as deep into it as Neil. So into it, drummer Ken Smythe recalls, that when they played, "Ken appeared to be in a trance— and there were no drugs involved."

Ken was an orphan who lived with this English family, the Claytons. I think his mom and dad had some problems and he didn't live with them—something about his past, there was some darkness somewhere— and he was in my room at school. He was one of the nerdiest and I was one of the geekiest. We hit it off.

We worked together well, supported each other. Ken was a good friend. He was always ready to go. And he was into it. There was a good bass player—when Ken was into it, he was pretty fuckin' cool.

The only thing I can remember is I used to get mad at him—sometimes he would take a while to answer. I'd go, "I'm talking to ya, what the fuck are you . . . " And he's still like that, only now I understand. I didn't understand anything at that point. I must've been quite a piece of work, apparently, heh heh. Who wouldn't look back on their life and say, "Wow, what a development." Or, as William Bendix would say, "What a revolting development."

Koblun and Young met at Earl Grey in Mr. White's math class. "Both he and I were suffering the same fate," said Koblun. "We were failing miserably just about all our classes." They also had one other thing in common: broken homes. "Ken didn't have parents and Neil didn't have a dad," said Allen Bates. "There was sort of a bond there."

"I thought Neil was cool," said Koblun. "I didn't think he was cool in the greasy-haircut sort of way. Neil was different—he had a brush cut. He was about the only guy in class who wore a sweater . . . I was a little disappointed he hung out with the guys who smoked." Being friends with

Neil came at a price in school. "I know some of our classmates were very anti-Neil," Koblun recalls. "I got in a fight with Sid Rogers once about Neil." Koblun doesn't remember Neil being in too many fights—"he was too sly for that"—although he does recall "there was one girl at the Earl Grey Community Club who said she was gonna beat us up. She was a hulk."

Koblun, an amateur guitarist who had already made his debut on local TV backing an accordion player, found out Neil was also a fledgling player. "I asked if I could come over and hear him play, and he was reluctant," said Koblun, who recalls Young playing a tune on his first real electric guitar, a secondhand Les Paul Jr. that Rassy had gotten him. "I said, 'That's good—what is it?' Neil said, 'It's something I wrote.' "

Young had already started a band at Earl Grey—the Jades: two guitars, vibes and the inevitable bongos. They lasted exactly one performance at the Earl Grey Community Club, playing the hits of the Fireballs and the Ventures. Then came a brief stint in a band called the Esquires.

Esquire Larry Wah has stated that Young performed so poorly he was fired. Not so, say the other band members, who recall that Young played about forty or fifty gigs with the band over a six-month period. Ken Johnson had been abandoned by his singing quartet, so with the help of drummer Don Marshall, a band was put together. Gary Reid not only had a guitar, he had a red and white '57 Olds that could serve as transportation, so he was in. Neil Young was enlisted to play rhythm. "First time I met Neil, I walked into his apartment at 205 Hugo," recalls Marshall. "He had a really cheap guitar, and he didn't have an amp, so he plugged it in to the record player."

The Esquires played their first gig at Churchill High School, a dance after a basketball tournament. Relieved by what initially appeared to be a mediocre turnout for their first public performance, the band was flabbergasted when the curtain opened to reveal a crowd numbering in the hundreds. "We about shit ourselves," said Reid. Playing a set of Shadows and Ventures instrumentals, plus a few rockers and pop ballads sung by Johnson, somehow the band got over. The Esquires began to get gigs, playing Saturday afternoons at a former country music nightspot called Paterson's Ranch House.

Johnson recalls Young as "the skinny kid with the brush cut who didn't quite look the part of a hip musician." Neil's ability on guitar was crude at best. "I remember feeling really bad for him, because he wasn't making it," said Ken Koblun. "I couldn't tell what to make of him," said Reid. "He was a lone wolf, off in his own little world—he did things his own way. I spent most of my time leanin' over his shoulder, yellin' at him: 'For God's sake, Neil, *change chords*!' "

Visiting Neil at Gray Apartments, Don Marshall got the impression Young was basically raising himself. "Looking back on it, I think he was alone more than he shoulda been," he said.

As far as the Esquires were concerned, Neil's mother was a force to be avoided. Ken Johnson recalls Rassy "really lit into me one time that Neil shouldn't even be in a band, that I was keepin' him out way late for someone his age, he's not even sixteen, he's gotta be in school. She was very tough. It scared the shit outta me."

Young's involvement with the Esquires came to an end after an escapade involving Neil and Don. "We heard on the radio that the Fendermen were playing out in Portage la Prairie, fifty-three miles away, so we figured, 'Hey, let's go,' " recalls Marshall. The pair hitchhiked, and a kind soul in a brown '64 Corvair station wagon took them all the way to the gig. On the way back they weren't so lucky. Stranded in the middle of Manitoba in the wee hours of the night, Neil called his mother. Don got the impression Neil hadn't even let her know where he was going. "Rassy came all the way out and picked us up, and she was not in a good mood. I don't think she talked all the way back. I think she thought I was leading her son astray. Back home, she told Neil to quit playing around with this shit because he'd never make any money out of it. So that was the last time we played with him."

When word got back to Scott that Neil had been stranded in the middle of the night hitchhiking, he let Rassy have it. In retrospect, Scott regretted his meddling. "Rassy and Neil's relationship—and Neil's approach to life—had gone far beyond what I knew, so I was wrong in that sense.

"Rassy would do anything in the world for either Bob or Neil," said Scott. "But it came with a price, and the price was a sort of unswerving loyalty—which I don't think would work very well with Neil. He's never said a word to me, but I just know.

"Rassy didn't keep any kind of a firm rein on Neil at any time, of course.

Eventually I came to understand he didn't need a firm rein. He knew where the hell he was going—instinctively."

When I grew up, Rassy was really all I had as far as bein' around. She was a big supporter during the early times, a very big supporter. We had a lot of fun. She was real emotional, though. If you'd get her too upset, she'd go off the deep end.

I love my mom, she was so wry and down. When people would say, "Your mother's crazy, she's really obnoxious," I would be going, "Goddammit—she thinks she's bein' funny." Her humor got so dry that she forgot it was a joke.

She had a boyfriend for a while. Bill Trebilcoe. He was her last flame, I think. Big, tall, bald guy—horn-rimmed glasses and polka-dot shirts. Great guy. Real gentle. That's the last time I really saw her flowering. She started wearing bright-colored clothes . . . she just changed. He got some disease and he died.

—Did Rassy understand you?

I don't think so. No. Does your mother understand you?

Rassy let that music grow, she let it do its thing. She tried to support it. And that really became her mission in life. I mean, she was on a mission from God. We'd practice in the living room. She was there, wandering around in her bedroom. Towards the end there, when a few of the guys were gettin' to be over twenty-one, she'd bring 'em beer, heh heh.

Rassy was pretty funny on TV. That was pretty out-there. I've had an innaresting family. My dad was on a quiz show, too. I'm breakin' the fuckin' chain. No quiz show. Gotta draw the line somewhere.

—Once Scott was gone, Rassy focused on you?

Yeah. And I think that something happened there that I wished hadn't happened. Meaning I think that she focused on me so much that it just made things kinda out of perspective with women. So I have all these built-in reactions because of the way my mom treated me. 'Cause my mom's biggest tool to get me to do things would be to cry. I think she used EMOTIONS to control me—instead of talking to me. If things didn't go right, she would start crying, and that always—I couldn't do anything. So now, to this day, if a woman starts crying, I can't—I can't—

I can't handle it. I just want everything to be all right, *whatever the fuck it takes. And that's probably not a good thing, because you get wishy-washy about things. So I've had to deal with that in my life. I was kind of* trained *to* cave *when she cried because I couldn't see myself dis-agreeing with my mother. Immediately I would feel like "Well, fuck, what have I done? What can I do?" And that just passed on to my rela-tionships with all women. I have a tough time holding a position that I may feel is* right *if they start crying. It's a problem. So really, my whole psyche with women came to the point where if they start to cry, I fuckin' cave. Which I suppose is not much different from any* other *guy, heh heh. I think it would've been different if my dad had stayed—but I'm not positive. In retrospect, it would've been nice to have had my father's point of view on some of the things that were happening. It woulda been nice to hear what* he *woulda had to say about it. That's somethin' I didn't get. But I got a lotta other really good things from my dad. So that's the balance.*

—What was the hardest thing for you to accept about Rassy?

Well, I think the hardest thing for me to accept about her—and still is—is that it's quite possible that during the entire time she was bringing me up, she was a raving alcoholic. Now, I still don't know if it's true, but now I think it's possible. *And that I just didn't recognize it.*

Despite whatever initial protests might've been made by his mother, Young continued to play in bands. In the fall of 1961, Young began attending Kelvin High School and Koblun went off to Churchill High School, but the pair still played music. The Stardusters, aka (perhaps) the Twilighters, played one known gig at a Kelvin dance in February 1962. The Classics lasted long enough to play a handful of gigs toward the end of that year. But it was over Christmas vacation, 1962, that Young would put together his first real band. They would have uniforms, a pile of shitty homemade equipment and even a fan club. The Squires (were the Esquires pissed off by the name? "You bet we were," said Ken Johnson) played everywhere, from gigs on the back of flatbed trucks in subzero cold to performances between wrestling matches. As Ken Koblun said proudly, "At one time we were third best band in the city."

Kelvin High was known as a school for Winnipeg's elite; it was Neil's attendance at Kelvin, coupled with a new address in the River Heights district, that prompts Randy Bachman to say, "I was from the wrong side of the river and Neil was from the good side." Toward the beginning of Neil's tenure at Kelvin, he and Rassy moved to 1123 Grosvenor Avenue, occupying the second floor of a nice old brick and stone home. The Youngs might have had the address, but they didn't have the money.

"Neil stood out," said Mike Katchmar, Kelvin's phys-ed teacher. "He was a tall, gawky-looking character—I always worried if there was a strong wind we'd have to put lead in his running shoes just to keep him down. Throwing a football at Neil? Well, you hoped it didn't hit him in the head. Kind of an awkward individual." And yet Neil managed to get Mike Katchmar's goat; Jack Harper recalls him coming to gym class in such getups as Bermuda shorts and street shoes. "Neil went to Kelvin for two and a half years and never had the outfit," said Harper. (When Young performed in Winnipeg decades later, during a 1996 Canadian tour, he dedicated a song to Katchmar, "Fuckin' Up," the chorus of which is "Why do I keep fuckin' up?" ad infinitum.)

"Neil was a nonconformist," said Katchmar, frowning at the memory. "He didn't mix with a lotta people. A loner is a good way to describe him." But he made friends with Harper, the gym rat who played drums—albeit only a marching drum—and was also friendly with Allen Bates. Class president and a varsity basketball player over at Grant Park High, Bates was classically trained on guitar and full of jazz licks that would never surface in Young's funky band.

Young, Koblun, Harper and Bates started playing in the drummer's basement. Young named the band the Squires, picked the material and, said Rassy, "Anybody who didn't make rehearsals was out on their ear so fast they didn't know what hit 'em." After a month of practice and a handful of gigs, Harper was out. "I remember saying, 'God, I don't think I can make practice—I've got hockey.' Neil said, 'Well, that's okay—we'll see if we can get another drummer.'" There was no confusion as to who was the leader. "It was Neil all the way," said Koblun.

"Neil was intense, driven and focused," said Allen Bates. "When he was eighteen he appeared to be twenty-five. He took control and he knew what the hell he wanted to do. Neil never showed any weakness in the time I saw him . . . he was hard as nails. You get that with kids whose fathers are gone. They feel sorta stranded in a way, so they gotta take over, they gotta have total control. That's the way Neil was."

Ken Smythe, another Grant Park student, took over on drums. The Squires' repertoire of instrumentals ran the gamut from old pop tunes and waltzes to the inevitable Shadows covers, as well as Neil's originals. Young's prolific output knocked the drummer out. "Right from the beginning, Neil had his own stuff. Half of our stuff, easy, was his own. It just kept comin', one after another . . . it seemed to be endless: 'Come to practice, I got a new tune.' And it always seemed to be catchy." Said Bates, "Neil was writing really nice melodies with nice harmonic changes in 'em. Something your ordinary run-of-the-mill guitar player wasn't doin'.'"

This lineup of the Squires would be the most stable, lasting a little over two years. The band played their first official gig on February 1, 1963, for the grand total of five bucks. Soon they had a small following, playing community clubs and CYOs around Winnipeg and hooking up with CKRC deejay Bob Bradburn. Five months after their first gig, they managed to snag a recording date. On July 23, Neil and the boys would enter the tiny studio of CKRC radio and lay down two instrumentals, with engineer Harry Taylor turning the big knobs on the primitive two-track console. Eight weeks later a two-sided single of "The Sultan" and "Aurora" would be released by V Records, a local outfit specializing in polka bands.

"I thought you'd go down, do three takes, pick the best one," said Smythe. "We didn't just sit down and play the songs—it was put together." The resulting single had some amusing touches, like Smythe intermittently hitting a gong and Bradburn whispering "Aurora," but sonically the record is so dim it sounds like it was recorded over the phone from Siberia. "Shakin' All Over" seems as polished as *Sgt. Pepper* in comparison. "The Sultan" was a likable surf number, and if you strain, you can hear in "Aurora" the crude beginnings of the dark, descending minor-chord Del Shannon–style mood pieces that would eventually lead to "Like a Hurricane." As exciting as it was to have an actual record out, what made more of an impression on Jack Harper was Young's continual frustration. "I remember Neil never being satisfied with the way things sounded. He was searching for the right sound. Neil was so driven."

• • •

Young was on his way, and another avocation bit the dust in the process. "I almost was a professional golfer," Young told deejay Tony Pig. "I used to wear alpaca sweaters, I was on a whole trip. . . . I came to a new realization about a lotta things when I turned eighteen, and I sold my golf clubs and bought another guitar which was good enough for me to play in front of more people."

That guitar was an orange Gretsch not unlike Randy Bachman's. Young had smashed his Les Paul Jr. after he received one shock too many, and after some maneuvering, he bought the Gretsch from Johnny Glowa. Now he had a band, songs and a worthy ax.

It was an innocent time. Koblun fondly recalls tooling around town in Rassy's blue Standard Ensign. "Neil was driving, I was sitting in the passenger side, had my foot out the window. It was a beautiful spring day, playin' hooky from school. 'Duke of Earl' was on the radio." The Squires were happening.

Harper. Bates. A character. We had a good time. He has a sense of humor, Bates. I love to go up to Canada and have a beer with Jack and Bates.

I remember the outfits the Squires used to wear—off-banana shirts, vests with ascots. We were some cool-lookin' dudes.

Bluegrass Bob and the Bobcats—that was the name of one of the bands that used to play at Paterson's Ranch House, where we used to play a dance party on Saturday and Sunday afternoons. One time we got a hundred people—that was our biggest crowd. We'd go there and play, and they'd advertise us on the radio and the guy charged people to get in. We'd get paid a percentage of the door, but then when you had to go talk to the guy, you felt like you were gonna get killed or somethin' just for bein' there. What a fuckin' deal.

I don't even remember what the percentages ended up being or anything like that, but I know I always had the feeling like "Wow—that doesn't seem right to me. But I'm not gonna say anything to that guy." Big potbellied guy, I think he had a gun or somethin' in his desk. I was fifteen or sixteen. Fuck.

• • •

"You knew when you went out with Neil that you had to bring money," Fran Gebhard told John Einarson. "And you had to carry his equipment, too."

Young had plenty of female friends in his early years—Susan Kelso, Jacolyne and Marilyne Nentwig, Fran Gebhard—but in matters of teen romance, he wasn't exactly lucky. Edna Stabler, a friend of Scott Young's, recalls Neil visiting for the weekend and taking the girl next door out for a walk. "She was a pretty little blonde, and he got a little bit fresh—not too bad, wanted to kiss her—and she slapped his face." Neil was so flustered, said Stabler, "he forgot his gray flannel trousers."

One girl in Winnipeg would become his sweetheart: Pam Smith. A vivacious blonde—"Neil loved my hair very short. I used to cut it with a razor blade every day"—Pam and her twin sister, Pat, were spending the summer at their family's cottage in Falcon Lake, a vacation spot east of Winnipeg. Neil and his buddies Jack Harper and Jim Atkin also headed out there late in the summer of 1963, and one day Neil moseyed into the drugstore where Pam was working.

"Neil had a very nice smile," said Smith. "He struck me as a very sincere person. Outwardly, he'd present an attitude of being very lighthearted, laugh a lot at things—he seemed like a leader with the group of friends he was with. But I think underneath it he had a much more serious side. I felt his mind was always working. He was a loner.

"I liked Neil best on our own. When Neil told you certain things, you sort of felt privileged—you just knew he wasn't telling everybody. He didn't talk carelessly about certain things in his life."

Young confessed to Smith his anguish over not being athletic. "It was something Neil wasn't capable of doing—he almost felt apologetic about it. Neil was insecure as a person—I think that's why playing music was so good for him. He had all the confidence in the world in that role, whereas in the person role he had so many misgivings. . . . He wanted to be a regular guy, he wanted to fit in. He didn't feel that he did, and even if you told him he did, he wouldn't believe it. Neil knew he was different."

Young was particularly sensitive about the frail body that polio had left him with. "Neil wouldn't swim. Part of that was he didn't want anyone to see him without his clothes on. He was uncomfortable about his body being skinny."

Neil also discussed his parents' breakup, telling Pam that when it happened, "He had to go to court. He was asked which parent he wanted to live with—it was just an awful situation for him." More than once he would regale Pam with recollections of the pancake breakfasts he had with his dad. "He was wistful about it. Neil dwelled on those memories . . . he needed a father in his life."

Smith got a thrill jumping in Rassy's broken-down car and accompanying Young to gigs at bohemian coffeehouses like the Fourth Dimension. "I just loved it—it was the kind of place my parents wouldn't allow me to go to," she said. She knew Neil was deep into the music when his leg buckled in and out. "It was almost a quirk, the old knee—you'd loosen the bolt and there it went. I found that endearing. Neil was so committed to his music. I was so proud, I could hardly stand it. . . . I always believed in him and I always encouraged him to go for it."

Neil was a gentleman. One night when the pair stayed out too late, Young accompanied her to her door rather than dropping her at the curb. "It was so great . . . my mum came out right away, and he apologized for having me home late and the reason why. I didn't get in heck at all. Neil was always a responsible person."

But after five months, Young abruptly broke off the relationship. "He came over one night and asked for his ring back," she said. "I was kind of dismayed by it." A few months later, Young tried to rekindle the relationship. The always broke musician took Pam out to the local Dairy Queen. "This was a big deal—Neil was buying ice-cream cones. He touched my hand and looked at me and told me he loved me, simple as that, out of the blue. I didn't know how to handle it, didn't know what to say . . . I said, 'You love me and I love ice cream!' Isn't that awful?"

The pair wouldn't get back together, but Pam Smith would linger in Young's mind for a long time to come. Aside from that relationship, his ability to connect with the opposite sex remained dismal. Future Squire Terry Crosby recalls one night out on the road when things were so dire that another Squire-to-be, Doug Campbell, "offered his girlfriend to Neil because Neil didn't have a girlfriend. I think Neil was driven by a lot of problems he had in his life—the polio, his parental breakup. Things just didn't seem to work out. He was hung up on girls, scared of them."

The one woman looming large in Neil Young's life—Rassy—had little desire to discuss the subject. "Neil didn't have any girlfriends," she said tersely. "He was too busy playing music."

I was living on another world. A music world. Everybody else's life centered around girls and dances and sports. My life centered around music. If I was gonna go to a school dance, it was because I had a gig. I was gonna make fuckin' seven-fifty that night, or the band was gonna make twenty-five bucks. That's why I went to the dances—to play. So the social part of it I missed.

After we finished playing, that's one of the first things you started workin' on! But we didn't have all night to get practiced at the art like everyone else who was out there hustling. It was an innaresting way to grow up. Went from not knowing anything about girls and not really knowing how to relate to them to havin' them all throwin' themselves at you when you're startin' to get famous. I didn't know what to think of it, but that was life.
—Was it easy for you to deal with women?
No it wasn't. I dunno where that came from—but it definitely wasn't easy. It had somethin' to do with my mother.
—How was Rassy about girlfriends?
She wasn't very supportive *of that side of life . . . I dunno. I don't remember any big advice coming from her about any of that.*
—Rassy was a very strong personality.
Very dominating—just like all the women I've known in my life. From Pam on. I like them like that. And strong personalities, I think, especially at a young age—I think they would do things and wouldn't realize the damage they were doing—they wouldn't realize what they were dealing with. I didn't really have any guidance to what a guy was supposed to be like— what you could take and what you couldn't . . . I'm still learning.

Girls would feel so incomplete *when they'd go with me to play music—it kinda leaves a void. It's like, I'm* gone. *What the fuck happened to* Neil? *And that's very disturbing.*
—"I Wonder," a Squires song, has to do with your girl ending up with another guy. Was that inspired by a real event? Pam remembers you coming over once and she had another boy there.
Maybe that had somethin' to do with Pam.

—There's a weird undercurrent of betrayal that runs through a few of your songs.

Yeah, well, that's true . . . I don't think it's Pam—although it may have been something that I buried. Something about it is unsettled, because I feel emotions when I talk about it.

—Is this a policy with you—anything unpleasant, cut loose from your mind?

It's not a policy—I think it's the way my subliminal mind works. I just remember all the good stuff. Maybe in my subconscious are these things that I don't even wanna think about, I don't even remember—because I've kept 'em so behind closed doors inside my own mind. And that might be the feed for a certain feeling that comes out of my music.

—Pam remembers reuniting with you at the Dairy Queen where you professed your love and she responded, "You love me—and I love ice cream."

Yeah. I'm sure I thought about that for a couple of weeks.

—Pam thought you had.

Heh heh. I can't think of anything about Pam that ever happened that wasn't a good thing. For instance, I know we must've broken up, but I can't remember that. I prefer to remember the feeling of those times without having to try to be specific, 'cause it seems like the more specific you get, the less the feeling . . .

Pam's just a real nice girl. Good person. We really had fun together. She was lighthearted, she was just fun to talk to, fun to be with—and beautiful.

She never ever did turn on me, heh heh. That's what I like about her the best, 'cause I remember she always had a kind word for me.

I'm too intense. I made Pam nervous. All I remember now is that I know she loved me as much as I loved her. She may not have been able to say it, but I know.

"I was playin' tennis, and Neil came over and said, 'I just heard these guys—they wear their hair way down on their forehead, they're called the Beatles,' " recalls Allen Bates. "He was all fired up."

The British Invasion took Winnipeg by storm in early 1964, and as usual, first to pick up on the trend were the Reflections, who began doing

Beatles tunes in their set, turning the Squires on to the new sound in the process. Young's hero, Randy Bachman, went as far as trading in his beloved Gretsch for the mop-top instrument of choice: a Rickenbacker. Beatlemania would force another major change besides bowl haircuts and boots, for the Squires' instrumental-only sound was no longer enough to make it on the Winnipeg scene—you had to have a singer. In the era of Paul McCartney, Cliff Richard and Roy Orbison, Young's high-pitched warble definitely stood out. As Ken Smythe recalls, Neil's first attempts at vocalizing during rehearsals in his basement didn't exactly set the world on fire. "My mother was a music teacher, and she used to think we sounded pretty good down there . . . then Neil started singing."

"Neil wasn't sure he could sing," said Koblun. "I think it was the economics of the situation that actually drove him to sing, because if we got a singer, that would cut down the share of each person in the band." Neil's first memory of singing in public is doing Beatles covers in the cafeteria at Kelvin High. Somewhat later, at the Squires' next CKRC recording session on April 2, 1964, the band recorded a batch of Young's originals, among them a vocal entitled "I Wonder."

After the session, engineer Harry Taylor bluntly told Young, "You're a good guitar player, kid—but you'll never make it as a singer."

I just wanna tell ya, Harry—you're absolutely right! But unfortunately, for monetary reasons, I'm gonna have to sing. That was a major factor—when you consider we were makin' twenty dollars a night for four guys, to add another guy would cost you a buck. I figured, well, I'll try to do it and see what happens. It wasn't because I really wanted to be the singer that I thought, "Oh wow, I can't wait to get out there and sing."
—What reaction did you get to your singing?
Well, it couldn't have been overwhelmingly great, okay? The first time I actually stood up and sang in front of everybody, that was a fuckin' trip. I still remember the day. I was scared shitless. We played at a school— set up our shit and played right there in the cafeteria. I think we did "It Won't Be Long" and "Money." And went to class.
—Did you feel less scared shitless after you sang?
Uh-huh. After exposing myself in that way, I think I heard the odd cry of

"*Boy, don't do* that *anymore." Heh heh. I don't really remember the re-action, though—I remember more how I felt. I felt great, 'cause I'd* sung.
—And you were gonna sing more.
Yeah. I wouldn't characterize it as a test—that I was gonna sing, and if it worked I would do more, heh heh. When you start singin'—unless everybody yells at ya, "Don't ever do that again"—I think you keep singing. I kept trying to sing. I was trying *to sing, heh heh. My own voice is a fuckin' mystery to me. I don't know where it is. It sounds so different all the time. I can sing soft and it sounds like one guy, I can sing loud and screamin' and it sounds like another completely different guy. I got several different voices in me. And the looser I get, the more I sing—the better I get.*

Canada was pretty musically aware. You got a lot of off-the-wall records in Canada that didn't even make it in the States. For instance, the early Beatles records. We were into them way before they did the Sullivan Show. *The Beatles were number one across Canada* before *the States. All the real early ones, "From Me to You"—"She Loves You" was number one, and it never made number one in the States. So we got all the English stuff immediately.*

But I think I was more into a lotta the funky music I liked. Wolfman Jack. Dick Biondi, he was the fuckin' big deejay back then in Chicago. WLS. You'd pick it up in Winnipeg. American Bandstand . . . Shindig *with Leon Russell, we had access to all of those things. I saw the Crickets after Buddy Holly died. Glen Hardin on piano, Sonny Curtis, Jerry Allison—they were great. They just didn't have Buddy with 'em. They played in a roller rink at Winnipeg Beach. I remember watching them set up their own stuff. They had a Cadillac and a U-Haul. Those were the days.*

I saw a Dick Clark Caravan of Stars with Fabian as the MC. This is after he'd already come and gone. He kept comin' out sayin', "Don't worry. I'm not gonna sing." I saw Roy Orbison at the top of his fucking game in '61, '62. Winnipeg. Roy and the Candymen. They kicked ass.

The Beatles were exciting because they were a group. They made bands popular—that's how the Beatles affected me. I was really im-pressed with them at first, but they didn't stay together for very long, so you kinda lost touch with what they were doin'. The Beatles made a real fast contribution. Heavy. A lotta stuff dumped.

What did I think of John Lennon? I thought he was great. Innaresting character. So idealistic. Never did get to see him play live. I wish I could've gotten a chance to play with him. Probably would've been good.

The Rolling Stones, now there *was somethin', because they kept goin'. They didn't just last for five years. It took them longer to make a great contribution. The Beatles made their contribution in about five years, bang, gone—right? The Rolling Stones came out with "Miss You" way after, years after the Beatles broke up—and when you think of the Rolling Stones, that's one of their best things, that* Some Girls *album— and that's with Ron Wood, y'know. They'd gone through a lot of changes. I liked the fact that the Stones lasted so long and kept making vital music.*

What I really really liked about the Stones was Brian Jones and Keith Richards playin' together. Even though Brian Jones was just kind of a bratty, sub-blues kind of guy, he still had the exuberance. Brian Jones was a very funky part of that band in the beginning, man—all the slide shit and everything? He was really wild, Jones. Too bad he was so crazy. A druggie. They were all young, goin' through a lotta changes real fast. Brian didn't make it.

"Satisfaction" was a great record. "Get Off My Cloud," even better record. Looser, less of a hit. More of a reckless abandon. "Get Off My Cloud"—I know it's not as good of a song, and I know that the perfor- mance is probably not as good as the "Satisfaction" performance, maybe it is—but the thing about it is it's obviously *just such a fuckin' throw-together song that they came up with on the way to the studio or the night before, y'know? That's what I liked about it. It really sounded like the Rolling Stones.*

I remember hearing one of the real early ones—"I'm a Man." It was really rough and crude. . . . It was when yer learning how to play, checkin' out songs, learnin' songs. You kinda look at things different, not so much what the song's saying as, is it hard or easy? If it is easy, does that mean they can't play? Are they good or bad? You're still working those things out. And then you can get so hung up playin' a bunch of chords and changes that you lose the thing. . . . You don't realize that the easy stuff is the hardest. To make the easy stuff be great.

• • •

*In the early days, when I was in high school, I was tryin' to fig-
ure out what I was doin'. . . . I thought maybe I'd like to be one
of those rockers that could bend the strings and get down on my
knees and kinda make everybody go crazy. And then I wanted to
be that other guy, too—just have a little acoustic guitar, kinda
sing a few songs, sing about things that I really felt inside myself and things I saw goin' on around me.*

*And then I saw Bob Dylan, then I saw so many others, Phil
Ochs, Tim Hardin, Pete Seeger, and it all started comin' together for me—but I still couldn't forget about that other guy
with the guitar, jumpin' around. . . . I saw what I wanted to do
with my life.*

—From Neil Young's speech inducting Woody Guthrie
into the Rock and Roll Hall of Fame, 1988

"Neil had just discovered Bob Dylan," said Joni Mitchell. "He was going
from rock and roll to a folkie direction. The concept of writing more poetic
lyrics had just occurred to him, so he was checkin' out the coffeehouse
scene." Joan Anderson was another aspiring folksinger making the rounds
when she first encountered Neil Young at the Fourth Dimension in mid–
1965. Way on the outskirts of Winnipeg near the university, the club was
part of a chain, a "little circuit of three or four cities where you could go
and play all the 4-Ds in a row," said Randy Bachman. For a young Squire,
the experience was pretty bohemian. "Low lights, lotsa candles and incense, lotsa chicks with no brassieres," said Allen Bates.

Mitchell and Young were kindred souls of a sort; both young, intense
and painfully unique. It must have been like two aliens recognizing each
other out on the prairie. Although never as tight as some have imagined—
both are essentially loners—the two artists would frequently cross paths in
the years to come. "Neil and I have a lot in common: Canadian; Scorpios;
polio in the same epidemic, struck the same parts of our body; and we both
have a black sense of humor," said Mitchell. "Typical Canadians." Mitchell
recalls ending up at a sporting event with Neil, watching Rassy curling.
"Rassy was brassy. Tough prairie stock."

Mitchell never got a chance to see the Squires at the 4-D, which was too bad, because once Young talked the club into taking a chance on a little rock and roll, the band got the beatniks in a tizzy that February 1964. Band members recall that the Beatles covers scored big, even with Young's tentative vocal attempts. "When we did 'It Won't Be Long' at the 4-D, we actually got a hand," recalls Bates. "Neil came back later and said, 'They liked it! They liked it!' He was really fired up."

The 4-D would become a favorite hangout and, for the perpetually destitute Young, a source of free meals. Undoubtedly all the exposure to folk music was putting ideas in his head, expanding his musical vocabulary beyond fifties-based rock and roll. He would never forsake his roots, though. Part of the beauty of Young is that he cut his teeth in a geeky instrumental band that lived to play "Rumble" and mean it, and unlike many of his folkie contemporaries, he would never forget or dismiss the intensity of the great big fucking noise that had blown his mind in the first place. There was room in Young's soul for "Bop-A-lena" and "Don't Think Twice, It's All Right," for the serious guy with the acoustic guitar and the string-bending rocker—sometimes in the same song. In the next year or so, Young would find that while he was in the fourth dimension, he could be both.

I was innarested in the Kingston Trio, Peter, Paul and Mary at the beginning. Way back there when it was popular, a college thing—then Dylan. Folk music, the coffeehouse thing. I liked it. Music all the time. People. Hang out, smoke cigarettes, drink coffee. It was fun. I'd go to the 4-D and hang out. Never had enough money. I could always get in for nothing.

"Four Strong Winds" by Ian and Sylvia. It meant a lot to me. I remember playin' it down at Falcon Lake where Jack and Pam and Pat and I were, listening to it over and over. Just the song, melody, the whole thing. It had a message too, y'know—leaving things behind. That feeling of something's not gonna work. There's a feeling in the song that I related to.

—Who first turned you on to Bob Dylan?

Bob. He just came over the airwaves—in Winnipeg. This is when I was tryin' to figure out a way to get a visa to go to the States, some way to go to L.A. directly from Winnipeg. I was hangin' out with these kids who went to this private high school that I couldn't go to because we couldn't afford a private school. Some pretty cool people who were older than I was. They had Freewheelin' *or his first album. That's when I heard it first. I was diggin' it.*

I said, "This guy's a real character." First time I heard it, I knew I liked it. His voice was so different. I never heard anybody sound that different. Guess if I had been listenin' to my own voice, heh heh . . . There have always been a lot of weird voices. How 'bout Ray Peterson— "Tell Laura I Love Her"? Now there's a weird voice. Roy Orbison's got a weird voice. Beautiful—but weird. Opera-velvet kind of a sound.

I liked Bob's voice when I first heard it. I just said, "Hey, there's a guy who sounds different doin' this thing, too—I really like this guy. I can write songs."

Since the family split, Scott had become a distant figure in Neil's life. For the most part, communication consisted of Rassy's irate phone calls for more money. "Rassy was difficult," said Scott's second wife, Astrid, who recalls an operator actually disconnecting a call due to her foul tongue. Astrid also remembers Scott being frustrated by the lack of information concerning his son's academic career. "There were a lot of demands made with no information given," she said.

Both Pam Smith and Jack Harper recall Neil's nervousness over the infrequent meetings with his father. "He seemed so distressed about it," said Harper. "I remember saying, 'Gee, do you want me to come with you?' No, he said, he was gonna handle it himself." It was during such a visit in May 1961 that Neil first told his father about his interest in music, giving him a card for the Esquires, the band he'd shortly be fired from. Scott admitted that Neil's love of music didn't sink in at the time. "I couldn't fully comprehend it; I wasn't with him all the time, hadn't been there to see and hear," he writes.

According to Rassy, the freedom to pursue music would've been impossible under his father's rule. "Neil would've never been allowed to practice all those hours if we hadn't separated. Heavens. No way. Too noisy." Bob agreed: "I think it was very good that Neil had somebody there that didn't get on his case because of what he didn't do in school. A lot of creative spark is killed by parents who play it safe."

Visitors to the Toronto home of Scott and Astrid at 280 Inglewood Drive recall an atmosphere that was conservative to the point of stuffiness, and many attribute that environment to Scott's wife. "Astrid had no sense of humor," said June Callwood. "She was very Icelandic, only wore black and white—ever. She made us all think color was vulgar. None of us were able to warm to her, and Scott took that as meanness on all our parts." Once again, Scott stood by his mate, said Callwood, just "like he did by Rassy." *

The subject of music came up during a weeklong visit to Scott's home in the summer of 1962, as Neil's grades in Winnipeg continued to plummet. "It was almost as if Neil was just putting in time just so the financial situation would carry on," said Astrid, referring to the $100 a month Rassy was getting as long as Neil stayed in school. "Neil said, 'I can't concentrate on school . . . I'm so interested in music that it just goes out of my head,' " recalls Scott, who suggested his son drop out and attend classes at the conservatory of music. But Neil was disinterested in the offer, according to Astrid, who recalls, "He said, 'No, if I'm ever gonna make it, this is the time. I can't take the time.' "

If the idea of the barely communicative rocker attending music school seems well meaning but misguided, the proposition was certainly greeted with derision in Winnipeg. " 'Would Neil like to go to a conservatory in Toronto on a hundred bucks a month?'—*that* would've been interesting," said Rassy. "Scott lives in a dream world."

Unquestionably, Scott was the more conventional parent, stressing success in school and a career to fall back on. "My father had a tendency to attach whatever he would do to whatever grades were achieved by whoever he was dealing with," said Bob. "My mother would look at the school system and say, 'These blockheads don't know what they're doing.' She would not only say it, she would *tell* them if they prodded her."

This clash of values came to a head over an amplifier. Early in May 1964, Scott received a letter from his son requesting a loan of $600 to buy an amp. "I'm doing better in school and am finally beginning to settle

---

*Said Astrid Jr. of Astrid Sr. and Rassy: "They both drank a lot, and they both had the same drink—rye whiskey and water. Neil and I used to laugh—'What does our father do to these women?' " Fourteen years later this marriage would also come to a dramatic end. "One morning Dad left the house," said Astrid Jr. "I think he went across the street to get a newspaper, still in his bathrobe—and he decided not to come back."

down," Neil wrote, unaware that Scott had already phoned the school for his grades—four failures, which was one more than at Christmas. On May 9, Scott wrote a very blunt reply, chastising Neil for being dishonest and offering to cosign a loan for the amplifier if his grades improved that June:

> I'm not trying to discourage you, but obviously you have a grave need to face facts. If I had read that letter you wrote me without knowing the facts, I would have thought everything was going great. Unfortunately, I don't see you often enough to know how you are in day to day life, but to get anywhere, in anything, you have to be able to distinguish between what you HOPE is going to happen and what really is true. I think that if you dig in at school you can make the grade—but that means DIGGING, not sitting there saying you're doing better when there are four failures out of seven subjects staring you in the face . . .
>
> I am pleased by your interest in music and by your apparent proficiency, but that is not as important right now as getting through school as rapidly as possible. Your mother gets $100 a month to see you through school, unhampered by outside needs for making money . . .
>
> I don't want to indulge in any lengthy discussion of this matter: You haven't time. Exams must be upon you, and every hour at the books counts. Now would be a good time to show what you are made of. I know that from when you were a boy, you were always an optimist, but also had guts and determination when you needed it. I think that you need it now. I would be the happiest father in Canada if you could wave those report cards, or card, at me in a few months and say, "Okay, Dad, I'm ready for the amplifier."
>
> Love, Dad

A buddy of Neil's, Pete "The Magic Dragon" Barber, was with Young the day he received the letter. "We were walkin' home after school and he had the letter with him. Neil was disappointed, hurt—you might even say angry. It was a painful thing."

Scott's letter didn't prompt one in return from his son; instead, he writes, "it drew a long letter in reply from my ex-wife, who said that was the trouble with me, I was always measuring things—her, our sons, everything—in terms of money. As a diatribe, it would stand up anywhere. World class." Writing in his *Globe and Mail* column about the incident— and others involving his ex-wife and son—Scott created the alias James Reilly Dunn. "You could really be frank about your feelings toward your fellow human beings if you're writing through somebody else," said Scott, sounding much like his son would years later, describing writing songs from another character's point of view.

"James Reilly Dunn was my doppelgänger," said Scott. "He was a good character—he had holes in his socks, drank a little too much. At this time I have a son I really love out in Winnipeg, I'm gettin' shat upon by people who were sympathetic to Rassy and who were unsympathetic to me, which is okay—but a lotta times, things would happen that there was no way I could explain, even to myself, let alone to some other friend, so if it was somethin' that James Reilly Dunn could solve in seven hundred words . . . in fact, I was sort of justifying, in some of the columns, the course of action that I had taken that I suspect a lotta people in that situation take or might take—so it angered people and it interested others."

One of the people it angered was Rassy, who took the columns—which were fairly harmless—as a direct assault. "I don't know what Scott had in mind, but he sure used to write these god-awful columns about what a crud I was, lettin' Neil do all this. My lawyer said sue him for every dime he's got, *Neil* didn't want me to because I woulda made a big mess."

For Rassy, supporting her son's dreams was undoubtedly a way to undermine her ex-husband. "Scott sure didn't approve of me letting Neil do this. Not that he could stop me." That Christmas, Rassy would scrounge together the funds to buy Neil his amplifier. Scott would forever be known as the ogre of this story, but he maintains in *Neil and Me* that "I'd do the same thing again. It's one of the ways I operate; value for value." (Years later, when Scott's daughter, Astrid, started showing interest in music, she soon received a gift from her half brother Neil: an amp.)

Certainly there is no denying the devotion of Neil's mother. As out of control as she must have been at times, she stood out of the way and let her son do his thing. Rassy, as son Bob wrote in a 1971 *Maclean's* article, "was Neil's first fan, his greatest supporter, and he needed her. She battled on his behalf, and, too often it seemed, the battles were with my father."

I don't remember that much of it. I wanted an amp. I asked my dad if he'd lend us some money to buy an amp. He said my grades weren't good enough. If I got good grades, I could get an amp. My mom freaked out—that was just one of their arguments, y'know. I probably woulda done what my dad did. Hard to say.
—Your dad thought that you weren't alone when you wrote that letter to him.
I can't remember—I'm sure that Rassy saw the letter. How could she not see the fuckin' letter? She saw the answer to it. She knew I asked him. Men are not going to like hearing from their wives through their son's mouths in that situation.
   My dad deserves credit for bein' my dad and helpin' out, but he wasn't there as much as my mum thought he should be, so she was takin' it very personally. . . . Anyway . . . that was their deal.

That August, up at Falcon Lake, Young had a revelation. "Neil saw this band, the Crescendos, come down to the lakefront and plug in to the concession stand—just plug in to an outlet with a couple of amps and start playing," said Harper. "I think that sort of tweaked Neil's mind—'Hmmm . . . *touring.*' " Young talked the hotel management into booking the Squires for room and board, then excitedly called his bandmates and told them to get their asses up there. Unfortunately, Smythe and Bates had other plans for the weekend. "Neil got pretty upset," recalls Smythe, still uncomfortable with the memory over thirty years later. "He was angry. *Angry.*" Young fired the band— except for Koblun, who had been ready to go to Falcon Lake and was equally ready to join Young when he quit school a month later.

   "I think Rassy had—well, call it ESP," said Nola Halter. "I think she knew it would be exhausting to turn him 'round to something he wasn't. She really believed in him."

   Rassy's sister Snooky was in Winnipeg to visit an ailing Pearl in the hospital when Neil came by to inform her of his plans. "I said, 'Neil, you're nearly finished—why don't you wait and get your high school degree?' He said, 'I can't, Aunt Snooky—my music, it *has* to come out.' He was driven by this mysterious music."

Of course, there was one person Rassy had to fill in on Neil's scholastic progress. "Dear Scott," she wrote in a letter to her ex-husband that September, "Neil has decided to follow your advice and become a dropout."

School was secondary to music. I can remember Mr. Hodgkinson—vice principal at Kelvin—took me in and said, "Neil, waddya wanna do with your life?" I said, "Well, I'd like to play music in a bar." And he said, "That's a flash-in-the-pan kind of a thing, y'know. In the music business, people come and go real fast. Look—you hear about somebody one year, and the next year they're gone."

Well, that made a big impression. That wasn't gonna be me. But I took that information in and I figured, well, y'know, if that's the way it is, that's the way it is. This is what I wanna do. I still wanted to be a professional musician so bad it didn't matter. None of the shit that people would say, tryin' to convince me not to do it—none of those things would matter. I never stopped.

The professional musician now needed some new band members. Bill Edmunsen, who lived across the street, was brought in on drums. Loud, soulful, and a ladies' man, Edmunsen was a breed apart from previous Squires—"a real wing nut," said the departing Allen Bates. Rassy bailed Edmunsen out of trouble a number of times, most notoriously when he "borrowed" a flag from the Pan American games and hid it in Neil's apartment. Edmunsen was the first in a long line of characters whom Young would gravitate to again and again in years to come: a wild-ass musician with a little too much heart and soul to survive the nine-to-five square life.*

---

*When Young returned to Winnipeg in June 1987 for Shakin' All Over, a reunion concert of Winnipeg rockers, Bill Edmunsen was nowhere to be found. "The people who put it together didn't invite him—they went outta their way to make *sure* he didn't come," a still angry Young told me. "They were just blackballing the guy for some reason—he definitely did not fit their program. I thought that was terrible." Young managed to locate Edmunsen, and on June 27, there was an impromptu reunion at a local restaurant. "We're the Squires," announced Young to the audience. "This is our first gig in twenty years."

Young added pianist Jeff Waukert and, apparently inspired by John Lennon's harmonica work on "I Should Have Known Better," started playing harp. Young also made a subtle change in the name of the band. Sitting in a restaurant one day, the drummer recalls Neil saying to him and Koblun, "I'm gonna be in this business the rest of my life, guaranteed. Do you mind if I put my name in front of the band—Neil Young and the Squires?"

Young also needed a set of wheels for the band to travel in, and Rassy loaned him the money to buy his first car, a '48 Buick Roadmaster hearse he christened Mortimer Hearsebug, aka Mort. Mort was heavy iron: big and black, sporting blue broadloom carpeting, black curtains and gold tassel trim. "You open the side door and the tray whips right out onto the sidewalk," Young told Cameron Crowe. "What could be cooler than that? What a way to make your entrance. Pull up to a gig and just wheel out all your stuff on the tray." Unfortunately, the hearse also attracted the attention of local police. Rassy remembers Neil getting caught behind a funeral, second hearse in the procession. "I wonder how many people they thought were dead," said Rassy, who maintained that her son was impervious to any foul-ups. "Nothing ever fazed Neil. You couldn't faze Neil. He was doin' what he was doin', and that's what he was gonna do."

After a month of playing gigs around Winnipeg, Young decided to head out of town. He picked Fort William, a working-class city five hundred miles east of Winnipeg. On October 12, the band set out by train, minus Waukert, whose family wouldn't let him go. In this improbable location many important things would happen for Neil. It would be in Fort William that he would first start playing his weird brand of rock-folk, getting lost on his electric guitar in the process. It was also in Fort William that Young would encounter Stephen Stills for the first time. What was most important to Neil about Fort William? "Independence."

•   •   •

Thunder Bay is one of those surreal, end-of-the-earth places peculiar to Canada. Fort William and Port Arthur, originally two cities, were joined as Thunder Bay in 1970. Located on Lake Superior not far from the Canadian/U.S. border, Thunder Bay is a grimy little town with soul. Trains rumble through the old downtown, and the dilapidated Sea-Vue Motel—where, once upon a time, Neil and his band lived on SPAM and crackers—still rents rooms. The port even raised its own grim celebrity: TV bandleader Paul Shaffer. There was also this unknown folksinger from nearby Hibbing, Minnesota. "We threw Bob Dylan out of the radio station," claimed local legend Ray Dee. "He walked over the border, guitar on his back, wanted to sing on the radio. Producer told him, 'We don't do that here.' "

Young urged me again and again to talk to Ray Dee, which was unusual since he seemed ambivalent about most everybody else. "You've *got* to talk to this guy. He's the original Briggs," he said, referring to his longtime producer David Briggs. From Neil there was no higher compliment. Ray Dee's vibe was a heavy one, and he took no guff. I got the feeling he'd tell Shakey to take the trolley back to Chinatown if he thought the guy was being an asshole.

"I don't have a lotta close friends," Dee told me. "I'm very emotional and sensitive about things. Neil was the same way—he keeps his things inside a little bit. I'm a Taurus—I don't dick around, and I do not carry anything on a sleeve. I have to let it out." Dee had the ingredients Young seems to require in people: a certain innocence, a lot of passion, some sort of craziness and a large dose of sadness.

· · ·

Ray Dee (aka Ray Delatinsky—"nobody could pronounce Delatinsky on the air") was a nineteen-year-old Russian-Ukrainian deejay making $185 a month at CJLX when he walked into the Fourth Dimension and first laid eyes on Neil Young and the Squires.

"There's a band on the stage, three guys whackin' away," recalls Dee. "Neil's about nine-feet-twelve, all legs and neck, he looks like Ichabod Crane. He did things back then I thought were different—he did not just pick. He beat the guitar up sometimes, that's the only way I can describe it. He goes at that goddamn thing like 'You SOB, I'm gonna win, I'm gonna beat you.' When Neil came out of Winnipeg, he brought something different to Thunder Bay that nobody had ever seen or heard—right away I said, 'This is interesting.' " The ornery deejay was less impressed with other aspects of the band. "That fucking drummer, he used to piss me off. He was too busy looking at the chicks. So I'm saying to myself, 'We get rid of the drummer, there might be a band.'

"Neil was gonna be a success, damn the torpedoes. That was the first thing that attracted me to this guy—the fact that he had a mission." Ray Dee became the Squires' big contact in Fort William, producing their next record as well as booking gigs. A hundred and twenty bucks bought you the Squires plus their deejay/manager. "We'd go up to the North Shore and play a school and come out thinkin' we were the Rolling Stones," Dee recalls. "I'll never forget driving two hundred miles to get to a gig in this stupid hearse—laying in the back with a big bass laying down one side, and on the other Ken Koblun laying beside me like a dead man. You couldn't sit up."

. . .

As soon as the Squires hit town, they landed a gig, earning $325 for five days at the Flamingo Club. The band was such a hit that they were immediately asked to return by the cigar-chomping, peg-legged Scott Shields, who ran this nightclub fallen on hard times. "What a place!" recalls Edmunsen. "First time we'd ever played in a liquor joint. We were underaged—all these babes start comin' in, hairdresser babes, a lotta women . . . I saw an awful lot of female action 'cause it was comin' and goin'. Neil wasn't really interested."

All Neil was interested in was music, and if the Squires weren't playing, they were rehearsing in their shabby hotel rooms. Edmunsen said that by this point the band was playing only a little over one-third instrumentals and recalls Neil being particularly obsessed with the vocal harmonies. Both Kenny and Bill sang harmonies into two mikes plugged into a Fender Tremolux amp, and, according to Edmunsen, the vocals were never good enough.

"Neil's a tough guy to work for," he said. "If you made a mistake onstage, he'd give ya a look that would peel paint. He'd hurt your feelings, break your fuckin' bones, then he'd walk away and say, 'I'm sorry.' " Young's drive made an impression. "One of the hardest workers I've ever met in my life," said Edmunsen, shaking his head. "He's like a tank. You can't stop him."

After a brief return to Winnipeg to score some much needed union cards, the band returned to Fort William for a two-week residency at the Flamingo beginning November 2. Away from home, turning nineteen, holed up in the Victoria Hotel, Young would write "Sugar Mountain," a lament for innocence lost that would become a staple of his solo acoustic sets. Young and the Squires also began playing afternoon hootenannies in exchange for free food at the local chapter of the Fourth Dimension.

Run by entrepreneur Gordie "Dinty" Crompton, the 4-D was a much hipper joint than the Flamingo. As Ray Dee recalls, it was a "nightclub turned coffeehouse, first and only one Thunder Bay ever had. Crompton bought it for peanuts, took a can of paint and painted the whole thing black—walls, ceiling, everything." There was a tiny stage and, said Dee, "all these people sittin' around drinkin' coffee and smokin' the latest mari-juana that came into Canada."

It was at the Fort William 4-D, playing the trash-rock hit "Farmer John," that Young first got gone on guitar. "Not much of a tune, but we made it happen," said Edmunsen. "We kept that song goin' for ten minutes. People just never wanted it to end." For the first time, Neil fused with his guitar in a way that was transcendental. "We just went nuts, Kenny, Bill and I," Young told John Einarson. "That's when I started to realize I had the ca-pacity to lose my mind playing music, not just playing the song and being cool."

I think the first real connection with an audience was in Fort William . . . there were some other times before that where we really got it going, but it started happening more when I left Winnipeg. We really started gettin' the audiences off. Because being the unknown, being from out of town, makes the mind open wider. People look at you, they have no precon-ceptions. You have virtually a fuckin' clean slate to work with, so you can go anywhere. But if they all know who you are when you walk out there, then yer limited by who you are to some extent, because they have preconceptions of what to expect. And they have an opinion.

—Edmunsen said Fort William was great—"We can drink, we can fuck." Bill was big on the fuck part.

—Was he different from the rest of the Squires?

Yeah, oh yeah—'cause he was big into the fuck part. We still hadn't even picked up on that . . . that's when all that started happening. When we left town.

There were a few bands playin' Fort William. Donny and the Bonn-

villes and they were pretty good. But we were the new kids in town and we were pretty hot. Chick Roberts of the Cryin' Shames, he told me, "That is one of the greatest songs I've ever heard." That was just after I'd written "Sugar Mountain." It was the first time anybody had ever said anything like that.

The first time I really got off playin' a guitar, I just went nuts. We were playing "Farmer John"—something happened. I went completely berserk. I just got lost in it. And then when I came off the stage, people were looking at me different. Heh heh. There was this other guy who could really play great guitar. He was in the Rubber Band, and he was really a good Telecaster player, really a lot better guitar player. He was just lookin' at me—"I didn't know you could play like that! Where did that *come from? What were you* doing?*" And I'm goin', "Well, I really got into it. I dunno." It made an impression.*

I was probably pretty intense for eighteen, nineteen years old. I was just startin' to find myself.

November 23, 1964, at 409 Victoria Avenue. A former movie theater, now the studios of CJLX. Second floor, in the back. Ray Dee was at the helm. The song was called "I'll Love You Forever," a ballad Neil would admit was for his old flame in Winnipeg, Pam Smith (Dee would also cut a beautiful version of "I Wonder" complete with slightly countrified touches from Neil's Gretsch). A tiny studio, with rudimentary equipment—a McCurdy board, two Ampex tape decks, a Bogen amplifier for a mixer and one exceptionally fine Telefunken tube mike. Dee isolated Koblun and his bass in the hallway and stuck Neil and his guitar in another wing. Drummer Edmunsen sat in a news booth.

Unlike the Squires' past two recording sessions, the band was recorded playing and singing at the same time. Dee: "What we tried to do was come up with something as close to reality as possible. A live session—mix it and hope for the best."

Unfortunately, the best wasn't good enough. Dee felt Young's vocal needed to be stronger. "If I told him once, I told him a thousand times: Neil couldn't carry a tune in a handbag. I looked at him and said, 'Neil, this is coming out flat and sharp and shit. What we have to do here, son, is double-track ya.' He said, 'Double-track?' Neil didn't wanna sing. He was petrified." But Dee talked him into overdubbing a second vocal.

The other concern was a couple of flubbed drumbeats. "Okay, you've got a glaring mistake—you didn't have to be a rocket scientist to know you had to cover this up somehow," said Dee, who grabbed a sound-effects record and overdubbed crashing surf and thunder to hide the mistake. "I rode that bloody thunderclap and Neil's eyes got as big as saucers." Ping-ponging between recorders, Dee did the overdubs in a couple of passes, also adding some delicate touches from Neil and his Gretsch.

Listening to the song today, you can come to only one conclusion: Neil Young had his trip down early. The minimal yet vivid lyrics, the emotion, the ethereal quality of the music—it's all there on "I'll Love You Forever" and Ray Dee captured it first. It would be years before Young would capture it again.

"I'll Love You Forever"—there was somethin' about that. That was the first one. That was kinda trippy.

Ray Dee—a great producer. The records we made, we had fun making. He believed in us. As I remember, he turned down the lights in the studio and did all this shit. It was very creative with Ray—it was a feeling and a mood. He was into that part of it. There was a mood.

After that, I went to places and we didn't have the trip. Like the stuff we recorded in the basement in East Kildonan—"(I'm a Man and) I Can't Cry" and "I Wonder"—they're not happening like the Ray Dee stuff.

Billy Edmunsen, he was a great guy. He was my friend in school and he had a lot of soul. Ray hated him—he wasn't a great drummer, okay? But I liked him—I still like him. He's soulful. He had a feeling. Even though he lost the beat—he was just beginning, heh heh—he'd get excited and do rolls and shit, radadadada—"What the fuck's goin' on?" But he was so into it, it was like "Wow, what great energy—I'll go with this guy."

Edmunsen couldn't go to Fort William the second time because he had this girlfriend, Sharon, who worked at the radio station, who he met during our recording session. Bill never went anywhere where he didn't end up with a girlfriend, so he had a good time. It's funny all the things that happened tryin' to get these bands together in high school—just when you wanna leave and you finally go, "Now I got the guys—we're gonna hit the road," one of 'em goes, "Oh, I can't go." They were all great, and they shoulda gone. They shoulda given it a shot. But things happen for a reason.

Ray Dee sent a tape of the session to Capitol Records in Winnipeg, where it was promptly rejected—although, thanks to Dee, it got some airplay in Fort William, where Edmunsen remembers "I'll Love You Forever" being played in a phone-in contest called "Voice Your Choice." "We were beatin' the competition from the U.S. of A.," he said proudly.

Back in Winnipeg that December, Young added Doug Campbell, a hotshot guitarist who had built his own FuzzTone. Campbell was in the Dimensions with ex-Squire Ken Smythe, whom Neil had asked to sit in at a gig for the increasingly unreliable Edmunsen. During intermission, Young let Smythe's band play a couple of numbers.

"Next thing I knew, Doug was playing with Neil," said Smythe. "He stole him from me. It happened very quickly—if Neil didn't talk to him that night, he was on the phone with him the next day, 'cause that was Neil." Young then had to fire Edmunsen. "Drummers are all crazy—I came home one day and he was ironing his hair," maintained Rassy, who admitted, "It was a little awkward, to put it mildly. Edmunsen lived across the street."

—How did you handle firing guys?
Poorly. I didn't like it. But I did do it. It's real difficult to tell somebody you've been working with that you don't want to play with them because you think the group will be better without them. Streamlining the group. How do you say it? It's not easy. You do the best you can. I've probably done worst at that of everything.
—You don't like confrontation?
Sometimes I'm really down for confrontation. It's kind of like a changing thing. I don't know why.
Must be something that makes me differentiate between things I want to be straight-ahead about, and things that I don't want to be straight-ahead about. I think that most people have that mechanism. But some

people handle it differently—they just go, "Well, this is something I don't wanna do that I gotta do." Some people think, "This is something I don't wanna do that I'm gonna do—but kinda half-assed." I think I fall into that *category, heh heh heh.*

Quite honestly, I think it's probably my problem. I carry things around for a long time, just little things. . . .

A string of drummers would replace Edmunsen, most notably Randy Peterson, who, along with Doug Campbell, would participate in the last known Squires recording session, which produced two cuts, a rocker entitled "(I'm a Man and) I Can't Cry" and the slickest, most up-tempo version of "I Wonder." Unfortunately, this lineup crashed quickly, as neither Doug nor Randy were allowed to go out on the road. The Squires reverted to trio status, with a new drummer, Bob Clark.

In the middle of April 1965, Neil Young and the Squires packed up Mort and moved to Fort William. Fourth Dimension owner Crompton was now splitting the meager take from the gigs with the band, and for the next couple of months they scraped by. The music Young and the Squires were experimenting with at the 4-D was by all accounts truly weird. Young was taking familiar old folk tunes like "She'll Be Coming 'Round the Mountain" and giving them rock and roll arrangements. David Rea, a formidable acoustic guitarist then working with the Allen Ward Trio, heard Young for the first time as he threw himself into a particularly doom-laden version of "Tom Dooley."

"I remember it just like it was yesterday," said Rea. "I walked into the 4-D and Neil was doing this incredibly outré version of 'Tom Dooley'—he was working with his guitar and voice in what I recall were parallel thirds, fifths and seconds. Really wild stuff, very heavy sound, very heavy plangent, plunging chords, like a dirge—imagine being in this little cinderblock club in the Lakehead, teenage customers sitting around . . . it was really somethin' else." At that time Rea was a bit of a folk purist, yet the electricity Young added seemed perfect for the ancient murder ballad.

•   •   •

The strange sounds Young was laying down in Fort William caught the ear of another visiting musician that April. Born in Dallas, Texas, on January 3, 1945, Stephen Stills was a brash southern boy. Mother Talitha was an omnipotent force not unlike Rassy; father William worked in construction, lumber, molasses and real estate. According to Crosby, Stills and Nash biographer Dave Zimmer, he "would shift from job to job, making a fortune, losing it, then making it all back again."

Stephen grew up mostly in Florida and Latin America, attending military school and listening to the blues, Latin rhythms and early rock and roll, although he felt Elvis lost it after "Blue Moon of Kentucky," "because he was always being told what to do." One thing is certain: No one has ever been able to tell Stephen Stills what to do.

Learning drums, guitar and piano, Stills played frat rock in Florida bands like the Radars and the Continentals, then folk as part of a duo in New Orleans before landing in the midst of New York's Greenwich Village folk scene in 1964. There he became a member of a New Christy Minstrels–style nine-member vocal group called the Au Go-Go Singers, cutting a bland record for Roulette. A mutated version of the group, the Company, somehow wound up playing Fort William.

"They were more folk-rock; we were more rock-folk," said Koblun. Stills and Young hit it off; each had something the other lacked. Stills had an accessibly "great" voice, Young was already writing his own material. Among the things they shared were complicated relationships with absent fathers, overbearing, impossible-to-please mothers and a drive to get somewhere that bordered on demonic. But there would be one important difference between them: Young excelled at self-preservation, Stills at self-sabotage, and while Neil would periodically recharge his batteries by escaping into nonmusical avenues (perhaps at times to the point of distraction), a guitar rarely left Stephen's hands.

That was all a lot further down the road. Right now they were just a couple of hungry kids tooling around in Mort, drinking beer and sharing dreams. Koblun felt that seeing Stills had a marked effect on the Squires. "We heard Stephen singing 'Oh Susannah' with a new arrangement. It sort of influenced Neil to arrange other songs like 'Clementine.' "

No. False. Stephen and the Company did "High-Flyin' Bird." "Clementine" was influenced by seein' the Thorns—they did "Oh Susannah." The Thorns came through playin' in nightclubs that we were playing in afternoons. They were the original folk-rock band, okay? Tim Rose and two other guys—no drums, but they had bass, two guitars, I think it was. They did some really nice stuff and sang really well. One of my favorites was "Oh Susannah"—they did this arrangement that was bizarre. It was in a minor key, which completely changed everything—and it was rock and roll. So that idea spawned arrangements of all these other songs for me. I did minor versions of them all. We got into it. That was a certain Squires stage that never got recorded. Wish there were tapes of those shows. We used to do all this stuff, a whole kinda music—folk-rock. We took famous old folk songs like "Clementine," "She'll Be Comin' 'Round the Mountain," "Tom Dooley," and we did them all in minor keys based on the Tim Rose arrangement of "Oh Susannah."

I'd like to get recordings of the Thorns—and a recording of Two Guys from Boston doin' "C'mon Betty Home." I met them at the 4-D in Fort William. They used to be kinda a ragtime duo, wore suits. They were funky. And then their record came in, and I thought it fuckin' sounded great. *We were listening to it for the first time. They were expecting to get some ganja from New York and they were waiting for it—anxiously. I didn't even know what it was. I said, "What's a ganja?" They started laughing.*

I learned a lot from all those musicians that came through town. Sonny Terry and Brownie McGhee—I learned more about playin' harmonica from Sonny Terry than Jimmy Reed, 'cause I could watch Sonny night after night. I saw them in Fort William, I saw them in Winnipeg and I saw them at New Gate of Cleve in Toronto. I'd go out of my way to see them, anytime . . . Brownie was the funky one, man.

Stephen was great. He had a cheap old red Guild guitar and he sang this song, "High-Flyin' Bird." I never heard any little white guy sound like a black guy before. That funky southern soul thing. His voice—I loved the way it sounded. I thought he was just a great fuckin' singer. He also had an ear for harmony. Stephen had been trained by this guy who was the musical director for the Au Go-Go Singers. He was a big influence on Stephen, and Stephen learned a lot from him. Stephen knew a lot about harmony structure. That was valuable information.

And Stephen was a rocker. *Definitely more of a rocker than the rest.*

Big fish in the very small pond of Fort William, Young and his band began to stagnate. Augmenting their pittance from the 4-D was a three-day, $150 gig at the bar in Smitty's Pancake House, plus the occasional one-night stand. But the band, now living at the local YMCA, was starving. In the wake of Stills, the group tried a new moniker: the High-Flying Birds, after the Billy Wheeler song they'd copped from the southerner. The new name wouldn't last more than ten minutes, due to a wild turn of events involving a musician named Terry Erikson who sat in with the band on occasion.

"Neil met this guitar player, Terry Erikson, and was kind of infatuated with him," said Koblun. "Terry said he had some stocks or bonds he was gonna sell—the plan was he and Neil were gonna go to Liverpool to the Cavern Club. It fell through." Erikson's next plan, almost as implausible, didn't. While sitting around at the Y with Young, Ray Dee and a couple of the Bonnvilles one night in June, Erikson mentioned that he had a gig hundreds of miles away in Sudbury and conned Young into driving his dilapidated hearse on the perilous highway along the edge of Lake Superior.

"The day Neil left, he was gonna see his dad and put together enough money to go to Los Angeles—but he was coming back," recalls Dee, who loaned Young $30 to make the trip. "We had a booking that following weekend at the Circle Inn. He came to me and said, 'Look, I'm headin' outta town, gonna go see my dad. I need some money, I'll see ya when I get back.' I had a funny feeling that that might be the last time I'd see him, and it just about turned out that way." Perhaps fearing Erikson and Young were shooting for Liverpool, Koblun was equally suspicious and borrowed Young's guitar as insurance. "I just wanted to make sure Neil was comin' back," he said. He wouldn't be.

It wasn't a mission destined for success. Young and Erikson's fellow travelers were Bob Clark and two members of the Bonnvilles, Tom Horricks and Donny Brown. Five funky musicians, with varying degrees of long hair—one wearing a Nazi helmet, another sporting a cape—and little more than a dime to their names, packed, along with guitars and amps, into a decrepit, seventeen-year-old hearse. The journey would prove to be Mort's last stand.

Just outside of Ironbridge, Ontario, the transmission literally fell out of Mort onto the highway. The surreal sight cracked up the intrepid bunch. "I don't know why, but we were killing ourselves laughing," Young told John

Einarson. "Here was my car, my whole life was in this car, falling apart on the road, and we're rolling around laughing." Mort would be towed to Bill's Garage in Blind River, where, despite repeated attempts at resurrection, it was the end of the line. "Dear Rassy," Neil would write his mother on a postcard, "please cancel the insurance as Mort is dead."

Unable to locate a new tranny for the hearse, the five were forced to depart. The two members of the Bonnvilles and High-Flying Bird Bob Clark barely managed to get back home, hitchhiking part of the way; Neil and Terry Erikson, on a Honda motorbike Erikson had stuffed into the back of the hearse, headed for Toronto.

Koblun, stranded in Fort William, was forced to live off of an advance check for the Smitty's gig the band would never play. "Scott had to pay 'em back," said Koblun. "He was pissed." Young would soon send for Koblun and Clark, but the Fort William days were over. Outside of Smitty's Pancake House, the marquee read THE BIRDS HAVE FLOWN.

· · ·

"That's the way I was brought up—to keep changing," Young told Johnny Walker in 1992. "I went to twelve different schools before I finished grade eleven or whenever I dropped out, and my family moved around a lot. All the time, there was always different things happening. So in my life, I can roll with that." Others often got rolled over in the process.

For Ray Dee, the man who first captured Young's sound on tape, there would be no phone calls, no letters, no explanation. Unfortunately for those who loved Young, this would be typical of the way he handled certain situations deemed too intense or complicated to face. "He never came back," said Dee. "I was really hurt by that. I tried everything I could do to make this guy a success back in those days. The guy was a friend—that meant more to me than anything, I suppose. I always wondered what the hell had gone wrong. That's what you're left with—you're wondering whether you screwed up. What did you do wrong . . . what did I say? Christ, I gave the guy thirty bucks."

What happened is I just went on to Toronto instead of going back to Fort William. It completely screwed everything up. I dealt with it by going on instead of going back. That's what kind of person I was at that point. I wasn't really that worried about anybody else. I didn't really consider Ray Dee, and I didn't consider the other guys in the band. But I thought I was coming back, okay?

Of all the people that I left behind on my journey, Ray Dee got screwed more than anybody. I don't know why, 'cause he was great. *But I think I was just so irresponsible that I didn't realize what I was doing.*
—Ray was really hurt.

Oh . . . *And I'm really sorry. I had no idea what I was doing—or the effect I was having—or how much other people really cared about what was happening. I'd never seen anybody really care before, so I didn't really pick up on it, y'know? But Ray did. Ray was there for me at the beginning. He really cared about it, and he could've ridden the whole thing all the way. I couldn't go back to Fort William. I had to keep on goin'. I felt without the car to get around in . . .*

Mort was real important. My first car. It was part of my identity. It was like this weird thing—The Band and The Car. I remember getting the hearse. A hundred and fifty bucks. Kinda gave the group something that made them different.

It's like a cowboy and his horse, know what I mean? That's your horse. Remember Hopalong Cassidy, Roy Rogers and the horse? If the guy lost his fuckin' horse, it would be like "Wow, what a fuckin' bummer. What are we gonna do with Roy now? He doesn't have a horse!" The idea of getting another horse never crossed anybody's mind.

Rassy Young appeared as a quiz show panelist on the show *Twenty Questions* when she and Neil lived in Winnipeg. "Rassy was pretty funny on TV," said Neil. "My dad was on a quiz show, too. I'm breakin' the fuckin' chain. No quiz show. Gotta draw the line somewhere."

Scott Young on the cover of his 1994 autobiography, *A Writer's Life*. "He's a *real* writer," said Neil. "He'd force himself to do five pages—some days they came real easy and some days it was like pullin' teeth."

Neil and Rassy. CSNY end-of-tour dinner, Minneapolis, 1970.

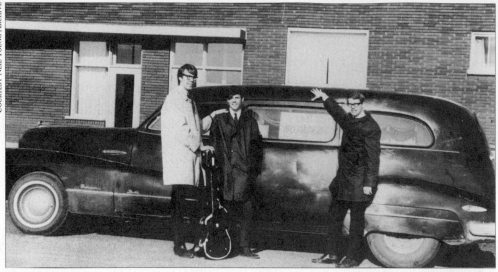

"Mort was real important.
. . . It was part of my identity . . . like a cowboy and
his horse." The Squires—
about to depart for Fort
William—alongside Mort,
the hearse, April 1965.
Left to right: Ken Koblun,
Neil Young, Bob Clark.

Ray Dee, producer of the
Squires' 1964 recording "I'll
Love You Forever." Ray was there
for me at the beginning," said
Young, who referred to Dee as
"the original Briggs."

"Buffalo Springfield
started out to be
what it was with all
of us. . . . Bruce was
beyond. He was the
soul of the whole
thing." Buffalo
Springfield publicity
shot, 1966 (left to
right: Dewey Martin,
Bruce Palmer, Richie
Furay, Stephen Stills
and Neil Young).

Crosby, Stills and Nash, Miami, 1977 (left to right: Stephen Stills, David Crosby and Graham Nash). "They were treated like royalty wherever they went," said tour manager Leo Makota.

Crazy Horse roaming the streets during sessions for their first Young-less LP, fall 1970. "The band members seemed kind of quasi-criminal to me," said photographer Joel Bernstein (left to right: Ralph Molina, Billy Talbot, Nils Lofgren, Jack Nitzsche and Danny Whitten).

Crazy Horse, before the funk: The a cappella Danny and the Memories (left to right: Billy Talbot, Ralph Molina, Ben Rocco, Danny Whitten). Danny always said, " 'Make sure our shoes are shined,' " recalled Ralph.

David Briggs "looked like the devil," said agent/manager Larry Kurzon. "He was from Wyoming—where they thought Jews had horns."

The dark prince—Jack Nitzsche, fall 1970. "Jack believed in my music," said Young.

Frank "Poncho" Sampedro alongside his new compadre for the last few years— highly acclaimed guitarist and songwriter Kevin Eubanks.

Danny Ray Whitten, fall 1970. "Danny could never close up. He predicted he would die before the age of thirty," said Terry Sachen.

The late, great Rusty Kershaw circa *Now and Then,* the 1992 album that reunited Kershaw and Young for the first time since the 1974 masterpiece *On the Beach.* "Rusty's amazing," said J. J. Cale. "He's so natural, man, that it *hurt* him."

"I was searching for something that I never really got." Neil Young and the Stray Gators (Ben Keith, Tim Drummond, Jack Nitzsche, Young and Kenny Buttrey) reconvene for tour rehearsals shortly after Danny Whitten's death, December 1972.

Neil Young, circa 1971.

Carrie Snodgress in *Diary of a Mad Housewife,* 1970. "I fell in love with the actress," wrote Young in "A Man Needs a Maid."

"Tequila and hamburgers. That was the input." Neil Young and Crazy Horse (left to right: Ben Keith, Billy Talbot, Ralph Molina and Young) at the dawn of the *Tonight's the Night* trip, Topanga Corral, August 1973.

Partners in crime: David Briggs and Neil Young backstage at the Roxy, *Tonight's the Night* tour, September 21, 1973. "I miss that guy. There is no one on the planet that compares to him. Not a day goes by without a thought of David."

a big blur of images

A large man in jeans with the zipper broken and a muslin shirt, both garments white, wanders around a big white Caddy with the engine running. We're in the wilds of Topanga Canyon outside some woebegone hippie house, past its prime and oozing that Manson vibe. He's annoyed, motioning for me to hurry. It takes me a minute to realize that the man is Bruce Palmer, the extraordinary bass player best known for his membership in Buffalo Springfield.

Palmer is in a mood. He leads me around the messy house, bitching about losing a bet to his old crony Rick James the night before. "By the way—it is a wig," he says of the funk clown. Big tanks of unnamed compounds lie askew on the floor, and in the corner is a Martin guitar bequeathed him by the late Tannis Neiman, a folksinger who had made most of the journey to California with Neil and Bruce so many years before. Palmer says he has to run an errand and will be right back. "Don't go in the bathroom," he says with a snicker. "That's where I hide my dirty needles." Bruce is making a little joke. Back in the sixties, his frequent drug busts would hasten Springfield's undoing.

When Palmer returns several hours later, his mood has not improved. He proceeds to shake me down for money to do the interview, getting about an inch from my face and demanding $500 an hour. "I'm a professional musician and that's what my time is *worth,* man," he screams, his hairy face going crimson. "Are you a narc? Are you with the U.S. government?"

Late in the afternoon, a bunch of longhairs show up to jam. Apparently part of the latest shadow of the Springfield—this one called "White Buffalo"—they're a motley bunch with bloodshot eyes. A pipe is passed. All I remember is some guy playing a wind instrument with his nose. In the hazy background, some haggard woman tends to the kitchen. Bruce hunches over his bass, huffing and puffing as he plucks strings, his eyes closed, lost in space. Legend has Palmer blasting off for Dimension X in the sixties and never really coming back, but for a fleeting moment he looks innocent, even blessed.

"Playing with Neil onstage is probably the most intense experience . . . when you play with Neil, you're playing for *him,*" Palmer told *Mojo* magazine in 1997. "You're playing at such a high level of expectancy from him—you'll never play with anybody else that's so in tune with the way it should sound. And if you vary from what it's supposed to sound like—if you go off into your own little world and start articulating something other than what he's used to hearing—you'll *hear* from him, in no uncertain terms, whether onstage right at that moment or later, when he gets you alone, haha. It's quite intense. You either do it right and his way, or not at all.

"It was always total control, never loose. The fine line that you walked was: It has to *sound* loose. Very loose . . . but he has to be able to know and be able to depend on every note that everyone plays. I'm not kidding— everything from the drummer on, he listens to it all at once. If I put in one extra note out of a thousand, he would pick up on it and he would mention it. You'd change that note, that one note—you'd just shake your head, and say, How did he *know*?"

Neil would speak more highly of Palmer than just about any other musician, and indeed, he must've been something back in '65. Rail-thin, with long hair and granny glasses, shy—but fearless when it came to music. "Brucey bassey," the girls called him. Palmer would be a major catalyst in the life of Neil Young, but Neil would have to slog through the muck and mire of the Toronto music scene before finding him.

•   •   •

"I know about old cars now, Comrie." Those were Young's first words over the phone to his old bongo-playing cohort, Comrie Smith, early one night in July 1965. Smith, who now had a band of his own, the Zen Men, was surprised. After Neil's one scrawled letter shortly after he left for Winnipeg, Comrie assumed he'd been forgotten. Now Young was back in Toronto, apparently staying a night or two at the home of an old Lawrence

Park friend, Rick Mundell, before heading to his father's. Smith drove over to Mundell's, where a party was going on and Neil was watching everybody get drunk. "He was really down on it," said Smith, who recalls Young lecturing, "Look at all these people—they're all sitting around here drinking. I can sit with one beer, I'll sip this for an hour while these guys all get blasted." Comrie was struck by how serious Young had become. "He was so much more mature."

Comrie listened to Young's tales of Fort William and Mort, and for the next eight months they would be pals again, although Comrie noticed his friend had become somewhat reclusive and mysterious. "Neil just disappeared," said Comrie Smith's then girlfriend and future wife, Linda Smith. "He never answered to anybody . . . he did what he wanted when he wanted."

. . .

Young summoned Ken Koblun and Bob Clark, starving back in Fort William, and soon his scraggly bandmates started arriving one by one at his father's house on Inglewood Drive. The writer's fancy home must've looked slightly surreal after all the dumpy motels and hotels of Fort William; Terry Erikson remembers Scott pushing a button to reveal a hideaway bar. "He was very friendly but businesslike," Erikson told John Einarson. "There wasn't a closeness between Neil and his dad, but he was courteous and offered to help us out." Some friends felt that Young's visit was more than a pit stop. "I think when Neil went to Toronto he was really looking for approval to continue on," said Ray Dee. Neil was respectful of his father's rules, issuing a one A.M. curfew for his bandmates and chewing them out when it wasn't adhered to. "He ran that band like Field Marshal Kesselring," said Scott.

For the next few weeks, Scott put up his son and a couple of his bandmates. He also found the group a place to rehearse and put $400 in a trust account that Neil could draw a $40-a-week allowance from throughout the summer. Neil also contacted the manager of the Allen Ward Trio, Martin Onrot, who agreed to represent Young's band. But Toronto proved to be very different from the supportive, insular scenes of Winnipeg and Fort William.

. . .

"Toronto is a wanna-be city," said Joni Mitchell. "It wants to be New York." Few Canadian musicians I talked to had pleasant things to say about the place. Mitchell was struggling to make a living in coffeehouses around the time Young arrived. "The folk scene was very competitive, and it took a hundred and sixty dollars to get into the musicians' union, which I didn't have, and as a result you couldn't work at all. I mean, union men used to show up at these little gigs where you'd get fifteen minutes, fifteen dollars a night—and they'd show up in trench coats for their cut. It was really small-time thuggery."

Yet music was thriving in Toronto, particularly in a section of town called Yorkville. "There wasn't really one Yorkville scene, there were several," said folksinger Murray McLauchlan. In a two-block stretch between Avenue Road and Yonge Street lay a clutch of coffeehouses like the Penny Farthing and the Purple Onion that catered to a beatnik-turning-hippie scene that revered such homegrown stars as Gordon Lightfoot and Ian and Sylvia.

Bar-band rock and roll flourished in joints like Le Coq d'Or, where Ronnie Hawkins and the Hawks (soon to be nabbed by Bob Dylan) had been tearing it up. Le Coq d'Or was "more Damon Runyon than hippie," said Murray McLauchlan. "Heroin users who wore sharkskin suits, had pomps and looked like Waylon Jennings." Toronto, said Bruce Palmer, was "the most hard-rocking city of its time." But musical camps were strictly divided, and there would be no outlet for the weird crossbreeding Young had been developing in Fort William. "I didn't see much folk-rock in Toronto," Young said decades later. "It was either folk or rock."

•   •   •

Young showed up a lot that summer at Comrie Smith's Toronto home at 45 Golfdale. He was piloting a new piece of heavy iron: Tinkerbell, an old Buick convertible with a clattering engine and a rusted-out exhaust. It also sported a tube radio, which invariably seemed to be blaring "Good Vibrations" upon his arrival. "Neil was adorable," said Linda Smith. "He was a con of the first order. How else could he get fed? He didn't have a cent."

Young had come a long way since miming along on the ukulele to Danny and the Juniors. "Gee, Comrie, you started playing guitar before I did," Neil told his old friend. "Now I'm better than you are." Comrie watched in awe as Young serenaded his sister with a weird version of "Clementine" that left her spellbound. "It was hypnotic," said Smith. "He'd stare you right in the eye, every word. It was like Neil put the notes directly into your brain." Young made his time in Fort William sound like Robert Johnson's trip to the crossroads. Comrie said he and his bandmates "were thinking of heading to Thunder Bay. There was this mystique because of Neil."

Still a bit of a record hound, Young was obsessed with two in particular that summer: "Thou Shalt Not Steal" by Dick and Dee Dee, and an eerie girl-group record by the Jaynettes, "Sally Go 'Round the Roses." "Neil was really enthusiastic about harmony," said Smith. "Just two voices singing together with his acoustic would do it. He had this feeling you could get this big huge sound." Smith recalls that Young wanted to put together an Everly Brothers–type duo with him and began playing his electric guitar with a capo while in Toronto. "Neil got more influenced by the folkies there," said Koblun, dismayed by this state of affairs.

Tinkerbell—'47 Buick convertible . . . that was a great fuckin' car. I bought it for seventy-five bucks, and it was worth every dollar. I didn't have enough money for a) a license or b) a registration, but I still had a good time. Just a cool fuckin' car. Finally had to just abandon it somewhere. You know how it is when you're nineteen? Couldn't quite keep it going, so I just left it. I don't even know where. Too bad. I'd love to have it today.
—Was Yorkville a burgeoning hippie scene?
No—it was an old beatnik scene. It was turning into a folk scene.

The Yorkville scene. I'd never seen anything like it. Music was everywhere. Two years before the Summer of Love. It was like this big deal, Toronto in '65.

I was just growin' up. It was a great experience. I loved it. It was freedom.

The Riverboat was an upscale thing—people who played there were really making a living. There was the New Gate of Cleve, which was just down the street—that's where I saw Lonnie Johnson. And I think I saw Pete Seeger there, too, and Sonny Terry and Brownie McGhee.

"Sally Go 'Round the Roses"—dangerous. Fuck. *That's a wild record. Hey, you take that song, put that with* any *Dennis Hopper movie. I think you'll have somethin'.* *

Two of the folkies Neil Young was hanging around with were David Rea and Craig Allen. Allen felt Young was turned off by the hokier aspects of the acoustic trip. "Neil could never come to terms with the sort of long-haired, lanky folksinging stuff. We sort of shared that, because my background was more country/western. He was interested in me for the western harmonies. We were each trying to learn the different guy's style—he'd show me the rock stuff up the neck and I'd show him the block chords down the bottom and the finger picking." From David Rea, Young learned tunings. "I believe I was the first person to show Neil the open-D tuning," said Rea.

As a rocker in the Toronto folk scene, Young would be something of an anomaly. "That's what was odd about Neil in this group of friends," said Craig Allen. "The rock people lived down the street." Allen felt it wasn't a case of Young denouncing rock and roll and going acoustic; he just wanted to adapt elements of the folk approach to further his own trip. "When Neil came to Toronto, he sucked in everything as he went through," said Comrie Smith. "I think what he got out of Yorkville at that time was he sort of adapted his rock style into a folk thing. I don't think it was ever an either/or for him. I didn't get any sense of a struggle."

While Neil was learning from the folkies, nothing was happening with his group. Their new manager apparently had great faith in Neil's talent but little understanding of his band, which he'd given a snappy new name, Four to Go. "Marty Onrot was a real Hollywood kinda guy," said folksinger Vicky Taylor. Friends felt Onrot was pressuring Neil to dump his group and go solo as a folk artist, and both Terry Erikson and Bob Clark soon departed, replaced by still more new members. Four to Go never got beyond rehearsals. "I never played one of my own songs with a band in Toronto," Young told John Einarson.

---

*Young has a penchant for pop songs sporting idiosyncratic femme vocals. During our interviews he would praise Blondie's "Heart of Glass," Kim Carnes's "Bette Davis Eyes," Suzanne Vega's "Luka" and also the vocals of Victoria Williams and No Doubt's Gwen Stefani. He was less than crazy about Liz Phair and Melissa Etheridge.

Young ended up in a room at a shabby boardinghouse down by the tracks. Ken Koblun recalls Young's stay at 88 Isabella as a bleak time, full of introspection and sad, sad songs. Whether it was depression or drugs or just the advancement of his own strange psyche, something was happening to unlock in Young a peculiar ability to write a new and different kind of song.

Toward the end of September, Tinkerbell was gone and so was his beloved Gretsch, which some friends say he was forced to pawn to start paying his father back (Young maintains it was to buy a Gibson twelve-string). Comrie Smith saw a change pass briefly over Neil, a fleeting attempt to conform, settle down, maybe in an attempt to please his father, whom he told, "I gotta get a job." Scott took him down to Mr. Ivan's, got him a $4 haircut, and Neil promptly landed the first job he applied for. "He had always been self-sufficient," said Scott. "Neil always had money that he made himself, delivering papers, whatever it was. So I always thought him walking down the street from the barbershop straight into Coles and getting a job as a stockroom boy was fairly typical."

Koblun visited Neil on the job and, feeling sorry for his frail friend, wound up moving heavy boxes of books. "I remember Neil sitting in the basement smoking while I was doing the work for him," he said. Five weeks into his new career, Neil came down with a mysterious illness that landed him under his stepmother's care for a few days. The last few years had brought the first glimmers that Young's internal chemistry could suddenly go awry. Koblun remembers one gig in Winnipeg where "we were playing a song and I could start feeling his vibrations. He was really weird—he started playing guitar and couldn't stop. I had to knock him on the arm."* Jack Harper remembers having to drive Young home when his vision abruptly blurred. As Young's life and career intensified in the coming months, so would these incidents.

The sickness cost him his job. "I kept phoning Coles, saying, 'Neil can't come in,' " said Astrid. "Finally they said, 'Don't bother.' "

I was a stock boy. I wasn't very together. I used to stay out late and come in in the morning . . . I wasn't meant for that kind of life.

---

*When I repeated Koblun's description to Young of his being unable to stop playing guitar after everyone else had stopped, he quipped, "I learned how to use that later on."

I remember sitting on the floor and writing "Clancy." And for sure "Peggy Grover" and "Don't Pity Me, Babe."
—Difficult period?
I don't remember things in that frame. It was part of the deal. Just another chapter. I'm sure I didn't enjoy it, but I knew I was by myself, anyway. On my own. Things weren't going that great, but still—what have you got to lose—you're nineteen, who gives a shit. At that point I had nothin' to worry about, compared to the kids who are growin' up out in this mess.
—Were you gaining an awareness that songs could be as complex as you wanted to make them?
Yeah. About the last eight months I was in Toronto. When I wrote "Clancy." I thought it was pretty good. Because obviously there was so much to it. I knew it was long.
—Did anything provoke "Nowadays Clancy Can't Even Sing"?
I don't know. It's just a product of my life at that point. That's all I can say. There was a lot on my mind.
—What do you think you were trying to accomplish with that song?
I don't know. Just writin' a song. It's so long ago. I don't remember much about Clancy. I really don't . . . except what he looked like, a little . . . He's an incidental character who somehow had his name in it—no more important than all the characters that didn't.

"Nowadays Clancy Can't Even Sing" was a landmark for Neil Young, one of the first major works in which he blends opposed realities in the peculiar way that would become a characteristic of his more abstract songs. Young cuts up time and place in a way not unlike the films of Nicolas Roeg or the writing of William Burroughs, but their methods are perhaps not as powerfully primitive or emotional as Young's. In Young's hands, it is not an intellectual exercise, and there is a naïve, almost preposterous beauty to many of his cutup songs. He uses lyrics to replicate the inner experience. The images rush out the way feelings do, imperfectly, veering from high to low without a road map and sometimes without logic. Listeners can dig all sorts of meanings out of the ambiguity, finding jagged little bits of their own lives poking through.

"Hey, who's that stompin' all over my face / Where's that silhouette I'm tryin' to trace." "Clancy" is a strange song, full of surreal imagery that conveys some sense of dreams being fucked with, even stopped: "Who's puttin' sponge in the bells I once rung." But lurking within are glimpses of real events and real people. Part of the song relates to Ross "Clancy" Smith, someone Young encountered back in Winnipeg while at Kelvin High. Smith, who suffered from multiple sclerosis, rode his bike to school, sang in the hallway and endured the derision of his fellow students. Clancy was just the kind of misfit Young admired and empathized with.

The last verse of the song deals with betrayal. Young once explained the lyric to his then manager Brian Stone, going into great detail about how he actually looked through the floorboards somewhere and saw his girlfriend with another guy. All stitched together, the song conjures up confusion, frustration, alienation and paranoia. Recorded the following year with Buffalo Springfield, it would resonate deeply with many embarking on the murky and explosive journey of the sixties.*

In 1967, Young would give an interview to Los Angeles reporter Jeffrey C. Alexander, talking in detail about the song. "Many people I know tell me they don't understand 'Clancy.' They can't figure out all the symbols and stuff. Well, I don't think it's possible at all for them to know who he really is. For listeners, Clancy is just an image, a guy who gets comedown all the time.

"He was a strange cat, beautiful. Kids in school would call him a 'weirdo' 'cause he would whistle and sing 'Valerie, Valera' in the halls. After awhile, he got so self-conscious he couldn't do his thing anymore. When someone who is as beautiful as that and as different as that is actually killed by his fellow man—you know what I mean—like taken and sorta chopped down—all the other things are nothing compared to this.

"In the song I'm just trying to communicate a feeling. Like the main part of 'Clancy' is about my hang-ups with an old girlfriend in Winnipeg. Now, I don't really want people to know my whole scene with that girl and another guy in Winnipeg. That's not important, that's just a story. You can read a story in *Time* magazine. I want them to get a feeling like when you

---

*The most powerful version of "Clancy" I have heard is a November 10, 1968, solo acoustic performance from the Canterbury House unearthed by Joel Bernstein for Young's Archives project. Ever the perverse one, Neil told me he doesn't want to use the take because it's too good. "I was too on it," he said.

see something bad go down—when you see a mother hit a kid for doing nothing. Or a frustration you see—a girl at an airport watching her husband leave to go to war. . . .

"Just because I wrote a song doesn't mean I know anything. I don't know very much about all the things that are going on around here, all the scenes, all the questions. All I know is just what I'm writing about. And even then I don't really know. I'm just trying to convey a feeling."

Probably the first time Young had ever seriously addressed songwriting, this interview—just a couple of paragraphs buried deep in a newspaper column—is about the most specific he has ever gotten concerning a lyric. Neil Young would rarely be so revealing of his intentions again.

> *I don't know where it comes from. It just comes out. . . . Seems like even when I'm happy, I write about bein' lonesome. I don't know why.*
>
> *And you're askin' about images I write, like "the burned-out basement" and all that—I really don't know where that comes from. I just see the pictures. I just see the pictures in my eyes.*
>
> *And sometimes I can't get 'em to come, y'know, but then if I just get high or something, and if I just sit there and wait, all of a sudden it comes gushing out. I just gotta get to the right level. It's like having a mental orgasm.*
>
> —Interview with Elliot Roberts,
> Wim van der Linden film, 1971

> *The song comes out. . . . You don't make up a song. The song comes through you . . . if I'm in the right place, the song comes through me on a piece of paper. It's not that I sit and think, "I'm gonna make up a song now."*
>
> —1982 Italy press conference

> *You read the newspaper and you watch the television and you go to sleep and you wake up and write a song. Twenty people become one person . . . if you break it into this is this, or this is that, it doesn't make any sense. The whole idea is a confusion.*
>
> —1987 Rome press conference

Neil Young has been remarkably consistent on the subject of songwriting over the years: It happens, I don't understand it, I'm grateful and it's pretty pointless to talk about it. I pity the poor fool who attempts to crack the meaning of his lyrics as if breaking a code. It can't be done—not with Young's help, at least, and he doesn't care. Although he'd never put it this way, I get the feeling Neil Young views songwriting almost superstitiously, like a conjurer's gift. Define it—question it—fuck with it too much, and it might just go away.

I don't feel the need *to write a song. It's not like that. It's almost like the song feels the need for me to write it and I'm just there. It's not like I'm not doing a job.*

Songwriting, for me, is like a release. *It's not a craft. Crafts usually involve a little bit of training and expertise and you draw on your experiences—but if you're thinking about that while you're writing, don't! If I can do it without thinking about it, I'm doing it great.*
—You've written songs that feel well crafted, like you've worked at them.
Yeah—and they are the most boring *songs that I've ever written, probably.*
—So you don't write songs, you just get the fax?
I don't know how to describe what I do. I'm *waiting to see what I'm gonna do next. That should give you some indication of how much planning goes into it.*
—How important are lyrics?
Well, it depends on the song.
—What about an abstract song like "Cowgirl in the Sand"?
The words to "Cowgirl in the Sand" are very important because you can free-associate with them. Some words won't let you do that, so you're locked into the specific fuckin' thing the guy's singin' about. . . . This way it could be anything.

The thing is, as long as there's a thread that carries through it, then when you imagine what it's about, there's gonna be a thread that takes you to the end, too. You can follow your thought all the way through if you happen to have one—or if you don't, you realize it doesn't matter.
—Do all the songs you write make sense to you?
No. That's not a requirement. It doesn't have to make sense, *just give you a feeling. You get a feeling from something that doesn't make any sense. It*

doesn't make sense—it kind of gives you a sense. Like "Last Trip to Tulsa"
or "Rapid Transit" don't make a lotta sense. Some do, some don't. It's not
important to me.
—So are your songs autobiographical?
It's not about information. The song is not meant for them to think about
me. *The song is meant for people to think about* themselves.

   The specifics of what songs are about are not necessarily constructive
or relevant. Songs come from a source and the source may be several . . .
It could give credence to the theory of reincarnation, where you've been a
lotta different places but obviously you haven't. What the fuck am I doing
writing about Aztecs in "Cortez the Killer" like I was there, wandering
around? 'Cause I only read about it in a few books. A lotta the shit I just
made up because it came to me.
—And you were open enough to receive it?
Yeah . . . I believed in myself enough to let it come in.
—Does believing in yourself have a lot to do with writing songs?
I don't know. Did Kurt Cobain believe in himself?
—How does stream of consciousness work in your writing?
If it's a steady stream of consciousness for me, and I can follow the picture
all the way through, you can just go smoothly through it on another level.
You're listening to the sound of the words and the pictures and the
melody—and they go together. It transcends any one of the elements—so
y'know, you just keep going. *You're not thinking about this word or that*
word, you just get a big blur *of images. That'll happen with me when I'm*
singing the song and I'm seeing some image that's unrelated to the
words—-seemingly unrelated. If I see it and keep seeing it, y'know, the next
time I sing it, it may come back. Keeps coming back for years sometimes,
a little glimmer of something. If that happens with me, then I think that
everybody is gonna have their own identifying place with the song that's
gonna carry them all the way through, too, and they're gonna think I'm
singing directly to them.
—Any songs of yours cut the closest?
Nope.
—Not "Will to Love"?
It was a good song, but its weakness is it was a one-shot deal. I mean, that
was it. I can't even sing *it. I can't* remember *it. I can't remember the*

melody. *I can't even . . . that's perfect. To have it like that—so every verse is different and it's all just comin' out. It's real good to get it like that. But uh . . . I don't think that's the only one—several have that vibe . . . "Goin' Back" is one of my all-time favorites.*

—Did smoking pot have an effect on your writing?

Yeah . . . I was just writing, I don't know if it had to do with smoking any grass or not smoking any grass. I don't think it mattered, but it had an effect, yeah. What it was, I don't know. 'Cause I can write both ways. Y'know, I can write in a car, I can write while I'm asleep. And all of a sudden I've got a melody or words or both—the whole fuckin' thing. . . .

—Do you have a policy on song editing?

Well, try not to edit. Sometimes you write too much. You take a verse out, whatever. The time *to edit is the only important thing. Try not to judge and edit yourself unless you've completely finished what you've done. Because to start second-guessing yourself as it's coming out of you, you're gonna jam it up and it's not gonna come out. Thinking in songs—that's where it gets lost. Either playing it or writing it.*

—Has your writing changed over the years?

I think it has—it's the same basic kind of writing . . . it's evolved. I've gotten more sure of things. Less thinking.

—Ever think you're guilty of preaching in your songs?

Probably I am—but I'm preaching to myself. Ya gotta remember that. The person that I talk to in my songs is mostly me. When I say, "You gotta blah, blah, blah," I'm talkin' to myself.

—Are you preaching in "Throw Your Hatred Down"?

I don't think I'm preaching. I'm reflecting. *Maybe talkin' to myself—I dunno. I hate to take responsibility for every word that I say.*

—Francis Bacon once said, "I can't be held responsible for the products of my subconscious."

I agree with that. That's what art's all about—if you wanna get it out there.
Well, I think that applies to songwriting, but it doesn't apply to life. I'm not sure how far that goes.

—More than a few of your songs mean completely different things to different people.

Open ambiguity. It's not stated, it's understood. Something's there that's understood, but you can't put your finger on it. It's a feeling you have that "Yes, I'm not hearing it all, but I can put it together from what I'm getting." Y'know what I mean? So that's part of what happens in my writing naturally. I think that's my style. What comes out of me is full of those things—where you leave out the connection and assume that the person knows the connection just subliminally. Just keep on goin'. Leave out key words and stuff and it still makes perfect sense—but it doesn't mean literally what it means . . . if you read it out word by word, it means one thing, but if you say it all in a line, it means something else—that's what I think songwriting is. That's the mystery. The mystery of art.

One day in the fall of 1965, Neil had Comrie drive him by all their old Toronto haunts. There were glimmers that Young was feeling the pull of his dreams, feeling the urge to move on. He insisted they stop at their old school, Lawrence Park. "I have to do this, Comrie," he said, and then sat on the steps with his guitar and played song after song.

Driving around, they ran into one of the woeful characters Young had defended back in grade school: Gary Renzetti. As Smith tells it, "Neil's in the backseat and goes, '*Look,* there's Renzetti! *Stop!*' I stopped the car, and Neil jumped out the back door and yelled at the top of his lungs, 'Renzetti, you *old fart*!' Neil runs up, shakes his hand, got back in the car and said, 'Someday he'll remember this. Neil Young'll be somebody.' "

One night at 45 Golfdale, Young and Smith, guitars in hand, tromped up to the third-floor attic and made some music. Neil embellished a couple of the songs with what he called his "Dylan kit"—a harmonica in a holder hanging around his neck. Comrie set up his reel-to-reel recorder and let it roll. The tape, which Smith held on to all these years, is a revelation.

There are six Young originals and one cover, "High-Heeled Sneakers," and they run the gamut from folk to R&B. "Betty Ann," with a dual vocal by Neil and Comrie, points to the sort of folk-duo ideas Young was toying with. "Casting Me Away from You," "Don't Tell My Friends," "There Goes My Babe," are all forlorn ballads of lost love. "My Room Is Dark 'Cepting for the Light of My Cigarette," is an angst-ridden coming-of-age song ("Who's to say my hair's too long?") with a weird, rolling-rhythm guitar part that's pure Neil.

But the frenetic performances of "High-Heeled Sneakers" and "Hello,

Lonely Woman" are particularly illuminating, conclusive proof of the depth of Young's feeling for rhythm and blues. Few white people can pull off singing about wighats convincingly, but Young, only nineteen years old, does just that in "High-Heeled Sneakers." I had falsely assumed it was Crazy Horse's Danny Whitten who uncorked Neil's really raggedy-ass side, dragged it out of him and made him work it. But in Young's life, there are surprises everywhere, and "Hello, Lonely Woman" is one of them.

For the first time, you can hear everything Young absorbed from those late-night transistor-radio sessions, lying there transfixed by the other-worldly Jimmy Reed. "Just come in when you feel like it," Young directs Comrie, his nasal voice sounding nervous and a bit under the weather. Then they lurch into "Hello, Lonely Woman," and I do mean lurch, be-cause at times the guitars are extremely tenuous and the song sounds ready to swallow itself, but the suspense excites in the same way Crazy Horse would years later, when you wonder if the band has a prayer of making it to the end of the song without totally collapsing.

"I know you, lonely woman, I know what's on your mind / I won't ask you any questions, I'm familiar with your kind," mutters Young in a men-acing growl, stomping his foot in time. The harp solo—nearly four min-utes long—falters a bit, like everything else, but there are moments where the playing so completely unhinges, it is every bit as thrilling as anything Young would later achieve. Young might have first experienced his signa-ture trance-out while playing "Farmer John" during an afternoon show in some dive in Fort William, but here he was, getting just as gone, learning to summon it up at will on a song he created, with Smith there to record it. It was, as Comrie compared it to the old days when Neil would nervously flick his fingers and go flush, a real "red-faced night."

Not everyone found Young's abandon so exhilarating. "Neil was up there chanting away," recalls Comrie, "and my mum said, 'Y'know, there's somethin' about Neil, somethin' about his eyes tonight that really worries me.' " Then Young disappeared into the night. Smith would spend much of the next month trying to find him.

.   .   .

On October 30, 1965, Young's band would play their one and only gig since leaving Thunder Bay, and they would have to venture into the States to do it. Wobbly Barn was a ski resort in Killington, Vermont, looking for a band to play the winter season. Four to Go lasted exactly one engagement.

Young and Koblun headed for New York City, where they looked up Richie Furay, a friend of Stephen Stills. Born May 9, 1944, in Dayton, Ohio, Furay was a harmony addict who had grown up on country music and early rock and roll, and in late 1964 wound up in New York City, where he joined Stills in the Au Go-Go Singers. Furay was a rare commodity in the music business: a nice, uncomplicated guy. And he could sing like a bird. Young played Furay some songs, including "Nowadays Clancy Can't Even Sing," which Furay started performing as a solo folkie. The two would soon meet again.

When he got back to Toronto, Young broke up his band. Smith recalls driving Neil around as he fumed, particularly upset about telling Ken Koblun it was over. Young seemed especially furious with Martin Onrot, complaining that the manager never understood the first thing about the music he was trying to make. Out of the gloom came a prophecy. "One day, Comrie, it'll be Neil Young. It'll just be me. I'll be alone out there on the stage."

Koblun was handing out flyers in front of the Riverboat when Young told him the news. He had followed Neil through thick and thin all the way from Winnipeg, and it had led nowhere. "I was upset," Koblun said with characteristic understatement. Ironically, Koblun got a job doing the lights at the Riverboat, and when Neil showed up at a hootenanny for one of his first solo appearances, playing songs on an unamplified Gretsch, Ken was manning the spotlight.

Somehow around this time Young snagged his first audition for an American record company, Elektra. Undoubtedly excited, he returned to New York City, but if the performance preserved on tape is any indication, it was a dismal experience. Young nervously rushes through seven songs, including "Clancy," playing second banana to a shorting amplifier during one tragically funny performance of a song entitled "I Ain't Got the Blues." Nothing came of the ordeal.

"Just turn it on and let it run." That's what the guy said at the beginning. Judy Collins was doing something in the studio. I thought I *was goin' in.*

Turned out I was goin' in the tape vault to do this demo in there. In New York, in a little room by myself, with my guitar. Sitting on an amp. Couldn't even record in a real studio. Went all the way there and they gave me a fuckin' tape machine. Told me to press start. I could've done that at home. But then, bless them, they didn't sign me. So things do work out.

It was a humbling experience. A slow, sinking feeling as I realized, "My shit's not very good—but I'm here. I'm here playin' it and it's not too good. My shit's no good." All by myself, makin' a tape for nobody. The funny fuckin' thing was, I was sitting in the tape library with all these Elektra masters, on an amp with a speaker in it—a magnetic *speaker. They put me in there—nobody said, "Don't put it near the tapes."*

"I Ain't Got the Blues"—Now, if I'd done that song with a band and had it developed a little farther, it probably woulda been more innaresting— but as it was, it was definitely just at the very beginning of my songwriting. It was like "I'm gonna write a song that has the word 'blues' in it," y'know what I mean? When you look at your early stuff, it's really funny. But as embarrassing as it is, those things have a place.

Onrot wanted to do the best he could. He just didn't know what the fuck he was doin'... I don't know what his real job was. But at least he was interested in managing me. Felt that I had something going. He wanted to be a manager, and I wanted to be an artist. Neither one of us really were what we thought we were—but we wanted *to be. So the two of us were a good match.*

First I wanted it to be a band. And then I just decided, "Well, fuck, I'll try it on my own." And I went back and forth on that a couple of times before I got out of Canada. If there wasn't a band, I was alone. If there was a band, I was in the band. If it was my band, it was my band.

Breakin' up the Squires—that was a decision I never shoulda fuckin' made. What a stupid asshole. That's too bad. Son of a bitch. We went the wrong way again.

Legend has it that Neil Young first encountered folksinger Vicky Taylor as he was being ejected from a Toronto Folk Guild hootenanny. "Take your squeaky voice and get outta here," said Riverboat owner Bernie Fiedler to

Young, who responded, "Someday you'll beg me to come back here." Both Fiedler and Young insisted the story was false.

Taylor claimed she witnessed the event, then took Young back to her place. "Neil had a vision," she said. "He was very focused, and it was like you could feel this energy and talent coiled inside. I got the impression he wasn't extremely healthy—that in spite of his burning talent, there was a very fragile spirit there. I wanted to protect him from life."

Taylor was a raven-haired singer with a rapid-fire vibrato whose big number was entitled "The Pill" and, according to her friend Janine Hollinghead, "it was twenty verses long—she could get through half a set just on that song alone." Taylor earned fifty bucks a week as the resident folksinger at the Mousehole, a club run by Bernie Fiedler's wife, and lived in a $90-a-month flat above the Night Owl on Avenue Road that served as a communal home to many starving musicians. Neil Young, Joni Mitchell, John Kay of Steppenwolf (known then as the Sparrow), David Rea and Craig Allen all passed through Vicky's apartment, sleeping on the floor, jamming with other musicians and subsisting on a no-budget concoction Taylor whipped up called "guck." "I was kinda like the mother hen," said Taylor.

"Vicky was the only one on the folk scene that was nice to me," said Joni Mitchell. "Every time she went to an audition, Vicky would insist on dragging me along. Vicky fancied that she looked like Cher. She had long black straight hair and bangs. She was thin and pale and I guess she was neurotic—she was the first person I met that went to a shrink. People in Canada didn't go to shrinks, and she had to go out of town to go."

Taylor's adventures in mental health led to poor treatment at the hands of professionals, in addition to access to endless prescriptions. Pills weren't the only drugs plentiful in the Avenue Road flat. Draft dodgers were flooding in from across the border, many of them carrying pot. Denizens at Taylor's began experimenting. "A friend of ours came back from Israel with a four-dollar Hershey bar of hash in her brassiere," said Craig Allen. "And we proceeded to clean it up. We lost three months with that brick of hash."

Taylor described Neil as vulnerable and wary. "He was like a brother to me. But he didn't have a lot of trust in women. I think he just felt so different inside that he was terrified of people. Neil and I shared a fear of

that fine line between sane and insane." Taylor recalls Young having "anxiety attacks, but they were probably precursors to epileptic attacks. I would
give him some Valiums or something. . . . I always had a thousand of those
kinda things." Impending visits with his father often seemed to bring on
the panic. "Neil was very intense. There was a little invisible wall around
him. He would sit there in the corner, writing songs, and nobody ever bothered him. He was just tuned out." Young immersed himself in Taylor's collection of folk records, listening to people like Bert Jansch, Phil Ochs and
Hamilton Camp.

Writers have gotten much mileage out of a Stephen Stills quote claiming Vicky Taylor "convinced Neil that he was Bob Dylan." During this period Young did start to perform around town solo, with little success.
" 'Clancy' is sort of a narrative, now it sounds okay," said Craig Allen.
"But in those days it was so vague, club owners didn't want him to sing
that kind of rambling stuff." Complicating matters was Young's insistence
on featuring mainly original material. "I'm sure he could've gotten jobs if
he would sing Bob Dylan stuff and Phil Ochs stuff," said Taylor. "But Neil
wouldn't bend."

Young also played Monday-night hootenannies at the Riverboat as part of
a folk group with Vicky Taylor, Donna Warner and Elyse Weinberg dubbed
the Public Futilities, but that was strictly for laughs. Young was mostly a
nonentity on the folk scene. "I was by myself, just me and my guitar traveling alone, just showing up at these places," Young told writer Nick Kent. "It
was quite an experience. The strong image I have now of that period is one
of me walking around in the middle of the night in the snow, wondering
where to go next! A part of me was thinking, 'Wow, this is really out on the
edge!' The other part of me was thinking, 'What the fuck do I do now?' "

*In Toronto I went out and played a whole bunch of gigs by myself.
The twelve-string gave me a chance to do that. They weren't very good
gigs. . . . I played one night when somebody was not available at the
New Gate of Cleve. And they knew a couple of days in advance, so I
filled the bill—for that one night they let me in. Somebody was down
there and reviewed me. It wasn't a big review. My first review said that
my songs were cliché-ridden.
—How did that strike you?*

"Marty, what's a cliché?"

Then there was a place in North Bay—the Bohemian Embassy. That's where I first did "Oh Lonesome Me." I had the arrangement before I left Toronto—that same arrangement, the chord changes and the rhythm. I did other songs that I wrote myself that I can't remember.

I couldn't get paid to play—I had to go for an open mike. Some kinda situation where I could be brought in if somebody was sick or something. I wasn't in the union, so that was a problem, too. In Canada, y'know, it's very complicated. Now it looks simple when I look back on it. But I'm sayin' for me in Canada it was very complicated, heh heh. Once I made it all the way into the States and got stopped by U.S. immigration at the bus depot in Detroit. They sent me back. Tryin' to get back and forth between the United States and Canada, my first run-in with the border. . . . I remember sleepin' in this one chick's basement. It was nighttime, it was too cold and I didn't have anywhere to go. She brought me back to her house and her parents were there. She convinced them I was okay. I got up and left before they woke up. I didn't really know where I was, though. I don't know how I got outta there.

I couldn't get into Detroit once because I couldn't get across the bridge with my guitar. Tried to sneak across, take the bus across. I think on my way back I went and visited my uncle Bob who lived in Windsor. Stayed there a couple of days, then I did a show there. Pretty big place. Those were like my first solo shows.

I had a series of gigs—maybe Joni and Chuck Mitchell might've gotten these gigs in the Detroit/Ann Arbor area—solo acoustic, before the Mynah Birds. Chess Mate coffeehouse, an old folk club in Detroit, Livernois and One-eleventh. Very near there is where the White Tower is. "The Old Laughing Lady"—I was having some coffee and wrote it on napkins. I don't know what prompted it. It came out on a napkin, no guitar. Hangin' out in a coffee shop.

—Did you feel part of the folk scene in Toronto?

Almost. I really didn't get too much of a chance, 'cause I wasn't there that long. I was at the bottom, kinda like the new guy. I wasn't that good, y'know. My songs were pretty dumb. You can hear 'em on that Elektra tape . . . they were what they were.

Vicky Taylor was just a good friend. She had an apartment above the

Night Owl—I lived there a little while. She was a little bit crazy. She would get real sad about things . . . but not for long. She was a real party girl. Had a little bit of money, liked to have a good time. Let me sleep on her floor—me and John Kay. The original Sparrow were great—Dennis Edmonton on guitar: Mars Bonfire. They had that Toronto sound, funky and good. John showed me funky little guitar things—little finger-picking things on the bass guitar strings. A lot of the basis of my rhythm-playing came from John Kay.

Vicky Taylor had this record—Bert Jansch, his first album—and I used to listen to that all the time. Some of the greatest guitar playing I ever heard. I could go on for years about this guy, how fuckin' talented he is. Every note destroyed me. Bert Jansch—great acoustic guitarist, unreal. Him and Dylan—same thing. Bob Dylan's a great *guitar player—a really good acoustic guitar player, a great rhythm guitar player and he's gettin' to be a good lead guitar player. He's just very expressive.*

—Who turned you on to Phil Ochs?

I've always been aware of Phil Ochs. Since the early folkie days in Toronto. Great singer/songwriter. Very melodic. Innaresting character.

The Allen Ward Trio—they were good. They were kinda like a Peter, Paul and Mary thing—sometimes they had David Rea playing with them, and that made them cooler. David Rea was pretty far out. I kinda looked up to them because they had a real job. They could go play clubs—not all the time, but occasionally.

That's where I got high the first time. In David Rea's apartment, with some members of the Allen Ward Trio—Craig Allen, Robin Ward. Hash. It was fun. A revelation.

—About what?

Y'know—about getting high. Just fun. There was nothin' serious *about it, I'll tell ya that, heh heh.*

• • •

---

*"Melodically speaking, Phil Ochs was a big influence on me," Young told deejay Tony Pig in 1969. "I really think Phil Ochs is a genius. . . . He's written fantastic, incredible songs— he's on the same level as Dylan in my eyes."

"My mother was an oil painter, my father played violin in the orchestra and sang through a megaphone," said Bruce Palmer. Born September 9, 1946, Bruce was introduced to jazz and R&B through his brother Stephen. "He was probably the first guy ever in Toronto to live with a Negro and brought her home to dinner," Palmer recalls.

A love of B. B. King, Lightnin' Hopkins and John Coltrane led Palmer into music. He was playing with a band called Jack London and the Sparrows when he saw Ricky James Matthews III, much later to become pimp-funk freak show Rick James, singing in an outfit called the Mynah Birds. "I saw him perform and it was the real deal," said Palmer, who actually traded bands with their bass player to get in the group. James, born James Johnson in Buffalo, New York, fancied himself the next Mick Jagger, a claim particularly ironic since he was black, although as Palmer told Scott Young, "as far as we knew he was white then."

The Mynah Birds—in black leather jackets, yellow turtlenecks and boots—had quite a surreal scene going. The band was financed by John Craig Eaton of the Eaton's department-store dynasty. Legend has it he poured money into the band, establishing a bottomless account for the band's equipment needs. "We used to walk into Eaton's department store, take the elevator up to John's office and say, 'We need about seven hundred dollars for lunch, John. Thanks.' " Apparently Eaton enjoyed being a rock and roll impresario. Outfitted in a trench coat, Eaton would march into the dressing room and, as Palmer told Scott Young, "stride up and down like Knute Rockne, telling us to go out there and knock 'em dead."

Into this rarefied atmosphere stumbled Neil Young. Palmer recalls bumping into him as Neil was wandering down the street carrying an amp. The Mynah Birds had just lost a guitarist, so, said Palmer, he told Young, "Come and join our band—there's a Negro lead singer, we do rock and roll and hey, who cares that you can only play a Gibson twelve-string and sing like a fag?"

So Young became a Mynah Bird. For the first time, he was a mere sideman. Those lucky enough to see any of the band's few gigs say they were electrifying. "Neil had just the acoustic twelve-string with a D'Armond pickup on it, stuffed with newspaper to kill the feedback," said Comrie Smith, who remembers a showstopping Young/James original—featuring the two of them singing harmony—called "Hideaway." "Neil would stop playing lead, do a harp solo, throw the harmonica way up in the air and Ricky would catch it and continue the solo."

Young and James were running buddies for a brief minute. "Neil always described Ricky as having built-in soul," said Smith. He and Young shared an apartment with James at 88 Charles Street, living on bakery deliveries James would lift in the wee hours of the morning. Their pad was your typical no-furniture musician shithole. "There were dustballs rolling like tumbleweed across the floor," said Linda Smith. "Neil would just open a door and tell me to sweep 'em into the closet." James also instigated Young's short romance with amphetamines.

The Mynah Birds were happening. Young helped himself to a new Rickenbacker six-string via the Eatons, and the band landed a recording contract. "We went from playing little clubs in Toronto to recording an album for Motown," said Palmer. A white rock act fronted by a black singer, the Mynah Birds were given the full treatment. "Motown would issue membership cards that would buy anything," said Palmer. "And if you got popped, you wouldn't have to pay—you'd just go, 'Motown recording artist.' " During sessions all the Detroit heavies wandered in and out, including Berry Gordy Jr., Smokey Robinson and Holland-Dozier-Holland. "If they thought we weren't strong enough, a couple of Motown singers would walk in," Young told Cameron Crowe. "And they'd Motown us!"

Unfortunately, everything screeched to a halt when James was busted in the studio for being AWOL from the navy. "We thought he was Canadian," said Palmer. "Even though there are no Negroes in Canada." A single, "It's My Time," was allegedly pulled the day of release, and the album recordings were shelved and remain unreleased to this day. The band's manager, Morley Shelman, ran off with their $25,000 advance and promptly overdosed.

—*What was Rick James like to hang out with?*
Intense. Ricky was great. He was a little bit touchy, dominating—but a good guy. Had a lot of talent. Really wanted to make it bad. Runnin' from the draft. I wasn't a driving force behind the Mynah Birds—I was the lead guitar player, Ricky was the front man. He's out there doin' all that shit and I was back there playin' a little rhythm, a little lead, groovin' along with my bro Bruce. We were havin' a good time. Up until

the time I went to Toronto, I think the Beatles were my favorite of the English groups, but when I went to Toronto, the Stones kind of moved in— along with Rick James. He was really into the Stones. "Get Off My Cloud," "Satisfaction," "Can I Get a Witness"—all these songs we used to do. We got more and more into how cool the Stones were. How simple they were and how cool it was.

We had a funky band. I like bein' in the band. You don't have to sing all the time. It's a lot like playing with Bob. There's somethin' about that that's cool.

We were the only white band at Motown. We didn't do too well in etiquette and choreography—how to be cool, how to move. I thought we fit in pretty good, considering.

I think I met Bruce down at David Rea's apartment below the Riverboat. Bruce was great. Bruce was one of the best guitar players I've ever heard in my life. Blues guitar. Neither Stephen or I played guitar half as well as Bruce. But he didn't play guitar—he played bass. Bruce used to sing and play, and it was funky as hell. Funky blues man. He had an old Kay. He can still play the blues, just like that.

—What did amphetamines do for you?

Kept me up. I loved everybody. Stand in front of the mirror, look at myself and get happy. We used to pop amyl nitrates—but I didn't do that for very long. It's not good for ya.

—Comrie felt when he visited your apartment something was going on he didn't know about.

Heh heh—when he visited the Mynah Birds? Oh, yeah. Whoa. I'm sure there were things goin' on there that I didn't know about.

Back in Toronto after the Mynah Birds fiasco, Young bided his time playing checkers with Palmer at a joint called the Cellar, an all-night basement coffeehouse run by a half-dozen hipsters that was, as Comrie Smith put it, "a horrible Yorkville dive." The ringleader of the bunch was Tannis Neiman, a rail-thin black-haired folksinger who was half Cree Indian and apparently a bit of a handful. "She was a cranky old broad," said Janine Hollinghead, who, along with Neiman and an artist named Beverly Davies, helped run the place.

Young, usually dressed rather mod in a snappy white shirt adorned by one large pink polka dot, sometimes played solo at the club. Beverly Davies remembers him performing one unforgettable number entitled "It's Leaves and It's Grass and It's Outta Your Class." For a while Young lived with Davies in an apartment on Avenue Road a few doors down from Webster's, a twenty-four-hour restaurant and hangout.

Tall, pale and sullen—not to mention painfully mysterious—the twenty-year-old loner had everything required to be a heartthrob, but most admirers soon became frustrated over Young's seeming disinterest. "Neil was beset by women in those days," said Hollinghead. "I think that everywhere he turned, he found adoring women, and he really didn't know what to do with it or how to deal with it—Beverly was in love with him, Judy was in love with him, Tannis was in love with him. Neil seemed to attract women like magnets—and yet he repelled 'em like crazy."

Meanwhile, the enormous and inescapable cultural pull of the Beatles was beginning to spawn weird hybrids in the States, as folkies and jug-band rejects plugged social consciousness and snips of real poetry in to the big beat. In mid-1965, teens and college-age kids were absolutely ripe for the stuff, and massive success came seemingly overnight for the likes of the Lovin' Spoonful, the Mamas and the Papas and, at the very top of the heap, L.A.'s Byrds. "The Byrds were the beginning of 'not straight,' " said writer Richard Meltzer. "It was about drugs. It was music to accompany the smoking of pot." The Byrds, Young said years later, "taught me about cool."

Dylan upped the ante with a shambolic howl called "Like a Rolling Stone." Haphazardly recorded in New York City with a band of up-all-week accidents on the ride of their lives, this was surely one of the most cathartic records ever unleashed. Shattering the three-minute limit twice over, it was Dylan's first Top-Ten hit, reaching number two at the end of August—and music that elicited catcalls from the hard-line folkies at the Newport Folk Festival on July 25. But petulant traditionalists couldn't stop the impending tsunami. "By '65, there was something happening," said Meltzer. "It was just immense. It was a world cultural thing."

Young must've felt like the world was passing him by. He had bombed as a folksinger, he owed everybody in town money and he was tied to a band whose leader was now in jail. Things weren't exactly looking up. His father remembers running into him that winter, walking down the street, his hands bare in the subzero temperature. Scott offered to buy him gloves, but Neil declined and wandered off. They would not see each other again for three and a half years.

Young hatched a plan with Palmer for an escape. They now had a friend in the States, Stephen Stills—supposedly in California, although nobody really had a clue as to where he actually was. Beverly Davies remembers the prophetic day they were all hanging out at Webster's, and the Mamas and the Papas' "California Dreamin' " wafted out of the jukebox.

"Let's go to California and become rock stars," proclaimed Young.

That sounds like a Canadian story to me. That sounds too real to be true.

I had a goal. First I wanted to quit school and go to L.A. Then I modified my plan—quit school, go to Toronto. I thought that if I made it in Toronto, it would be easier to make it in L.A. So I went to Toronto and I couldn't make it. So I said, "Fuck Toronto—I'll go to L.A. and make it. If I make it in Toronto, all I am is big in Toronto. If I go to L.A. and make it, then I'm big in the fuckin' WORLD." Then I'm talkin' to more people—I got a bigger audience, and an audience is where it's at.

The more of an audience, the more experimenting you can do, the bigger you are and the bigger chance you have for a lotta people to like ya, even if they all don't. I was aware of it right from the beginning— why spend a lotta time making it big in a place that it didn't matter? If you're gonna make it big somewhere, why not go where if you make it big, it matters right away?

I thought the Byrds were great. They looked different, y'know—it was like "Wow, must be a trip down there." I don't know that I wanted to go down there and look like them, but I did want to go down to L.A. and see what the fuck that was all about.

They were the new thing. They were the marriage of folk and rock and roll. All the folkies were gonna start playing electric music. Some of them were scared and some of them weren't. But they all knew that there was more to a song than just The Songs and The Lyrics, and that was scaring some of them. Because when you do it with a band, it puts a third thing that's just as big right up there with it. So that was what I heard when I heard the Byrds, and it didn't scare me at all because I already knew how to play the electric guitar. I felt good about it.

—Dylan has described his music as "attempting to do something that's never been done before."

Well, I think he's done that. How 'bout me? No, Bob *did it, heh heh. I don't know . . . I don't know.*

For me, *Dylan is the greatest that ever lived in the singer/songwriter/poet vein. He's an original, like Woody Guthrie. From a literary sense? This guy's over the top. He's like Longfellow or one of those fuckin' guys, that's what Dylan is. He even named himself after a poet. He knew who* he *was, heh heh.*

There was a time when his essence was coming out strongly—really strongly—so it affected this whole generation. Everybody related to his voice, what he was saying, and you could really get into it. Not many people had that kind of impact—Woody Guthrie had that kind of an impact. Hank Williams.

He was a heavy influence on me at the beginning. The thread of his music—not so much the musical thread, but the soul of what he was doing . . . what he was putting together. His music was a unique kind of music, too, like Jimmie Rodgers, Woody Guthrie. Plus, at that point in my life, the whole thing of "Who do you want to emulate? Who do you want to be like?" That makes a big mark on ya.

Early on, when Bob decided to play with a band, everybody else perceived it as a radical change. I thought it was great, I was fuckin' knocked out. . . . I had already played rock and roll and folk music. I was goin' back and forth from one to the other, so to me it never made any difference. I couldn't see what the big deal was. You play electric guitar, you play acoustic guitar, who gives a shit? What's the big deal? Only the people that try to put a label on it. They try to label you—they all thought they had him figured out.

He'd always been a folkie, he had this following and they all hated rock and roll music. They were intellectuals, they were the beatnik hippies, they were cool. They weren't goin' for this rock and roll shit.

That's a classic case of someone trying to nail you into a corner. He just did what he did—he played folk music up to a point, made records, sang, became a folk hero, did the whole thing, then decided to move on—so there really wasn't that big of a deal. The big deal was the reaction to it.

The audience was upset because they knew that other audiences had been upset, so they were gonna get upset, too. It's like the Trans *thing, when I wore the vocoder and people booed me. That was on a much lower scale than what was happening with Bob, but that's what I can relate it to.*

They were exposing themselves—the audience. For not being free-thinking. For being closed-minded. Heh, heh. Bob just kept playing. He'd seen people expose themselves before, so I don't think it stopped him at all. Pretty funny.

Bob had a great band, too. That first band was awesome. Mike Bloomfield. Al Kooper. Man, that was bad. *Mike Bloomfield especially. What a guitar player. I can remember hearing "Like a Rolling Stone" on the radio. I was walkin' down a sidewalk, I think I'd been up all night—I was comin' home from the Eatons' house, walkin' back to Yorkville either by myself or with Rick James. A walk through the city, and I heard it. I was out on the street. I think it was on a transistor radio, I'm not sure. I'm hearing all these great lyrics come pouring out over this track, all these images and everything, and I'm going, "That is the coolest shit I've heard." It was out there. "Like a Rolling Stone" was over the top when it came out.*

And I was relating to it big-time. I just loved it. Made me wanna keep doin' it. Great words, great beat—the whole emotion of the whole thing was very much like a lotta these bands today who sing their songs, and they're seemingly abstract? It's the same fuckin' thing, it's exactly the same thing, the same feeling. I can relate to "Like a Rolling Stone" the way these kids can relate to Eddie Vedder or Nirvana or Soundgarden.

I always listen. There isn't a record that he's made that I haven't listened to. Dylan's somethin' so good you don't wanna have too much of it. I mean, I think I liked Bob's music so much that at one point I actually had to consciously not listen to it because it affected me so much. I realized at one point, "If I listened too much I'd become like him." Because I'm like a sponge.

There's a song that I wrote because I heard "Positively 4th Street" that's terrible. . . . *What the fuck was the name of that song?* * *There was this chick that was kinda leading me on and then wouldn't fuck me. And I left her. And I got all fuckin' bent out of shape and wrote this song. It was a nasty song, it wasn't very nice. I realized you could be an* asshole *in a record and tell somebody exactly what you thought of them. I realized all this* new *territory that could be covered. . . .*

After Bob moved on and became a band member as well as a singer/songwriter, then basically he kind of advanced along. He's made some radical changes, but Bob really has been pretty steady. His changes aren't as radical as Bobby Darin's. He's still my favorite when I listen to writers. "Tom Thumb Blues"—I love that song. I like the melody and I like the words. The girl. The guy. Images of the housing project. It's almost like a movie, that song. Real free-floating. Typical Dylan, lettin' it go. Lettin' it out. Heh heh.

I'd like to do a tour with him someday—where we both play in the same band—his band. You could record a great album with Bob in about three days.

Dylan. He's so funny. He came up to me in Europe, first time we ac-tually shared a concert bill and not a benefit. He'd just done a great fuckin' set. *They just slammed. Bob came over and whispers—"Well, I got 'em all warmed up for ya" . . . Oh God. I like him.*

He's a brutally honest guy. He loves to tell the truth, heh heh. He even enjoys *it.*

"All of a sudden Neil phoned me up one Sunday," said Comrie Smith. "I hadn't heard from him. He said, 'I gotta deliver this equipment to the Tee Pee Motor Inn in Pickering. Is there any way you can help me?' " Smith whizzed over to Charles Street, where Young was loading stacks of the Mynah Birds' equipment into a clapped-out red Econoline van. The left-overs were stuffed into Comrie's '41 Plymouth. Unbeknownst to Smith, Young and Palmer had decided to sell the equipment Eaton had bought

---

*Both Joel Bernstein and I think the song Young is referring to is "Lover in the Mirror," an unrecorded work that a manuscript exists for, dating from September 1966: "You look an awful lot older than you did before the dawn / Is it your eyes are getting colder or your makeup has broken up wrong?"

them to subsidize the trip to California. "I didn't have a clue," said Smith, who cheerfully drove the hot goods out Highway 401 to the drop-off in Pickering.

Smith finally got wise. "On the way back, I said, 'Neil, what the hell's going on?' " Young avoided the unsavory details, but as the ubiquitous "California Dreamin' " slithered out of the old tube radio in Comrie's car, he did let on about his plans for the future: "Well, Comrie, I can hear the Mamas and the Papas singing 'All the leaves are brown, and the skies are gray . . . ' I'm gonna go down to the States and really make it. I'm on my way." Smith recalls Neil shouting out the window, "Today North Toronto, tomorrow the world!"

Young next got a new set of wheels for the journey—a '53 Pontiac hearse he christened Mort Two. Since Comrie had never ridden in the original Mort, Young took him for a spin, revisiting all their old haunts, stopping at the old spot overlooking Yonge where the pair had smoked their pipes and dreamed of being rock stars. Smith didn't know it, but Young was saying goodbye. Linda Smith, along for the ride, didn't sense much remorse in Neil's looking back.

"Neil was totally confident, very focused. You knew he was gonna make it. I think he had it all planned . . . he knew what he was doing. I don't think Neil did anything spontaneously—he appeared to be reckless and spontaneous, but I think he plotted it all out and just kept his mouth shut. I think he's that way with his whole life."

Those people need to take a pill or something. Get a life. Think clearly, heh heh. How far in advance was I plotting? That's the key question. One step? Two steps? Prebirth? *When was the Plot Laid and the Deed Done? Heh heh. That's what I'd like to know. I'm not talking about Linda—it's more general than that. You can plot your whole life ahead and have it be spontaneous? Because very rarely did I do anything that I didn't want to do. I'd come to a point and make a decision—but did I think about the next decision, or the one after that, very often? I guess the longer it went along, the more I'd look down the road to make a move. But did I know I was gonna make a move? No. Not till somethin' happened. Always somethin' would happen. . . . You got a new thing, where ya gonna go? Waddya gonna do? That's how it happened, that's how I moved through that whole period—and my whole life.*

They left Toronto from the Cellar. Young's group now included Bruce Palmer, Tannis Neiman, Janine Hollinghead, a nonmusician named Mike Gallagher who had some funds and a redhead named Judy Mack who apparently also had a few dollars, which cut Beverly Davies and her empty pockets out of the journey. "Beverly is the girl who got left behind," said Hollinghead. "The six of us left her on the sidewalk."

Hollinghead recalls Young not being thrilled to leave town in another funky old hearse, and said that Davies had a lot to do with boosting his confidence. "Beverly practically engineered this trip. She talked Neil into trying it again." Palmer gave the teary-eyed Beverly his last dollar, then Neil took her sleeping bag with the tepees and Indians on the inside, telling her "when he had the money, he'd send it."

One ramshackle hearse packed to the gills with six scraggly kids, a bunch of guitars, amps, an autoharp and, on Palmer, a couple ounces of pot, which, said Hollinghead, "he shared for a while." According to Hollinghead, they left on March 22, 1966. Young planned on five days to get to Los Angeles. First they went west, curving way up out of the way because Young, paranoid about crossing into Detroit, wanted to cross at Sault Ste. Marie. His hunch paid off; arriving at the border in the wee hours of the night, they encountered some lone geezer in a rocking chair who bought Young's bullshit story about shortcutting through the States to visit his mom in Winnipeg.

Once safely across, the group promptly got lost in Hiawatha National Forest, where they spent what sounds like the only peaceful night of the trip. This was not a harmonious bunch. Visions of the original Mort no doubt dancing in his head, Young freaked out whenever anyone other than he drove. "I'd be laying at the back of the hearse trying to sleep, but listening instead obsessively to the transmission," Young told Nick Kent. More than one person told me that Neiman became furious with Young, accusing him of indulging in Vicky Taylor's downers to get him through the trip. "Tannis's mother had killed herself on painkillers," recalls Beverly Davies, who said Tannis claimed Young "was popping pills all the way down there."

Somewhere in Ohio, Young short-circuited. "We'd been on the road two and a half days pretty much nonstop," said Hollinghead. "Eating garbage food, spending more money than we had, not even a third of the way there yet, and Neil just got a little nutsy one morning and pulled off. He just basically said, 'Out, out, everybody out,' and he just tore out everything, threw it all out on the ground. He just emptied the hearse. I think at one point Neil was considering leaving us and everything there and driving away. He just stood there with his shirttails hangin' out, his eyes all bloodshot, lifted his arms to the gods, screamed to the ozone, 'AAAAGGHHH!' and got over it. We all got back in and drove away."

*The girls, they were all fighting and everything, I think it was gettin'
nasty. So I just said, "Fuck all of you if you can't get along." I can't see
how I would take a downer and drive. I think the only thing involved in
the trip would be weed, but I may have blocked that out of my mind. I
wasn't doin' speed then. No. Tannis mighta just been shocked at what I
was really like. 'Cause I was nervous as hell! I was twitchy. Jumpy . . .
That's why I couldn't smoke grass in those days . . . I was still . . . tuning it up. And I was way outta tune.
—What fears did you conquer?
I don't think I conquered any fears. Maybe I wore down some so that
they're not as real.
—Such as?
Driving. Driving up and down hills. That used to bother me. Changing
altitudes did something to my head. Made me feel . . . funny. Disoriented. But I overcame that. I don't know how. Somehow I struck a deal
with this thing, okay? But it's not conquered—it was bigger than me.
   I was always worried. I was hyper-worrying that the car wouldn't
make it. I think Tannis drove it rough. I could hear it. . . . I'd already had
one go out on me, see, so I was pretty fuckin' paranoid about this Pontiac. And it was really a similar kind of sound like with the other hearse.
I could tell it was gettin' worse. It was just a U-joint.
   Route 66 was a gas. I just loved traveling. I got hooked on those kind
of trips when I was five, six, years old when my dad used to drive us
down to Florida. The highway bug. Four-lane highway, long thin lines*

through the desert, goin' into these towns, the gambling, all the neon lights. I went, "Wow, this is so wild!" Pretty far-out.

In Oklahoma the scraggly travelers managed to float a free meal out of a southern couple who saw Neil's Beatle haircut and Neiman's long black hair and thought they were Sonny and Cher. In Texas there were some tense moments when the ever fearless Palmer mouthed off to a state trooper. "Bruce used to always carry his pot in his shirt pocket in a bag," said Hollinghead. "It was flappin' in the breeze, and this trooper's standin' there askin' these boys for draft cards." They managed to escape.

Struggling up an incline east of Albuquerque, the hearse began to falter. Nerves frayed. "Neil started yellin' at me about second gear, lugging his vehicle," recalls Hollinghead. "I said, 'Y'know, Neil, this car's never been outta second gear, it's a fuckin' *hearse.*' We were yellin' and arguin'. Tannis was in one of her huffs and started haulin' suitcases out." Along came another unsympathetic state trooper to complicate matters. Everybody wound up back in Albuquerque, stuck in a motel while Mort Two was being fixed. According to Hollinghead, weird tests were going on out in the desert, and looking out of the motel-room window one night, she thought she saw a "friggin' mushroom cloud." It was an ominous sign, for Young's nervous system was experiencing explosions of its own.

With a sleeping bag pulled over his head, Young holed up in his room, unable to eat. He "basically just turned into a chattering, blooming idiot," said Hollinghead. Palmer said Young "went into convulsions, for what reasons we didn't know. For days he was on the floor and I was tending to him." Despite what sounds like the first onset of epilepsy, Young was determined to make it to Los Angeles. Soon the hearse was back on the road—minus Janine and Tannis. "They dumped us in Albuquerque," said Hollinghead.

We left Tannis and Janine 'cause they were drivin' us fuckin' nuts. These chicks were fuckin' nuts, they had bad vibes. But who knows. My tolerance level wasn't very high. Ran out of steam in Albuquerque. Had to stop there a couple of days. I was really exhausted.

We got all the way down to L.A. It was, like, nonstop, smoking weed, driving down the road. Really a trip. Comin' down the hill from San Bernardino and bein' scared—I mean, it was so steep, we're comin' down in the hearse, it was like "Whoa!" And we were fuckin' exhausted. We really were burnin' it. Mort Two got me there. Made it to L.A. Phenomenal.

—Did you have an idea of California in your head?

Not really. 77 Sunset Strip, Route 66 *and* Dragnet. *TV shows.*

When I went, I didn't have any intention of anything. I didn't know what the fuck I was doin'. We were just going—like lemmings. I knew what I wanted and I knew that's where I had to go to get it, but what was I gonna do after that? Would I stick around to enjoy it? I didn't have the foggiest notion.

Foggy . . . everything was foggy. It was a foggy day in L.A. when we got there. April Fool's Day. We were punchy from the trip. I think Bruce and I drove straight from Albuquerque to Los Angeles. I remember drivin' by Juanita Street. Bruce and I were pretty giddy by then. We must've said "JUAN-EEE-TA STREET" two hundred times, laughing our asses off because we were so tired and giddy.

We stayed on this street parallel to Laurel Canyon, I think it's called Holly Street. We parked the hearse there and slept in it a couple of nights. Then we found this old friend, Danny Cox—a black folksinger, a really cool guy I met in Winnipeg at the 4-D who went to breakfast once with Koblun and I and told us about Hollywood and California. He put us up for a night or two.

We made enough money to live on by selling rides in the hearse. There were two restaurants that were happening, one was called Huff's, the other was Canter's. We would hang out at one and charge people a buck to go to the other. We'd load up, go back. That's how we made our money, Bruce and I.

L.A. was just real big. Bruce and I were walkin' down Sunset, we found a roach on the sidewalk and we smoked it. And that stuff got us so wasted . . . I don't know what it was.

"For a time we were all free in the sixties," said Ken Viola. "For a time. I don't think our parents were ever free . . . ya know?"

I talked to many fans while writing this book. I interviewed most all of the people in Young's inner circle. At times I even consulted that most loathsome bottom-feeder, the rock critic. And nobody understood Neil Young's art like Ken Viola.

Ken Viola lives in a nice house in the New Jersey suburbs with his wife and two kids. He wears his salt-and-pepper hair and mustache short. Ken's a big guy, and with his imposing frame and machine-gun raps, for a minute you think you're talking to a teamster. A pretty decent disguise. Because once his vibe hits full force, you realize you're dealing with a poet, a *psychedelic* poet. If you come through a round with Viola without a question raised—or your consciousness altered—you'd better have your karma inspected back at the factory, pal.

Take that dough set aside for a trip to the Rock and Roll Hall of Fame and blow it on a bus ride to Ken's instead. Hopefully he'll let you in, because there's nothing you really need to see in Cleveland—it's all in Ken Viola's attic. Records and tapes are everywhere, huge posters of Neil Young cover the ceiling, file cabinets bulge with thirty years of clippings. Viola possesses one of the world's great collections of pop-culture ephemera, but this is no anal-retentive keep-it-in-the-plastic-bag-and-don't-touch collector's nightmare. Viola *uses* this stuff—to live. To teach. And to search for an alternative to the way things sometimes are.

Ken Viola still believes in the power of rock and roll. And the rock and roll he believes in more than just about anything else is that of Neil Young. Viola has listened very closely to Neil Young for over thirty years, buying every record, digesting every song, relishing every phase with the fevered enthusiasm of a kid who's just bought his first 45—all the while retaining a critical overview that borders on mystical. It is in this ability that he stands alone.

Lemme tell you something about Neil Young fans—the *real* fans: They're all a bunch of fuckin' maniacs. You have the ones that prefer the mellow acoustic side, like Scott Oxman, a proud Christian who heads the Crosby, Stills, Nash, and Young archives out of his well-appointed Los Angeles condo and organizes yearly get-togethers with like-minded fans for sing-alongs of "Helpless" and "Teach Your Children." He's disdainful of the freakier side of Young's work, the complete opposite of Crazy Horse fanatic Dave McFarlin, a blue-collar kid who discovered Young in the mid-eighties. McFarlin thinks anything Shakey does without the Horse is lame, no-edge bullshit—Neil Young Lite. Then there's Jef Michael Pielher, who specializes in arcane discographical inquiries. He gingerly studies the label of a single with the cold eye of a lab technician analyzing a bacterial smear under a microscope. He can rave over the "obvious" superiority of an alternate version of "Like an Inca" that Young dropped from *Trans* and has written detailed-to-the-verge-of-the-subatomic articles on variations in pressings and album versions for *Broken Arrow,* a quarterly fanzine put out by a European-based organization called the Neil Young Appreciation Society.

Broken Arrow publishes the mind-numbing ramblings of fans, plus whatever arcane details of Young's life they can ferret out, like their in-depth article—complete with footnotes—on the 1952 Canadian polio outbreak that struck Young as a child. Once, the publication was endearingly crude, a few mimeographed sheets stapled together. Now it's a real magazine with computer graphics and full-color cover, a little too slick and worldly—but maybe that just reflects something of its subject. The NYAS seems benign compared to the Rusties, a group of self-appointed experts spawned by the Internet.

None of these divergent strains seem to agree on anything—they all think they have the one correct answer. Just like me. I'm sure it would fill Young with glee—if he bothered to pay the slightest attention.

Ken Viola is an exception. He's been able to sidestep the pitfalls of being a fan, avoiding becoming obsessed in an unhealthy way, and although at odd and sometimes amusing junctures in his life he has bumped into his hero, Viola takes it in stride. He doesn't expect anything from Neil Young. The way he sees it, Young has already given him enough. Each new album, says Ken, is "like a letter from a friend I don't have to write back to."

Somehow Ken managed to become a fully functional adult without throwing his records away, and without becoming a square. For a while Viola tried being a musician himself, even gaining Young's permission to cut one of the master's unreleased songs. Then for many years Ken made his living overseeing security for the Grateful Dead, watching the culture he loved become big business, seeing many of the musicians who so inspired him act in a less than flattering manner or, worse, completely self-destruct. But Ken has remained uncynical about it all. In what has to be the ultimate tribute, he named his two sons Dylan and Neil. Coming from anybody else, that alone could make me throw up, but with Ken, it's just more proof of how serious the guy is.

Rock and roll changed Ken Viola's life, and it all began with Neil Young and Buffalo Springfield.

•   •   •

The year 1966 remains sacred for many who went through it at an impressionable age. As culture hound Charlie Beesley put it, "There you are, heading out after school in the family Buick, scanning the AM dial, when the Yardbirds' 'Happenings Ten Years Time Ago' hits you square in the face and lifts you into the squall of a whole new universe being born. All the way to Burger World."

"You had this, in a way, totally disposable thing—you had trash, in a sense," said writer Richard Meltzer, then a twenty-one-year-old Yale grad student immersed in the music and writing about it like no one else. "Something where, yes, it had its emotional urgency and all that, but basically it was disposable—something that could be blown away in the night merging with the eternal, infinite . . . universe-manifesting disposable shit.

"I was taking courses in philosophy and religion, and it seemed to me it was a greater example than Jesus Christ for something of the moment equaling the forever. Before producers came up with the formula sound, it was really about hearing that tentative attempt to come up with new sound—to come up with *something*. Sound for sound's sake.

"It was about discovery—you have the artist, you have the artwork, you have the audience—and I'm not gonna say that we were all one in the fabulous sixties, but those three things were in tandem: the artist, the work and the audience. It was a dance."

The original explosion of rock and roll—Elvis, Jerry Lee, Bo Diddley, Chuck Berry, Little Richard and so many others—had petered out by the tail end of the fifties. "Everybody I know who came outta the fifties couldn't have made it to the end of the fifties without rock and roll," said Meltzer. "In the fifties, you had all this regional music that suddenly became national. I think that it was something that had been brewing forever that finally got exposed. Whereas the sixties were an accident that was even more massive than the fifties. The sixties were the fifties with chops."

Meltzer clearly remembers November 1963 and the frenzied soundtrack that accompanied the wake following John F. Kennedy's assassination in Dallas—"Surfin' Bird" by the Trashmen and the Beatles' first album. "The Beatles were the suggestion of infinite possibility in a music that really wasn't thinking very big. You felt that rock and roll had been reborn, and one of the clues was that teenage girls were screaming again—that was to me the most spine-chilling fact. Not since the beginning of Elvis had there been that kind of frenzy about it."

The Beatles begat the British Invasion: the Stones, the Kinks, the Animals, the Zombies; the Byrds brought it back to America with "Mr. Tambourine Man." Then Dylan went electric, and he and the Beatles headed an intense period of experimentation that crossed rock and folk and soul with exotic bits of Eastern, jazz and music-hall pop to arc toward the future. The Kinks' *Face to Face,* Love's *Da Capo, The Velvet Underground & Nico*—each, as Meltzer put it, "strip-mining a new continent." And this cyclone of innovation couldn't help but feed off the chaos tearing through social structures.

"Put the music together with all the social stuff going on—you have a civil rights movement, you have a lot of people taking the same drugs, you have a peace movement—a bunch of guys who wanna get out of the war because otherwise they're gonna die," said Meltzer. "Here were kids who pretty much stuck their necks out, put their head on a guillotine block— 'I'll stand for who I am right now. Kill me.' Certainly lots of bullshit took place during the sixties, and certainly most of the participants were bourgeois middle-class white-bread assholes, but it was their finest hour. It did help that you had fear of death, combined with drugs, combined with music that worked.

"Because of the fact that so many of the people involved were doing the same things—you had an ideology of some sort, you had a war, you had these drugs—you had people that were coming to the music with a full head of steam. Without the music, drugs would've delivered nothing, the Vietnam protests would've delivered nothing. Music was the cutting edge of everything. And the music was great. It was like an anthem for rejecting the house with the picket fence, Mommy, Daddy, let's sit down for some roast beef and talk about nice things or whatever the American myth was supposed to be. . . . It was like the beast that controlled everything was losing its grip."

As Elvis, the Beatles and Dylan reconfigured the world, Neil Young listened and watched from the sidelines. Now he would be thrown directly into the eye of the hurricane—Los Angeles, 1966. Buffalo Springfield would be critically acclaimed, gain a rabid following and influence much music that followed but the band itself never got over, and the story they left behind is so tortured, it's amazing Neil Young survived it at all. "Kind of hopped up" is how he described himself during the Springfield days to Karen Schoemer in 1992. "Not on drugs, but kind of amped out. A little out of control. And too open. Wide open."

•　　•　　•

Buffalo Springfield met on the road. Chance has played a big part in Neil Young's life, and it was chance that brought the Springfield together.

The Byrds phenomenon had drawn Stephen Stills—now free of the Au Go-Go Singers—out to California in the fall of 1965. There he hooked up with Barry Friedman, aka Frazier Mohawk, a music business eccentric with many odd involvements, among them producing such outré artifacts as Nico's *The Marble Index* and *The Moray Eels Eat the Holy Modal Rounders*. He would play an integral part in the early days of the Springfield, and would promptly get screwed over in the process.

At first, Stills hadn't exactly set Hollywood on fire; he'd even failed an audition for the Monkees. He did succeed in conning his friend Richie Furay to fly out and join him, bullshitting that he had a band together.

Furay stepped off the plane to discover the band Stills touted had exactly one member: Stephen Stills. It was a grim time, although Friedman managed to get the pair a publishing deal with Screen Gems that kept them alive.

It was around this same time that Neil Young and Bruce Palmer, having spent days looking for Stills, were thinking of leaving Los Angeles and heading for San Francisco. The details of the unlikely event that happened next depend on which participant tells it, but the outcome was Buffalo Springfield.

"We were in this white van," Furay told writer Dave Zimmer, "stuck in traffic on Sunset Boulevard. I turned to brush a fly off my arm, looked into the other lane and saw this black hearse with Ontario plates going in the other direction. Then Stephen looked across and said, 'I'll bet I know who that is.'" Furay swung a quick U-turn and gave chase. "We hear *honk! honk!* and all this screaming and yelling," said Bruce Palmer. "We turn around and there's Stephen and Richie.

"They were going that way and we were going this way," said Palmer. "Karma turned Richie Furay's head."

We didn't have a plan. I hung out at the Trip tryin' to find Stills. Asking people did anybody know Steve Stills—just people on the street. Couldn't get anything together in L.A. Hadn't met anybody we could get together with, so we were on our way to San Francisco. We knew music was happening up there, too. Later that day we were gonna leave. I don't exactly know what we had to do to be ready, heh heh.

It just so happens we met Stephen in a traffic jam that day. I just remember them yelling at us in traffic. Turned around and came up behind us. Stephen recognized the hearse and Ontario plates—even though it wasn't the hearse I had before. He thought that must be us.

We went to Friedman's house because it was a place to stay. We started playing, and right away it seemed like it would be a good thing to start a band.

The name started out as a joke. We saw it on the side of a steamroller. Me and Stephen and Van Dyke Parks were walkin' along and we saw this Buffalo Springfield steamroller parked right outside Barry's house. "What the fuck are we gonna call our group?" Either me or Stephen said, "Buffalo Springfield." I think it was me, but I can't swear to it. Then we started tryin' drummers—Dewey Martin and Billy Mundi. Billy was really good, but I liked Dewey. I still like Dewey. I like playing with him. He's a sensitive drummer—same way Ralph Molina's sensitive. Sensitive. *You get harder, he gets harder. You pull back, he pulls back. He can feel the music—you don't have to tell him. Eye contact. Signals. All natural. To me that's worth its weight in gold. I guess I didn't feel that with Billy—although he may have been a better drummer.*

Born September 30, 1940, Walter Dwayne Midkiff, aka Dewey Martin, the third Canadian to join the band, already had a reputation as a professional musician: he had gone out on the road with the likes of Patsy Cline, Faron Young and Roy Orbison. After fronting an ersatz, Seattle-based British Invasion band called Sir Walter Raleigh and the Coupons, Martin had made his way to Los Angeles, playing in an unsuccessful rock version of bluegrass outfit the Dillards. Out of work, he heard about some hot young band in need of a drummer, so he called Stills, who promptly informed Martin he could drag his kit over to Fountain Avenue and audition.

"I'm going out on an *audition,*" grumbled Martin, still indignant decades later. "I didn't have to audition for Orbison or Patsy." A few years older than the rest of the Springfield, Martin was perhaps the most incongruous addition to a band full of mutual misfits. Cocky, aggressive and sporting mod attire, he behaved more like an extra from a cop show than some folk-rocker. Dewey liked showbiz: He'd be the only Buffalo to appear as a contestant on *The Dating Game.*

"After the first rehearsal, I said, 'What are you gonna call the band?' " he recalls. "They went over and pulled out this sign, BUFFALO SPRINGFIELD. I said, 'Great, man—a *steamroller.* You got a heavy sound. Let's go for it.' "

"There was no downtime," Young would later tell his father. "Everybody was ready. These were people who had come to L.A. for the same reason, identical, all finding each other. . . . It didn't take any time before we all knew we had the right combination. Time meant nothing. We were ready."

And in retrospect, Young felt they were all equals. "It was the best of the bands that I've played with in my life, because of the fact that there was no one in it that was any more than anyone else," he told David Gans in 1982.

"Everybody was the same; we were all in a band together. That gave an urgency to the music which I haven't experienced since."

On April 15, 1966—approximately ten days after getting together*—the Springfield began a short tour of southern California with the Byrds that Barry Friedman had arranged. "We went from rehearsing in the living room to opening for the Byrds," said Palmer.

•　　•　　•

When I asked Arthur Lee of Love to give me a feel for what Los Angeles was like in 1966, he laughed wearily. "I think that feel is gone, friend—it was a more loving, sharing-type feel, and not so much drive-by shooting, y'know what I mean? It was real free."

Part of the freedom involved drugs. "It's a shame to have to talk about drugs in a way today—the connotation," said Henry Diltz, then a member of the Modern Folk Quartet. "I remember it was just kind of dream time where everybody was just so idealistic. . . . I was smokin' grass all the time, and it kept you in this constant state of idealism and this wonderful sort of euphoria—not an escape kind, the kind where you say, 'Why is there war? Let's be friends. Let's put down the guns and hug each other for God's sake. Life is beautiful.' I remember thinking if only we could get the president to smoke some grass, we could have world peace."

Rock music took over Los Angeles, and most of the action centered around a flock of clubs on Sunset Strip, a scene galvanized by the overnight success of the Byrds. "The Byrds were the absolute paragon of what it meant to be hip in the sixties," said Peter Lewis, songwriter/guitarist for Moby Grape. Omnipresent in the L.A. scene: rebel Byrd David Crosby. "David smoked a lot of really fine grass," said Henry Diltz. "I remember him walkin' through the Trip in his Borsalino hat with a whole box

---

*According to recent recollections, Young maintained that Buffalo Springfield's first public gig took place at a Monday-night hoot at the Troubadour on April 11, 1966. The Springfield era remains the most chaotic period of Young's life. Trying to ascertain a specific date for many events during the Springfield era remains a convoluted nightmare, and I have attempted to avoid it unless there is some corroboration. So many rumors have swirled around the Springfield—such as "Stampede," a mythical *second* LP. "Buffalo Springfield was a mirage," said Young. "Only those who were there know what happened and we're not too sure."

of Bambu rolling papers you couldn't buy anywhere, just handing them out to people."

As influential as the Byrds were, they still suffered from "the lingering stink of folk," said writer Richard Meltzer. "They came from the very squeaky-clean folk scene. . . . Nietzsche came up with this dichotomy for music—Apollonian and Dionysian. Dionysian is drunk and falling down and of the flesh; Apollonian is ethereal, the music of the spheres. The Byrds were totally an Apollonian band without exception, until the more hard-core psychedelic period—I don't think before 'Eight Miles High' they had one song with much Dionysian oompah—but the Springfield had a lot of that Dionysian thing in them, because they came from rock."

Three veteran folksingers gone electric, with a rhythm section made up of a bluegrass mandolin whiz on his first Fender bass and a notoriously erratic drummer whose only previous experience had been playing bongos on Venice Beach, at the time they played with the Springfield, the Byrds were, as bassist Chris Hillman recalls, "so 'lacksadaisical' we were on the verge of collapsing." In the studio, the Byrds were miraculous, but live, the situation—exacerbated by clashing personalities and drugs—was hopeless. A Byrds show was more a happening than a listening experience. The reverse was true of the Springfield, who would triumph onstage and fumble in the studio.

"Live, we cast a spell on people," said Dewey Martin. No one had ever heard anything like it—three guitars, three singer/songwriters and an extraordinarily funky bass-and-drum combo. "A bunch of folkies backed by a Stax-Volt rhythm section," is how fan John Breckow puts it. "The Springfield blew us off the stage," said Hillman. "It was tough to play with 'em. They were hungry and young and they just had the goods."

From the beginning we were really good. I think Chris Hillman really helped us out in the beginning. I thought the Byrds were great, too. Michael Clarke—I thought he was a great *drummer, I didn't think he was a* bad *drummer. He lost the beat every once in awhile—but that didn't make him bad. He was a* funky *drummer. I remember the Byrds being really fuckin' good. The fact that they were sloppy didn't bother me. They were still the Byrds, and they sounded like the Byrds. The only problem they had was that sometimes they were* too *high. Crosby would start talkin' or they'd get disoriented or somethin'. But they all sounded great to me. I loved it. I was happy to be there.*

The L.A. music scene. The Doors. Used to play with them all the time at the Whisky. One week it would be the Doors with the Springfield, the next week it would be the Springfield with the Doors—for weeks on end. Play every night. Crowds would come. The Doors were fuckin' great. A little weird. Kinda arty. They were over my head at the time—I didn't even realize how great they were. I didn't see it till a lotta time had passed. Love—they were cool. Pretty "out there." They were just bad enough and fucked up enough to make fun of—but they were so good, too. They were just off-the-wall—they weren't really respected for what they were doing by the other musicians. But Love was a great band—when you look back on it, they were really awesome. "Orange Skies." "I just got out my little red book. . . ." Those fuckin' songs, what the hell is that? Great stuff.*

I loved the Beach Boys. I hung out with Mike and Dennis—Dennis and I were real tight. Brian's a genius. Ever heard this song Brian wrote called "A Day in the Life of a Tree"? Great song, man.

The Seeds—they were one of those great bands that were terrible. *Didn't matter—their records cooked. "Mr. Farmer"—that's a good one, man. Buffalo Springfield wasn't as "out there" as those bands. With the Byrds, the energy may be similar—the music isn't. But the Byrds' records sounded better.*

•   •   •

Impresario Barry Friedman took credit for encouraging the band to develop distinct onstage personalities. "I copied what the Byrds did, really," he said. "Each one had their own individual trademark."

The engine of the Springfield was Palmer. "There was a mystique around Bruce," said record mogul Ahmet Ertegun. "He was like a guru, a musical guru. The rest of the band all idolized him."

---

*At one point Young was going to produce Love's second LP with engineer Bruce Botnick, and it has long been rumored that he had a hand in arranging some of their songs. Member Bryan McLean claimed in a recent interview that Young had a hand in arranging their side-long opus, "Revelation." Arthur Lee told me Neil might have had something to do with "Daily Planet." "Nope," said Young.

Silent, gangly, with psychedelic shades and the longest hair in the band, at this point Palmer looked like, as Dewey Martin put it, "a cross between Alfred E. Newman and Ichabod Crane." Palmer would stand with his back to the audience, seemingly oblivious of everyone and everything around him, start fingering the four fat E strings he'd stuck on a beat-up violin-bodied bass, and whip out James Jamerson Motown-styled melodic runs that would propel the band into the stratosphere. Seeing the Springfield became, in the words of soon-to-be aide-de-camp Richard Davis, "going down to hear Bruce."

Furay was the nice midwestern guy, at first considered the band's lead performer. "Richie didn't have much to do with the music," claimed Davis. "They gave him a twelve-string guitar and told him to strum along. But he contributed quite a bit in terms of stage presence. I don't think you could say Stephen or Bruce or Neil had a lot of stage presence, but Richie did. He sort of charged around on his toes backward, screamin'."

Stills and Young: what a combo. Outfitted in cream-colored pants and cowboy hat, Stills was the white-soul blond southerner, determined to lead the Springfield with the firm grip of a plantation owner. But Neil Young was a force to be reckoned with, onstage and off. "Neil always had presence," said David Crosby. "Stills would try too hard. Neil would be more laid-back, and everybody would go, 'Oooh, what's *Neil* gonna do next?' "

Young dressed in a buckskin fringe jacket, a Comanche war shirt and some funky jewelry. As he would tell Robert Greenfield, "The group was Western, the name 'Buffalo Springfield' came off a tractor, so it all fitted. I was the Indian." The Hollywood Indian would turn out to be the band's wild card. Initially his role was that of lead guitar and songwriter, though getting his idiosyncratic ideas across to the band was a struggle. "The rest of us probably thought his stuff was the weakest of everything," proclaimed Dewey Martin. "I still don't understand a lot of his songs. They're so weird."

Young grew dissatisfied with his assigned role, and some observers felt he was frustrated from the outset with others performing his compositions. "They wouldn't let Neil sing his own songs," recalls Donna Port, a friend of the band. "That really hurt him."

*I started singing a little later, 'cause the other guys could really sing.
The harmony thing I wasn't too good at . . . I don't think I could be
counted on for a good harmony. I played lead guitar—which is what I'd
done in the Mynah Birds. I didn't care all that much that Richie sang
"Clancy." I wasn't pissed. It didn't make any difference. I thought,
"Well, we're doing my song." I wasn't dyin' to sing every song. I could
sing other songs. I could write more songs. Richie didn't write that
many songs, and he was a good singer. So to be in that band, somebody's gonna have to write the songs Richie's gonna sing. It was all
wide open then—no preconceptions.*

*In the beginning, the Springfield lived at the Hollywood Center Motel on
Sunset. We had this double-story house back there. All of us living in one little house, top and bottom. And Bruce lived in the closet. Bruce said, "I'll
take* this.*" This big closet. Fuckin' set up all his shit in there. It was perfect.
We had a little dollar-a-day allowance we were gettin' from Barry Friedman.*

*We woulda done a lot better if we'd stayed with Barry. I firmly believe
that. He made some recordings of us. They sounded* good. *No one knows
where those are. His sound was better. See,* he *shoulda produced the Buffalo Springfield. Barry was much more artistic than Dickie. That's the
guy—he shoulda had it.*

Energetic, gung ho and a bit of a hothead, the diminutive Richard "Dickie"
Davis ran lights at Sunset Strip clubs like the Whisky A Go-Go and the
Trip. He was also Barry Friedman's neighbor, and when Friedman began
to negotiate the publishing deal with Screen Gems, Stephen Stills called
him over to take a look at the contract. After surveying the low royalty
rates and finding out the band would lose the rights to their name, he told
the Springfield not to sign. The end result was, Davis said, "Barry never
spoke to me again, and the Springfield were sort of my responsibility."

On the strength of Chris Hillman's word, the Springfield got a gig opening for the Grass Roots on May 3 (or possibly May 2), 1966,* at the Whisky,
the hottest club on Sunset Strip. There, amid bikinied dancers in cages, the

---

*This date, the subject of much dispute in recent years, came to light only when, over thirty
years later, Susan Mayer, aka Jennifer Starkey—a fan who interviewed the band and
crudely taped some of the earliest live performances—surfaced during the eleventh hour of
work on the Buffalo Springfield boxed set.

Springfield wowed all of Los Angeles (except the lion king himself, David Crosby, who initially told Hillman they "sucked"). A fight to sign the Springfield ensued, and the discussions were navigated by Richard Davis, a novice to the music business. The Springfield came close to signing with Lenny Waronker at Warner Bros.—Davis said he met with him to discuss Jack Nitzsche producing the band—but at the last minute, the notorious management team of Greene and Stone entered the picture. Overwhelmed by the deal machinations, Davis had called upon them for advice, and they quickly took over. It would change everything for Buffalo Springfield. "Greene and Stone," said Bruce Palmer with a sigh. "They were the sleaziest, most underhanded, backstabbing motherfuckers in the business. They were the best."

•   •   •

"Reckless Abandon—they're the 1993 version of the Buffalo Springfield. This kid plays as good as Neil Young, Jimmy Page and Jeff Beck. You're gonna freak. Geffen is going crazy over 'em." Charlie Greene is on the phone, talking a mile a minute in that thick Brooklyn accent, demo tapes of his latest discovery blasting in the background. You gotta love Charlie. I'm trying to interview him, and he's hawking some band like I'm Ahmet Ertegun. A true manager.

Greene and Stone, Charlie will tell you, were the greatest fucking managers that ever roamed the earth. Greene and Stone gave the world Buffalo Springfield, Iron Butterfly *and* Sonny and Cher. Greene and Stone were the first to smoke bananas. Listen to Charlie's rap on how he brought "heavy" into the lexicon of hippie lingo: "The Butterfly had this new album called *Heavy*. So I take it in to our deejay at KRLA, the 'Real' Don Steele, and I say, 'Look—after you play a Beatles record, just say 'HEAVY.' When you play anything that is really happening, say 'HEAVY.' 'Why?' 'Do me a favor—just *do it*.' And all of a sudden, 'heavy' became something other than *a measure of weight*. I *invented* heavy." The hype is so fucking funny, who gives a shit if it's true.

Greene and Stone were happening guys on Sunset Strip in 1966. They had a *limo*. An $18,500 Lincoln limousine with a Blackglama mink interior, a bar with full sterling silver service and a goddamn eight-track player to boot, all presided over by an elegant white-gloved black chauffeur with a sideline in all sorts of contraband.

Inside their headquarters at 7715 Sunset Boulevard, chaos reigned twenty-four hours a day. Band members, bill collectors and supergroupies all took turns trying to get past June Nelson, the hip, manic secretary who was usually on the phone to some deejay, plugging the latest Greene and Stone sensation. Back in their respective offices—connected by means of a secret door—were Charlie and Brian, dressed in some outrageous approximation of hippie chic, wired on God knows what and jazzing some beleaguered record exec on their next big thing.

They were the classic good cop/bad cop routine. Short, tightly wound Charlie, a walking explosion of hype, twirling a trademark drumstick between his fingers with a gun never out of reach;* and tall, too thin Brian, the quiet bookkeeper who waited for the dust to clear, then drove home the terms. "I'd dance on the desk and he played the businessman," said Greene proudly.

Despite the roach-clip personas, the pair certainly weren't hippies, but they were far from square. Greene and Stone held the keys to a world many mid-sixties rockers found unfathomable: establishment showbiz. "We weren't really rock-and-rollers," said Stone. "We came from the school of dressing like Sammy Davis Jr. and Bobby Darin—New York sharp. Me and Charlie came out of a whole other milieu."

As teenagers they had broken into the publicity racket running errands for stars. They opened their own agency in 1959, amassing bills all over Manhattan in the process. They fled to California the following year and, after a series of mishaps found themselves broke and homeless—until they snuck onto a huge production lot known as Revue Studios one drunken night. From an empty dressing room furnished with office supplies from the prop department, the pair operated an on-the-lot publicity firm right under the noses of studio executives, until they were thrown off the premises by security guards. "I remember they forced us to take the typewriter," said Stone. "It was their typewriter."

---

*Greene had occasion to use the firearm during an altercation over money with Esquerita, a notorious New Orleans singer/pianist with a propensity for women's clothing, and who had also taught Little Richard a thing or two about being a rock-and-roller. "Esquerita was a big fuckin' guy—six-three," said Greene. "He wanted an advance—he grabbed me by the throat and I broke it by sticking my hands up. Then I ran into my office, took out a gun and stuck it in his mouth." R&B crooner Barry White was present for the event and disabled Esquerita by grabbing him from behind.

The dynamic duo then decided to open a folk/jazz nightclub, the Hootenanny. The club was miles from nowhere and the employees robbed them blind, leaving Greene and Stone to contemplate another career change. "The day the club closed we thought, 'What are we gonna do now?' " said Stone. " 'Hey—how about the *record business*?' "

Greene and Stone began bankrolling sessions for producer/arranger Jack Nitzsche, and it was at a Darlene Love recording date that they first encountered Sonny and Cher. Masterminding a meteoric ascent, they sold the duo—together and separately—to every record executive in town, including Mo Ostin at Warner Bros., who already had them under contract (albeit unsigned) as Caesar and Cleo. It was Ahmet Ertegun who wound up with "I Got You, Babe," a monster hit that cemented Greene and Stone's relationship with Atlantic Records. "Sonny and Cher was Ahmet's first white rock and roll act *ever,* other than Bobby Darin," said Stone.

Sonny and Cher had hit after hit, yet somehow finances remained shaky at 7715 Sunset Boulevard. "The back offices overlooked the parking lot, so Charlie and Brian could watch their cars getting repossessed," recalls Marcy Greene, Charlie's wife. "I'd be standing in front of the window going, 'Oh, Charles, there's a man getting into your Corvette.' He'd buzz Brian on the intercom and say, 'They just got the car—we gotta go get another one!' In an hour they'd be back, and now they had a Caddy convertible." Things got so desperate that Charlie had their royalty checks sent directly from BMI to Martoni's, a music-biz watering hole. "I was buying drinks for every motherfucking disc jockey who lived," he groaned.

Even while Charlie and Marcy were getting married at the ritzy Plaza Hotel, a prestigious event attended by Atlantic executives Ahmet Ertegun and Jerry Wexler, the IRS was padlocking Greene and Stone's Los Angeles offices for back taxes. After the ceremony, Greene had to go to Wexler and ask for a very sizable loan. "The man just attended our wedding, and now Charlie needs seventy-eight thousand dollars," said Marcy. "I mean, this is a very expensive night."*

---

*Jerry Wexler: "Greene and Stone were constantly hitting on us, and we were constantly bailing them out. They came to the well again and again until the pitcher broke. Listen, we were completely aware of their hype—it was a deal where *they* knew that we knew that they knew that *we* knew. But the bottom line was, it was a very productive relationship. Also— we enjoyed them. We enjoyed the scoundrel, scamp, aspect of them."

• • •

Tumbling into this insanity came Buffalo Springfield, five naïve kids hungry for success. According to Charlie Greene, it was the limo that got them. "Stephen once told me, 'I saw you driving down Sunset Boulevard in that limousine and I knew I had to have you. That's what I wanted, man—those fucking guys in the limo.' " Added Richard Davis, "Greene and Stone were all flash and sizzle. They had the act down. Being counterculture business types, they were one of us . . . so it seemed."

So it seemed. Greene and Stone immediately hyped the band to Atlantic. Jerry Wexler remembers getting the call. The renowned producer of much of Atlantic's R&B and soul had a profound distaste for dealing with what he called "the rockoids" and passed the information on to his partner, Ahmet Ertegun. Balding, goateed, Ertegun was a rare commodity in the low-rent world of the music business: a gentleman.

"When Ahmet walked into the room," Young told the Rock and Roll Hall of Fame audience in 1995, "you got good." The son of a Turkish diplomat, Ertegun was capable of charming everyone from Otis Redding to heads of state, and beneath the gravelly hipster voice lurked a killer businessman. New York–based, Atlantic Records had become famous for the sophisticato R&B of such artists as Ray Charles, Ruth Brown and the Drifters, but in the mid-sixties Ertegun was anxious to expand into the burgeoning white rock scene. After Greene and Stone delivered the gold mine of Sonny and Cher, Ertegun was all ears, and once in L.A., he was knocked out by a short demo tape the Springfield had cut at Capitol with Barry Friedman—Ertegun recalls Young's "Flying on the Ground Is Wrong" as one of the songs—and met with the band at Greene and Stone's office.

"There were other people interested in the Springfield," said Ertegun. "I had to make a really strong pitch to get them, and it wasn't over money—it was over 'Who's going to understand our music.' And they finally believed in me.

"I remember I sat on the floor with them and we chatted. We hit it off. . . . I think they liked the fact that I sat down on the floor. When I like an artist, I treat them like a star, and to me these guys were exceptional stars. I thought they were going to be a revolutionary kind of group. It was fantastic to have three great guitar players who were also three outstanding lead singers."

Ahmet was in, and he would remain an ally to the bitter end. Over the next two years he would forge a particularly tight bond with Stephen Stills. Ertegun didn't deny that Neil Young was a bit difficult to figure, both personally and commercially. "Neil was a very, very different person," said Ertegun, who recalls that Young had one last question before that first meeting was over. "I'm a golfer," he told the head of his new label. "Can you get me in a country club out here?"

"Stephen's poetry was earthy, based more on the blues, with a penchant towards Latin grooves," said Ertegun. "Neil's music was much more abstract. He had a lot of musical thoughts which didn't make sense to me right away. His voice was odd, shaky. It's like looking at a Cubist painting in 1920—if you just look at one Picasso, you would say, 'I don't know what this is.' But when you see the whole body of work, it's a great thing."

On June 8, 1966, the band entered into a contractual agreement with Greene and Stone. In a deal that mirrored Sonny and Cher's, Buffalo Springfield were leased to Atlantic's subsidiary label Atco, but actually signed to Greene and Stone's label, York/Pala Records.

Included in the deal was a publishing arrangement that would cause some acrimony down the line. Atlantic wound up with 37.5 percent of the rights, as did Greene and Stone, through their company Ten East. Through Springalo Toones, a publishing company created by the managers, the Springfield wound up with only 25 percent, which was to be split six ways (Richard Davis, considered an auxiliary member of the band, was given a share).

Greene and Stone set the band up with instruments, apartments and expense accounts, enabling Young to buy another Gretsch and pay for a $12.50-a-week one-room apartment in Commodore Gardens, a complex not far from Hollywood Boulevard. Lastly, Greene and Stone appointed themselves producers of Buffalo Springfield's records. "They slowly talked us out of Jack Nitzsche and into themselves as producers," said Davis. "It was probably the biggest mistake that happened."

The buzz on the Springfield spread like wildfire. John Hartmann, an excitable young William Morris agent, went with Greene and Stone to a gig in San Diego and "decided to put my entire reputation on this act." Returning to the staid confines of his very uptight agency, Hartmann and fellow agent Skip Taylor concocted a notorious interoffice memo that nearly got them fired. According to Hartmann, it read, TO ALL AGENTS: THE COAST, NEW YORK, CHICAGO. RE: BUFFALO SPRINGFIELD. PLEASE BE ADVISED THAT THEY ARE THE NEXT BIG THING TO HAPPEN TO THE WORLD. BUT DON'T WORRY—THEY'RE IN OUR HERD. At the bottom of the memo was the real blasphemy: a buffalo, with the William Morris logo tattooed on his posterior.

"I got yelled at by my boss," remembered Hartmann. "I said, 'Yessir—I won't do it again.' He didn't know I'd already sent out the second one." Hartmann would snag the Springfield a gig opening for the Rolling Stones at the Hollywood Bowl—a neat trick for a band that didn't even have a record out—and lined up six guest shots on the conservative *Hollywood Palace* TV variety show, unheard of for a rock band at the time. "John Hartmann," as Young put it, "was on the side of the Buffalo."

Hartmann threw his weight behind Greene and Stone, and this, along with the clout of Ahmet Ertegun and Atlantic Records, should've pushed Buffalo Springfield over the top. Instead, things immediately began to fall apart. Stephen Stills would say ruefully, "That's when we peaked, at the Whisky, and after then it was all downhill."

—Was your apartment at Commodore Gardens a cool place?
It was for me. It was really my first own place. Everything was kinda psychedelic. I had a blue lightbulb in my refrigerator. Got this bamboo wall-covering stuff at Pier 9. Went down with Donna and Vicki and bought a whole shitload of stuff. Grass mats on the wall. Very funky. My apartment looked like the dressing room at the Fillmore.

That's when we were playin' the Whisky A Go-Go. I was able to pay for my own place for a while—that was a first. It was fun. I got so far in arrears that I skipped out on the rent.

I wrote "Out of My Mind" and "Flying on the Ground Is Wrong" at Commodore Gardens on Orchid Avenue. "Flying on the Ground" wasn't written for anybody in particular. It's about drugs. It's about bein' straight and takin' drugs—mixed in with life.

If you want to know me and you don't wanna get high, you won't get

to know me. That's kinda what that song's about. We can't be together
because we're too different. It's like "I love you, but you're not with me."

"Stephen is the leader but we all are," it said ominously on the back of the band's debut album. This nebulous organizational concept would lead to trouble, but early on Stills was considered the driving force of the group. "Hey, listen, as far as I'm concerned, Buffalo Springfield was Stephen Stills's band," Richie Furay has said over and over. "His creativity at the time was incredible."

Eve Babitz, a writer who created two of the Springfield's distinctive collage album covers, was involved with Stills briefly and remembers his maniacal intensity. "Stephen used to play Buffalo Springfield records over and over on my horrible mono record player so he could hear how it would sound on a car radio. He told me from the day I met him, 'I want to write great songs, be very popular and have lots of groupies.' "

"Success, stardom—Stephen wanted to hang out in London with the Beatles as soon as possible," said Richard Davis. Unfortunately, Stills was in a band with Neil Young, whose methods and goals were considerably more ambiguous. The cowboy and the Indian were soon at war. At one Whisky rehearsal, Davis remembers Stills saying, "I want to do *my* song"; "I don't know why, but it struck me. It was the first time I heard an attitude." Stills not only saw his role in the band as singer/songwriter, but "Stephen wanted songs where he could play lead guitar," said Davis.

"There were major fights at the Whisky," said Donna Port. "Screaming matches. Stephen would pick on the stupidest little things—'You missed a note!' Neil was not that petty. He'd have to think to come back at him." Port and her friend Vicki Cavaleri, both waitresses at the club, had instructions from the band to listen very carefully to the two musicians during each set so they could agree or disagree in the dressing-room battles that followed. "It was like we were supposed to keep score," said Cavaleri.

As long as the friction between Stills and Young played out in front of an audience, it could produce artistic dividends. "He's on top of the beat and I'm on the back of it," Young told Sylvie Simmons in 1996. "It was a constant battle." Those fortunate enough to see the Springfield in their heyday recall the call-and-response between the two guitarists as thrilling, with Stills provoking incendiary leads out of Young. "Neil would just fuckin' smoke amps," said roadie Miles Thomas. "He'd be on eleven every night."

But Young wanted to sing the songs he wrote, and his strange vocal abilities weren't a hit, particularly with Stephen. "Stills was out of his *mind* if Neil was singing," said Brian Stone. "The band didn't even want him to sing harmony."* Donna Port remembers one gig where Young nervously approached the mike to sing a song and Stills, in an attempt to be funny, apologized to the audience in advance for his bandmate's voice. "After the show, Neil went into the dressing room and broke down," she said.

Many feel it was Stills's insecurities driving the conflicts. "I always felt Stephen had something to prove, that he was as good or better than Neil Young," said Nurit Wilde, a friend of the band. "I felt Neil didn't have to prove who he was musically. I don't think Stephen understood his own talent."

Wilde believed that once the band got into the studio, Charlie Greene "really tried to encourage a rivalry between Stephen and Neil. It wasn't like 'Okay, today we'll do this Buffalo Springfield song,' it was 'Today we'll do *Stephen's* song. Tomorrow we'll do *Neil's* song.' I think Charlie felt he'd get optimum work out of it. Instead there was competitiveness."

Intensifying the conflict was backseat driving by the dominating mothers of the two musicians. "Rassy would come up to me and say, 'My son's the star of the group, they should do more of Neil's stuff, they never let Neil sing,' " recalled Elliot Roberts, who attempted to manage the band briefly. "If there was a pamphlet or an article that said, 'Lead guitar, Stephen Stills,' she freaked. Stephen's mother was the same way." Both Rassy Young and Talitha Stills were prone to drink, and their quarreling often turned, in the words of Roberts, "bitter, cutting, drunken, mean."

The more difficult things became, the more Stills fought to control them. "I was trying to be boss cat and keep the thing in order," he told writer Allan McDougall in 1971. "You gotta dig that part of my upbringing in the South was very militaristic. I was in this military school and

---

*It appears nobody wanted Young to sing. He told deejay Tony Pig in 1969, "Our producers Charlie Greene and Brian Stone used to think my voice was pretty funny, and it made me pretty paranoid—and I just didn't sing that much."

being taught to be an *officer*. A lot of the ways I relate to situations like that is to simply take command—because *someone* has to. . . . That is the only thing that will work, and of course somebody like Neil or Bruce is instantly going to rebel. So there was chaos."

Stephen was the group leader. He also had arrangement concepts that were solid, and he knew a lot about harmony structure that was very valuable. Stills was a great musician then—before cocaine. He knew about the groove. Stills was always counting things off, saying this guy can't rush, that guy can't drag—it was then I became conscious of the groove.
—Donna Port feels you probably buried a lot of the conflict between you and Stephen because it would be too painful to recall.
Maybe she's right. I know there was a lotta conflict in the group, but I don't know why . . . that's true. There was that turmoil there I kinda buried, I guess.

Stephen truly felt that it was very important that he tell everybody what to do. He had a vision for the band. The only thing wrong was that Bruce and I resented being told what to do. It just didn't work, especially with Bruce. I was more quiet about it, more brooding. But Bruce didn't take any shit at all.

Bruce would just imitate him. Stephen would do something, and Bruce would be right in his face. Stephen would say, "Well, play it this way," and Bruce would go, "Well, play it this way—you diggee?" Bruce would get right up in his face, look him right in the eye, and say, "You diggee? You're NOWHERE, man!"

The fact of the matter was that no matter how crazy it was—no matter how domineering Stephen could be to do what he thought was the right thing for the band—believe me, this guy was trying to do the right thing for everybody. It broke his heart when the band broke up, because he knew how good it was.

With Stephen and I, it was two young guys—two musical forces—tryin' to coexist in a band that we knew was really good. But neither of us had planned on the other being a force.

I don't think I ever did what anybody told me to do. But that's the way it's always been. That's the way it is.

—Did you and Stills grow simultaneously on guitar?

I guess so. I think I could play a little better than him when we first met, especially electric, because he was just learnin' it. But then he caught up. For a while he was really good. And he's still really good.

—Are you a competitive guitar player?

I don't think so. Stills and I used to get into playing what could be termed competitively, but not really. It's more like we're building this thing together, y'know.

Patti Smith told me how she saw Bobfest and we were doin' "Knockin' on Heaven's Door" and I kept playing . . . I didn't realize I was making the song longer. *She could tell some of the people onstage thought it was just crazy—"What the fuck is this about? What are they doing?"*

But hey, it's all in the spirit of the thing. It's funny—I never looked at it like that, 'cause I had my eyes closed. I was just thinkin', "Wow, we're really fuckin' groovin', hah hah hah. Everybody's gettin' off."

That's where music's funny. What one person likes, another person might think is really not cool.

—Did you see any of yourself in Stephen?

Yeah. Just the maniacal egomaniac guitar player/singer/songwriter— but I didn't think I was an egomaniac until he pointed it out to me. Then I realized, "Maybe he recognized me."

I didn't even know the word "ego" until I got to Los Angeles. Ego— what do you mean? *Of course you wanna do something because it is* you. *I mean, fuck, "ego" all of a sudden became this byword. Kind of like paint-by-numbers psychoanalysis through marijuana. "Ego trip." People were talking like that—paranoia, ego—"Oh, he's paranoid, man." Looking ahead . . . is a form of paranoia. If you wanna look at it that way, everything's paranoia.*

However entertaining Greene and Stone may have been as managers, many failed to take them seriously as record producers. Phil Spector summed it up on Les Crane's radio show when he turned to Charlie and Brian and said, "There's *Beach Blanket Bingo,* which is you guys, and there's me—Fellini." When the Springfield went into Gold Star Studios to begin cutting their first album, problems began.

"When we got to our first session and we went into the studio and cut this one song, the voice came over the talkback saying, 'No, that's too long. Play it faster,' " Stills told writer Joe Smith. "Neil and I looked at each other and said, 'We better learn how to work this shit ourselves.' "

There was no mystery to the way Greene and Stone recorded the band: First they built the band track, then they overdubbed vocals. In the process something was lost. "The Buffalo used to arrange songs so they'd go somewhere vocally and instrumentally," said Richard Davis. " 'Clancy' got shortchanged in the studio because we ran out of tracks for the backing vocals." Tensions began to mount.

•   •   •

In the mid-sixties, harassment by law enforcement was an occupational hazard for longhairs, and the Los Angeles police seemed to have a particular ax to grind. "The cops were terrible, man," said Charlie Greene. "All of a sudden all these longhaired guys were walking around in flowered pants, a little zoned out, but not causing anybody any trouble. The cops didn't know what to do. It was culture shock."

On July 10, 1966, Young got caught in the cross fire. Driving around town in his Corvette, he came across Richard Davis being hassled by cops over a parking infraction outside the Whisky. When Young stopped to help, the cops turned their attention to him and dragged him off to jail.

When Greene and Stone arrived to bail Young out, Charlie promptly got into an argument with one of the officers behind the desk. Not liking the looks of these two hipsters any more than the musician already behind bars, the cop ran a make on Greene, found out he had an outstanding warrant for a traffic violation and threw him in the cell with Neil.

"Charlie started screaming, 'Call my attorney! Call my attorney!' " recalled Stone. "So I said, 'All right—*I'll* bail him out.' And the cop said, 'Can we have *your* ID?' Now, I'm not an idiot. I saw what they did to my partner, so I refused. Finally they said, 'We're gonna arrest ya.' And I said, 'That's the only way you're gonna get my ID!' Now we're all in jail."

In the wee hours of the morning, all three were bailed out by the managers' wives. Back at Charlie Greene's house, a doctor tended to Young's wounds, which, according to legal papers Brian Stone filed as part of a lawsuit he eventually won, included "lacerations, head injuries and a broken bridge in his mouth." Young shrugs off the incident today, but those around him say it took its toll. "Neil was pretty shaken up," said Stone. "He's not a big tough guy and they really worked him over."

I got stopped drivin' my '57 Corvette and I didn't have a license. I wasn't supposed to be there. I didn't have a fuckin' visa, I didn't have anything, but I had a car. I had a lot of things and I didn't have a lot of things.

They took me to jail. They were running a make on me, whatever. Fuckin' guy walks by and calls me a filthy animal, this cop. He had on these big horn-rimmed glasses and a brush cut. I told him he looked like some kind of fuckin' insect, a grasshopper. He came in the cell and beat the shit out of me.

—When I look at pictures of you when you were in the Springfield, you look like you were scared of everything.

I was—that's why I have such a healthy respect for everything. A lotta things scared me. But I was just growin' up. I was a late bloomer.

—Some people link what happened with the cops to your seizures.

Well, I don't know about that. I don't know if there's a correlation or not. I don't think so. I think that was my trip.

I was gonna go on that trip anyway.

This was yet another complication that would have an impact on the Springfield, not to mention Young's psyche: epilepsy. Without warning, just as things were starting to happen for the band, Young began having seizures.

Bruce Palmer was there for the first recognized one, standing next to Young at a Teen Fair at Hollywood and Vine sometime in the summer of 1966. "When I turned to say something to Neil, he wasn't beside me," Palmer told Scott Young. "Then I saw him on the floor having convulsions. I was scared as hell."

The seizures—which went undiagnosed for a brief period—began occurring with alarming frequency. During a gig at the Melodyland Theater in Anaheim in early September 1966, Young had to be carried offstage on a stretcher. John Hartmann witnessed one the first time he saw the Springfield, in San Diego. Early in the set Young bolted from the stage midsong. "I turned to Charlie Greene and said, 'Is this part of the act?' " Stills rushed offstage after Neil, and the crowd swarmed toward the exit door after them. Out in the parking lot Young was sprawled across a Corvette, convulsing. "Some woman who turned out to be a nurse had her hand down his throat tryin' to keep him from swallowin' his tongue."

"The seizures were sort of an event," Richard Davis recalled. "We'd have a system. If Neil was gonna go down, I could always tell—we'd slap the lights on and somebody would grab him and get him off." Poor Richie Furay was the one assigned to get Neil's Gretsch. "I hated bein' the guy to get his guitar on the way down," he said. "He would sense this thing comin' on and he would hand me his guitar. Our guitar grounds would never be the same, and I'd get a jolt."

Not everyone took the seizures seriously. "Stills always thought Neil was full of shit, having one of his phony spells," said Brian Stone. "It was like 'He doesn't want to play the date and now he's fainting.' "

"It seemed like some of the attacks were staged—maybe they weren't, but it *seemed* like that—for dramatic effect and attention," said Dewey Martin. "He'd always get some babe rubbing his forehead with a cool towel." Richard Davis concurred: "Neil did me out of a couple of women by having the occasional seizure or coming close to it. He was ruthless."

This kind of attitude infuriated Donna Port. "I wanted to kill them. See, it was all supposed to be that Neil was faking. He wasn't doing it to get attention! With epilepsy, people under great stress can have more attacks, so it became a real catch-22, because the more crap they gave him, naturally the more problems he had. Neil was exposed in the worst possible way."

Just the feeling that a seizure might be coming on could provoke panic for Young. One night at songwriter Tandyn Almer's house, Young suddenly bolted out the door. Vicki Cavaleri followed and found him inside a car, shaking. It took him almost half an hour to calm down. "He kept saying, 'Hold me, but don't touch my head.' "

A neurological condition that produces brief disturbances in the electrical functions of the brain, epilepsy can cause more than twenty different types of seizures. The mental-health professionals I contacted suggested Young's episodes were very much in keeping with complex partial seizures—what the Epilepsy Foundation of America calls "a disturbance which occurs in just one part of the brain, affecting whatever physical or mental activity that area controls." The psychic symptoms for these seizures can include sensations of déjà vu, unreality and depersonalization, fear, panic and hallucinations.

Many epileptics experience a preseizure warning state known as an aura, which can produce its own anxieties, even if the expected seizure fails to materialize. "When they happen, you actually forget who you are, but you feel something wondrous and holy is at hand," writer Thom Jones said, "and when it passes you get frightened."

Certainly some creative people have been epileptic—van Gogh, Dostoevsky, plus such musicians as Jimmy Reed, Robert Johnson and Ian Curtis. There are even those close to Neil who dare to suggest some of the more abstract aspects of his songwriting might have been influenced by the seizures. Sandy Mazzeo, the artist whom Young would grow close to a few years after leaving the Springfield, recalled discussing this once with him.

"Neil told me about going into other lives. He'd go to this same place every seizure, and all these people would go, 'Oh, haven't seen you around—how ya doin'?' He was called by some other name. Neil was just in another world, another reality, and just about the time he started to adjust and adopt to that reality, he'd get yanked out of that one and find himself back in this reality again. It was really strange, because he didn't want that other place to be all that familiar to him because he was here. But then he was there. It was out of his control.

"I think that's why he writes such weird shit. That's the strength of his creativity—he's been to all these far points where he's had only himself to talk to. Most of his songs are just Neil talking to himself, really. The voice inside himself."

Did I get songs from the seizures? Probably. To go somewhere else and you're there and you're talkin' to people and you're part of the thing and you are *somebody else. Then you realize, "Hey, wait a minute, I'm not—" You don't know who you are because you know you're not the person you seem to be. And you start waking up. Then you find out who you are by looking around.*

Having to learn my own name—I had to do that a couple of times. Learn who I was. Get familiar with it. Then hear the first LIE—or the first thing somebody would say that wasn't exactly true—it would be like a fucking terrible trauma to me when I was coming back from these seizures. It's like being a baby. Anything that's not pure, you go, "What the—" because you're starting over again, regrouping. Everything's coming back together.

I can remember one seizure at the ranch in 1974 when this doctor took my blood before I went out on the road with CSNY. Probably the last big one I had. It was mind-blowing. I faint regularly from having my blood taken—not because I'm scared of the needle, but because the blood leaving my body does something to me. I can feel my life leaving me, and I go under and I have a seizure sometimes. Just from having blood taken.

I had just had a grand mal seizure and I went for a walk—and I had just barely figured out that it was my ranch—and this doctor was with me and he was sayin', "Now, we're not gonna tell people this happened, because it will upset them. The only people who need to know about this are you and me and Russ Kunkel"—a drummer who was there, too.

So it was like bein' born again and wakin' up and seein' everything is beautiful—seein' things for the first time—and then having someone tell you, "Well, this is not what it seems. We're not gonna tell. People are not gonna know what happened." So it's a lie. Why *should there be a lie?*

When you're born, I don't think you can conceive of telling a lie. But if you can imagine being born, and within ten minutes after you're born, you're introduced to the concept of a lie—y'know, you've only been alive *for five minutes, and now they're teaching you how to* lie.

So there's something that happens there. I don't know what it is. It doesn't happen anymore hardly at all because I just have such control over it. But it used to happen all the time back then, because I was running hot.

I think at some point the seizures became an escape for me. Some of the seizures probably weren't real. I would think I was gonna have one, and then I'd get myself kinda into havin' one—"Oh, I'm gonna have one"—and then I wouldn't.

You gotta remember, I was, like, twenty years old. So there was a lotta escape hatches, and the seizures were an escape hatch. Now I know I had several seizures that were real, so what can I say? I outgrew the seizures. They gave me Dilantin and I took it for a couple of years and then I tapered off of it. Then I controlled the seizures like I control everything else—mind over matter.

Control. Inner control. I can't explain it. It's not a matter of the psyche or controlling your actions so much as it is controlling the velocity that you're working at inside yourself. Slow down that thinking process, because you know that you could burn out. Take a little more time. Be able to pull out of things.

I used to be the kinda guy, if I smoked anything—or even sometimes if I didn't—that if I was lookin' at somethin' for too long, I would get so far into it that I would have trouble gettin' out of it. And that's what would happen when I would have a seizure—I would keep lookin' at somethin' for so long, like I'd be readin' a book and I'd get to a certain word and I'd just start lookin' at the word. And I'd start getting right into the letter. And right into the granules on the page. And pretty soon I was gone.

I've learned to control that. I don't let those things happen. Maybe that's why I was able to see where I was going and pull back so many times—I would say, "Okay, you've gone far enough, you've made your point. Now is the time to stop." And it's not conscious. I think I learned something, dealing with that condition. It's helped me in other ways. So consequently, I think once you start controlling that, then you control all kinds of things. Maybe that's why I'm still here.

The A-side of the first Buffalo Springfield single was supposed to be "Go and Say Goodbye," a jaunty Stills song featuring a lick taken from an old bluegrass tune Chris Hillman had shown him. Unfortunately for Stephen, the flip side—Young's "Nowadays Clancy Can't Even Sing"—was chosen instead.

" 'Clancy' was probably the worst fucking song that I ever heard in my life," said Ron Jacobs, then promotion director for L.A.'s top-forty station KHJ. "I heard it in the parking lot at Gold Star and I almost threw up." But whatever Greene and Stone's deficits might have been as producers, they got the band heard by the world. "Charlie and Brian really lit the fuse that allowed Buffalo Springfield to at least start moving," said Jacobs. "They worked their asses off to get things happening. There's no way that group would've ever gotten played at KHJ without Charlie and Brian." In late August 1966, "Clancy" debuted on KHJ, reaching a high of number twenty-five there.

Nationally, "Clancy" stiffed, and everyone has an opinion as to why. Some say the lyrics were too abstract and contained the word "damn." Others say the song was too long and the odd time changes threw people. There are also those who think that Richie Furay, despite his good intentions, just couldn't convey the very subjective feelings of Neil Young.

Vicki and Donna remember sitting a very confused Furay down and explaining Neil's lyrics word by word (Young himself, thank God, wasn't present). Rassy Young remembered a live show where Furay mangled the words to "Clancy" by singing "Who's putting *bells* in the *sponge* I once rung." "Neil turned around and looked at him," recalled Rassy, laughing. "Richie hadn't realized he'd done it."

Whatever the reason, when "Clancy" showed signs of bombing, "We all panicked and started climbing on Charlie and Brian's back," Furay told the Los Angeles fanzine *TeenSet*. Continuing to work on their first album, the group eventually gave up on Gold Star's four-track, following the Byrds over to Columbia's new eight-track studio B, but studio trickery couldn't mask the fact that the magic hadn't been captured in the first place. Meanwhile, Atlantic was pressuring them to get the album finished.

Greene and Stone claimed that the band's inexperience in the studio was a major factor in the delays. "You reach a point where you say, 'That's it,'" said Stone. "We'd been in the studio a long, long time just holding hands with them. We used to spend enormous time doing and redoing vocals, because really the lead singer was Richie."

When the record was finally done, the Springfield took an acetate over to a friend with the best stereo system in town, gathering around the speakers in anticipation. "It was awful," said Richard Davis. "It sounded so good in the studio, but when you put a needle to it, it wasn't there. Everybody knew it. It was a devastating moment."

When we heard the record, we said, "Fuck, this isn't what we wanted. This isn't what we did." The stereo mix was done in a day and a half— and we weren't even there.

I was pretty frustrated, because we had to play—then sing. I watched a lot of sessions for other groups, trying to figure out why the Buffalo Springfield records were so fuckin' terrible compared to the real thing. I'd already made records with Ray Dee that were better than the first Springfield records—they may not sound *better, because the musicians weren't as good, but the concept of how to make them was better. On the Springfield records, we didn't ever really play. Everybody put everything on one thing at a time, trying to be the fuckin'* Beatles *instead of the Buffalo Springfield. We got off on a tangent. If we'd had a little bit of direction . . .*

See, Ahmet Ertegun's the only guy who's heard Buffalo Springfield recorded. A musician's businessman, Ahmet. He knows music. Ahmet always said, "This record's not as good as the fuckin' demos, man." Before the first Springfield record, we had made demos, and the demos were fuckin' great. It was very early on and we cut demos of "Go and Say Goodbye," "Clancy" and "Sit Down, I Think I Love You." Ahmet heard those demos and, based on hearing those demos, signed us to Atlantic. And then Charlie and Brian made a record with us that was nowhere near *as good as those fucking demos. See, the demos were done the way we played it. We did 'em live. We just went in and played, sang, did everything all at once.*

Those demos were ours, but "Doc" Siegal, the Gold Star engineer who recorded the first album, didn't get paid, so he took them to hurt Charlie and Brian. So we got the shaft on that one. He had all that shit in his garage, and when he died they didn't know what to do with it. They sold the acetates to some record store, the record store apparently sold them to somebody in Japan who collects acetates, and we've never been able to find 'em. Probably sittin' on somebody's shelf—some Japanese guy who's proud of how many acetates he has and doesn't even know what's on 'em. Now I can't find the guy. Don't know where the tapes are. Bummer.

The acetate listening party for the first album produced grim results. The next day, according to Brian Stone, "the Springfield called us and said, 'We have very bad news. This record has to be destroyed. It has to be burned. It's a piece of *shit*!' "

Nearly thirty years later, Greene and Stone were still sensitive to claims that they botched the production. "Listen, at that time we had probably made a thousand records, and these guys knew nothing about making records," said Stone. "These guys played live, and they expected to hear back what they played. We tried to *improve* their sound. We spent eight hundred million hours mixing that thing, and all *six* members were present. I think the record stands by itself."

The record does stand by itself—anyone who gives even the most cursory listen to *Buffalo Springfield* can hear why the band was so unhappy. On songs like "Pay the Price," the rhythm section feels a football stadium away from the guitars. The recording is thin and crappy, and it never sounds like a group of people playing in the same room. The mono version of the album, which Stills and Young reputedly spent ten days mixing, was an improvement, but few would hear it.

The band demanded to recut the record. Charlie Greene's response: "Go fuck yourself."

Stills, who had grown dubious of the duo's production abilities early on, went ballistic. "Stephen really took on Greene and Stone while they were in the driver's seat," said Richard Davis. "Stills insulted Charlie and Brian, made enemies of them—he really drove a wedge between them and the group, and maybe rightly so.

"I was in a position of trying to make things work. I used to tell Stephen, 'You wanna fight these guys, just make sure you can win—they've got your *contract*.' But Stephen was impossible. 'Reason' wasn't a word you used."

∙   ∙   ∙

Epilepsy, band problems, management hassles, arrests—if you want to know how Neil Young was feeling circa mid-1966, pull out that beat-up copy of *Buffalo Springfield* and play "Out of My Mind."

"Tired of hangin' on / If you missed me I've just gone," sings Young, the terror apparent in his voice. With its death-knell drumbeat and trembling Gretsch fed through a Leslie, this circular song without a chorus clearly chronicles the tortured times its creator was going through. His first album, and already Young was disillusioned with the whole trip. As Ken

Viola put it, "The audacity to write a song about bein' a star—before he even *was* a star."

The Beatle-esque pop of Stephen Stills dominated the first side of *Buffalo Springfield,* finally released in November 1966, but the most original material on the record belonged to Neil Young. "Burned" was his first tentative vocal with the band. As Young would write in the liner notes to his *Decade* anthology, "The boys gave me uppers to get my nerve up. Maybe you can hear that." Furay sang three of Young's songs, Neil only two, but the quality and range of his writing was auspicious: "Out of My Mind," "Nowadays Clancy Can't Even Sing," "Do I Have to Come Right Out and Say It?" and the magnificent "Flying on the Ground Is Wrong," perhaps the most sophisticated piece of writing on the album.*

Despite the band's misgivings over the production, *Buffalo Springfield* would gain them a loyal following beyond Los Angeles and in the burgeoning rock press, where Paul Williams at *Crawdaddy!* and Judith Sims of *TeenSet* spread the word. Ken Viola was obsessed by *TeenSet.* "I'd be at the candy store at six A.M., waitin' for them to snap those bundles open so I could get the latest issue and read about the Springfield."

Ken Viola remembers his first glimpse of his new spiritual adviser. Just fifteen years old, he turned on the TV one day in his family's New Jersey home and "here's this guy in a Confederate uniform, which to me was such a statement, like 'Down with the old, in with the new.' It was so heavy." The guy was Neil Young, the band was Buffalo Springfield and Viola ran right out and bought their first album.

"It's so strange, if I think back, I can remember that exact day, the exact feeling when that connection happened. I had a strange habit of playing the second side of a record first, so the first thing I heard was a Neil Young song, 'Flying on the Ground Is Wrong.' I knew from the second I heard it that this guy was plugged in to everything. It was somebody speaking directly to me. Everything about it was so right, when everything in my life up to that point had been so wrong. I mean, he *understood.*"

Hiding in the sanctuary of his bedroom, Ken would sprawl out across

---

*In a rare admission, Young would tell deejay Tony Pig in a 1969 interview that the song was partially inspired by the work of his hero Roy Orbison: "That's where 'Flying on the Ground' came from . . . the idea of the melody came from 'Blue Bayou.' "

the bed and play record after record, listening on headphones to avoid drawing the attention of his father, a fruit-and-vegetable man who sold his wares off a truck he drove through the streets of Hackensack.

His parents thought rock and roll would be "the ruination of me. I knew something was happening, and they were trying to keep me from going in that direction with everything they had." When Neil Young became the focus of Ken's attention, he became Public Enemy Number One. On the morning of Ken's twentieth birthday, his mother would march into his bedroom, waking him up at six A.M. by screeching a Neil Young lyric: "You can't be twenty on SUGAR MOUNTAIN!"

the red-haired guy

The sixties ended for Donna Port on November 28, 1968, when a van driven by a famous L.A. guitarist sailed off a cliff in Mexico. Donna, a passenger in that van, never walked again. Since that accident, life has not been easy for Port, but the painkillers and countless operations haven't dulled her spirit. She lies in her bed and shares withering insights—usually about any member of the Springfield except Neil—and then giggles like a schoolgirl, quickly covering her missing front tooth with her hand. Donna is one ornery critter. I'm sure she's driven the few friends left by her side crazy.

Vicki Cavaleri stands by the bed, and Donna, despite her often helpless condition, still mothers her friend of nearly twenty-five years. The two will disagree over some arcane detail of the distant past, then Donna will pipe up, "No, Vicki, it was Commodore Gardens, not the Saint Regis," ending the matter forcefully. Port doesn't hold back her opinions of Neil, good or bad; Vicki—who was writing a largely autobiographical screenplay named after the Springfield song Young dedicated to her and Donna, "Expecting to Fly"—is more reserved. Donna hasn't seen Young since her accident and she's pissed off about it, much to the dismay of Vicki. "Oh, Neil can't pick up the phone, he's so goddamn special? I mean, Neil doesn't shit roses," said Donna indignantly. "I'm sorry, Vicki—he's not God."

There we sat, in a shabby Los Angeles apartment that Donna would eventually have to vacate due to dwindling funds, and as one of her sons—a serious-looking adolescent with a pet rat on his shoulder—darted in and out of the room, Vicki and Donna took me back to 1966, when they were wide-eyed innocents in bell-bottoms and moccasins, working as waitresses on the Sunset Strip, and an oddball named Neil Young entered their lives.

.   .   .

"People thought we were a threesome," said Port, shaking her head. "We were a nothing-some," added Vicki. "We weren't his groupies, we were just good friends."

Donna brought Neil home one day to Commodore Gardens, a low-rent apartment complex around the corner from Hollywood Boulevard run by a grouchy old woman who would get drunk at night and throw everybody out, only to invite them back the next morning.

"I remember Neil's reaction to the bowl of marijuana we had," said Port. "He wasn't used to it. He was very green. You gotta remember how young we all were. We were all babies. Neil was not this worldly creature off the streets everyone envisions. He was just a kid from Canada who was exceptionally talented. *Thank God* he had this talent, because I don't know what would've happened to him without it.

"Neil was looking to hang on to something in every direction. That's one of the things that first attracted me—his vulnerability. He was so timid and fragile—he didn't hang out with the band. That's why he stayed with us all the time." When the girls first met Neil, he was staying with the Springfield at the Hollywood Center Motel. "He hated being there," said Cavaleri. "Neil didn't really want to be with the guys."

"Neil made sure he had relationships with females that were platonic," said Port. "It's really odd—Neil might as well have been a girl at times, in the sense of closeness and comfort." Young began showing up nights at their Commodore Gardens apartment. Often they'd wake up in the morning and there Neil would be, curled up in a ball, asleep on the floor. During the early days of the Springfield, the trio were inseparable. "We were the three musketeers."

Donna, a few years older than the other two, was the protective one, out battling the world; Neil and Vicki were like two scared kids who had retreated into their own little protective bubble. "Those two were the biggest dreamers I ever came across," said Port. "I'd come home from work and these two are watching cartoons and playing with *blocks*. The place was a mess. Goddamn it, I was twenty-two years old—I didn't want kids!"

The three of them shunned what they considered the phony Hollywood scene, preferring instead to haunt toy stores or scour Los Angeles to find Young a pair of kittens. "We went to every shelter until we found the right ones," said Cavaleri. "Neil knew *exactly* what he was looking for." Neil christened one kitten Orange Julius and the other Black Cat Plain, after Rassy's favorite brand of cigarettes.

Neil's family was a sensitive subject for him at the time. "He had a big scene with his mother and father," said June Nelson, Greene and Stone's secretary. "He wasn't speaking to his father, and he didn't want to speak to his mother. He used to tell me, 'I don't wanna talk to her.' "

Donna Port remembers putting quarters in a pay phone and dialing Rassy long-distance because Young was unable to do it himself. "He really loved his mother, but he was scared to death of her. Rassy came down to sign the Buffalo Springfield recording contract—at twenty, Neil was underage—he begged Donna to come along. He was looking forward to that like a cyanide pill. He could not go alone."*

Port also remembered Rassy calling Commodore Gardens, her voice booming out of the phone for all to hear. "Neil would sense the looks in the room and how everything went quiet. Once he got off the phone, he'd be very upset. He'd either go off to the guitar or listen to records."

Donna didn't discuss it with Neil. "It was an area you didn't want to probe, because the guard came up and you knew you were upsetting him just by bringing it up. He always tried to get her approval. I don't know to this day if he has it."

> *You know, you start out and everything's groovy. Then you get popular and you get money, and when you get money all of a sudden you get all these dumb chicks hanging around the group with nothing to do but use any excuse to try and climb into bed with a guy in the group—any guy in the group, it doesn't matter—and they're called groupies ... ten, fifteen steady groupies hanging around and picking out some guy they want to make it with, and starting to tell him he's the best, he's the greatest, he should be making it alone—and the other guys start to get jealous, and it creates a real hassle.*
>
> —Interview with Marci McDonald, 1968

---

*For a brief period, Young's mother relocated to California while he was in the Springfield. "Rassy always came after Neil," said Elliot Roberts. "Even when Neil left, Rassy followed. She lived her life through Neil—to the point that she could."

One night at the Whisky, Barry Friedman and Doors producer Paul Rothchild saw the Springfield perform. "We were sitting there watching the whole thing. I said, 'How are we gonna know if they're really it? How can you tell the difference between *really* it and maybe it—the difference between a hype and success?' Paul said, 'Oh, that's easy—by the quality of the women that surround them.' The women around the Springfield were very high-quality."

Now that he was a pop star, Neil Young was routinely surrounded by willing partners, but how involved he got with any of them remains a mystery. "That's a tough one," said producer Jack Nitzsche. "Neil's relationship with women has always seemed strange." Writer Eve Babitz felt that Young was a bit sinister and said she was afraid of him. Elliot Roberts stated that Young was "very, very relationship-oriented," but, recalling seeing Neil with a well-known groupie, added, "he wasn't a homebody, either."

Others portray him as just the opposite. "Neil worked at being frail," said Denny Bruce, a pal of Nitzsche's. "Jack and I would go to the Whisky, because we could usually get laid there. Neil would say, 'I have to go home and take my medication.' We were always talking about it—'Does he do it to make girls like him?' With Neil, girls would have to come up and fawn over him."

It is interesting to study Young's portrayal of women, because it's as convoluted as anything else in his world. He sounds desperate to connect in songs like "Flying on the Ground Is Wrong" or the wistful "One More Sign," an unreleased demo from the Springfield era. Unreleased until 1977, the Springfield's "Down to the Wire" is an overwrought portrayal of a soul-sucking vampire who is omnipotently seductive. You can find a lot of fear in Young's songs and, in "Mr. Soul," a hostility that borders on hatred. A little more complicated than "All You Need Is Love."

Some on the L.A. scene felt pushed into all sorts of sexual freedoms they were ill equipped to deal with. "It was almost forced on you," said Nurit Wilde. " 'You gotta be free—you can't be afraid—you gotta go with this one or that one.' There was a lack of freedom in that, I think. I know it was hard on me. People from Toronto were behind schedule."

The pressures seemed particularly hard on Young. "Neil was very shy about women—extraordinarily, painfully, tragically shy," said Donna Port. Vicki and Donna both remember an odd ritual they'd go through with Neil:

When he was to meet some female admirer, they'd be instructed to show up exactly forty-five minutes into the date to announce that he was late for wherever they were going. Neil didn't seem to want anything to happen.

Port attempted to fix Young up with one of her girlfriends. "She couldn't figure out what was wrong. They'd spend the night together, but he'd never take his clothes off. She'd come home crying, 'He doesn't like me.' She'd get too close, and Neil would freak out. He was tortured. Here's this sex idol onstage and . . . you can imagine the pressure."

When Young spent the night on the floor at Commodore Gardens, Port—ever the mother hen—would try to get him up off the floor, out of his clothes and into a warm makeshift bed on the couch. "As soon as I got the belt off, that was the panic zone. It was always 'No, I'm more comfortable with my clothes on. I don't mind sleeping with my clothes on.' "

Port suspected there was more to it than that. Young's frailty seemed familiar. Noticing how self-conscious he was over his skeletal frame, she began to wonder if he might have had polio. The disease had affected her family when she was a child.

"His legs were like toothpicks, and one day I just asked him," said Port. "The look of terror gave me the answer. Then it just flowed out. He was wrapped up in a blanket at the time, crying. It was a huge emotional scar to him. We talked about how cruel kids are when you're growing up. It explained a lot.

"This guy had a heavy load, physically and emotionally. Neil didn't fit. He never felt he fit. He wanted to desperately, but it always eluded him. Neil was always bleeding inside."

My point of view was really different. Where I came from—Canada—was just different. I didn't know how to relate to women that well. I mean, all these girls and everything . . . I was so innocent sexually. It was just too fast for me. Too much, too soon. I didn't understand it. I wasn't ready.

Everything was so fuckin' far out down here. Everybody was so far ahead of me socially. I was just goin', "Wow—this is really fuckin' somethin' else. Where's my guitar?" Took awhile. But like all good Canadians, I eventually caught on.

With Vicki and Donna, it was just a really good friendship that was happening at a magical time in our lives. We were all living this thing together. I was able to relate to those girls—they were really cool. So hangin' out together was fun—they were more like my friends. Donna's a great lady. I should see her. I keep missing all the chances. . . .

I was just so into what I was doin', I wasn't really focusing on women that much. I wasn't worried *about it—I just wasn't into it. There were other things on my mind.*

—So much went wrong for you during the Springfield. Did you ever feel rejected?

AHAHAHAHAHAHA—I gotta get a drink. *Whew. Oh man. Have I ever felt rejected? I don't think it's ever been a major thing, know what I mean? Or maybe it has—and it's so* obvious *I can't even see it. I think everybody's felt rejected . . . but I don't think I've ever been* bothered *by feeling rejected.*

Behind on his rent at Commodore Gardens, Young needed a new place to escape to, and Donna Port helped him find one: 8451 Utica Drive. It looked like something out of a fairy tale: an old, rough-shingled house with a wrought-iron gate, tucked away in the hills of Laurel Canyon. The one-room knotty-pine guest house Young lived in was perched behind the house at the end of a long trail of steps, nestled in the treetops and over-looking the canyon. It's still an eerie place today—you expect an elf to pop out from behind the trees and whisper a dirty limerick. "It's outta the way," drawled Young laconically. "You had to go through something to get there. You had to *wanna* go there."

Overseeing the property was the late Kiyo Hodell, an exotic, raven-haired half-Asian astrologist who mistrusted musicians and refused to rent to Young until she did his chart. "This woman had some kind of power goin' for her," said Linda Stevens, a friend of Young's. "Gorgeous long hair piled on top of her head, always very intense. She was a Leo, and Scorpio was her opposite, so she thought Neil was wonderful."

"Kiyo was a good witch," said musician Jim Messina. "She invited me to her house for tea, and I remember this mass of bees rolling out of her fireplace. It was like somebody spilled honey. She lived that way." Consider-ably older than Young, Hodell became a buffer between him and the rest of the world. "She was a tremendous protector of Neil," said Donna Port.

Visitors to Utica Drive remember it as a difficult time. "Neil was very intense to be around," said musician Robin Lane, who lived with Young for a few weeks. "He had a purpose. Neil didn't talk much about himself or what he was feeling. He was removed and in his own world. He was strange, mysterious—he sort of floated above the earth, but at the same time had his feet planted on the ground."

.　.　.

"We hated each other a lotta the time" is how Young would describe the relationships in the Springfield to Tony Pig, and the friction wasn't just between Stills and Young. Dewey Martin provided his own unique frustrations. "There were times when everybody wanted to replace him," said Richard Davis, who remembers a secret audition at the Whisky with the drummer from the Grass Roots. "We all felt very sheepish about it. Nobody knew how to do it."

"Dewey would always say the wrong thing at the wrong time," said roadie Chris Sarns. "Right about the time Stephen and Neil were calming down, he'd say something to fire 'em both up again." Martin didn't deny his own obnoxiousness, blaming the copious amounts of amphetamine he was ingesting. "I know I got on a lotta people's nerves, 'cause I like to rap, rap, rap. Here's a guy who's *already* hyper, takin' uppers."

But with Martin it wasn't the chemicals that people remember most, it was the alcohol—a very unhip substance to abuse in the sixties. Charlie Greene's wife, Marcy, remembered telling the drummer just that one afternoon at the Beverly Hills Hotel. "I said, 'Dewey, if you ever get busted, they're gonna find a bottle of Scotch in your drum kit. You're an *embarrassment* to the music industry.' "

Then there was Bruce Palmer. Once he hit Los Angeles, he was lost to another dimension. "Bruce became psychedelicized overnight," said Donna Port. "Bruce could not say no. He opened Pandora's box. We had to have people literally follow Bruce in cars to make sure he wasn't arrested or killed in an accident, because he was driving under the influence of God knows what. I can't tell you how many rented cars that guy wrecked. Bruce wrecked everything he touched."

At his best, Palmer was an otherworldly creature. Charlie Greene remembers how they'd stick a mike over him as he lay on the floor, oblivious.

"If you said, 'Excuse me, Bruce,' he couldn't give you the time of day—but the minute the music started he'd play perfectly."

"Bruce was very aloof and off on his own trip," said Dewey Martin. "Dropping acid and playing sitar for twelve hours at a time." Withdrawing more and more into his studies of Eastern music, religion and karate, Palmer began to blow off sessions, showing up late or not at all. "We were always waiting for Bruce, it seems," said Martin. Palmer, the driving musical force of the band, was slipping away. "As Bruce became more and more difficult, Neil felt more and more protective," said Richard Davis. "He took care of Bruce."

Getting high was a prerequisite in the Los Angeles rock scene, but drugs were something Young had grown extremely cautious about. Robin Lane recalled Neil bawling her out for smoking a joint in his car. Linda McCartney—then Linda Eastman, a photographer on the scene—remembered being in a car with Neil, some of the Jefferson Airplane and LSD guru Owsley Stanley. A joint was passed, and Young frantically rolled down the window to get away from the smoke. "Before he was the king of dope, Neil was scared to death of marijuana," said Jack Nitzsche. "Just to be around the smell of it."

I was crazy anyway. It didn't matter if I did the drugs or not.

Crosby said somethin' to me once, 'cause he knew I couldn't smoke as much weed as other people that he knew—I had the seizures and whatever—he just said, "Your chemistry is just different—you're different. You can't do this. Be careful."
—R. Crumb said taking LSD profoundly altered his work. Did any drugs do that for you?
I don't think so. Debatable, though. Y'know, I really find the one thing that always works if you've really gotta do something is to be straight.

But like anything else, that'll change. I'll take it right to a point, and then one day I just won't do it anymore. That's the way I am.

Live one way, live another way. Change modes. See things a different way.

In the summer of 1966, Young's nervous system short-circuited. "Neil was real sick," recalls June Nelson. "He'd have these shaking fits. He called me in the middle of the night and said, 'June! You have to come over—I'm gonna die!' " Nelson packed him into her car and took him to UCLA Medical Center.

Young was in the hospital for ten days, during which a battery of tests was run, including, according to Charlie Greene, one procedure where they opened his skull. "I'll never forget it. They drilled a fucking hole in his head to release pressure."

Then came the pneumoencephalogram, a torturous procedure designed to check abnormalities in the brain. When it was over, the doctor asked him if he'd ever taken LSD. Young said no. According to Neil, the doctor replied, " 'Well, don't ever take it—*you'll never come back.*' That's what they came up with." Young was put on Dilantin and Valium to minimize the chance of seizures, then sent home. Charlie Greene felt that the turmoil of the previous few months, culminating in his surreal hospital stay, left Young shell-shocked and depressed.

"You could see the fear in his heart about this success being thrust on him with fuckin' limousines and shit. He was in a quandary. He didn't understand what was goin' on."

The pneumoencephalogram was like God's answer to the Spanish In-quisition. Y'know, "What can we do to fuckin' really make somebody go nuts—break 'em down to primal scream, let's do that."

You're completely strapped into this thing, leather all around you, then they put a needle in your back, give you a shot and start feeding in this radioactive dye—and it hurts. You can't be sedated for this, you have to be totally awake. That was pure fuckin' hell. *The worst. Strap you in, do all this shit, shoot all this radioactive dye up and down your fuckin' back, into your brain. Track it. With all these little instruments, satellite receivers and stuff going around in the room. It was killing me. Very painful. Very, very painful.*

And then you have a headache for a couple weeks after that while the air bubbles dissipate into your brain from the intrusion of this foreign substance into your body, and that air rises, tryin' to get out, seeking the highest level, like a bubble would in water—and gets caught in the top of your brain—until the air actually dissolves and goes away. Had a headache for a week, bubbles of air in my head. Fuck. And every time you move your head, it kills you. But that's nothing compared to the pain of having the procedure done. It reduces you to a complete fuckin' animal.

They never really figured out what was wrong, either. Kind of a medical limbo dance. They don't do it anymore—they decided it was inhumane. I got in just under the line, I guess.

Definitely that whole trip was major. I'm sure that had a big effect. A seminal happening in my life—big-time pain.

—Were you curious about LSD?

No, I never took LSD. Nobody ever gave me any. I never wanted any.

—Why not?

Doctor told me not to take any. That was the message: "Don't take LSD." He inferred that I was a little bit too far out there to take LSD and that I might not make it back. Even if I smoked some grass, I was liable to get too high, so I wasn't ready to go off the deep end on some psychedelic drug. Everything seemed to be psychedelic already. When people talked about things bein' psychedelic, it didn't seem that I was missing that. Y'know, I could relate. So I was thinkin', "Well, y'know, maybe this is a bonus. I get this for nothing—without taking the drug."

—Is your music psychedelic?

Some of it. Depends. What's psychedelic to you might not be psychedelic to me. It's transcendental, trandscending the moment. What's psychedelic about my music is the fact that when the music is really happening, we're all just tuned in to some force that's fuckin' driving us and we're all going together—that's psychedelic. Even last night when our performance was as mediocre as it was, it still had a semblance of that. We got hung up. Getting hung up is part of psychedelia. Things repeat. The same thing happens over and over again.

I do that in my thought processes. Sometimes I do it in my music. When I do it in my music, I love it, when I do it in my thought processes, it drives me fuckin' crazy. In music I can control it, but outside of music, when you start thinkin' about the same thing over and over again and you can't get it out of your head, that turns into a negative. In music it's a positive. You don't try to control it and you have total control over it—it's like . . . psychedelic.

Free from the hospital, Young must've felt despair. He'd come to L.A. to make music, be a rock star, and had slammed into a wall.* He was fighting his managers, his band and now his brain. Young took this tangle of feelings and set it to music. It came out in one shot, unedited, and it was called "Mr. Soul." The song was a turning point. Written on a twelve-string acoustic, the original version of "Mr. Soul" circa fall 1966 was, according to those who heard it, a slow, moody folk number with a dark edge intensified by Young's D-modal tuning.

Both Peter Lewis of Moby Grape and critic Paul Williams told me they were more impressed with the original arrangement of "Mr. Soul" than the released version. "It was a completely different thing," said Lewis. "That one was *really* mysterious." The unrecorded "Mr. Soul" was the first Neil Young song known to utilize D-modal tuning, also heard in "Ohio," "When You Dance," "Cinnamon Girl" and "Don't Let It Bring You Down." Young said he liked "the way it just sustained. I liked the drone."

The recorded version of "Mr. Soul" is propelled by a riff Young nicked from the Rolling Stones' "(I Can't Get No) Satisfaction"—an appropriate touch for a song rife with sexual tension and "respectfully dedicated to the ladies of the Whisky A Go-Go and the women of Hollywood." But the rock version of "Mr. Soul" with the Springfield was months away. Things would have to get a little more insane before the band could record it.

Open to a thousand interpretations, shot full of mystery and dread, "Mr. Soul" is the first glimpse into the darker side of Neil Young's psyche. Whatever it was that had descended on him, the feeling in "Mr. Soul" is that he's just made it out from underneath. There's an ironic distance new to Young's lyrics, and a creepy black humor. "Stick around while the clown who is sick does the trick of disaster"—perhaps a reference to epileptic attacks and hospital stays, but like much of what Young writes, subject to endless debate.

Young reflects on the relationship between his audience and himself, his observations reaching a climax in the last verse. "Hearin' that tune at the

*Around this time, Young reached toward his past, writing Pam Smith an eleven-page letter—since destroyed in a flood—describing his torment. "I think it was a plea for help," said Smith. "Neil wasn't coping well. In one part, I was almost worried he felt like throwing in the towel. . . . Neil sounded worn out. He wanted me to write him every day. . . . I told him I wouldn't write back until I heard from him." Neil never responded.

time was so heavy," said Ken Viola. "There was a lot of talk at the time about the soul, the inside of a person. To me, the whole point of the song is: What's externally on the face of a person—how does that juxtapose with what's in their soul? And that last line—'Is it strange I should change / I don't know why don't you ask her?'—I remember at the time thinkin' how nasty that was."

The Faustian aspects of show business and the machinations of fame simultaneously repulsed and fascinated Young, but no craziness—not his own nor that of others—would prevent him from forging on. And continuing to mutate.

Almost thirty years later, Young would open his *Unplugged* taping with "Mr. Soul." Trapped in an appropriately garish, hyper-real MTV set, he looked like the weird psychedelic spawn of some itinerant bluesman, his blank face made even more inscrutable by the omnipresent ink-black shades, a grizzled visage that looked older than time. The old man of the mountain had come down to the Colosseum and, staring into the TV eye, waited for the lions to be set loose. His vocal had a walking-dead quality, the guitar a drone. The backup band, there to play along on most of the rest of Young's ditties, had to sit this number out. This was a solo trip.

I asked Young about the song many, many times in the course of our interviews. Around in circles we went.

"Mr. Soul" takes me through all those times—the Springfield era. It really typifies the end without really being near the end or knowing what the end was about. That's a song that is somehow semiprophetic and semiretro. It seems to make more sense the more I play it. I don't know where it came from, but it really tells the story of my life at that time, and strangely enough, *it still seems to be true.*

I remember bein' up in the middle of the night writing it—I don't know why.* I wrote that on the floor in my little cabin. With a felt-tip pen. On the floor on newspapers in the bathroom, smokin' some bad grass. That's what I really like, writing on newspapers. It's so easy and

---

*Robin Lane, who was around Young at the time, remembers "Mr. Soul" as somehow being inspired by the death of Lenny Bruce on August 3, 1966. Young didn't recall any connection.

it looks so good. You write in black on top of it, and it's hidden because of the black-and-white background. The words can't come out and assert themselves that way. They lay in there, so you're not intimidated by seein' them so clearly. Even if you glance at them, they're not that clear. They're in there. If you wanna spend time findin' them, they'll be there, but you don't read it instantaneously. They're, like, a fuzzy thing.

—*Was the Stones riff your idea of a little joke?*

Never even entered my mind, really, that it was that *similiar to "Satisfaction"—until it was pointed out to me and I went, "Yeah, it is, you're* right*." But I wasn't gonna* change *it because of that. So then I guess I kind of exaggerated it. If it's there, you gotta go with it.*

—*Who's Mr. Soul?*

Everybody has their own Mr. Soul. So even if I could—which I don't think I can—point out to you who Mr. Soul is to me, it defeats the purpose.

—*Is there a coldness about "Mr. Soul"?*

I don't think so.

—*Sometimes I hear a deal with the devil in it.*

Maybe—but I don't think so. I mean, there's nothin' you can say about the song—the song is a combination of the lyrics and the beat and the sound of it when it's bein' sung. Breaking it down any more than that takes away from its meaning. It's basically a guy talkin' to himself— talking to his conscience.

—*What does the guy singing this song want?*

He wants to be heard.

—*"Out of My Mind," "Mr. Soul"—they seem like the darker side of the sixties.*

Well, that was sort of like still not feeling I was part of it. Outside looking in. I was groovin' on it—it wasn't like I was bummed or anything. It was just a part of growing up, those songs. Growing up in a band that people knew about, playing in front of audiences . . .

You take things very heavily when you're that age. You don't realize you're gonna live through it. Of course, sometimes you don't live through it.

—*"Mr. Soul" sounds like you almost didn't make it out.*

Yeah . . . I think sometimes when you have some kind of an experience

*in your life that makes you feel like you're lucky to still be alive, that
makes you look back into what makes yourself tick.*
—Have you ever been close to death?
*I don't think so. But I've felt the presence of it enough to know . . . during my seizures that I had around that time, afterwards, when you look
at how disorienting things are and the first couple of times it happened,
I mighta felt like I was threatened in some way. As far as having a life
goes, y'know—as far as* living. *When you have a seizure, you go off . . .
it kind of feels like you lose yourself for a while. Somehow you're still
there. All these things happen to your body, but you don't have any recollection of it—and it wasn't an accident, where somebody hit you. It
came from inside.*
—Did you wanna destroy your audience as soon as you got it?
*Turnover. Like in clubs where they turn over the audience? Did you ever
notice that if the same audience stays, the second set usually isn't as
good as the first set? But if they turn the audience over, the second set
could be better than the first set? Because with me that's the way it is.*

In July 1966, Vicki Cavaleri and Donna Port abruptly left Los Angeles for
San Francisco. A well-known gnomelike pop star, angry that Port had
spurned his advances one night at the Whisky, had threatened to have her
"taken care of." Given money by one of the star's handlers and advised to
leave town until things cooled down, Port scooped up Vicki and headed
north. The pair wound up in an old Victorian mansion in Haight Ashbury
with members of the newly formed Jefferson Airplane. It was there in late
October that Vicki and Donna received an unexpected guest.

"We hear this little knock on the door and it's Neil with his two kittens,"
remembers Port. "I don't know how he got there or how he found us. He
said, 'I've got two weeks off and I had to get away from the guys. I've had
it. I don't care if I ever see those guys again.' "

Six hours later there was another knock at the door: Stephen Stills.
Within a few days, the entire band—along with Greene and Stone, complete with limo—had shown up. "There was no furniture in the place," recalls Stone. "Everybody was completely stoned, lying on the floor."

Although the Airplane's Marty Balin persuaded concert promoter Bill
Graham to give the Springfield a shot at the Fillmore that November 11

through 13, their stay in San Francisco was a dismal one. They were so broke Richard Davis had his parents wire $500 so the band could eat. Tensions were at an all-time high. "Stephen and Neil were not getting along," said Port. "There was no flow in that band whatsoever."

In addition, Young was very self-conscious about his Los Angeles address. "There was this big thing about San Francisco being San Francisco and L.A. being L.A. . . . and if you're from L.A. you're *phony* and if you're from San Francisco you're *real,* y'know," Young told Tony Pig in 1969. "And here we were—the other groups happening from L.A., from our town, were the Association, the Monkees. . . . I was very aware of the difference between the two cities and how one was real or trying to be real and the other one was in its own reality—not real at all."

There was one San Francisco band with whom the Springfield would form a brief but significant bond: Moby Grape. Led by Alexander "Skip" Spence, a maniacal Canadian who had been the original drummer for the Airplane, the Grape had just gotten together and were playing a Sausalito dive called the Ark.

Moby Grape shared the Springfield's unique structure: three singer/songwriters, three electric guitars. "It was a real stunner, because instrumentally it was a mirror of the Buffalo," said Richard Davis. For the few weeks they were in San Francisco, the Springfield alternated sets with the Grape at the Ark. "Richie used to sing, man, and when he'd get to those high parts, his neck would bulge out like a stomped-on toad frog," said Grape guitarist Jerry Miller.

Even in terms of personalities, the Grape and the Springfield had their parallels, with blond redneck blues singer Bob Mosley offsetting the dark and mysterious Peter Lewis. Offstage they hung out with their doppelgängers—Mosley with Stills and Lewis with Young. Son of actress Loretta Young, Lewis found the distance between Neil Young and his bandmates reminiscent of his own situation.

"I came from a completely different background from the other guys in the Grape. I was in the band, but I didn't feel as in the band as they were, and in that respect I identified with Neil a lot. Because I think that the Buffalo Springfield did that to him, too. They would all get much more loaded than he did, so there was this thing about him bein' sorta on the outs. I didn't really see Neil as bein' on the inside in that band." For a brief moment, Lewis said, a trade was pondered: Lewis into the Springfield for Young joining the Grape.

Moby Grape would quickly self-destruct in a morass of management and personal problems even worse than the Springfield's. They were "too aligned with the whole sixties trip," as Ken Viola put it. But they would leave behind something that had completely eluded the Springfield: a perfect debut album, *Moby Grape*.

There are those who were present at the Ark that claim the Grape's tough sound had a big impact on the Springfield. Lewis said that the Grape "used guitars much more aggressively." The records the Springfield made after their San Francisco trip belie a possible influence, but one has to keep in mind the Springfield's insistence that their live sound had always been much heavier than their debut would indicate.* Whatever the case, the Springfield would return to Los Angeles and, on December 5, 1966, record a song some feel was directly inspired by their time with the Grape, "For What It's Worth."

—*Did going to San Francisco have any effect on you musically?*
I don't think there's anything that didn't *have an effect on me. That was just a different situation up there . . . the band playin' in a communal kind of club. I wasn't really part of it. We were on the outside. It was open and great if you were from San Francisco, but for those of us less fortunate, from Los Angeles, it wasn't quite the same.*
—*You have that way of categorizing music—'This is the Beatles, this is the Stones.' Where did psychedelic music fit in?*
Closer to the Beatles, but in between—because there was a lot more improvising in that psychedelic music than there was in the Beatles' music.
—*Did you like it?*
I didn't mind it. Didn't really get to me. Because the songs *didn't get to me. I'm a song kinda guy, so I do love Jefferson Airplane. "Today" by Marty Balin is a great record, and I think* Surrealistic Pillow *is real good. It had a vibe. That's the one that does it for me.*

---

*Complicating the matter is the fact that there are not that many live tapes of the Springfield and virtually none of any real quality that appear to document the original lineup with Bruce Palmer.

—Did the Grateful Dead make an impression?
Not a musical impression that much—their thing was real subtle. It took
years to grow on me, even just to realize what it was. They just played
and jammed, and they weren't great. They were just so real—*as musi-*
cians, they grew into greatness.
—Tell me about recording "For What It's Worth."
Two of our engineers did that record. Stan Ross, a really well-respected
Hollywood engineer, and Tom May, an engineer at Columbia. Old-
timers. Tom May was doin' the session. Bruce played on it. Really cool
song. Stan came in and said, "You gotta do this one thing to the drum,
the snare." Took a broom, a guitar pick and mixed that in so it's got that
sound of a guitar pick goin' through a broom, on the straw. That
was it.
  Again, that was done without Charlie and Brian. They *don't remem-*
ber that, though—I guarantee ya.
—So what effect did Moby Grape have on Buffalo Springfield?
The same effect Buffalo Springfield had on Moby Grape.

"While we were gone, the shit hit the fan on Sunset Boulevard," said
Richard Davis. "A bunch of teenagers had flipped out over being rounded
up at ten o'clock every night. They'd run down the street burning cars,
smashing windows, screaming and yelling, protesting their own mistreat-
ment."

In an attempt to control the long hair and drugs overrunning Sunset
Strip, local authorities had instituted a ten P.M. curfew for those under eighteen. The neon-purple Pandora's Box, a dive bar not far from the Whisky,
was ordered to close down, which resulted in mass demonstrations and
three hundred arrests. By the time the Springfield got back to town in November, rioting had turned violent and protesters had banded together to
form CAFF: Community Action for Facts and Freedom. Two of the members were Greene and Stone, still burning over their jailhouse debacle with
Neil.

Out in Topanga Canyon, Stephen Stills wrote a song about it. According
to Richard Davis, he'd been messing around with a jam based on two
Grape songs: a 4/4 blues called "Murder in My Heart for the Judge" and a
never released Peter Lewis song called "On the Other Side" that featured

an unusual stop-time chorus ("Stop! Can't you hear the music ringin' in your ear").

Musing on the Sunset Strip situation—after, Dewey Martin noted, ingesting hallucinogens—Stills wrote a new song based on the jam "but done up in a more folky, gentle manner," said Davis. Charlie Greene remembers Stills in the back of his limo, picking up an acoustic guitar and saying, "Let me play you a song, for what it's worth." Time was booked immediately in Columbia's studio B and, Dewey Martin claimed, "an acetate was being played on KHJ within four days."*

It was a landmark session for the group, their first time recording as a real band. Young contributed his own bit of genius on guitar—spare, bell-like harmonics that took the edge off the "heavy" lyrics and added so much to the record's ominous, day-of-reckoning feel—but the moment belonged to Stills. He captured the paranoia in the air, circa early 1967. Dennis Hopper would proclaim to me that " 'For What It's Worth' and 'Dancin' in the Streets' by Martha and the Vandellas were the two most revolutionary songs of the time."

When the session was over, maintained Charlie Greene, Stills complained he didn't have a title. "Yes you do," said the manager. "You said, 'Let me play you this song *for what it's worth.*' For once Stephen agreed with me." Ahmet Ertegun didn't, hence the convoluted original title: "(Stop, Hey What's That Sound) For What It's Worth." According to Greene, Ertegun also requested that Stills change the line about the "man with a gun over there," but he refused.

No one in the band thought the song would be a hit, least of all Stills, who worried that the Springfield would be pegged as a protest group. Some claim he didn't seem to think much of the song at all. Peter Lewis remembered seeing him in San Francisco shortly after the session. Stills said sheepishly, "Man, we just recorded this song—and when we were done we realized it was a compilation of two of your songs."

·   ·   ·

*Longtime Atlantic engineer Tom Dowd maintained that he mixed "For What It's Worth" at Atlantic's New York studios, a claim that Greene and Stone vigorously denied. "Not true," said Greene. "And if I see Tommy, I'm gonna punch him in the nose."

Atlantic Records felt strongly enough about "For What It's Worth" to pull the Springfield's debut album out of the stores and add the song to a new pressing.

In December and early January 1967, the band went to New York City to play Ondine's, a small showcase club on the Upper West Side. During their engagement, "For What It's Worth" started to climb the charts, and it looked like the band was headed for success after all. Ertegun recalled the gigs with excitement. "When they performed there, man, there was no band I ever heard that had the electricity of that group. That was the most exciting group I've ever seen, bar none. It was just mind-boggling." Otis Redding, Mitch Ryder and Odetta all showed up to jam.

But the Springfield would crash hard in New York. While Greene and Stone stayed at the Plaza Hotel, the musicians were crammed like sardines into a two-room suite at the Wellington. Tempers flared. At one of the Ondine's shows, Stills and Palmer got into a fight over the volume of the bass, and Palmer, as Stills would later recall to writer Allen McDougall, "slapped me across the face. So I went completely purple with rage and put him through the drums . . . everyone was very shocked. . . . We all just flipped right out, man. Neil, Bruce, me, the lot of us."

At this point Stills and Young were like "chalk and cheese," as Linda McCartney put it. "It would really make me angry, because Stephen pushed Neil back constantly. Neil was painfully shy. I thought, 'Well, he just doesn't stick up for himself.' "

Young was having his own problems. After one show he experienced a severe seizure. "I could see Neil holding on for dear life," said Nurit Wilde. "Near the end of their last song, I could see Neil was gonna have an episode. He was struggling so hard against it. As soon as the band finished the song, the audience started to applaud, and Neil ran right off. I ran after him."

Ondine's had no dressing rooms, so Young made it to an empty hallway and collapsed to the floor in the throes of a grand mal seizure. Wilde stuck a pencil in his mouth so he wouldn't swallow his tongue, and gradually Young came to.

"He was kind of dazed, like 'What am I doing here?' " she said. "I'll never forget how he ran for that hallway to get away from everybody and collapse. Anybody else would've just fallen down and had a seizure."

To top it all off, Bruce Palmer got busted for pot at the Wellington.

While the rest of the band returned to Los Angeles, Palmer was sent to jail and then back to Canada. His repeated legal problems would wreak havoc with the Springfield.

"Bruce was always getting thrown out and we were always getting him back in," said Charlie Greene. "Bruce had the longest hair of anybody, so we snuck him in as a woman once. He looked like an ugly Veronica Lake. Then we cut his hair, gave him a briefcase and pince-nez glasses and got him in as a businessman."

As the Springfield struggled to replace him, the momentum of the hit single was lost. Despite a host of substitutes—Jim Fielder, Ken Koblun, Bobby West, Ken Forssi and Jim Messina—the band would never recover from the loss of Palmer. "Bruce," as June Nelson put it, was "the glue that kept the Springfield together."

Buffalo Springfield started out to be what it was with all of us—as far as I was concerned, when we changed the people, it was somethin' else.

Bruce was beyond. He was the soul of the whole thing. He wasn't in-hibited by anybody, and he knew he was probably better than any of these guys—because he was. It was Bruce that made it so great, because his bass playing was like nothing I'd ever heard before. It was just in an-other world.

The band was just about to start happening when we lost Bruce. That was real tough. That was the end of the real thing—the real dream of what it was gonna be like as Buffalo Springfield.

But before Palmer slipped into the ozone, the band slipped into Atlantic's New York studios and cut "Mr. Soul" on January 9, 1967. It was a fitting choice for such a demented time: The paranoia of the lyrics seemed to mir-ror everything the band was going through.

The session was directed by a forgotten red-haired engineer smart enough to record the band live. Young wrenched wild sounds out of his Gretsch; Palmer whipped out a frantic, punishing bass line; Martin chugged along like a diesel puffing uphill; Stills's and Furay's ghostly high harmonies gave the lyrics a disquieting edge. Stephen finished it off with an odd backward twelve-string-guitar overdub. Unlike other Springfield records, it was recorded and mixed all at once.

"Mr. Soul" is the Springfield's *Rashomon;* no two people recall the session the same way. Charlie Greene remembered that his relationship with Stills finally exploded. "I hit him in the mouth. Stephen just got me so fuckin' pissed I finally whacked him. Y'know, in my eyes I'm doing my best—I took the Springfield from street urchins to a point where the entire industry thought they were devastating. But Stephen was such an irritating piece of shit I couldn't believe it. Stephen thought he *invented* the notes." Greene was furious. "We had to give Charlie one of Neil's pills to calm him down," recalled Dewey Martin.*

Some involved say Otis Redding, who had sat in with the band at Ondine's, was present at the recording, and Dewey Martin claimed that Redding wanted to cut the song, feeling it was a natural follow-up to his version of "Satisfaction." "I *gotsta* have that song, man," Redding told Martin, who then relayed the message to Young. His terse reply, according to Dewey: "Tell him I'm cutting the song."

I don't remember Otis ever sayin' to me he wanted to cut it. I remember Atlantic wanted him to cut it. Greene and Stone weren't there—just this red-haired guy who was the producer. I can't remember his fuckin' name. One night's work—the definitive take of the song. That's the real Buffalo Springfield. Creative production, everybody a part of it. Really a unified trip—everybody had their idea, and we all did 'em, and it worked. And it sounded good—you listened to it and it sounded good. But no one said, "Next song." There was no continuity. That guy was gone after that night. We never had him back.

That record is so fuckin' much better than the ones that are out with Buffalo Springfield, it scares me. It's better than all the other versions of it combined. The tones, the guitar groove . . . We got a good sound with that red-haired guy.

Engineer Bruce Tergesen—"the red-haired guy," whom I finally tracked down after five years of searching—has his own version of "Mr. Soul"

---

*Brian Stone on Charlie Greene: "Everybody liked Charlie to start, but as time went on, he wore on people. Every time he got mad, he'd punch his fist through the wall. He was a very volatile character, kinda like the manager's equivalent of Stephen Stills."

events. He doesn't remember Redding being present, nor does he recall a physical fight between Stills and Charlie Greene. But the friction between Stills and Young that night made an impression. "Stephen wanted to be productive and go ahead," said Tergesen. "Neil was being very moody—he had misgivings about what was going on and his cautions were not being heeded. It left him looking at the floor."*

Although Greene and Stone would be credited with the production of "Mr. Soul," they would never be involved in another Buffalo Springfield recording session. Back at Ondine's, everyone gathered to hear the song over the sound system, but "nobody was talking," said Greene. "It was grim. *Grim.* I went back to the Plaza and got drunk outta my tits. I knew that was it. That was the last time I ever talked to Stephen Stills." Greene and Stone would continue to be involved with the band off and on until late 1967, when the acrimony became so great it had to be settled legally. The Springfield—and its future publishing—were free to go as long as their managers were repaid expenses. Greene and Stone would remain villains in Springfield mythology for years. "Manager!" Young hissed to Jean-Charles Costa in 1971. "What kind of cat is a manager, anyway? . . . They legally stole $60,000."

"I never really thought of them as producers," said Ahmet Ertegun. "Look, don't get me wrong—I like Greene and Stone. They were funny. They were also hustlers. And y'know—you don't want to have a hustler hustle you."

Charlie and Brian were good managers. They were bad record producers. It's like if Elliot wanted to produce my records, I'd fuckin' kill him. But these guys went in and mixed the stereo version of Buffalo Springfield—without telling us. So that's where they made their big mistake, as far as I'm concerned. Not in ripping off our publishing. Hey— how are the poor fuckin' guys gonna make any money? They're makin' us into big megastars, connecting us with all these fuckin' heavies, getting us a recording contract . . . so they're entitled to their part of the

---

* Interestingly, Tergesen—who was unaware of the controversies—also insisted it was he who mixed the tapes for the Springfield's dismal first album, a claim that Greene and Stone refuted.

publishing until we get smart enough to figure out it's ours and have enough energy to fight and get it back.

Greene and Stone were good guys. They really were. They wanted us to make it. They were into it a hundred percent. Unfortunately, that didn't leave anything for us—they had the hundred percent. But that's okay. If we'd made it big, we woulda made some money and it woulda been okay. But we didn't make it big. Sour grapes. We blame everybody else. That's my viewpoint now.

Charlie and Brian were sincere. They wanted to do the right thing. They were jive, but that was part of their personality—that didn't mean that they didn't have soul.

Young took the tapes of "Mr. Soul" back to Los Angeles and started tinkering, replacing the guitar parts with overdubs of his own. When Stills heard the finished track, he told Neil he preferred the original. This apparently haunted Young, because in the late eighties he enlisted Ken Viola to track down a copy of the only existing acetate of the original. Upon hearing it, Young immediately picked up the phone, called Stills and told him, over twenty years later, "Ya know that version of 'Mr. Soul' with the backwards guitar? You were right. I put out the wrong one."

Stills didn't like the "Mr. Soul" that came out as much as the original, and he was RIGHT. The way we did it in New York was the best recording Buffalo Springfield ever made—because it was done by somebody who knew what the fuck they were doing. Then I did overdubs in L.A. and ruined it. Some stupid dickhead with too much time on his hands got a chance to do something, and I had to play the role. I completely fucked it up.

I can't find the original tape. The only copy I have of the original session is a scratchy fuckin' acetate—you can barely hear it—but it's still the one. So that's that. Either I find it or I don't. And if it's the only one I can find, I'm gonna put it out. I don't give a shit how fucked up it is.
—What do you think about when you hear that demo?
I think about how you can lose it when you already got it.

I worked all night on "Mr. Soul." We did it all in one day. What did I do after that? I fucked it up—so what did that teach me? It teaches me that WHAT YOU DO FIRST IS THE RIGHT FUCKIN' THING AND JUST MOVE ON.

Don't start until you're sure you can finish. Whatever it is you wanna do makin' a record, DO IT. Stay right on it. Don't change your head. That's what comes from "Mr. Soul."

Hiring Ken Koblun to replace Bruce Palmer, the Springfield embarked on its first real tour and this, too, was a disaster. Headlining a package show featuring a weird assortment of stale fifties groups and current novelty acts, the Springfield would alternate closing the show with IQ-challenged trash-rockers the Seeds. After a few dismal Los Angeles–area dates in early February 1967, the tour moved through New Mexico, then Texas, where the band jumped ship over a money dispute.

Although "For What It's Worth" would get as high as number seven on the pop charts, "the record never seemed to get any national push," said Richard Davis. "It was really big in some places, other places wouldn't know who we were." Charlie Greene's theory is that "For What It's Worth" was like "Kate Smith singing 'God Bless America'—it was one of those things everybody heard and loved but nobody bought." It was frustrating to all involved. Said Ertegun, "I couldn't figure out why we weren't selling more records, because we were working that group very hard."

Broke again, the band returned to Los Angeles. Neil holed up in his little house on Utica Drive. He started missing rehearsals and gigs. "Neil was going through a real weird period," said Ken Koblun. "He'd sleep all day and stay over at Kiyo's place instead of staying at his own house. She had some influence over Neil, but I think he wanted to have it under control."

I was pretty sick. Got real sick for a while. There was somethin' really fucking wrong with me. Couldn't get up. Kiyo took me to this herbologist, Dr. Kanower. I could hardly walk, I was so weak. I went in there in a robe and pajamas—I didn't have the strength to get dressed.

Dr. Kanower said there had been several radiation tests and that several people had come in feeling down and he thought it had something to do with Los Alamos. Then he gave me this shot of green stuff, right under my rib cage, and I got a hot rush. He said, "This is not gonna hurt you at all." And he said, "Just lie here awhile and you'll feel yourself getting better right away." I came out walking, *not all hunched over. The next day I was up. There was something really wrong with me and he fixed it. I have no idea what it was. But I still feel it every once in awhile when I get tired.*

For the fourth Springfield single, Stills wanted the A-side for his new song "Bluebird"; Young wanted "Mr. Soul." Neil would lose this battle. "Clancy" had bombed and so had the follow-up, Young singing "Burned." Stills now had the edge—he had provided the band with their first hit in "For What It's Worth." His tracks were everything Neil's weren't: accessible, commercial and sung by a voice radio could understand. "The sound of the Buffalo Springfield was really Stephen Stills's voice," the Turtles' Mark Volman told John Einarson. "Neil was kind of like Frankenstein's monster."

Tensions continued to mount. Robin Lane, staying with Young at the time, remembers Stills showing up, enraged over Neil's increasing belligerence. He picked up Lane's Epiphone acoustic guitar and threatened to smash it over Young's head, screaming, "You're ruining *my career!*"

The more Stills demanded control, the more the elusive Young withdrew, a pattern familiar to those close to him. "Neil is very passive/aggressive," said Donna Port. "He sees conflict and hides under a chair. And when there's aggression, believe me, it's passive. It's called *hide.* It's 'Okay, I won't come to your party.' " Young could be contentious about being himself, sometimes humorously so. When Furay got married, he implored Young not to wear his fringe jacket. Young acquiesced, showing up in a Confederate uniform instead. "That's just the kinda guy he was," said Furay. But nobody was laughing in the spring of 1967, when Young suddenly quit Buffalo Springfield.

Following the success of "For What It's Worth," the Springfield's booking price had climbed to $1,000 a night; they were scheduled to play at the landmark Monterey Pop Festival in June, and the Newport Folk Festival wanted them as well. Even Johnny Carson's *Tonight Show* offered a spot. "That's when the Carson show meant something *big,*" said Dewey Martin. "Do his show and you would've made it." A little before June 1, Young set up a meeting with his bandmates.

"Now, we never called meetings," Richard Davis told writer Jerry Hopkins. "Sometimes maybe we'd run into each other. But Neil called a meeting. So we walk into Greene and Stone's office and Neil said, 'I'm leaving the group.' "

"The reason Neil quit was, he wanted to release 'Mr. Soul,' " recalls roadie Chris Sarns. "Stephen didn't, because he thought it sounded too much like 'Satisfaction.' It broke up the group." Young had also begun to work on his own with Jack Nitzsche. Whatever the particulars, Young wanted out.* Stunned, the band talked him into staying through Monterey Pop.

Arrangements were made for some East Coast dates before the *Tonight Show* appearance, but just before they were supposed to leave, Young vanished. "I couldn't believe it," said Davis. "He just stopped taking our calls and disappeared."

His bandmates felt shafted. "I think Neil always wanted to be a solo artist, and I can't hold it against him," Richie Furay told writer Dave Zimmer. "It just seems there may have been a different way to make the point clear rather than not show up."

Forced to carry on without him, the band played Boston, enduring screams of "Where's Neil?" from the fans. Arriving at New York's JFK airport, Dewey Martin, stoned on two hits of Purple Haze, got on the pay phone and made a last-ditch attempt to save their appearance on *The Tonight Show* by inviting Otis Redding to sit in. Unfortunately, Redding had a gig at the Apollo Theater, and once again all momentum was lost. "That's when Neil had to quit," Stills told writer Allen McDougall, "exactly at the time when it meant the most."

I fucked everything up, no doubt about it. I was takin' a lot of Valium for the seizures 'cause I was so high-strung. I would go off—real easy. But y'know—if I hadn't fucked it up, somebody else would've. Bruce did, too. I was only a ripple in a pond.

---

*Bob Young wrote a letter to a friend in Canada on June 26, 1967, stating that Neil was already out of the band by June 1 and working with Jack Nitzsche. He confirmed the rejection of "Mr. Soul" as one of the reasons Neil left. Writes Bob: "Neil's music was criticized frequently by Steve Stills . . . Neil was beginning to lose confidence in his music . . . the group had also been recording a new LP and Neil at one point told me he'd be lucky to get two songs on it."

For me, it was over when the Springfield wanted to do the Johnny Carson show. What the fuck were we doin' the Johnny Carson show for? That was just another of Stephen Stills's things, and he was right—*if the Springfield was gonna make it, people had to see them—but I didn't wanna be seen doin'* that. *I didn't wanna do it that way.*

Once the Buffalo Springfield were doin' this lighthearted afternoon TV show—hosted by Woody Woodbury. We were trying to get exposure, the managers wanted us to do it. So we're doin' this stupid show, and we played a song, and we were gonna be back later to play another song. We were sittin' in the back—all the other guests are in the front, and we were supposed to sit in the row behind 'em because they didn't really want to talk to us other than say "Hello" and "Who are ya," that sorta thing.

So Rona Barrett comes out, she's on the panel there and they're talkin' back and forth. She's talkin' about this person and that person and their private lives—and I said, "Now wait a minute. Just a minute here. Is it true that what you do—what you do—*is expose other people's* private lives? *And try to unearth their own* personal secrets *and try to* share them *with everybody else—that's how you make a living, right?"*

That was a dark moment for TV. We weren't invited back.

The Smothers Brothers, *Tom Jones,* Hollywood Palace, *all those shows I did when I was . . . crazy. These music shows were pretty cool, they were for kids, they were for our audience, but we weren't there to be on* The Tonight Show *with all these fuckin' stiff old farts that had nothin' to do with anything. It wouldn't be right. We're not entertainment for the masses.*

—What's your feeling about performing music on television?
I hate it. It's unnatural. Anything that you can turn off, turn up or adjust as it's going down live I don't like. Someone else is making the TV show, you're just passing through. I'm not controlling the situation. Anything could happen. What I do shouldn't be exposed to that.

We screwed the BBC once. I was gonna do a couple of songs, and then when I got down there, they said the last *song I would be doing would be while the credits were rolling at the end of the show. And I said, "No, I can't do that." They said, "You* will *do that." And I said,*

"No, I'm leaving. Fuck you people. I'm outta here." It was a live show, and I just left, heh heh.

TV has an effect on you. I can't just block it out or use it for background . . . I don't have the talent to do that. If it's on, I can be distracted by it. I can focus on anything, *so the more things that are on, the harder time I have focusing on one given thing. I would be okay if there was no television, but I'm not the only one in my house . . . I wish I didn't have to see it.*

I once asked Young if any musicians on the Los Angeles scene had influenced him at all. He remained silent for a long time—so long I thought the question had been ignored or forgotten, and then he offered one name only: Jack Nitzsche.

"Jack believed in my music, and his belief in my music was reinforcing enough to me to go out on my own—and leave Buffalo Springfield."

growin' up, blowin' up

Jack Nitzsche sits in his home in the Hollywood Hills, looking, as always, a bit awkward. Those harsh features, the long, graying hair and, behind thick glasses, piercing, pained eyes—sometimes Nitzsche, now in his sixties, resembles an agitated Indian shaman; others, a hip Amish farmer. There are nights Jack can look older than a ghost. Demons plague him, and he's known depths lower than any submarine. Jack's heart was broken long ago, by a singer/songwriter whose music he never even liked.

Nitzsche's had a hand in decades of rock and roll: arranging a long string of hits for Phil Spector, playing furious rhythm piano on such Stones tracks as "Have You Seen Your Mother, Baby," composing landmark movie scores for *Performance* and *One Flew Over the Cuckoo's Nest,* producing everyone from the Neville Brothers to the Germs. And there's his idiosyncratic solo records, among them *St. Giles Cripplegate,* a 1972 album of Ives-inspired original orchestral pieces recorded with the London Symphony Orchestra, and a wild 1963 big-band version of "Rumble" that actually inspired Link Wray to revamp the arrangement of his trademark song. Nitzsche touches other musicians in a way that's hard for civilians to understand. "Jack's one of the modern-day masters," Neil Young told Gavin Martin. "His creations are on par with Mozart and the composers of the Renaissance."

On and on it goes, but even on a good day you get the feeling Jack thinks it's all a load of shit. Everybody warned me about Jack—friends, enemies, even family: Jack's evil, Jack's an asshole, Jack's the devil, Jack will eat you alive ten seconds after meeting you. . . . Now, Jack can be cruel. I've heard tales of Nitzsche telling people things that peeled their skin off. He once reduced Carly Simon to tears merely by commenting on the equestrian nature of her face.

Yet there is something pure about Jack. Take him to a record store and he'll blow a fortune looking for some new sound to love, whereas everybody else in this fucking story retired from listening to music in 1974. Nitzsche has loved rock and roll ever since the Penguins' immortal 1955 doo-wop hit. "Once I heard 'Earth Angel' it was all over," he said. "That's the first one that really, really grabbed me hard and made me cry. . . . It had death in it. Death is always a part of the music that I make. Death means a lot."

Nitzsche lives up to his name. He can be devastatingly cynical about the music business, the world and himself. To him, rock and roll, all of it, including whatever he's created, was stolen from the black man. "Jack's prejudiced in reverse," said his son, Jack Jr. "He hates white people."

Jack has a reputation for being scaldingly candid and has remained on a very short list of people who will tell Neil Young what he thinks without fear of reprisal. Their lives have intertwined both professionally and privately, and Nitzsche never holds back his opinions of what went down—no matter how much of an asshole it makes him seem—and it scares people. "Jack's brutally honest," said his old friend Leslie Morris. "He uses it as a weapon."

• • •

In 1955, Jack Nitzsche drove his two-year-old Studebaker across the country to attend music school in Los Angeles, leaving behind a miserable childhood in Michigan. Nineteen years old, he wanted to be a jazz saxophonist but realized he'd never be good enough. Copying lead sheets at Specialty Records for A&R man Sonny Bono led to a partnership with black-music impresario H. B. Barnum and Jack's first modest hit as a producer/arranger, "Bongo, Bongo, Bongo," the follow-up to the immortal Preston Epps hit, "Bongo Rock."

The arrangements for Spector began in 1962 with the Crystals' immortal "He's a Rebel," a number-one smash, and ended with Ike and Tina Turner's ill-fated "River Deep, Mountain High." During those years Nitzsche would be omnipresent on the pop charts. His work with Greene and Stone began in 1964 with an all-star session featuring Darlene Love on a droning version of "Yessir, That's My Baby." "Jack was the first guy I ever saw with long hair," said Charlie Greene. "He was a nerd, but a cool nerd."

Nitzsche—so enamored of the beatniks that he blackened his entire apartment with Rit die—was similarly entranced by the burgeoning hippie movement "until they put it on TV and it all became a costume."

It was Brian Stone who first played demos of the Springfield for Nitzsche. "I didn't think they were so great," said Nitzsche. "But Neil's songs stood out. I loved his songs and that squeaky fucking voice. Stills would complain about how squeaky his voice was. I told him, 'That's what's gonna make Neil a star.' "

After spending a night with Young at the Whisky heckling the Nazz— "Neil kept yelling, 'There's only one Mick Jagger! You're not the Rolling Stones!' "—Jack recalls that the musician invited him back to his home to hear a new song. Nitzsche followed Young's car up Laurel Canyon Boulevard and, drunk on a bottle of Lancer's, plowed into a head-on collision, smashing the windshield of his Caddy convertible with his cranium. Nitzsche was hauled off to jail, where, much to his mortification and embarrassment, Young harassed the cops who'd detained him by shouting, "Do you *know* who you arrested tonight? This is a heavyweight ya got here." Thus began a very unusual friendship.

Nitzsche and sidekick Denny Bruce soon completed the pilgrimage to Utica Drive. Inside the house, beneath a picture of Marianne Faithfull pinned to the wall, Young picked up a twelve-string guitar to play an as yet unrecorded song, "Expecting to Fly." Halfway through the ballad, Nitzsche exclaimed, "Fuck—what a great song!" That one of the more powerful figures on the music scene had just complimented him was less important than the fact he'd been interrupted, and Young admonished the producer sharply, "Shhhh! Just *listen*!" "I thought, 'Fuck, I am listening,' " said Nitzsche, impressed—arrogance was a subject he knew something about.

· · ·

"Jack Nitzsche was the Yoko Ono of the Buffalo Springfield," said Denny Bruce. Bruce Palmer recalled that the band members were constantly searching for Neil, and the path inevitably led to the producer's house. One day Nitzsche came home to find a nervous Young hiding in Jack Jr.'s bedroom—"If Stephen comes looking for me, tell him I'm not here and that your kid's taking a nap." Young had fled the group and Stills had stolen his beloved Gretsch White Falcon to lure him back. "Neil was afraid Stephen was gonna hit him over the head with it," said Nitzsche.

Stills would be rebuffed by Jack when he asked him to produce his opus, "Bluebird." "I'm too busy with Neil," said Nitzsche, infuriating Stills, who then snagged Ahmet Ertegun to coproduce.

Using layers of virtuoso acoustic/electric guitar, Stills concocted an unrelenting folk-pop-blues confection: just the sort of meticulously crafted studio creation Young would soon be running from. Live, the song was a showcase for Stills/Young guitar exchanges, and some observers feel that the Springfield's "Bluebird" excursions were a direct result of exposure to the noodlings of San Francisco groups. An overwrought nine-minute version, complete with Stills's moaning-groaning bluesman posturings, mercifully went unreleased until 1973, but it hardly constitutes any kind of real jam—Young's intermittently berserk guitar was overdubbed.

"Neil and Stills had an argument, because it was Stills's song and it was getting down to 'Well, it's *your* song, *you* should do it,' " remembers engineer Bruce Botnick. "And Stills was saying, '*You're* the lead guitar player.' He worked Neil up to the point where he had an epileptic seizure right there in the control room. When he came out of it, he played the solo."

Nitzsche, present at the session, remembered Ertegun gently admonishing the quarreling musicians by stating a bit of music-biz reality in that low, gravelly voice of his: "You will have to stop this. This is ridiculous. You see, this is Jack Nitzsche over here, and if he picks up that guitar over there and hits me in the head with it, that goes in *Cashbox* magazine— front page. If you two guys beat each other bloody, no one cares. No *Cashbox* magazine. Understand?"

•　　•　　•

Once out of the Springfield, Neil Young found a home with the oddball crew around Nitzsche, which included Jack's long-suffering wife, Gracia, a member of the backup vocal trio the Blossoms (until they joined the cast of *Shindig* and the TV people didn't want a white girl standing between two black ones); his highly amusing teenage sidekick, Denny Bruce; an effete aspiring actor named John Hunter; and Chris Varez, a strapping scarfaced German whom KHJ had fobbed off on the public as a spear-carrying

Hawaiian deity known as the Big Kahuna.* Varez supplied grass that was "beyond anything we'd ever experienced," said Nitzsche. "It was like acid."

Nitzsche and Denny Bruce sometimes snickered over the idiosyncrasies of their odd new friend. No matter what restaurant they went into, Neil would insist on ordering the same thing—a hamburger. At home, all he cooked was french fries, cutting the potatoes into big hunks "so he wouldn't have to peel 'em," said Bruce, adding that physically, Young was "never healthy at all. His gums were always bleeding, and the jar of big yellow pills for his seizures was never far from reach." Social activities invariably seemed awkward for Young. He went along on Hollywood Boulevard excursions for miniature golf or Ping-Pong, but "he had no athletic ability whatsoever. You could see he kind of hated it if we were having fun."

One night in 1967, Denny Bruce went with Neil to see *Don't Look Back,* the acidic D. A. Pennebaker documentary on Bob Dylan's 1965 tour of England. "It blew Neil out of the water so much he said, 'Denny—can we stay to see it a second time?' " Nitzsche recalls that Young was obsessed with the Rolling Stones and constantly quizzed the producer about them. "Neil later told me in these words: 'I knew what I wanted and I knew how to get it'—cross Bob Dylan with the Rolling Stones. He tried to become a meld of the two."

Nitzsche began taking Young to sessions, cutting covers of his songs with other artists and even writing songs with him. He tried to get his own label off the ground with Young as its premier artist. Engineer Bruce Botnick remembers Nitzsche's excitement: "Jack kept saying, 'Wait till you meet this guy.' Neil came in looking like an eagle—he had this leather jacket that was a little bit large on him. When he'd hold his arms out, the fringe went almost down to the floor."

However fast Nitzsche got Young into the studio, it wasn't fast enough.

---

*The Springfield recorded an unusual surf-tinged instrumental for one of KHJ's radio spots, "Kahuna Sunset." Cowritten by Stills and Young, it brings to mind the Shadows (and the Squires).

In the credits for Young's self-titled debut it says, "A John Hunter contract." Hunter filled out the contract forms for the sessions. Young—always one to enjoy spreading a little mystery—told Jack, "We'll put it on the record—nobody will know what the fuck it means."

"Whenever Neil wanted something, he wanted it now," said Nitzsche. "Who did he think was gonna pay for the sessions now that he was solo? He never once gave consideration to that. He just said, 'Book the studio, book the musicians.'" Denny Bruce remembers picking up the phone at Nitzsche's when Young called, demanding to know when his studio time with Jack had been scheduled. Nitzsche had an appointment book filled with his session dates and Bruce said he'd check it. Young became impatient. "I'm not just some name in a book! I'm NEIL YOUNG!"

.   .   .

Nitzsche had happened into Young's life at a crucial moment. Although the Springfield had continued working in the studio since the release of their debut album, by the summer of 1967 the sessions were becoming less of a group thing, and not just because of their squabbles.

Released in the U.S. on June 2, the Beatles' *Sgt. Pepper's Lonely Hearts Club Band* altered the way rock bands went about getting their ideas onto tape, as well as the ideas themselves. Four or five guys standing there cranking it out was suddenly "old-fashioned." There was a whole universe of juicy sounds out there, and to make an album without strings, sitars, segues, sound effects and spoken-word sections became almost unthinkable.

By Christmas of that year, stores would be full of overblown concept-album "masterpieces" impossible to duplicate for a live audience. Leonard Bernstein spent an hour of prime time extolling the virtues of the Left Banke's "Pretty Ballerina" while Brian Wilson previewed "Surf's Up" on a grand piano. Record companies, sensing that highbrow credibility could open up vast markets beyond pimple-faced teens, threw unlimited funds at neophyte bands and let them run wild. Seemingly revolutionary at the time, much of this *Pepper*-inspired stuff was pretentious kitsch with a shelf life of thirty days or less. For each album like Love's *Forever Changes,* there was a truckload of hogwash like the Electric Prunes' *Mass in F Minor* and Sonny Bono's *Inner Views*. Predictably, the only one who didn't lose his head was Dylan, who retreated to Woodstock with the Band to record the most unproduced, spontaneous and truly psychedelic music of his life: *The Basement Tapes*. "I didn't know how to record the way other people were recording and didn't want to," said Dylan to Matt Damsker in

1978. "The Beatles had just released *Sgt. Pepper,* which I didn't like at all. I thought that was a very indulgent album. . . . I didn't think all that production was necessary."

But Young and Nitzsche brought a little genuine art to the party with the stunning "Expecting to Fly." Completed for the most part before *Pepper* hit the street, "Expecting to Fly" leans more toward Brian Wilson and his *Pet Sounds* in its hallucinatory lushness, where everything seems to be taking place underwater. Strings are the first thing you hear, but on a long, slow fade-in that wobbles and veers sharp just as a solo violin opens up out of it like a time-lapse rose blooming: "There you stood on the edge of your feather, expecting to fly / Well, I laughed, I wondered whether I could wave goodbye," sliding into a woozy 3/4 time signature on "goodbye." On a snare hit, the stereo pans from one side to another, and the song ends with what Nitzsche dubbed "the pancake," an eerie in-unison shimmer of female voices that leaves you hanging in the Twilight Zone. Longing, but not getting. Young's fragile voice supplies a very different perspective on the Summer of Love from Grace Slick yowling "Don't you want somebody to love?"*

Nothing like other Springfield records—or any other record, for that matter—Nitzsche created the perfect introduction for Young the solo artist. When I asked Jack what he thought the secret of the record was, he said one word only: "Epilepsy." I don't think Nitzsche's being a smart aleck—the out-of-kilter sense of time in the arrangement captured the je ne sais quoi of Young's electrical system.

Nitzsche built the track while Young was still touring with the Springfield, employing session players Don Randi, Carole Kaye, Jim Gordon, Russ Titleman and the Johnny Vidor string section. ("They were the hip string section in town," said Jack. "Johnny wore a lot of felt hats.") Then Young came in to overdub his guitar. But when faced with doing his vocal, suddenly his "I'm-not-a-name-in-a-book" bravado evaporated.

---

*Nitzsche said Young told him at the time the song was about "fear of making it with a girl"— that he grew apprehensive as he approached his Utica Drive home because Robin Lane was waiting for him inside and he might have a seizure. "I knew he had epilepsy," said Lane. "But I never saw it . . . Neil didn't talk about anything personal." She wound up fleeing from Utica Drive. "I just left . . . it wasn't gonna work out. We weren't communicating, and I think he got real upset with me one time when his grandmother died and I felt bad for him."

"When it came time to sing, Neil was scared to death of the microphone," said Nitzsche. "To the point of saying, 'Maybe this isn't such a good idea.' He didn't have much confidence in his voice. I tried to encourage him any way I could. That strange thing in his voice—all that quivering and shaking, like you think the guy might have a nervous breakdown in front of your eyes? I told him that was appealing. I said, 'You sound *different*—it isn't a matter of can you sing like Stephen Stills—you're a nonsinger. Look at Bob Dylan.' "

The record took weeks to create, giving Jack and Neil a reputation for obsessive tinkering in the process. Bruce Botnick remembers "a lot of trying to make guitars sound like they were on clouds." Many attempts were made at an ending before coming up with the pancake—overdubbed and slowed down—sung by Gloria Jones, Merry Clayton, Gracia Nitzsche, Brenda and Patrice Holloway. The pair mixed and remixed the record. As Jack said, "Those were the good old days. We kept going back until that mix was fucking perfect."

As evidence of the all-pervasive influence of *Sgt. Pepper,* Young changed his own record after hearing it. "I'll tell ya where the beginning of 'Expecting to Fly' came from," Young told deejay Tony Pig. "It was supposed to be the end . . . that whole fade-in and that low rumble, we did that before 'A Day in the Life'—and that was the last note. . . . You can hear a splice in the end just before those chicks' voices come in doing that big *'Oooh'* note. . . . The first note of the song played backwards is the last note . . . and it lasted like about half a minute on the record and we had it all ready to go and the Beatles came out with 'A Day in the Life,' so we just went back into the studio and changed it around, started it off with it, faded it in."

Later, when Young returned to the Springfield, he brought "Expecting to Fly" with him, and while the record failed as a single—Atlantic put out a pointless truncated version—it had a tremendous effect on Young's peers. Graham Nash, then of the Hollies, called Nitzsche from England to sing its praises and when the producer played the record for Keith Richards and then girlfriend, Anita Pallenberg—fresh from a trip to Disneyland and high on a fat Kahuna joint—they were rendered speechless. " 'Expecting to Fly' was a great record for smoking pot," said Nitzsche. "Each time you listened to it, you could discover something new."

—*"Expecting to Fly"—overdubbed, but good?*
That's JACK. His dedication to feelings—getting the feelings on tape. It was a collaboration. Jack and I were working away peacefully with no distractions. "Expecting to Fly" has a sound. It's overdubbed and yet nothing's missing. It's possible to overdub. But the longer you overdub, the harder it is to do.

Jack. What a fuckin' character. He was just great. I think I met Jack at a press party for Buffalo Springfield. I loved the Phil Spector records that he'd been a part of. Jack had a whole scene. He was a player. "Expecting to Fly" is the best thing we did.

Bruce Botnick played an important part in that record. He was an artist. He would set up the board and if he didn't like it, he would just fuckin' erase the whole thing—the Botnick sweep.

We worked on it really hard. It's probably one of the best records that I ever made. It took thirty days. That's a long time on one song. But with Jack we got the real shit. 'Cause Jack could bring it out—he wrestled it out of me line by line, word by word . . . he reinforced it. My *believing in me.*

—*Did "Expecting to Fly" have anything to do with the Summer of Love?*
Yeah, that must've been it. I remember the girls came up, I don't know if it was Donna, Vicki, somebody came up and listened to "Expecting to Fly" over and over again on acid for hours. Got way *into it.*

I don't think I was there.

With "Expecting to Fly" in the can, Neil Young concocted a new plan of attack: Take England by storm. Neil was going to move to the land of the Beatles and the Stones, and he convinced Nitzsche and Denny Bruce to go with him. According to Bruce, Young had it all worked out, down to the costume: a black velvet suit with white patent-leather boots that matched his White Falcon guitar. Neil had heard they hadn't seen *Roadrunner* cartoons in England, so he'd bring those, too. And they didn't have Waterpiks yet, so, Bruce said, "Neil was gonna take one with him and squirt Mick with it just to blow his mind."

Unbelievably, Nitzsche and Bruce went along with the plan and prepared to leave the country. They got passports; Nitzsche even sold his house. For a very brief period the three of them lived together at 7776 Torreyson Drive in a place called the Chemosphere House, aka "the bubble house": a climate-controlled curiosity built into the side of Laurel Canyon that had been featured in *Life* magazine. "It lasted three days," recalls Nitzsche. "There were two variations in the bubble—hot and hotter. You'd go to bed and the next day it was a hundred and twenty degrees."

It was on that last day the trio had breakfast at the International House of Pancakes on Sunset Boulevard. Despite the bubble-house fiasco, spirits were high—after all, they'd be in England soon, squirting Mick with a Waterpik. They were driving home in Jack's blue Cadillac convertible listening to the radio when B. Mitchell Reid played "Mr. Soul." When it was over, the deejay dramatically intoned an epitaph: "When Neil was with 'em, baby."

Young suddenly lurched over the front seat. "*What* did he just say?" Nitzsche repeated it blankly. "No, no, no—what was the *exact tone* in his voice?" Young insisted. "Now I'm doing it and Jack's doing it," said Bruce. " 'When Neil was with 'em, baby.' That snapped something in his mind right there. You could see Neil thinking. And all of a sudden we're not moving to England and he's back in the fucking group."

· · ·

"I got the feeling back. I guess I really need you guys." That's how Dewey Martin remembers Young announcing his return when he came to sit in for a gig. "Neil was very humble," said Martin. "Still Neil, but very humble. He was scruffy, hunched over—he looked like he'd been living in a cave for a couple of months." Replacement Doug Hastings was ousted and Young was back in the band.

The Springfield had struggled without Neil. They had made a dismal appearance at the Monterey Pop Festival augmented by an ever egomaniacal David Crosby, who played with both the Byrds *and* the Buffalo, all the while providing preposterous onstage commentary on LSD and the assassination of JFK. In August the Springfield had toured the Midwest with the Monkees, then moved out to a Malibu beach house just down the road from Moby Grape. For a minute or so, Young moved into a room built underneath an outside deck.

The house had been rented by Stephen Stills, enjoying royalties from

"For What It's Worth" and becoming a bit of a rock star. "Stephen wore as much Saint-Tropez stuff as he possibly could," said writer Eve Babitz. "He looked like a rich person. I just figured he was trying to be like Ahmet." Stills had bonded with the biggest kahuna of the Los Angeles scene: David Crosby. "Stephen and I had a lot of the same attitude," said Crosby. "Egotistical, punk young guys. . . . Neil was in general more intelligent than we were."

Stills had also welded himself to Jimi Hendrix, the opening act on the tour with the Monkees. Stills followed him around like a puppy. "Jimi was my guru, man," Stills told writer Dave Zimmer. "Some people thought we were fags or that I was a groupie. But hey, it wasn't like that at all. It was like I was going to music school, learning how to play lead guitar."*

The beach house was the location of numerous jam sessions, most notably an acid-infused get-together with Jimi Hendrix and Buddy Miles. For Young—who was so gone on his own trip he wouldn't really get into Hendrix until years later—this kind of celebrity circle-jerk was more overblown rock-star bullshit that had little to do with making real music.

Stills went berserk. He had to play the fuckin' guitar behind *his head, play it with his teeth, all this shit—and he couldn't* do *it. So he would do it anyway, and it sounded like* shit. *All of a sudden you'd hear this fuckin' awful sound, and Stills is over there playin' guitar behind his head. He was just goin' through a phase, but to me it was real important—that was belittling to the Springfield as far as I was concerned.*

I didn't like this . . . social playing. I liked to really play. I didn't

---

*An odd coda to the Hendrix/Stills relationship: While living in London in 1970, Stills recorded his hit song "Love the One You're With." Agent/manager Larry Kurzon was knocked out by the original acoustic demo and witnessed Jimi Hendrix overdub a wild solo on the song. "It was a one-take electric lead—he just dropped his guitar and walked out the door. It was an animal, this record," said Kurzon, who went all over London raving about the performance. He was stunned when he heard the finished record weeks later. "There was no more Hendrix . . . [Stephen] replaced it with a steel drum that he played himself." Bassist Greg Reeves claimed that the lost overdub "was the last guitar solo Hendrix ever played" before his death on September 18, 1970. Stills dedicated his first self-titled solo album to Hendrix. "When Jimi died," Stills would tell Dave Zimmer years later, "I almost quit the business."

*like to hang out at parties and the Hollywood trip. And Stephen . . . it
bothered me how he was so impressed with these fuckin' people. I know
Hendrix was great, but let him be great. What the fuck did we have to be
like Hendrix for? That wasn't us.*

In addition to "Mr. Soul," and "Expecting to Fly," Neil Young contributed
another heavy hitter to the Springfield's second album, *Buffalo Springfield Again*—"Broken Arrow." Recorded in the fall of 1967 at the peak of
Pepper-mania, "Broken Arrow" stuffs the whole bag of tricks into its six-
plus minutes.

Comparing "Broken Arrow" to "Expecting to Fly" gives a pretty fair
picture of how *Pepper* affected pop music: a slide from narcotic dream-
scapes to vaudeville, from Brian Wilson to Vanilla Fudge. The absence of
Jack Nitzsche is sorely felt: Where the enigmatic "Expecting to Fly" is understated, elegant and spare, Young's labored solo production on "Broken
Arrow" displays all the subtlety of a William Castle exploitation movie.
Sound effects, tempo changes, a clarinet—all that's missing is a buzzer
under your seat. Young's as yet unreleased acoustic demo is a small trea-
sure, but the song became something else in the studio.

Framing the sections of "Broken Arrow" are such amusements as
Dewey Martin bellowing a self-referential snippet of "Mr. Soul," complete
with screams borrowed from the Beatles at the Hollywood Bowl; a cheesy
stadium-organ rendition of "Take Me Out to the Ball Game" that dissolves
into an acid-distorto wash; and the big finale, a lite-jazz combo fading into
an overamped heartbeat. As Charlie Greene would say, "Heavy."

Of course, Ken Viola thinks I'm full of shit. The record changed his life.
" 'Broken Arrow' was the ultimate fragmentational history of the sixties
encapsulated in one song," he said. "It was so unlike anything I'd ever
heard . . . I must've listened to it a thousand times. The first verse was a
continuation of 'Out of My Mind' and 'Mr. Soul,' but the second verse is
what pushed it over the top for me.

"For a vast majority of young people, 'A Day in the Life' was the turning point—'I'd love to turn you on.' Well, I was already turned on, and for
me the turning point was 'Broken Arrow,' specifically the second verse, because it was a rallying cry to the youth to cast off the bullshit that their par-

ents were handing them—and it was a validation that everything we'd been feeling was *right*.

" 'Eighteen years of the American Dream'—you were eligible for the draft, but you couldn't buy a drink. You could get killed in the war, but you couldn't vote. . . . It was like eighteen years of bullshit and then you go, 'Ma, I heard about trippin',' and she goes, 'A trip is a fall and don't mention babies at all.' It's everything that was happenin' at the time—trips, free love, something alternative—and your mom's goin', '*Forget* about it. Don't come home and tell me you got this girl *pregnant*.' That verse was the whole essence of growin' up, so simply put.

"And the third verse—how could I not help but feel it was about the Kennedy assassination? And I was *not* alone. However far-fetched the allusion was, it fit, which made it all the more relevant. Then the jazz refrain—truly American music. And it ends with the heartbeat—the lifeline—the very nature of our existence. It was life-affirming, exhilarating, and I got *way* into it."

So into it that when Viola was called upon to choose a classic poem to explain to his tenth-grade English class, he mimeographed the lyrics to "Broken Arrow," stuck Robert Frost's name at the bottom and proceeded into a very manic rap on the song for his peers. "It was like 'Stump the teacher.' He couldn't get what the song was about or what I was saying. It was *great*."

We did "Broken Arrow" in sections. Each verse, one at a time. A hundred takes of all of the pieces—they were all cross-faded. Could've been better. Well, maybe I'm not bein' fair when I say that. Could've been more of a group *record. The only reason Jack and I didn't do it is I got back in the group. Too bad. It woulda been fuckin' great.*
—Why did you dedicate the song to Ken Koblun?
He tried to make it, but it didn't work out. He didn't fit into the Buffalo Springfield like Bruce did. Very tough—tough for all of us—but that's growin' up. That's what it's all about. You find out a lotta things. Nothing is forever.

To me, "Broken Arrow" was the end of something—and the beginning. Transition. From one struggle to another. Some kind of milestone. The sign of peace at the end of an Indian war. "Now we can talk." Arafat

and Rabin—they could've broken the arrow. See, I wrote "Broken Arrow" right after I quit Buffalo Springfield, right? So there's the end of something right there.
—What did you think of Sgt. Pepper*?*
It was great—at the time it was way out there.
—It had a strange effect on rock and roll.
Well, it made people take it real seriously. Everybody started doing these overblown, gigantic—everybody had their version. In the long run it had a negative effect, 'cause it made us all into record producers and geniuses and we really should've just been in the band playing.
—What's your deal with Indians?
I like all kinds of Indians. Good ones and bad ones. I relate to them. I don't know why.
—Not in your blood?
There's nothing of any consequence to make you assume that I have any Indian blood—a chance? Yes. Concrete evidence? No. So I don't know.
But it doesn't really matter. What matters is for some reason I love native peoples. How they *used to live. What did they do before civilization and organization came to a point where things got so convenient that the real essence of life was being destroyed? Innaresting . . .*

Released in October 1967, *Buffalo Springfield Again* would be the band's greatest recorded achievement, an ambitious but naïve southern California folk-rock take on *Pepper*.* The band produced much of *Again* themselves, and had control down to the delicate Eve Babitz collage cover. On the back was a list, hand-lettered by Henry Diltz, thanking all their friends, influences and groupies. The record was dedicated to their forgotten first mentor, Barry Friedman.

On just his second outing, the twenty-two-year-old Stills had already mastered his particular brand of folk-pop concoction in "Rock & Roll Woman" and "Bluebird." "Hung Upside Down" is one of Stills's finest

---

*Leave it to Young to dwell on the failure of their first album. "The only good album we made was the second one," he would tell writer Pete Johnson in 1968. "But the first one was better than the second one . . . if the production on the first album had been anywhere near the production on the second one, we'd have had a much better thing."

moments: a guitar-laden blues reverie about one helpless to overcome self-destruction that in retrospect seems to foretell his own tortured future.

Overdub beyond perfection might have been the modus operandi of Stephen Stills, but for Young it was an exercise in frustration. And while he dwelled on the failures outside of his collaboration with Nitzsche, "Mr. Soul," "Expecting to Fly" and "Broken Arrow" hint at the many directions Young would take in the years to come. "Those three songs on that record represented the whole sixties," said Ken Viola. "Neil Young did it all in just three songs. If I ever had a shred of doubt about him—which I didn't—that record told me I was right about this guy. I knew *this guy* was gonna be the one."

Viola was so convinced that he hitchhiked to California, determined to meet his favorite artist. After a handful of gigs, Richie Furay befriended him, and Viola eventually found out where Young was staying. Summoning up all his courage, the fan knocked on the door of the man who had written "Mr. Soul," and Young "just about slammed the door in my face. He was very high-strung, paranoid and not really a nice guy . . . it was very devastating at the time."

• • •

In November, the Springfield toured with the Beach Boys and the Strawberry Alarm Clock. Bruce Palmer was back in the band and more unwieldy than ever. Dewey Martin recalls Palmer—dressed in a full-length monk's robe and beret—walking offstage in the middle of a show.

"Bruce liked his LSD," said Martin. "So he walks up to the mike and said, really loud, 'WILL YOU GUYS GET THOSE FUCKING GUITARS IN TUNE?' They still kept tuning. Bruce took his bass off and just threw it down on the stage really hard. Of course, the bass fed back, and Bruce just went into the wings and wouldn't come back on. He just stood there, looking over those sunglasses with his finger in his mouth." A livid Stephen Stills had to finish the last half of the set playing bass.

"Bluebird" would usually close the second set, "Mr. Soul" the first. "There were quite a few seizures during the end, and it was "Mr. Soul" that would do it," said Davis. "It was a pretty violent end to the set. I used to literally see him startin' to fall, and somebody would get him offstage. The audience would think it was some sort of strange finale."

• • •

Armed with a tremendous second album, the Springfield should have reaped some rewards, but things disintegrated faster than ever before. Three singles were released, and none really hit.

On January 26, 1968, the tension between Stills and Young turned physical, and Dewey Martin had to break up a dressing-room scuffle between the two. Heading home from the gig, Palmer—driving his Camaro without a license and accompanied by an open bottle of booze plus an underage girl carrying pot—found himself in deep shit with the law once again. Out on bail, he immediately got busted a second time. Back to Canada he went, and Jim Messina, who had engineered parts of the second album, was brought in to substitute.

The band lost Richard Davis next. After a concert in Fresno, Davis got into an argument with Dewey Martin and quit. Enduring a succession of would-be managers, the Springfield stumbled ahead without any real guidance. Sessions began for a third album, but it was, as Young told Gary Kenton in 1970, "pieced together by Jim Messina because neither Stills nor I gave a shit."

"It was very difficult," said Messina. "I couldn't get everybody in the same place at the same time. Stephen Stills would bring in Buddy Miles and they'd play, just the two of them. Then we'd have to lay a bass down and whatever else on top of it. It wasn't like making music with everybody together." In an effort to focus the band, Messina moved the sessions to New York. Young didn't show.

In April 1968, the band embarked on another tour with the Beach Boys, this one far from successful. "We were touring the South and it was a nightmare," said Messina. At the Veterans Coliseum in Jacksonville, Florida, Rassy and Neil's brother, Bob, were present for a major meltdown.

"It was really hot, and Dewey took off his shirt and jumped into the audience," recalls Messina. "He was trying to be a good performer, but he was inebriated that night, and this big southern cop came over, grabbed him by the hair and said, 'The concert is *over.*' Then he turned to the rest of us and said, 'Unless you boys wanna rot in my jail, you'll get your asses off this stage, into your cars and outta my county.' "

The band fled the stage—except for Young, in the throes of an epileptic fit. "I saw Neil laying there," said Messina. "I went over to make sure he was still alive and I noticed this one tear in his eye. He was totally silent. And I thought to myself at the time, 'I think we've embarrassed him. His family was there to see him and this happens.' I felt bad. I bet that night was a deciding factor in Neil's life to get away from the Springfield." A few days later, Martin Luther King Jr. was assassinated and the tour was postponed, creating a deep pile of debt for the band.

On March 20 came another bust involving nearly the entire band. Stills had relocated to a ranch in the wilds of Topanga Canyon, and Eric Clapton showed up to jam. "They were partyin'," remembers friend Linda Stevens. "The Marshall amps were stacked. Clapton and Stephen were playing so loud the mountains were ringing. One of the neighbors didn't think it was so cool."

The musicians were warned to crank down the volume, but didn't. Late that afternoon, Dewey Martin started home to Encino. "As I'm driving down Old Topanga Boulevard, I see this patrol car comin' up. It was too late to warn the band." To ice the cake, recalls Chris Sarns, "These three or four girls came busting in the door and said, 'The police are right behind us—here, hide this dope!' "

"They started pulling this shit out of their purses—like five containers of smoke—and I'm going, 'Oh my God!' Being the road manager, they handed it all to me. I tried to flush it down the toilet and the toilet backed up. The cops came running in the bathroom and I'm sitting there looking at this pot floating around. The sheriff came in and I just looked up at him and went, 'Aaaah, *shit*!' He said, 'Why don't you go sit in the other room?' "

Inside the house it was bedlam, with cops and longhairs scattering in every direction. "It was very heavy," said Linda Stevens. "They came in on us from the front and the back. It was like being storm-trooped."

Everyone was arrested except for Stills, who slipped out a window and ran to call for help. "Stephen had the attorneys on the phone before we even hit Malibu," said Stevens. Prebooked in Malibu, then taken to the L.A. county jail on the prison bus, "It was guys in back, chicks in front. We started singing 'For What It's Worth.' "

Inside the jail, the men were stripped down and sprayed with DDT. Clapton's long hair and pink boots seemed to particularly amuse and anger the authorities, so they made him—naked except for his boots—stand separate from the rest. "They set him out in front of us to humiliate him, I guess," said Messina. "It was a time when long hair was not cool." Chris Sarns remembers that Clapton "handled it beautifully. Typically British stiff-upper-lip: 'Oh, well, we've got good lawyers. We'll be out of here by morning.' "

Everyone worried about Young. "Neil was afraid of having an attack because they denied him his medicine," said Sarns. "They separated him from the rest of us and put him in a tank with a bunch of drunks."

Despite the initial fears of conviction—and, for Clapton and Young, deportation—the lawyers took care of everything. All were found guilty only of disturbing the peace—except the unlucky Chris Sarns, who wound up literally holding the bag. "Three hundred bucks and three years probation," he said glumly. "It was kind of a piss, because there was no one left to get the money from."

There was no one left because Buffalo Springfield was on the verge of disintegration, and the bust was yet another nail in the coffin. Expecting to fly, the group had never really gotten off the ground. There was a crazed final gig in Long Beach on May 5, 1968; five days later, Buffalo Springfield called a legal meeting announcing their demise. Ahmet Ertegun was devastated. "I think it was one of the few times I cried, because I just thought that I had the historic group," he said. "Bands didn't make it in those days without hit singles, but my attachment to that group had nothing to do with commerce. The Buffalo Springfield were ahead of their time. They were too artistic." Ertegun would hang on to Stills as a solo artist, releasing Young to pursue a solo career at Warner/Reprise.

"I had to make a choice," said Ertegun. "I don't think Neil and Stephen wanted to be on the same label, and it was a tough decision, but the decision was made for me by Neil, who said he wanted to go on Warner's with Jack Nitzsche and make some records that I thought could be financially disastrous—uncommercial and expensive. I figured he and Neil would go off on a wild tangent, so it seemed to me I had a very good shot with Steve."

· · ·

In August 1968, the band's final effort, *Last Time Around,* was released. Young contributed only two songs and criticized the sound of the album, telling Tony Pig, "Jimmy Messina did a miserable job of mixing it." Commenting on the cover shot, he said, "I quit the group—as a matter of fact, the day that photo session was being taken, I was meeting with Mo Ostin at Reprise . . . I just didn't want to have anything to do with the group anymore." Young was later pasted into the photo—facing in the opposite direction from his bandmates.

Last Time Around betrayed its lack of collaborative effort. "I remember thinkin' to myself, 'Wow, this sounds like a bunch of solo tracks,'" said Ken Viola. "It no longer had that group thing to it." Young contributed his first foray into an explicitly country-tinged sound, "I Am a Child," a song that seems to celebrate childhood while looking a bit wryly at those who bring us into the world. Some took the number as a response to Furay's critique of Young's petulant ways on the previous Springfield album's "A Child's Claim to Fame." Young said no, but Stills would later claim the bittersweet "On the Way Home" was addressed to him, and Young doesn't deny it. Sung by Furay, it could be taken as the story of the band—and also as goodbye.

"Maybe 'On the Way Home' is the coolest rock song written during that period," said Moby Grape's Peter Lewis. "That song made me smile when I heard it, because if you can write that way in the midst of the battle, then, y'know, you've *got* it. There was tremendous competition in that band—they could've destroyed Neil's self-confidence. But what I hear in 'On the Way Home' is a guy who went through all that stuff without becoming cynical. That's what's amazing to me."

Buffalo Springfield wasn't the only thing coming to an end. "Nineteen sixty-eight was the year the whole political edge hit the wall," said writer Richard Meltzer. "The Democratic convention. It was the heaviest casualty period in Vietnam. That was the year Martin Luther King and Robert Kennedy both got killed—and Andy Warhol was shot. That was basically the year the powers that be decided, 'Hippies EAT SHIT. If we don't kill ya, we'll make it pretty tough.'

"It was somewhere in sixty-eight you realized nobody was listening. . . . It woulda been nice if everything worked, if the ideology had delivered on a certain level, but I don't think that it did—the only thing to me that succeeded about the sixties was the music. The fact is, the music was, for a moment, good."

In the wake of mega-events like Monterey Pop and *Sgt. Pepper,* rock would only get bigger, bigger, bigger. But for some, the thrill was already gone. "The music ran out of steam . . . there was no thrill in it anymore," said Meltzer. "The Beatles, Stones, Kinks—even the major ones ran out of new turf. It seemed like it was too soon for everything to dry up, but it dried up." Rock would move away from groups into hype-laden superstar configurations and singer/songwriter confessionals. Buffalo Springfield had lasted two years and one month, the end flameout of a turbulent but relatively innocent time. "When the Springfield broke up, it heralded the end of the magic," said Ken Viola. "I was completely devastated."

For Neil Young, Buffalo Springfield remains a painful memory, linked forever to epilepsy and inner turmoil. "We were good, even great—I thought when we started we'd be together forever," Neil Young would tell his father years later. "We were just too young to be patient, and I was the worst. I was having these seizures, and I was sure—I'm sure now—knowing more about it, that the way I felt and acted was mostly because of nerves, the seizures. It got so I didn't care. I didn't *want* to make it with them. I didn't want to be a slave to the medication I was taking for epilepsy. I couldn't stand the way I was feeling. My thing, I figured, was to keep going, doing something else. I know I should've been happy, but in some ways it was the worst time in my life. . . ."

•   •   •

After Buffalo Springfield, Stephen Stills would be the architect of the un-relentingly successful Crosby, Stills and Nash; Richie Furay would have success in Poco before becoming a minister; and Neil Young would go on to do a million things. Dewey Martin and Bruce Palmer, after releas-ing a solo album apiece, didn't fare so well. Almost immediately after the Springfield's demise, Martin would gather up a bunch of musicians and start advertising his group—which included a tuba player and two drummers—as "the New Buffalo Springfield." This did not endear him to Young and Stills, who took him to court. Martin wound up giving away his stake in the Springfield for the ability to advertise his band as "The New Buffalo." It quickly faded away. Martin would file a lawsuit in 1974 to get back the rights he gave away in 1968, then would settle out of court. It left him with considerable bitterness, particularly toward Young. "Certain things that went on with the Buffalo Springfield gave me good reason to drink myself to death, cocaine myself to death," said Martin, who credits a religious experience in 1983 with saving his life. Other than playing the oldies circuit in Buffalo Springfield Revisited with Martin, Palmer has remained nearly invisible, although both Martin and Palmer have still played occasionally with Young.

In the late eighties, respected archivist and producer Bill Inglot began laying the groundwork for a Buffalo Springfield boxed set. Young immediately quashed the project. He has hoarded nearly every tape of the Springfield, and in the fall of 1998 finished the definitive four-CD set, which was finally released in July 2001.

There was a private Springfield reunion in 1986 at the home of Stephen Stills, a videotape of which has escaped into the hands of fans. The performances are unremarkable. The best moment comes after the songs, when the musicians pose for a group shot. "We should try to re-create our earlier album covers," says Young. Furay shouts out, "You weren't even in 'em!" as Stills pretends to strangle Neil.

There was another reunion a few years later that Young failed to show for. The band waited around, eventually learning that Neil was off in the studio—with Jack Nitzsche. "Some things never change," said Richie Furay, who had flown in for the occasion and was so irate that he demanded Young reimburse him for his ticket. "They don't call him Shakey for nothin'," quipped David Crosby, present for the no-show. In 1997, Young, protesting the crass television event the Rock and Roll Hall of Fame awards ceremony had become, failed to show at the last minute for the band's induction. "So, Rich," said Stills, turning back to Furay as he began his acceptance speech, "he quit it again."

But Neil Young was just starting on his journey when he left Buffalo Springfield. What he had to give couldn't be contained by any one band, and Young would not only go on, he would prevail—alone.

Perhaps unconsciously, Young learned some lessons from his tumultuous time in the Springfield. He would never relinquish control over his music—or much of anything else in his life—again. By his very next record, he would have both a manager and a producer who would protect him ferociously, and he would physically extricate himself from the Los Angeles scene. Never again would Neil Young be so "wide open."

Denny Bruce remembers the long limo ride back to Los Angeles from the Springfield's final gig in Long Beach: "Jimmy Messina hung his head and cried the whole fucking way back. He couldn't speak, look up, nothing. Neil was in a pretty good mood. I sensed a little relief on his part that it was over. The feeling was that it certainly wasn't over for Neil."

People were very emotional, because they knew that was it, and those people had been with us since the very beginning. That was our base. Too bad. But hey—that's the way it goes. Too many problems. I took it as a sign of "Good—it's over now. I don't have to worry about it. I don't have to do this over and over again." Somethin' was wrong, *y'know?*

Dewey was tryin' to keep Buffalo Springfield going. He put some time into it himself, so he felt it was part his. It was part his, but it wasn't his to destroy. *It was his to live with, like the rest of us have to.*

Dewey gave away all his shit two or three times. I just keep givin' it back to him. Then he wants to sell it. At one point I think Bruce was tryin' to sell his interest in stuff that was gonna be in the Archives. Fuck, it's not even out yet.

I feel sorry for them—not even sorry, I feel *for them. I just think it's not my problem anymore. I mean, maybe I felt a little guilty five years after the group broke up and I'd been in Crosby, Stills and Nash, doin' all this shit and doin' great. But fuck, man, I've outlived my lifespan several times, so I don't owe anybody from way back there anything. I've started over several times.*

Buffalo Springfield never achieved their potential. Poorly made records. Shoulda had more direction. Real direction from somebody who knew what the fuck was goin' on. If we'd had a real producer, that band woulda been huge, and—more importantly—we would've made some great music that you could listen to today.

We had a couple of records that sounded good—"Hung Upside Down," "For What It's Worth"—Stan Ross. "Mr. Soul" with the red-haired guy. But there was no continuity. We didn't have a producer that forced us to be a band. Forced people just to play and shut up—all of us. Somebody who would have it so when we came in, it sounded great. We never got the elation of playing a great take and walking in and hearing it. Everything always sounded shitty. No one knew what they were doing. Never recorded hardly anything live. Everything was over-dubbed, all the vocals. Never got that feel. When we were playin' live and cookin', that's what blew everybody's fuckin' mind. "Bluebird," man—I used to pull the strings off my guitar. I can remember looking down and having the spring in my hand. We were doing that in 1968.

But you'll never hear it. It's not on the fuckin' records. That's why Buffalo Springfield is so mythical. You listen to the record and go, "I know this is great," but the truth is, it's not there. It's just not there.

You gotta remember Buffalo Springfield was a major force in music and it didn't reach fruition. It never happened the way it should've. Buffalo Springfield was a failure. I was pretty intense back in the Spring-field. Everything was intense. There wasn't anything lightweight goin' on. Everything was blown out of perspective. People were either growin' up—or blowin' up.

·   ·   ·

I went back to Commodore Gardens awhile ago—just to kinda find my-self. It's no longer the Commodore Gardens. I don't know what it is now, but when you drive down that street, it looks completely different than it used to. Commodore Gardens, heh heh. It's only in my mind. I saw some people who were obviously in a band—they were sittin' on the porch of what used to be Commodore Gardens. I stopped, got out of my car and they recognized me. So I got back in the car and left.

the no men

"Artists are manipulated by business all the time," said Neil Young in 1992 to Johnny Walker. "A lot of artists are *weak* when it comes to their own direction and their own future. Many of them just put themselves in other people's hands—and then feel frustrated that things aren't turning out right. They really have no one to blame but themselves."

Few rock and rollers have Young's acumen for wheeling and dealing, and it leaves many of his peers awestruck. "His sense of business is extraordinary," said Dennis Hopper. "He's a cutthroat in a cutthroat business. . . . Neil demands certain things that if anyone else demanded them, they would say that they were outrageous—and he *gets* them. It's a business manipulation, not an artistic manipulation, and very few artists ever have it. They may have the same ideal and approach it the same way—but they ain't gonna get it. Neil gets it."

Over and over again in our interviews, Young would credit his longevity to the extraordinary people around him. "The reason I'm still here today is not so much because of me. Most teams are not as solid as my team. I need that," he said, adding quickly, "with other people who are just as crazy as I am. They have to be—or it doesn't work."

As Buffalo Springfield fell apart, Neil Young would meet two men who were indeed just as crazy as he was, and they would become his two most important allies: Elliot Roberts, his manager, and David Briggs, his producer. Control freaks who seemed to covet the power the other had, each would prove the other's greatest adversary. And they protected Young with a Rassy-like intensity that could be frightening to outsiders. There is no question that each was occasionally frustrated and maybe even heartbroken by Young's mercurial nature—just as there is no doubt that both loved him unconditionally.

First to arrive in Neil Young's life was Elliot Roberts.

. . .

I went to Lookout Management's shithole of an office—at that time just a bunch of rooms not far from the beach in Santa Monica. Crap piled everywhere, spare and unpretentious. On the walls were prints by M. C. Escher—cold, analytical art befitting a former chess player.

I wasn't looking foward to this. Months and months spent trying to get this book off the ground had degenerated into screaming matches between Roberts and me over the phone. Most recently Elliot had crept behind the back of my agent and started negotiations with publishers himself. Crazily enough, Elliot would invite my agent back into the deal many months later, but at the moment I was without representation or a dime to my name.

Soon enough, Elliot swept into the room, a blur of white hair under a cloud of pot smoke. Immediately he lunged into his rap—how *he* was gonna represent me, how he didn't have a contract with Joni or Neil, don't worry, he was gonna take care of me. I interrupted him: "All right, Elliot, cut the crap." He frowned, and I wanna tell you: There is nothing worse than the Mama Soprano frown of Elliot Roberts. NOTHING. But I pressed on. "How bad am I gonna get fucked?" Elliot paused for a millisecond. "Maybe a finger or a little tongue, Jimmy—but not full penetration."

Now he had me laughing, so I was really helpless. Within minutes my head was spinning. The rap went something like "Sure, Jimmy, go ahead with the book—you can always do the unauthorized if the authorized doesn't work out . . . *but* if you do a book like that, we will have to sue you, of course." It was classic Elliot—making me feel good and bad without really telling me anything at all.

At times Elliot acted like this book was a threat to his client, but in the end it was Elliot Roberts who got me the most crucial interviews with Neil. I could never figure him out. Period.

There have been other infamous artist/manager teams in rock and roll: Dylan and Albert Grossman. Ray Charles and Joe Adams, Bruce Springsteen and Jon Landau—and, of course, Elvis and Colonel Tom Parker. Elliot Roberts definitely resides in that hall of infamy—and is the only human capable of guiding Neil Young's career.

HARLAN GOODMAN, Geffen-Roberts employee: I'm on the road with America. I'm in New York, Carnegie Hall. I'm standing by the side of the stage—I'm on stage right, Elliot's on stage left. All of a sudden a bottle comes out of the crowd, hits the stage. As I look over to Elliot, he's gone. I grab two security guys. We get into the hallway and I see Elliot moving up the stairs. We get to the top of the stairs just as I see a door close to a private box. I throw open the door and Elliot's got a chair raised up over his head, screaming, "I'm gonna *kill* you, you motherfuckers!" These kids are in tears, I say to security, "Take 'em into custody." Elliot turns to me and goes, "Pretty good, huh?"

WILLIE B. HINDS, aka BABY JOHN, former Geffen-Roberts employee: Filmmaker Robert Downey was about to make *Greaser's Palace*. Elliot was handling Jack Nitzsche at the time and Downey wanted Jack to do the music. He comes into Elliot's office. Elliot wasn't there yet, so he went into the office to wait. When Elliot walked in, Downey was bent over the desk with his pants down and he said, "Go ahead, Elliot, get it over with—do it to me now."

AHMET ERTEGUN: Elliot is one of the most soulful managers. He's not just a manager, he's a very music-oriented person. He has great regard for whoever he represents and he's also very financially savvy, so he protects his artists and does what he thinks is best for them. But he's also a person who cares. A humane person.

GERALD V. CASALE, member of Devo, former client: Elliot can tell ten people ten stories in one hour and they'll all believe them. It's amazing— he could pass a lie-detector test. He could be a murderer and absolutely convince the judge he was home with his wife. Elliot was well aware of what his talents were, and he used to let me witness it—sit in the office and watch him tell some guy at the record company, "Neil's livid, he doesn't even wanna fucking *talk* to you," then call up some agent and go, "Look, I'll get Neil in line." Elliot knew if I ever said anything, he'd just deny it. He's the best liar I ever met, and I don't say that with any judgment, because to be in this business you have to be an incredibly creative liar.

JOHN HARTMANN, former Geffen-Roberts employee: Once I came down on him. I said, "Elliot, you tell too many unnecessary lies. You don't have to tell these lies." Elliot said, "No, man—they *want* ya to lie for 'em." So I learned that from Elliot. I would never lie. Now I'll lie if it's good business.

DAVID BRIGGS, producer: Elliot's a great manager—not for me or for Crazy Horse, but for Neil.

Neil is the boss, Elliot is his henchman. That's all. Everybody tries to blame Elliot for all the problems they have dealing with Neil. Elliot doesn't make Neil's decisions for him. Neil makes his own decisions and Elliot carries them out. That's the way it goes.

GARY BURDEN, art director: Elliot's a frustrated actor. He's driven because he always wanted to be Neil, he wanted to be Joni—and in a way, he was. He's a very endearing character, even though he would cut your throat in a minute. No, let me amend that—five seconds. When Elliot was being a prick, I always used to say, "Elliot, you should just stay funny. You're really good as a funny guy. You aren't worth a shit being a prick."

LESLIE MORRIS, former Geffen-Roberts employee: Elliot's got such a great sense of humor—if it wasn't for that, this man would be dead . . . *any* of us would've killed him.

DEAN STOCKWELL, actor: I love Elliot. I've always felt a good thing with Elliot. Why? Does he hate me?

JIM JARMUSCH, director: I used to scream and swear, "Who is this Elliot Roberts? Why can't I get to Neil?" Now I see what kind of job he has. Elliot doesn't know either what Neil's gonna do next. Elliot doesn't control him. And Elliot's often put in a position of having to speak for what Neil's going to do.

JEFF WALD, childhood friend, fellow manager: Elliot's had a longer marriage with Neil than with any of his wives. I keep tellin' him, "Elliot, don't ya fuck him and get him pregnant."

HARLAN GOODMAN: This is a man who loves and worships his children, probably to a fault. That's all he has to do—invoke one of the names of his kids and I go, "All right, Elliot, I'll do it. What?"

LESLIE MORRIS: Elliot wastes money like you wouldn't believe. He didn't wash socks, he threw them out and bought new ones. He'd leave a rental car running in front of the airport and they'd call three days later. He doesn't care. He just doesn't care. That was always the thing about him.

WILLIE B. HINDS: Elliot doesn't tell you how he feels, he doesn't say what's on his mind. Nobody knows what he's thinkin'. And he prides himself on that. He doesn't crack. You could beat this guy over the fuckin' head, he does not crack. And it's killing him.

RON STONE, childhood friend, former Geffen-Roberts employee, fellow manager: Somehow Elliot made Neil's agenda work. He took Neil's most insane moments and he made it work. Five years later, everybody thought *Tonight's the Night* was a great idea.

You don't really manage Neil—you help Neil do what he's decided to do. I think one of the reasons that relationship has lasted so long is because Elliot gets it. He understands what Neil is trying to do.

ELLIOT ROBERTS: You need a vision. You gotta see what's different about this guy playing from everyone *else* that's playing, because everyone else has the same instrument in their hands. Is this someone unique, special, one of a kind? That's all I try to get involved in. Because it's a long-term thing. You don't make any money in managing for the first two, three, years of an act. You put in more than you get out. There aren't that many people who are willing to take the time to let it happen and not sell it out.

You need a great artist. I can't just do it with everybody. I've done it with a lot of people, I've failed a lot of people . . . it's the artist, ultimately. I couldn't write all those great fuckin' albums for Neil, or have the pain that he has so he could get those emotions out. I can protect him, I can showcase him, I can make sure when it's special, everyone knows. It's not all "This is great, everything outta this guy's mouth is the best." I don't hype every album.

Neil has the privilege of doing things and creating without any governor at all. And that's somethin' I *give* him, that's not somethin' anyone else gets. Took us a long time to get that—and we fight for that every day still.

You gotta always be very honest, 'cause the only thing you have in your relationship is honesty. In a manager/artist relationship, he's gotta count on that—that this *is* important, that it *is* happening, this *is* how it's perceived, that *is* what's going on. You really have to have that belief, that bond. That whatever else, his best interest is at heart—win or lose, good or bad, mistake or failure, that's your intent. His best interest is your first thought. Success and failure will happen—you will fail, you will succeed, you will make mistakes, but you can't live a lie, *because that always brings the relationship into question.* It's like the first time you get caught cheating by your girlfriend or your wife. It's just never, ever the same again.

I think of myself as this mad-professor kind of manager. I don't like managers who are very together, because they tend to really *suck.* Because that's not what managing's about. You can get an accountant or a bookkeeper to keep you in order, but that doesn't help you break an act. That doesn't help you maintain a record. The secret to really good management most of the time is to do nothing. It's got nothing to do with neatness or your portfolio or your briefcase or how many phone numbers you've got. It's circumstance, stroke-of-luck. It's about seeing an opportunity and taking advantage of it.

I'm a tough negotiator. Everyone has to negotiate through me. I make everybody's deal. I make David Briggs's deal. So when he wants more money or thinks he deserves more and I say no, we clash. Then there'll be a period of two or three years where he'll hold a grudge. That's just a fact of life . . . but I do that with every musician we play with.

That's what makes you a tough negotiator—when you don't give a shit. If you can just say, "No, I'm sorry, thank you very much for coming," you're gonna get what you want more often than not. I was always willing to pass. And Neil is *always* willing to pass. Always, from the beginning.

I think I'm tough. Have you ever met a guy in my position who *thought* he was a pussy? I'm tough, but I'm fair. . . . No—I think I'm *way* tough, and I don't think I'm fair at all. Fairness comes into the equation sometimes, but when I deal with Neil for Neil, I don't care what's fair—I only care what Neil wants. Not what's fair.

I'm too nice. I am. I'm too artist-oriented. My artists own everything and always have. All the other managers own all the continuing participation in their artists and took their publishing and did all that shit and at least are partners. I've never ever done any of that. Grossman probably defined what managers are. Albert was a great manager. Beat all his clients, though.

Has Neil ever let me down? Are you kidding? I could've got off the hook this summer with the IRS if that cocksucker would be touring. As a friend he's always been there, every time I've ever asked anything of him or needed him to be my friend—on a my-relationships-are-falling-apart-divorces-my-life's-in-shambles level, he's never let me down.

Neil's let me down professionally sometimes when he's committed to things and I've made plans and he changes his mind—and I look like an *idiot*. Where I've given my word that we'll do this, 'cause he's *told* me to do it. He's done that about thirty times. As a matter of fact, thirty would be undercutting it. Nine hundred.

You never know which Neil you're dealing with. Some Neils give me great latitude, some Neils want to see each and every thing that goes out. You learn over the years. I know when I can push him . . . or can't.

It's funny. Neil and I used to have this joke—whenever we were asked to do anything, a commercial, even a TV show—I would say to Neil, "What would Bob Dylan do?" From, like, the very beginning. That's how we made our decision. And years later I'm managing Bob, and some decision came up, he turns to me and goes, "What would *Neil* do?"

Now I'm an elder statesman. I've lived one of the great lives, I'm one of the luckiest motherfuckers that ever lived, so I don't lie awake goin', "I wonder what sales will be like tomorrow? Will KROQ add the record?" None of it can get to me at this point.

• • •

Elliot Roberts was born Elliot Rabinowitz in the Bronx on February 25, 1943. His father was a waiter at the Waldorf-Astoria, president of the local union and active in civil rights; his mother was a homemaker who seldom strayed from the Bronx half-block that was home to so many other Jewish refugees. Both parents fled the Nazis, and eleven of Elliot's relatives died in Auschwitz. "Leo and Mitzi, they were tough," said his friend Jeff Wald. "You didn't come from where they came from in Eastern Europe, in the era they came here, without being tough. Elliot's mother never understood his involvement in show business. After Elliot became a millionaire, she'd say, 'Tell him to quit this stuff with the long hair—he should go to the garment center.' " Added Roberts, "Rassy and my mother were very much the same. She was real dominating."

Roberts attended DeWitt Clinton High School, where he was the only white kid on both the track and basketball teams and learned to use humor as a defense. "I was gawky. My nose was broken eight times 'cause I played basketball with guys who *hurt* you. I was never like this great-looking guy, and I wasn't a tough guy. So I was funny."

As a teenager Elliot was in a gang called the Fordham Daggers ("Back then being in a gang meant you carried an antenna") and sang in an a cappella group, the Crestones. After a brief, fruitless tenure at Bradley University (attained via a basketball scholarship), Roberts returned to New York. He decided to study acting and began hanging out at the Cafe Au Go-Go in hopes of becoming a stand-up comic.

While working as an NBC page and dealing pot on the side to augment his income, Roberts was asked to represent a fellow page and aspiring singer. Not having a clue as to what an agent did, he turned to the owner of the Au Go-Go, Howard Solomon. "Howard told me that the guys he respected were not agents—they're all slime, they have to *sell* shit—but managers, they're the clever guys, they get the money. Managing is where it's at—you get control, you tell people, 'Fuck you!' Agents can't, because they gotta deal with the guy again. Managers can say 'Fuck you!' I always remembered that. Now I wanted to be a manager."

While peddling the singer's demo tape, Roberts met Hal Ray, a William Morris agent who got Elliot, now turning twenty, a $65-a-week job in the agency's highly competitive mail room. It was there that Elliot encountered David Geffen.

"All these other William Morris guys were like dorks, unbelievably square. Everyone was afraid of Geffen except me—he thought I was funny. His vibe, even then . . . David was *beyond.* The very first time I ever went over to David's house, he played me a Buffy Sainte-Marie album,

Now That the Buffalo's Gone. By the second song he's in tears. Literally. Tears are running down his face and I had to hold him."

Roberts's pot-smoking—and general lax behavior—drove Geffen crazy. "I couldn't smoke in front of David. I would have to go out, even when I was over at his house. It freaked him out. He was incredibly straight—no one knew he was gay, nor was he very into guys. David wasn't into *any-thing*. He was into planning and thinking and seeing who was out there that he could get."

Geffen took the rather green Roberts under his wing. "David taught me shit from the first day. He told me, 'Elliot, first—this coming in at eight o'clock! You meet me here at five-thirty, we'll have coffee, we'll be in the office at six, and I'll show you how you use the mail room.' David Geffen would get in at six in the morning and steam open *everybody's* mail."

Roberts was present for an infamous episode in Geffen's climb to the top: He had lied on his application, claiming to have graduated from UCLA with honors, and when UCLA wrote back to William Morris informing them Geffen's credentials were false, Geffen intercepted the letter. "We went to Forty-second Street together. He had the stationery duplicated, typed in what a great student he was, put it *back* in and delivered it himself—to the head of personnel."

Roberts was stunned. "It never entered my mind that you could do that—*do* it—never mind that it was, like, the thing to do. To David it was the way to go. And I went, 'Wow, this man's *awesome*.' David instinctively knew he wasn't gonna be anybody's patsy. He was no one's chick, as they say."

Geffen set a record at William Morris by getting out of the mail room in six months; a feat he pulled off, once again, by steaming open mail and finding out that Danny Thomas wanted a new agent. Posing as just the William Morris agent Thomas needed, Geffen nabbed the star, then used his new clout to get promoted to head of TV packaging. Roberts was right behind him.

Bob Chartoff and Irwin Winkler were managers heading out to Hollywood and looking for someone to run their talent stable, which consisted of a bunch of stand-up comics and folksinger Buffy Sainte-Marie. Roberts got the gig and in the process got close to Sainte-Marie, who turned him on to a tape of a folksinger named Joni Mitchell, whose "Song to a

Seagull" Sainte-Marie had just covered. A maverick talent, complicated beyond belief, Mitchell would be a galvanizing force in Roberts's life as well as the California rock scene.

Mitchell was appearing at the Cafe Au Go-Go, so Roberts went to check her out, "and she blows me away. I stay for two sets, and after that I go back to Joan and say, 'You kill me. I think I'm in love with you. I'd do anything to manage you.' " Mitchell, who had just split from her manager/husband, Chuck, was booking all her own gigs at the time and, as she recalls, "I said, 'Why should I cut you in? I'm doing quite nicely.' " The next day Mitchell had to head out for a show at the Checkmate club in Ann Arbor, Michigan. She invited Roberts to tag along—if he paid his own way.

In Michigan, both got high in their respective rooms before the gig, without telling each other. "We all smoked pot back then, but nobody told each other," said Mitchell. The club was directly across from where the pair were staying, but Elliot, a manager for only about seven days and stoned out of his brain, proceeded to get his artist lost—inside the hotel. "We couldn't find our way out," said Mitchell. "We went through soup kitchens—and all the time Elliot was makin' these jokes. He had me in stitches."

Arriving at the gig forty-five minutes late, Mitchell got a standing ovation after the first number, and "I grinned so wide that my upper lip stuck to my gums. My mouth was dry from pot, and Elliot was the first one to pick up on it. He started doing shtick in the audience and made me laugh all the more. So I said, 'Okay—I'll cut ya in. Just for the jokes, y'know.' I was his first racehorse."

Mitchell and Roberts were a real team. "They could finish each other's sentences," said Jeff Wald. "Elliot knew every nuance of who Joni was and how to make it work so she could overcome some of her innate shyness."

The pair went out to L.A., where Roberts unsuccessfully pitched Mitchell to every record company in town and put the artist through such mishaps as auditioning for *The Tonight Show*. "Joan managed *me* for the first year. I didn't know much about management—I never thought of negotiating, I'd take first offers. I was just very, very lucky. Joni was very gracious—I made a ton of mistakes, but it was fine with her, she didn't give a shit. In my career, Joni was my big influence. Joni taught me how you build a legend—that singer/songwriters were gonna happen, that you didn't need singles. Joni taught me everything—not Neil."

Roberts finally made a deal for Mitchell with Mo Ostin at Warner Bros. At the same time, Mitchell, out on the road in Florida, encountered David Crosby, who had left the Byrds. Their brief fling would lead to the next catalyst in Elliot's life. As Roberts recalls, "Joan calls me up and said, 'Listen, I'm fucking a Byrd.' I go, 'Excuse me?' "

•   •   •

David Crosby. Sooner or later the name elicits an expletive or two from his friends, although they're usually said with a smile. People love this character—especially Neil Young.

David Crosby was born in Los Angeles on August 14, 1941. His parents came from New York high society and show business. Father Floyd was a Hollywood cinematographer who shot everything from *High Noon* to *How to Stuff a Wild Bikini.* A jazz and folk fan who looked down his nose at most rock and roll outside of the Everly Brothers—"I didn't dig Elvis at all," he told Dave Zimmer—the plump teen came to the realization that folksinging increased his opportunities with the opposite sex and started performing in Santa Barbara coffeehouses in 1958.

In the early sixties, Crosby would wander all over the country, discovering the joys of marijuana in Los Angeles and learning the finer points of acoustic guitar from Fred Neil in Greenwich Village. He did a brief stint in an ultra-square folk outfit called Les Baxter's Balladeers, and then in early 1964, after a solo gig at the Troubadour in L.A., Crosby found himself in an informal jam with two other disenfranchised folkies, Roger McGuinn and Gene Clark.

This led to full-blown stardom via the Byrds, and Crosby would prove to be their feistiest, furthest-out member, contributing such truly weird pieces of work as "What's Happening?!?!" and the infamous "Mind Gardens." Being a maverick blowhard would eventually alienate him from his bandmates; things finally came to a head when the band refused to record his ménage-à-trois ode "Triad."

In the Los Angeles music scene, Elliot Roberts quickly found that all roads led to David Crosby. "No one was cooler than the Byrds, and David was the guy kicked *outta* the Byrds. It made him the rebel king." Introduced to Crosby by Mitchell, Roberts found himself mesmerized by the singer. "He was like no one I'd ever seen before. Because he's wearing this Byrd hat and cape and the Byrd glasses—and he had long, flowing hair, this long mustache. He always dressed like an album cover so you knew who he was. But he was very forceful in town. David was dynamite. Dynamite. And more obnoxious than any seven people you could imagine. So full of himself—and beyond arrogant. I found him to be incredibly funny. I could not stop laughing at him."

In the ego-overload triumvirate of Crosby, Stills and Nash, it would be David Crosby who called the shots. "Crosby was bigger than life," said Roberts. "David ran things—even though Stephen produced the sessions, David was always the motivator. Everything that you were afraid to do, he made you do it. Whether it was mescaline or that girl or this stage, whatever it was, he egged you on—but he would do it *first*. He was the bravest, he was fearless and he was the leader. Without question.

"David was very wise about the biz in those days. He was the one who had the concept for CSN, the whole vision of what it could be. When Geffen and I were plotting and planning, Crosby was right in there. He got it."

Crosby would inevitably up the ante with the contraband he carried, particularly a potent, seedless brand of pot. "It was devastating weed," said Roberts. "He'd break it out at meetings and go, 'Before we say anything, let's all smoke this so we're all on the same page.' Everyone would go, 'WOOOOOOOOOOH!' Then David would go, 'Okay, *here's* what we're doin'.' "

At Crosby's behest, Roberts relocated to Los Angeles, living—along with Crosby and Mitchell—at the home of KMET-FM's B. Mitchell Reid, who would be greatly influential in the careers of CSNY and Joni Mitchell. Crosby's romance with Joni wouldn't last, but David would produce her debut album for Warner Bros. "Crosby produced my first record solely not to produce me," she said. "He said, 'They're gonna want a producer in there,' so Crosby brought me my freedom from the beginning."

· · ·

Since the demise of Buffalo Springfield, Stephen Stills had pinballed from project to project, playing and touring with then girlfriend Judy Collins, chasing after Hendrix and recording the *Super Session* album with Mike

Bloomfield and Al Kooper. In the spring of 1968 he met up with Crosby, who was down in Florida, floating around on a boat with Jefferson Airplane lunatics Paul Kantner and Grace Slick. Crosby, Kantner and Stills would conjure up the hippie anthem that would be one of the centerpieces of the first Crosby, Stills and Nash LP, "Wooden Ships." By that summer, Stills and Crosby were thick as thieves. A sing-along in the backyard of Cass Elliot of the Mamas and the Papas prompted the pair to start recording demos at Wally Heider's Hollywood studio.

"Mama Cass was the Gertrude Stein of rock and roll," said Gary Burden, who would design many of CSN's and Neil Young's album covers. "I met more people in her living room. . . . I used to be an architect—I was this guy still wearin' a three-piece suit and bow tie, sneakin' off to get high. She convinced me I could do artwork." It was Cass who would also, as they say, turn Graham Nash on, administering the first doses of pot and LSD to the English pop star, who was growing increasingly unhappy with the uptight attitudes in the Hollies.

Graham Nash would complete Crosby, Stills and Nash, and would perhaps prevent the ensemble from ever being anything really rock and roll. He filled the Paul McCartney slot in the trio, providing such bland but radio-friendly pop fodder as "Marrakesh Express," "Our House" and "Just a Song Before I Go." He also held things together when things got nuts. "Graham kind of mother-henned the whole thing," said Mitchell. "He was the diplomat, the smoother-over, the one who tried to hold the family together. He's the only one that valued the team.

"I fell in love with Graham. Not initially, because initially he was not a warm person at all. There was always a thin, icy barrier between him and anybody. Charming, genteel and gentlemanly and all, but very withholding. Withholding of his heart. English reserve, perhaps."

.   .   .

"When Neil gives his word, it's right there—*if* it suits him." It's December 12, 1991, and Graham Nash is sitting in his well-appointed Tudor-style southern California home. Graham Nash and Neil Young: an odd combination in any sense. It was Nash who initially resisted Young's addition to the group and Nash who sold his CSNY songs for use in TV commercials, against Young's protests. In the nineties, one could even purchase a car stereo with a curious twist: "You'll never have to look to see if you've hit the right buttom again! JVC's Voice Support audibly confirms each operation with the voice of Graham Nash!"

"Neil didn't agree with that stuff, but fuck him," said Nash. "I can do with my music whatever the fuck I want. In these days of college educations and all that kinda shit, where somebody offers you a half a million to use three bars of something you wrote twenty years ago and don't particularly care about anyway, who cares?"

Today Nash was relating Neil's noninvolvement in the 1991 Crosby, Stills and Nash four-CD career anthology. "With the box set, it was a chance for me to establish a true history of the band—and whatever you say, Neil was very much a part of this band. So I called Neil and he said, 'You can use anything you want, man.'

"Then Elliot calls, saying that it's all changed—we can only use seven or eight things with Neil. It was a very different story, and I could never pin down exactly who was responsible . . . at first I was pissed at Elliot . . . I thought Elliot had convinced Neil to only let us use a certain amount and save the best stuff for *his* box."

Months later Nash confronted Elliot. "He said, 'Wait a second—you, Graham, of all people, should realize that nobody tells Neil what to do with his music.' And Elliot tells me that the very next day after Neil's talk with me, he calls Elliot and tells him he's committed to this stuff—and for Elliot to get him out of it. It's the same old shit with Elliot and Neil, good cop/bad cop . . . they play it brilliantly, and it's devastating."*

Nash grew livid recounting the memory. "As easily as Neil called me up and said, 'I'm into it, I'm gonna do this,' he could've just as easily said, 'Graham, I'm uncomfortable with this. It's not what I want.' And I would've said, 'Fine.' What I was upset at, it appeared once again that management came in the way of the *music*."

---

*Elliot Roberts on the CSNY boxed set: "They had made a shit deal for themselves and wanted us to be part of the shit deal and it was too late to change their deal, so we were in for a quarter of a piece of shit. Then they were totally using Neil, putting 'and Young' on the box cover prominently, and Neil would end up having the bulk of unreleased material . . . I denied permission, even though Neil had given it to Graham. I said, 'Well, you shouldn't have gone to Neil—that's why he pays me big fuckin' bucks.' Graham was never close to me again."

Ah yes, The Music: That's the strange part of the story. In the history of Crosby, Stills and Nash as joined by Young, there's not a whole lotta music: three studio albums, a live two-record set and a handful of other tracks.

After a few years of gargantuan commercial success, Crosby, Stills and Nash unraveled in clichéd rock-star excess. As Crosby and Stills wigged out on substance abuse—with Neil Young occasionally popping in to confuse and terrorize everybody—Nash carved out a niche as Mr. Sensible, the one who took care of business and didn't go crazy.

"It's very strange," he said. "In many ways I don't think I fit in this band . . . in that they all don't like themselves. I once met a friend of David's in Santa Barbara and I said, 'Tell me something about David when he was a kid.' He said, 'I'll tell ya one thing. David came home one day from school and there's a note on the refrigerator. The note said, "Chip"— Chip is David's brother—"your supper's in the fridge. And David—stay out of here, fatty." '

"I spent a lot of time not liking myself, but it was basically a product of too much cocaine. I've come to grips with my frailties and weaknesses— I know I'm not perfect, but I'm trying to be the best person I can be. . . . I don't have the self-hatred that I see in David during his drug days or that I see in Stephen—or that I feel looms large in Neil's life.

"Neil scares me a lot. I don't understand him. I don't understand his ability to change his mind ruthlessly . . . it *still* scares me that he can do some of the stuff he does.

"A happy guy? I don't think so. I don't think he's ever been happy with himself . . . it might be too painful to look at. God knows Neil's wanting for nothing—he's got all the music he wants, all the wealth and fame, all the material trappings—but I don't think he's fuckin' happy. He's a very strange human being . . . very strange."

I certainly don't hate myself. Most of all I don't hate myself for anything that I did with CROSBY, STILLS and NASH, heh heh heh.

I don't agree with that—but I don't have another opinion to offer, either. I just don't agree with it.

What happened with the boxed set was Elliot was makin' the deal for my archival project and talking to Warner Bros. about it at that time. When I talked to Graham, I thought just purely on a CSNY level, certain things would have to happen—that it would have to be realistic to work. So we agreed. But then Elliot said to me, "Well, listen, you're makin' the deal for the Archives and all the shit. That's yours, you shouldn't give it to them. You should keep it for the Archives. That's worth a lot."

But that happens sometimes. I say one thing and then Elliot said somethin' else—and he had a good reason for it. It's business.
—Nash was pissed. He wanted to know why you didn't call him and tell him you changed your mind.
He's right. That's my fault. I probably shoulda done that. However, *the conversation that Elliot had with Graham was not something I knew about, okay? Until way after. That wasn't* me—*that was Elliot. A lotta time goes by and I don't even know the fuckin' discussion has happened. I don't even know if they're working on the CSN box set yet. To me it was just a hypothetical idea we were talkin' about. I hadn't seen the final song list or anything, y'know.*

A lotta people think that I talk to Elliot and then he calls, but that's not the way it is. Elliot acts on his own.
—That can be problematic for some of the people involved with you, Neil.
It's been the cause of a lotta fuckups over the years—but I still wouldn't trade Elliot in on a different manager because of that. It's like you got a car, and there's a knock. *But that fuckin' motor goes like hell. It uses a little bit of oil every once in awhile, more oil than it should— but the fuckin' thing goes like hell. What are you gonna do—get a new motor? No—I* use *this fuckin' motor. It's not perfect, but it's* mine. *That's how I feel about it. I back up Elliot. He's made more good decisions than bad ones by* a lot.

Crosby was the catalyst in CSNY—he was the guy who made it happen, the spiritual leader of the band. Stills was musical director. Graham was kinda like the CEO. We all thought we were doin' great. Everybody was lovin' us.

Turns out I was just passing through.

Graham Nash was born on February 2, 1942, in Manchester, England. His father worked in a foundry, and his mother was an office administrator for a local dairy. Nash, like David Crosby, was an Everly Brothers fan, and with grade-school chum Allan Clarke, he started playing in a variety of outfits, which led to the formation of the Hollies in 1962. Known for tight three-part harmonies, the Hollies first gained success with pop covers of American R&B hits. The motive for writing original material came about, as Nash told Dave Zimmer, "not to reach people's souls. The reason was there was *money* in it."

It was on the Hollies' first trip to Los Angeles that Nash met Mama Cass. "She opened my mind to opening my life," Nash told Zimmer. Elliot also introduced him to David Crosby, whose off-the-wall behavior fascinated Nash. With repeated exposure to the American scene, Nash's songwriting became more experimental, and his increasingly psychedelic outlook didn't sit well with his more conservative bandmates, who were "still the five-pints-every-night lads."

Fleeing band frustrations and a bad marriage, Nash found solace in Cass Elliot, and it was during a July 1968 trip to Laurel Canyon—at either Elliot's or Joni Mitchell's house—that an informal jam took place, and Crosby, Stills and Nash sang together for the very first time.

While Nash extricated himself from the Hollies, CSN moved to England for a few months to work on material and figure out whom to approach for management. Underwriting their expenses at the time was Larry Kurzon, a William Morris representative who had grown close to Nash. When Kurzon heard a two-song demo the band had cut in New York with Paul Rothchild, he flipped. Nash wanted Kurzon to manage them. "When the group was forming in London, Crosby was holding out for Elliot Roberts," said Kurzon. "Nash wanted me, and Stephen would go along with whoever."

A meeting was arranged in New York City at the apartment of William Morris executive Hal Ray, where the trio would "audition me and Elliot Roberts simultaneously," said Kurzon, who considered the up-and-coming Roberts no threat. "I kept sayin' to these guys, 'You're gonna cost me a friend, you're gonna make me go against him because he can't compete with me, he's got a lot to learn.' Elliot was not ready."

Kurzon had underestimated Roberts. On the second day of the meeting, Elliot showed up with David Geffen. "I didn't know what Geffen was doing at the house, 'cause he was as close a friend to me as anybody. I didn't realize that Elliot brought him as a one-two punch." Kurzon would quickly find out what a lethal combination Geffen and Roberts were. "Geffen got right in the middle of it and blew me out of the water. I said something to him on the q.t., and he repeated it to Graham Nash."

What Kurzon let slip was that the trio had also been considering Dylan's all-powerful manager, Albert Grossman, and had been to see him that week. "Graham *flipped*. He came to me and said, 'Why are you putting our business in the street?' I was standing there with egg on my face. There's nothing like making a mistake around David Geffen—he'll make you pay for it."*

Kurzon's weakness was Roberts's strength. Elliot could simultaneously handle Crosby's titanic ego, Mitchell's emotional hurts and Young's weird, reclusive ways. The artist was always right and no demand was too great—he'd take the four A.M. phone calls, come to the studio and smoke a joint, even get busted with you if need be. Elliot was "our pal, our buddy," said Crosby. "Back then he was like part of the group." He would be the only outsider invited into CSNY's preshow-huddle ritual. He also had a power over the foursome that some found unearthly. "Elliot was a Svengali," said Nash associate Mac Holberg. "I saw it again and again. He would mesmerize them into doing what he wanted them to do."

Roberts was feared but loved, Geffen feared. He was unrelenting. As Ron Stone put it, "Elliot had a life—he had wives and kids. David had business." Said Roberts, "Even when we were partners, I never thought for one second that we were equal. I always relied on David's business acumen. I would say, 'Let's ask for a million,' and he would go, 'You are a fuckin' moron—ask for five, we'll get three.' I went, 'No *way*—there's no more than a million there.' He'd say, 'Elliot! SCHMUCK! *Ask for* five! You'll get three.' And every single time, without exception—*without exception*—he was right. In all the years that we were together, David was never wrong once. When he told me how somebody would react, that's how they reacted. Every time. His sense of people, his sense of what motivated them—*past* what they projected—was just uncanny. He's an alien."

---

*Some dispute Kurzon's story. Said Nash, "I don't believe we had a meeting with Albert Grossman, nor did we ever want to. This is all clouded in the history of marijuana. . . . Larry did have a shot at managing us and was blown out of the water by Elliot and Geffen."

Geffen was formidable enough to engineer a trade that gave Crosby, Stills and Nash the freedom to record in the first place. He got Nash out of his contract with Epic Records in return for Richie Furay—who was still under the Springfield contract to Atlantic and wanted out to record with his new band, Poco—then engineered a deal for Crosby, Stills and Nash at Atlantic with Ahmet Ertegun. "Ahmet was a fan from the very beginning," said Nash. "He gave us the feeling he would protect us." Released in June 1969, *Crosby, Stills & Nash* was tailor-made for the exploding FM market and immediately shot to the top of the *Billboard* charts, where it would remain for over two years. Hippiedom had reached critical mass, and CSN, dubbed the "American Beatles" in the press, was its voice. "Crosby, Stills and Nash were *it*," said tour manager Leo Makota. "They were treated like royalty wherever they went."

Crosby, Stills & Nash was a Stephen Stills tour de force. He was a maniac in the studio—arranging, rearranging, playing every instrument in sight. "It's getting to the point where I'm no fun anymore," he wails in the album's opener, "Suite: Judy Blue Eyes," an intricate swirl of acoustic guitars and harmony. It was like a folkie version of the Spector wall of sound, and Stills had created it almost single-handedly, aided primarily by Dallas Taylor—a sullen-faced drummer on the rebound from Elektra also-rans Clear Light. Taylor would be one of Stephen's major sidekicks until drugs knocked him out of commission. "We hold one of the records for being in the studio and staying up the longest," Taylor said. "Five days without sleep. We didn't get much work done, but we had fun. A lotta cocaine."

The chemistry of the original trio suited Stills's vision. Although Crosby was a respectable rhythm guitarist, he and Nash were nowhere near as instrumentally proficient as Stills, and they were content to let him run wild and fill up every empty space. While things would change radically when Young entered the picture, CSN's debut was completed quickly and without controversy. "The first album was a breeze, the music was effortless," said Taylor. "We'd go in, spend days in the studio doin' the tracks. Then David and Graham would come in, sing their parts and leave, and we'd continue to fuck with the tracks."

Driven by acoustic guitars and three-part harmony, CSN was a novel idea, but not all fans of sixties rock were convinced. "Squeaky mouse music," said Richard Meltzer. "Dog food. There was nothing Dionysian about them—they were the worst aspects of the Byrds, the Hollies and Buffalo Springfield."

Crosby, Stills and Nash's instant self-importance also left something to be desired. Whereas Buffalo Springfield seemed almost innocent and naïve, CSN were nothing of the sort. They were Superheroes of Rock, Out to Save the World. Ever the comedian, Dylan would have the best line on CSNY in 1997, when a reporter from *Der Spiegel* commented that the quartet were convinced they had stopped the Vietnam War. "I believe that immediately," said Dylan. "They were those kinda guys."

Crosby, Stills and Nash would also enjoy the dubious distinction of being openly associated with cocaine. Early on, deejay B. Mitchell Reid dubbed the trio the Frozen Noses. "Frozen Noses—I didn't even know what that meant," said Joni Mitchell. "I just knew Graham was getting skinnier and skinnier and staying out all night. I thought it had to be another woman. No wonder they call it the Lady."

. . .

With Joni Mitchell and various members of Crosby, Stills and Nash constantly flitting about, the scene in Laurel Canyon was a rich one. But Neil Young wasn't really part of the gang. "Neil never dealt with *anyone*," said Elliot Roberts. "Neil very rarely called anyone and never socialized—Neil just doesn't go to parties. He will go a year without talking to you, 'cause he doesn't initiate phone calls."

Roberts would first encounter Young during the tail end of the Springfield. "Even then, you knew he was his own person. Neil didn't hang with the band, wasn't friendly with the band, wasn't nice to the band—'cause they weren't cooperating with him. They were always afraid of Neil. He had this vibe like Clint Eastwood—he was like death. You saw him ride into town. You didn't know a thing about him, but you knew not to fuck with this guy. Everyone was petrified of Neil."*

But Roberts detected a frailty that others missed. "Instantly—from the first day—I knew that Neil was physically very, very weak. Neil was sickly. He was so vulnerable—you could blow him away with a word, you

---

*When I asked Roberts where he thought Young got this vibe of doom, he had a one-word answer: "Rassy."

could hurt his feelings with the drop of a hat. It was so easy to get Neil—so fuckin' easy—it was really sorta weird."

Although Joni Mitchell was Elliot Roberts's "first racehorse," it was Neil Young who would go the distance. Ironically, Mitchell put the pair together. She was in the studio working on her first album when she discovered her cohort from the Canadian folk scene, still in the Springfield at the time, was recording in the next studio over. Mitchell called Roberts, telling him, "You've got to meet Neil Young. He's the only guy who is funnier than you are."

The pair so hit it off that Roberts—still sleeping on B. Mitchell Reid's floor at this point—got an invitation from Young to stay in his Laurel Canyon guest house. By this time the Springfield were without a manager and floundering. Roberts badly wanted to manage the band and accompany them on a southern California bus tour as sort of a test run. It was just before his first gig with the Springfield that Roberts discovered how difficult a client Young could be.

"Neil fired me 'cause I took off a half hour to play golf. We went to the hotel and right next to the hotel was a driving range. Everyone goes to their rooms and I go to the golf range. I don't know it, but Neil's not feeling well, he's calling around for me to get him a doctor, and when I get back, Dickie Davis said to me, 'Well, you can split. Neil fired you. He doesn't want a manager who's playin' golf—he wants a manager who's lookin' after the band.'

"And Neil won't see me. I'll tell ya what a lunatic this guy was—Neil won't see me, but I'm *there,* I'm on the bus! So I hang out, try and avoid him like the plague. Neil won't look at me. And that's how he treats me all night long—like I'm dead. The other guys are talking to me, but to Neil I'm not even in the *room.* I'm tryin' to get in his good graces—'Can I get you somethin', some aspirin? Do you want some water?' Neil doesn't turn around. I don't exist. When he needed me, I was playing golf."

Somehow Roberts slipped back in Young's good graces, or so he thought, and put together a management contract for the Springfield through Chartoff-Winkler. But when the time came to sign, the deal fell through—because of Young. "Neil refused to sign, even though the band voted four to one," recalls Roberts, thoroughly confused and hurt by the artist's behavior. He was still living with Young, who hadn't offered a word of complaint on the deal. "He *drove* me to the meeting," said Roberts.

Undaunted, a day or two later, Roberts tracked the Springfield down to a rehearsal at the Variety Arts Center in Santa Monica. "I go to the rehearsal and it's just the band and Dickie. And Neil stops playing and said to me, 'Get the fuck outta here.' I walk all the way up to the stage and I go, 'Neil, please don't do this'—I'm yelling now, 'Don't do this, I *know* I can make this band happen.' And Stephen is like 'Let Elliot talk.' Neil said, '*FUCK* Elliot! Fuck him!'

"Now I start to cry. I really loved the Springfield, and I had gotten to really like Neil—and I can't believe he's doing this to me. He was so bad to me I was *crying in front of the band*. I couldn't believe it, it was so off the wall. Neil's screaming at me—he said to the band, 'Either he leaves now or I leave now. You wanna play, or you wanna listen to this fuckin' shit?' Now everyone's stopped, they're all staring, and Neil's cursing me and telling me to just get the fuck out. And the band goes, 'No, we wanna play.' I'm in tears and I leave.

"A week later Neil shows up. At one o'clock in the morning, there's a knock at the door—and it's Fuckface. I go, 'What do *you* want?' I didn't know if he wanted to hit me or if he heard I bad-mouthed him—which I had. And he goes, 'I wanna talk to you for a few minutes.' I go, 'FINE.' He comes in and goes, 'I want you to manage me. I left the Springfield. I told them today. I didn't want you to manage the Springfield because I knew I was leaving and I'd rather you manage *me* than manage the Springfield.' I go, 'This guy's like *Geffen*.' "

First of all, I fired Elliot from Buffalo Springfield because he was out playing golf. I was in a bad mood or somethin'. It was just before the Springfield was gonna break up, so everything *pissed me off. So you could even say I was like a spoiled little brat or whatever and it would probably be true. No problem with that. Because I know how long it took me to learn some things—to grow up.*

But still—my feelings were "This guy's a fucking jerk." I liked him, but he was a jerk. No way I wanted him to manage Buffalo Springfield. Then later, when I quit the Springfield, I was looking for a manager, and

I remembered, "This guy's pretty good." But when I said, "I don't want him to manage the band," I wasn't thinking to myself, "I'm gonna get this guy. He's gonna manage me."

Now, to tell ya the truth, I don't exactly remember every detail about this. It's twenty-six years ago—what the fuck do you want?

How did I know Elliot was the one? It was obvious. He was a lotta fun. Just like that.

As long as I give Elliot good direction, he does what he has to do to protect me. Elliot, he's a character, boy. Hard to find. One in a million. He's a soulful guy. That's all. Elliot's got soul.

The night Young came knocking on the door, "he ended up staying, just smoking pot and talking about his hopes and his fears, what he really wanted to do," said Roberts, who described the Young of those days as a primitive, instinctual artist without the savvy of a Joni Mitchell. "Joni really had a much clearer vision. Neil was into his thing and thought that being too much into the business end of it perverted you. He only knew that he had more to give than he was able to give."

Folksinger Dave Van Ronk—playing a gig at the Ice House in nearby Pasadena—was staying at Roberts's house, and the next night Elliot convinced Young to open for him. "Neil was scared to death—he wanted to do it, but he didn't have the balls to do it," said Roberts, who maintains that this impromptu gig was a turning point.

Young "played all these new songs and kicked ass. Everyone loved him. Had they booed him, life would've been a hundred percent different. It was after that night that Neil's vision became clearer, because he was resolved that he could do his own material better than anyone else—and that there was an audience for it."

Roberts took Young to Reprise (Jack Nitzsche also deserves credit, having talked up Young to label head Mo Ostin every chance he got). Under the guidance of Ostin and Lenny Waronker, Warner/Reprise was thriving on the singer/songwriter boom of the early seventies. "You could be sort of ugly and not have a traditional voice and it was okay," said Reprise veteran Randy Newman. With its counterculture advertising and hip roster, Reprise was the record company of the era. "Of course, Reprise was never as different as it purported to be—they always cared about sellin' records—but they left us alone," said Newman. "Lenny was passionate about music."

Roberts would make an unusual deal for Young at Reprise. "We took very little money, and I took a lot of points. Everyone else was front-loading their deals, taking short points and taking the bread up front. I really thought Neil was gonna sell big records. I believed in Neil."

Young's first record would flop, but within a year he would link up with Crosby, Stills and Nash and, with Elliot Roberts's careful orchestration, emerge a superstar. In the meantime, Neil Young would meet his greatest producer, David Briggs, and his greatest rock and roll band, Crazy Horse.

•   •   •

Santa Cruz, a day or two past the full moon. I call on David Briggs. We head to the Sea Cloud, a hangout off the Santa Cruz Pier. Accompanying David, as always, is his wife, Bettina, a blond German sprite whom Briggs met on the 1986 Crazy Horse European tour. Once nicknamed Little Mike—after Tyson—for her feisty demeanor during dice games, Bettina is a lively match for David and the only woman he would ever marry.

Also along for the ride is Briggs's foreign houseguest; let's call him the Fanzine Editor. The Fanzine Editor is pals with Crazy Horse bass player Billy Talbot, has cut a few demo tracks with him and has the audacity to play Briggs these wayward warblings and make him guess who it is. David, who has been producing Billy Talbot for the last twenty-five years, doesn't wanna play "Name That Tune" and in fact gets it in less than two notes. He's been letting it fester for the last couple of days, and now a constant supply of Mexican coffees enables Briggs to get a little more intimate and relaxed with his houseguest.

"Billy Talbot can LICK MY ASSHOLE, you FUCKING IDIOT," he screams. "Playing me fucking BILLY TALBOT music in my own home . . . I SHOULD KILL YOU RIGHT here and now, you WORTHLESS, NO-GOOD FOREIGN MOTHERFUCKER."

After deconstructing the guy verbally, Briggs slinks off to the bar, where, as usual, he pays the tab for all of us. Back at David's bungalow, the fury continues. Briggs proceeds to eject the Fanzine Editor—and the man's wife—out of his home and into the street.

The little guests scuttle about, snatching up their things as their host rants and raves. In the middle of it all, David pauses for a moment, looks at me and says with a smile, "How'm I doin'?" Taking my gales of laughter as approval, he starts right back in on the hapless pair until they run into the night, Briggs slamming the door behind them.

Then he starts in on me. I once made the mistake of describing David as looking like a cross between Peter O' Toole and a beaten dog in a worthless article for *Spin* magazine, so he now does ten minutes on what a shitty piece of writing the story was (correct), and how I'm lucky he doesn't kill *me* at that precise moment. He then begins pawing my girlfriend, cooing about some nearby hot tub. Amid the abuse, he slinks off to the bathroom to chip away at the requisite eight-ball of cocaine. Booze and coke. It fueled Briggs for decades.

Pit stop completed, David grabs the phone, ringing up Young archivist Joel Bernstein to give him a full report on this evening's merriment. Then, standing in his boxer shorts, teeth chattering, eyes rolling back in his skull, he threatens to kill me, my girlfriend AND ALL THE BABIES in the town where I live if I write a SINGLE FUCKING WORD in my FUCKING BOOK he doesn't like. In many ways, David was my biggest ally. He's gotten me into places I shouldn't have been, given me information I shouldn't have had. But that didn't mean I wasn't an asshole just like the rest of them.

Briggs suddenly demands to see a Little Richard boxed set I have just bought. Visions of shattering vinyl filling my head, I am reluctant to hand it over to this stoned maniac, but David gingerly cradles it as if it contains nitroglycerine. Gazing at the manic visage of Little Richard, he begins to weep, then wanders out of the room. I follow. There, alone in the kitchen, a crumpled and deflated Briggs is sobbing. For a moment it is hard to reconcile the wounded individual before me with the raging lunatic in the other room.

"I was just a boy . . . just a child," he moans. "Little Richard was my God, he was my *fucking God.* Don't you see?" As he looks up at me, I notice David has the saddest eyes of any man I've ever met. Bogart eyes, lonesome beyond words. I don't know what it was Briggs saw, but I was glad I hadn't.

NILS LOFGREN: David was not only a producer—he was an audience, a cheerleader, engineer and brother all in one. He wasn't the kind of guy who would be there with ya for twenty minutes and go make phone calls and do another deal—I mean, he was down in the trenches with ya the whole time.

David is a real gentle soul, but he had a real tough life. He was never able to be a kid.

LINCOLN BRIGGS, son: He's a spiritual atheist, a scientific realist. He doesn't believe in an afterlife. It's like, "This is it. This is my chance and I'm gonna go for it. I've got no time to waste, and nobody's gonna tell me what to do." That's a real powerful stance to be approaching life with.

JOHN HANLON, engineer: David doesn't give a shit about money. He's had it, he's lost it . . . he doesn't seem to be motivated by it at all. He wants to make art—group art.

JOHN LOCKE, keyboard player for Spirit: If *anybody* is rock and roll, it's David Briggs. As a producer, as a lifestyle . . . If we'd stayed with Briggs, Spirit would've been huge . . . but he ran off with our guitar player's old lady.

FRANK "PONCHO" SAMPEDRO, Crazy Horse guitarist: David was the master of committing women to slavery by putting them in left field . . . a true master of administering pure pain and gaining true love, HAHA-HAHA. David fuckin' had the women on their hands and knees. He cleaned up the fuckin' floor and then washed the walls with them, twisted 'em up like a pretzel and filled their head full of fog and haze. And I think he said "I love you" now and then . . . just to make it real.

LESLIE MORRIS, Geffen-Roberts employee: An asshole, an arrogant asshole . . . Briggs came off as *such* an asshole.

DAVID BLUMBERG, arranger: David chased Manson off the grounds of his Topanga house. Manson wanted his truck. David told him he'd shoot him if he didn't get lost. Manson was *scared* of Briggs.

BOBBY MORRIS, cohort: Get on his wrong side, forget it—he'd probably kill you before he'd fight you. Just shoot you dead.

KIRBY COHEE, childhood friend: You put a hand right in front of David's face, you'll get a lot of respect out of him immediately. His mouth has written a lot of checks his ass couldn't cash. David, despite his persona, is a very frail man.

SHANNON FORBES: David doesn't like families . . . I think the minute I became a mother, it went to pieces, 'cause he doesn't like mothers—starting with his own. He didn't even go see her when she was dyin'. She'd send letters, he wouldn't write back. David has a hard time being happy. He's not used to it.

LARRY KURZON, agent and manager: Briggs was evil, an evil individual. He *looked* like the devil.

There was this anti-Semitic thing I used to get from David Briggs. He wasn't too crazy about Jews, David Briggs. He was from Wyoming—where they thought Jews had horns.

JOEL BERNSTEIN, archivist: Once I said to Neil, "Well, you and Briggs have always been into that quasi-criminal thing." That just completely riled him. He gave me that look and said, *"Quasi?"*

SAL TRENTINO, amplifier expert: With Briggs and Neil, there's always this thing going on that's very powerful. I've been around electric fields all my life, and I know what they feel like—and when those guys work together, it literally feels high-voltage. If you stand between them, you feel the twenty-seven thousand volts pulling at your hairs. It's like being in a vortex.

NIKO BOLAS, engineer, producer: One thing about David Briggs—even when you thought he was completely gone, he was a hundred percent there. He may have been there a hundred percent stoned, a hundred percent out of his mind, a hundred percent lost on some fuckin' trip, but he was there. The one thing I got from David is "Be great or be gone." Briggs's job? I think he kept the chaos happening.

SANDY MAZZEO, artist: Neil thinks creativity can come from harmony and order. Maybe it's because Neil's an epileptic that he fears chaos, because his brain goes chaotic. He fears that. Lack of control.

That's why he and Briggs had an on-and-off relationship, because Briggs put fire into it. Briggs believed in chaos.

JEANNIE FIELD, filmmaker: I think when people who work for Neil get into it, he likes the theater—as long as it doesn't take over. Neil lets it happen. He thinks it's funny.

ELLIOT ROBERTS: Neil gets bored. He'll put Briggs and I next to each other when he knows we're fighting. I'm always saying, "Why do you *do* that?" That's why Neil's bands are crazy—he purposely does that. He likes to see people mixed up.

I think one of the things Neil's very successful at is that he keeps a lotta the same people around, and those people are far from yes-men—if anything he has, like, no-men. There are constantly people in his face about what he's doing, and David is the ultimate of that. I had a great relationship with Briggs. We had different motives. It was very combative. And the records he makes with Neil are easily the best records. I respected David a lot. David lost a lotta jobs 'cause he was an asshole. David was very much like Stills, who, again, had no father—the one recurring thing in all these guys: They all had no father and they all had failed relationships. In David's case, it was worse. Neil at least knew his father, Stephen at least knew his father—David didn't know who his father was.

He's very much like Neil. I remember David and Neil not being very physical at all. A hug would be a big thing, or physical with relationships—kids, women, any of that stuff. Later on, David loosened up like Neil did.

Neil is a very lonely person. All his strong friendships are still musically based—me, Briggs. Neil's very, very lonely, and he isolates himself. And then he gets further isolated by his scene and who he is.

That's why David Briggs is so fuckin' cool, because David still has the same attitude towards Neil that he had in Topanga—if Neil's an asshole, it's "Hey, asshole—I don't take this shit. FUCK YOU."

And when he did that, Neil listened.

RICHARD KAPLAN, engineer: People may think Neil took care of David—and it may have even looked like that—but David took care of Neil. Loving care. David was the one guy who would say, "No, that wasn't good enough, Neil," when everybody else was kissing his feet.

PONCHO SAMPEDRO: David knew Neil had rock and roll in him and he just tried his best to get it out.

DAVID BRIGGS: I can teach you everything I know in an hour. Everything. That's how simple it is to make records. Nowadays, buddy, the technician is in control of the medium. They try to make out like it's black magic, or flyin' a spaceship. I can teach *any*body on this planet how to fly the spaceship. If you look at the modern console, there'll be thirty knobs— high frequency, low frequency, midfrequency, all notched in little tiny, tiny, *teeny* tiny degrees—and it's all bullshit. All this stuff doesn't matter, and you can't be intimidated. You just ignore it—*all* of it.

I walk into studios with the biggest console known to mankind, and I ask for the schematic and say, "Can you patch from here to here and *eliminate the* ENTIRE *board*?" I just run it right into the tape machines. All the modern consoles, they're all made by hacks, they're not worth a shit, they sound terrible. None of it touches the old tube stuff—like the green board from Heider's. It has *two tone controls*—high end, low end and a pan knob—and that's *it*. I had great good fortune when I was a kid and started makin' records. I made 'em at Wally Heider's, Gold Star, so all the people that taught me were Frank Dimidio, Dave Gold, Stan Ross, Dean Jensen— these guys were the geniuses of the music business, still are.

They taught me more about sound and how sound is made and the principles of doing it, and it's *unshakably correct* what they said to me: You get a great sound at the source. Put the correct mike in front of the source, get it to the tape *the shortest possible route*—that's how you get a great sound. That's how you do it. All other ways are work. The biggest moment of my life—the one I haven't been able to get past ever, really—is 1961, when I first got to L.A. I got invited to Radio Recorders to see Ray Charles, and I walk into the studio, and Ray's playin' all the piano parts with his left hand, reading a braille score with his right hand, singing the vocal *live* while a full orchestra played behind him. So I sat there and I watched. And I went, "*This* is how records are made. Put everybody in the fuckin' room and *off we go*." In those days everybody knew they had to go in, get their dick hard at the same time and deliver. And three hours later they walked out the fuckin' door with a record in their pocket, man.

Of course, in those days they didn't have eight- , sixteen- , twenty-four- , forty-eight- , sixty-four-track recording, ad nauseum, to fuck people up, and that is what fucked up the recording business and the musicians of today, by the way—fucked 'em all up to where they'll never be the same, in my opinion. People realized they could do their part . . . *later*. Play their part and *fix it* later. And with rock and roll, the more you think, the more you *stink*.

It's very easy for people to forget what rock and roll really is. Look man, I'm *forty-seven years old,* and I grew up in *Wyoming,* and I *stole cars* and drove *five hundred miles* to watch Little Richard, and I wanna tell you somethin'—when I saw this nigger come out in a gold suit, fuckin' hair flyin', and leap up onstage and come down on his piano bangin' and goin' fuckin' nuts in *Salt Lake City,* I went, "Hey man, I wanna be like *him.* This is what I want." Even *today* he's a scary dude. He's the real thing. Rock and roll is not sedate, not safe, has truly nothin' to do with money or anything. It's like wind, rain, fire—it's elemental. Fourteen-year-old kids, they don't think, they feel. Rock and roll is fire, man, FIRE. It's the *attitude.* It's thumbing your nose at the world.

It's a load. It's such a load that it burns people out after a few years. Even the best of 'em burn out. People get old—they forget what it's like to be a kid, they're responsible, they're this and they're that. . . . You can't have it both ways. You're a rock and roller. Or you're not.

I wanna tell you somethin': Neil's never been insecure about anything in his fuckin' life. First among equals is Neil Young, and it's *always* been that way. When Neil's got his ax in hand, it's like the Hulk. His aura becomes solid—he becomes eight feet tall, six feet wide. The only guy other than John Lennon who can actually go from folk to country to full orchestra. The *only* guy. I think when it's all written down, he will unquestionably stand in the top five that *ever* made rock and roll.

Elliot and I get along really well. He's a witty guy. But he and I stand at opposite poles of one of the great artists of rock and roll. My trip is further, like Ken Kesey said. Go more out there, be more dangerous, risk it all. Out there is where the great artists should be.

Elliot sits on the other side of that.

I never wanna be Neil's employee, and that's what allows me to be his partner. I do the work, and when I'm done, I'm done, dude. And I don't care about the money, and they all know it. I'll say "Fuck you" and walk away—or I'll work for a year for nothin'. It scares them, especially Elliot. I'm a very dangerous guy. If I'm in control, he knows I motivate Neil like nobody else in the world. And if I motivate him within what Elliot thinks are acceptable boundaries, we get along fine. When I think it should go farther—big sparks. When people ask, "Oh, you produce Neil Young's albums?" I'm not ashamed to say, "Only the best ones." When Neil was starting to put together his Archives, he gave me a computer printout of what he thought it should be. Hundreds of songs. I thought he was asking for my opinion, y'see? I took it and I crossed off *every fucking song* that I didn't produce and I gave it back to him. And I meant it. Neil looked at me like I was being . . . arrogant.

Neil's a funny guy. Once he told me, "If you agreed with me all the time, there wouldn't be any need for one of us. Guess which one?"

.　.　.

Manning Philander "David" Briggs was born in Casper, Wyoming, on February 29—the day exists only in leap years, so he claimed one quarter his age—1944. He knew little about his real father except that he had a sense of humor: In recent years, David started receiving mail for another David Briggs, a professional gambler who turned out to be his brother. Apparently his father liked the name. "It's a franchise deal," quipped Briggs. "There's probably a million of us all over the country."

There was little else amusing in his bleak childhood. "I left home and started workin' at thirteen. I had a very bad home life, the brutal step-father . . . things I don't like to talk about much." He worked in uranium mines and on oil wells, moving in with the family of a friend, Kirby Cohee. "David's mother had married a man who despised him," said Cohee. "They threw him out. He had no place to go."

With Kirby, David discovered rock and roll. "We had the largest record collection in the entire state," boasted Cohee. They were also members of a car club, the Vaccaros, and had turned into the kind of teenage hoodlums girls love. "We had a reputation. We were the criminal element in town. The more they bad-rapped us, the bigger our reps got." Driving David's green '41 Ford street rod, the pair cruised the Casper A&W and hung out at Joe's Pool Hall until "we were asked to leave the state," said Cohee. "I got thrown out for fighting, David for raising hell."

Briggs and Cohee left Wyoming on Christmas Day, 1961, and hitch-hiked to Los Angeles. "I was a player," Briggs said. "When I was seven-teen, eighteen, years old, I just realized I could never play guitar like I wanted to—I started way too late. I didn't have the physical tools, it just didn't flow for me. Gettin' past it was a big deal for me." What he wound up doing was making records, "great records that nobody ever heard." His first major production was for comedian Murray Roman—"I did the first record that ever said 'fuck' on it," claimed Briggs. It led to a job as staff producer for Bill Cosby's Tetragrammaton label. Briggs made a handful of records no one heard, and then one fateful day in 1968 he met Neil Young out on the highway.

"I was driving my army personnel carrier. It's meant to hold twenty peo-ple, and I'm thundering down the road. I looked at this guy and said, 'Hey, dude—wanna ride?' It's kinda the way we both started off. We both liked cars, y'know?"

I was hitchhiking. He stopped to pick me up. I just wanted to check out the vehicle. Briggs was a unique individual. He was as crazy as I am. I called him Mr. Briggs most of the time. Monsieur Briggs.
—Why did you take a chance on him?
Just the energy. He was there. He wanted to do it. We just went through it together—learning how to make records. David didn't know much more than I knew. But he knew how to keep on top of me and keep things organized. Give me an objective opinion. Learned all about me so he could get the most. His ways of getting things out of me were probably more subliminal . . . mentioning certain singers at certain times. People that he knew I thought were good, like Roy Orbison or somebody like that. He would mention their names in a conversation the day or the afternoon before a session. Just to bring people into my mind, remind me of my roots.

—How did you get the best out of Mr. Briggs?

Just by bein' his friend and bein' together with him. Lettin' him do what he could really do best and always tryin' to come through when he needed it. When you see how into it David was, it made you wanna do it. The guy wanted to help me get to where I needed to go. He'd do everything he could to help me get the music. If I really had the music, he was gonna really help me get there.

Briggs went on the trip—whatever it was. Stayed with it. As long as it was happening, he was there. Hard to describe, really. The thing is, he knew how much work went into this. If it was a record or a song or somethin', he knew the effort that went into making it right and the care it took. He understood. That that was more important than a lot of other things. Very few people understand that. Particularly very few people around me. He was as tenacious as I am. Maybe even more. When he got an idea in his head that somethin' was fucked, it was fucked. He wasn't gonna change his mind.

—How did Elliot and David get along?

Terrible.

—Why?

I don't know. It's not my business. Briggs could've told ya—but he probably didn't wanna. I mean, more than three or four times. It's all water under the bridge, it's all old hat. The only time we had a problem with Briggs is when somethin' went wrong—usually somethin' was wrong financially somewhere—and he didn't mention it until it was time to explode. Because he didn't wanna talk about it. Just like all the other guys—they don't wanna talk about money.

Briggs and Elliot worked well against each other—but at the end, it was kinda a love thing between them. They really liked each other. It grew to that over twenty or thirty years from the other extreme. The majority of it was David didn't like Elliot. But David didn't like ANYBODY. So that's okay.

—There were periods where you and David didn't talk.

Uh-huh. Like brothers. We had a love/hate relationship. Y'know? I couldn't do every record with Briggs.

It was not a bad thing for Briggs when we got away from each other. It was good for him. If we were together for too long, we fought. Like any other close relationship, after awhile, y'know, it almost becomes its own worst enemy, heh heh. It's so familiar, it's scary.

There's a lotta relationships like that. Where you just go out, come back, go out, come back—that's the way Briggs and I were. What did we do—seventeen albums? That's a lotta fuckin' albums. From the time I was twenty-three right up until forty-nine. That's a lot of fuckin' time.

I believe David had more fun with me than he had with anybody. When we were havin' a good time, there was nobody fuckin' laughin' harder than us. I always kinda felt that David might be one of the early ones to go. He was so destructive when he wasn't around me, y'know. Self-destructive. He was a tormented guy.
—No idea what tormented him?
Not really. There was a lot he didn't share. He didn't really reveal much of his inner self to anybody. There was always somethin' that you didn't know about David. I'm not sayin' that he ax-murdered *his* original family *or anything like that, please don't get the wrong idea—heh heh heh—it could've been . . . quilt-making. But it was something we didn't know about.*

Something bothered him, something hurt him somewhere. David was a fun-lovin' guy. He didn't let it get him down for long . . . but it would always come back.

Most of the records David Briggs would coproduce for Neil Young would feature one band: Crazy Horse, originally with Danny Whitten on guitar, Billy Talbot on bass, Ralph Molina on drums. Whitten would be replaced on guitar in the mid-seventies by Frank "Poncho" Sampedro.

The history of Crosby, Stills and Nash is well known: countless books, documentaries, magazine articles. You have to rattle a few garbage cans and look under rocks to unearth the story of Crazy Horse. Only recently have they turned up in music videos or mainstream interviews, and they've never appeared live on network TV. For close to thirty years they have toiled in the shadows.

This is a band like no other. Muffed changes. Tattered harmonies. Tempos that slow down, speed up or collapse altogether. Guitar passages that last longer than a lifetime. Songs about nothing that never end. Repetition to the point of lunacy. Those who love the Horse can't live without 'em, but those who hate the band are equally passionate. It is the antithesis of the smooth California soft-rock sound churned out by Young's peers.

"If I would go into a little bar to go dancin', I'd say, 'What a great band.' But presented in concert?" Joni Mitchell said with a sniff. "That should not be elevated to the concert level."

Tim Drummond, bass player for Young's most commercial and traditional band, the Stray Gators, echoed an opinion I heard more than once; Crazy Horse's lack of musicianship eliminates a threat. "I think Neil's afraid of a band that will kick ass. He'd rather have Crazy Horse around so he can yell at 'em—'I like playin' with Crazy Horse 'cause I can yell at 'em and they'll take it.' Neil told me that right to my face."

Graham Nash chimed in. "That's the difference between Crosby, Stills and Nash and Crazy Horse—Crazy Horse only plays what Neil tells 'em to play, always. No extra stuff, no experimenting . . . that's terribly confining for a creative musician. I can see exactly why Neil plays with them— because he completely controls everything, and God forbid they should ever have an opinion. Neil's got such a single-minded direction that it does not allow for the creative process from other people, because sometimes when you're being creative, searching, you fuck up. If you fuck up with Neil, it's terrifying."

The mere mention of Crazy Horse sent David Crosby into a twenty-minute rant. "What does Crazy Horse give Neil Young? A clean slate. They should've never been allowed to be musicians at all. They should've been shot at birth. They can't play. I've heard the bass player muff a change in a song *seventeen times in a row.* 'Cinnamon Girl'—he still doesn't know it! And the drummer—boom-boom thack! Boom-boom thack! I'd say to Neil, 'What the fuck are you doing playing with those jerks?!' He'd say, 'They're soulful.' I'd say, 'Man, so is my *dog,* but I don't give him a set of drums!' "*

I can always tell a musician—because a musician said, "Why the fuck do you play with those guys? I can play that good. Any*body can play that good."*

No—they couldn't. Nobody can do that—except Billy and Ralph and

---

*Crosby would actually join the Horse onstage during the 1996 Farm Aid. He appeared to be enjoying himself.

Poncho. They're all equally fuckin' great, and I really would not be able to do what I do without them. It's an intangible. What can I say? It's the Horse. Had a major effect on American music—while being musicians that most musicians thought couldn't play.

—What do you get out of that rhythm section?

It sustains me. Keeps me goin'. It's not just a rhythm section, either. The guitar player is also very fuckin' important. Poncho—you look at him and you look at Billy and Ralph and you go, "Oh fuck, why don't you get new guys? What's special about them?" What's special about Poncho and Billy and Ralph and me is that it's a band.

Crazy Horse is a great, great thing. You can never go out and play a whole show with a band that's gonna be more fun through the whole thing than Crazy Horse, because it's so real.

It's not that they fuck up that makes them great. That's a by-product of the abandon that they play with. They're not organized. No matter how fuckin' much we practice the song, Billy can get so into the groove he'll forget to do the change, y'know? And Ralph may turn the beat around. It happens. Or I can start playin' the guitar, and Ralph can pick it up on the wrong beat and play it backwards—that happens all the time. Never happens with real professional groups. With our band this shit happens all the time. But what really happens all the time is that it grooves—even if it's not in the groove, it's in a groove. You hear it and you wanna hear more.

—The Horse haven't had a lot of big moments with you in terms of a certain visibility. Was that intentional on your part?

I like to keep 'em outta that shit. Might disturb them. I don't wanna spook 'em.

—And that's part of the reason they're still here with you . . . right?

I protected them. Hard to tell, though, the amount of damage I did to them. Heh heh.

—It's a tough gig.

Oh, yeah—it's a tough gig for them, it's a tough gig for me. I gotta keep 'em going without having them feel I'm taking care of them, y'know. That they've gotta be their own people. They don't do much when I'm not with them. They do, but it doesn't make them a lot of money. But they're true to their craft.

—So where does the Horse sit in your art?
Top o' the heap. I mean, for me, I love Crazy Horse. But if I hear a sound
in my head that's not Crazy Horse, I wanna go there. Try it.

It's utter pandemonium at Billy Talbot's house. Music blasting from the stereo, his soon to be ex-wife, Laurie, hovering over a pot of pasta in the kitchen, Billy on the phone haggling over the price of some fancy new doors. The ranch-style southern California home is a pastiche of the very expensive amid the very broken.

Four kids burst into the living room, home from school, and Billy, suddenly looking down at the joint he's been absently sucking on, rasps, "Oh, no! What am I *doing*?" and quickly stabs it out. Wiry and dark, with a prominent proboscis not unlike an eagle's beak, Billy sprawls in a chair next to the stereo he keeps fidgeting with. He's playing me rough mixes of *Weld,* the live set from the Young and Crazy Horse 1991 *Ragged Glory* tour, and I'm anxious to hear them, only Billy keeps turning it off to play *Left for Dead,* a Horse-alone record from 1989. I can't stand the fuckin' thing. Without Neil and Poncho, it sounds more like Toto than the Horse.

I try to be polite and keep my opinions to myself, but Billy is UNRELENTING. He squeezes out every nuance of the way you feel about something, and if he sniffs out an opposing opinion, watch out—he'll talk you into changing it even if it takes hours, days, weeks, months. Billy wears you down. The guy should have been a manager. "I love Billy," said former Horse member Nils Lofgren. "But sometimes you just want him to shut up and play."

Talbot is Crazy Horse's bass player and, to say the least, a real wild card. He puts the Crazy in the Horse. "Billy Talbot is horribly inconsistent," said David Briggs. "Nobody hates it worse than me, because I'm the guy in the studio who has to say, 'Billy, hey, you fuckin' *blew* it. I actually had him say, 'Oh yeah? You know so much, let's hear *you* play it.' I play left-handed, right? I walked into the fuckin' studio, took his bass away from him, turned it upside down and played his part to him—*upside down*—and said, 'Okay, MOTHERFUCKER?' "

But it must be said that some of the greatest Neil Young/Crazy Horse projects happened because Billy picked up the phone, hunted Neil down and got him excited about the Horse again. "Billy brings enthusiasm to Crazy Horse," said Lofgren. "Billy's a cheerleader."

Talbot lives, breathes and sleeps music like a teenager in his first band. Without Billy you don't have the magic, as Briggs himself attested. "The greatest example I can make is this: on 'Lotta Love,' Billy Talbot played two notes that aren't even *in* the chords. Two notes, like, one here and one there. Terrible fuckin' notes. I just left them in. When it got to that part, I just ducked the notes a little bit.

"Well, when Nicolette Larson covered the fuckin' record, 'son, they wrote the charts, and guess what? Billy's two bass mistakes are *written in*. What you gotta remember is this: *Billy Talbot's the guy who played on all these great fucking records.* He's part of the band. It's an emotional thing. It's tribal. Can you dig it?"

When you discuss Billy, it's inevitable that you arrive at drummer Ralph Molina. They're a package deal. "Ralph tempers Billy, he's the voice of reason," said Lofgren. "Where Billy runs amok, Ralph is the deadpan guy."

• • •

Not fifteen minutes away from Billy's house sits Ralph Molina, the dead-pan guy, a ubiquitous baseball cap atop his head. Curly black hair peeks out from under, and with his dusky complexion and slightly sour expression, he resembles a stern Chico Marx. His duplex apartment is immaculate— his wife, Barbara, once caught Ralph crouched on his knees with flashlight in hand, searching under the furniture for suspected cobwebs.

So here Ralph sits, admonishing his dog, Cody, for barking, or clawing, or even breathing. As usual, he doesn't seem very excited to see me, but that's Ralph. Crazy Horse can play the greatest, most transcendental set of their lives, and Ralph will come offstage bitching and moaning about how he missed a Dodgers game on Channel Nine. "Ralph never gets excited," said Nils Lofgren. "He lowballs everything."

Ralph keeps time for Crazy Horse, and from so-called professional musicians you'll get the same disparaging comments: He slows down, he speeds up, blah blah blah. It's all a load of shit. Ask Neil Young: "Ralph? The greatest drummer in the world. What can I say? Number one. *Numero uno.* For my music, he's fuckin' great."

"Ralph's genius is that when Neil goes wandering away into dreamland, where he creates out of the cosmos, Ralph's there to catch him when he hits the brick wall," said Briggs. "That's what allows Neil to go sailin' out where no other people go but him, 'cause when he gets to the end of it all and falls off, there's Ralph. He's like the catcher on a trapeze act."

For Molina, recalling the past is bittersweet. He liked it better when they were all young nobodies. "Back then it was just four guys playing music— if I made two hundred bucks, I was happy. I loved those days. I think when you get to where Neil is, for instance, it's, like, *staying there*. Getting there is the fun. We're still getting there."

Unlike Billy—who gets into everything—Ralph doesn't know much about the technical side of music and wishes he were more ignorant about plenty of other things. "I didn't start getting aware until my thirties. I'm glad—you get too aware, you get fucked up. They say you can't turn back the clock . . . it's a fuckin' drag."

As I perused the framed memorabilia on Ralph's walls, one thing in particular caught my eye: a lyric sheet for "Look at All the Things," a classic Horse song written by Danny Whitten, who was Billy and Ralph's driving force until 1972. Ralph saw me looking at it, and, turning to stare out the window, he sighed. "If Danny had never died, who knows what woulda happened."

• • •

People remember funny things about Danny Whitten. Nils Lofgren recalls that Danny took pride in maneuvering his car around the speed bumps on the highway. Willie B. Hinds remembers the psychedelic nickname he gave Whitten: the Golden Lizard. Robin Lane recalls how encouraging Danny was: he "didn't have an ego, the self-esteem that would've enabled him to be a somebody—he was always a sideman." His buddy Terry Sachen remembers, "We coined a word for Danny: He had 'verballs'— verbal balls. He didn't mince words." "Danny was the one that everybody wanted to hug," recalls his sister, Brenda Decker. "I always thought he'd make a great comedian. Danny could say the awfulest thing and it would come out funny." David Briggs could pick up a guitar and play unreleased Whitten songs that were twenty years old. Everybody gets a little quiet remembering Danny, a little sad. No one has forgotten.

He was born Danny Ray Whitten on May 8, 1943, in Columbus, Georgia. His mother, Dorothy, worked round-the-clock as a waitress to feed her two kids. The family was fatherless and poor. "Danny used to tell me in his house you could see through the floor to the dirt on the ground," said Billy Talbot.

When Danny was nine, Dorothy remarried and moved the family to Canton, Ohio. It was there that Danny discovered teenage rebellion. "Danny and his sister were really great dancers," said friend Larry Lear. "So were my girlfriend and I. We used to end up in a lotta contests together. We were kinda wild—hoodlumish—and we loved rock and roll."

Danny formed a vocal group, the El-Cadins, whose specialty was "In the Still of the Night." Danny and Larry were soon skipping more school than they attended, preferring to hitchhike into town to steal 45s. "We'd hit all the record stores and come home with bagfuls of the hot new records," said Lear.

Doo-wop, R&B, soul—Danny loved black music, and he and Larry were often the only whites in a nightclub called the Baby Grand. "Danny always ran around with an older crowd," said Brenda. "At fifteen he used to slip into my stepdad's closet, slip into his air force uniform, then go downtown and get served."

Much to the relief of his mother, Danny quit school at seventeen and joined the navy. Studying to be an air traffic controller, he rose to the top of the class, but it was not to be. "He was in the navy six months and his knees got big as basketballs," said Brenda. "They found out it was rheumatoid arthritis. He was in the hospital four months. They said he'd probably be in a wheelchair by the time he was forty." For the rest of his life, Whitten would blame a sadistic commanding officer who had made him stand watch overnight in subzero weather.

At eighteen, Danny took a trip to California. "When he came back, he started hypin' me on the Rivingtons, all that," said Lear. "So we left for California, Labor Day weekend, 1962." Within a few months, Whitten wandered into a popular Hollywood dance spot—the Peppermint West—and met a sexy black dancer named Marie Janisse.

"I was thin and gorgeous—just a real hot number on the scene," recalls Janisse. "And in walks this pumpkin-headed country boy. The minute he walked in, we all knew he wasn't from Hollywood. He looked like they had just scraped him off some corn patch. All the girls thought he was cute, but you knew he wasn't hip. He just wasn't a part of the 'in' crowd."

Determined to break into the gang, Danny crashed a party one weekend at Marie Janisse's. "The thing was, if I didn't invite you, you didn't dare show up. And here comes Danny knocking at my door. I said, 'What the hell are you doing here?' " Danny conned his way in, and the pair became fast friends and dance partners.

The black sex kitten and the blond hillbilly from Ohio had a show-stopping routine: Marie would pull a long scarf out of her sleeve, and Danny would charge like a bull. "Danny was hot. We won contest after contest." Yet his arthritis continued to plague him. "His joints were getting so bad they said he'd drop right on the dance floor and they'd have to carry him off," said Brenda Decker. "He'd just get right back up and dance again."

Marie Janisse introduced Whitten to a small clique of Peppermint West dancers that included her brother, "Three-Finger" Joe ("Gimme five and I'll give you back two"), and Don Paris, who would infuriate Janisse by sneaking Danny off to a gay bar across the street. It was at the Peppermint that Danny met another doo-wop fan by the name of Billy Talbot.

· · ·

Billy Talbot was born on October 23, 1943, in New York City. His mother, Verna, was a struggling nightclub singer who barely kept the family together. "My father was a frustrated musician," said Talbot. "He used to drink a lot. My early childhood was emotionally unstable—funky at best."

For most of his preteen years, Billy and his brother, Johnny, were shuttled between foster homes. When the family reunited and moved to New Jersey, Billy started singing in vocal groups. "I got into hard-core doo-wop—the Penguins, Lee Andrews and the Hearts. A lotta groups that were funky and soulful, even a little bit weird."

When Talbot was sixteen, his mother and brother moved to California. Billy's music career went nowhere, and while wandering through Times Square, he saw a billboard advertising one-way fares to California for $360. "I thought, 'What the hell,' " said Billy, who headed for the promised land, where he soon encountered Danny Whitten.

"Danny was a James Dean guy," said Talbot. "A rebel. He wanted to be an actor." Discovering their mutual passion for doo-wop, Whitten and Talbot sang together at a party with two other guys, Lou Bisbol and Pat Vegas, then formed a vocal group. Even though Vegas was committed to another band, the quartet recorded a demo, "Mirror, Mirror on the Wall." "We decided it was gonna be a hit," said Talbot. "We needed another guy in the band, so we called Lou's cousin—Ralph."

•　•　•

Another product of poverty and doo-wop, Ralph Molina came into the world on June 22, 1943. He was born in Puerto Rico and raised on Manhattan's Lower East Side in a housing project at the foot of the Brooklyn Bridge. Ralphic was an a cappella fan, but his real love was the angst-ridden castrato pop of Frankie Valli and the Four Seasons. At fifteen, Molina moved to Florida and sang with a group called the Enchanters. Five years later, his cousin Lou called and asked him to "come out to California and sing the high part," and in August 1963, Danny and the Memories were born.

The group haunted the Peppermint West, where, said Molina, "Danny would dance in contests, win twenty-five bucks and we'd eat for a week." Billy and Ralph weren't really dancers, but it was five bucks a night and all you could drink to stand around and make the club look busy. "What a funny bunch of guys," said Janisse. "Here was Danny—Mr. Blonde—surrounded by these short little dark guys who looked like Italian thugs."

In between dances they sang in the club's alley, grooving on the echo. It was there they met Sal Mineo look-alike Bengiamino Rocco, aka Dino, who replaced Lou Bisbal. "As soon as my voice got into the other three, we had a sound," said Rocco. "We started jamming vocally. We did Mills Brothers, Four Lads, show tunes, rock and roll—and we did 'em with a unique flavor, not really doo-wop. We had this falsetto lead thing that Danny did."

They dressed in green velvet pullovers, black pants and boots, chosen by Danny, the group's leader. "He always used to say, 'Make sure our shoes are shined,' " said Molina. "Danny was smooth, man. He was so together. He looked like a surfer." "Danny was real serious about music," said Ben Rocco. "Maybe more serious than any of us."

The group lived in adjacent apartments in Mark Manor, an $80-a-month complex not far from Hollywood Boulevard that was run by Verna Talbot. "I remember when I first got to California and stepped into the courtyard," said Ralph. "The first thing I saw was this lady with all this long black hair staring at me through the window. The impression I got was 'Wow, a witch.' Turns out it was Billy's mom." An eccentric who ran her own religion, Verna would function as den mother to many a starving artist at Mark Manor.

Danny and the Memories secured few gigs—spending most of their time gathered around the courtyard fountain, serenading the denizens of Mark Manor—but in spring 1965 they would release one single, "Can't Help Lovin' That Girl of Mine" on Valiant Records. The group sexchanged the old Jerome Kern show tune and sailed it into the air, with Whitten's dreamy lead floating above killer harmonies that hint at the Crazy Horse sound still years away. As Molina said, "We sang the shit outta that song, man." The record went nowhere and neither did the group, although they were too young to care. "What we learned with Danny and the Memories was how to be together, how to be a team, that kind of shit," said Molina.

Sometime early in 1965, Danny got a job promoting a pre-MTV filmclip jukebox called Scopitone (a great clip exists of an ultra-cool Whitten and the boys lip-synching "Land of a Thousand Dances"). The gig took him to San Francisco, with Billy and Ralph following close behind. They lived in bohemian North Beach, off of money their girlfriends earned from topless dancing. " Sixty-five—that was the crazy year," said Ben Rocco. "We were in San Francisco when it happened."

Much of what was happening involved mind-altering substances of one kind or another. Whitten and his cohorts had already begun smoking cheap Mexican pot back at Mark Manor. "It was garbage," recalls Molina. "We used to put it in strainers and strain the shit out of it. It was like smoking dirt. We were so naïve back then." Said Talbot, "It was nothin', but we'd get high—and we'd sing a lot more then."

The boys quickly lost their naïveté in San Francisco, getting heavily into pot and LSD, although psychedelics didn't sit well with Ralph. One night the gang hung out with Margo St. James, soon to be infamous for founding COYOTE, the hookers-rights organization. Everybody dropped acid, then Danny, Billy and Rocco split, leaving Ralph to navigate his one and only acid trip alone. As he recalls, "Margo's naked on the floor, getting her pussy sucked by this guy in a suit who looks like a cop, right? Then all of a sudden she's throwin' fuckin' flowerpots out the fuckin' window, screaming, 'Let's call Khrushchev and tell him we love him.' That was one of the worst experiences of my life, man."

Despite Ralph's abstention, acid opened the group up, as did the new wave of sixties music. Ironically, it was the band of confirmed Horse-hater David Crosby that inspired Whitten and crew to move beyond a cappella. The Byrds played a North Beach club called Mother's, and as Talbot reported, "We went, 'Whoa—what's goin' on?' So we decided to play instruments." Ben Rocco, who had done a brief stint in the Marine Corps before heading to San Francisco, remembers how his friends started mutating. "Danny and Billy and Ralph had long hair now—Billy especially—and it was real strange, because there weren't a lot of longhairs. Danny had a guitar. I thought, 'Well, this is a new era.' "

The group began writing their own material and called themselves the Psyrcle, aka the Circle. "It was a play on psychedelic," said Rocco. "We thought it would be commercial, but at that time people in the record business did not want to be associated with drugs. Of course, we were associated with drugs, so it was all right with us. We were hippies before the word was used."

The Psyrcle recorded one single, "Baby, Don't Do That," produced by San Francisco deejay Sly Stone. Written by Whitten and Talbot, the song captures a metamorphosis in progress—vocal hepcats being thrust into the psychedelic sixties at the speed of light. "Baby Don't Do That" was the only release on Lorna Records, named after Barbara "Lorna" Maitland, an exotic dancer and actress whose spectacular chassis was central to two of Russ Meyer's infamous flesh melodramas, *Mudhoney* and *Lorna*. Maitland was married to Ben Rocco and bankrolled the group's effort. Unfortunately, the record flopped, and Maitland would soon become one of the first acid casualties. "Lorna fuckin' flipped," said Molina glumly. "I heard she ran through the courtyard completely naked."

Broke as usual, the Psyrcle returned to Los Angeles, moving into the San Ramone, another low-rent complex run by Verna Talbot. Whitten moved into a tiny L-shaped basement apartment and, according to cohort Willie B. Hinds, "locked himself in there for six months and came out a guitar player." Molina started drumming on cardboard boxes and phone books with spaghetti strainers. Somehow Billy got ahold of a bass.

Neighbors Pat and Lolly Vegas—later famous as seventies Native American funk curiosities Redbone—gave them lessons. "They couldn't play a lick," said Pat. "Redbone has always been tom-tom rock, we never strayed from that. We taught 'em the basics of a feel—just hold the pocket, and if you get a good groove, hold it. We showed 'em some scales and a couple of runs—man, when they got ahold of those scales, you can forget it—they wouldn't let go. Twenty-four hours a day—dum-dit-dit-dit-dum."

Around this time Ben Rocco quit the group, disenchanted with the decidedly nonshowbiz turn the former vocal band had taken. He said his bandmates blew many opportunities and he grew tired of the endless pontification and procrastination. The addition of mind-altering substances into the equation only made things worse. "Our association with drugs was the demise of our group, no question about it," said Rocco. "Too much pot."

For a brief time the entire band fell apart. Whitten headed out to Topanga Canyon and became half of a duo called Bonnett and Mountjoy. Talbot also relocated, to a house in Laurel Canyon where a scene started to congeal around a couple of oddball musicians he had met.

The son of Russian-Polish immigrants, Bobby Notkoff was a violinist who would perform with the L.A. Philharmonic, then jump into his smoke-belching '41 Ford and head for Talbot's to rip into screeching rock and roll runs on his fiddle. "He was an incredible musician, just incredible," said Talbot, shaking his head in awe. "He could play anything. Bobby was like a reborn Paganini—the consummate emotional, crazy violin player. He told me, 'There's only eight notes in music. Don't be afraid.' "

The mysterious Leon Whitsell was a guitar player with a mystical bent. "Leon was into sitars, Eastern music and bein' alone," said Molina, who remembers how the reclusive guitarist would set his amp in the room with the other musicians, then take his guitar into another room to play. "You didn't see Leon. You just heard his amp."

Talbot began organizing wild, psychedelic jam sessions with Molina, Whitsell, Notkoff and any other weirdos who happened by. "Some of the jams were monumental," said Willie B. Hinds. "I remember this guy walked in once in a suit and whipped out a harmonica—he made Sonny

Boy Williamson sound like a kid. He came in with this big six-foot-five guy called the Monster who played blues guitar like crazy. Things like this happened all the time."

Talbot recalls it was at one of these jams that "Danny came walkin' in, and that's how the Rockets started." Their name was copped from the "rockets' red glare" line in "The Star-Spangled Banner." The band's line-up grew to seven members after Leon quit in a huff as recording began on their only album and his brother, George—an R&B-styled guitarist—came in to replace him. "After a day or two, Leon wanted to come back and they said, 'We'll keep you, too, George,' " recalls George Whitsell, who would contribute what some consider to be the Rockets' theme song, "Pills Blues": "I wake up in the mornin', can't find my mind / Drop a little pill, baby, and I wash it down with wine."

The band was now three guitars, bass, drums and electric violin. Notkoff and the Whitsells were accomplished musicians; Whitten, Talbot and Molina were anything but. Together they made a heavy sound. "Everybody was layin' down the rock," said George Whitsell. "It was screamin' stuff. Some people were callin' us the American Stones, because the raw energy was there."

Billy Talbot's house was christened Rockets Headquarters, and the Rockets became a true garage band, playing mostly in Billy's. The house was located on a sharp bend of busy Laurel Canyon Boulevard, and the garage where their jams took place was so close to the street that Notkoff almost fell into the traffic more than once while leaning into a solo with his eyes closed. Traffic backups provided the Rockets with a captive audience. "Everytime you drove by that corner, there'd be this music that was so *loud,*" recalls Robin Lane. "I went there to visit and never left."

Rockets Headquarters was notorious. "We'd go over, hang out, drop acid and jam on blues for twelve hours," said George Whitsell. The standard hippie crash pad, crawling with musicians, their girlfriends and countless dogs. A pile of R&B 45s like Betty Wright's "Clean-up Woman" provided a soundtrack. "I prided myself on my old records," said George Whitsell. "I'd put on two or three of the right singles, get everybody dancin' and we'd go for a day or two. It was hot times for sure." Pot was sold out of the house and undercover cops were forever trying to bust the joint. "We were really just a bunch of crazy psychedelic guys," said Talbot innocently.

The Rockets played some gigs at the Shrine Auditorium, opening for the likes of Jeff Beck as well as their old crony Sly Stone, but their reputation far exceeded their exposure. "They weren't popular—it wasn't even like they had a clique they were so underground," said Danny Hutton. "They were professionally self-destructive, 'cause they didn't care—'Go and do that gig? No man, don't wanna—going out to *eat.*'" Hutton was so impressed with Whitten that he briefly considered him for one of the lead-singer slots when he was putting together Three Dog Night, who would cover Danny's song "Let Me Go" on their 1969 debut album (along with Young's "The Loner"). "We were workin' to pay the rent," said Hutton. "They were a real band—one that actually sits and plays and doesn't make any money at it."

Former Electric Flag member and Dylan sideman Barry Goldberg was equally awestruck. To him, the Rockets "were the cognoscente, the inner hip, the cool guys," and as a West Coast talent scout for Atlantic Records, he talked Ahmet Ertegun into letting him produce the band—until, Goldberg claims, Ertegun attended one of the sessions and heard the lyrics to Whitten's "Mr. Chips," which concerned "a dirty old man" with "a shiny head" who "washed his hands in money."

Although the song was not about him, the band believed the lyrics alienated Ertegun, who withdrew his support. The Rockets' self-titled debut was eventually released in the summer of 1968 by a much smaller independent, White Whale, known primarily as the home of the Turtles. The company was at a loss as to how to promote such psychedelic crazies; Willie B. Hinds said the Rockets "scared White Whale outta their pants." The one time they did a local radio interview was a typical disaster. The deejay warned them not to say the two words deemed obscene by the station. "Now, we're on the air, and this was the first time I'd taken downers," said George Whitsell. "I said, 'What were those words—*shit* and *fuck?*' We were out-there."

Out there they remained. Their greatest commercial success would come when Goldberg's cover of Whitten's "Hole in My Pocket" reached number thirty on the L.A. charts. Today *The Rockets* is nearly forgotten, despite being a great psychedelic R&B record and—in terms of Young and the Horse—a revealing landmark. Listening to Whitten's "Let Me Go," with its minimal, evocative lyrics and long, extended jam built around Notkoff's incendiary fiddle, one can hear the roots of Young's own "Down by the River"—although he would drain out the R&B and slow everything down to sixteen rpm.

Danny Whitten was the band's spark. "Danny brought up a band any time he was in one," said Hinds. "Everybody around him got raised up." In the Rockets, Whitten really came into his own. "I got a hole in my pocket / I had a dime but I lost it," he sings, wailing like a deep-soul singer, his songwriting sly, sad and funny. "Danny didn't say a lot, but he was a colorful guy with language," said Talbot. "He had a knack for putting things in street terms and saying it just right. He was sarcastic in such a beautiful way."

•   •   •

The Rockets and Crosby, Stills and Nash were at opposite ends of the spectrum. Young would walk into both outfits and take over. He destroyed one band in the process and forever disrupted the chemistry of the other, but also pushed each group to some of their highest musical achievements. Elliot Roberts would orchestrate CSNY's superstardom, David Briggs would corral the Horse into creating "group art." For Neil Young it all caught fire in Topanga Canyon.

I'm waiting for Louie Kelly, "the canyon reprobate," as Shannon Forbes, the one-time companion of David Briggs, puts it. Louie's ramshackle two-story house sits nestled in the trees just a few yards from Topanga Canyon Boulevard, one of two main roads that bisect the canyon's rocky terrain. Beer cans litter the front porch, and on an old picnic table is a copy of *Playboy,* its glossy pages flipping in the wind.

After awhile a white van sputters around the corner, its side emblazoned with Louie's logo: IF IT'S SMELLY, CALL KELLY. Louie now works as a plumber. He wisely toned down his first motto, YOUR SHIT IS OUR GOLD. Out of the van jumps a tall, skinny fellow with long, stringy hair and—under a rather sizable nose—a fading mustache. Giddy, almost manic, he could've popped off the pages of some old underground comic.

Kelly didn't know Neil Young all that well—few in Topanga did—but Louie was a part of the canyon spirit. His parties were infamous, and he remains a charter member of the Topanga All-Stars, a loose congregation of fifteen or so roughnecks who functioned as Topanga's answer to the James Gang.

Louie Kelly is an endangered species in Topanga Canyon. Skyrocketing real-estate values and changing times have driven many of the old-timers out, leaving an influx of humorless professionals in their place. "I have to pay to have a party now—get a permit or be arrested," Kelly says with a snort.

He cracks open a beer. "My greatest memory of Neil is watchin' him feel free. He was just gettin' into ridin' motorcycles, and I tell you, it was the funniest thing I ever seen in my life."

At some point, another musician pulled up alongside Young and grabbed his throttle. "It scared the fuck out of Neil." He putted away into the wilderness. "Everybody was worried," says Kelly. "He was lost. It was 'Where's Neil?' " Louie, alone on a hill having a smoke, spied Young down below, riding around in circles. "He forgot which way to go," says Kelly. Young finally managed to climb the hill. "He rode right up to me and said 'Wow!' To me that was *'I did it!'* We smoked, watchin' everybody lookin' for him."

·　·　·

Topanga Canyon is a mere twenty-five minute drive from Hollywood and, in the late sixties, was a universe apart from the glitz of Sunset Strip. "I hated it," said writer Eve Babitz. "It was like I was on speed and everybody there was on downers. People wore capes in Topanga."

Situated in an isolated stretch of the Santa Monica Mountains between Los Angeles and Malibu, Topanga has long been a hideaway for outcasts. Its original inhabitants were Indians and Spanish settlers, and during the fifties, McCarthy-accused communists hid out there from the FBI. "Topanga has always had a very liberal faction and a very conservative faction," said longtime resident Max Penner. "The neat thing about it is they live together in harmony."

Not in the beginning, said David Briggs. When he first moved there in the mid-sixties, "you couldn't go out without being arrested. I got rousted every day for years." Floods and fires brought rednecks and hippies together, and the concentration of longhairs would earn Topanga the moniker "Haight Ashbury South." "It just exploded," said actor Dean Stockwell, who claimed Topanga's geographical limitations protected it from getting too overrun. "It's inaccessible except for one road, so it became a microcosm of the best of the sixties."

There were theater groups, nudist colonies and communes, plus a small but thriving music scene centered around the Corral. Originally a country/western hole in the wall called Mickey's Hideaway, the Corral was revamped by architect Ral Curran into a hippie nightclub, complete with a large painting of a naked couple, entitled *Pisces Dancing,* hanging over the dance floor. Canned Heat, Taj Mahal, the Flying Burrito Brothers and Joni Mitchell all played the Corral, along with Neil Young and Crazy Horse. Biker gang Satan's Slaves also called the Corral home, as did R&B great Big Joe Turner, who was booked into the club by beatnik "Topanga" Dick

Ludwig, infamous for his T-shirt proclaiming TOPANGA DICK IS NOT A SO-
CIAL DISEASE.

"There were times we had to lock the door to keep people from comin'
in," said Topanga local Jimmy Dehr. "People would walk out into the
parking lot with pitchers of beer, there'd be drug connections up the street,
people screwin' in the bushes. It was just nuts." But if Neil Young was
at the Corral, he was probably onstage. For the most part he would remain
an invisible man in Topanga. "Everybody's goin' out and havin' fun / I'm a
fool for stayin' home and havin' none," Young states in his morose version
of Don Gibson's "Oh Lonesome Me," a cut from his archetypal Topanga
album, *After the Gold Rush.* "Neil was real," said neighbor, friend and occasional art director Tom Wilkes. "He didn't have that music-star crap
goin' for him at all . . . the guy was real private. He just seemed very lonely
and withdrawn a lotta the time."

"Neil didn't play with the boys," said Elliot Roberts. "He seemed much
more adult. Neil had a vision of what being a man was—he was more responsible, moved out to Topanga alone, got married very early." Despite
his seclusion, or maybe because of it, Young remained eerily in touch with
the times. As Max Penner put it, "Neil watched us all go crazy and wrote
about it."

Another Neil emerged in Topanga. No longer as exposed or vulnerable
as he was in the Springfield, he had a manager and a producer, and within
months a wife and home were added. His paranoia subsided, as would his
seizures, which became so infrequent Young was able to jest about them
after one light-show-induced attack during a dance at the Topanga shopping center. "We kidded him forever," said Shannon Forbes. "Two beers
and a strobe light and he's out."

Apparently marijuana no longer made Neil twitch all that badly. Jack
Nitzsche, amazed at the prodigious amounts of pot the once apprehensive
musician could now consume, asked what had happened to make this possible. "Success," answered Young.

*I was kinda on my own. I survived the Springfield and headed out to
Topanga—farther away from Hollywood. That was a heavy scene. At
that point it was too intense for me. And I knew I wanted to do a solo
thing—I didn't want to be part of another group. That was liberating.*

—There was a lot about L.A. you didn't like.
Well, y'know, I liked my place, I liked where I lived. I just didn't like
the hustle and bustle of the entertainment business. Once I made it, I
didn't like to be there at all. Once I got to a certain point, I didn't have
to be there. I really couldn't relax there. A little too fast. I'm fast—but I
have to have slowness around me. I have to have space. I have to have
room.

I didn't hang at the Corral that much . . . it was cooler for everybody
else than me, probably. Those places are hard for me. I was pretty high,
probably why I don't have any memories. I remember one night I went
to the Corral and when I came back the next day, I had no hair. Heh heh.
My hair was gone. I wasn't married at the time.

At some point Young—along with a white mutt named Winnipeg, who
would share the cover of *Everybody Knows This Is Nowhere*—parked his
ass on the couch at David Briggs's ranch at 1174 Old Topanga Road, formerly the site of the final Springfield bust. Also congregating on the property were a motley bunch sometimes known as the Topanga All-Stars:
Bobby Morris was the ranch manager when he wasn't totaling Briggs's
newest car; pals Louie Kelly and Ron Denend lived out in the barn; and
actor Danny Tucker was always good for a bad joke or a fierce right hook.
"All of us had long hair, but we were the furthest thing from hippies you
can imagine," said Morris.

Briggs and Tucker liked to gamble, so high-stakes card games were a
ritual for the clan. "They'd frisk ya when you came to the table to see if you
were holdin' drugs or guns," recalls Denend. "Drugs stayed, guns went in
the locker. They'd get me to bring a couple newcomers into the games. I
knew it was a turkey shoot. They'd play all these weird games, like if the
third deuce dealt is a red one it's wild. The rules changed as they went
along. How can you play with guys like that?"

Den mother for the bunch was David's companion at the time, Shannon
Forbes, who stayed busy feeding the troops pineapple upside-down cake
and sketching everybody from her kitchen easel. Nils Lofgren, who would
soon be making records with both Briggs and Young, felt that it was a real
boys' club. "They treated women like dirt," said Lofgren, laughing. "That
whole macho cowboy thing—walking into a restaurant and calling some

woman 'sugar' or 'babe.' I never heard anyone before refer to a woman as an 'old lady.' "

Amid all this testosterone, Young was the sensitive longhair. "Neil was very kind," said Shannon Forbes, remembering a shy, quiet Young hunched over the shabby old upright piano, picking out notes around the missing keys. "He was tall, thin—Neanderthal man with an oddball voice."

In addition to all the other Topanga crazies Young was meeting, at some point in 1968 he encountered Charles Manson a few times (curiously, Young and Manson share a November 12 birthdate). The two were introduced by Dennis Wilson, a friend of Young's since the Beach Boys tours. Manson lusted after a recording career. "Helter Skelter" was months away.

This meeting of the minds has provided much fodder for interviews, with Young telling journalist Nick Kent that Manson was "great, he was unreal. . . . I mean, if he had a band like Dylan had on 'Subterranean Homesick Blues'. . . " Young wrote a wild number inspired by Manson in 1974, "Revolution Blues." Manson returned the favor, telling a 1995 interviewer from his Vacaville, California, prison cell that his music-celebrity friends from the old days "didn't give me shit"—except for Neil Young, who bequeathed him a motorcycle.

Charlie remembers me too, huh? Everybody else ripped him off, I gave him a motorcycle. I turn out to be a good guy.

We just hung out. He played some songs for me, sittin' in Will Rogers's old house, on Sunset Boulevard. Dennis had the house there, and I visited Dennis a couple of times . . . Charlie was always there. I think I met him maybe two, three times. Spent the afternoon with him, Dennis and all those girls—Linda Kasabian, Squeaky Fromme.

The girls. They only paid attention to Charlie. Dennis and I felt like we weren't there, okay? Now that may not seem that unusual, but—it is. Because both Dennis and I were known. These girls couldn't see us.

He seemed a little uptight, a little too intense. Frustrated artist. Spent a lot of time in jail. Frustrated songwriter, singer. Made up songs as he went along, new stuff all the time, no two songs were the same. I remember playin' a little guitar while he was makin' up songs. Strong will, that guy.

I told Mo Ostin about him, Warner Brothers—"This guy is unbelievable—

he makes the songs up as he goes along, and they're all good." *Never got any further than that. Never got a demo.*

Glad he didn't get around to me *when he was punishing people for the fact he didn't make it in the music biz. That's what that was all about. Didn't get to be a rock and roll star, so he started fuckin' wipin' people out. Dig that.*

—*What would've happened if he got signed?*

Well, he probably woulda gotten pissed off at them. He was an angry man. But brilliant. Wrong, *but stone-brilliant. He sounds like Dylan when he talks.*

He's like one of the main movers and shakers of time—when you look back at Jesus and all these people, Charlie was like that. But he was kind of . . . skewed. You can tell by reading his words. He's real smart. He's very deceptive, though. Tricky. Confuses you. Crosby was scared to death of doin' "Revolution Blues." He didn't think it was safe to do it. Didn't want people to get the message, y'know, about rock and roll stars being worse than lepers, heh heh. Didn't want that vibe out there.*

—*Are some people just evil?*

Some people's lives *are evil. I think people are receptacles—evil and good are out there. We either pick up on one or the other. I can't see a little kid being evil.*

—*You believe in the death penalty?*

Yes. An eye for an eye. It makes absolute *sense. I mean, if somebody does something like that . . . y'know, okay, they're* crazy. *They're crazy—that's a reason why it's okay? We're gonna spend the rest of their lives trying to change them—and they've already committed this heinous crime, taken away somebody's life? Those people don't really deserve an* investment. *I make the call for the death penalty, 'cause it's* cheaper. *Too many little kids out there need that money.*

Some were intimidated by Susan Acevedo. Guillermo Giachetti, who worked as a roadie for both Young and Stephen Stills, recalls Susan

---

*Actress Charlotte Stewart, who was at drummer Dallas Taylor's the night of the LaBianca murders, recalls a panicked Stephen Stills and David Crosby barging in armed, saying, "They're killin' all the people with estates!"

dressed head to toe in black, tearing around town in Neil's black Mini-Cooper. "Susan was a wild one. She didn't look like a mellow, easygoing person—she was a city chick." Willie B. Hinds—who washed dishes in the Canyon Kitchen, said, "Susan was maybe the first women's libber. She was in hate with men."

"Susan was a tough broad—I liked her," said Tom Wilkes of Young's first wife. "She was kind of overpowering."

"Susan was much tougher than Neil," recalled Elliot Roberts. "Real smart, real strong, very much like Rassy. Neil was always dominated by women. I think he respects women more than men—he thinks they're smarter and tougher. It seems to me all great artists pick very strong-willed women who are combative so they can draw into their art to get away."

An earthy, strawberry-blond Sicilian approximately a half-dozen years older than Young and raising an adolescent daughter from a previous relationship, Susan Acevedo ran the Canyon Kitchen, a bacon-and-eggs hangout in the tiny Topanga shopping center. Longhairs would gather to soothe last night's mescaline hangover with some of Acevedo's homemade bread. "Susan showed me the merits of brown rice and tofu," said Wilkes's ex-wife, Lynn. "She always knew who did the best tie-dye."

Young seems to have a special affection for waitresses; they figure in several of his songs. "Neil wasn't into sitting at a table with eight girls and seven guys," said Elliot Roberts. "But you put a waitress at his table alone, and she's gone." Romance bloomed in the Canyon Kitchen. "Susan set her cap for Neil and absolutely pursued him," said Shannon Forbes.

"Susan cooked, took care of things, fielded the calls—she kept everything calm and smooth for Neil," said Lynn Wilkes. "Susan was definitely a bit of a mother figure to him. At times I got the feeling that was ninety percent of their relationship—very respectful and kind to each other, but not terribly demonstrative."

Jeannie Field, who would work on a number of film projects with Young, remembers that when she first met Neil, "Susan was painstakingly ironing this white tux shirt with all these ruffles. I couldn't believe it—I was so nonhousemaking at that point, and here's this beautiful red-haired woman. I think she spent the entire visit ironing Neil's shirt." With an eye to Young's epilepsy, Acevedo weaned him off hamburgers and onto a healthier diet.

Young had moved into his own house in August 1968, using his entire cash advance from Warner Bros. to purchase the property. "I said to Neil, 'So tell me what the least amount is you need to get this house,' " recalls Roberts. "He said, 'Fifteen thousand.' It turns out with tax and commissions it was seventeen. So I went back to Mo Ostin—'Mo, I fucked up. I was supposed to ask for *seventeen.*' He thought I was so naïve and stupid he gave it to me."

"I always seem to live in placces people can't find," Young mused in his first Warner Bros. bio. The house at 611 Skyline Trail was typical Neil: a redwood box situated on top of an extremely steep hill overlooking the canyon. "It's a totally ridiculous piece of architecture," said Tom Wilkes. "Three stories, skinny, straight up like a quart of milk. I can't believe it hasn't fallen down the hill."

The house was quintessential hippie: cats, candles, antiques. Down one embankment sat a trashed TV set Young had apparently pitched out in a rage. The road up to the house was so treacherous that one night Young's Mini-Cooper slid off the drive and nearly demolished a neighbor's house.

Neil and Susan were married there December 1, 1968. "During the wedding the whole house shook," recalls Louie Kelly. "I thought it might fall down." Neil wore a white suit, Susan a white satin dress. Scott Young was invited at the last minute but couldn't attend; nor was Rassy present. "I never met Susan," she told me. "I sent her a thing out of the paper on epilepsy and she gave me hell for even mentioning it."

Presiding over the ceremony was George Herms, an artist whose wild hair gave him the look of Rasputin. After Susan's daughter, Tia, entered carrying a ring on a pillow, Herms—an ordained minister in the Temple of Man—blew a horn, then read a long poem he'd written the night before. "Neil," Herms asked solemnly, "do you wish to be the solar light upon this lady's path? And Susan, do you wish to be the moonbeam of devotion to this man's light?"

Too bad it didn't take. It was beautiful while it lasted.

Something about me caused my first wife to say that she hated *my mother—heh heh—and* never *wanted to meet her and would never meet her.*

—Rassy had differences with every woman in your life.

Yeah. None were spared. The smartest one was Susan. She wouldn't allow her *to come and visit me. She said, "Neil, I know you, and I know your mother because I know something about you, and I don't want to meet your mother—ever." Heh heh. I went, "Hmmmm."*

—What do you think it was?

Well, it was a magical combination of her being thirty-one and me being, like, twenty-three—a young *twenty-three. The start that I had in sexuality was basically being on the road, heh heh . . . a different start— but* hey, *it was* mine.

—How did the relationship between you and Susan begin?

I used to come to the Canyon Kitchen for one of her breakfasts: the one-eye. One egg and a couple pieces of Canadian bacon. It was pretty good.

Susan was my friend. She was cool. A real ball of fire. I think we loved each other. A great, great lady—very strong. My life is better for havin' known her. Met Russ Tamblyn and Dean Stockwell through Susan. Dean—very cool guy. Turned me on to Devo. Into Bowie way early.

Susan introduced me to people who were artists—George Herms, Wallace Berman—those guys were friends of my wife. Susan really loved them, she knew all about them. Susan introduced me to the concept of art.

For many it's impossible to talk about Topanga's glory days without invoking the name of Wallace Berman. As of 1997, Neil Young was planning to use an image of himself from one of Berman's collages for the cover of his Archives boxed set. An influential assemblage artist, Berman created collages with an early photocopying machine called a Verifax. With his hatchetlike nose and long steel-gray ponytail, Berman was part beatnik, part pool shark and all art. "Wallace Berman was as pure an artist as there ever was," said longtime Topanga resident Dean Stockwell. "He was the funniest motherfucker that ever lived, the greatest cocksman that ever lived . . . a big magus, the big affector . . . Wallace Berman was the Monster Mash."

Berman was known to be eerily prescient, even predicting his own death at the age of fifty in 1976. Stockwell recalls seeing the future at the Berman household in 1958: "One day I noticed a decal on his backdoor window—an American flag, and at the top of the thing were the words 'Support the American Revolution.' All of a sudden it was like someone said my mother was a hooker. . . . It bothered me. It struck me so heavily I couldn't even confront Wallace with it. So some years go by and I *see the fuckin' revolution happen, man.* I see everything in the world change around me."

A Stockwell photo of Berman would appear in the lineup on *Sgt. Pepper,* and both he and George Herms were fixtures on the Topanga scene. Herms, an eccentric who made mournful sculptures out of shopping carts and old car parts, was another natural for Young. As actor Russ Tamblyn put it, Herms was "a junk artist. It's unfortunate that what George found beauty in was rust—that doesn't make it with a lotta people."

Both Herms and Berman encouraged Young as an artist. Herms first encountered Young's music during an acid trip at Dean Stockwell's house, when the actor played him "Expecting to Fly." "Neil was this Canadian with this incredible cowboy side to him," said Herms. "He was like this jewel that was just blossoming. One thing Neil said was he did not know where those lyrics were coming from. We all said, 'Don't worry, man—let 'em come.' Because that's always been a tradition in the arts—that we don't know where it's coming from."

Both Dean Stockwell and Russ Tamblyn were former child actors who had turned their backs on Hollywood, save for the occasional exploitation movie to buy groceries. Both were involved in the Topanga art scene, and Tamblyn, who lived right up the hill from Neil, was making a go of it as an artist himself.

"I was very anti-entertainment, and I sort of resented the fact Neil was living next door to me—fans used to camp out on the side of the road, and I'd have to go by 'em to get home. I was really into my art and not the friendliest guy in the world. Neil used to come up and sit in my studio. We hardly talked at all . . . sometimes he'd sit there for hours." Years later, working on Young's film *Human Highway,* Tamblyn apologized for being so uncommunicative back in Topanga, and Neil told him how much he'd enjoyed the silent times. "I was probably one of the few people who *didn't* talk to him."

Stockwell, a music aficionado, was an early champion of Young's work. "There was a great awareness of the talent of Neil Young being amongst us. I just think he's on another level—I thought that when I first laid eyes on him. Neil's a tormented person of towering strength and huge creative power. If he didn't have creative talent, I don't know if he would be with us. I also sensed that Neil was a real good guy and very straight with people—and that people were straight with him. . . . I saw nothing but admirable qualities in him from the get-go.

"Neil's always fun to be with . . . whether you're on a bummer or your car broke down or you're in a limo. I just love him deeply, and maybe I value him even more." As to why he's been able to remain friends with Young all these years, Stockwell said, "I don't ask him questions about himself. I never have. Maybe that's one reason Neil likes me, if he does . . ."

•   •   •

"My first album was a really lonely experience," Neil Young would tell deejay Tony Pig. Producer David Briggs didn't remember it that way. "We had a lotta fun making that record. We'd get up, smoke a joint, cruise down Mulholland all the way to Hollywood. We'd work in one studio for three hours, then go to another . . . in those days, Hollywood had great studios—Sunset Sound, Wally Heider, Gold Star, TTG. It was beautiful."

It was around August 1968 that Young and Briggs plunged into work on the first album. Three cuts coproduced by Nitzsche featured soon to be top L.A. sessionmen, including a young Ry Cooder, then Jack's protégé. The rest were cut with a rhythm section consisting of Jim Messina on bass and drummer George Grantham from Messina's new band, Poco. Messina, who admired Young during his time with the Springfield but never felt close to him, was surprised to get the call. "I wasn't sure he liked me. Neil was very aloof."*

---

*Although *Neil Young* was overdubbed piece by piece, glimmers of the Briggs/Young "the more you think, the more you stink" ethos were already in evidence. Jim Messina once stepped up to the mike to record a song and found out he'd already done it. "As I was warming up—learning the chart—they recorded me," said Messina, still annoyed. "I said, '*Wait a minute*—I want to do it again.' Neil said, 'No—it's fine the way it is.'"

Neil Young sticks fairly close to the eclectic mix developed in the Springfield. Each side opens with an instrumental overture and ends with an epic, with shorter, more straightforward numbers in between. Only Shakey would begin his solo career with an instrumental, but "The Emperor of Wyoming" finds many of his trademarks already in place: a simple, classic melody line; a relaxed, loping beat; the distinctive bent-vibrato guitar. Once the prairie feel is established, Young adds another layer to his mystique with "The Loner." With lyrics more Mickey Spillane than sixties rock—"He's the perfect stranger, like a cross of himself and a fox"—the song is tough and driving, full of the attenuated guitar squeal that vibrates throughout the album.

"I've Been Waiting for You" is another bomb: massed guitars churning out a killer riff as Young searches for "a woman to save my life." At the end of the chorus, hallucinatory pipe organ pushes the bass and drums to a dizzying crescendo full of such tension and menace it feels like Young's grown tired of waiting and has taken to stalking instead. Then the riff kicks back in, exploding in a crazed, squalling solo. "That record is a masterpiece of tones," said Briggs proudly of the album. "We got tones nobody's ever got except Hendrix."* Jack Nitzsche's measured orchestration in "The Old Laughing Lady" closes out side one, featuring sweet, sad countermelodies passing from strings to French horn with beautiful restraint. The track employs a vocal-muting technique Nitzsche stumbled on to called pre-echo, which made Neil sound, in his words, "a million miles away but right there." On most of the record, Young sounds like a small, wounded animal—inward, fragile, barely able to yelp the words out.

Not everything works. Nitzsche's use of a soul chorus feels overwrought, as does Young's first released solo acoustic performance, the

---

According to Jack Nitzsche, many L.A. session players looked down their noses at Neil Young, and Ry Cooder was no exception. "Ry hated Neil and let it show and I hated him for it, because Neil was so scared."

*According to Briggs, the psycho guitar noises featured on both "The Loner" and "I've Been Waiting for You"—where it sounds like Young is sticking the instrument into a garbage disposal and shredding the strings—were made by "putting Neil's guitar through an organ Leslie, not even through an amp, just the Leslie into the board."

almost endless paranoiac barrage of "Last Trip to Tulsa";* but you have to admire Young as he stretches in more directions than Plastic Man. The overall impression *Neil Young* leaves with you is of the sound itself— submerged, smothered, desperately controlled. All the jagged edges are overdubbed away, as if this would somehow conceal the hysteria in Young's vocal cords. Music made by a terrified kid cowering in a closet, playing keening, demented guitar solos through layers of gauze.

Neil Young shows Briggs and Young in a conventional L.A. studio setting: building tracks piece by piece, playing around with string sections, echo chambers and limiters; making the smooth, seamless, professional record expected of them. Who knew it would be their last?

•   •   •

Now facing the music press as a solo artist, Neil Young made clear he was no longer the Hollywood Indian of Buffalo Springfield lore. Putting on the beloved fringe jacket "just got ridiculous," said Young in the record company bio. "People expected me to wear that all the time." He told journalist Pete Johnson that he "never wanted to be in a group" and that the only reason he returned to the band was because management problems had him "starving to death." I'm not that guy, Young suggests, and maybe I never was. The chameleon act was just beginning.

Young made clear that distancing himself from Los Angeles was no accident. He ranted about what he'd been put through in Hollywood. "The Strip! The Whisky A Go-Go! It's just a big phony scene," Young told writer Marci McDonald. "A bunch of people trying to make it and they don't care how. Those idiots, they have no taste. They're not sensitive. They have no idea what real art is. Sure I sound bitter about it. I'm one of the most bitter people I know when it comes to the Hollywood music scene."

Neil Young was released in December 1968 (or January 1969, depending on the source). Despite a typical Warner/Reprise counterculture ad campaign that promised fans a free sample of Topanga dirt, the record flopped.

---

*Apparently Young thinks the nightmarish lyrics of this song are a laugh riot. "I always thought there was a funny side to my music," Young told Nick Kent. " 'Last Trip to Tulsa' . . . that's my idea of a really funny song."

Those involved in making it put a lot of the blame on an experimental mastering process called Heico-CSG that was supposed to allow stereo records to be played back on still existent mono equipment. Unfortunately Heico-CSG also muffled the dynamics of a record featuring vocals that were difficult enough to hear without it. (Young said he found out his solo debut was a guinea pig for the process only after it was in the stores and managed not only to talk Reprise out of using the process, but also to rerelease a new version of the record. "It was too late," said Elliot Roberts.)

Neil Young's title-free original cover was a garish head-on painting by Topanga artist Roland Diehl of Young against the mountains, a cityscape surreally jutting out of his body. According to Jack Nitzsche, Young hated the cover at first. "What am I supposed to do?" Neil told Jack. "My wife asked the guy to paint it."

No, no—I liked the cover. I just didn't know what to make of it. It's like a straight-on picture of me right in the camera, but it wasn't me—it was a painting. I dug that. Not really commercial, though. We're not selling an image here. It's not like a David Cassidy cover or something.

One of the hardest things to do is look through pictures and decide which ones you like. I could live without it. I've seen too many pictures of myself. Figure out how many pictures I've seen of myself compared to you. *I think I've got my fuckin' quota already.*

I love parts of the "Piece of Crap" video [1994]. I like to have a great thing that purposely leaves the rough edge in and goes, "Fuck you." I like it to be purposely shitty. One verse of the video is the back of the grip's head. *You can't see fuckin' anything. Till the very end—he moves his head, and I'm like "PIECE OF CRAP!" That's me, okay? That's the way I like it—you know I'm there, you can feel it all over the place, but you can't get enough. You always feel like you didn't quite see it.*

—You've never made another record like Neil Young *since.*

No.

—Drove you crazy?

Exactly. *We got into that one—don't know if we'll do it that way again. It was intense. If I had left it alone at an earlier stage, it woulda been better. Like a lot of that Buffalo Springfield stuff—I went on working and fucked it up. I don't do that anymore. Thank God I got that out of my system at an early age, heh heh.*

—You once said, "My first record was a lonely experience." Why?

Because I wasn't playing with anybody. A labor of love is another way to look at it—it was either a lonely experience or a labor of love. But there's not that much difference between the two. It's something I had to do. I was really glad when it was over, because it was so technical, it took so much thinking. That's when I learned how hard it is to construct something when you can actually just play *it.*

Briggs and I used to drive home in this old Bentley I had. Had a great time makin' that first record. The actual doin' it was great. Near the end, the responsibility got to be pretty heavy for what we'd done. And then to have it come out with the Heico-CSG process. Here I was, a brand-new artist, my first record, hadn't had any hits, and I'm screamin' and yellin', "You're fuckin' crazy if you think this is good—don't tell me it's better, because I know it isn't." And it wasn't.

—What did you learn about overdubbing on the first record?

There's almost no overdubbing on the second record. Heh heh. You could do it for a little color, a little bang now and then—but not as an integral part of the music.

When I first got freedom in the studio, I abused it. I played almost everything on that first record myself. That was the kind of thinking that was goin' on in the Springfield. We shouldn't have been allowed to do that. It was wrong. And that's as well as I could do it at the time with the technology I had, and it's really cool and it felt great when we made it— but it's not rewarding. Everybody Knows This Is Nowhere—*now that's rewarding.*

No one remembers exactly how Neil Young stumbled upon the Rockets— probably through Robin Lane or Autumn Amateau, both friends of Danny Whitten. At some point early in the Springfield days, Young wound up in Laurel Canyon at Rockets Headquarters, sitting in Talbot's bedroom playing the original D-modal version of "Mr. Soul" with Danny and Billy singing along. There were some hazy jams. Neil told Tony Pig that playing with the Rockets "changed my mind about a lotta things . . . I heard a lotta things that I'd forgotten. We used to get together and really get stoned and play to all hours of the morning . . . there were about thirteen or fourteen of us . . . sitars, tabla . . . Ralphie hadn't started to play drums . . . Billy had just bought his bass, he didn't know how to play."

When the Rockets album came out in March 1968, they made the trek out to Topanga to play it for Young. He loved it, and one night during the Rockets' engagement at the Whisky—August 11 through 15, 1968— Young sat in with the band. "I didn't know who Neil was," said Molina, typically blasé. "He was just another guy who sat in with us." But Talbot recalls that Young's big guitar sound "blew George Whitsell's away. He was kind of overshadowed."

Young came to the gig armed with the weapons that have become crucial elements of his rock and roll sound: Old Black, a 1953 Gibson Les Paul plugged into a 1959 Fender Deluxe. The guitar came from Jim Messina, who found the instrument's monstrous sound uncontrollable. "Neil's the kind of guy that if there's an old scraggly dog walkin' down the street, he'd see somethin' in that dog and take it home. That's kind of like that Les Paul—I liked the way it looked, but it was just terrible. It sounded like *hell.* Neil loved it," said Messina.

Young bought the Deluxe for approximately fifty bucks in 1967. As Young told writer Jas Obrecht, he "took it home, plugged in this Gretsch guitar and immediately the entire room started to vibrate. . . . I went, 'Holy shit!' I turned it halfway down before it stopped feeding back." The Les Paul/Deluxe combo, which remains the cornerstone of his sound, would make its thunderous debut in Young's music on his very first record with Crazy Horse, *Everybody Knows This Is Nowhere.**

After the Whisky gig, Talbot said, "the wheels started turning in Mr. Young's head." A Topanga jam session was arranged but limited to only three members from the six-piece Rockets: Whitten, Talbot and Molina. Young booked studio time almost immediately. There would be no false starts or missed opportunities like there had been with the Springfield.

---

*Young first used Old Black for some uncredited wild guitar on a 1969 Tetragrammaton record Briggs produced for Elyse Weinberg, Neil's old friend from his Toronto folkie days.

"We got together, started rehearsing and we went right in," Young told writer Jean-Charles Costa. "That whole album was like catching the group just as they were getting to know each other . . . we didn't even know what we sounded like until we heard the album."

"That's when a change came over me, right then," Young would say of *Everybody Knows* a few years later to deejay B. Mitchell Reid. "I started just tryin' to be real instead of fabricate something. . . . Since then I've just been striving to get realer and realer on record. As in More Real."

·   ·   ·

At the beginning of the seminal "Running Dry"—most likely Young's first live studio vocal with a band—you can hear chattering as the tape starts rolling. David Briggs, not a man given to looking back, recalled with gusto the origin of the impromptu babble: "I knew the band was hittin' it, so I turned around and said, 'Fire up the machine!' " said Briggs, exhilarated by the memory. "These guys didn't act like they were in the studio, they acted like it was the end of the world. GIVE IT ALL."

In the middle of January 1969, Young and the Horse began recording at Wally Heider's in Los Angeles, cutting two landmark nine-minute-plus jams—"Down by the River" and "Cowgirl in the Sand," and two short, funky rockers—"Cinnamon Girl" and "Everybody Knows." Twin archetypes of the Crazy Horse sound: long, guitar-heavy epics and compact, country-tinged numbers, both so instantly familiar they seem to have come down from the ancients.

In March the band went back in the studio—this time Sunwest—to cut a plaintive country ballad with beautiful harmonies from Danny called "The Losing End," and the moody, magnificent "Running Dry," featuring spine-tingling electric violin work from Rocket Bobby Notkoff. Unlike the labored creations of the Springfield and the first solo record, the music on *Everybody Knows This Is Nowhere* was recorded and in the can as quickly as it happened. Robin Lane said Young ambushed her on "Round and Round." "I thought we were rehearsing. I didn't even know what I was singing. . . . Neil was the original punk rocker."

Young named the new band Crazy Horse, although he couldn't remember when or why. The Rockets were history. "My understanding was Neil was gonna use the guys for a record and a quick tour, bring 'em back and help us produce the next Rockets album," said Whitsell. "It took me a year and a half to realize my band had been taken."

"Big pictures, wide-open spaces" is how Young described his music to writer Paul Zollo in 1991. The Horse left wide-open spaces in which Young could go berserk on Old Black and the frequently minimal lyrics he wrote painted big pictures. His imagery was sometimes over the top on *Everybody Knows*. "Purple words on a gray background / To be a woman and to be turned down," Young sings in the truly obtuse "Cowgirl in the Sand." What the hell does that mean? "My songs are pictures," Dylan once said. "And the band makes the sound of the pictures." In Crazy Horse, Neil Young had found his own picture-sound band.

Everybody Knows This Is Nowhere was a fusion of all Young's influences, not only Dylan and the Stones, but country music, the Shadows and Orbison. "I remember Crazy Horse like Roy Orbison remembers 'Leah' and 'Blue Bayou,'" Young writes in his 1977 liner notes to "Down by the River" on *Decade*.

Captain Beefheart once described Jimmy Reed's music as one-head music. A group of players coalescing into something indivisible. Crazy Horse was a one-head band Jimmy Reed could love: crude, simple and loud, in the groove one minute and ready to fall apart the next. No fancy licks, no extra stuff. These guys were incapable of it—they'd barely *played* outside their goddamn garage. "Crazy Horse weren't musicians," said Briggs. "They weren't musicians at all. They were a bunch of dudes that hit a simpatico, a rapport, an emotional thing. Neil was the musician."

According to Billy Talbot, it was figuring out how to play "Down by the River" that gave birth to the moronically perfect Crazy Horse backbeat. "At first we played it double-time, faster, like the chorus is now. It was almost a jazz thing. George Whitsell had showed me and Ralph a basic James Brown beat the first time he taught us how to play—boom-boom tak! boom-boom tak!—and I said to Ralph, 'Let's try it with George's beat, except real slow.'"

To hear what a difference the Horse made one has only to listen to "Everybody Knows This Is Nowhere," a song cut at the *Neil Young* sessions in August 1968 and then five months later with the Horse. The *Neil Young* version is typical of those sessions—jaunty, restrained, polite, complete with a rooty-toot-toot Moog solo. The version with the Horse is a real pip.

"Everybody seems to wonder what it's like down here," Young muses, his caustic tone making it clear that for him, the entire Los Angeles scene might as well fall into the sea. Young's Les Paul guitar leaps out of his amp and directly into your heart. It's a garage/country sound, ragged but right, with guitars, vocals and drums smack-dab in your face. By the end of the song Young is absently moaning the song's refrain over and over, while Danny and Ralph's wistful, slightly sarcastic sha-la-las provide just the right edge. "Cinnamon Girl" is another kick—irresistibly melodic, with ridiculous but great lyrics, funky hand claps and a Johnny-one-note solo that had axmeisters everywhere cringing. Young and Whitten's vocals, truly a dual performance, not harmony, blend beautifully and drive the song like a motherfucker. When Whitten lets out a "Whooo!" as Young slides into the ringing solo—each note bent ever so slightly by his Bigsby wang bar—it feels so good, you have to laugh.*

Who was making music like this? Long songs were not uncommon: San Francisco bands had their endless spacy jams, New York's Velvet Underground had their harsh, metallic ones; but Crazy Horse was out in the barn, rooted in melody and wobbly, repetitive rhythms. "Everybody thought San Francisco music was druggy," said aficionado Charlie Beesley. "Crazy Horse was *really* druggy—bleary, laid-back, stoned. Nobody played that slow."

Then there are the warhorses, "Down by the River" and "Cowgirl in the Sand." "It's a cry—a desperation plea" is how Young described "Down by the River" to Robert Greenfield in 1970. "There's no murder in it—it's about blowin' your thing with a chick." The song oozes dread. Opening with shaky, nervous electric guitars, Ralphie picks the beat up to a stoned rumble, and then Young warbles, "Be on my side, I'll be on your side /

---

*There exists a single version of "Cinnamon Girl" that band members sounded less than thrilled with. The 45 contains a "different vocal performance," said Young. "The parts are switched, Danny is on the bottom and me on top. That was so you could hear my voice clearly, which Reprise wanted for the single. We left the album version alone because it was better and we knew it."

The vocals for the *Everybody Knows* title track were recorded directly onto tape, without even passing through a mixing board. "We were tryin' to get all the bullshit out, so we figured directly into the machine would be better," said Young. "Actually, the way we did it there was an impedance mismatch, which made it kinda spitty-sounding. We kinda liked that . . . gave it an edge. It could cut through anything."

Together we can get away." The feeling is that this pair is headed straight for the electric chair. "I shot my baby, shot her dead, shot her dead," Young howls. The guitar playing is violent; as one critic put it, "He draws out notes with a sound that might remind one of a man taking his own blood with a knife."

"Neil Young does with his guitar what Dylan does with his voice," said Ken Viola. I agree. It is futile to try to link either Young's songwriting or his voice to much of what came before, but his guitar sound carried clear links to the past: the gutbucket emotion of Link Wray, the hypnotic rhythm of Jimmy Reed, even Floyd Cramer's slip-note piano. It feels traditional and yet sounds like no one else. Young had forged something wholly his own, as instantly identifiable as a few notes from Jerry Lee's piano or a phrase from the lips of George Jones.

Even though nearly all the vocals on *Everybody Knows* were over-dubbed, one hears the tremendous confidence Young had gained as a singer.* As Briggs said, "After everybody told him he shouldn't sing at all, he went from his first record—where his singing isn't that projected—to bein' the fuckin' man right there in front." High, trembling, full of vulnerability yet somehow strong, "It's not a classical voice," said Emmylou Harris. "His voice has a real innocent quality, like a choirboy, but it's almost scary. It's very haunting, other-worldly."

Everybody Knows This Is Nowhere was released in May 1969, and although it took awhile to gather steam—"Cinnamon Girl" was a minor pop hit, and FM radio made "Down by the River" a stoner anthem for an army of teenage boys eager to mangle its three chords themselves—Neil Young, for the first time since Ray Dee, had captured his vision without interference or disappointment.

Peter Lewis, Young's friend from Moby Grape, remembers stopping by his Topanga Canyon home and listening to an acetate of *Everybody Knows* while Neil sat proudly on the thronelike chair featured in many of the pictures inside the album. "He was waitin' for me to say somethin', and there really wasn't much to say. The thing is, I knew he did what he wanted

---

*There's an alternate version of "Down by the River"—same track, different background parts, different mix—with a very intense scratch vocal (done the night of the band recording) that hints at just what a challenge singing was to Young.

to do. With the Springfield stuff, I always felt it wasn't exactly what he wanted to do. That's why I was so happy for him. He finally got the thing he wanted out of his music."

I liked Everybody Knows. *I knew that was a good record. I also knew that it was raw. I knew that it was us.*

We practiced at my house. That's where Crazy Horse first played. That's when I discovered Old Black and the Deluxe—in the living room of my house, rehearsing. It was great. A small room with my Deluxe on a chair.

There were no effects, it was just the guitar and the amp. Very clean. I didn't have it turned up all the way. Volume's not really that important. It's the size of the room and the relationship of the sound to the enclosure it's in that makes a difference.

I remember lookin' over at Ralph once, havin' Ralph look up at me, and he was just so into it. It was like "Yeah, this is great. We're right *in it." It was fabulous. And I remember the Buffalo Springfield guys comin' over and makin' me nervous every once in awhile.*

The direction change between the first and second album was pretty radical. The difference is, I wanted to play with people. *But that shows radical direction changes were possible and were probably gonna happen—as early as between the first and second records. So what I was doin' in the eighties was nothin'. Absolutely nothin'.*
—*What did you hear in the Rockets?*
It wasn't so much hearing as feeling. Just a vibe—funky, honest and soulful. Direct.
—*How different were they from the Springfield or other musicians?*
A lot deeper. Not that the lyrics were deeper, but there was this . . . depth. *The sound. Something was going* on *there, I don't know what it was. 'Cause none of 'em could hardly play at the time—I mean, they weren't very good, but they were great in their own way. That White Whale record they did was pretty fuckin' cosmic shit. It sounds exactly like they do now. Almost the same, Billy and Ralph. A little simpler.*
—*Did you break the Rockets up?*
I don't think so. I just wanted those three guys to play with me. It didn't mean they couldn't play with the Rockets.

—You wrote some of the Everybody Knows *songs from a sickbed?*
Sometimes if I get sick, get a fever, it's easy to write. Everything opens
up. You don't have any resistance—you just let things go. Your guard is
down. I wrote "Round and Round" up in my cabin. It was written for
Buffalo Springfield—that's when Danny and Robin and I used to sing it
at Billy's house.
—Did you have a concept of doing longer songs?
It just happened. We just started playin' instrumentals and we didn't
stop. The energy was right. We just kept going.

See, before that, the big instrumental was the ending of "Bluebird"
by Buffalo Springfield. That was a big long jam that ended in crashing
guitars, broken strings and all this shit . . . the long jam at the end of
"Bluebird" lasted like eight minutes or something. So I guess the next
thing for me was "Well, that was really cool—why not have one of those
after every verse." Then I started figuring, "Well, shit, we can have one
of these all the way through. There can be three verses and three instru-
mental journeys. It could be a big thing and a lotta fun to play. Really
explore the lyric with the guitar."

"Down by the River" was really edited. We got the vibe, but it was
just too long and sometimes it fell apart, so we just took the shitty parts
out. Made some radical cuts in there—I mean, you can hear *'em. But*
Danny just played so cool on that. He was playin' R&B kinda things. He
made the whole band sound good. Me and Billy and Ralph sounded like
Crazy Horse right away. All I had to do was come up with the songs and
the riffs. I started realizing how long we could jam. *It was fantastic.*

Crazy Horse was really mellow. I really liked them all right from the
very beginning. It was more of a camaraderie. It was much more mellow
than hanging out with Buffalo Springfield.

Those guys were my *band. That was the difference. I called the shots.*
Plus I had Briggs—that's important.
—What did Briggs bring to Everybody Knows?
Stability. The singing had to be coaxed outta me. Learning to sing live.
Learning the need. Learning why to sing live. I was still overdubbing,
because I wanted it to be really right—yet I was overdubbing. I didn't
know what I was doing wrong. Relearning the simplest basic thing—
that music feels good—and should feel unified.

—Where did the inspiration come from for the hand claps on "Cinnamon Girl"?
Remember "My Boyfriend's Back"?
—Is there a link between Jimmy Reed and Crazy Horse?
Yeah. Groove.
—Nitzsche said you told him over and over, "I wanna cross Dylan with the Stones."
Probably that was about the time I had already met Crazy Horse. That wasn't really an idea—heh heh—it was like, you had me *and you had* them.

I wanted to break out of that perfection thing. In reaction to Buffalo Springfield, Crosby, Stills and Nash, my first solo album, all that stuff. Buffalo Springfield was always trying to make clean records, make "real" records, and then my first record with David was the same kinda thing—tryin' to make a great record of, y'know, craft.
—How important were the Stones to you?
Very important. *In the early times, I never thought of what was funky and what wasn't. It was all music—either you liked it or you didn't. There wasn't a funky music or a black music or a white music, it was just fuckin'* music. *I never* categorized *it. And then when I got down to L.A., there's like black music, funky music, white music, R&B and soul. Get down there and they're talking about all these different kinds of music. I'd go, "This is all the same shit I've been listening to. What are they talking* about?*"*

So when I joined Crazy Horse and we started playing, it became obvious to me that this *band was much* funkier *than all the* other *bands I'd been in. And I noticed that some of the musicians that I'd played with in the* other *bands didn't think these guys were very good. Yet I liked* them. *Even more, as a matter of fact. I was having a really good fuckin' time playing with them. Where else could I go and play my guitar for fuckin' seven minutes, sing a verse and play another five-minute solo? Not in Crosby, Stills, Nash and Young. But even more than that, it was a simple thing—everybody just wanted to make the music and nothin' else mattered. It wasn't like "Whose name is gonna be on the record?"*

So then I realized, "Hey, these Crazy Horse guys are a lot *closer to the Rolling Stones. More than Buffalo Springfield was the Beatles."*

So I'd taken rock and roll and divided it into two categories, Rolling Stones and Beatles, okay? And I realized that if you divided into those two categories, color made no difference, what part of the world made no difference. Beatles are on one side, Rolling Stones on the other side, everybody else line up, okay? Crazy Horse and the Mynah Birds, they were on the Rolling Stones side.
—Buffalo Springfield were the Beatles?
Yup.
—CSNY?
Beatles.
—Pearl Jam?
Rolling Stones.
—The Harvest *band, the Stray Gators?*
Beatles, heh heh . . . See, it's just like that—pretty simple.
—Where did Dylan fit in this equation?
Where did he fit in? Rolling Stones. Dylan was never as tight as the Beatles.
—Was the fact that Crazy Horse couldn't "play" a big attraction for you?
The most important thing to me was that they really *loved playing. And they were a hundred percent into it. Second most important thing was that they couldn't play for shit—so that left a lotta room for me to play very little and have it sound fuckin'* phenomenal. *If a good musician plays with me, they play way too much. They always play too much. Always trying to show me how great they are.*
—Nitzsche said, "Neil has a death wish when it comes to rhythm sections." What does he mean?
He means that I like playin' with Billy and Ralph, heh heh.

  Billy's a mystery, isn't he? Billy's great. *Billy's the reason why Crazy Horse is great, and Billy's also the reason why Crazy Horse has never had a hit record. 'Cause Billy's great but not* "I can dance to it" *great, know what I mean?*

  It's like as sensual *as Billy is, his bass playing is not sensual. His bass playing is fuckin' heartfelt and big. The notes are huge. It's teenage guys. You can see it in all of our big hits—it's like a bunch of guys in flannel shirts goin' out of their minds, "LET'S GO THERE NEIL,*

*ARRRGGGGGGGHHHHH!" It's not so much a bunch of chicks goin',
"Hey, wow, this is cool" and gettin' into the groove. . . .*

*I mean, I don't know what it is—but it's never been about a hit record.
And the only record that Crazy Horse ever had that was really truly a hit
record was "Cinnamon Girl." That's the only one. All the other ones
have been underground hits. "Cinnamon Girl" had a groove to it, a different kind of groove. And it had Danny.*

"Danny was a world-class singer," said Briggs. "So all of a sudden Neil
had right up in his face a guy who could really sing his fuckin' ass off *and*
play the best guitar of anybody who ever played with Neil. That's how you
get good—by being with people who are good." Many point to Danny
Whitten for bringing Young out as a vocalist and guitarist. "Danny gave
Neil the blackness he lacks," said Jack Nitzsche.

Whitten's hillbilly/R&B roots helped the Horse avoid any airy-fairy
hippie clichés. His second-lead playing on "Cowgirl in the Sand"—to call
it rhythm guitar would be an insult—shows an understanding of Young's
music that borders on telepathic (all the later versions I've heard without
Danny fail to fly). "Danny was one of those guys who played less, and you
can hear it on *Everybody Knows,*" said Willie B. Hinds. "It's the notes he
didn't play that were important. Danny was actually the backbeat of the
rhythm section. The rhythm guitar usually follows the drummer, but not in
this case. Everybody followed Danny."

Yet there were none of the ego clashes that had soured the Springfield.
"Danny really supported Neil," said Robin Lane. "See, Danny really took
a backseat to anyone he did anything with. He never played me anything
he wrote. He'd go, 'So play me a song, Robin.' "

"Danny Whitten," said Briggs, "was the Brian Jones of Crazy Horse."

*What did Danny bring to Crazy Horse? The glue. The glue that held it
together. Danny was funny. I can't really describe it. He had a lot of little things he would say that were really fuckin' funny—most of them at
Billy or Ralph's expense. And he definitely ran the show. Everyone listened to Danny. He was basically the leader of the Rockets, from what I
can tell.*

That's what was so great about Crazy Horse in those days—Danny understood my music, and everyone listened to Danny. He understood what we were doing. A really great second guitar player, the perfect counterpoint to everything else that was happening. His style of playing was so adventuresome. So sympathetic. So unthoughtful. And just so natural. That's really what made "Cowgirl in the Sand" and "Down by the River" happen—Danny's guitar parts. Nobody played guitar with me like that—that rhythm. When you listen to "Cowgirl in the Sand," he keeps changing—plays something one and a half, maybe two, times, and he's on to the next thing. Billy and Ralph will get into a groove and everything will be goin' along and all of a sudden Danny'll start doin' somethin' else. He just led those guys from one groove to another—all within the same groove. *So when I played these long guitar solos, it seemed like they weren't all that long, that I was making all these changes, when in reality what was changing was not one thing, but the whole band. Danny was the key.*

I was singin' by myself on the first record. I was by myself. *Danny influenced my singing and especially my playing—his rhythms. Danny was ahead of Billy and Ralph at that time, but they were catchin' up fast. Danny was more like me—he just* played. *Some people just have it.*

We did a tour of clubs when we first started—all I had was the Deluxe, Billy had a little amp and Danny had the Bandmaster—very little stuff. No big crowds. No excitement. We'd just be back in the dressing room smoking weed and getting ready to go out there and play "Losing End," "Cinnamon Girl," "Everybody Knows" and "Down by the River" or "Cowgirl in the Sand"—never the two of them together, because we didn't think it was a good idea to do that much playing in one set.

We were a fuckin' funky bunch, between me being stoned on grass and everybody else doin' whatever the hell they were doin'. It's really a trip that most of the band is still here.

Danny was great . . . everybody loved Danny. I liked hangin' out with him, but what I really liked was makin' music with him. The very beginning of the first Crazy Horse was great. Great. *But there's no way to get that particular thing back. That's not gonna happen again.*

Young took Crazy Horse on the road immediately, in between the January and March 1969 recording dates and again in May. Talbot remembers a test gig somewhere in the Valley. "It was a typical gig, Neil Young–style. Nobody knew we were playin' there."

Young had already hit the road solo for a few dates the previous October and November. On November 10, at the end of a two-day gig at the Canterbury House in Ann Arbor, Michigan, he made his first known live recordings as a solo artist, which resulted in the definitive "Clancy" and the "Sugar Mountain" that would soon become a B-side staple.

At the end of January and in early February, he appeared solo in Canada, first at Le Hibou coffeehouse, then for a six-day stand at his old haunt, the Riverboat in Toronto. The Canadian shows were all taped and contain a number of gems, particularly a note-perfect "Flying on the Ground Is Wrong."

"The Riverboat series is very important, unquestionably," said archivist Joel Bernstein. "Neil has that very innocent, soft voice that is not really present in the Springfield. His guitar playing has improved immensely. I think he was really comfortable being solo, playing in small clubs—he doesn't have an urge to be in a group, he doesn't want somebody singing harmony—he's retelling all the Buffalo Springfield songs in a way that's very poignant."

But a band would join Young directly after these shows, at the Bitter End in New York City, beginning February 12. Young would do a short acoustic set, then Crazy Horse would crowd onto the Bitter End's tiny stage. To hear intimate acoustic performances—followed by Young and the Horse bashing away at as yet unreleased jams like "Down by the River"—must have been mind-bending.

Ken Viola recalled seeing the band play to a handful of people on the bottom of a quadruple bill (topped by Deep Purple) at New York's Felt Forum in May. "Hearing Crazy Horse was like standing on a mountaintop and breathing in all that fresh air. It almost hurt to experience it, it was so pure."

Playing dives, the Horse stayed in cheap motels, splitting the meager take after gigs, Susan and Neil cooking in their room. Ralph Molina remembers playing a high school gym in San Diego where Young was too stoned to go on. "Neil was lying back in the locker room, man, and he was paralyzed. They had to make an announcement." One night at a Mafia gambling joint in Providence, Rhode Island, the band got so gone playing

"Cowgirl" that they didn't even notice a drunken brawl had emptied the house. "It was really groovy," Young said of the tour to Tony Pig. "Six weeks on the road and not one argument."

Innocent, happy times, but they wouldn't last. Toward the end of the Crazy Horse tour, a couple of visitors showed up—Stephen Stills, along with CSN drummer Dallas Taylor. Stills came to talk to Young about going on the road with his new outfit. "After our set, they'd sit in with Neil," said Molina. "They wanted Neil bad." What happened next would hot-wire Young's career and test the sanity of everyone involved. "How can I bring you to this sea of madness?" Young would sing on one of the few CSNY tunes that kind of rocked. "I love you so much, it's gonna bring me sadness."

the guy with the balls

"That boy can flat *yap*," said David Briggs, exhausted after a session with Joel Bernstein. There are those who will forever see Bernstein as the kid, the fan who crossed over, and his ability to endlessly pontificate can send the more-you-think-the-more-you-stink members of Young's tribe over the edge. Bernstein's devotion to his heroes has led to a sometimes lonely life. "Joel hasn't been able to mate," said Joni Mitchell. "Part of it is, he's the court historian."

Bernstein was fifteen when he discovered Joni Mitchell doing "Circle Game" on a Philadelphia radio station in 1967. "It was way past my bedtime. I'd never heard a song in a nonstandard tuning before, and I taped it on my dad's Dictaphone. I stayed up all night learning to play it."

When the unknown Mitchell came to play a small local coffeehouse, Bernstein was there. "He was still in braces," she said. "His mother used to take him to the club and pick him up." Joel began to haunt Mitchell's East Coast gigs and, being an aspiring photographer, took reams of pictures. By 1969, Elliot Roberts was summoning him to document Mitchell's Carnegie Hall gig and Neil Young's appearance at the Bitter End. Five days into Joel's college education, Mitchell called, asking him to fly out to Los Angeles to take publicity shots. He fled school and moved to Topanga Canyon. Bernstein had memorized his musical heroes' every move, down to the weird ways they tuned guitars. "Joel did my tunings," said Mitchell. "Then everybody wanted him."

Bernstein went on to work with Dylan, Prince and scores of others, but it is Neil Young with whom he's stayed the longest. His technical knowledge of Young's work is unassailable; if Neil farted in a bathtub in 1964, Bernstein knows the date, location and whether it was recorded in stereo.

At the time I started this book, Neil called Joel in to start work on the

Archives boxed set, and, sentenced to dealing with each other, we fought like cats and dogs. What a fucking know-it-all, I thought, and a longhaired folkie to boot. To him I was Mark David Chapman with a pen.

But like so many other odd couples in Young's orbit, we became allies. We shared war wounds: While Neil had given his blessing to both projects, he seemed to delight in throwing as many obstacles our way as possible. Joel would hit the wall more than once with Young on Archives, just as there were long periods when Neil refused to talk to me at all.

I thought Joel might help me appreciate CSNY, like Ken Viola had with Buffalo Springfield, but after experiencing his idols up close, and wading through a mountain of archival tapes, Bernstein had seen his teenage worship give way to deep disappointment. His final analysis: "Bombastic, self-absorbed superstar group that showed great promise and had, in fact, some moments of gelling. But ultimately? A failure."

> *At that time I was really excited, because I hadn't been doin' really well. I had a couple of records out, neither one was really too successful,* Neil Young *and* Everybody Knows This Is Nowhere, *and neither one of them were doin' super-good, y'know, and then I joined Crosby, Stills and Nash and did that tour with them and my records started takin' off—*Everybody Knows *started doin' better and better, hung in there for a really long time. So I guess it helped me on all levels, joining them. Besides making what I thought was really great music that was really getting me off, more people were getting to know me as an artist and get interested in what I was doing. So it was a really good thing for me.*
> —Radio interview with B. Mitchell Reid, 1973

"I'll never forget our ride in the limo on the way to see Neil," said Dallas Taylor, recalling a 1969 Crazy Horse gig on Long Island they were crashing. "Stephen said, 'How would you feel about Neil joining the band?' 'Wow, great—except isn't that why the Springfield broke up?' He said, 'Oh, no, man—it's gonna be different this time. It'll be cool.' But there was this tone of doubt in his voice."

With their debut album topping the charts, Crosby, Stills and Nash were faced with the necessity of performing live—a bit of a problem, since so much of the record had been overdubbed by one-man-band Stills. Crosby and Nash wanted to keep the live presentation acoustic, but Stills had a fatal desire to hear the trio rock. Many possible musicians had been discussed and even approached before Ahmet Ertegun, at dinner with Stills and David Geffen, suggested the obvious choice: Neil Young.

At first Young was wanted only as a sideman. Ever the master manipulator, Elliot Roberts laid down the law: full partnership, equal songs. "He'd have to be a Y," Roberts demanded. Graham Nash balked. "We'd spent a lotta time getting this beautiful harmonic sound together. I mean, Jesus Christ, wasn't the album a huge multiplatinum success? I didn't feel like we *needed* anybody else."

Nash had never spent time around the reclusive Young, so the pair met to discuss matters over breakfast in New York City at Bleecker Street Café, near where the group was already in rehearsal. Young charmed Nash instantly. "Neil absolutely won me over. I came out of that breakfast two eggs over easy."

This put Neil Young in an amazing position: He could reap the hype benefits of a smash album he didn't even play on and in the process expose a gigantic audience to his own music. "CSNY was definitely not hurting Neil," said Roberts. "Neil never had a downside in any of this, never. It could only help us. What we were asked to do is take something soft and give it balls. . . . Neil's got balls dripping from his shoulders, there's balls in his hair, there's balls comin' down his back—he's got balls everywhere."

Young was definitely the guy with the balls. He gutted one band— the Rockets—to create his own, then walked into a supergroup with full membership status and continued to work with Crazy Horse. "Neil made it clear that CSN was not his first priority," said Roberts. "The *work* was the priority. So the seeds of discontent were always there."

Once Young was in the group, his power continued to swell. "As soon as they started to rehearse, it was clear Neil was gonna be in charge," said Roberts. "Everyone was afraid of Neil. Because Neil walked. When Neil said, 'Fuck you, I'm leaving,' Neil *left*. Everyone else goes, 'Fuck you, I'm leaving,' and they go to the bathroom, roll a joint and come back. But when Neil said anything, he did it. He really *did* back out of Monterey. And this was terrifying to these guys, because they were full of that—every other thing was 'I'm not playing, I'm not showing.' Like little kids. Neil wasn't into that. It was serious business."

All CSNY needed now was a bass player. Bruce Palmer was in the band briefly but was unable to stomach the ego parade and was deemed too unreliable by Nash and Crosby. On Sunset Boulevard one day Young ran into Rick James, his old friend from the Mynah Birds. With him was a fresh-faced kid named Greg Reeves.* A protégé of Motown bass legend James Jamerson, Reeves had been making $38 a week as a session man on such hits as the Temptations' "Cloud Nine" before heading to California. Both Reeves and James had just been fired from Ray Charles's studio after the blind musician's manager caught the pair rolling Charles a joint. Reeves auditioned for CSNY, and his fiery, idiosyncratic playing won the band over.

But Reeves, who told me that he lied about his age and was practically prepubescent at the time he joined the group—would have a hard time making his way through the vortex of rock stardom. He took to wearing capes onstage and casting spells on whoever entered his hotel room. "Greg went completely bats," said Crosby. "He decided he didn't like being a handsome young black kid. He was gonna be an Indian. Then he was gonna be a witch doctor."

"Greg Reeves we all loved," said Roberts. "Neil especially liked him, because he was so crazy. He had the same balls that Neil had—from second one, he was in your face rocking—but he was really a psycho. Greg had this sack with his sacred feather that he did all his prayers with. And coming into London, the customs guy wanted to look in his feather bag and grabbed it out of Greg's hands. Greg said, 'This is sacred stuff—my God, you've desecrated it! OOMAH! OOMAH!' And he starts dancing and chanting. We're all in line, and now they're coming from all angles—and we all had grass. Everybody was arrested."

Drummer Dallas Taylor and Young would never quite mesh. "Neil would freeze him with a glance," said Elliot Roberts. "You rush one or two

---

*"When Bruce Palmer found out I was takin' his job, he flipped right out," said Greg Reeves. "He swung a guitar at me. [CSNY] gave him a D45 guitar with mother-of-pearl inlay and $5,000. I felt bad for him." Neil Young on Palmer: "He couldn't learn the songs fast enough, and they didn't have the patience. He was kind of a rough runner—always made a few mistakes, like Billy [Talbot] does. Didn't stop me."

times with Neil, and he glares at you. He gets *in your face*—he doesn't, like, *hope* you're seeing him from across the stage—he goes up to the drum kit and does the time for you. And you're embarrassed. When Neil glared at people—much bigger people who could kill him, and I knew a lamb chop could hurt Neil—they backed down. When he glared at you, it was like 'WAAAAAAGHHHH! UGGGHHHH!' "

Four singer/songwriters with a rhythm section: CSNY was now complete, but it would never be a cohesive musical unit. As Graham Nash stated, "I never considered Greg or Dallas part of CSNY. I considered them hired hands—always."

Equally tenuous for some was Neil Young's place in the outfit. His presence certainly increased the supergroup hype factor, but many felt the addition was aesthetically wrong. Young could spin out lightweight pop as well as the next guy, but for the most part his talents ran to the deeper, darker side of things. "It was like Muddy Waters sitting in with the Rolling Stones," said writer Richard Meltzer. "Crosby, Stills and Nash is great, but why did they ask Neil to join?" said Chris Hillman. "It didn't make any sense to me."

—*Lie to me and tell me you joined Crosby, Stills and Nash for the money.*
It was Stills. Stephen came out and asked me to play in the band. I said, "Sure—we can do somethin' as good as the Springfield was." That's what I was lookin' for. But I never really got that. That was gone.

Ahmet and all those guys found out what it would be like with me in it, as opposed to without *me. We went through a little period where they were tryin' to decide if my name should be on it. At the beginning, when Stephen came and asked me to play with them—he never really put it to me that it was gonna make it CSN and Y—but he never said it wouldn't, either.*

Stephen's heart wasn't in it being just CSN—that's how I feel about it—but Graham's probably was. Y'know, they had already done this big hit record. What the fuck do they need me for? That's the way they were lookin' at it. Now—if my name hadn't been on it, and I'd been another guitar player in CSN, that woulda worked out great. But when they found out what they needed me for, *then it became a different thing. They all realized if they were gonna have to have* me *there, they were gonna have to say I was there. Or I wasn't gonna be there.*

CSNY was pretty good—some nights it was really good—but we had a little trouble staying *good after the beginning. It was always a little too much. I was kinda like a third foot in that band. I loved those guys. We went through a lot of shit together. And we were into it—but we were into it for ourselves as well. Everybody was tryin' to do their own thing. I don't think it was ever supposed to be a band. It* wasn't *a band. That wasn't ever a part of it. It's like the Mamas and Papas weren't a band, either.*

So it didn't work. But we tried. I had some good times with 'em, especially with Crosby. Crosby's a great singer. I learned a little bit about singing from CSN, but their sense of harmony and my sense of harmony were not quite the same. I heard things a different way.

Live, it was more exciting, because Stills and I had somethin' goin' on. When he was on I was on, and we were happening, it was a great thing. Because Stills and I still had memories of Buffalo Springfield— how great that was, that we could take that farther. We tried to re-create it, but it never really happened. Instead of havin' one guy who was pretty laid-back, didn't really play a lot—Richie Furay—we had two guys who didn't really play electric guitar at all. Crosby and Graham, they were both acoustic-guitar players. Strap on an electric and it just kinda got in the way of Stephen and I. There was never enough room.

*It had to be during the 1970 CSNY tour that I somehow got turned on to Coltrane, 'cause I had a Sony cassette player and some John Coltrane—*My Favorite Things, Equinox—*and I used to listen to that shit* all *the time. Nice melodies, the bass player was really good . . . I thought Coltrane was great.*

It gave me refuge. I would go into my room, turn up my jazz records really loud and nobody would come in there. Not that I didn't wanna see 'em, but sometimes I'm just not ready. I have to get ready to see people. I do okay for small amounts of time with spontaneous visits—after a while I gotta get back in my hole and have that long tunnel so I can see people comin'.
—*What's that about?*

I dunno. That's the way I feel comfortable. Maybe I'm shy. It's just the way I am.

"A bunch of dopes in the mud not even paying attention," said Richard Meltzer of Woodstock. He left on the first day. "Woodstock was just the first time the middle class got hip to the whole rock scene. By the time you had that many people doing it in one place, it was closer to an Alan Freed show . . . it was minus the sixties consciousness. It was just entertainment value." Ken Viola, also present, was similarly disenchanted. "As a communal event it was a big success. But I remember being at Woodstock and saying, 'It's over.' "*

Crosby, Stills, Nash and Young's first two live performances were on August 16, 1969, in Chicago. To give an idea of how big the hype around them was, Joni Mitchell—already an established artist who had played Carnegie Hall—opened for them. ("Neil took me aside and said they should be opening for me," said Mitchell. "He was kind.") Just two days later, CSNY joined The Who, Jimi Hendrix, the Band and Sly and the Family Stone at Woodstock, and despite the competition, many felt it was CSNY's gig. As Grace Slick told writer Dave Zimmer, "They represented the Woodstock sound—whatever that is." They would also later record a cover of Joni Mitchell's "Woodstock," which Young complained Stills overdubbed the juice out of. In hindsight it seems appropriate: an overblown performance of an overblown song for an overblown event.

Although Crosby, Stills and Nash's overwrought performance is intact, Young—who played only two of his compositions, "Mr. Soul" and "Wonderin' "—isn't seen in the *Woodstock* documentary (although he's more than occasionally visible in recently surfaced outtakes). "To this day, I have no idea why Neil did not want to be part of that," said Nash, indicating a real lack of awareness of what Young's all about.

---

*One musician would be conspicuously absent from the event. "Woodstock—I didn't want to be part of that thing," Bob Dylan said in 1975. "I liked the town. I felt they exploited the shit out of that, goin' up there and gettin' fifteen million people all in the same spot. That don't excite me. The flower generation—is that what it was? I wasn't into that at all. I just thought it was a lot of kids out and around wearing flowers in their hair, takin' a lot of acid. I mean, what *can* you think about that?"

The CSNY phenomenon spread across America like an unchecked virus, but for many observers they peaked as a live entity during their first concert dates, from August 1969 to January 1970. Everyone had new songs, the egos and drug habits hadn't mushroomed out of control. An audience tape from their seven-day stand in Los Angeles at the Greek Theatre contains an understated acoustic version of Young's "I've Loved Her So Long" with Nash providing stunning harmony, showing how effective Young could be within this configuration. Electrically, things tended toward the grandiose, as evidenced by their first TV performance, a live "Down by the River" for *The Music Scene* taped in September. Fans of the outfit revere this performance, but the bombastic Stills/Young guitar duels and the hopped-up vocals leave me yearning for the simplicity and spook of the Horse.

September 6 also brought a surreal appearance on the *This Is Tom Jones* variety show, featuring Jones himself bellowing lead vocal on Crosby's "Long Time Gone." "It was very highly rated, sold a lotta records, but in retrospect it was embarrassing, just a bad call," said Elliot Roberts. "Neil went, '*The Tom Jones Show!* What possessed you? It's that shit.' He always used to say 'that shit.' Crosby had this weed of doom . . . Neil never forgave me for that. He ripped me about it for a very, very long time. Years."

Footage of the Big Sur Festival from September 13 provides another prime cut of unintentional CSNY hilarity. Some nut in the audience starts to harangue CSNY for being rich rock stars, and Stills, who would later explain that he was in a sour state because the group was playing for free, bolts from the stage, high as a kite in an outrageous fur coat, and goes after the guy as Crosby pleads for "Peace and love, peace and love" over the microphone. After an embarrassing tussle, Stills returns to the stage and launches into a muddled apology. "Y'know, we think about what that guy was sayin' and we look at these fur coats and pretty guitars and fancy cars and say, 'Wow, man, what am I doin'?' "

That December, CSNY would provide the only comic relief at the event Richard Meltzer describes as "the evil embodiment of Woodstock"— Altamont, infamous, of course, for the death of audience member Meredith Hunter. CSNY provided a moment of absurdity before things turned murderous.

What was really memorable for me about that gig was, the CSN portion of it was just fuckin' nuts. I'll just give you a picture, okay? These gigs were all ridiculously unorganized, and we showed up there and there was no way to get to the stage. We were on the other side of the crowd. So we get this pickup truck, and we're driving this pickup truck through the crowd. I think everybody was pretty high. Crosby and Stills were standing on the front of the truck or on the running boards, yelling, "CROSBY STILLS NASH AND YOUNG!" Just like, y'know . . . parting the sea.

I thought it was Fellini-esque. I mean, he's standing there yelling the name of the band in the crowd—how much fuckin' recognition do you need?

A lotta times CSNY was pretty crazy, and I couldn't understand why. Maybe it had more to do with drugs than I realized. I mean, everybody was, like, toasted. I *wasn't doing drugs, but drugs were starting to surface in other places—and were having a negative impact, I might add. Was I naïve? I think so. Crosby'd probably be laughing like hell if he heard that. He'd be rolling around goin', "Maybe you were a little naïve . . . that's all right, Bernard."*

See, Crosby's a real person. I always like to be with him. Crosby's the heart and soul of the whole thing. CSNY was at its best when Crosby was right there in the middle of it. Crosby's a musical guy. He loves to play music, show ya his songs, talk about words. It's real important to him. He's an individual who has his own point of view. It's so refreshing, somebody so much on their trip. You can count on Crosby.

Big Sur was funny. Stills went nuts. I don't know what the fuck happened—he picked a fight with somebody in the audience. *Oh man, so many crazy things happened—what the fuck was going on? What the fuck were they doing? I still have no idea.*

—What effect did Woodstock have on music?

That's when the market got big enough for the marketers to realize that they should go for it. They could isolate this whole group of people, target them as a consumer group—and they did. They used the music. That was the beginning of rock and roll being used in commercials. That's the long-term effect.

Woodstock was a bullshit gig. A piece of shit. We played fuckin' awful. No one was into the music. I think Stephen was way overboard into this huge crowd. Everybody was on this Hollywood trip with the fuckin' cameras. They weren't playin' to the audience as much as to the cameras—these fuckin' cameramen were all over the stage. It was a distraction.

I thought TV was a sellout. You get used to it after a while, and you even start getting into filming things to keep a record of it, but at first I never thought of being filmed while I was playin', and I could see everybody changing their performances for the fucking camera and I thought that was bullshit. All these assholes filming, everybody's carried away with how cool they are. . . . I wasn't moved. I wouldn't let them film me, that's why I'm not in the movie. I said, "One of you fuckin' guys comes near me and I'm gonna fuckin' hit you with my guitar. I'm playing music. Just leave me out." Peace, love and flowers. That's where I was at when we did Woodstock. So I was there . . . but I wasn't. I left an imprint.

You gotta look at these events in rock and roll history as shit, okay? Woodstock was a big piece of shit, and there have been several pieces of shit all the way down the line since the beginning of rock and roll—it's all waste.

The event is nothing. It's what made *the event happen—which is no longer where the event* is. *The event is the leftovers—it happens so the entity, the spirit, or what made the shit happen can move on.*

So all these events, no matter what the hell they are, are nothing. What is meaningful is what is left and gone beyond that. So all we have is people standing around a pile of shit, looking at it. You wouldn't expect the thing that shit to go back and sit in the shit, would you?

The sudden, monstrous success of CSNY unleashed the demons within. "Stephen and I were druggies together," said Crosby. "Cocaine, acid and pot. In Neil's case it wasn't coke—that was never his drug—but me and Stills just went right out the window on it."

Poor Stephen. Stills was now the superstar he always wanted to be, but unfortunately he had invited company. "After a long CSN set, they'd leave and Neil would come on by himself," Elliot Roberts recalled. "From then on it was 'Wow, who's the heavy guy with these three poseurs?' " Young's seemingly effortless ability to control situations sent Stills over the edge. "Neil started making all the decisions, all the calls. Stephen would speak and then everyone would look at Neil. It killed Stephen, who had started it all. It still always shocks me that it was Stephen's call to invite Neil back into the fold when he knew he wouldn't be able to intimidate him."

"Stephen was always intensely, obviously, juvenilely competitive with Neil," said Crosby. "He always wanted to be better than Neil but never could. Neil would never respond at the same level. Stephen would get loud, Neil would be loud enough to be heard, but he'd make a joke out of it. Stephen would have stacks of Marshall amps and Neil would have two little tiny amps and be *louder*. It would drive Stephen crazy."

With drugs fueling his paranoia, Stills would stretch his live CSNY solo segments by way of an excruciating, endless piano medley of "49 Bye-Byes" and "For What It's Worth," complete with topical Nixon/Agnew references. "Stephen overplayed," said Roberts, who frequently clashed with Stills. "He was so high he was missing notes. . . . He would destroy himself by thinking, 'This is how I get on top, this is how I get on top.' . . . You knew Stephen was tortured. You felt sorry for Stephen all the time."

Larry Kurzon told a story about Stills in England after the tour. "Stills was dyin' to play with Paul McCartney. He just bought a Ferrari to go see McCartney. Stills paid cash for it, $12,500 cash in a shoe box. I led him to McCartney's house. It was teeming out, an unbelievable Friday night in London where it was rainin' like the world was comin' down. I said, 'Ring the bell, he'll either answer or he won't answer. You gotta ring the bell, I ain't playin' groupie.' McCartney never answered the door. I left him there in the pouring rain with his brand-new Ferrari. Three days later he totalled it."

"Do I think that cocaine destroyed CSNY? Absolutely," Neil Young told Nick Kent. "Cocaine and ego."

> *I'm trying to make records of the quality of the records that were made in the late fifties and the sixties, the Everly Brothers and Roy Orbison records and things like that . . . It's just a quality about them, the singer is into the song and the musicians were playing with the singer and it was an entity, y'know. It was something special that used to hit me all the time, that all*

these people were thinking the same thing and they're all play-
ing at the same time.
—Interview with Elliot Blinder, 1970

Thinking the same thing, playing at the same time. Listen to Young and the Horse's 1969 version of Don Gibson's 1958 country hit "Oh Lonesome Me" and you can feel what Neil is talking about. Gibson's classic original is smooth, up-tempo country; Young's version is doom-laden, funereal. From his crying bursts on the harmonica—WAAAAH!WAAAAH!—to Ralphie's hit-you-in-the-gut kick drum on the breaks, to Young's withering bee-sting solo at the song's climax, this is astonishing stuff. "I've thought of everything from A to Z," wails Young, sounding ready to crack.

"You could compare CSNY to the Beatles and Crazy Horse to the Stones," Young said to writer Gary Kenton in 1970. "Another thing I'll tell you: The Rolling Stones are my favorite group." Young went on to add, "The CSNY thing supports Crazy Horse. Without the other trip, Crazy Horse wouldn't be doing this . . . that's why I joined."

In the early seventies, CSNY was omnipotent, inescapable. *Rolling Stone* and the rest of the burgeoning rock media fawned over their every move—throughout Young's seventies interviews, the emphasis was on CSNY. Crazy Horse just didn't exist—there's no press, no filmed performances, hardly any good live tapes and no real interviews with Danny Whitten. They were invisible—a point that, in retrospect, seems in their favor. Young could toil in the shadows, making great music with the Horse, while the universe hung on CSNY.

Although most of the music remains unreleased, the studio recordings from Sunset Sound/Larrabee/Topanga and the taped live shows from the Fillmore in March 1970—the great lost period of the original Horse lineup—is some of the finest rock and roll ever made.

Recorded, unbelievably enough, during the day while Young was rehearsing with CSNY at night, this music was completely different from the garage mysticism of *Everybody Knows*—short songs, countryish, more traditionally based, perhaps in a tiny way reminiscent of the Band. These sessions would begin Young's long-standing tradition of recording during a full moon. "There are certain times to record," Young would tell writer John Rockwell in 1977. "For the longest time I only recorded on a full moon, and it always had the same intensity. . . . Everybody would get crazy."

Young and the Horse cut "Everybody's Alone," "Oh Lonesome Me," "Wonderin'," "I Believe in You," "Birds," an exquisite version of Whitten's "Look at All the Things," as well as an epic ballad called "Helpless" that failed to make it to tape. "We were doing it live, everybody playing and singing at once, and we did about an eight- or nine-minute version of it . . . with a long instrumental in the middle," Young told writer Jean-Charles Costa. "And the engineer didn't press the button down. It was much more free than anything I've done onstage."

Young's live singing on these sessions is completely unrestrained, gut-wrenching, and the instrumentation is exquisite: just Danny, Billy and Ralph, with Neil on guitar and piano, plus a few tasteful overdubs— ringing acoustic guitars, muted electric solos placed low in the mix and spare touches of vibes (not the first instrument that comes to mind when you think of the Horse) that add the spook to everything.

"Songs are supposed to be heroic enough to give the illusion of stopping time," Bob Dylan once said. Well, "I Believe in You" knocks the clock off the wall every time. Ralphie smacks out a sad, empty drumbeat—it sounds like he's back to banging cardboard boxes, for chrissakes—and Young comes in with that eeriest of first lines, "Now that you've found yourself losin' your mind, are you here again?" The song creeps along, and as Young picks out a forlorn note on the piano—dit-dit-dit—he utters a question unspeakable in any relationship: "How can I place you above me? Am I lyin' to you when I say"—now the piano ascends dramatically—"I believe in you." He moans over and over, his voice soaring to unearthly heights, a singing apparition, the Horse la-la-la-ing in the background. The sound of Neil with Danny and Ralph on harmonies . . . I've never heard anything remotely like it. As for those pained by Young's voice, on this track I'd put him up against Elvis, Roy Orbison, *anybody.*

What emotions come to mind listening to "I Believe in You"? Fear, paralysis, complete doom. Just because you believe in somebody doesn't mean you're going to stay with them, and one wonders what thoughts went through Susan Young's mind the first time she heard this little ditty. The honesty with which Young addresses his own will chills me to the bone. As Young wrote of the song in his 1977 *Decade* liner notes, "I think this gets to the heart of the matter and as Danny Whitten once said, 'I don't want to talk about it.' " Powerful, raw stuff, some of the best—and already some of the last—the original Crazy Horse would make. Unfortunately, Young returned to the CSNY circus, and while it was a jackpot in terms of exposure, in terms of his art it paid meager dividends, as his first venture into the studio with the lineup would attest.

· · ·

In October 1969, Young joined his infinitely more famous friends at Wally Heider's San Francisco studio to record the album known as *Déjà Vu*. The band stayed at the Caravan Lodge Motel, a dump in the middle of the Tenderloin district. Young was accompanied by Harriet and Speedy, two bush babies purchased from a Topanga pet store that unsettled Nash. "Neil never had his room cleaned because the maids wouldn't go in. You'd be talking to Neil, and all of a sudden this thing would go BING! and leap right across the room onto his shoulder. You know how dogs start to look like their owners? Neil started to look like these fuckin' bush babies. It was insane."

Emotionally it was not a good time for CSN. Stills was reeling from a breakup with Judy Collins; Nash and Joni Mitchell were about to go kaflooie; and Crosby had lost his girlfriend, Christine Hinton, in a head-on car collision. He began missing sessions, snorting heroin. "I would come into the studio, just sit on the floor and cry," said Crosby. "It wasn't a big upper."

Dealing with Neil Young in the studio presented its own problems. "Trying to get through *Déjà Vu* was a nightmare," said Dallas Taylor. "See, the formula that we hit on during the first record—with Stephen in the driver's seat—worked. That didn't work when Neil came into the picture. You can't have two presidents."

"Neil was very Neil during *Déjà Vu*," said Nash. "He never played us all his songs—he was obviously doing his own solo record—and he would take his CSNY tracks down to the studio, do overdubs and mix 'em himself. Once again, it's part of Neil's insatiable quest for control. I was physically moved to tears at least once."

Only one non-Young cut would be done as a live band track—Crosby's "Almost Cut My Hair," a hippie meltdown expressing fear of the barber's chair that has an Ed Wood Jr.–like intensity. Most of the recordings reek of Overdub City, which Young bitched about in the press—a criticism Nash felt was two-faced. "If it's so fucking much to have the band in one room playing, why did Neil do all the overdubs on 'Country Girl' himself? He's full of shit." Recording dragged on, with Stills grandly claiming that *Déjà Vu* took eight hundred hours of studio time to make. "Eight ten-hour days," Young later cracked to his father.

One can't deny *Déjà Vu*'s outrageous commercial success—upon its release in March 1970, it shipped two million copies—but it contained little of what made CSN's first album unique. The one great pleasure is the cut Young failed to capture with the Horse, "Helpless," a ballad so spare not even Crosby, Stills and Nash could muck it up. William S. Burroughs once said, "The function of art and all creative thought is to make us aware of what we know and don't know we know. You can't tell anybody anything he doesn't know already." Primordial, aching, trancelike, "Helpless" is something you already know, and it makes you believe Young is only the messenger of his work. It's the only one of his songs I could actually imagine Otis Redding singing.

The rest of *Déjà Vu* sounds like a lead turd by comparison. "I remember being very disappointed by that record and feeling it was overblown and pompous," said Joel Bernstein. The extravagant leatherette paper cover said it all—an old-timey photo of the group as sullen hippie aristocrats, decked out in period regalia. It was a long way from Little Richard and Chuck Berry.

But the money rolled in. Dallas Taylor, who went from wretched poverty to paying for Porsches with fistfuls of cash, tasted the ennui of stardom. "I can remember one night after one of our better shows, watchin' our roadies Bruce and Guillermo packin' up the equipment and putting everything in cases. I just wished they could pack me away in a case until the next show.

"What started out as our goal to be the world's greatest rock and roll band became trying to be the world's richest rock and roll band. It seemed to happen overnight. In the beginning, nothing mattered but the music. Then nothing mattered but the money. Once that happens, you're doomed."

I think that Crosby, Stills and Nash made great records. Crosby, Stills, & Nash *is better than* Déjà Vu. *"Country Girl" is overblown. It's over-done. It's my fault . . . parts of* Déjà Vu *are as good—but they're the parts that I'm not on.*

The rest of it . . . I don't really know what to say. Dallas was right.

The best records were when Stephen and Dallas were making the tracks. They really had a unified thing happening. My thing was "We gotta play it live. We gotta play it together," and that was like, fuck, it didn't fit. Different approach. That's okay. CSN is still together.

—What do you think of the Crazy Horse Sunset Sound sessions?

The electric version of "Birds" with vibes turned out to be great, but it was only half the song. After the first verse I stopped. "Wow, that's great." "Neil—you stopped." Forgot the second verse, heh heh. Good shit. If I hadn't been distracted by the CSNY thing, I probably would've made a whole record like that. But things have a way of doing what they do.

—How did the Horse feel about you and CSN?

Hey, lemme put it this way—it didn't bother them at all. It wasn't the same on the other side.

—Did you explain it to CSN?

No. Crazy Horse was hard for anybody to understand when I was in CSNY. CSN couldn't understand. "What the fuck do you need Crazy Horse for?" There was very little understanding of what the hell was I doing with these people. Why would I waste my time? CSN were fulfilled with what they were doing, and I guess they couldn't understand why I wasn't. But I had already had this other thing going before and I wasn't gonna give it up. I had to keep going. I liked it. Everybody Knows was good, because even though CSN thought it was no good—it wasn't, like, theirs, it wasn't CSN—in the long run, it hung in there. It stayed on the charts. It was like, y'know, a constant reminder to them.

All the different ways that I could express myself with all these different groups of people . . . I had twice as many possibilities as the other guys. But CSN had their own thing. And y'know, it's funny how many more people liked that. Isn't that funny?

—Speedy and Harriet made quite an impression on Graham Nash.

I bet they did. Go back to my room and there're MONKEYS in there. I was ahead of Michael Jackson on that one.
—Your spare taste in drums might not have been Dallas Taylor's trip.
It was *his trip at five o'clock in the morning after playing "Helpless" about sixteen times. . . . I had to wait until it was real late and keep on playin' it with 'em for a* long *time. They got so fuckin' tired, everybody got slowed down—they could actually play it without goin'. . . too fast.*

Dallas couldn't play my shit for crap. That was hard for me, because I liked Dallas. He had to work to play my stuff, 'cause he had to lay back. I really gave him a rough time. It was like he felt I shouldn't be in CSN, and I felt like he couldn't play my music. It's funny—I didn't even know he was on junk at the time or I woulda said, "Go out and get high—because it might slow you down a little." Dallas really was Stephen's drummer, so they had their thing goin'. And their thing was playin' a lotta notes, okay? I'd been playin' with Ralph. It was a different thing.

The Crazy Horse "Helpless" was just like all those other ones at Sunset Sound—it had the big cymbals, guitars. When I missed recording it with Crazy Horse, I took that as an omen. I said, "Well, that's why I did it with CSN."

When Briggs and I started workin' together, I was harder than Briggs about certain things. *About people hangin' out in the studio. About rolling from the very beginning, not stopping the tape in between takes. As soon as I started figurin' out where I was really at and started to grow as a performer in the studio, I said, "Let's not stop. We just gotta keep on goin'. I don't wanna wait for anybody—it's time to go." So that's when we started rolling tape all the time, getting sounds. And that's because I was an* animal *if we didn't get it. I don't know why the fuckin' machine wasn't on when we did that great take of "Helpless," anyway. What's the use of havin' a machine, paying thousands of dollars, if you don't turn the fuckin' thing* on. *People who save tape* piss me off. *Savin' tape. Fuck. Why do you have to fuckin' get all into music and then stop and talk about whether you're recording or not? I always figured,* record *everything. The only time they should mention it is when it's* not on. *But it's not a perfect world. A lotta people miss the opportunity to record something great waiting for it to start.*

"They have no sense at all of being onstage," said exotic folk-pop singer Buffy Sainte-Marie to Jack Nitzsche after watching Young and the Horse play the Fillmore East. "That's Crazy Horse," said Jack. "Whatever clothes they woke up in, they wear onstage."

Compared to the CSNY extravaganza, Crazy Horse was gutter trash— pot, pills and a couple bottles of cheap red wine. Joel Bernstein recalls the vibe: "I'm a white kid from Philadelphia. At the time, the band members seemed kind of quasi-criminal to me." Whitten gave the teenager a joint, which Bernstein smoked, "and the next thing I knew I was on the floor in a fetal position, stupefied."

In February and March 1970, Young would do a tour of small theaters with the Horse, augmenting the band with an explosive new player: Jack Nitzsche. Nitzsche—one of the very, very few "professional" musicians who doesn't spook the Horse—played electric rhythm piano, and his sparse, soulful notes added just the right color to new songs like "Winter-long" and "It Might Have Been," an ancient ballad Young had learned at a church dance. Nitzsche wasn't a Horse fan and quickly grew tired of their limitations. "Billy used to say, 'Crazy Horse isn't a band, we're a basket-ball team,'" said Jack. "I tend to agree." But the interplay between Nitzsche and Whitten was electrifying. "Danny was the only black man in the band," reiterated Jack.

On March 6 and 7, the band played a quartet of sets at the Fillmore East, two of which were recorded for a projected live album, and these record-ings capture the Horse in all their glory, including a torrential version of "Down by the River" that more than matches the original studio take in in-tensity. Young's maniacal solos hint at future greatness as Nitzsche sup-plies a jazzy blues underpinning that's shockingly complex for the Horse.

Young sounds happily stoned out of his mind between songs, assigning band members all the wrong hometowns, prefacing "The Loner" by wryly quoting from a review of the single in *Cashbox* magazine: "This little ditty should send Young rising phoenix-like from the ashes of the Buffalo Springfield."

You can actually see it in a photo Bernstein snapped of the band on-stage: Head back and eyes closed as he wangs some brain-sick scream out of Old Black, Young looks lost in the stars. Behind the scenes, though, not everything was groovy. "C'mon, baby, let's go downtown," Whitten sings on his one contribution to the Fillmore shows, and he was alluding to the new passion in his life: heroin.*

At some point either a girlfriend or a roadie introduced Whitten to the narcotic and it quickly took over his life. His friend Terry Sachen felt Whitten had gone through such heavy transformations in his experiments with LSD that, when the sixties ended, "Danny could never close up. He predicted he would die before the age of thirty—he said that a few times. Danny was pained by life because people are so shitty. He needed a vacation from the world. It was just too much for Danny."

Ralph Molina said that Whitten nursed a persistent unhappiness over his role in the band. "Danny did say that Neil was holdin' him back. He was in the background and he didn't dig it. But he wasn't bad-mouthing anybody—he had more class than that."

Whitten's incredible talent went largely unrecognized, and it had to have stung. "During that period, I liked some of Danny's songs better than Neil's," said David Briggs. "Danny had some great songs—powerful, emotional music. I knew he was a star. I knew that *he* knew he was a star. Everyone around him knew he was a star, just the *people* didn't know he was a star. I remember tellin' him, 'Danny, you can't pick your own time—that's picked by other people for you—you just gotta keep being yourself.' Danny was a great guy. He was just a great *tortured* guy."

Whitten began nodding out, even onstage, which led to moments of black humor at the Fillmore. "I looked up from the piano and fuckin' Danny Whitten had stopped singing," said Nitzsche. "His eyes were closed and he had a real big smile . . . Danny was enjoying the show. Finally Neil just yelled at him—'Danny! SING!' " Backstage, according to Nitzsche, Young reamed out the rest of the band, yelling, "All right—who scored for

---

*In 2000, Young pointed out that his contribution to the song was the lines "Sure enough they'll be sellin' stuff when the moon begins to rise / Pretty bad when you're dealin' with the man and the light shines in your eyes." "Not that it matters now, but Danny was more subtle and I was more surface," he commented.

Danny?" "I wanted to say, '*Danny* did,' " said Jack. " 'Do you think any-body else in *this* band knows how to score smack in the middle of the night in Manhattan?' "

"I've seen the needle and the damage done / A little part of it in every-one," Young scrawled out on the road somewhere at the time. These days, after ten million performances, it is sometimes hard to appreciate "The Needle and the Damage Done" outside of its Official Cautionary Tale des-ignation, but in the early seventies next to no one (at least in song) was writing about the death-trip flip side of feelin' groovy; leave it to Young to shine a particularly bare light bulb on the urge for self-destruction. Randy Newman maintains that it's Young's greatest song.

Encouraged, no doubt, by Young's frequently downbeat demeanor, the public would so fixate on this song that whispers of heroin abuse would follow Neil for years—a ridiculous charge to anyone who knows him. Frank "Poncho" Sampedro, who would eventually replace Whitten in the Horse, recalls copping some heroin while driving around with Young in Europe in the mid-seventies. When he figured out what Poncho was up to, "Neil literally jumped out of the car," said Sampedro.

There would be no Horse for a few years, and Young would head off in another direction—much more singer/songwriterly, much less rock and roll. Crazy Horse was at the height of its powers, but Whitten was already slipping away. Once the tour finished, Neil fired the band.

We had a meeting at the Clear Thoughts building on La Cienega Boule-vard to try to bring things into focus. Those kind of things never help. I think it's been proven now that intervention is not a good idea. You can't stop someone from doing something by taking things away from them. That only makes them do it more. "Tough love," as Courtney Love would call it, doesn't work.

We knew what we had. We all knew it was really good. Then to see it get fucked up was really depressing. Seeing drugs come in and fuck it up, seeing the whole thing just go downhill. The inexperience of not knowing how to deal with heroin use, not knowing what it was, being too young for certain kinds of decisions. But that was the hand I was dealt at the time. The destruction of Danny's life . . .
—Heroin. What did you notice about that drug?

I noticed it killed people. I don't know much about it. It's the worst kind of drug. Heroin wasn't for me. I never tried it. I didn't see any reason to try it. I never shot up anything. It's not my deal. I never asked for it, it's never been offered.

I guess after I wrote a couple songs about it, then people who might've offered it . . . didn't.

•   •   •

"Neil was very aloof," said Dennis Hopper with admiration. "He had a princelike quality about him."

In the wake of *Easy Rider*'s success, Hopper had a deal at Universal "where, if I put up twenty-five thousand dollars, they'd match it." Dean Stockwell had been in Peru with Hopper making *The Last Movie* and took up his invitation to write a script.

"I was gonna write a movie that was personal, a Jungian self-discovery of the gnosis," said Stockwell. "It involved the Kabala, it involved a lot of arcane stuff." Though the *After the Gold Rush* script is currently missing, Shannon Forbes recalls that it involved a huge tidal wave coming to destroy Topanga. "It was sort of an end-of-the-world movie," she said. "At the very end, the hero is standing in the Corral parking lot watching this huge wave come in and this house is surfing along, and as the house comes at him, he turns the knob—and that's the end of the movie." Russ Tamblyn was to play an over-the-hill rocker living in a castle; others vaguely recall some scene of George Herms carrying a huge "tree of life" through the canyon.

Young got ahold of the script and told Stockwell he was interested in producing the soundtrack. "Neil told me he had a writer's-block thing, and Warner Bros. was after him to do something," said Stockwell. But it all came to naught once the studio executives paid a visit to Topanga. "These suits came out from Universal," recalls Tamblyn. "Dean was trying to show 'em around—'This is Janis Joplin, she's gonna be in the movie.' And the Universal guys were like 'Oh, swell—who are these jerks? Neil who?' "

None of this stopped Young—even though there wasn't a movie, he went ahead with the soundtrack. (Despite what the back cover said, Young, over twenty-five years later, could recall only two of *After the Gold Rush*'s cuts actually being inspired by the movie: the title cut and "Cripple Creek Ferry.")

Gold Rush would be the first album cut outside the confines of a commercial studio and the first featuring live vocals exclusively. The main sessions were recorded in the tiny basement studio of Young's house on Skyline Trail. Neighbor Louie Kelly and a couple of cronies carried a huge hunk of lead up the steep hill to soundproof the room. "We're lucky we're not dead from breathing the fumes," said Briggs, who would be sent over the edge more than once in fulfilling Young's whims. For these recordings, Young used players from CSNY and Crazy Horse: Ralph Molina on drums and Greg Reeves on bass (a move that Reeves said infuriated CSN). One new player was added to this nucleus—a diminutive, scrappy East Coast guitarist named Nils Lofgren.

· · ·

"I was a young kid, confident and arrogant in a nervous sort of way," said Lofgren, who at age seventeen snuck backstage at Young's 1969 Washington, D.C., appearance at the Cellar Door. Lofgren had been taught a few tricks on guitar by his neighbor, blues legend Roy Buchanan, and wanted Young's advice on how to get his band, Grin, into the record business. "Finally Neil just said, 'Well, if you think yer so hot, you must have some songs—why don't you play me some of 'em?' and handed me his Martin guitar," recalls Lofgren, who proceeded to perform what would end up being the first Grin album in its entirety.

Young took the musician under his wing, buying him a hamburger and Coke before the show. Lofgren—who really didn't know Young's work outside of Buffalo Springfield—panicked. "I was like, 'Oh my God, this guy's so nice, I hope I like his music.' " Young and the Horse live blew Lofgren away, and a few days later the teenager got a phone call. "My mom hands me the phone and said, 'It's some guy named Neil.' He said, 'Nils, I've just talked to Ahmet, and I think I can get you a record deal at Atlantic.' I'm like 'What did I do to deserve this guy?' It's been like that ever since."

A few weeks later, Lofgren flew to Los Angeles. "Neil never gave me his address—he just said, 'When you get there, look me up. I live in Topanga Canyon,' " said Lofgren, who, unable to get a lift hitchhiking with his huge suitcase and guitar, proceeded to walk the whole way. Arriving exhausted late that afternoon, he finally got someone to point out Young's home, then climbed the steep driveway only to find Neil about to get in his car. Young was typically nonchalant. "He said, 'Oh, Nils—great to see ya. I'm goin' into town to record. Why don't you come by tomorrow?' " Too shy to tell Young of his incredible journey, Nils turned around and hitchhiked back to L.A.

Soon Lofgren was staying in Topanga with David Briggs, who believed in the musician so wholeheartedly he would produce the first Grin sessions on spec without a record deal. Lofgren, who grew up in the suburbs of Maryland, recalls that his first night in Topanga was like something out of the Wild West. "David was in the kitchen with Louie Kelly, Danny Tucker and Billy Gray playing cards. Booze, cigarettes, piles of money. *Serious* gamblers."

Sprawled out on a mattress on the floor of the next room watching this surreal scene as he drifted off to sleep, Lofgren noticed "somethin' movin' on the floor, crawlin' towards me. I realize it's a scorpion. I freak out, screaming, 'David, what the fuck is a *scorpion* doin' crawlin' in my face?' He goes, 'Aaaah, that's just a little one,' and kills it."

· · ·

"It was very strange," recalls Greg Reeves of the *Gold Rush* sessions. "It was just me, Ralph and Neil in the cellar of his house with the recording equipment. It was so cluttered and tore up only the three of us could fit in there." Somehow Lofgren squeezed in to join them, noting Reeves's eccentricities in the process. "One day Greg shows up and he's gold. Gold. I was like 'Hey, Neil, is, uh, Greg gold or somethin'?' Neil said, 'Yeah, he's doin' his Indian thing.' I took it in stride."

Within this minimalist context Reeves truly shone, playing amazingly weird, soulful bass parts on songs like "Don't Let It Bring You Down." "Greg Reeves was kinda like James Jamerson gone mad," said Lofgren, referring to Reeves's Motown mentor. "Greg had this ability to play way too many notes, the kind of thing where you'd bet anybody—especially Neil—would say, 'That's too much, you're overplaying.' And just before you were about to say, 'Stop bein' so busy,' not only does he start playin' the simplest, funkiest rhythmic thing, you realize what you just heard was beautiful. It was like 'How did he do that?' To this day, no one knows."

Young would subject Lofgren to a special trial by requesting that the guitarist play an instrument he didn't know at all: piano. "I was taken aback," said Lofgren. "Let me play guitar, Neil—I can't play piano," he told Young. "Yeah, I know—but I want you to play piano on this record," Neil replied.

Terrified, Lofgren spent day and night practicing at Spirit keyboardist John Locke's house. Even on a session lunch break, Lofgren kept working on "Southern Man." "I used to be an accordion player, and accordion's all 'oompah, oompah,' so I started doin' the accordion thing on piano. Ralphie came in and starts double-timin' it and we get into this great jam. I said, 'Neil, check this out.' I banged into this solo, minus his guitar. He said, '*That's* the solo.' I said, 'Really?' "

"I can't play piano"? Perfect. That's the sound I was looking for. I didn't want to hear a bunch of fuckin' licks. I don't like musicians playing licks. The only guy who could play licks on that record was Greg Reeves. He could play whatever the fuck he wanted to, and you couldn't hear it anyway—it was just like this big rumble down there. Greg Reeves is the only bass player where it didn't bother Ralph not to be playin' with Billy. He just moved right along. Greg's a great bass player—had his own style and there was a lotta room. There was a shitload *of room on those records, because there wasn't anything else goin' on—rhythm guitar, rhythm piano, bass and drums—that's all there was. It was a good concept I had on that one. The song was it. The song spoke, everything else was supporting it.*

That was a real small studio. Had a very funky little sound goin' on. After the Gold Rush *is the only thing we ever did there.*

Nils is fantastic—if all it required was energy, Nils would be number one. And he keeps growing. Some of that stuff he played with me on different records is really fantastic, especially his keyboard stuff. Nils is the fuckin' classic barrel-roll piano player—put a cigar in his mouth and a white hat on his head and let that boy go. He'll fuckin' be gone all over those eighty-eights.

—What was it about recording studios that you had to get away from?

Factories. I didn't like seeing other musicians in the hallways. I didn't like hearing other music. I didn't feel like "I'm workin' on my record, they're workin' on their record." Fuck that. I want to be by myself. I don't want to be affected by social bullshit. Don't want to have anything to do with it. We're not part of that, heh heh.

Cinema verité? I got into audio verité. The concept of capturing the moment on the camera? I just translated that right into the recording studio. And when I started doin' it, I found all these other reasons why I was doin' the right thing. But the original thought was audio verité. Why not make records like that? Capture the moment.

More than a few people told me that Young was unsure of the direction he was heading on *Gold Rush*. There are apocryphal tales of Neil playing the album in its entirety live on piano and guitar for visitors. Out on the porch of his house between takes, Young expressed his doubts to Nils Lofgren. "We were about halfway through *Gold Rush* and Neil was like 'God, it really sounds good to me, but it's been so easy to do. I wonder if people are gonna get it.' "

A patchwork of songs quilted together from different sessions, *After the Gold Rush* was primarily the mellower side of Young, consisting of eight songs from Topanga, two songs from the August 1969 Sunset Sound sessions—"I Believe in You" and "Oh Lonesome Me"—and an overly polished solo rendition of "Birds." There were funky touches everywhere: You can hear the band *talking* during the solo on "When You Dance I Can Really Love," and two of the songs feature French horn. The dry-as-a-bone flatness of the cramped Topanga studio created a sound like no other record on the radio. There's no echo on those songs, as Briggs noted, "because we didn't *have* any."

"Don't Let It Bring You Down" is a doomy work with a mood that recurs throughout Young's music: hope in the face of total despair, which somehow doesn't sound like hope at all. "Tell Me Why" showcased Young's spartan but unerring rhythm on acoustic guitar. As Ken Viola stated, "Neil has a unique way of playing acoustic which is solely his. It's a perfect combination of melody and rhythm. It's not just chording—the melodies are married to the words in a strum relationship that's not just simply played—it's very calculated, designed."

Lyrically, "Tell Me Why" illustrates both the virtues and the flaws of *Gold Rush*. The verses are incredibly evocative and simple, and then you get to that convoluted hippie doublespeak chorus: "Is it hard to make arrangements with yourself? / When you're old enough to repay and young enough to sell." "It sounds like gibberish to me," Young admitted to writer Scott Cohen in 1988. "I stopped singing that song because when I get to that line, I go, 'What the fuck am I talking about?' You know I don't edit my songs."

Young's most accessible—and most popular—work rarely qualifies as his most interesting. One wonders if a little of CSN's finger-pointing didn't rub off on Neil on "Southern Man." Despite its rocking groove and insect-guitar soloing, this is Young at his least subtle lyrically. " 'Southern Man,' 'Alabama' are a little misguided," said Randy Newman, a long-time admirer of Young's work. "It's too easy a target. I don't think he knows enough about it. Neil's Big Issue things—'Ohio,' or where he's pissed off about people selling his songs—I don't like as well. It's not his best stuff." The late great Ronnie Van Zant would zing off the best retort to "Southern Man" via a much more powerful song, Lynyrd Skynyrd's 1974 hit, "Sweet Home Alabama": "I hope Neil Young will remember / A southern man don't need him around, anyhow."*

Toward the end of the sessions, Jack Nitzsche joined the Horse for the unbelievable "When You Dance I Can Really Love." Jack's piano playing on the song is truly nuts—he bashes away at the keys with fevered intensity, adding dark, furious rhythms that give the song a twisted edge. Lofgren remembers Nitzsche as incredibly cranky, "a little looped, and not convinced he should be playing piano on this song. One minute he would be up for it and just love the music, the next it would be 'I'm not gonna do it.' Neil had to keep talking him through it." Equally unforgettable are the song's lyrics. " 'When you dance, I can really love'—I mean, that's a stu-

---

*Always game for a good joke, especially one that put his name on the radio, Young would laud "Sweet Home Alabama" in a 1975 interview, telling Bud Scoppa, "I can't do songs like 'Southern Man,' I'd rather play the Lynyrd Skynyrd song. That'd be great." Van Zant was a huge Young fan; the cover of the last original Skynyrd album, *Street Survivors,* shows him wearing his omnipresent *Tonight's the Night* T-shirt. Hearing the news that Van Zant and members of the band had been killed in a plane crash, Young played a medley of "Alabama"/"Sweet Home Alabama" in tribute during a November 12, 1977, concert in Miami. Rumor has it that Van Zant was buried in the *Tonight's the Night* T-shirt.

pid thing to say to a girl," said Randy Newman. "It's really low-end IQ—it isn't above a hundred—and Neil is not a low-IQ guy. He did it on purpose. That's funny."

"When You Dance" is a funky record. Me and Billy and Ralph and Danny and Jack. They were all crazy. Jack plays great—I was pushing him. A lotta leakage, boy. That's a unique take, 'cause that's the only take ever done in the studio by the Horse with Jack playing. That group actually didn't work as well as I would've liked. It was nice havin' Jack with us, but some of the stuff, he was in the way tonally. Crazy Horse was so good with the two guitars, bass and drums it didn't need *anything else.*

"When You Dance" is probably the last record with Danny that we played together on. That was done near the end of the sessions. When I did all the other stuff, Danny wasn't on it—Nils, Ralph and I did the singing. Stills came up and sang, but I didn't like those vocals, so I redid them all with Danny. Danny kinda got himself together, did the overdubs . . . He wasn't lookin' too good at that point.
—Who inspired all the dancing-women songs?
I don't know . . . I remember this one girl, Jean "Monte" Ray—she was the singing partner of Jim, Jim and Jean, a folk duo. Had a record out called "People World," and she did a lot of dancing with finger cymbals. She was really great. Might've been her. Good chance. I kinda had a crush on her for a while. Moved nice. She was real musical, soulful.
—So is she the Cinnamon Girl?
Only part of the song. There's images in there that have to do with Jean and there's images that have to do with other people.
—Are you preaching in "Southern Man"?
No. I'm warning. Warning. "Southern Man" was an angry song. I wrote "Southern Man" in my studio in Topanga. Susan was angry at me for some reason, throwing things. They were crashing against the door 'cause I was down there doin' I don't know what the fuck. We fought a lot. There's some reason for it, I'm sure. It was probably my fault . . . everybody can relate to that.

"Southern Man" was more than the South—I think the civil rights movement was sorta what that was about. The far North and the deep

South are not very different. They're extremes. Look at Robbie Robertson— an Indian from Canada who wrote a lot about the deep South. I'm sure it's the same kinda thing.

Southerners, northerners, they're extremists. I mean, look at the people who live up in Canada. And look at the people who live in the deep South. They're out there. I love Canada, with the hockey games and the fuckin' spirit—everybody gets so fuckin' into it. It's so real. And there's that real family thing about the South—everybody gets together and has barbecues, ya know what I mean?

"Southern Man" is a strange song. I don't sing it anymore. I don't feel like it's particularly relevant. It's not "Southern Man"—it's "White Man." Heh heh. It's much bigger than "Southern Man."

—People recall you were very unsure of your direction with After the Gold Rush.

I always feel unsure about stuff that I like. But I knew that I liked it, I could hear *it—I could stand outside, listen, and it made me feel good. I want the music to feel like I'm immersed in it. You* know *it's right, you know you got the take of the song. That's what I'm looking for.*

Released in August 1970, *After the Gold Rush* was "the spirit of Topanga Canyon," Young would tell Cameron Crowe. "It seemed like I'd realized I'd gotten somewhere."

Young's album packaging was becoming more personal: *Gold Rush* included a foldout insert of handwritten lyrics, plus—just to make everybody wonder—a list of the songs that *didn't* make the cut. There was even a credit for Susan Young's patches, featured in the back-cover close-up of Neil's ass. Joel Bernstein took the pictures and was shocked by Young's choice for the front cover: an odd, accidental shot of the musician walking through Greenwich Village passing an old woman. Joel considered the shot scrap-heap material—he had even solarized the print in order to hide its soft focus. Young glanced at it and immediately announced, "*That's* my album cover." The eighteen-year-old thought it was a joke until he walked into a record store and there it was on display.

Coming after *Neil Young, Everybody Knows* and the work with CSN, *Gold Rush* was another completely different piece of the puzzle and a smash success. "Only Love Can Break Your Heart," an infectious ballad said to be inspired by Nash's split with Joni Mitchell, provided Young with his first top-forty hit. "*Gold Rush* really did make the turn for us," said Elliot Roberts. "It was a soft record and much more writerly. It propelled Neil into that writer class with Leonard Cohen, James Taylor and Joni."

But Neil Young was a whole lot odder than his peers, as evidenced by the album cut that resonated most deeply for many, "After the Gold Rush." Accompanied by a mournful French horn, Young tickles the ivories and sings a tale of time travel that culminates in an exodus to another planet. Spaceships, archers, Mother Nature's silver seed . . . it's the sort of cornball shit Dylan wouldn't be caught dead with, but it was completely original and, for better or worse, completely Neil. In 1992, Young would describe the song as being "about three times in history: There's a Robin Hood scene, there's a fire scene in the present and there's the future . . . the air is yellow and red, ships are leaving, certain people can go and certain people can't . . . I think it's going to happen."

The inherent mystery of the song appealed to Dean Stockwell, who was flattered that Young gave eternal life to his abandoned project. "Sit down and listen to the lyrics of that tune itself—tell me what it means. I mean, you can't do it. And no one could tell what that screenplay meant either. But Neil got it."

The song has been a staple of Young's solo sets over the years as well as one of his most covered.* "I would listen to Neil singing that all the time when we were on the road," said Linda Ronstadt. "I would think, 'This is the future. Neil's seeing humans leave the planet and go off to start a new space colony.' I've always felt that Neil had a great deal of really uncanny prescience in his writing."

What appealed most to Ronstadt was Young's imagery. "With a record you don't try to make music, you try to make your story clear. As strange and surreal as a lot of Neil's lyrics are, they're very clear—'The archer split the tree.' His images are much more precise than Bob Dylan's. There's a clarity that grabs you by the collarbones and just shakes you. 'After the

---

*Dutch group Prelude would score an improbable a cappella hit with the song in 1975; Linda Ronstadt cut it accompanied by glass harps. Even Dolly Parton (solo and in a Grammy-winning cut with Ronstadt and Emmylou Harris) tackled the surreal lyric, asking permission to change the song's infamous, crowd-pleasing lyric about getting high to "I felt like I would cry."

Gold Rush' is evocative, like the I Ching is evocative, or a powerful mandala. It evokes a feeling in you."

Randy Newman found the song's charms more inexplicable. "I can't *believe* I liked 'After the Gold Rush,' because it doesn't hold up to analysis. I can't stand that sort of 'meadow rock' thing—Neil's doing it, and writing about a big issue in a simplistic way, but I still like it. I *love* it. It just sounds good. There's some kind of alchemy going on. It's an artless type of thing—not to imply that Neil's some kind of idiot savant, he's certainly shrewder than that—but you have to listen to the records to realize how really great he is.

"You can't put those lyrics down on the page and say, 'Look! This guy's great!' They lay there like a turd . . . if you look at it close, his songwriting seems so artless. It's very simple—'bad' rhymes with 'sad,' 'mad' and 'glad,' and he'll do it *again* in the third verse—it's like a child grabbin' around and pickin' the first thing he finds. But between those grabs there's a high IQ at work, making it all turn out.

" 'After the Gold Rush' is very evocative—'thinking about what a friend had said, I was hoping it was a lie.' That's great—Neil doesn't tell you what the friend said, you don't know what it is, you *never* know what it is—it has nothing to do with *anything,* but I like it. 'After the Gold Rush' is sort of a primal urge for a simpler, better time—which may never have existed, but Neil thinks it does. 'Sugar Mountain,' same thing: same kind of nostalgia for childhood, spaceships, knights. For something else."

I love nature. To me, nature is a church.
—Are all living things sacred?
Everything. Every living thing. Smallest to the largest. The cancer cells, the spirogyras . . . It's all there for a reason, possibly because if it wasn't there, something worse *would happen.*

What if they found out that cancer could be cured—but that if you got this other *thing, that not only was it not curable, but it was contagious. Okay—that's what cancer did in the balance of nature. Now, doesn't that fit in with a lot of the things that nature does? Protecting itself? So if you get back far enough and look at any part of nature, there's a reason for it. So living within the balance of nature—like eating organic*

foods and doing all the right things—you've got more of a chance of ac-
tually making it.
—Does it make you angry the way man has polluted this planet?
What makes me angry is people planning *to do things that will pollute*
the planet. That makes me angry. What has already gone down is a prod-
uct of many things we have no control of. . . . I look at the planet and all
you see is proof that we need to change.
—I get the feeling you see space travel as organic.
I think so, yeah. I don't know how we're gonna do it, but we're gonna be
able to travel all over the fuckin' universe. Without using fuel. Perpetual
motion. Get in a vehicle and just go to another planet.
—The "silver seed" in "After the Gold Rush," it's like farming—
Civilizations. Dropping seeds. Races. Blending. Species getting stronger.
Like plants do. I see it all as the same thing. Who knows how big the
fuckin' universe is? How can there be an inside or an outside or a
boundary to this? I mean, this whole planet could be a fuckin' seed.
—Would you like to go into outer space?
If I knew I was goin' all the way. I'm not just goin' to the fuckin' moon.
I'd like to take my family. . . . I think I could talk them into it. And
y'know—we might not come back. *It might be nice out there. In twenty*
years, rock and roll might be the biggest fuckin' communication medium
in the universe. Who knows? Invaded *by people from another fuckin'*
planet—and all they want is the musicians.

I'd go up on my bus. I'd be playing with the All-Insect Orchestra by
then. I'll just go in my bus, open up one of the doors. We could make a
very grand *entrance, like the King of Egypt—the thing comes down, a*
little fanfare, my son Ben rolls out, says a few words on his communica-
tion device, then back on the bus, heh heh.
—When did you become interested in the environment?
"After the Gold Rush" is an environmental song. . . . I recognize in it
now this thread that goes through a lotta my songs that's this time-travel
thing. And the reason I recognize it now is that I heard it in someone
else's song and I said, "Wow, that was trippy, that kinda sounded like
somethin' I did." Then I realized that I *did that.*
—Do you have a feeling you were here in a previous life?

I don't think that I need to be here in a previous life. . . . Suppose there's just many dimensions to the same life—things are just going on all at once, everywhere, all at the same time. All different times, all different places, everything's happening at once instead of having time go by. Only the people are moving, time is standing still. What I see when I look out the window, the first thing that comes to my mind is the way this place looked a hundred years ago. Then I see the city. I can look out there and I know that there's an airport, but I always, in the back of my mind, see what it looked like before. I try to figure out what was here be-fore all this. I don't know why. It's just the way I am.

When Neil Young returned to CSNY for the *Déjà Vu* May through July 1970 mega-tour, things were wackier than ever. First, Greg Reeves, who'd been recording solo material with Young and Briggs, wanted to do a song with CSNY he had written called "Stop." Stills and Young were for it, Nash and Crosby said no. "It was a big confrontation," said Crosby, who fired Reeves. "I said, 'Hey, kid—it ain't good enough. It has to be great. You're a good fuckin' bass player, you're not great. Kiss your ass goodbye.' "*

Reeves was replaced by Calvin "Fuzzy" Samuels, a bowler-hatted Ja-maican who was homeless and sleeping with his bass on the couch at Is-land Studios in England when Stills hired him for his first solo album. On May 12, 1970, CSNY played their first tour date in Denver with Fuzzy, and it was a very surreal show.

Samuels—who would later claim to have spent the entire tour on acid—fumbled songs left and right, and the electric set was nearly all Stills songs, since he maintained that there wasn't enough time to teach Samuels any-

---

*During the argument with Crosby, Reeves remembers, "Neil turned right around to me in the middle of all this heat and told me, 'Regardless of this thing, I still want you to play with me. You and me still got somethin' goin'.' I want it to be known that whenever Greg Reeves wanted Neil Young to come and record, he would always come. He was super to me, man. Success brings out the prick in everyone, but Neil's very good at keeping a hold on that. He's a very good motherfucker. Solid as a rock."

Later, Young sent Reeves $10,000 to get him out of a bad situation in Mexico. Both Reeves and Dallas Taylor have taken CSNY to court over their one royalty point apiece on *Déjà Vu.*

thing else. On top of this, Stills spent the entire show hobbling around on crutches due to a ski injury, which, Nash said, "we all knew was bullshit, because we were in the dressing room and Stephen was walking around."

The group was reportedly awful and Young stormed off the stage midshow. Backstage, Dallas Taylor—who had sunk into a major heroin habit hanging out with Stills in Europe—overheard a heated group discussion during which Young delivered an ultimatum: "Either Dallas goes or I go." Tempers remained so hot that, after arriving the next day for a date in Chicago, Crosby, Nash and Young all fled the tour for Los Angeles. "Stills went to the sound check and he's standing onstage, plunking away, ready to go," said Nash. "He goes, 'Where are the other assholes?' Our road manager, Leo Makota, said, 'They're in Los Angeles.' Stephen goes, 'Fuck you! I saw 'em this morning.' Leo goes, 'Stephen, they're *gone*. They ain't in Chicago.' I don't think Stephen's ever forgiven us—to this day."

I don't know what the hell was goin' on. See, that'd be it—we'd have a tour to do and Stephen would show up completely zoned. I realize now that maybe he'd been up for a couple of days and was just completely out the window. He'd get so wound up about goin' on the road, nervous about goin' out with these guys. He's a real sensitive guy—sensitive. He had to get himself together, and how he gets himself together is he tries to take over the world.

But I'll tell ya, he was just nervous. I could see that. You take away all the insecurity and all the things that have made Stephen do some of the stuff that he's done over the years—and there's a wonderful human being who's right there. Just one thing gets in the way of it—or did in the past.

But I always see the real Stephen in there, and he's a really great guy. A wonderful guitar player, great singer and really a good friend. I love Stephen. In his heart, he's a really loving guy, an individual, a really good parent. A good family guy.

Stephen just has personal torments and demons that are constantly on him, and a lotta the things he's done in his life are a result of that conflict he has with himself. He has, in his own way, been his own worst enemy. Without Stephen *to get in his way, he would be great. We would still be making records today.*

Back in Los Angeles, Dallas Taylor was fired. Taking his place on drums was Johnny Barbata, formerly with the Turtles. Rehearsals with the new rhythm section began immediately on the Warner Bros. soundstage where the dance-marathon drama *They Shoot Horses, Don't They?* had just been filmed. On the wall facing the band was a leftover prop, a huge banner that read ominously, HOW LONG WILL THEY LAST?

The tour finally began again with a six-day stand at the Fillmore East in June. CSNY arrived in regal fashion, with their own light show designed by flamboyant Woodstock luminary Chip Monck, their own sound system and a documentary film crew. A phone-book-sized contract rider demanded all sorts of ridiculous perks, including a Persian rug that had to be placed on the stage just so.

For some on the Fillmore crew—mainly young music-loving longhairs—the coming of CSNY marked the beginning of the end. As Fillmore light-show creator Joshua White told writer Robert Greenfield, the group "were stoned and sang flat and the audience went nuts. To me that indicated that times were changing. We were now applauding the *presence* of the artist. Rather than the performance."

Joel Bernstein, fresh out of high school, attended most of the shows and was dazzled as only a young fan can be. Listening to tapes of the shows years later for Young's Archives project left him disappointed, particularly when he compared them to the CSNY's first Fillmore appearance nine months earlier, during which, he said, "They still had something to prove. By June it's superstars, American Beatles. They didn't rehearse as much, their vocals weren't as good." Nash would oversee a two-record set from the tour, *4 Way Street,* which was released to huge commercial success in April 1971. Stills would disown the album in the press, deeming it "atrocious" because the group didn't overdub away the rough edges. But no amount of overdubbing could save such a dud. Jams that might've seemed exciting in person sounded interminable and self-indulgent on vinyl.

During the Fillmore engagement, Stills was up to his usual antics, sneaking three extra songs into his solo segment the night Dylan showed up. Backstage after one show, Bernstein naïvely snapped a close-up shot of Stills "watching his friend take a hit of blow the way a hungry dog watches another dog eating. I didn't realize Stephen was completely drunk. He staggers over and grabs me, whips a buck knife out of his pocket, and sticks the point in my neck and said, 'That better not be a *wide-angle lens* on that camera.' "

.   .   .

Neil Young sailed serenely through this sea of madness. Bernstein recalls visiting Young in his room at New York's Gorham Hotel, which he had personalized by draping a scarf over the lamp, burning some incense and sticking up on the wall a ridiculous drawing of Crosby that some fan had done.

"Neil had more of an elfin quality then than he did with Crazy Horse. Magic, otherworldly—not in a spaced-out way, but a dreamy way. He was scarecrow-like, lanky, but his frailty was belied by the intensity of his eyes. His eyes are different now—he's lived a lot. They were wider then, more open to the world, but getting wiser all the time. To the rest of them, CSNY was the biggest thing in the world, but Neil took it with a grain of salt."

Young pulled out a worn acetate of the new CSNY single and played it for his teenage fan on "this rinky-dink kid's turntable. That D-modal drone comes through the speaker and from the first bar I was electrified. I knew what kind of effect that was gonna have on the country."

On May 4, 1970, four students had been shot dead by the National Guard at Kent State University. Crosby, hanging out with Young at road manager Leo Makota's place in Pescadero, California, handed Neil a copy of a magazine containing the infamous picture of a Kent State student grieving over the body of her dead classmate. Neil "looked at it, got out his guitar and wrote the song right there in front of me," said Crosby. "On the porch in the sunlight. I called Nash—'Book the studio. *Now.*' I'm sure it wasn't twenty-four hours before we were in the studio. I remember gettin' nuts at the end of the song, I was so moved. The hair was standin' up on my arms—I was freaked out because I felt it so strongly—screaming, 'Why? *Why?*' Ahmet was in Los Angeles, we gave him the mix, and he got on the red-eye and it was out—BANG!—while it was still fresh in everybody's mind." According to Chrissie Hynde, then a Kent State student, Jeff Miller—one of the slain—had been a big Neil Young fan.*

Cut live with the new rhythm section on May 15, 1970, "Ohio" flew up the charts to number fourteen, passing Nash's odious "Teach Your Children" on the way. In ten lines, Young captured the fear, frustration and anger felt by youth across the country, and set it to a lumbering D-modal death march that hammered home the dread.

"Ohio" was the best record I ever made with CSNY. Definitely. That's the only recording that I know of where CSNY is truly a band. It's all live. And it felt really good to hear it come back so fast—the whole idea of using music as a message and unifying generations and giving them a point of view. That's what I brought to that band. That song. And that song gave the band a depth that the band didn't have without that. Aside from that one thing, I was a hindrance to their progress—except live.

I always felt funny about makin' money off that. It never has been resolved. I think I resolved it by the way I treated other things after. That was about the first time I had to have a conscience about something like that.

There's nothing I did before "Ohio" that would be in the same category—and very little since. Because it's kind of a political song as well as a feeling song, and it's dated to a particular incident, kinda like "Rockin' in the Free World." I just don't write that many of them. It's not personal like Tonight's the Night *is personal.*

Events like that don't happen every day, so you gotta have an artist at a point in his or her life where the artist is vulnerable, open and feels completely what has happened so they can put it into words or some sort of expression. All those things gotta come together. You can't have a cynical artist. That's my whole thing—to try to stay open. With all I know and all I've learned, to try to keep it in perspective, be

---

*Not everyone was so fond of "Ohio." Devo member and future Young cohort Gerald V. Casale, also a student at Kent State, knew two of the four students shot. "At the time we just thought rich hippies were making money off of something horrible and political that they didn't get. I know there were big, screaming arguments in SDS meetings about Young being a tool of the military industrial complex. I just said, 'Well, it wasn't a very good song.' "

open to what's really happening and feel it. That's really the essence of youth.

During his Fillmore engagement with CSNY, Young told Joel Bernstein about a piece of property near San Francisco that road manager Leo Makota had shown him. "It's just incredible. There's a log cabin, a pond with red-winged blackbirds. It's paradise." Young paid $340,000 cash for the 140-acre property and moved there around September 1970. He named it Broken Arrow Ranch.

Susan would not be going with him. So much had happened in the last year and a half: three solo records, two tours with Crazy Horse, *Déjà Vu,* three tours with CSNY, "Ohio." Young's career had exploded, and one casualty would be his marriage. Young would later tell Bernstein that the cover shot of *Gold Rush*—where he walks by an old woman heading in the opposite direction—symbolized the end of the relationship.

"Susan was older than Neil, so she was very insecure about that and tried to be very possessive—*wrong!*" said Crosby. "Trying to be real possessive with Neil is like trying to hold on to a greased snake."

"For Susan, life was nothing but hard work and raising children, and Neil swept her off her feet and put her in this beautiful house," said Linda Stevens. "But she couldn't take the pressure from other women—and there were a lot of us around."

Young's celebrity status drove Susan off the deep end. "When Susan would go to a show, the girls would just kinda push past her to get to Neil, and she just couldn't handle it," said Russ Tamblyn. "She'd talk about how these girls would come in the dressing room and fall all over Neil, totally ignoring the fact that he had a wife sitting there. It became a real problem. This was a very strong lady, with lots of identity, who was suddenly no longer Susan Acevedo but Mrs. Neil Young.

"Her personality changed. She started to hate everything Neil was. I remember this one time right before they split up—this was at a point when Neil was out front in the press and Susan was screamin' at him because of his popularity—it was like 'Get unpopular.' I know she used to scream at the fans—'Get outta here!' It was bizarre, really bizarre."

"I'll tell you only one thing about Susan," said Graham Nash. "I shot a portrait of Neil in 1969—a really great shot. I made Neil a print of it. I went out to his house in Topanga, and Susan had pinned it up on one of those little corkboards by the refrigerator. She'd pinned it up with two pins through the eyes. That's where Susan was at."

Susan never took advantage of me. Never ever was lookin' out for Susan—always lookin' out for me. Even afterwards. She never wanted to rely on me or take advantage. Very, very independent. She had a lot of pride in herself. I still have a piece of patchwork she made that I keep up in my study, and a little cup from our wedding day. . . . I keep these things.
—Were you mature in that relationship?
Not really. I was in over my head. I wasn't ready. It just wasn't the right time. It was a good combination, but the time frames were outta sync.

Success was hard to handle. Both of us had a hard time handling it. But Susan even more, because being older than I was, I think she was a little bit insecure about that. It's different when a woman's older than a man. All these chicks around and everything . . . naked women in the house. It was just too fuckin' much. It was not meant to succeed. But it was fun trying.

Whenever I think of Susan, I wonder what it would be like to sit down and talk to her a little bit now and see how she's doin'.' I think about her daughter, Tia—what a little sweetheart. I wasn't able to take the responsibility—if I could've stayed, I could've probably been a good father for Tia . . . it just didn't work out.

I was busy. Had a lot of music in me. Topanga got pretty wild. Not much privacy left. That's when I realized it was a little too out in the open. You never knew what was gonna be happening when you went home.

Young split from Topanga, staying briefly at the Chateau Marmont before moving to his new ranch. Leo Makota remembers a frantic phone call from Susan demanding to be taken to the ranch. When he refused, she became hysterical. She never made the trip.

Longtime friend Gary Burden bought Young's Topanga home. "Neil didn't want it. He wanted to get away from the vibes of the house, that's why he sold it to me. It was real painful—he wanted to break up, he didn't want to break up."

I told Burden that, as I understood it, Susan thought she was moving to the ranch, too. "I'm sure that's true. And that's why Neil was so stressed out—because he's capable of making ruthless decisions, but at the same time has this side of himself that feels real bad about it—or maybe not," he said, laughing. "Neil knows the pain he is causing, but he does it anyway."

Ralph Molina recalls tension between Neil and Susan at the beginning of work on *Gold Rush*. "I was in this booth in the studio, and Neil got this phone call and I remember him saying, 'Fuck, Susan, all I have is $250,000, and you can have every penny of it. Just leave me alone!' I'll never forget those words." According to court records—which state that Young left the Topanga residence on August 20, 1970—Young paid Susan $80,000 for court costs and medical expenses. Susan filed for divorce on October 9, 1970.

"Susan Acevedo was very classy," said Elliot Roberts. "Didn't want an accountant to go over Neil's figures. She needed eighty grand for a restaurant. That's all she wanted, not a penny more, and never came back. I mean, we saw her through the years, but never for a reason. She never came back, never asked for anything, never once."

Young was loath to criticize Susan in any way, and it was only after prodding that he expressed having felt the need to escape the relationship before her jealous rages went any further. I got the impression that he fled quickly and without explanation. Acevedo took the separation hard. She went on a particularly bad post-breakup trip after ingesting some hallucinogens with Jack Nitzsche and Denny Bruce at Nitzsche's Mill Valley home. Said Jack Nitzsche: "A bunch of friends were over, and we all got high and everyone was doin' fine, except at one point she asked me, 'Do you think Neil will ever come back to me?' I said, 'Never.' My God, she freaked out. Y'know the theater masks of comedy and tragedy? She froze into a tragedy mask. For like five minutes. You should've seen that mask of tragedy."

Young would move on to another new life. Alone.

—Your relationship with Susan ended abruptly?
It didn't end that *abruptly. We had divorce proceedings. It was just . . .*

late. It was over. Y'know, at that point in my life it was easier for me to walk away from that *than it was to walk away from my career—and the two of them were not gonna go together, okay? It was one or the other.*
—Can I find Susan in any of your songs?
Something about ribbons. It's not there. I can't remember. *
—You mean "Running Dry." You also refer to shaming yourself with lies. Somehow I don't think you remember what those lies were.
Yeah, I don't. I'm sure I've lied, your honor. I confess to having lied at some point, heh heh.
—So you knew then it was heading south?
Probably. Yeah.
—To be an artist, do you have to be ruthless?
I do. Hey, you can either be true to your art or be a good public relations man.
—When did you leave Topanga?
As soon as I finished After the Gold Rush. *When I broke up with Susan.*
—How did you get so driven?
Well, I didn't get *that way . . . I* am *that way. It didn't start at any given point. There's no time of day or year that it starts.*

    It was just . . . there.

---

*I left my love with ribbons on and water in her eyes . . .
  I took from her the love I'd won and turned it to the sky
    —"Running Dry (Requiem for the Rockets)," 1969.

cut to the lizards

"Look at his eyes," Young said. "Is this guy a wizard or what?" As usual, Neil was on the money: The light in Mazzeo's blue eyes glistens like fire on the sun. A big dirty-blond creature who pads about with the awkward gentleness of a bear pawing something out of an overstuffed garbage can, he is described by Neil's half sister, Astrid, as "the surf bum from hell. Just the fact that Maz can consistently come up with these seventeen-year-old girls boggles my mind."

Mazzeo is a fabulous artist. He's worked in every medium, even cardboard, but is most beloved to Young fans for the twisted naked women and prehistoric-bird pen-and-ink illustrations on the 1975 *Zuma* album, which enjoyed the distinction of being chosen one of the all-time worst covers by *Rolling Stone*.

Jim Mazzeo, aka Sandy Castle, aka Sandy Mazzeo, has been Young's off-and-on running buddy for many years. Defenders maintain he's an artist who helped Young tune in to his muse, while critics describe him as a con artist who attaches himself to Young—and his money—like a lamprey eel. Others see Mazzeo more as an equal-opportunity chaos maker. "Sure, Maz would take your car and crash it," said Frank "Poncho" Sampedro. "But it doesn't have to be Neil's car—he'd do it to *anybody*."

Mazzeo didn't flinch in the face of such accusations. "Well, I've always tried to substantiate those claims whenever possible," he said with an innocent grin. On one tour, rumors flew that Mazzeo had picked up a disabled girl and attached electrical wires to her brace to see how she jumped when he plugged her in. Maz not only didn't deny the untrue story, he embellished it. "I try to tell 'em something so awful that even *I* don't believe it."

• • •

At the time Young moved into his ranch in the fall of 1970, Jim Mazzeo was inhabiting a nearby stretch of land that he and fellow artist James McCracken had given the name Star Hill Academy for Anything. Sixteen hundred acres of redwood forest surrounding an abandoned sawmill, Star Hill was presided over by a young conservative named Jimmy Wickett, whose freethinking father had donated the land for an artists' community.

The first inhabitants were Mazzeo and McCracken, who moved to the property in August 1968. A hulking giant in wire-rimmed glasses who would soon be wreaking havoc in everyone's life, including Young's, McCracken was "the greatest artist I've ever known," said Mazzeo. "He was able to create thunder in the middle of a sunny day." The pair created all manner of art together, McCracken carving giant faces out of wood and Mazzeo forging gnarly sculptures out of scrap metal.

Star Hill "was an extraordinary place, with all these weirdos up there," said Johanna Putnoy, who later lived in a geodesic dome on the property. She recalls one of the unique power sources for the enclave: a methane-gas generator. "They got this big canister with a hole in the top, and you'd sit on this canister overlooking the hills and everybody took their shit in this big canister. One night it blew sky-high. Luckily no one was on it, but there was shit all over the place."

Mazzeo also managed to con the phone company into putting a pay phone on the wilderness property, then pirated the electricity for a number of abodes, including a seven-room tree house perched a hundred feet up in a towering redwood. A pulley-and-rope cable car very tenuously made its way from one of their workshops up to the tree house, and it was Neil Young's bad luck to show up the day after the contraption had been completed.

Young had already made a couple of neighborly visits to Star Hill, and Mazzeo—aware that Young was an aficionado of odd art—led him to the trolley. "He didn't know it was a gondolier car, he thought it was some kinda sculpture, some kinda art. I go, 'Hop in. Check it out. Ya gotta sit in it.' Neil was takin' all kinds of medication—he was really frail, really weak, his back hurt, so he's bein' real careful. I go 'Click!,' the wall swings open and *Wham!* We launched him!" Mazzeo watched as a terrified Neil Young shot up through the air, gripping on to the car for dear life. "He spent about four hours in the tree house before he took the cable car back."

Such was the chaos Sandy had to offer, and he and Young became fast friends.

Star Hill would soon become more of a bona fide commune rather than a retreat for oddball artists, and when Young added another six-hundred-acre parcel to his ranch, Mazzeo moved to Broken Arrow, converting an old blacksmith shop into a welding studio where he made Young stoves, art and, recalls Larry Johnson, "weird chandeliers that are great to look at but still don't work. You shock yourself trying to turn them on."

I didn't like L.A. Topanga. Too busy. Too many weirdos. I like the country better. Somebody's comin' at ya, you can see 'em. And then if they do somethin', they got a long way to go to get away from where they were when they did it.

The ranch was great. First place I looked at. I liked the road—getting in, getting out. The view. I was so happy I had my own place. Everything was new.
—Did you have a plan when you moved to the ranch?
Nope.
—Did you know you were gonna build?
Yeah. I didn't know I was gonna build as much. . . . I just loved the ranch, and it grew with me.
—Were you a hippie?
Well, y'know, I wouldn't call me a hippie, but I think anyone else would've. You see a lot of kids walkin' around today that look almost exactly like I did then, down to the fuckin' boots, jeans, plaid shirts and long hair. It's unbelievable. Don't know what that means.
—You should've copyrighted that look.
I feel good about lettin' it go.

The first few months on the ranch were quiet. Young lived in a small house with meager electricity and heat. "It was this little old funky ranch—the living room was half the house," said craftsman Morris Shepard. Indian blankets decorated the walls and a tree stump served as a coffee table. Out in the driveway were a couple of old Cadillacs and a Willys Jeepster nicknamed "Old Yeller." The property was sparsely populated at first: Drummer Johnny Barbata lived with Young for a month or so, then roadie

Guillermo Giachetti moved in for a while. Louie Avilla—the Portuguese ranch foreman—and his wife, Clara, lived nearby. Avilla would find himself immortalized to some degree in "Old Man," a moody meditation on age, love and everything else Young was feeling at the moment.

At the end of November, Young played some acoustic solo gigs at the Cellar Door in Washington, D.C., then two prestigious dates at Carnegie Hall in New York City on December 4 and 5. Young sold out both performances without the benefit of either CSNY or Crazy Horse. Carnegie Hall didn't smooth Young's mercurial temperament one iota—he angrily stormed offstage after some noisy fans snuck into the packed house via the fire exits. "It was intermission," Young would tell writer Bud Scoppa. "I just took it a little early." Both Rassy and Scott attended, on separate nights.

Although most of the material performed consisted of career highlights from as far back as the Springfield days, there was, as usual, a handful of new songs: "Old Man," "See the Sky About to Rain" and "Bad Fog of Loneliness," one of Young's more revealing relationship songs. The droll first line said it all: "Bad fog of loneliness / Put a cloud on my single-mindedness." It was written in the aftermath of his marriage to Susan, and you can hear the agonizing dialogue in Young's head as heart tries to over-rule mind. "So long, woman, I am gone / So much pain to go through / Come back, maybe I was wrong," he cries, then plunges into a sad little jig on guitar.

Relationships were on Young's mind. As he sang in "Old Man," "live alone in a paradise / that makes me think of two." He would encounter the next woman in his life while in traction, confined to a hospital bed. Directly after the Carnegie Hall show, Young wrenched his back severely while moving a slab of walnut at the ranch. For nearly a year Young would live in a back brace, frequently under the influence of a powerful muscle relaxant called Soma.

First time I got in trouble with my back was from working in the garden in Topanga, doing a lot of work with a shovel. Then I got stuck in my car and I couldn't move. I went to the chiropractor, got straightened out, was kinda okay, then within a year I was movin' somethin' else heavy, some big pieces of wood. The next day I got in my car to go somewhere and my leg wouldn't come up—I put my foot on the clutch, on the brake. I had to lift it up. So I went to the doctor and they put me in the hospital.

It wasn't good. It wasn't a happy thing. Soma compound.
—How long were you on Soma?
Too long! Long enough to make some really stupid mistakes. Soma compound and Michelob—the combination is just unbelievable.

I made some erroneous decisions based on that stuff.
—Can you, uh, tell me exactly what decisions you're referring to?
No. If you could find decisions that I've made in my life that are obviously *erroneous—chances are, you just put the time together with when I was takin' the Soma compound, you can figure it out yourself. I can't say.*
—Not the best grounds for starting a relationship, you being in a neck brace and on painkillers?
No . . . that was the grounds for starting the relationship. That's the shaky foundation it was built on.

"I do everything backwards—I get an Academy Award nomination to start out with, and I end up in B pictures."

Carrie Snodgress is behind the wheel of a beat-up white Caddy. Dressed in a flimsy white shirt and white jeans, she blasts Tracy Chapman on the stereo and sings along without really knowing the words, talking a mile a minute in her infamous voice, a rasp that sounds like a thousand cigarettes have been ground out on her vocal cords. Her sinewy, spare figure betrays her midwestern roots, and her features are worn but sturdy—a classic American look, Pippi Longstocking by way of the Carter Family.

The Caddy careens down the road like a bumper car broken free of its orbit. At the very least, riding with Snodgress is exhilarating. You sort of cover your eyes and hope for the best. And although the song wasn't written for her, Carrie really is like a hurricane. The minute I hop in the car, she's on me like a searchlight, picking my brain, hugging me, invading my personal space.

With Carrie you think you're long-lost buddies, then months pass with phone calls unreturned. Then you see her roar by in the Caddy, which is invariably a little more dented, with a neighbor's baby in a car seat at her side. That's Carrie. Always helping everybody but herself.

Snodgress was not a popular figure with many in the Young camp. While taking Young to court for child support, she aired her grievances in a sensational and inaccurate *People* magazine article. Then there was the lurid court case with Jack Nitzsche, which had many questioning her role in the whole affair. "She's an actress," I would hear over and over from those who knew her, as if that explained away some affliction worse than death.

We made our way through Hollywood to the home Young provided her and their son. Zeke was in his room, glued to his computer, deep into his current project: logging in the lyrics to every one of his father's songs. He was up to Young's 1975 album, *Zuma,* which was blaring from a stereo system Zeke seemed to know every working detail of.

Zeke suffers from mild cerebral palsy, and Carrie is obsessively devoted to him. The slightest whimper from his lips had Carrie up fixing whatever caused it, as Zeke's wry observations pricked holes here and there in his mother's nonstop monologue. I wondered what would happen when Zeke was full-grown and mother and son would have to separate. It wasn't going to be easy for either of them. "It isn't what you'd call your average mother-child relationship," she said with a grin.

Carrie was a million laughs, but a hellhound always seemed to be on her trail. Every time I saw her there was some new catastrophe going on in her life: car crashes, strange people hanging around the house, harassing phone calls in the middle of the night. Typical was the unappreciative soul she took in who turned out to be a crackhead and took her for everything she had. "Police said he must've pulled a truck up," Carrie said with a tired chuckle. In the process she'd lost a hand-carved antique heart of gold, one of her few mementos from the long-gone relationship with Young. She was always racing around putting out fires, and occasionally you couldn't help but wonder if the match was in her own pocket.

·   ·   ·

Carrie Snodgress was born in Barrington, Illinois, on October 27, 1946. A tomboy among three brothers, Carrie said her role in the family was "the clown, the little kid who would put on funny outfits and do little skits to make everybody laugh when things were bad. What my parents gave me as a toolbox to live with was a joke—I had screwdrivers with no handles. I didn't have a clue to identify my feelings. How the fuck was I supposed to figure out if I was sad, glad, mad?"

Her father was "the most honest car salesman in Chicago," she said. "If you bought a used car from Harry Snodgress, you knew what you were buyin'." Her mother, Carolyn, was a severe alcoholic who would test the love of her children by feigning suicide on a regular basis.

"She was so funny. She'd have the gas going, then she'd announce, 'I'm going to kill myself, everybody. So if anybody wants to see me alive in the morning, *maybe* you'll do something about it.' Well, we all heard it so many times we'd all go back to sleep. Next thing you know she'd be sayin', '*Goddamn it* isn't *anybody* gonna get up and come downstairs? I've been down here for fifteen minutes, for chrissakes. I could be *dead* and nobody cares. NOW GET DOWN HERE!' We'd all flip coins to decide who was gonna save her. Oh my God, it was too funny."

Abandoning an original plan to become a nurse, Snodgress got a master's degree in acting from the prestigious Goodman School of Drama. By 1968 she had moved to Hollywood and begun acting in television. Signed as one of the last contract players at Universal, Snodgress burst into the limelight with her portrayal of a neglected mate in 1970's *Diary of a Mad Housewife,* for which she would win two Golden Globe Awards and be nominated for an Oscar. Snodgress had to endure five screen tests to win the part. Director Frank Perry was "hostile and cold," she said. "Oddly enough, I took that as a stage direction: 'Maybe that's what he wants— nothing.' "

The result was an unnervingly real performance, and among the many viewers captivated was Young's roadie Guillermo Giachetti. "I had seen this movie and just fell in love with this person—I wanted to save her from this asshole husband," he recalls. While on the road in Washington, D.C., he took Young to see the film. Young was similarly smitten, and upon returning to Los Angeles he discovered she was appearing in a play at the Mark Taper Forum. Giachetti and fellow roadie Bruce Berry were dispatched to slip backstage and check her out. "The next day there was a note on the table saying, 'Call Neil Young,' " said Snodgress. "Of course,

I didn't know Neil Young from Neil Diamond." Her roommate Gigi filled her in, Snodgress called back and a date was arranged for the following month.

When the time came, Young was bedridden at the Chateau Marmont, seeking medical attention for his back. What Snodgress remembers most from their first encounter was the incredibly potent marijuana. "That Panama Red! Jesus, that was strong pot. I got about halfway home and had to pull over and go to sleep. I got lost goin' home."

The next day Young was hospitalized, and Snodgress, with roommate Gigi di Piazza in tow, came to visit. Snodgress was on her way out of town on a lengthy publicity tour for *Diary,* and Young was headed back to the road as well, but another date was arranged, this time for lunch at a fifties coffee shop called Ship's. Snodgress showed up with her cocker spaniel, Timer. "I told him I went everywhere with my dog. Neil said, *'Every-where?'*" Young was in fragile condition. "He had this real old-fashioned lace-up brace on, with metal bars diggin' into his hips to keep him straight—it was gruesome. My choice was being an actress or a nurse, so Neil was right up my alley. I just got to nurse the hell out of him." Snodgress would tell Jeannie Field, "I fell in love with Neil's pain."

The simplicity of Young's life impressed Snodgress. "When I first met him, he was on tour with that little bamboo case. I said, 'Is that it?' He truly was what he represented himself to be—the man with the single suitcase and two pair of jeans." Snodgress visited the ranch and the romance blossomed. "I had something to offer him in the beginning, which was to keep it simple. To go look at sunsets. To say fuck the phone and pull the jack out. Neil loved it—management didn't.

"We were in this cocoon of intensity. Neil and I were uniquely in the same position at the same time, having overwhelming success facing us." Much more savvy than Snodgress when it came to dealing with the success, Young quizzed the actress on her finances and counseled her on how to cope with fame. "Neil was the one who pointed out to me the edge I was walkin' on. I was goin' so goddamn fast I don't think I knew how to sit down." When Snodgress complained about being scrutinized by the press, Young maintained that pleasing reporters wasn't necessarily part of the job. "Neil had a concept that the media could screw ya, and he'd have nothin' to do with that."

Young and Snodgress were like "a royal couple," said Elliot Roberts. "He was the big pop star, she was a movie star nominated for an Academy Award. Wherever they went it was a big thing. *Diary* was a big women's film—people looked at Carrie like she was this incredible political figure. She was what Jane Fonda wanted to be." The quintessential hippie in granny glasses, Snodgress didn't seem to care about money, spoke out against the Vietnam war and had a menagerie of characters she looked after. "She would have all these people who didn't have places to stay just sleeping in the downstairs room, and Neil thought that was just so cool," said Roberts. "She devoted herself to the poor and the tired." For the inward and remote Young, it must've been overwhelming. "Everything he couldn't be, she was."

. . .

Accompanying himself on piano, guitar and for the first time extensively on harmonica, Young spent January and February 1971 on a solo tour of small halls that took him through the United States, Canada and England. It was a small production with a four-man crew. Young tuned his own guitars because roadie Guillermo Giachetti didn't know how. These were intimate shows. At the end of the Edmonton performance, Giachetti remembers, "The windchill factor went down to sixty below—all the autos were frozen. The people came back in the theater, and as we were tearing down, Neil played some more."

A raft of new songs shot out of the love-struck musician. This would be by far his most popular incarnation: the lonely, lovelorn boy (he looked and sounded oddly adolescent) with guitar. Most of the songs were ballads—simple, accessible tunes like "Journey Through the Past" and "Love in Mind." "Heart of Gold" was the archetypal Young lament: restless, romantic, intent on getting what he wants, even though you wonder if he'll still want it when he has it.

At first Young performed "Heart of Gold" on piano coupled with another new song, "A Man Needs a Maid." The "Maid" lyrics were remarkably honest in expressing a typically paralyzed male point of view on relationships: "Just someone to keep my house clean / Fix my meals and go away," yearning for something more, but incapable of intimacy. "To give a love, you gotta live a love / To live a love, you gotta be 'part of,'" he sings, acknowledging he is part of nothing. The line that was perhaps most revealing was cut when the two songs mutated into separate entities: "Afraid," he cries, "a man feels afraid."

In an era of women's lib, "A Man Needs a Maid" would be number one on the hit parade of Male Chauvinist Pigs everywhere. "Young was tired of cowgirls," said writer Richard Meltzer. "He just wants to limit what a woman is to him to those few things that can be managed without falling apart, so let's begin very simply—the first thing he wants is a maid. He needs love, he needs pussy, he needs excitement, but primarily he needs a maid. I thought that was just so thrilling."

∙   ∙   ∙

The solo tour was a tremendous success, with triumphant shows at the Dorothy Chandler Pavilion in Los Angeles and at London's Royal Festival Hall. Joel Bernstein attended a handful of the California dates and remembers the Los Angeles show, and meeting Carrie Snodgress, vividly. "She was disarmingly down-to-earth—beautiful, elfin, slight. What they both had was that combination of frailty and strength. They were madly in love. That show was played for her."

Bernstein found Young's performance "riveting. You never took your eyes off him. He was on a whole other roll, he wasn't the 'Loner' guy or the Crazy Horse guy or the *After the Gold Rush* guy. And when he was funny, you could hardly believe he was cracking a joke, because the last song had so much pathos. It startled you, he could be so wry." The show would be widely bootlegged.

You can see exactly what Bernstein is talking about, watching a live concert shot by Stanley Dorfman for British television's *BBC2 in Concert* on February 23. This is the great visual document of the *Harvest* period: Dressed in a flannel shirt, lace-up boots and a seen-better-days brown suede jacket Briggs had given him, Young looks half woodland creature and half nineteenth-century engraving. He belts out "Old Man" and "Heart of Gold" with a ragged intensity missing from the studio recordings, singing so jubilantly you fear he might hurt himself. He seems uncharacteristically relaxed throughout the performance, the mumbled between-song patter about cars and TV so offhand you miss it on the first viewing. "Forget it," he says with a crooked grin after some particularly corny shtick. "That's a line." There is a feral, wounded quality about the Young of this period that is mesmerizing. No wonder an army of teenage girls fell under his spell. He seemed not unlike them.

In February, a Dutch documentary crew came to the ranch and filmed Young driving around in his Jeep, hanging out with Louie Avilla, lying around in his house looking very stoned and doing an impromptu performance of a new song he would soon cut in Nashville—"Out on the Weekend." "Think I'll pack it in and buy a pickup," he sings, chuckling over the cornball lyrics.

"I feel more free now than I've ever felt before," Young said during a short interview conducted by Elliot Roberts. "I don't find it hard to sing for any one person anymore . . . last night I sat down at the piano and played three songs for Carrie—I've never been able to do that before." Tellingly, the one new song Young couldn't play for Snodgress was "A Man Needs a Maid."

•   •   •

In the first week of February 1971, Young went to Nashville to appear on *The Johnny Cash Show*. That weekend he found himself in a Nashville studio, and it would be a watershed session for many reasons: It would yield Young's only number-one hit, "Heart of Gold"; begin an association with a new producer, Elliot Mazer; and introduce him to a new band of professional musicians dubbed the Stray Gators.

Four years Young's senior, Elliot Mazer was a self-described "long-haired Jew intellectual" who had worked with a variety of folk acts and Janis Joplin before battling his way into the very conservative Nashville music scene. Mazer was part owner of Quadrafonic Studios, where he had recorded such Nashville outsiders as Joan Baez and Tony Joe White, and it would be there that Young would start recording the *Harvest* album on February 7.

Mazer had a reputation as an excellent engineer who lacked a certain soulfulness in dealing with the players. Most musicians considered David Briggs a brother, even when they wanted to punch him out; Mazer got a more indifferent response. He was always the guy on the other side of the glass.

Like so many of the crucial events in Young's career, everything about the session came together by accident, including the producer's involvement. Mazer—who had no awareness of Young other than that of being driven crazy by a girlfriend who played *After the Gold Rush* incessantly— was a friend of Elliot Roberts and by chance ran into him with Young at a dinner party. Young mentioned that he had some new songs he wanted to cut, and a session was hastily arranged. Mazer had to bump another artist to get Young studio time, and since most of the studio musicians went fishing on the weekend, none of his first picks were available.

The Stray Gators "were the other side of Nashville," said Mazer. "They were not part of the establishment." They were also all characters Young could truly appreciate. On bass was Tim Drummond. The mention of Drummond's name elicits a chuckle from even the most jaded, for everybody has something to say about T.D. Nicknamed "the jive midget" by drummer Kenny Buttrey, he's called "The Moth" by detractors due to his propensity for the spotlight. "More balls than a tennis court," said David Crosby. Percussionist Joe Lala fondly recalls Drummond out on the road in his red silk pajamas, ordering up two complete meals for breakfast. Why two breakfasts? asked Lala. "So I can walk around the table and not miss a bite," Drummond said.

Squat, balding and bearded, Drummond sports a mug straight off a post-office wanted poster and speaks in a wry, froglike croak. The only man who's managed to snag cowriter credits out of Bob Dylan, Neil Young and J. J. Cale, Drummond reminds me of a carny huckster at the game of chance—first he steals your money, then your girlfriend. There's frequently some shadowy, amusing activity on the side with Drummond, and he has a sometime reputation as a shit-stirrer. If there's a band uprising, Drummond usually isn't far from the action.

Born in Bloomington, Illinois, on April 20, 1940, Drummond conned his way into Conway Twitty's group before joining the Daps (allegedly short for Dapicetic, a sleeping pill popular with the band), famous for backing James Brown on his mind-blowing two-sided single "I Can't Stand Myself" / "Licking Stick." Drummond was the token white in Brown's touring band, which is where Young copped the name the Stray Gators: Drummond and Brown's legendary guitar player, Jimmy Nolan, would amuse themselves by watching some of the more stoned members of the band staring into space. "They'd be flashin', seein' stuff in the sky," recalls Drummond with a laugh. "We'd say, 'Lookit him—he's lookin' at some gators, and here comes a stray.' "

Young chose to use pedal steel guitar for the first time on record, and tall, rangy Ben Keith answered the call. It is hard to find a musician more loved or respected. "Buddy Emmons may be the best steel player," said J. J. Cale, "but Ben's my favorite." Drummond put it this way: "Y'know how when you're in San Francisco and the fingertips of fog crawl in from the ocean and cover the city? That's the way Ben Keith plays."

Aka Long-Grain, aka King, Ben Keith was born March 6, 1937, in Fort Riley, Kansas, but raised in Kentucky. As a teenager he practiced guitar so much that one of his fingers had to undergo surgery. Switching to laptop steel, Keith soon made a name for himself with the likes of Faron Young and Patsy Cline—Cline's immortal "I Fall to Pieces" would be Ben's recording debut. There are few Neil Young albums Keith doesn't appear on, and it is hard to come up with a musician more perfect for that universe—steeped in tradition, but open and soulful enough to get down with the Horse. As Young said in 1973 introducing Keith onstage, "I swear to God, I love every sound he makes—no matter what the fuck it is."

Keith's quiet personality matches Young's to a tee, and he steers clear of band squabbles and other controversies. "I don't remember Neil ever sayin' one cross word to Ben," said Kenny Buttrey. "They're like brothers joined at the hip."

Kenny Buttrey's sparse, rock-solid drumming would be the cement that held *Harvest* together. As Mazer said, "He made the song sound like one person." Buttrey loved R&B and drummers like Memphis legend Al Jackson; he'd also been the metronomic bedrock of Dylan's *Blonde on Blonde*. Mazer describes him as "a hundred-percent asshole character—a guy living in Nashville who hated country music." Buttrey smoked cigarettes with his name embossed on them in gold and wore "jeans that were pressed," said Jack Nitzsche, who felt that Buttrey was a little too much of a southern man for Young.

"Basically every drum part that I ever did with Neil are his drum parts, not mine," said Buttrey. "He said, 'I don't want any right hand'—no cymbals—which was really tough for me, because I was havin' to think about what I was playin' instead of lettin' it come natural. 'Less is more' is the phrase he used over and over. Only lick I ever came up with on my own is the high-hat on the 'Heart of Gold' verse . . . Neil tells everybody what to play, note for note. If you play somethin' he doesn't like, boy, he'll put a look on you you'll never forget. Neil hires some of the best musicians in the world and has 'em play as stupid as they possibly can."

Although Young's minimalism drove Buttrey crazy, the drummer was impressed by the way he kept time. "It's just ultra- , ultra-simple, a laid-back kinda thing nobody but Neil does, and if you're right with him it sounds great, and it sounds awful if you're not. If I can't see Neil's right hand when he's playin' guitar, then I'm not playing. His rhythm playing is just perfect—it'll feel like he's slowing down, but it's just the Neil Young feel. No drummer should ever hold Neil to a certain tempo, because if you put a metronome on it, you kill the Neil Young feel."

This band would cut "Heart of Gold," "Old Man" and an as yet unreleased version of "Bad Fog of Loneliness." Young was ready; as Mazer said, "More than any artist I've worked with, you could sense when it was gonna be the take. Neil'll teach the band the song, but he'll hold back until he knows everything is together." With the Stray Gators, the songs fell together quickly. Ben Keith would tell deejay Redbeard there was "no runnin' 'em down—I didn't know 'em till we recorded."

Equally impromptu were the vocal contributions of James Taylor and Linda Ronstadt, also in town for the Cash show. "We wound up on our knees around this microphone," Ronstadt recalls. "I was just shrieking this high harmony, singing a part that was just higher than *God*."

A queen of the layered California seventies-rock sound, Ronstadt was amazed by Young's approach in the studio. "The way Neil makes records, oh my gosh. I have a very, very meticulous way of working. I'm an oil painter—I take a long time to get all the parts real in tune, get 'em right with multiple tracking, doing it over and over. With Neil you don't get the chance—you're lucky if you've figured the part out, he does things so fast. Neil's a sketch artist. He just washes the color over it, it's done and it's brilliant. He's really got an uncanny instinct to go for the throat."

Taylor also laid down the jaunty six-string banjo picking on "Old Man." "I don't think I played on one before or since," said Taylor, who was untroubled by Young's rough-draft methods. "Neil likes to be present in his own life, as in-the-moment as he can be. And that's how he plays, that's how he writes, that's how he sings. He's present. You don't get the feeling he's mapped out this area of music that he wants to learn everything about . . . he just does it."

The crew worked all weekend, and by the wee hours of Monday morning the session was complete. "It was snowing in Nashville, which was very unusual," recalls Mazer. "Ben's windshield wipers weren't working, so he had to drive his Triumph home backwards." Mazer was excited; he was certain "Heart of Gold" was a smash hit.

"We all knew there was something very special going on," he said of the session, and yet like so many others, Mazer didn't think he got that close to Young. "Looking back, I don't really think I felt at ease with him, even though we spent hours and hours in the studio. The serious amount of pain he was in and his mood shifts—greatly controlled by drugs—kept everybody at a distance."

Harvest *was just easy. I liked it because it happened* fast, *kind of an accidental thing—I wasn't looking for the Nashville Sound, they were the musicians that were there. They got my stuff down and we did it. Just come in, go out—that's the way they do it in Nashville. There were no preconceptions. Elliot Mazer was in the right place at the right time. He let me do my music and recorded it. He's really good at what he does, but he doesn't work with me like David.*
—Buttrey said you came up with all his parts.
I wouldn't say that. I don't like musicians playin' licks. Buttrey's got a real good feel—he can get a pocket goin', he's very organized and he does take direction really well. He's an incredible drummer. He and Ralph* are the best drummers I ever played with.

I wrote "A Man Needs a Maid / Heart of Gold" on the road. Piano. It was like a medley, the two went together. You should see the video with the London Symphony Orchestra live. There's a take of it that's great. *It's not the one we used. It's not quite as together. "There's a World" is overblown. "A Man Needs a Maid" is overblown, but it's great. There's a difference.*

---

*Reviewing these remarks in 2000, Young added a third name to the list: Jim Keltner, known for his session work with Bob Dylan, Ry Cooder, Richard Thompson, Eric Clapton, J. J. Cale, the Traveling Wilburys, Leon Russell and many others; an unusual choice for Young, who tends to prefer more minimal drums.

Harvest *and* Comes a Time *are probably as much me as anything I've done with the Horse. "Harvest" is one of my best songs. That's the best thing on* Harvest.

I was in love when I first made Harvest. *With Carrie. So that was it. I was an in-love and on-top-of-the-world-type guy.*
—*All those relationship songs—it's "I want to, but I can't."*
Right. Good thing I got past that stage.
—*How did you do it?*
Time, I guess. Gettin' the right woman. That was a good thing.

Although they would never marry, Young asked Snodgress to join him on the ranch sometime in 1971. As Carrie recalls, "I said, 'I have a problem—I got my own family.' Neil said, 'I don't think there's anything that can't be worked out.'" One wonders if Young knew what he was in for, because with Carrie came a small but growing army: what Nitzsche snidely refers to as "the Snodgress people." At one time or another, living on the ranch were her parents; her brothers, John and Mel; Betsy Heimann and Gigi di Piazza, a couple of girlfriends from Chicago; and a Vietnam vet named Jim Love whom Carrie had taken under her wing. Perhaps most significantly for Neil, the Chicago gang also included Tim Mulligan, who would become an indispensable member of Young's technical team.

Carrie's family was a touchy-feely bunch, much to Young's discomfort. He would complain to Jack Nitzsche that one Snodgress or another was continually hugging him. "The Snodgress people, they were everywhere, they just took over," said Nitzsche. "Her family, they were all *big*. They scared us all. Neil and I used to goof about that one—'They could take over.' All of a sudden they could walk in and go, 'Okay, little people over there, the big people are here now.' Her brothers? Two of the scariest people I've ever met. Frightening."

Rassy would be the first of Young's parents to visit the ranch, and craftsman Morris Shepard recalls that it put Neil "on edge." Rassy was "almost putting Neil down and making fun of him because he was a big star, and not in a kindly way. Neil tried his best to treat her respectfully and not to lose his temper, but it was real hard. He didn't like having her around."

According to Carrie, when Rassy arrived, Neil would immediately disappear, leaving Snodgress to fend for herself as Rassy bitched about his absence. "Rassy didn't like me, never ever ever, from the beginning to the end. Her inference was that I had created this monster—that basically I had something to do with Neil turning against her."

But on the whole, the early part of Young's relationship with Carrie sounds like an idyllic time. After some Nashville sessions, the couple meandered back to the ranch, burning through old automobiles. Young would go "into a lot and buy a three-hundred-dollar car," recalls Guillermo Giachetti. "And then when the car would break down he'd go to another lot. Neil went from lot to lot, buying old clunkers." Carrie seemed unaffected by Young's fortunes at the time. Friends recall her agonizing over spending $5 on a pair of salt shakers.

Snodgress left motion pictures behind when she went to Broken Arrow. She became pregnant and, much to the dismay of her agents, began turning down roles. Neil's world viewed the Hollywood scene with disdain, which led to problems when Snodgress received an Oscar nomination for *Diary* and was expected to attend the ceremony. Young wasn't thrilled with the prospect. Nitzsche remembers him grousing about having to wear a tux. Snodgress ended up staying home. "We were all anti-establishment and she had the guts to thumb her nose at Hollywood," said neighbor Johanna Putnoy. "It was really considered very ballsy of her." Whatever political points it earned Carrie at home, it sealed her fate in Los Angeles. Her days as a star were over. "I always felt for Carrie, giving up her career for the love of a man," said Guillermo Giachetti.

Carrie was the hippie matriarch of Young's scene and dressed the part. She recalls that it drove Elliot Roberts's business partner crazy. "Geffen used to take me aside and say, 'My God, you guys have money. Look how you dress—combat boots and Mexican minidresses! You look like a wreck—why are you doing this?'" Giachetti noticed a curious aspect to Snodgress's attire. "Carrie looked like a guy—flannel shirts, Levi's. She started lookin' just like Neil."

.   .   .

Young initiated many projects in the early days of Broken Arrow. He started building roads and populated the ranch with livestock as well as more exotic creatures. He constructed a studio. "Neil wanted to build a clone of Quadrafonic on his ranch," said Mazer. "Same console, same feel." Morris Shepard was enlisted to craft elaborate wood cases for the equipment in the control room, dubbed the Redwood Rocketship due to its meld of the high-tech and hand-carved.* Young also began to delve into film, acquiring both the very first Magna-tech high-speed dubbing system and one of the first KEM editing machines in the country. Broken Arrow was becoming a little empire unto itself.

"We had a closed world," said Johanna Putnoy. "You live on two thousand acres and only the people you want to see come and go. Money means nothing." Joel Bernstein, visiting the ranch for the first time in February 1972, declared it "a Ponderosa for sensitive people." The center of this world was Neil, with everybody else vying for his attention in one way or another. "There was always someone who could replace you," said Putnoy. "Someone waiting in the wings to kiss ass. There was enormous competition to be close to him."

Young was not that easy to get close to. Despite all the activity swirling around him, he remained unapproachable to many. "You gotta understand that Neil would send out this vibe, like 'STAY AWAY,' and a lot of people walked around on little cat's feet because of that," said filmmaker Jeannie Field. "I think at that point Neil was just living in his own head, which is why he had gone to the ranch in the first place. He was a private man. He was not accessible."

The portrait of Young that emerges during this period is of a prolific, driven artist, a recluse who followed his whims and avoided confontation at all costs, insulated by layers of people happy to do his bidding. David Briggs would have a falling-out with Young early into the *Harvest* period. In January, Briggs had recorded two Massey Hall solo shows in Toronto, but now that Young had recorded the new material in the studio with

---

*When Shepard expressed his frustration at not being able to create full-time, Young underwrote his living expenses and got his career off the ground. As Shepard recalls, "Neil said, 'I make a lot of money and I can't think of anything better to do with it than give it to you.' I was stunned. It changed my life."

Mazer, he wouldn't even listen to the tapes. Briggs wouldn't work with Young for another two years.*

•   •   •

Young's back problems would draw out completion of the *Harvest* album. In March, Young went to London with Jack Nitzsche to record a pair of songs live with the London Symphony—"A Man Needs a Maid" and "There's a World." In April, Young returned to Nashville to cut "Harvest." September would bring the first recordings done on the ranch, with "Words," "Are You Ready for the Country?" and "Alabama" cut by backing up a remote-recording truck to a dilapidated old barn on the property, where Nitzsche would join Young's Nashville outlaws for these sessions, playing piano and, for the first time in his life, slide guitar.

Poking around an instrument shop, Young caught Nitzsche eyeing a vintage 1936 Epiphone amp and an old Kay guitar. Young bought them for Jack on the spot and, after overhearing Nitzsche fumble around with an ancient blues lick he'd copped from a Howlin' Wolf record, Neil soon appeared with "Are You Ready for the Country?"†

Much to Nitzsche's embarrassment, he was soon sitting amid bales of hay accompanying Young on the Kay guitar he barely knew how to play. Bernstein would capture the barn vibe in a photo Young used for the back cover of *Harvest:* all the Stray Gators, hands at their instruments, staring apprehensively at Young bent over his guitar, his long mane of hair totally obscuring his face, indifferent to their attention. Look at me, I'm not here.

Vocal overdubs were added by Young's CSN buddies, giving him yet another chance to weird out Graham Nash. "I'm down at the ranch and Neil goes, 'Hey, Willie, wanna hear something?' So we go down to the lake and row out to the middle in this rowboat and I think, 'Jesus Christ, this guy's been a fuckin' mystery to me all my life—if he wants to talk to me pri-

---

*Those who have heard the Massey Hall shows say they're tremendous. Twenty-five years later, when Young finally got around to listening to the tapes for his Archives project, he realized how great the recordings were, but David Briggs was no longer around to thank. "What Neil told me was, David was furious at him because he never listened," said Young's studio engineer John Nowland. "Neil sat here and heard it. . . . It was pretty intense."

†"The image in my mind was the Uncle Sam poster lookin' out, sayin', 'Are you ready for the country, because it's time to go,' " Young told Ralph Emery in 1984 when asked why he wrote the song.

vately, surely there's more places to do it than the middle of a fucking lake in a rowboat.' What he'd done is he'd wired his house as the left speaker and his entire barn as the right speaker, and they played *Harvest*. And at the end of it Elliot Mazer comes down to the shore of the lake and goes, 'Neil, how is it?' Neil turns around and shouts, *'More barn!'* "

On August 11, 1971, Young was operated on by Dr. Peter Lindstrom, undergoing a laminectomy that removed a couple of discs in his back. He was welcomed home by Carrie's parents. "My mother made this nurse's hat, my father a stethoscope. Talk about corn. Neil loved it." The months of physical debilitation were about to come to an end. Young was particularly relieved to get off the pills. "Neil hated those Percodans," said Snodgress. "He's not a man who likes bein' on dope consciousness."

Finishing *Harvest* was complicated by Young's health problems and the fact that he wanted to mix the record at home. The ornately lettered Tom Wilkes cover was another unending nightmare for the record company. Much care was given to finding just the right kind of oatmeal paper, initiating a Neil Young tradition of self-destructing album covers that drove the pressing plants crazy.

Finally the record was complete, comprised of the Mazer sessions, the two Nitzsche cuts and a live performance of "The Needle and the Damage Done" from the solo tour recorded at UCLA. "Heart of Gold" hit number one on the *Cashbox* charts on March 18, 1972 ("Old Man" would reach number thirty-one on the *Billboard* charts in June).* The album shot to number one on the *Billboard* charts and would stay in the top forty for twenty-five weeks.

Ironically, "Heart of Gold" would be bumped from the charts by a clone—America's moronic "Horse with No Name." Young even received a congratulatory phone call from his father, who heard the record on the radio and assumed it was his son. Amazingly, Elliot Roberts immediately signed the band to a management contract, a bit of information that both Nitzsche and Mazzeo would use to wind up Neil. Mazzeo: "I remember

---

*Although Young and Elliot Roberts disagree, Mazer claims both he and Young rejected copies of test pressings to delay the album's release until after the single caught fire, much to the dismay of Warner Bros., who wanted to release the single and album simultaneously. "I still think at that point they didn't figure Neil in this top-forty genre," said Mazer.

him callin' Elliot, yellin' and screamin'—'Waddya spendin' time with this copy band when you've got the original right here, Elliot?' "

Jeannie Field recalls Young showing up for dinner one night around this time. "I was really surprised. He didn't usually hang out with us—it was so unusual. Well, I found out later that Elliot had brought America up to meet him, and Neil was so pissed off there was no way he was going to meet them. He was just hiding out."

Young might've been momentarily annoyed, but by most accounts the musician was unimpressed with his massive success. "I remember coming up to the ranch one day and 'Heart of Gold' had just started on KFRC, the big top-forty station up there, and I grabbed Neil and set him out in the rent-a-car," said Elliot Mazer. "He was disappointed, hearing his song on the radio."

—Hearing your own hit song on the radio didn't thrill you, I'm told. What else is new?

—Do you have a philosophy about fame?

It's part of my life now. I can get away from it with my family—Pegi gives me a nice kind of hiding place from fame, gives it reality. There's no recipe for how to deal with fame, there's no book. I think you just gotta do what you gotta do and not be a prisoner of it. Don't try to do things just to satisfy other people—or fame can really eat you.

But, y'know, I think I focus maybe too much on that aspect of life.

I spend too much of my life thinking about fame and what's hard about it. . . . I've covered that, I've gotten into that, I've tried to figure it out. May have learned some things—I don't know how to articulate them—about how to survive.

You can't dwell on it. You can't take it seriously. You can't believe too many of the good things that people tell you. Nobody should be told that many good things about themselves. Makes you kinda cold, kinda gets so you don't feel it. Because if you feel all those things, you just can't help but get addicted to "You're different."

—Do you have a philosophy about money?

Keep it moving. Don't hoard. Money's no good, get rid of it. Turn it into people doing things. Turn it into jobs. Turn it into happiness.

—You get off on that?

Oh, I love that. The more people I employ, the happier I am—that means my money's goin' into other people's lives, and if I can give 'em somethin' to create that they can be happy with, that's great. Now that all sounds fantastic—unless you happen to work for me. The idea's great— "Okay, I work for Neil, I make records, I take care of his ranch"—but the truth of the matter is that I'm very remote.

—What was the result of Harvest?

Seclusion was a big part of it. I liked the idea of bein' able to get away. Control that part of it. Not be on the front lines all the time.

Despite its mass appeal, *Harvest* didn't fare so well with the critics. Even *Rolling Stone,* which Young has had in his pocket most of his career, panned it (to be fair, it should be pointed out that the magazine was on a bit of a roll: They had been lukewarm on *Gold Rush* and would torpedo the *Journey Through the Past* soundtrack). But *Harvest* was another important piece of the puzzle.

Mazer and the Stray Gators bring a little polish to Young's sound on *Harvest,* adding mathematical precision to his standard boom-boom tak. Consciously or not, Neil had hired Nashville pros and made 'em play like Crazy Horse. Restraining players from their licks created a palpable tension: Listen to Buttrey sneak in the tiniest variation in "Out on the Weekend," hoping the boss doesn't catch him adding the dreaded extra stuff.

"Heart of Gold" and "Old Man" were irresistible: extremely well executed, commercial country-pop of a sort Young hadn't attempted before but instantly mastered. Even these songs had some dark shadows within— who else but Young would slip into "Old Man" such an unsettling line as "Does it mean that much to me / To mean that much to you"? Was it directed at somebody in particular, or Young's entire audience? "The audience is definitely who I was going after," Young wrote to me in 2000.

"Neil has those classic elements of sturdy song construction," said Linda Ronstadt, "but still gives you something new and unique. There's just some completely classic support structures in his chord progressions—that often seem to run off the key of D—that are just so sturdy and so right, like Greek architecture. The strength of the classic traditional stuff, even though they're completely unique, they're all completely Neil."

The London sessions were Nitzsche and Young at their most over the top: The bombastic reading of "A Man Needs a Maid" gave it a pretension not present in the naked solo performances. So much of the *Harvest*-era material that seemed so heavy at the time is just that: heavy. As in *turgid, man.* Like the overly simplistic "Alabama." You might skip this one altogether if it weren't for that gorgeous howling guitar.

But then what's a great Neil Young track without the flaw? The unreleased Briggs-recorded solo demo of "See the Sky About to Rain" is one of the gems of the period, with stark, powerful lyrics just this side of Hank Williams; that is, until the excruciating end line, where Young whines about "the man" breaking his fiddle "down the middle."

Some expected more from Young. Ken Viola, who had been somewhat disappointed by what he felt was the lighter direction of *After the Gold Rush,* felt cheated by *Harvest.* The lyrics were full of "surface vagaries" and "simple chord changes"; there were none of the mind-altering surprises Viola had come to expect from his hero. Joel Bernstein preferred the bootlegs of the solo shows to what ended up on record.

Hiding out in Phoenix at the time, Bob Dylan was driven crazy by "Heart of Gold." "I used to hate it when it came on the radio," he said to Scott Cohen in 1985. "I'd say, 'Shit, that's me. If it sounds like me, it should well as be me.' . . . There I was, stuck in the desert someplace . . . I needed to lay back for a while, forget about things, myself included, and I'd get so far away and turn on the radio and there I am, but it's not me. It seemed to me somebody else had taken my thing and had run away with it, y'know, and I never got over it."

The one truly great moment on *Harvest* is "Harvest." Accompanied by the empathetic and evocative piano work of John Harris, Young explores the darker side of the Snodgress clan: The way Carrie tells it, Young pumped her for details of her bizarre family life as she and a friend tripped on acid. She revealed her mother's many false-alarm suicide attempts, which Young perhaps refers to with: "Did she wake you up to tell you that / It was only a change of plan?" "Harvest," as Briggs would say, had the spook, and Carrie's mother, Carolyn Snodgress, would burst into tears when Young invited her to the studio to hear it. Carolyn would be dead within a few years and, eerily enough, so would John Harris.*

---

* Young, of course, backed away from any commitment when I asked if Carolyn inspired the song. "She's in there," he muttered.

•   •   •

It was during the *Harvest* period that Young's film company, Shakey Pictures, was born. Young had already toyed with moviemaking, fooling around with Super-8 equipment in Topanga. The first Shakey Pictures project would be a pseudo-documentary entitled *Journey Through the Past*. Did Young work from a script? No, nothing so conventional. "I have a list," Young would tell Larry Johnson, his principal collaborator, and with a crew consisting mainly of Fred Underhill, Jeannie Field and veteran cameraman David Myers, Young ran around the country shooting mostly sixteen-millimeter footage relating to weird ideas on his list and whatever other odd ideas popped out of his skull in the process.

A man who's funny, fast and takes the weirder aspects of Young's scene with a grain of salt, Johnson said *Journey Through the Past* "was very experimental, and that to me is the strength of Neil and why he's great to work for—because he will try stuff that other people more knowledgeable than him would never think of trying, because they know all the pitfalls. Neil's the naïve explorer." Much of the film was straight-documentary footage of Young in various locations; the rest consisted of symbolic reveries that Mazzeo claimed were extrapolated from Young's dreams. The film was then augmented with bits of CSNY footage shot the previous year (much to the chagrin of Gary Burden, who felt Young hijacked his never completed documentary).

Featured in the film were some of Young's more eccentric neighbors. Richard Lee Patterson "lived in a heart-shaped hole carved in the side of a hill," said Mazzeo. "He put sod back on the roof so you couldn't tell he was there." Patterson played "The Graduate," a character who wandered silently around the desert through most of the film. Young also enlisted Gary Davis's participation. A nomad with long gray hair and a drum named Bob, Davis has floated in and out of Young's world for years. "Scary Gary—he was just this weird freak who decided he was gonna clean our studio for the rest of his life for free," said Mazzeo. "He sat around the first year just quoting the Bible—and we were rather far from the Bible." Mazzeo pinpointed the moment Young realized Davis had star potential. "I remember we were driving, and Gary said, 'You know, I find a lot of personal solace talking to my truck.' Neil went, 'You talk to your truck?' " Davis was quickly before the camera, conversing with his vehicle—and the truck, in a voice dubbed by James McCracken, talked back to him.

McCracken, who also appeared before the cameras, spent hours and hours building elaborate miniature adobe buildings housing salamanders, and then promptly destroyed them. "Mac was drunk and he didn't think Neil responded appropriately—like he was totally blown away—so he just walked all over 'em," said Mazzeo. "Neil would go, 'No! No!' and Mac would step on another one." (The incomprehensible salamander footage would give Young an out when constructing the equally incomprehensible movie; when things got too confused, he'd command Johnson, "Cut to the lizards.")

What's *Journey Through the Past* about? "About ninety minutes," quipped Johnson, and that's the kindest analysis I've ever heard. Many viewers found it unwatchable, but if you have a road map for the characters involved, *Journey Through the Past* is a valuable (if grimy) artifact of some of the more surreal and ridiculous aspects of Young's hippie lifestyle circa the early seventies.

You get to see Graham Nash haughtily lecturing someone on how to handle his master tapes. Stills wanders through a field, guitar over his shoulder, looking high out of his mind and spouting meaningless psychobabble about how in the future "the reassurance by way of words won't be necessary." Crosby, looking equally dazed, and as arrogant as ever, mumbles his own convoluted soliloquy: "I mean, man, on one side you've got a set of values that's doom, death, degradation and despair, being dealt out of the cards of the bottom of the deck by a gray-faced man who hates ya. And on the other side you've got a girl, runnin' through a field of flowers, man, half naked and laughin' in sunshine. Now you offer those two alternates to a child, and a child is too smart to make that mistake, man. It's not gonna go for that gray-faced dude with the cards."

Thankfully, Young is somewhat wittier, doing some old-car shtick in a junkyard, but it's hard to sit through endless nonscenes like the long shot of Carrie and Neil driving an old jalopy across a bridge at the ranch, then stopping to smoke a joint (which Carrie bogarts, by the way) and drink from a jug. (There is said to be a mountain of outtakes from the film, including an amusing scene where Young wanders into a record store and, as

Sugarloaf's "Green-Eyed Lady" blares in the background, claims one of his own bootlegs and walks out without paying.)

The symbolic sequences are even more inexplicable. Hooded men on horseback carrying crosses come to a 2001-like obelisk on the beach that's being circled by Gary Davis's truck. The hooded men surround the post, straining to stroke and worship it. The Graduate is handed a Bible concealing a syringe, then shoots up (this scene would contribute to the film's being banned in England and also would arouse the ire of Topanga artist Wallace Berman, who walked out of a screening angered by what he felt was Young's cavalier handling of narcotics).

The climax of all this is Young, sitting at the piano next to a billowing sawdust burner, performing a song called "Soldier": "Jesus, I saw you / Walkin' on the river / I don't believe you / You can't deliver right away." We encounter a limo containing a trio of new characters, a general, a robed religious figure and a mafioso guy who contemplate a little silver cross, then get out of the car. The end. "I can't say what the theme is," Young told one of the few audiences to see the film. "It speaks for itself."

—Do you have a beef with organized religion, Mr. Young?
HAH HAH HAH. Yeah—I do.
—What is it?
Well, y'know—there's good and bad, just like anything else, okay? The thing about religion is, it preys upon people's weaknesses. If you take that kind of power and use it in the wrong way—that's really bad. And that song "Soldier" was written to represent the subconscious of the Graduate guy movin' through his decision-making process about what he was gonna do with his life or the kinda person he was gonna be. That was the decision—to go either to drugs, to religion or the army.
—I have a feeling you see them as Let's Make a Deal—*"Don Pardo, what's behind door number one?"*
Heh heh. That's right.
—What's your concept of God, if you have one?
It's not a little guy in a white coat.
—Okay. We've ruled that out.
That's where the Bible loses all credibility.
—Why?

God created man in his own image?
—What is it to you?
What is it to me? What is God to me? God is faith that there is a higher
power. It's an understanding.
—Heaven?
It's bollocks. That's nothing. That's a story.
—Hell?
They're stories.

A responsible organized religion is one that reaches out into the con-
gregation and helps people. Uses the money, sends it back. The ones
that are just into it for the buck, go the other way—they take advantage.
Those are probably the ones that give you the most doubt *about whether*
the system is even workable.
—Do you believe in karma?
Karma's much easier to believe in than heaven and hell.
—Why?
It makes more sense. It happens. But the heaven and hell story—those
are just big metaphors for "You go up *or* down." *Y'know—"What did*
you do? How did you fare?" All that stuff. That's just a way of measur-
ing whether you're a good person or a bad person. They gotta give you
a conscience—tryin' to organize this conscience to be responsible.

Define faith *and* conscience*—it's very hard to do. So people write*
stories. To explain what they are. The Bible is one of them. None of them
are perfect. They all got mixed reviews. Some people like one, but they
don't like the other. Nobody likes all of them. So in the end these
stories—heaven and hell and Adam and Eve—the whole fuckin' thing is
no more than this year's crop of movies. They're just stories to hang
your hat on.

Once completed, *Journey Through the Past* was screened at the ranch for
John Calley, vice president of production at Warner Bros. and, according
to Larry Johnson, "a young, hip guy who understood." But apparently
Young's vision wasn't easy for even Calley to decipher. "It was the shock
of his life," said Johnson. "He was wide-eyed and sorta . . . left. I think
that's when Neil realized it wasn't commercially viable." The film was also
shown to executives at Universal, where Snodgress was still under con-

tract. After seeing the actress puffing on a joint in the movie, the suits terminated her immediately. "Clever Neil," said Snodgress.

Warner Bros. took the two-record soundtrack—a mishmash of source music and such must-haves as a sidelong workout on "Words"—and dumped it on the marketplace before the movie was out. "They chickened out on the movie because they thought it was weird," Young told Cameron Crowe. "That's the only instance of discooperation and confusion I've ever had with Warner's. . . . They fucked me for sure."

The film premiered at the U.S. Film Festival in Dallas on April 8, 1973. It then ran at a couple of art houses but received scant notice, none of it positive. "To be charitable, Neil's filmic odyssey, a $400,000 home movie, makes any of the old 'Francis, the Talking Mule' films seem absolutely incisive," wrote critic Henry Armetta.

Graham Nash associate Mac Holbert recalls attending a special screening for Young's peers. "At dinner, nobody said much about it . . . I remember everybody walking away very confused. They were all a little embarrassed, because maybe there was something they should've caught—'There must be something there, because Neil did it.' " Young was apparently unfazed by the apathetic response. "Neil got in his car and left. He didn't give a shit what people thought about it."

I bought this Beaulieu Super-8 and I was workin' with it. And I worked with it and worked with it. Then I went to Hawaii and I shot stuff in a zoo. Filming the animals and filming the flowers, filming everything—with all these jungle sounds like you were in the Amazon. I think the concept was that, "It's a jungle," y'know, but you could always see a little litter. . . . You could never see fences *or anything, but you always knew, heh heh. I'm better at ideas than I am at actually doing things.*

Later, I shot a commercial. Hyatt Hotel. Jeannie Field got me the job. I was just hired on as Bernard Shakey, cameraman. I had my assistant who knew how to set up the camera—which I didn't. I can remember doing a long pan over these suitcases outside on the street with the traffic going by and, like, two hundred suitcases, and this one guy standing there with a red outfit and a hat. I pulled back to the Hyatt—that was my big payoff shot.

It was like "When you arrive in L.A., stay at the Hyatt," so I went to the airport, went into one of the revolving restaurants, and I was shooting all these people in the restaurant. You're not supposed to do that, they really didn't want me in there. I told them, "We're doing a commercial for Hyatt." I got thrown out of the fucking revolving restaurant at the L.A. airport, me and my assistant. It was great. I shot a bunch of footage. They didn't use much of my shit. . . . I don't think they used any. *It had a little bit of a slant.*

Super-8 made me ill. I got sick. I think I musta OD'd on it or somethin'— I was so into it, I got a fever. It was like you eat something poison and you get sick, you never wanna have it again? After that, every time I thought about filming I got sick. That was the end of it. I didn't want to have any more to do with the camera.
—*Sometimes* other people *feel sick when they see* your *movies.*
HAH HAH HAH. That's right.
—*Most people I talk to think* Journey Through the Past *is a self-indulgent piece of shit that doesn't make any sense. Does that bother you?*
No. That wasn't why I did it. I didn't make the film to teach anybody anything or to preach to anybody. I made it to express myself. So in that way it was pretty selfish. But I had this dream. I had this image of the way these things went together and I just couldn't stop myself from doing it.

It's pretty obscure. I haven't seen it for years. Years. There should be some funny stuff in there—drunk debutantes singing "Let Me Call You Sweetheart" while lizards are invading this little castle somewhere with an electric chair in it and all this shit Mac made. . . . What a nutty fuckin' movie. See, I wasn't intimidated by anybody. Nobody could stop me at that point. Now I probably wouldn't do that kinda movie. I'd have to really open up to do that. I really would. And I think there's room for that kind of movie—little metal people, trains and shit. Lizards . . .

I thought what was happening in my life was very innaresting. Should be documented—heh heh—and then I found out that, y'know, I had no perspective and was an egomaniac because I did that. But I had to make that movie to find out. Heh heh.

It's a little like windsurfing. I was really into it. I got all the equipment, and I windsurfed a couple of years. I thought about it a lot. Read windsurfing magazines. Finally one day I realized, "Fuck, I could just be doin' this for the rest of time, just buyin' equipment—new equipment comes out every four months. Windsurfing's great, but I'm not really *very good." I never was able to get a jibe down. So I stopped. But I did* *it for two or three years. It totally distracted me. And when I made films,* *that was a major distraction. For years. From music, okay? It enabled* *me to* come back *to music.*

"You're the only friend I have, because you're the only one that tells me the truth," Young would say to Jack Nitzsche on their car rides through the ranch. "So I played that role," said Nitzsche. "I told Neil he was an asshole—not realizing I was being an asshole myself a lotta the time."

Nitzsche had become the most improbable addition to the ranch bunch, living with his wife, Gracia, and son, Jack, in a house he rented from El- liot Roberts. Jack Jr. recalls that living at the ranch wasn't the brightest time for the Nitzsche family. His father was obsessed with voodoo, and "he would use this shit to scare me. He once got me in a car when I was a kid—he was pretty drunk—and he started screamin' at me that he was the Angel of Death."

The arranger quickly grew weary of playing second banana to Young. "It was stifling, because I was there for Neil, and that started to get to me," said Nitzsche. "I started drinking heavy, doing a lot of drugs and becom- ing more abusive to Neil."

Few understood the relationship. "The ridicule Neil suffered at the hands of Jack's opinions was ruthless—and that's what turned Neil on," said Snodgress, who felt Nitzsche was acting out of envy. "I mean, look at all the music Jack Nitzsche's written, and who knows who Jack Nitzsche is?" Nitzsche reserved his most potent venom for Carrie herself. "I didn't get along with her at all. I said to Neil immediately when I met her, 'This is the biggest phony I've ever met in my life. What an asshole this woman is—she's constantly lying, she's an actress.' "

Nitzsche's main running buddy was James McCracken, who was get- ting more and more out of control. "Neil tried to hang in there, but McCracken wore out his welcome everywhere he went," said Mazzeo. "He always bit the hand that fed him, really hard." One night he pulled up to Young's door at two in the morning, drunk out of his mind, demanding that Neil buy ten of his paintings and give him thousands of dollars immedi- ately to "fix his magic carpet." Young declined, and, according to Mazzeo,

McCracken "pulls out his dick and pisses on Neil's brand-new oriental rug that cost, like, sixteen thousand dollars."*

Rogue behavior like this only further endeared him to Nitzsche. And, according to Mazzeo, "It was suicide hanging out with those guys. You'd hop in the car and they'd both be drinking and they'd start arguin' in the front seat, and Mac would just take the wheel and the car would go off the road into a cow field. Nitzsche would be very indignant 'cause now he didn't know where the road was." Nitzsche and McCracken would try to out-macho each other by throwing knives and grinding their hands into broken glass. Needless to say, the peace-and-love types were terrified by these two.

At some point McCracken ventured off to the desert and—painting with the whiskers of a dead mouse he'd accidentally overdosed on hash—created a Bosch-like image of a horse skull to adorn Nitzsche's album of classical music for Reprise, *St. Giles Cripplegate*. Recorded with the London Symphony Orchestra and produced by Elliot Mazer, the record didn't even feature Jack's name on the cover. Surely it ranks as one of the most bizarre releases by a major label. "After you deliver something like *Harvest* to the record company, they'll let you come in their mouth," said Mazer.

Nitzsche felt Young had gotten a little carried away in lording over his empire. "Neil would've made a terrible southerner," cracked Jack. He began to feel sorry for Neil, who he felt was besieged by the scene he'd let happen. "When Neil took Carrie, he took a whole fucking load of people, a commune of his very own. Carrie was treated like a goddamn queen, and these stupid hippies would talk about 'the inner circle' . . . it was so ridiculous. 'Ohhh, far out'—that's the most profound thing anybody ever said. What could I do but rant and rave, surrounded by that kind of assholery?"

Jack watched as Neil grew weary of the situation. The last straw came when Carrie's parents parked a trailer directly outside Young's kitchen door. "I couldn't figure out how Neil could take it. And one day he came up in one of his old cars and came in the house and said, 'Man, if some-

---

*Now sober and creating art in Maine, McCracken has little memory of his antics with Young but doesn't deny they happened. "I used to drink so much I had blackouts—didn't remember what I'd done. Neil was mostly very gracious when I would get crazy and do stuff—I probably woulda said, 'Hey, that's enough. I don't ever wanna see you again.' I stepped outta line a lot with that guy. I had no respect."

thing doesn't change pretty soon, you're gonna see flying Snodgresses out here.' "

—*Was the ranch kind of a commune when it was first started?*
Not in my eyes. Maybe in Carrie's it was. When it first started, it was just a little tiny farm, a hundred and forty acres. Louie and Clara living across the way, me and Johnny Barbata and Guillermo Giachetti in the ranch house. So it wasn't a commune. It started to be a little like a commune when Carrie moved in. . . . Carrie had so many people around all the time, it was sick.
—*How did you put up with it?*
Well, y'know, I just wasn't very forceful. I was never an enforcing type of person. I give people a lotta slack, a lotta rope, and either they have a good time and a good relationship—or they hang themselves. That's basically it. But I'm not a controller that way. McCracken's a great artist. He was a little scary because he was so fuckin' out of it. Guy had to pee on my rug and ask for ten G. It's not my deal. I know I didn't owe him ten G. That was his trip.

I don't like to tell people what to do, what they should do to make me comfortable or whatever. I figure either they know or they don't. That's the way I was then—now I communicate a lot more with Pegi because, number one, I know Pegi would never lie to me. Pegi tells me the truth all the time. That's a big difference right there.
—*How did that affect you? Seems to me honesty's pretty important to you.*
Well, y'know, honesty's important, but I'm not that honest myself. I did a lotta things in my early relationships that I couldn't talk about where I was fuckin' around and everything. I'm as guilty as the next guy. So honesty's a matter of how you use the word. It doesn't have to do so much with "Oh he never told a lie" or "He never covered anything up." That's not honesty. Honesty's something else. I can't put my finger on it. Because I know I'm not. People tend to think I'm honest because I speak from the heart. If that's what honesty is, I'm honest. But if honesty's never telling a lie in your whole life, then I'm not honest. I'm as much of a fuckin' dishonest person as the next guy.

Louie—What did I get from him? Just a nice old guy. It was cool when he was there. Times were simple. I didn't realize for him it was the end of an era and for me it was the beginning of one. Too many things happened on the ranch. He told me he had to go. Too many changes.

"Whenever Neil's had a big success, he's had to do something to counter it or he can't appreciate it," said Elliot Roberts. "Always. His whole life. After every big album he'll do something inane—like put on blackface and do a minstrel show."

Young's own sheet music for "Only Love Can Break Your Heart" is adorned with a sketch illustrating the Neil Young of the early seventies— the forlorn, lonely troubadour with a guitar. With the massive success of his past two albums and the work with CSN, Young had created a persona that would prove so indelible some would never know him as anything else. But just as quickly as Young created, he would destroy, and the music that followed the radio-friendly *Harvest* would please few of those expecting some kind of consistency, whether they were his fans, the record company or the handlers and musicians around him.

It would take a terrible tragedy to send Young on his way. In 1992 Kristine McKenna would ask Neil what episodes in his life had forced him to grow up. "The birth of my children and the death of my friends," Young responded. The joy of his firstborn came on September 8, 1972, with the arrival of Zeke. Next Young would experience the death of a friend, and it would spiral him into the shadier side of life.

world on a string

"Everybody tried to save Danny—everybody," said Don Paris, stiff drink in shaking hand. "But hey—we're lucky we lived through the sixties. Shit happened.

"Danny was the dustiest guy, just the dustiest. He was too good, too damn good. He had a heart of gold. He gave too much. Shared too much. Bottom line—he loved too much. But Mr. Whitten's not gone—he's holdin' up the sky right now. He's here. Every day I feel him." As if on cue, Whitten's voice wafts up from a jukebox down below. Sitting in the upstairs office of his dingy Hollywood bar, Don Paris sighs.

Paris is one of those unsung heroes who support a band not because of fame or money but for the love of music. He was a dancer at the Peppermint West with Danny, and the two were running buddies until the end. For years after Whitten's death, he wore one of Danny's teeth around his neck. "Don Paris was Crazy Horse's spiritual adviser," said guitarist George Whitsell. "Don always had a joint down his boot and a couple of reds for the end of the evening."

"C'mon—I got somethin' I want you to hear." Paris leads me down through the bowels of the bar and into a grim parking lot out back. Ignoring the overflowing garbage bins, blaring radios and a lone stray cat, we get into an old beat-up car. Paris sticks a cassette into the deck and turns away. "I can't listen," he says, shaking his head. "Not today."

I know what the tape is before the music starts. For months I've been after Paris to play me the last demos Whitten ever cut, and now, after months of meetings, Don has finally decided I'm worthy. It's only four rough sketches, a small piece of the story, but I'm unprepared for the emotions the music draws out. "Oh Boy," the last song on the tape—and the last Whitten would sing in this world—is the clincher. "I think about the times that I was happier than now / Oh boy," he sings, worrying the "Oh boy" in a way few white men can. The words are so sad, the voice so weary, that you can reach only one conclusion: Danny Whitten knew he was checking out.

.   .   .

The year or so following *After the Gold Rush* was not easy for Danny Whitten. First came the Crazy Horse solo record recorded in the fall of 1970 that Jack Nitzsche produced with the help of Bruce Botnick. "Danny wasn't playing for shit," Jack recalls. "Every now and then he'd nod out and wouldn't play. So I stopped everything and said, 'Fuck it. We might as well not have a session today. 'Cause Danny's stoned out of his mind nodding off.' Danny said, 'Hey, man—I took a Valium and drank a vodka and it really got to me.' 'You haven't had any junk? You're not strung out?' He said, 'No, man, I'm totally clean.' Danny was real hurt and angry that I would ask and really made a fucking scene. He stormed out of the room. I thought, 'Oh my God, maybe I did make a mistake.' So I went into the men's room and there he was with a fuckin' needle in his arm. He said, 'Hey—this is good shit. Want some?' "

Figuring misery loves company, Nitzsche actually got high with Danny, then went on to finish the one great Whitten-era Horse document—*Crazy Horse*. Besides "Gone Dead Train," a rocker with lyrics Nitzsche and Russ Titleman cobbled together from scores of old blues songs expertly mumbled by Whitten, the album contains "I Don't Want to Talk About It," a haunting ballad coauthored by Nils Lofgren that would provide Whitten with a posthumous hit when Rod Stewart covered it in 1975.

Once the album was finished, Whitten continued to fall apart. During rehearsals for a tour to support the album, Ralph Molina fired Danny. "I remember being in a rehearsal studio in San Francisco and the shit hit the fan," Molina said. "Danny said, 'Okay, am I in the band or not?' Jack and Billy said it was up to me. Without any hesitation, I said, 'Danny, you're *out*. We can't even rehearse. You're too fuckin' gone.' I couldn't believe I said that. I think Billy and Jack were stunned, too. I remember Danny saying, 'Oh, so now *you're* Crazy Horse.' "

Back in Los Angeles, Whitten made several attempts at a methadone program and failed. He began to drink heavily and take pills, gaining weight and losing his surfer good looks in the process. There was an ill-fated trip to Maryland where he was to join Nils Lofgren's band Grin, but "Danny was just gone," said Lofgren. "He was just in too much pain to pull himself out of it." Lofgren sent Whitten back home, where he begged Molina to let him back in Crazy Horse.

Marie Janisse, his old dance partner from the Peppermint West, sent him a weekly roll of dimes with a note attached, imploring him to call. Whitten wouldn't see her. "He said, 'I love you too much. I don't want you to see me the way I am.' "

When he wasn't blasted on alcohol and pills, Whitten went on heroin/cocaine speedball rampages, terrifying his friends with the massive amounts of drugs involved. "Danny had a tolerance that wouldn't quit," said Don Paris. "A tolerance of three or four human beings. It was unreal." Whitten would hole up in his apartment, sitting in his bathtub mainlining for weeks on end. Whitten's hero, he now told people, was fellow addict Bela Lugosi.

"Near the end Danny was a different guy," said Three Dog Night's Danny Hutton. "He just turned into a stone junkie. You didn't trust him anymore." Whitten lived with Hutton until Hutton threw him out, then snuck back in and stole a guitar. Although cheap and beat to hell, the instrument had great sentimental value for Hutton, who had used it to write his first hit. "Danny must've gotten five dollars for it. It's like somebody stealin' a picture of your mother."

Whitten continued on his downward spiral, ripping off friends and burning bridges. For a while he lived with Rockets guitarist George Whitsell, who said, "Danny was pretty disillusioned and saddened by everything. He realized that he'd blown it with Neil, the Horse and the Rockets. He inferred it was the pressure of workin' with Neil, which to me was a cop-out. 'I'm a star, now I feel guilty, I broke up the Rockets'—this kind of shit. It didn't wash with me." Whitsell asked Danny to leave when he found him shooting up with a friend in the bathroom. "A week later, I got ripped off and found some of Danny's cigarette butts in the driveway."

Somehow Whitten managed to pull himself together enough to record that last four-song demo. Nothing happened with the songs, and Danny Whitten's light continued to fade. He made another attempt to escape heroin, heading off to Mexico with his old friend Terry Sachen. On the way, they stopped in Encinitas at the home of Whitten's vocal partner from Danny and the Memories, Ben Rocco, who watched as Whitten downed an entire bottle of Jose Cuervo Gold. "Danny was trying to kick heroin, so he was drinking tons of tequila," said Sachen. The trip was a disaster. "When we came across the border they asked if we had anything to declare, so Danny threw up on the guy."

. . .

It was in this state that Danny Whitten arrived at Broken Arrow ranch for *Time Fades Away* rehearsals sometime in the fall of 1972. Someone had convinced Young that Whitten was off drugs, and Neil put him on a $500-a-week retainer. Some say Young's good intentions only made it easier for him to continue the abuse. The real mystery is how anyone could've thought Danny was in good enough shape for any kind of tour.

Nitzsche was there when Whitten showed up. "I could tell he was using. I waited until Neil was gone. I said, 'Jesus Christ, man, you're fucked up.'" Once again, Whitten claimed it was only the vodka and Valium talking. Carrie Snodgress remembers Nitzsche showing up at the house that night to deliver the bad news about Danny's condition. "Jack just put on this curse that it wasn't gonna be any good, that you don't change a dope addict. He kept telling Neil, 'You're blind, you're blind, man, he's fucked up.'"

Arrangements were made for Whitten to stay at the white house with the rest of the musicians, but Danny requested his own place, ending up in an old Airstream trailer just outside the studio. "To Neil, that was already a little sign of trouble," said Snodgress.

Rehearsals went miserably, with Whitten in terrible shape. "It was just amazing," said Kenny Buttrey. "The guy was asleep standing upright. He'd be playing guitar right in rhythm—but *after* the song was over. I'd have to say, 'Danny, it's over now. We're finished.' I really didn't know who Danny Whitten was. I just thought, 'This guy can't play a note, man. What's he doin' in our band?'"

Nitzsche concurred. "Danny couldn't play anything. He just stood there. Neil would say, 'Danny, ya gotta play. Ya gotta learn these songs.' And Danny would go, 'Hey Jack, play "Be My Baby."' The vibe was, like, silence."

Nitzsche also remembered a communal dinner where Whitten, who had been drinking, launched into the story of the sadistic naval officer who had made him stand guard in subzero temperatures and how the resulting frostbite had caused his arthritis. "Danny said, 'Did any of you guys ever feel like killing somebody?' And the room was totally silent. All these hippie girls in calico dresses cooking 'healthy stew.' They all went silent, Neil included. I just laughed."

Whitten spent more and more time alone in his trailer. "I brought over a bunch of sandwiches and Danny wouldn't eat," said Carrie Snodgress. "He'd laugh about how hard it was to teach an old dog new tricks. He said, 'I can't do it, I can't do it. I just don't belong here.' And he cried."

Young refused to give up on Whitten. Between rehearsals, he'd go over to the trailer and try to teach him the songs one-on-one. "Neil was totally convinced that Danny was gonna be great again," said Snodgress. "Because up until the last minute, when they let him go, Neil was sayin', 'Maybe today, maybe today.' "

But Whitten got no better and Young, facing the biggest tour of his career, had to make a decision. Danny was fired. He was given $50 and a ticket back to L.A. Snodgress had a bad feeling as she watched him being driven off the ranch. "I said to Neil, 'I'm scared, I'm scared. This doesn't feel right.' But Neil had too much to do. Too much to think about. It was just so sad. So sad."

On the flight back to Los Angeles, Whitten reportedly became inebriated and had to be restrained. Later that same day—November 18, 1972—he wound up at a friend's house at 143 North Manhattan Place. That evening, Whitten called up Nitzsche. "Danny asked, 'Would you be there for me? No matter what?' I said, 'Sure,' and he said, 'That's all I wanna know,' and hung up." At some point, Whitten went into the bathroom and never came out. A female companion found him dead on the floor. An autopsy revealed that he had died of "acute diazepam and ethanol intoxication"—an overdose of alcohol and Valium.

"I always thought that was kind of ironic, 'cause Danny more or less taught me about drugs, and he'd always tell me not to take depressants when you're drinkin'," recalled childhood friend Larry Lear. "He was real explicit with that." Some say Danny's death was just one of those unfortunate accidents, while others, like Jack Nitzsche, believe it was suicide: "The third day Danny was up at the ranch, he said, 'I got a feeling Neil's gonna fire me. Man, if that happens, it's all over for me. That's just the end of the line.' The poor fucker."

"That night between twelve and one o'clock we got the phone call," said Snodgress. "It was the Los Angeles police department. They had found a white male, no identification, just a note with Neil's phone number. Neil was a mess. That was very hard for him. It's somethin' Neil will carry with him to the grave."

Brenda Whitten knew nothing of her brother's death until a telegram came from the Westwood Village mortuary, asking her to pick up the body. Out to Los Angeles she went. Brenda was given Danny's worldly possessions, all of which fit into a cardboard box. There was a clipboard, a couple of shirts, a few pairs of pants and a gold record. "I brought it home wrapped in newspaper. I stopped at the gate and the electronic thing went off and I created a scene. It was a real trip comin' home. I cried all the way back."

·   ·   ·

News of Danny's death circulated discreetly among the denizens of Broken Arrow ranch. "We never talked about it," said Kenny Buttrey. "It was like somethin' that didn't happen."

"It was horrible," recalled Jeannie Field, working in the editing room on *Journey Through the Past* at the time. "It was so serious. I don't think anybody did anything about it. I think that's the toughest part. I think if we'd had a memorial for him at the ranch—y'know, lit a fire or a candle—it probably would've been a lot better. Nobody was to think about it. It was as if it hadn't happened. Business as usual. It's very interesting that, for all the hippie values, there were some very unhippie things goin' down."

The death of Danny Whitten would cast a long shadow. "I loved Danny," Young told Cameron Crowe in 1975. "I felt responsible." Mazzeo was one of the few people to discuss the subject with Young at the time. "Neil told me, 'Hey, every musician has one guy on the planet that he can play with better than anyone else. You only get one guy. My guy was Danny Whitten.' "

—What effect did Danny's passing have on you?
A big effect. I felt responsible. But really there was nothin' I could do—I mean, he *was responsible. But I thought I was for a long time.*

—Ralph has told me over and over, "We should've been able to do more for Danny."
Uh-huh. That's right.
—You'd handle it differently today?
I think I would. I was very young at that time. I had very little experience—not that I have a lot of experience now. That was a tough period. It was a learning process.

Danny just wasn't happy. It just all came down on him. He was engulfed by this drug. That was too bad. Because Danny had a lot to give, boy. He was really good.

See, I had the whole Harvest *band together, and I wanted to get Danny into it. Y'know, it may be that playing with those guys is what got him so fucked up—that's a different thing from playing with the Horse. Maybe if he'd been playing with Billy and Ralph, he would've been less threatened and the music might've brought him out of it. But he was gone. Not in good shape at all.*

Last time I saw him, he was really wasted. Couldn't keep it together to remember what he was doin' in the sessions. I had to tell him he wasn't in the band. That was a drag. Then he went home and OD'd. That was devastating.

The day after Whitten's death, Young wrote "Don't Be Denied," in which he recounted the story of his life: getting beaten up in school, his father leaving, the promise of music and the moment that dreams can fail. Young had come this far and there was no turning back. "Don't be denied, don't be denied," he would scream out over and over on the next tour. Who was he trying to convince—himself?

"Don't Be Denied" has a lot to do with Danny, I think. . . . Any big event will inspire a song, and that indeed was a very large event. I think that's the first major life-and-death event that really affected me in what I was trying to do. Like when one of your parents dies, or a friend dies, you kinda reassess yourself as to what you're doing—because you realize life is so impermanent. So you wanna do the best you can while you're here, to say whatever the fuck it is you wanna say. Express yourself.

What did I learn? Well, I learned that I missed Danny. As a person. It was such a loss. You can't count on things. You just can't take things for granted. Anything could go at any time.

That's why things have lasted so long—because there's always been something in the way to stop things from happening the way they could have, the optimum. . . . Some people get it, and they get it so quick. The Beatles, the Stones, Led Zepplin, the Who—for years they had all their original guys, so they could go out and do it.

It never happened right with Buffalo Springfield. Bruce Palmer—lost him right away. With Crazy Horse, when the big success came, the band was gone—we lost Danny. Things like that happened a lot—for a long time. When it doesn't happen right away, it means you don't go too far too fast. So you keep trying. You don't give up. That's the positive *side of it.*

Young's troubles did not end with Danny Whitten's death. As rehearsals continued, the subject of money came up among the players. Kenny Buttrey—very much in demand as a Nashville session man—informed Elliot Roberts that he needed $100,000 to tour. Jack Nitzsche found out and relayed the news to Tim Drummond, who talked Jack into telling Neil that the rest of the band wanted the same.

"Of course, I did it with the worst timing—in the middle of rehearsal and a six-pack of beer," Nitzsche said glumly. "I was drunk as a skunk. Neil said, 'We'll talk about that later.' Instead of having manners, I made him name it. Oh God, Neil got so pissed off. 'Okay, you got a hundred thousand each—are ya happy now? Is that gonna make you play better?' I don't think things ever recovered after that."

My least favorite record is Time Fades Away. *I think it's the worst record I ever made—but as a documentary of what was happening to me, it was a great record. I was onstage and I was playing all these songs that nobody had heard before, recording them, and I didn't have the right band. It was just an uncomfortable tour. It was supposed to be this big deal—I just had* Harvest *out, and they booked me into ninety cities. I felt like a*

product, and I had this band of all-star musicians that couldn't even look *at each other. It was a total joke.*
—Interview with Dave Ferrin, 1987

"I'm singin' this borrowed tune / I took from the Rolling Stones / Alone in this empty room / Too wasted to write my own." Written in a Wisconsin hotel around the start of the *Time Fades Away* tour and performed solo on piano and harmonica, the barren "Borrowed Tune" set the vibe for things to come.

The first show was at Milwaukee Auditorium on January 5, 1973, a gray winter day. A terrified Linda Ronstadt was the opening act for the grueling three-month tour. Adding to her discomfort was a drunken, taunting Jack Nitzsche, who, suffering from his own stage fright, would make things interesting for everyone. "I was an asshole," he said, crediting Neil for putting up with him. "Anyone else would've had me thrown off, beaten up or killed."*

The band traveled in an old Electra prop jet. Ben Keith's wife, Linda, a redheaded former stewardess, roamed the aisles waiting on the band. "You could do anything on that plane you wanted. Anything," said assistant engineer Denny Purcell. "There was some really incredible dope people were smokin', the air you could hardly see through, and the door to the pilot was open. I got to thinking, 'Man, if those guys are as stoned as I am, I'm *scared.*' "

Much of the smoke emanated from Big Red, a homemade hookah built from an aquarium pump. "We called it, 'Gettin' the wagons in a circle,' " said Drummond. "It was like puttin' your mouth over the exhaust pipe of a car." Between the pot, pills, booze and coke, the band was blotto much of the time. "Halfway through the tour, after a crazy number of nights, I remember Ben coming in and saying, 'What key is "Don't Be Denied"?' " said Mazer. "This was a song he'd been playing for three months."

Carrie Snodgress floated in and out of the tour. I asked Elliot Mazer to characterize her presence. "Remember Monty Python—'Spot the Looney'?

---

*In Texas on February 24, Young and the band crossed paths with country-rock icon Gram Parsons, who was also playing a gig in Houston. Sharing a limo, Nitzsche appalled everyone by taking one glance at Parsons and muttering, "You look like Danny . . . and Danny's dead." Parsons would overdose just seven months later.

Carrie was always rolling joints and had this crazy band of characters around her. There was a certain vibe in that relationship which was very weird, and I don't think it made Neil particularly happy. Something wasn't right and I think he knew it."

Snodgress felt a wall developing between her and Young. "I'd say, 'Let's go for a walk,' and he couldn't, he was so tied up with the pressure. It was the beginning of booze, Cuervo Gold and a rock and roll tour that was overbooked."

Ken Viola, who snuck backstage at Boston Music Hall, had an unsettling encounter with his hero: "Neil came out and grabbed me by the lapels and stuck his face right in my face and said *'They're gonna win the war!'* " Young was more out of control than Viola had ever seen him, then or since. "Neil was boozed up. He let go of me, pushed the door open and ran outside. He was runnin' around out there until Elliot came and got him. Neil was way out."

Much to the consternation of the audience, a third of the songs performed would be dark new rockers that bore little relation to the gentle acoustic bliss of *Harvest*. Young—who had tried unsuccessfully to record a new album during rehearsals—decided at the last minute to record the new songs live on the road, and Elliot Mazer had to scramble to put a recording truck together. Young dubbed the traveling studio "His Master's Wheels."

Denny Purcell, manning an onstage video camera that fed to the recording truck, still remembers the intensity of Young's gaze. "Sometimes you'd zoom in on Neil and those lasers would come right through the camera. I didn't want to look through the lens." Purcell sensed no great love between artist and producer. "I never figured out why Mazer had the gig. 'Cause the most I ever saw Neil beam those looks was right at Elliot."

Mazer wasn't alone. "We'd have incredibly tense sound checks," said Buttrey. "Once, Joel brought out a review from the night before and it wasn't favorable. Neil just reeled around and, with his guitar neck, knocked the article out of Joel's hand—and all the mikes across the stage—and told him, 'Don't ever do that shit again!' "

When Young wasn't putting everyone through the meat grinder, he was unapproachable or out of sight. At hotels, he stayed on a separate floor. Anyone who tried to talk to him was chased off by his ever blustery road manager, Leo Makota. "There was always separation," said Nitzsche. "Neil was in the penthouse. Fuck him.

"Neil was such a jerk on that tour. Now he's a star, he's not easygoing Neil anymore. He'd yell at people. We'd get to a town and he'd say, 'I want everybody to stay in their rooms, 'cause we're gonna do a sound check and rehearsal.' So we'd sit in our rooms and sit in our rooms and we wouldn't hear anything until two hours before the show, and then he'd say, 'Well, there's not gonna be a sound check, just be ready to go.' It wasn't like 'Jesus, I'm sorry, you guys, we fucked up here.' It was as though he *owned* us. Since he was gonna pay us that much money, he could treat us like slaves."

When the sound checks did take place, things weren't any better. Young was playing a Gibson Flying V, an instrument that would not be seen again after the tour. He spent hours changing his guitar rig around, moving amps, tinkering with mikes, driving the band and the crew crazy in the process. "The Flying V sounded like shit," said Joel Bernstein. "Neil was never happy."

"There was always a lecture in the dressing room after the show," said Nitzsche. He'd say, 'I don't want you guys to play so stiff, I want you to loosen up, play what you feel, not what we rehearsed.' The next night we'd all stretch out a bit more, and in the dressing room a new lecture would come—'I can't let you guys just ramble and play whatever the fuck you want. I mean, you gotta stick to the arrangement.' Finally I said, 'Why don't you put *both speeches* on a cassette and tell us *which one to play* in our hotel room?' "

Nitzsche had terrible stage fright and turned to the bottle to cope. The more he drank, the more hostile he became toward Young. "We used to solo Jack's vocal mike in the truck," said Mazer. "He would do commentary, say shit into the microphone, editorializing. Neil would sing a line and Jack would answer him—'I don't believe that. *Bullshit!*' The audience wouldn't hear it because [soundman Tim] Mulligan had the mike off, but I was sitting in the truck hearing this shit and just getting hysterical."

Nitzsche found little humor in the situation. "I remember playing a big hockey arena somewhere and Ben's out there during the opening act, sitting on a folding chair just staring at the audience. He turns to me and said, 'You may not know it, but this is the greatest time in your life.' I said, 'If this is as good as it gets, *suicide* is a real viable alternative.' " Jack got so fed up with Neil at one drunken moment that he went up to Young's room and pissed on the floor. Neil was unfazed. "Aaaah, you just did that because McCracken did it," he told Nitzsche, whose whizzing was something of a trademark. "Were that it was just hotel rooms," said Carrie Snodgress. "His own home was the worst. Jack was always whippin' that thing out."

Jack was pretty steady. Really. He was just fucked up all the time. But he was pretty steady.
—He was givin' you a hard time.
Oh yeah . . . a hard time from Jack's not that bad. It's just like gettin' a hard time from Briggs, y'know. They're just doin' it to keep me real. In some ways, I guess Jack thinks that I sold out when I started playin' with Crazy Horse.
—Did he tell you that?
No. *I got that feeling—that somethin' I did somewhere along the line with my albums made him not respect me or not like me like he used to.*
—I think everybody goes through that feeling with Jack.
AHAHAHAHA. To tell ya the truth, I don't remember much about that tour. I don't remember bein' with anybody much. I was mostly alone. I've had some funny ideas in my time about what was the right thing to do. That was a big tour . . . I coulda made a big impression. But it just goes to show ya. Every time I've had a big tour, it's been a shitty tour. A tour where I took the wrong people.

Kenny Buttrey had the most miserable time of all. "I remember one of the rehearsals. It was after dinner, everybody had a couple beers. We were gonna count off the song we'd been workin' on all that day, and just for the hell of it I did some drum pickups. Neil stopped right there and said, 'That's what I *don't* want. I don't want you to *ever* do that again,' and he just proceeded to jump down my throat. From that day on, I never played one drum fill. I played just the licks Neil wanted me to play—I was just so damn afraid to add anything I felt."

Things got much worse out on the road when Young began complaining Buttrey wasn't drumming loud enough. "Two or three hours at sound check, Neil would just jump all over me. I was a studio drummer. I never had to play that loud in my life."

Bernstein saw Young grow so furious at one sound check that he plunged a drumstick through the snare and stormed out. Young kept telling Buttrey to get bigger sticks, until the clerk at one music store finally told the drummer, "Son, anything bigger than this is gonna have *bark* on it." Nothing worked, and adding to Buttrey's misfortune was the fact that Mazzeo—who knew nothing about drums—had been hired to be his roadie. "I wasn't an expert drum tech," said Mazzeo, smiling. "I'd tune these heads and go bam-bam, 'Well, close enough.' "

"I was playin' ten times louder than I had ever played in my life," said Buttrey. "I was tryin' thicker heads, bigger sticks. It was drivin' me crazy. I looked down at the snare drum one night and saw somethin' splatter. My hand would bleed, it was drippin' down the stick and formed a big puddle on the snare. And when I hit the drum, blood would fly through the air. I just said, 'Oh man, what's happening here? This is a damn nightmare.' It was the roughest time of my life. I wouldn't go through that again for ten times that amount."

Buttrey didn't have an easy time. I was not really groovin' on the music. Buttrey was not really cuttin' it for that kind of music. He was uncomfortable out there. There was nothin' wrong with the way Buttrey was, the problems stemmed from me. *It was* my *fault* the tour didn't come off. *I tried to get the band to do somethin' they couldn't do. I probably shoulda had Billy and Ralph out there with Jack and Ben—but I didn't know that at the time.*
—Did it get any better when Buttrey left?
A little bit. But not really.

I was searching for something that I never really got. It didn't get to the groove like I wanted it to. I never really nailed it. And y'know, you could blame anybody for that, but I blame myself. I don't think I put together the right organization.

It was a bad tour. I didn't feel good. Didn't have a great time. Not a lot of smiling. It wasn't like you would expect a tour to be at that point in my life. The music was not rewarding.

The whole thing was, I was finding out that it wasn't me *who made the records. The records I was making with Crazy Horse—I couldn't just go and do another record that was that good with just anybody. I didn't* know *that until I did the* Time Fades Away *tour. Because with Buffalo Springfield, then Crazy Horse, it was* there. *I had Bruce and Dewey and then I had Billy and Ralph—y'know, they all* moved. *As much as there were great players in the* Harvest *band, it wasn't the same kind of thing as Buffalo Springfield or Crazy Horse. So I think I was finding that out—that I was frustrated on that level.*

That tour was like payin' your dues. It was a long tour, hectic. It had a devastating physical effect on me. Flying in that stupid airplane—up and down in this dumb plane. Why I didn't take a bus, I'll never know.
—Why did you switch to the Flying V?
Old Black had lost its pickup. I loved Lonnie Mack,* and I thought if I had a Flying V that I'd get a lot of the same sounds, but I didn't. It wouldn't stay in tune.
—People shudder, remembering your sound checks on that tour.
I was tryin' to find it. Couldn't find where it went. Thought it must be the equipment.
—Any regrets about those times?
They were meant to be the way they were. The only thing I regret is, I wasn't on the road with Crazy Horse at that time. But Crazy Horse didn't have Danny—or Poncho. There was no Crazy Horse.

Somewhere in that tour I started drinking. A lot of tequila.
—I get the picture you were much more fucked up on the Time Fades Away *tour than, say,* Tonight's the Night.
Maybe after I started drinkin' tequila I was . . . Tequila kind of got me away from the reality of things.

All the people that were with me, all of a sudden they were on this new level of success. Sold-out concerts night after night after night. Nobody had ever seen success like that before. People went crazy. Everybody wanted more than they were making last week. More and more and more all the time. Everybody.

---

*Indiana-born Lonnie Mack—himself influenced by R&B guitar legend Robert Ward—combined a Gibson Flying V with a Magnatone amp to create wrenching ballads like "Why?" and intense vibrato-laden instrumentals such as his 1963 top-twenty hit, "Memphis." Young has also utilized Magnatone amps. "Good sound," said Young. "Low, funky."

—Who got you into the tequila?
Drummond. My experimenting with tequila proved to be quite innarest-
ing. It does something else to me than alcohol usually does.
—There's a tape from the Cleveland show . . .
Heard that tape? Heh heh heh. I got into drinking tequila that night.
—What effect did tequila have?
Well, you heard the tape. We started goin' the other way. That was
completely turning on the audience, turning on everybody . . . but still
playing music. It wasn't like we stopped.

Jose Cuervo became the sixth member of the *Time Fades Away* band on
February 11, during the encore at the Cleveland Arena. Frustrated by an
apathetic crowd who had undoubtedly come to hear the soft rock of *Harvest,* a drunken Young became unglued. After a hoarse dedication to those
in the audience who had come to see Young and Crazy Horse in their 1969
appearances at La Cave, a tiny basement coffeehouse, he begins mumbling
incoherently. "We got last dance tonight / C'mon turn on the light / Look
out mama, you're right / Can you *stand up* tonight?" Then Young and the
band lurch into "Last Dance," one of the unfamiliar new rockers featured
on the tour. There is a demo of the song recorded before the tour in which
the song sounds almost optimistic as Young implores listeners to take
charge of their lives and do what they want. By Cleveland, the hope is
gone. The performance is grating, the tempo molasses. Young, painfully
out of tune, his voice raw, screams at the audience to "Get up, Cleveland,
get up!" In between demands, Young free-associates. "TE-dium, BORE-
dom," he yells, spinning out a tone-deaf traffic jam on the Flying V. "I got
a woman I love," he insists, then howls, "No, no, no," over and over until
anyone listening wants to scream back at him to shut the fuck up.

It was also the worst guitar playing of Young's career. The only life in
the band comes from Ben Keith's out-there pedal steel parts that seem to
mirror Young's bent condition and Nitzsche's two-fisted rhythm piano,
which adds little glimmers of sunlight to oil slicks like "Last Dance" and
"Time Fades Away." To Young's credit, he didn't shy away from document-
ing any of it, and although *Time Fades Away*—released in August 1973—
is augmented by a couple of delicate solo performances, they do nothing

to blunt the grating headache of the electric material. The record was a big spit in the face to those expecting more hits.*

"Neil hated the audience's inability to follow him into the next phase," said Joel Bernstein, who admitted that the folkie inside him was equally shocked. "How does a guy go from being the mellow hippie smiling in the barn to the drunk, intentionally out-of-it guy screaming at the audience? The hippie's *gone*. The hippie took a plane home."

The Mr. Hyde taking Young's place continued to rant and rave. About halfway through the tour, Buttrey was replaced by Johnny Barbata, who'd replaced Dallas Taylor on the last CSNY tour. "Neil calls me up and goes, 'Barbata, waddya doin'? Buttrey's not makin' it.' I sped down in a Chevy wagon with my drums." Things improved a bit, but overall the band never gelled, and the pressure of the tour wore on Young. "Neil was petrified, very insecure," said Tim Drummond. "One night he said, 'Oh fuck, I can't take this shit no more.' The tour was so big it was beyond his grasp. He was scared to death."

The nightmarish quality of arena shows would make an indelible impression on Young. Months later, in a radio interview with deejay B. Mitchell Reid, he'd liken it to "gettin' together for a war dance or somethin' . . . it's a very primitive thing . . . people that are just shakin' and boogyin' to those loud sounds, having a *great* time—getting drunk, taking reds and downers and OD'ing in the audience. I mean, I've been to those places. I know there's an ambulance behind the stage, and those wheelchairs just fly back and forth all night, man. That's what's really happening, y'know. That's where it's really at."

To make matters worse, Young's voice gave out toward the end of the tour, and dates had to be canceled. David Crosby and Graham Nash were invited along to cover but only added to the cacophony. "Nash and Crosby had no business being in that band," said Bernstein. "There's not enough shit coming out of the speakers—we gotta add two more rhythm guitars and voices? It was abysmal." Graham Nash's presence on "Last Dance"

---

*Despite Young's assertions that *Time Fades Away* is his "worst record," it was far ahead of its time in its raggedy-ass nakedness. In 1996, R.E.M. cited it as an inspiration for their recorded-live-on-the-road *New Adventures in Hi-Fi*.

certainly added a surreal touch to Young's dirgelike rocker, as you can hear on *Time Fades Away*. "C'mon, everybody—sing along!" shouts Nash with the zeal of a game show host.

Nitzsche and Crosby also clashed. "When Crosby was onstage, you couldn't hear anything," said Nitzsche, who was constantly telling him to turn it down. "He turned around and said, 'Don't start tellin' *me,* man. I've been doin' this all my life.' I wanted to say, 'You'll be doin' it the *rest* of your life, ya fat fuck.' " Once again, Crosby's regal behavior didn't enamor him to the crew. At one of the final shows in Long Beach, a coked-up Crosby injured himself jumping around onstage. Elliot Mazer recalls the moment: "How I heard about it was my guy onstage called me and said, 'Crosby's down on the floor. He looks like he's in pain and everybody's having a really good time watching him.' "

· · ·

The *Time Fades Away* tour came crashing to a halt at the Oakland Coliseum on March 31. During the encore, the band lurched into "Southern Man" as it had most other nights on the tour. "Show number fifty-eight, having a pretty mediocre time, feeling like a Wurlitzer" is how Young later described his mood at the time. But the audience, undoubtedly excited that Young was finally playing a song they knew, rushed the stage, and a burly black cop began punching out one overzealous fan. Young stopped playing. "I can't fuckin' sing it with this happening!" he shouted. "I'm sorry, I just can't!" As Ben Keith oozed out a menacing, liquid note on the steel guitar, Young put down his guitar and proceeded to leave the stage. "I said, 'Where are *you* goin'?' " recalls Drummond, who was dumbfounded. "Neil said, 'We gotta get outta here right now, 'cause this place is gonna go up.' "

As the crew was pelted with bottles, the band ran for their lives. "I remember opening the door to my truck and watching the limo go flying out," said Mazer.

A few dates later the tour ended. "It was a terrible affair," Young told writer Ray Coleman a few months later. "It was like I was watching myself on TV and someone had pulled the plug . . . I said to myself, 'Who *needs* it?' Who needs to be a dot in the distance for twenty thousand people . . .

the circus might be all right for some acts, but it's not for me anymore. I'm tired of singing to a cop, that's all.

"Filling a twenty-thousand-seat hall is not rock and roll but rock and roll *business.* . . . I want to be able to see the people I'm playing for . . . I want to be able to live with myself . . . I just hope there is not a single off my next album."

Released in August 1973, the hitless *Time Fades Away* would more than fulfill Young's wishes, and his next three albums would contain some of his most extreme and least commercial music. Not that Young gave a shit. As he would write in the *Decade* liner notes, "Heart of Gold" had "put me in the middle of the road. Traveling there soon became a bore so I headed for the ditch. A rougher ride but I saw more interesting people there."

With the exception of the 1974 CSNY tour, the next few years would be full of weird records, raggedy tours and long silences. Now that Young had "made it," he retreated from the press, TV and most everything else that was out of his control.

> *Those huge concerts . . . I did it and it was great for my head, to know that I could do that . . . but y'know, even as much as I tried every night to get everybody in those barns off, I couldn't. Because I couldn't even* see *them, man, and I knew they couldn't see me . . . I had to cut off all the subtleties of my music and just project it out to eighteen thousand people. . . . My music is basically subtle . . . that's why I've gone back to just playin' clubs like the Roxy. And the Corral in Topanga . . . it gets me off. It makes me feel like I'm still a musician and not in a circus . . . the Allmans, Led Zeppelin, all those groups, they're great for those big events, y'know, but you take a guy like me and put me in those circumstances, it's just not right. I just don't belong there.*
>
> —Interview with B. Mitchell Reid, 1973

Before Young headed for the ditch, there would be a short, typically surreal side trip with CSNY. In late May through early June, the group made a trip to Hawaii that was part vacation and part "to see if Stephen could get off the coke, 'cause Neil didn't want to be with Stephen doin' the dope," said Carrie Snodgress. "So Graham and Crosby developed this to show Neil that everything would be okay to do a tour. We were gonna get Stephen sober, right?" The quartet began working on new songs, among them "Human Highway," Young's image-laden folkie ballad that was chosen as the tentative title track for the next album.

"They sang me 'Human Highway' over the phone in Maui," said Elliot Mazer, and once everyone was back at Broken Arrow, recording got under way. "Those sessions were a problem, 'cause Stephen wanted to do drugs and stay up all night recording. Graham and David wanted to get up early in the morning and watch the Watergate hearings, then play. Right about the time Stephen was waking up, they'd wanna go to sleep, so there weren't many times during those few weeks they were all together."

The fact that the record was done at Young's ranch was indicative of his omnipotent position in the group. Silently, subtlely, Shakey was once again in command. "Neil would drive up in a '56 Packard with a bad paint job," said Guillermo Giachetti. "The guy had his own style. I think they were all either jealous or they hated that he was a goddamn original."

Engineer Denny Purcell recalls the vibe surrounding the ranch sessions. "On one side of the studio was a whole bunch of Neil's guitars, and on the other side were all Stephen's guitars. I looked at one of his old Washburns and I said, 'Y'know, Neil's got one just like that.' And Stephen said, 'Yeah, but mine's *older*.' "

Young kept CSN at arm's length. "Neil didn't socialize with those guys," said Snodgress. "I remember all of 'em comin' to the ranch one day and Neil ran off with Elliot. They sat and waited for him all day long, until dark.

"There were so many times. Graham would invite Neil to the city and he'd say he was coming, then he wouldn't come. Or they'd plan a whole meal and we'd spend like thirty minutes. Neil would say, 'I gotta go, I don't feel so good. Maybe something's wrong'—the seizure stuff.

"Graham would say to me, 'Why can't we be friends? Why can't Neil come and be with us?' I'd say, 'Well, he doesn't like leaving the ranch.' But it was more than that . . . something not balanced, not equal. It was keeping people hungry for him."

. . . .

During the CSNY get-together in Hawaii, another tragedy would occur: the death of Bruce Berry, a young roadie who had worked extensively with CSNY. "Bruce was a wonderful kid" is invariably the first thing you hear when his name comes up. But Berry—along with his business partner Guillermo Giachetti—would get swept up in seventies rock and roll excess, and it would cost Berry his life. "Bruce and Guillermo," stated Neil Young, "were the dark side of *Wayne's World*."

Bruce Berry was part of a music-business family. His brother Jan had been half of the surf duo Jan and Dean. After Jan was seriously injured in a car accident, another brother, Ken, took his dormant equipment and started renting it out. Los Angeles–based Studio Instrument Rentals would quickly grow into a thriving business.

Bruce started working at S.I.R. as a teenager in the summer of 1968, along with his high school buddies Guillermo Giachetti and Richard O'Connell. "Bruce and Guillermo formed a team," said O'Connell. "I was the third musketeer."

Through their S.I.R. connections, Berry and Giachetti started working as roadies, which led to steady gigs with CSNY. "At sound check we'd play 'Cinnamon Girl' every day," said Giachetti. "Bruce played guitar, he taught me bass and another roadie played drums. It started sounding good, but CSN got upset and told us to stop—I guess 'cause it was a Neil tune."

The pair tooled around town in a white Ford Econoline van given to Bruce by his brother Ken. Two handsome young kids working for one of the most popular bands on the planet—the women were unlimited, and so were the drugs. According to Richard O'Connell, it was Danny Whitten who first turned Berry on to heroin. "Bruce said, 'Hey Richie, you'll never guess what I did.' So that was the beginning of the end for Bruce." Berry joined a small clique of roadies and musicians, among them David Crosby and Dallas Taylor, who were using the drug secretly. "Heroin was a no-no," recalls Crosby crony Debbie Donovan. "You did not associate with anybody who did heroin. It was kept very hush-hush."

Around this time Giachetti was doing ranch work for Young and Roberts. "I was making a hundred bucks a week—fifty from Elliot, fifty from Neil," said Giachetti, who was soon offered more money to join Berry working for Stills, living in England with his new band, Manassas. "It was like Neil lent us to Stephen for a couple of months—but we never came back."

The scene around Stills was much faster and Berry's friends say it had an effect. "After England, Bruce was a changed guy," said O'Connell. "That's when we lost Bruce. He was always like a light, and now there was a shade over that light. It wasn't out, but it was so dim. He never laughed."

Upon returning to Los Angeles, Giachetti and Berry broke up their roadie company. "It was a heartbreaker, 'cause the three musketeers had broken up," said O'Connell. "When Bruce came back he was just a junkie, man. A fuckin' junkie. He'd sell us dope that was beat. He'd burn his best friends." O'Connell shared a house with Berry on Beverly Glen. "I come home and there's fuckin' Bruce stoned out of his mind on dope with a Walther PPK, shootin' at my favorite cactus."

Berry's descent continued when Crosby hired him as his roadie for a Byrds reunion album. "He came back one afternoon and said, 'Hey, somebody broke into the trunk of your car and stole your Stratocaster,' " said Crosby. "Well, nobody broke into my car. Bruce had sold it for junk."

It was while CSNY were in Maui trying to dry out Stills that Bruce Berry showed up at the wrong time with some cocaine. Delivering drugs was part of the roadie's gig. "Bruce would've been one of the ones who went and got what was needed," said Debbie Donovan. According to Snodgress, Crosby and Nash tore Berry a new asshole for his muling. "They said, 'We're gonna tell your brother about this! You will not work in this business again! Get the fuck out!' Neil wanted nothing to do with it. Nothing."

. . .

Berry was soon sent back to Los Angeles to purchase more coke—let's just say it wasn't for Neil Young—and ran into O'Connell. "Bruce told me he had been doing coke in Hawaii. He hadn't slept for days." Berry bought the drugs and, according to O'Connell, "the dealer threw in a shitload of dope. We got so stoned I couldn't believe it. I used to have a high tolerance, and that shit knocked me for a loop. I didn't even do a whole one. I was used to doin' a whole bag of dope and nothin'. This was *boom!*" The potency of this heroin—combined with cocaine—would prove to be a fatal combination for Berry.

At some point, Guillermo Giachetti showed up, and he and Berry patched up their feud. O'Connell was ecstatic. "I said, 'God, it's great. The three of us are back together—this is a good thing, don't fuck it up.' " O'Connell departed for home, and Berry said he'd be in touch.

Three days later O'Connell still hadn't heard from Berry. It was June 7, 1973, a typically beautiful southern California day. After breakfast, O'Connell hopped into his pink and white '57 Chevy and headed over to Berry's Santa Monica apartment at 317 Ocean Park Boulevard and knocked on the door. No one answered.

"The place smelled awful. This fuckin' smell, it was death. I walked into the bedroom and there he is on the floor in one of those unnatural positions that you can only end up in if you go out, right?

"I was so freaked out, I ran to the phone and called the ambulance—'Ya gotta get here quick!' Fuckin' dead for three days, I'm callin' the ambulance. I also knew there were a couple of bags of dope in the bathroom, just laying there on the toilet—two bags of dope that woulda killed me. Him on a coke binge, that was *it*."

Suddenly frantic over what to do before authorities arrived, O'Connell ran into the bedroom and found Berry's hypodermic. "I ran outside and I threw it away, but I leave the bags of dope in the bathroom. Like, I'm really doin' great. The cops come in. 'When did you last see him? What's the deal? Roll up your sleeves.' There were some week-old tracks they didn't notice.' "

Detectives—along with minions of the aforementioned rock star, claimed O'Connell—initially suspected foul play because of the recent bad blood between Berry and Giachetti. "They had formulated this opinion that Bruce had come to the house and Guillermo and I had hotshotted him. In other words, I was a murder suspect for one of my dearest, closest friends. They came back two or three times. One day they sat us down and Guillermo was just fuming. He hollered at the cops, 'You get the fuck outta here!' After that I got an ulcer, man. Twenty-one with an ulcer. Guillermo and I won't even talk about it."

"Bruce killed himself by breaking the rules, which is to get high alone," said Giachetti. "I never knew Bruce was on heroin, I never fucking knew," said Nash, echoing the sentiments of many. "I never knew Cros was on it, and he was my best friend. Cocaine and dope were okay, but heroin was for *jazz musicians.*"

George Whitsell had seen Berry just days before his death at a night-club, dropping off a Hammond B3 organ from S.I.R. "First Danny Whitten, now Bruce Berry," he said. "They were droppin' like flies."

I asked Dallas Taylor, who also had a bad heroin habit at the time, what he thought when Berry died. "I didn't," he said, frowning. "I just shot dope. That's all I did for ten years."

The seventies. Hendrix, Joplin and Morrison had all checked out; now the grim reaper was paying visits to Young's inner circle. The death of Danny Whitten in November 1972 and the loss of Bruce Berry seven months later registered deep within Neil Young, inspiring a new record that would be much more unsettling than *Time Fades Away*. It would be a project that CSN—and Elliot Mazer—were incapable of understanding. So on the way to the sessions one day, Young decided to mosey over to David Briggs's place instead.

"There was a knock on my door and it was Neil. I hadn't seen him in years. He said, 'I've been doing this record with CSN and it's all wrong. I want to make a rock and roll record.' "

Crosby, Stills and Nash were left in the dust. According to Joel Bernstein, Young told them he was just too fatigued to start a new project. But almost immediately he was in Los Angeles with the remnants of Crazy Horse, working on his next record. CSN, who had planned the entire next year around Young, were understandably outraged. Whatever feelings were hurt, Young's decision to walk away from CSNY would turn out to be a good one, because he could now record his greatest—and certainly seediest—work to date, *Tonight's the Night*.

It was long past midnight on April 19, 1972, and the Doctor was definitely in. An orgy was under way in the Topanga Canyon house on Vision Drive. Outside, a drug deal was going sour. The stereo was cranked, so they wouldn't hear the shots.

"I was a big-ass coke dealer," said the Doctor, a member of the Topanga All-Stars, just a nice guy who got caught up in narcotics. "I was importin' pounds of cocaine outta Lima, Peru. Flyin' 'em into Ventura. Big guy, lotsa bucks. All of a sudden I was in a situation with five pounds and fifty grand."

Two others were involved in the deal. One was a friend; the other, a stranger supplying the drugs, would turn out to be "much heavier than I thought." It seems he was involved in pornography and had ripped off a hundred grand in a Texas transaction. "They had to make my deal to pay off another that went bad . . . they were settin' me up one way or another."

The Doctor had until midnight to come up with the cash and stopped by the party on Vision Drive to raise some. "I invited him to take off his clothes and stay awhile," one of the five people in the house would later testify. The Doctor was able to unload only two ounces, and with time running out, he called his partners, informing them he wouldn't have the money until eight the next morning. The connection got antsy and drove up to the house with the Doctor's partner. Out in the driveway, the Doctor approached the orange Porsche and the three men conferred. The connection didn't want to wait. He wanted his coke back and ended up firing on the Doctor's partner, putting a hole through the back of his head.

"The guy shot him twice," said the Doctor. "Because he put a second bullet in him, he missed me. I was standin' there, he dropped, the rear window of the Porsche splashed all over me. That's when I hit the dirt and ran. Bullets started flyin', I spun around and shot. It was over in less than a minute. A very big minute."

The connection fell to the ground, dead. The Doctor hopped in his Volkswagen and split, leaving behind a car full of cash and drugs that would be ransacked by one of the partygoers—allegedly a gofer on *After the Gold Rush*—before the police arrived. "I was so scared I walked away from thousands of dollars—dirty money," said the Doctor. "I took two reds and went to sleep. I lived through it. Not everybody did."

The folks in the house were oblivious to what had gone down outside until one of the women, looking out and seeing a man slumped over with the car door open, wandered out naked. "I thought he was drunk or stoned," she later told the court. "I was going to lift his head up and close the door so he wouldn't get busted when they patrolled. He looked dead." The woman came back into the house crying, but no one called the police, who finally arrived at 6:50 that morning, answering a complaint call by a neighbor who had also seen the "drunk" in the car. The man the Doctor shot had died instantly. His partner didn't pass away until later that morning in a Santa Monica hospital. It would be four years before the police, tipped off by a snitch, arrested the Doctor.*

News of the double murder traveled quickly. "I knew about it the next day. Everybody knew about it," said Briggs. The other Topanga All-Stars rallied to the Doctor's defense. One of them even disposed of the murder weapon, tossing it off the Santa Monica Pier. The crime cast a pall over the canyon scene. "It was heavy," said bass player Mark Andes, who left Topanga—and his band, Jo Jo Gunne—in part because of the event. "It touched the canyon in a very specific way. It really epitomized the dark side."

Neil Young was not around, not involved, didn't even know the full details, but he caught the vibe. The seventies had arrived, maaaaaaan. Close on the heels of the deaths of Danny Whitten and Bruce Berry, the Topanga

*A benefit for the Doctor—which Young attended—took place at the Topanga Community House in 1976, and once again Topanga's spirit would be demonstrated when a little old lady walked in and, hearing what the benefit was for, expressed her outrage over the Doctor's fate. "Of course he's innocent!" she declared. "No, ma'am, actually he's guilty," piped up one musician in the crowd.

drug murders would be the third grim event to inspire *Tonight's the Night,* in particular a song called "Tired Eyes."

In a bleary spoken voice Young looks at drugs and death, empathizing with one "who tried to do his best but could not." The recitation gives way to a grim melody. "Please take my advice," he pleads. "Open up the tired eyes." But somehow you know these particular eyes will never open again. The starkness of "Tired Eyes"—"as if Dylan did 'Wild Horses,' " is how Richard Meltzer describes it—is hard to shake. "I think it's the best song on *Tonight's the Night,*" said Briggs. "You'll never hear another song like it. The dreamy recitation, the lyrics are so abstract—Neil really caught dope murder, that kind of feel."

The Doctor agreed. I played him "Tired Eyes" out in the Topanga shack where he was living. He had spent two and a half years in prison for his part in the event, and the song—although Young smudges the details and throws God knows what other inspiration into the picture—definitely took him back. As the ghostly song echoed through the cabin, I asked him if I could tell the story. He didn't mind.

"I had to do what I had to do," he said, frowning. "I was in a defensive situation. I did kill somebody. What I don't want is to be made out as some heavy . . . I was victim to the romance of it all. I liked being in that position—the Doctor. I prided myself almost to the point of delusion, looking out for these poor little drug addicts, 'cause at least my shit was good. Ain't that sick?"

> *The sixties are definitely not with us anymore . . . the change into the music of the seventies is starting to come with people like David Bowie and Lou Reed . . . "Walk on the Wild Side." He's telling a story, a street story, and that's a reality in the seventies, heroin. . . . This is much more of a dope generation that we're in now . . . and that's what the approach a lotta these people have towards makin' records—is that homosexualism and heavy dope use and everything is a way of life to a lotta people—and they don't expect to live any more than thirty years and they don't care. And they don't care. They're in the seventies.*
>
> *What I'm tryin' to say is these people like Lou Reed and*

David Booie or Bowie, however you pronounce it, those folks—
I think they got somethin' there, heh heh. Take a walk on the
wild side!

—Interview with B. Mitchell Reid, 1973

The smooth sounds of California rock were fully entrenched by 1973, but other sounds were blowing in, and not very nice ones. Bowie, Lou Reed, the New York Dolls, the Stooges' *Raw Power*—it was all rude, crude and made by people who had little use for the hippie ethos. "I hated Woodstock," Iggy Pop said in 1996. "Still hate it . . . the worst. Crosby, Stills, Nash. Just so loathsome. Just not music." Uninterested (at least at the time) in finessing their guitar solos, overdubbing out mistakes or attending benefit concerts, these angry hooligans gave members of the status quo the willies. "I wouldn't even stay in the same hotel as the New York Dolls," barked Stephen Stills in 1974. Perhaps alone among his peers, Young hadn't forgotten that rock and roll was supposed to be made by misfits.

Nineteen seventy-three was a curious, potent year in music—Dylan was back in the studio with the Band, Roxy Music and Lynyrd Skynyrd were unleashing their particular visions of the world, and Jerry Lee Lewis recorded two late masterpieces in Memphis and London. Beginning perhaps in 1972 with Leon Russell's *Carney,* a new disillusionment with fame and celebrity began to ooze out of many singer/songwriters. Neil Young would outbleak all competition.

For his walk on the wild side, Neil Young turned back to Briggs and the Horse. Crazy Horse had stumbled along without Danny Whitten, enlisting new members for the vapid *Loose,* but "when we weren't playing with Neil, we were dogshit," said Billy Talbot.

Talbot, ever the instigator, called Young while he was in Hawaii with CSN. "I said, 'Remember Ralph and me? We're still here.' " Something clicked in Young's mind, because when he returned to the States, he played a two-day benefit gig at the Topanga Corral with the Horse in August 1973.* Young—who already had a handful of new songs, among them

---

*Young: "There were a few *Tonight's the Night* songs in the show, but it wasn't the *Tonight's the Night* vibe—it was the 'Walk On' vibe. We'd do 'Walk On' when we walked on, then we'd do it when we walked off. So that concept of doing the same song at the beginning and the end happened with 'Walk On'—then we dropped 'Walk On' and put in 'Tonight's the Night.' "

"Tired Eyes"—took the band into the studio later that month. "We went to L.A., checked in to the sleaziest motel we could find down on Sunset," said Briggs. At first, they stayed at the Hollywood Center Motel, the fleabag dump where Young had stayed when he first arrived in Los Angeles.

Adding Ben Keith and Nils Lofgren to the Horse rhythm section, Young returned to Sunset Sound, where he had cut such past triumphs as "I Believe in You." But after just a day, "I could hear it wasn't going anywhere," said Briggs. "Too stiff. I said, 'Man, if it's not going anywhere in this fuckin' studio, we gotta get outta studios entirely. I went down the street to S.I.R. and said, 'Do you mind if I knock a hole in your wall?' "

Studio Instrument Rentals was run by Bruce Berry's brother Ken, and down on Santa Monica Boulevard they had an innocuous black and gray building that functioned as a rehearsal space. Briggs backed a mobile recording truck into the alley next to the building, then someone actually took a twenty-five-pound sledgehammer and smashed a hole through. Cable was run into a cramped, closet-sized equipment locker that served as a control room. The band played on a small stage and was recorded live. It was a concert without an audience, save for Briggs. "When I'm in the room, I'm in the band," he said.

"He was down in the trenches with ya the whole time," said Nils Lofgren. "Briggs was the go-go dancer MC, shakin' his legs, snappin' his fingers, illustrating the music while we were playin'. He was the music video." Briggs and Young refused to let the musicians listen to playback of any of the recordings until it was all over. If Briggs liked a particular take, he'd mix it out in the truck.

A picture began to develop, and with it came more new songs. "We didn't go down with the idea, 'Let's make a spooky record,' " said Briggs. "The album just kind of evolved." Crew member Tim Foster remembers that the album's title song came from an offhand remark Young made the first day of the sessions. "They started workin' this thing out a cappella, everybody sitting around thumping the tables. The next day, Neil shows up with all these lyrics about Bruce Berry."

Mind-altering chemicals were an essential component of this particular trip, with alcohol at the top of the list. Ben Keith set the tone when he popped the top off a bottle of tequila and threw it to the wind. "We won't be needing that anymore," he quipped. "A drunken Irish wake," is how Billy Talbot described the sessions.

Getting loose enough took time. On the two-track masters, Young initially sounds uptight and impatient with the band, particularly over the background vocal parts for such songs as "World on a String." But as the days passed and the tequila flowed, so did the music.*

"We weren't stumbling or anything," recalls Ralph Molina. "We'd just get to a point where you get a glow, just a glow. The head was fucking great, man. When you do blow and drink, that's when you get that glow." The band shot pool and worked on their glow until the wee hours, then began to record. "No one said, 'Let's go play,' we all just knew it was time. We never talked about what anybody was playin', who's playin' what part or any of that kinda shit. It was so fuckin' emotional—it wasn't like we were doin' sessions."

The music created at S.I.R. began to conjure up spirits. "The mood was hangin' in the air. You could cut it with a knife," said Lofgren. "There was no need for Neil to lead us to the mood. We were all affected in our own ways by Danny Whitten and Bruce Berry dying. That's what that whole record was about—we didn't sit around and talk about 'Oh God, what a shame.' This was a chance for all of us to come together and get out of that stuff."

> What we were doing was playing those guys on the way . . . I mean, I'm not a junkie, and I won't even try to check out what it's like. But we'd get really high—drink a lot of tequila, get right out on the edge, where we knew we were so screwed up that we could easily just fall on our faces. . . . We were wide open . . . just wide open . . .
>
> I was able to step outside myself to do this record, to become a performer of the songs rather than the writer. That's the main difference—every song was performed.
>
> I just didn't feel like I was a lonely figure with a guitar or

---

* It had been over twenty years since the *Tonight's the Night* session tapes had been heard when Joel Bernstein and I listened to them in 1996, and it provoked one of those weird coincidences that seem almost routine around Neil Young. "Wow, man, I feel like I'm in 1996," Young mutters between songs on the tape from August 26, 1973. "I really do."

whatever the trip is that people see me as sometimes. I didn't
feel that laid-back. . . . So I thought I'd just forget about all that
and . . . wipe it out.

—Interview with Bud Scoppa, 1975

Spontaneous, ragged, and headed for a cliff, this music was much further out than anything Young had attempted before. "With *After the Gold Rush,* even though the recording was done as live as possible, at least we rehearsed things and got pretty on top of 'em before we recorded," said Lofgren. "On *Tonight's the Night,* Neil took it a step further. He was kinda rebelling against everything. I remember talkin' to him and he said, 'Hey, I've made records where you analyze everything and you do it three thousand times and it's perfect. I'm sick of it. I want to make a record that's totally stark naked. Raw. I don't wanna fix any of it.' "

Between songs, Young and the band would conduct rambling, drunken raps that were frequently hilarious. "I just wanna play, I don't give a shit," Young mumbles before lurching into a liquid version of "Everybody's Alone." "I don't care if it's out of tune, man, let's just play. *Fuck it.* . . . Cut that, will ya, that 'Fuck it'? Just cut it right out so it doesn't offend anybody, the 'fuck it' . . . from the top of the 'f' to the bottom of the 't.' Just cut that fucker out."

The band holed up in the rehearsal hall, getting tanked, wearing sunglasses all night and playing drunken sets of new songs for a nonexistent audience. "If I wasn't a part of it and I peeked in, I woulda gone, 'Whoa, what the fuck's goin' on in there. Who *are* these weirdos?' " said Molina. "It was like working in a bottle, but a great bottle," said Briggs. "It wasn't like onstage, where if you got too far over the edge you'd embarrass yourself in front of a bunch of people. It liberated everybody from the confines of makin' records."

Visitors to the sessions were dumbfounded by the grimy, film-noir atmosphere. "It was completely black inside, didn't matter what time it was," said Joel Bernstein, who was assigned the task of taking visa photos of the band for a proposed Japanese tour. "I had to get 'em in daylight. It was like doing a documentary on nocturnal animals pulled out from under a rock. They looked like little rodents when you shine a light in their eyes."

Art Linson—Briggs's partner in the Spindizzy record label—brought

Mel Brooks by. The director watched, somewhat nonplussed, as the musicians got more and more trashed, only to suddenly crawl out of the bottle at midnight and go to work. "You mean first they do that—then they do *this*?" Brooks exclaimed to Linson, incredulous.

Not all the musicians got it at first, either. "It was frustrating," said Lofgren. "It took me a while to latch on to the concept. As we learned the songs, we'd be recording. I'm sittin' there thinkin', 'Well, another five runthroughs and I'll have my part down,' and Neil would be like 'Okay, next song.' I'd go, 'Wait a minute, wait a minute!' " Young would show the band the chords, the words, and work out harmonies—all simultaneously. "Just as we were learnin' a new song and trying to sing at the same time, he'd be rollin' tape, lookin' for a final take. It freaked us all out. We were like 'Hey, c'mon, man, let's rehearse a little bit. Let's learn the song.' But Neil's attitude was 'I know the song—and that's all that matters.' "

They didn't even know the song—what could be better?
—What did you notice was going on with the way your peers were making records in the seventies?
They all took a dump.
—Why?
Technology. Too much control. Not enough creativity in the recording process, too much in the mixing. It wasn't about music. It wasn't about performing. Slick. Many overdubs. Cleanest, dinkiest, pissantiest-sounding records that could possibly be made . . . I hated that shit.
—What was it about—craft?
Yeah. Building things. Painting instead of taking pictures. I like the idea of . . . capturing something. Record something that happened. I'm a musician. I don't wanna sit there and build a record—I built a coupla records. Big deal.
—Tom Waits said, "Recording is so permanent, it's maddening."
He doesn't record enough. He should record everything, so everything becomes maddening and then he can deal with it. That's how I dealt with it. For years I wouldn't play unless the tape was running. I just recorded everything—all the tours, everything. Make it so there's no difference between playing and recording—it's all one thing. Then you forget you're recording, 'cause ultimately the music gets in your face, you

forget what your doing, and all of a sudden you realize, "Jesus, we recorded that." That's the ticket, that's the way to get it. So I just tricked myself into not having to worry about whether we were recording or not.

I don't worry about the permanence of the record. That's what's good about it. You make it, you got it, that one's too late to change, you do another one.

After the Gold Rush *was in a studio I had in my house. Then we realized how easy it was to build a studio* anywhere. *We built a studio in S.I.R.* Tonight's the Night *was the first record recorded in a studio after Danny died.*

"Tonight's the Night" I wrote in my head without a guitar—I just heard the bass line. Most of the other songs, I don't remember where they came from. "World on a String"—I like that one. But the singing is really out. *It's so outta key, it's terrible. We tried to fix it, but we couldn't, heh heh.*

I played a Broadcaster on all of Tonight's the Night. *I wanted a different sound—very funky-sounding, but clean. We were groovin'. We all liked each other and we didn't have anything else we were doin'. Just focused on that until it was done. It was a pretty funky scene. We'd go home down Santa Monica Boulevard every night, Briggs and I, back to the hotel, eat burgers, drink tequila. That tequila was very relaxing. Y'know—after you get into drinking it a coupla days in a row? It's a whole other thing. Tequila and hamburgers. That was the input.*

When I first started the record, I didn't know what the hell I was doin'. But I did get into a persona. I have no real idea where the fuck it came from, but there it was. It was part of me. I thought I had gotten into a character—but maybe a character had gotten into me.

I was twenty-seven when we did Tonight's the Night, *livin' down there in L.A., travelin' around . . . that's the time when you start realizing, "Hey, this isn't what I thought it was gonna be." Things happen and they hit you around that age . . . but you still have enough energy to go nuts.*

On August 26, Young and the band blasted through five performances that would form the core of the finished record—"Tonight's the Night," "Tired Eyes," "Mellow my Mind," "Speakin' Out" and "World on a String." They also cut a track with an unlikely guest star. "Somebody said, 'Listen, open up another mike, we've got another guitar player,' " recalls assistant engineer Andy Bloch. "We started rolling tape, and the most awful-sounding electric guitar came down the wires—a person slamming the strings as if it were a big twelve-string acoustic. It wasn't more than five minutes later we took a break. I wandered into the room, and there's Neil trying to teach Joni Mitchell the difference between electric and acoustic."

Mitchell had entered with Joel Bernstein and Young immediately handed her a Gretsch. Soon the band was plowing through a train-wreck rendition of Joni's "Raised on Robbery," complete with boozy off-key harmonies from Young. When Briggs later played Mitchell a tape, she winced, shaking her head over the racket. Briggs said he threw her out of his house.

The music recorded at S.I.R. is some of the top-drawer, big-time, hot-shit greatest rock and roll ever made. You could write a book on the bit of piano that opens *Tonight's the Night*. Just an offhand, uncertain tinkling of the ivories, but so ominous, so full of dread. It sets the tone for the onslaught to come—out-of-tune singing, bum notes, mike hits and some of the best, most beautiful noise ever.

These are dispatches from the other side—sublime, stream-of-consciousness poetry set to drunken Jimmy Reed rhythms; "Speakin' Out" is half Kahlil Gibran, half Fats Domino. "Oh tell me where the answer lies / Is it in the notebook behind your eyes?" croons Young, propelled by his chunky honky tonk piano and Lofgren's quicksilver blues guitar. "All right, Nils, play it!"—one of the only times Young will ever invite a musician to solo on record.

The unearthly "World on a String" sports lyrics that evoke all sorts of thoughts on success, purpose and mortality, and one couplet in particular could be tattooed on Young's heart: "It's just a game you see me play / Only real in the way that I feel from day to day." The doomed, resigned opening rumble of guitar tells you no happy face came up with this riff.

In the sly, soulful "Roll Another Number"—written on the spot in the studio—a well-oiled Young fumbled with the key to his ignition, then tells us he's "a million miles away from that helicopter day" of Woodstock and goes on to mourn those who didn't go the distance ("Though my feet aren't on the ground / I been standin' on the sound / Of some openhearted people goin' down"). At once funny and profound, the music is exquisite—loose, liquid and just short of falling apart.

Perhaps the most luminous playing is by Ben Keith, whose otherworldy steel lends just the right lonesome-prairie feel to songs like "Albuquerque." "I couldn't believe all that weird slide in *Tonight's the Night,*" said Lofgren. "All those shades of melancholy that were in us . . . it's almost Middle-Eastern, like 'Ben Keith Goes to East Cairo.' "

"If you don't live it, it won't come out your horn," Charlie Parker once proclaimed. Young was in the thick of it. Surrounded by friends, his subconscious unhinged, he had tuned in to the cosmos. Halfway through "Mellow My Mind," Young's ravaged voice cracks with emotion. "I still get chills when it gets to that fuckin' note," said Molina. "It's so real. I'll tell ya, man, Neil was right there with us. He was wide open."

The finished tracks were sequenced with drunken between-song raps, and toward the end of September—believing the record was near completion— the band played eight shows opening the Roxy, a Sunset Strip nightclub owned by David Geffen, Elliot Roberts, Lou Adler and Elmer Valentine. It was a flashy joint, with the exclusive private enclave "On the Rox" upstairs, and opening night attracted all manner of record-company slime and celebrity. Young and company gave them a show they wouldn't soon forget.

"Every night was like goin' for broke, like the end of the world" is how Bob Dylan described his infamous 1966 tour. Neil Young was about to add a mushroom cloud of his own by taking *Tonight's the Night* on the road.

• • •

"Welcome to Miami Beach, ladies and gentlemen. Everything is cheaper than it looks." This is the cryptic introduction Young would customarily use to open *Tonight's the Night* shows—after banging through the title song, a number the audience had never heard but would get to know painfully well before the evening was over. "Put a little light on that palm tree, B.J.," he'd call out, and roadie Willie "Baby John" Hinds— resplendent in Hawaiian shirt and beach baggies and looking like the tackiest Florida tourist—would pull the chain on a bare forty-watt bulb to illuminate a sad, sickly specimen with about four fronds.

"A lot of it just came about," said Tim Foster. "We stole the palm tree from the S.I.R. entryway. Then there was this guy who had an arts-and-crafts store on Santa Monica. Neil said, 'God, look at that wooden Indian—that would be cool on our stage.' So we went down there, cut the chain and left a note: 'We stole your wooden Indian. If you want your money, come to the Roxy.' " The Indian ended up onstage with a Gibson Explorer around his neck. At various points in the show, Young would talk to him. Before the first Roxy show, a woozy Ben Keith staggered over to Foster, pointed to the Indian and said, "Tell that guy to turn up. I can't hear him."

Then there were the platform glitter boots. Leslie Morris remembers getting a call at the management office the day of the Roxy show. "Neil decided that day he wanted these glitter boots. Nine hundred dollars' worth." A chorus line of the knee-high monstrosities was duct-taped around the edge of his grand piano, "Black Beauty." On every stop of the tour, more boots were bought. Briggs remembered snagging a shitload on Carnaby Street in London. "We went in and said, 'We wanna buy some boots.' They said, 'What size?' We said, 'It don't matter. We'll take ten pairs.' "

Even the way the band looked was from beyond. "The guys came out, they never shaved—I don't think they even bathed," said Hinds. Young was dressed for the party in a white Tinkerbell "Topanga All-Stars" T-shirt, patched jeans, scruffy beard, a pair of shades worthy of Elvis—Polaroid Cool-Ray 420 Fastbacks—and, to top off the ensemble, a thrift-store jacket: "a gray-and-white seersucker sport coat like a bad-news band would wear in the forties," as Hinds described it. Young pinched the jacket from Lofgren. "Neil said, 'Hey Nils, can I borrow your coat?' He never took it off." The overall impression struck some in the audience as border-line demonic. "He looked like Manson," said writer Mike Thomas.

Young might have looked like Manson, but his onstage patter was pure Shecky Greene. He rambled on about Miami, made obscure references to Bebe Rebozo and Spiro Agnew, then played new song after new song. "Here's one you've heard before," he would mutter toward the end of the night, and the relieved audience would start to applaud. Then he'd lurch into "Tonight's the Night" for the third time.

Young played only one or two familiar songs during the entire show, and that was just for the encore. The rest was all the unheard *Tonight's the*

Night material, and the band, finally getting to learn the songs they'd already recorded, played with an intensity that seemed to increase nightly. "The mood live was completely different," said Lofgren. "There was an angry edge the original recording didn't have. We were all pissed off about losin' a couple of people close to us and it came out."

Lofgren took the downer ambience as a personal challenge. "I was the most naturally up of the group, so to help me stay in the groove, I brought along giant combat boots and ankle weights beneath my jeans. To have that extra ten pounds on the bottom of my feet helped me stay more in the place Neil was in."

What place was Neil in? "Wasted out of his mind," said Dave Sigler, a sixteen-year-old fan sitting in the third row at the Roxy. The audience yelled at Young to take off his shades, and when he did, Sigler noticed "his eyes were just bloody-red pulpy slits. You couldn't even tell what color they were." Young smoked joints thrown from the audience and took occasional swigs from a gallon jug of Cuervo Gold he passed down to the front rows. But as bombed as he was, he wasn't depressed and self-destructive like he'd been on the *Time Fades Away* tour. "It was trashed, but in a controlled way," said Briggs.

Those who were a part of *Tonight's the Night* are quick to downplay the doom and gloom many rock critics have seized on when it comes to this period. "Even today, people come up to me and go, 'Oh man, that heavy, horrible *Tonight's the Night* thing,' " said Lofgren. "I'm like, 'Hey man, we had a party. We were releasin' all that dark stuff—on a nightly basis.' " "That's the first tour I ever saw Neil have fun," said Willie B. Hinds.

The final night at the Roxy was a wild one. Annoyed that industry weasels had scarfed up all the tickets for the first three nights, Young added an extra night for his fans, and when the second show started late, he invited the audience to have a drink on the house. "I had a tequila sunrise on Neil," said Dave Sigler. Young's handlers went ballistic over the expense.

Then, commemorating the Roxy's previous incarnation as a strip joint, Young offered a pair of glitter boots to the first topless woman onstage. Urged on by Ben Keith's wife, Linda, Carrie Snodgress started making her way to the stage to claim them. "I'm unbuttoning my little vest, and Roberts and Geffen are standing there. Elliot said, 'What are you doing?'

'Well, Neil said that the first girl who came out topless was gonna get a pair of those shoes, so I think my name's written on them.' Elliot said, 'You're not goin' out there! Snodgress, you must be tripping on acid to do an insane thing like this! Do you know what you're gonna do to Neil's reputation?' " Crew member Tim Foster was standing next to Elliot. "As Carrie was going past me, she hands me her shirt. Elliot was exasperated, tellin' me, 'Put that shirt on her!' I'm goin', 'Fuck you, Elliot—you put the shirt on her.' He was embarrassed. Nobody else was."

"The whole theme of *Tonight's the Night* was 'Let go of all the crap and get real,' " said Snodgress. "So I just came up behind Neil and put my arms around his waist—he just looked, started laughing, said, 'Oh my God,' and started playing 'Tonight's the Night.' Elliot didn't speak to me for days."

As game as Snodgress was for the antics at the Roxy, inside she felt that Young had left the building with Elvis. "That passion, that hunger, that rock and roll release . . . watchin' musicians get swept right up in it. Neil didn't belong in that world. *Tonight's the Night* was the beginning of sex, drugs, rock and roll, and it was the beginning of the end for my life with Neil."

· · ·

The *Tonight's the Night* circus gathered steam during a trio of Canadian dates one month later. "Briggs goes, 'Neil, I got the set. You'll love it,' " recalled Tim Foster. "And he pulls out all these hubcaps, speedometers and turn signals." The stage took on the appearance of an auto junkyard. Buick hood ornaments and rearview mirrors were attached to Young's piano, the speedometer onto Lofgren's amp and hubcaps hung everywhere. Cheesy trophies were stacked on the amps. "Anything that glittered and was kind of goofy," said Foster.

Briggs blew hundreds of dollars on crew T-shirts emblazoned with obscure in-jokes like EVERYTHING'S CHEAPER THAN IT LOOKS, EQUAL TIME FOR PAST, PRESENT AND FUTURE and HELLO, WATERFACE. Briggs got everyone involved. This was group art of the highest order. "It was like a buncha actors in a traveling road show, but the roles went on all day and night," said Briggs.

The Canadian audiences didn't get it at all. "The audience really thought they had come to the wrong building," said Joel Bernstein. "People were pissed off. It was not funny."

"It was so intense," said Briggs. "I'd look at the crowd going out, and I never saw such a drained bunch of people before or since. They looked like they'd gone ten rounds with Ali—all of 'em."

A week in England and Scotland began on November 3. Midflight, Young abruptly renamed the band the Santa Monica Flyers, donning a plastic Nixon mask Briggs had given him. Tim Foster awoke to a surreal card game in progress. "I remember looking up and seeing Nixon go, 'I'll bet thirty dollars.' " Foster had grown tired of hubcap duty, so Willie B. Hinds was called in as set dresser for Europe. He also snuck in some much needed spiritual supplies.

"When I flew over to London, I brought a case of tequila," said Hinds. He was allowed to bring in only two bottles, so he handed out the rest to fellow passengers, then collected it all back after landing. "I'm on the other side of customs and I'm tryin' to catch these people as they're walkin' off with my tequila." Some incredibly potent Hawaiian grass— Maui Wowie—was also smuggled over in a speaker case. "The case was impounded four days in customs," said Foster. "Next day you see nine guys with screwdrivers tryin' to get the back off the cabinets." To keep the Indian company onstage, there was now a suit of Samurai armor—wearing the Nixon mask when Young didn't have it on.

Also on the British bill were newcomers the Eagles, who were dumbfounded by the drunken buffoonery of their big hero. The English audiences were equally bewildered. "They think, 'We're gonna have an evening of really fine country-flavored rock and roll and folk rock,' " Young recalled to Cameron Crowe in 1979. "And then we just came out and . . . took 'em all to Miami Beach."

The assault continued. At the Rainbow Theater in London on November 5, Young guzzled tequila onstage, awarded the crowd a trophy and borrowed a camera from a concertgoer to take a picture of the audience. Impatient with such antics, someone in the house shouted, "Rock and roll!" "I'd love to see some," retorted Shakey.

The old, intimate theaters Young played in Britain were the antithesis of the cavernous arenas of his last tour. The band was flying, the music soaring higher and higher.* The set list was Young at his disillusioned best and included a short acoustic segment featuring a powerful, booze-soaked version of "Helpless" with Ben Keith on Dobro and, on accordion, Nils Lofgren, who—at the urging of Briggs—just stumbled onstage one night and joined in.

The versions of "Tonight's the Night" were also growing longer and weirder, expanding like some out-of-control amoeba. As the band vamped, Young launched into demented, impromptu raps about Bruce Berry's downfall, relating stoned-out dialogue between Berry and CSNY that was at once chilling and hilarious. Here's the one from Liverpool:

"So one day Bruce was pickin' up the guitars, y'know, for the band. That's what Bruce did, carried around the instruments, made sure everything was workin' good." Young trills a few notes on piano. "And, uh, one day he showed up with his station wagon." More piano. "Walked up to my friend David and said, 'I lost your guitar, man . . . I left it in the station wagon, but when I came back it was gone . . . I don't know what happened to it.' " The band plays a few bars.

"A couple of years passed, y'know . . . wasn't too much work for Bruce. . . . One day he came to us lookin' for work and he said, 'I'd like a job . . . I got everything together, man. I'd like to take care of your guitars for ya'. So we looked at him and I said, 'I'm sorry, man, can't do it. I mean, ya lost David's guitar, y'know. You don't know what happened to the guitar, it's gone. Ya lost his guitar, man, I mean, that's his ax. That was it. Ya lost it. That's your job and you lost it . . . ' " Young thunders the low notes on the keyboard. "You took that guitar and you put it in your *arm,* Bruce," he moans as the band charges back into the song.

Riveting stuff, but undoubtedly lost on an audience who hadn't heard any of the songs before and had no clue who Bruce Berry was anyway. Murray McLauchlan, the Canadian folkie who had the unenviable task of

---

*Curiously, for an artist who has documented his own career so obsessively, the *Tonight's the Night* tour is a bit of a blank spot. The only live shows Young recorded were at the Roxy, before the band truly caught fire. The best way to enjoy the tour is through audience tapes of the European and most of the American gigs. No tapes have surfaced of the Canadian shows. Joel Bernstein's thirty-five-millimeter shots of the Canadian tour were lost, as was Super-8 film Briggs shot at the Roxy.

opening the shows in America ("I was the human sacrifice on that tour") recalled it as an era "when university kids were drinking wine and eating quaaludes. There was a mindless, amorphous energy about it all. It was really insane—the audience was very druggy, very stoned, very rude. I mean, they were screaming for Neil Young *while he was playing*.

"And the tour was built around this one phrase—'Everything is cheaper than it looks'—which was Neil's laconic summation of what the entire music biz and most of life is all about. The more people would act like howling monkeys, the more it would vindicate that point of view. It was like 'Waddya here for, ya fuckin' assholes? I'm gonna stick somethin' ya don't even *want* right in your fuckin' face, and you're still gonna be here. Where are you at?' "

Things spun totally out of control at the Bristol Hippodrome, the second English show. "Neil will be right along," Young said to the audience, introducing the band as "Clark Kent and the Micronite Filters." Between songs, he carried on a nonsensical monologue about senior citizens in Miami Beach charging up their electric carts to go to a big nightclub show that culminated in an orgy. Bruce Berry, Young told the crowd, never got to attend the gig, so it was time to raise him from the dead. "We're gonna attempt to bring him right back here to the Hippodrome," said Young, fingering the chords to "Tonight's the Night." "Shake your opera glasses."

The impatient crowd grew more and more rowdy, until Young got so perturbed that he stormed off at the beginning of his acoustic set, vowing not to return. The audience went nuts, and Roberts had to plead with Young to finish the set before a riot started. Young angrily returned to the stage, and by the end of the show—"Tonight's the Night," of course—the band was going berserk. "Neil was freaking out on piano, just banging away," recalled Lofgren. "I wound up jumping on top of it and trying to break the strings with my combat boots, playing guitar with my teeth. Neil was just yellin' and screamin', 'Bruce, you took the guitar and put it in your arm!' The intensity was outrageous. All this for an audience that was hoping this was a bad dream and any minute we'd do 'Cinnamon Girl.' "

The crew watched the Bristol show from the safety of the wings. "I remember lookin' at Briggs and sayin', 'I don't care if somethin' breaks—I ain't goin' out there,' " said Foster. On a chaotic audience tape you can hear the crowd—what's left of it—getting more and more intense. "Piss off!" someone screams. Young plays on, unconcerned. "Elvis has left the arena, ladies and gentlemen," he drawls, tinkling away at the piano.

—*Tell me about your* Tonight's the Night *guy.*
One of the hardest-workin' men in show business.
—*People tell me* Time Fades Away *was bleak, and* Tonight's the Night *was more fun.*
Oh, yeah—Tonight's the Night *was a lot more fun. 'Cause I was with my friends. I was havin' a fantastic time. It was dark but it was good. That was a band with a reason. We were on a mission. That's maybe as artistic a performance as I've given. I think there was more drama in* Tonight's the Night *because I knew what I was doing to the audience. But the audience didn't know if I knew what I was doing. I was drunk outta my mind on that tour. Hey—you don't play bad when you're drunk, you just play real slow. You don't give a shit. Really don't give a shit.*

I was fucking with the audience. From what I understand, the way rock and roll unfolded with Johnny Rotten and the punk movement—that kind of audience abuse—kinda started with that tour. I have no idea where the concept came from. Somebody else musta done it first, we all know that, whether it was Jerry Lee Lewis or Little Richard, somebody shit on the audience first.

Elliot Roberts was stuck with the thankless task of trying to keep Young's career on track throughout the *Tonight's the Night* debauchery.

"Elliot didn't get it," said Lofgren. "We'd do this insane show and all be high off it and feeling great, we'd all get on the bus, all be drinkin' tequila, talkin' about the show and how wild it was, havin' a ball partyin', and sure enough, Elliot would always drag Neil to the rear of the bus and just berate him. 'What are you doing? You gotta cancel this tour now. You're gonna lose fifteen thousand dollars! Crosby, Stills and Nash are waiting.' Every night Neil would go to the back of the bus and let Elliot give his rap and try to calm him down."

Roberts, who still seemed pained when discussing this period over twenty years later, related an apocryphal tale concerning Ahmet Ertegun and his entourage attending one of the British shows. "Neil is really really drunk, and he comes off and said, 'Man, we kicked ass. We never played better. It's really coming together now. Let's go out and do the encore.' I say, 'Neil, do an encore to who? There's no one here but Ahmet.' 'Ahmet's here?' 'Yeah, he's got, like, this one row of people.' Neil goes, 'All right! That's who was applauding.' Neil actually deluded himself like that . . . he went out and did a three-song encore to Ahmet.

"And it cost us a lot of money to do that—it was in overtime. Not only was Neil being abusive and losing it, but the whole tour really hurt us in the marketplace. We couldn't tour Europe."

Although the press would come around quickly when the *Tonight's the Night* album was released eighteen months later, most of them were harsh on the tour. "Banal . . . off-key" is how Young's old Buffalo Springfield supporter Judith Sims summed up the Roxy shows in *Rolling Stone*. "Tedious," decreed *Melody Maker* of the London Rainbow show. "He talked too much about nothing and went on too long." One disgruntled fan who had attended the show wrote in to the paper declaring, "The real Neil Young is dead."

Best of all was a long piece by Constant Meijers, a Dutch correspondent who was allowed to attend only after he provided Young with numerous bottles of Jose Cuervo. "Neil couldn't hit any of the high notes. I began to lose all hope. What on earth was happening to Neil? Where had the magic gone? He talked a lot, drank tequila by the wineglass in one gulp . . . Jesus Christ, what a downer!" Meijers got even more hysterical after Young's inebriated performance of "Helpless." "And how helpless he looked sitting there, his hair hanging in his face . . . shaking on his stool, knocking the microphone in his fury and his fear. . . . Who was that man sitting there? What in the name of Jesus was he doing?"

Invited backstage, Meijers found Young's traveling circus much more upbeat. "They made a lot of jokes, always punning. Neil's a man's guy. Drink a beer, be around guys, go out for a meal—he wants to play. There were no girls around. This was not Elvis Presley time."

Young would eventually reprint the entire Meijers article, untranslated, in an insert for the *Tonight's the Night* album. "It seemed a good idea to print it in Dutch because nobody in the U.S. would be able to understand any of it," he told a writer in 1976. "Because I didn't understand any of it myself, and when someone is so sickened and fucked up as I was then, everything's in Dutch anyway."*

.   .   .

Despite the protests of management, press and the general public, the Santa Monica Flyers rolled on, returning to America for a handful of dates that began on November 15 at Queens College, which featured a magnificent graveyard-tempo "I Believe in You." An incandescent performance took place in Cleveland on the nineteenth, and with the next day came Chicago, where Murray McLauchlan caught an image out the tour-bus window that summed up the depravity of the entire *Tonight's the Night* experience. "It was just pissing down rain, and standing out on the sidewalk was a girl. This onetime hippie-looking girl, with long hair, the proverbial floral-print dress—but very bedraggled, because she's soaking wet and covered in speed zits, very wasted—with a sign around her neck hung with binder twine. Written in some kind of crayon on the sign were the words WHERE'S THE BAND STAYING?"

That night, an incredibly loose show had Young again berating a noisy audience. "Shut up!" he snapped. "Some of you people are fucked! You all scream out so much, why don't you stay home and listen to yourself talk. There's a lotta things you can say up here if you don't have to fight your way through a buncha idiots that are just yellin' to hear their own voices." Young went on to play a truly scary, surreal thirty-six-minute "Tonight's the Night," invoking the names of Ricky Nelson and James Brown as he preached. Again came the tale of Bruce Berry, with Young screaming over and over, "No . . . no . . . no!"

The last show of the tour was in Berkeley on November 23, and the band whooped it up. Willie B. Hinds surprised Young with an entirely new

---

*Typically, Young didn't ask Meijers permission to reprint the article—he just did it, and the writer found out only when he saw a copy of the album. "It blew my mind," Meijers said proudly. He became friends with Young, visiting the ranch a few years later. He attempted to write a book but felt in the end that Shakey had somehow snake-charmed him out of the project. "As a journalist, you can become someone's friend, and after that you can't be a journalist anymore," he said. "Neil got me in his pocket. As a journalist, he castrated me."

tourist outfit complete with white shoes, and when Young asked for the palm tree to be lit, Hinds was standing there dressed to the nines with a tray of cocktails in his hand. "Neil went without singin' the whole next verse, he was laughin' so fuckin' hard. I was sittin' there just totally Palm-Beached out. I got him good."

Young had one last joke to pull on the audience. When he introduced one of the opening acts, he wore the bearded shipwrecked look he'd perfected over the course of the tour. Then he went backstage, shaved and, when he returned to play his own set, as Tim Foster remembers, "nobody knew who he was."

•   •   •

Although Young had told audiences that the *Tonight's the Night* album would be coming out in January 1974, he continued to fiddle with it, much to the annoyance of David Briggs, who considered the project finished. "After we stopped recording I gave the tape to Neil. I said, 'Here's the record.' It was done. It was a masterpiece.

"Then we go into Neil's studio with whatever kind of pathetic console Elliot Mazer convinced him to buy, and I tried to mix *Tonight's the Night* with and without Neil, and he tried to mix it with and without me—but it was always through the Compumix." The Compufuck, as Briggs dubbed it, was the first computerized mixing console—an expensive, unwieldy piece of technology that had caused major problems on *Time Fades Away*. "That thing almost ruined *Tonight's the Night*," said Briggs. "What a fuckin' nightmare.

"This went on for months, for fuckin' months, and every time I'd do a mix I'd say, 'Man, this sounds like shit, what's the fuckin' matter here? Something's wrong here.' Finally I said, 'Hey, we gotta get outta here. Your studio sucks and your consoles suck. We'll go down to Heider's and mix the fucking thing.' Now, neither he—or especially me—had it in us at all to mix it again."

Young went on to record two other albums and complete a massive CSNY tour before returning to the project. By that time, the between-song raps were gone and new material added. Just bringing up the subject made Briggs livid. "To me, *Tonight's the Night* was a masterpiece when it was done. Then they put on these fuckin' feepy versions of songs and took all the raps off. Most people think *Tonight's the Night* is the real deal, but I know better—it's the watered-down version."

For Briggs, the original unedited S.I.R. version is the only *Tonight's the Night*. "It never let up. There was no attempt to make it nicer. It was unrelenting from minute one to minute last. I felt once you started that mood, you had to go all the way, a hundred percent, give it the full dose—to try and insert stuff into it was bogus.

"Tell you the truth, I can't listen to *Tonight's the Night* because of those things on it. I did the record, I thought it was fucking great, and Neil and Elliot and the record company backpedaled.

"They ruined the real *Tonight's the Night,* hid it away on a shelf, in a closet, like a monster thing. Pissed me off so much I didn't wanna see or speak to any of 'em."

Well, Briggs never mentioned that to me. Never said a thing about it. And Tonight's the Night *came out in the same year as two other records we did together. So we were together when that happened.*

The record was so out-there, I sort of held on to it for a while. In those days—1973—you could make a cassette copy, but they never sounded good. So I'd go home and play it back on a reel-to-reel. And at one point my son Zeke got a tape recorder, and he was playing with the masters of Tonight's the Night, *which he was rolling back and forth and having a good ol' time. For about six months he played with 'em. And the record never came out. We just held on to it.*

That record is very unusual. A lotta things happened to it. On the record, the mixes are original—they were all done on this two-track board at S.I.R. Briggs would do a rough right there as we were doing the record. Then when we tried to mix it, of course, it was too fucking late—it was already mixed.

The pure Tonight's the Night *was a nine-song deal.* It was great. But*

---

*The *Tonight's the Night* material went through an insane amount of different running orders, but the cassette Briggs played for me—which contained the raps—was a twelve-song version: "Tonight's the Night," "Mellow My Mind," "Bad Fog of Loneliness," "Speakin' Out," "Walk On," "Winterlong," "Albuquerque," "New Mama," "Roll Another Number," "Tired Eyes," "Tonight's the Night." "Bad Fog" and "Winterlong" were cut on February 5, 1974; the rest are from S.I.R. Eight of these songs would wind up on the released album, *the way it came out was a record. I diluted it. I had to. That's where the other songs came from. They held it together, but they diluted it a little bit. The pure, essential* Tonight's the Night *was more of a work of art than what came out, because it was the original shit—in order, the way we listened to it all the time with all the raps in it—mumbling shit, all kinds of weird stuff that entered into the songs and left off at the end. There was a whole bunch of that stuff, and it made it so eerie. It's just so fuckin' drunk and hysterical. We were really out-there—swearing, knocking the microphone, giggling and carrying on. It's funny how different it was.*

We had a rough mix of the whole thing—it had the raps and everything. Then somehow the raps got cut out. I don't know how that happened. If Briggs said he finished the record and that was it, that's not true. 'Cause if he thought it was done, we wouldn't have been fucking around with those masters.

We tried to put the raps back in. The emulsion, the magnetic shit, was scraped off of it—the sound on the tape had changed and we couldn't get it back. We couldn't make it work—we couldn't cut it, we couldn't cross-fade it, because we had a different mix of the raps. If we had been able to match the raps to the original mixes, it all would've been in there.

We could re-create the original Tonight's the Night *with digital. We could go and put it back together again and get the whole fuckin' thing, 'cause we got the masters and we got the raps.*

Ironically, it would be Elliot Roberts—the man made most distraught by the entire *Tonight's the Night* era—who came up with the key for finishing the record. Roberts briefly toyed with the very odd idea of turning the story of Bruce Berry into a Broadway show. Mel Frohman—husband of Elliot's secretary, Mary, and an award-winning writer—even wrote a surreal

---

two would be released on subsequent LPs, and one tremendous performance—"Bad Fog"—remains unreleased. "It really is one of my best recordings," said Young, who had cut a more polished "Bad Fog" nearly three years to the day earlier during the *Harvest* sessions. How frequently does a later version of a song top the first recording? "Almost never," he said.

At S.I.R., Young also cut versions of "Wonderin'," "Everybody's Alone," "Lookout Joe" and a solo acoustic take of the Springfield-era "One More Sign."

twenty-four-page treatment that had little to do with the actual participants. Berry became "Joey Superstar" and was joined by a girlfriend, "Hey Chick," plus black choruses "The Dudes" and "The Sisters." In the process, three older songs were added to flesh out the score—a live version of "Come On Baby, Let's Go Downtown" from the 1970 Crazy Horse Fillmore shows, plus "Borrowed Tune" and "Lookout Joe" from the *Time Fades Away* period.

Sandy Mazzeo was present when Young looked over the treatment. "Neil didn't really like the play, but he said, 'Look at this order of songs.' " At the time Young was finishing an album entitled *Homegrown,* he and Mazzeo were staying at the Chateau Marmont in the bungalow that John Belushi would later OD in. It was in this room that another catalytic event would occur.

"It was late at night. We were all pretty fucked up, listenin' to tapes, on the edge," Young remembered. Present were Richard Manuel and Rick Danko of the Band, the great Louisiana singer/songwriter Bobby Charles, Ralph Molina and Billy Talbot of Crazy Horse, maybe others—no one present for this hazy event is quite sure of anything. "Danko, Neil and me were sittin' around the piano singing," recalled Molina. "I think we'd done a little meth, because when you do methedrine, the fuckin' harmonies are so beautiful. We fuckin' sang and sang. It was Godlike." After they listened to *Homegrown, Tonight's the Night*—which happened to be on the same reel—came on. "Danko freaked. He said, 'If you guys don't release this fuckin' album, you're crazy.' " Young did just that, much to the consternation of Warner Bros., who were anticipating *Homegrown* as somewhat of a return to the commercial sound of *Harvest.*

Warner Brothers was kinda thinkin' it might not be that great of an idea to put Tonight's the Night *out at that point in my career, but they always said, "If you wanna put it out, we'll put it out. Whatever you wanna do." But that was the first time they said, "Well . . . you're sure you wanna put* this *out?"*

Everybody thought it was awful. Everybody I knew. CSN? Oh, they hated it—wouldn't even mention it. "That's not a record." Then you get guys like the Eagles, Glenn Frey especially—when we did that tour, they thought we were fuckin' crazy. Glenn would come over and say, "Why are you doing this to yourself?"

—He wasn't alone. Elliot thought you were nuts, too.

"What Elliot thinks is the right thing to do for my career is the last thing we give a shit about. It's like he thinks he's steering the ship, and when it gets out of control, he thinks he's not—and he doesn't know what the fuck's going on.

But y'know, Tonight's the Night *was just an attitude that was ahead of its time—or behind its time. For that time, that record was pretty wild. I just knew it was a good record. There's something irreverent about it.* Tonight's the Night *doesn't* care—*and that makes you feel good about it. There's no pretense.*

When you first listened to it you thought, "Oh my God. What's happened to these people—are these guys lost?" Real music—played by people who have nothing else to do than play music, not because they're recording, or anything. This shit had to come out. When they put out Harvest *on CD, I made* them *put out* Tonight's the Night. *I said, "If you wanna put out my biggest hit, I want you to put out my best record." So a lot of audiophiles get to hear tape hiss and fucking microphones popping and all kinds of shit that they wouldn't normally be able to hear— plus music that was out of tune and fuckin' crazy that they probably wanted to turn down anyway.*

—Some critics maintain it's an anti-drug record.

Anti-drug record, huh? [lets out a breath after taking hit off joint]

Sort of like "Kicks" by Paul Revere and the Raiders is an anti-drug record?

I think Tonight's the Night *is a druggy kinda record, but is it a pro-drug record? I dunno . . . I hope it doesn't* glorify *drugs. That's just the way I saw that story.*

The album jacket for *Tonight's the Night* is as ominous as the music inside it. On the front is a murky, high-contrast shot of a disheveled Young in his seersucker jacket and Fastback shades, waggling a crooked finger like a man selling French postcards from his trench coat. On the back is an equally demented Joel Bernstein photo of the band next to the hole in the wall. Young's handwritten scrawl is all over the place and everything about the album's look is pitch-black and grimy.

"There's a package that drove everybody crazy," said artist Gary Burden. "That was printed on blotter paper. It's meant to age quickly and fall apart, because I guess Neil was around a lotta things that were just falling apart." Inside the record is an odd leaflet with Meijers's infamous Dutch article, a blurry Bernstein shot of Young's '48 Buick speeding off to the Roxy opening and a typewritten letter to the mysterious "Waterface," who is also addressed in messages scratched into the run-out grooves of the record itself. "Hello Waterface," read side one; "Goodbye Waterface," said the flip.

The back page of the insert is perhaps the most obscure. The words to "Florida"—a strange unreleased recitation—are superimposed over the credits to *On the Beach,* a record Young had already released. To top it all off is a tiny picture of Roy Orbison that Young nicked from a dubious cassette he picked up on the road.

They put out one of these bootleg cassettes of Roy. I saw it and said, "Aw, fuck, look at this picture—Roy doesn't know this fuckin' record's even out." So we said, "Well, that's okay—we'll use the picture on our record, then." And it had all the credits from another record—now that was beautiful.

Everything had to be different with that record—even the label had to be a different color from all the other records on the label—it had to be black, like all the labels in the old, old days.

In the original Tonight's the Night *there was a little package of glitter in a plastic container, so when the whole thing opened, the bag of glitter fell out. And you'd open the bag of glitter and of course you'd get glitter all over everything. The platform boots and the tinsel in the album . . . that was our Bowie statement.*

They had to use so much fuckin' ink on that record. It's like they used enough material for twenty times as many records as they actually made. Blotter paper would just eat up the presses. But I knew what I wanted. I knew exactly how it had to be. It's hard with CDs. It's not expressive. What ya gonna do—put all that artwork into a CD? It's so fuckin' small you gotta have a magnifying glass to look at it.

See, Tonight's the Night *was the closest to art that I've come. But you really have to be detached. The whole thing was just me and it. You can't struggle to get there. It's just gotta happen—a set of circumstances that make those things take place, and if the circumstances ever come together for me again to do something like that, I'll do it.*
—Who is Waterface?
Waterface is the person writing the letter. When I read the letter, I'm *Waterface. It's just a stupid thing—a suicide note without the suicide.*

I vividly remember when *Tonight's the Night* finally came out in June 1975. The charts were full of pop confections like the Bee Gees' "Jive Talkin" and John Denver's "Thank God I'm a Country Boy." Hearing a blast of reality like *Tonight's the Night* was, oddly enough, a lifesaver.

For me, the seventies can be summed up by just three things: those grotesque early shopping malls, *Texas Chainsaw Massacre* and *Tonight's the Night.* Decay, but with a gleam in its eye. This was an album shockingly different from the output of Young's California folk-rock buddies, with their liberal niceties, babbling on about saving whales. Young was definitely a million miles away from the helicopter day of Woodstock, as well as just about everything else about the music business, which he made clear in interviews when the album was released. "If you're gonna put a record on at eleven in the morning, don't put on *Tonight's the Night,*" Young told Cameron Crowe in 1975. "Put on the Doobie Brothers."

"Art is supposed to take you out of your chair," said Bob Dylan. "It's supposed to move you from one place to another." Well, *Tonight's the Night* put me on the moon. Everything about the record moved me, down to the fuzzy blotter-paper cover. It looked so mysterious and sounded so real. I went through ten copies of the fucker, wearing out one after another. If I was in a record store and saw somebody with a copy of *Harvest* under their arm, I'd launch into a twenty-minute harangue on why they should put it back and buy *Tonight's the Night* instead. They usually did, too— probably out of fear I'd kill them if they didn't. I was fifteen, and the record would be my best friend for a long, long time.

You know how it is when you've been up too long, the apartment's trashed, everything is silent, the sun's about to come up and you're feeling like some germ stuck to a big cold rock hurtling through space—and somehow you don't mind? Here is a record that induces that state automatically. Hearing somebody so totally fucked up rant about the ills of extremism is liberating. *Tonight's the Night* made no judgments. Young knew the attraction—and the rewards—of being wasted out of your skull, and had no illusions about the price paid, which for some was the boneyard. The record was shot through with a sardonic humor that deflated any pretense of a Big Statement, which somehow made it even heavier. Unlike Briggs, I feel that the additional material helps tell the story. When gone-dead Danny Whitten's voice jumps out of the speakers singing "Come On Baby Let's Go Downtown," it just hits you in the gut that much harder.

Painter Francis Bacon once said, "The job of the artist is to deepen the mystery." You'd have to get into a diving bell to descend any lower than *Tonight's the Night*.

.   .   .

While the album sold poorly, the critics salivated in *Rolling Stone* and *The New York Times*. But the most interesting reviews come from Young's own parents. Scott Young devotes an entire chapter in his book to the record, calling it "essential" and describing his son as "a man on a binge at a wake, a long happy bout of not giving a shit."

Rassy was less complimentary. She attended the Berkeley show on the *Tonight's the Night* tour and "had a hemorrhage over it," she told me, frowning. When I asked her opinion of the album, her brow furrowed further. "That's the one about everybody dead? I can't stand it. No way. I've never played it all the way through and I ain't a-gonna play it. There's too many Johnny Rottens around. Ruins me. No thanks." Rassy refused to discuss it any further.

shit mary, I can't dance

"Ask Buttrey about Rusty skinnin' cats," advised Tim Drummond. Feline turned to canine by the next version. "I heard the dog was in pieces," whispered engineer Denny Purcell. "Somebody at the motel found the dog pieces and they got arrested."

Tales of animal sacrifice seem to hound Rusty Kershaw. Lawyer Craig Hayes said the stories originated back in the seventies when he extricated Ben Keith and Rusty from a sticky situation. "They had destroyed a hotel room in their tequila madness," Hayes said. "There's been a lotta subsequent rumors about everything from voodoo to dog mutilations." I can't even print the story Graham Nash recounted. Rusty busted a gut when I told him the tales. None of them were true. "I've had lots of stories pinned on me, shit," he purred in his syrupy Cajun drawl. But, he added, "I have a story about a *monkey*.

"This was back in the late fifties, early sixties. New Orleans. My brother Doug and I was on a country-music tour, people like Ernest Tubb, Roy Acuff, Jerry Lee Lewis—a whole slew of us. This chick, boy, she looked about as fuckin' crazy as I was. She came right to me and we went to a Holiday Inn and we just did a whole bunch a fuckin' 'n shit, 'n after we done a whole lotta that, I done me up a joint and drank me some fuckin' whiskey 'n shit, and I flicked the TV on and it was one of these movies that have a monkey in it, and boy, she went, 'Wooooh—look at *that*!' And I said, 'What?' Y'know—I wanna know 'bout *this*.

"And she says, 'Well, when I was real young, my husband wanted to be kinky and he got this monkey. And this monkey had these great big soft furry lips and this great big, long tongue. I didn't wanna do it at first, but he kept remindin' me about these great big ol' soft lips and that great big ol' long tongue—and it worked out for a while.' And I said, 'Then what happened?' She said, 'Well, my husband started gettin' jealous of the monkey'—hee hee. And I said, 'Then what happened?' She said, 'He beat the shit out of the goddamn monkey.' And I said, '*Then* what happened?' 'I ran off with the monkey. That's the fuckin' truth.' I said, 'Ahllll *right*!' "

Rusty Kershaw is a wild man straight from the Louisiana swamps. Born into a musical family on February 2, 1938, Russell Lee Kershaw started performing at the age of nine, perfecting his formidable guitar style a few years later in a band his mother formed after his father shot himself. Rusty recorded with the likes of Lightnin' Slim, and in the mid-fifties, he hit it big on the country charts as half of the swamp-pop duo Rusty and Doug, recording up-tempo hits like "Louisiana Man" and aching ballads like "I Can't See Myself." In 1964, after much touring and hell-raising, the brothers split. "I just couldn't stand the grind of the tourin' and the same set every night," said Rusty. "I like to play from the top of my head. Once you practice and get all the parts stuck together, that's what you've done—you're stuck. It takes the life out of it. To me, it's 'Oh man, we gotta play this motherfucker *again*?' Just do it—Nike's got a good one with that."

Doug Kershaw would go on to solo fame as the hyperactive hippie fiddler; Rusty would wander down a much darker road. "Rusty's amazing," said J. J. Cale. "He's so natural, man, that it *hurt* him." In 1970, Cotillion issued a barely noticed solo album with liner notes detailing Rusty's battles with the bottle. By the time 1974 rolled around, he had mutated into a big, hairy psychedelic swamp rat in bib overalls. Rusty would wield tremendous influence over Neil Young's next album, getting everyone fucked up on a noxious concoction called honey slides and hurtling Young into a musical space even further out than *Tonight's the Night.* Young had blown everybody's mind on that record by recording material the band barely knew, but Rusty Kershaw would go one better—he wanted to record Young's songs without knowing them at *all.*

Rusty's on to that thing. He wants to get that moment—just sit down and "I'll start, then you start goin' and we'll get it." Some people, once they discover that, they're so into it that it's all-encompassing. Nothing else matters. Rusty's one of 'em. I was, too, at one point.

He's a cool cat, Rusty's fine. He's wild, boy—he probably never listened to Nirvana, but he probably woulda liked Kurt.

—What kind of shape were you in at that point?
Searchin' for the muse, I think. Pretty dark. Not really that happy. I think it was a period of disillusionment about things turning out differently than I had anticipated. I think I was starting to realize what a fucked-up life I had chosen for myself with Carrie. It wasn't really happening. So I was outta there.
—When did that relationship end for you?
Right about then. That was just about it.
—What effect did that relationship have on your art?
It had a good effect. Because I was able to get a lot of it out in my art. It was like adding fuel to the fire.

Early in 1974, Young began recording new material with David Briggs at the ranch. In February and March he cut "Walk On," with its great duck-walking guitar figure (a song allegedly inspired by Jack Nitzsche's repeated trashing of Young; Young doesn't remember), a hopped-up remake of "Tonight's the Night" with Greg Reeves on bass; "Traces," a ballad best forgotten; a sluggish "Winterlong" that was done far more successfully by the Horse with Whitten; a wonderfully inebriated "Bad Fog of Loneliness"; and, most significantly, on March 8, a surreal ballad called "For the Turnstiles." The way others recall the song's origin reveals a Warholian quality in the way Young would snatch art from anywhere: Carrie Snodgress remembers walking around the house whistling the tune Young copped for the melody. Sandy Mazzeo recalls telling Neil that day about his infamous friend and prostitution-rights advocate Margo St. James, who had invited all of them to her Hooker's Ball, where tickets were a then exorbitant $10.

Young worked fragments of the conversation into "Turnstiles," and by that afternoon he was in the studio, playing banjo opposite Ben Keith's Dobro, both singing twisted harmonies that sounded positively Appalachian. Keith recalls, "I'd sing these off, weird harmonies, and Neil'd go, 'Oh, that's cool—do *that.*' I didn't know I could sing that high—I still can't. I must've been sittin' on a crack and got my balls in there."

The downbeat mood of "For the Turnstiles"—which for me has always suggested Young's disillusion with the faceless arenas of the *Time Fades Away* tour—would set the tone for *On the Beach.* Unfortunately Briggs, who coproduced the cut with Young, didn't make the rest of the sessions.

"I got so deathly sick the second day—sickest I've ever been, hundred and five temperature—and they just kept recording. Just threw me away because Neil was hot. Pissed me off so much that I didn't have anything to do with him for a long time."

Ben Keith would make the rest of the *On the Beach* journey, guiding Young into a strange scene with heavy players. Keith brought in the Band's rhythm section, Rick Danko and Levon Helm, and last but not least, Rusty Kershaw, whom Ben had met when he first came to Nashville back in '56. Some were apprehensive about the direction Keith sent Young in. The steel player would "steer Neil into the weird," said Elliot Mazer. "Ben can go to the moon."

According to Tim Drummond, *On the Beach* officially began with a Lincoln Continental and a bottle of Mateus Rose. Drummond was in Los Angeles working with Graham Nash when Young showed up. Young and Drummond left the studio together and spent the night cruising around Hollywood in the "Confidential"—a big white pimpmobile Young had rented—while demolishing a bottle. When Drummond returned home the next day, he found a message from Young. It was time to make some music.

The sessions took place at Sunset Sound and the players began to congregate at the Sunset Marquis Hotel. It was a nonstop sleazefest, with odd visitors popping in and out. One night it might be one of the Everly Brothers, the next a Playboy bunny or two. Even porn star Linda Lovelace—whose picture graced the back of Drummond's Fender Precision bass—made an appearance. "We were all crazier than shithouse rats," said Drummond fondly. "Hollywood Babylon at its fullest."

• • •

The nucleus for the L.A. sessions was Ralph Molina, Ben Keith and Tim Drummond, plus a motley array of guest stars. George Whitsell, the Rockets' old guitar player, was summoned out of the blue. "April Fool's Day 1974, I get a call at midnight sayin', 'Neil wants you to come down and record with him right now.' I stayed for a month." But almost before Whitsell knew it, his sole musical contribution—guitar on a demented number called "Vampire Blues"—was over. "We played that song for about fifteen minutes. I said, 'That was pretty good. You wanna try one?' Neil said, 'You wanna hear the playback?' He took the rehearsal and spliced it together."

These were loose, foggy sessions, with musicians trading off on instruments they had far from mastered: Ben Keith played bass, drums, organ, piano; guitarist Rusty Kershaw played lap steel and fiddle.

Hanging over everything was the furry shadow of Kershaw, and with him came the honey slides, cooked up by his wife, Julie, at the rate of a pound a week. "I think me and Rusty came up with it," recalls Keith, who said you start off by frying some weed in a skillet just until it starts to smoke. "When that stuff started smokin', boy, it would stink like hell. The studio smelled like a marijuana farm!" Then you add the honey, and "it just all looks like cowshit, heh heh. You take a spoonful of this cowshit and you eat it. And in about twenty minutes you start forgettin' where you are."

The high was debilitating. "People passed out," said Elliot Roberts. "This stuff was, like, much worse than heroin. Much heavier. Rusty would pour it down your throat and within ten minutes you were catatonic." This might account for the ultra-low slow-motion D-chord drone of the L.A. sessions. None of the songs were under four minutes, and two— "Ambulance Blues" and "On the Beach"—were seven minutes plus.

"It was Kershaw's record, not Neil's," said Willie B. Hinds. "This is a funny thing to say about Neil—people have had influences on him, like Danny Whitten or Kershaw. Ralph and Billy didn't, Rusty Kershaw did." Roberts, to whom *On the Beach* would be dedicated, watched Young float away with understandable concern. "Ben's advertising Rusty as the new messiah—and Neil, if he has a problem, it's that he wants to be a good ol' boy too much. *Too* much."

Once on the expense account, Kershaw made himself right at home at the Sunset Marquis. "One morning I saw this guy pushing in cases of wine and boxes of Fritos, shit like that," Drummond recalls. "I said, 'Wow, you gonna have a room-service thing here?' He said, 'This is going to Mr. Kershaw's room.' I mean, Jesus Christ!"

Room One at the Sunset Marquis soon registered the effects of Kershaw's debauchery. Red-wine stains covered the carpet, which was also dotted by cigarette burns commemorating the Cajun's drug-induced nods. Visitors were awestruck by the extent of the wreckage. "It was like cannibals had been livin' in there," said Drummond, who witnessed Elliot arguing frantically with the hotel manager over a settlement price for Kershaw's demolition job. Julie Kershaw said her husband's vibe was intensified by the fact that he'd been on a six-week jag without sleep. Finally he just collapsed—after attaching a one-word note to his bedroom door via his pocket knife. "It just said DON'T," said Rusty. "Not 'Don't do this, don't do that'—just DON'T."

Kershaw hated the cold, impersonal studio atmosphere of Sunset Sound. "I said, 'Shit, this is too spiffy. We gotta get this like your livin' room, man, sittin' real close together. Like we're at home. Either that or let's put on some *suits.*' " Hinds was sent out to scour thrift stores for furniture, inaugurating another Neil Young tradition.

Old overstuffed chairs and floor lamps were arranged in a circle, the room's non-lighting limited to a few candles wrapped in tinfoil. Kershaw had one last request—that he be in close physical proximity to Young when they started. "I said, 'Neil, when it'll move me the most is the *first* time you play it. You're gonna do it your very best then—and I can play it with you the first time. We only have to sit real close together.' "

Young was blown away by the fact that Kershaw didn't care to rehearse a song before recording it. "Neil said to me later, 'How in the hell do you know how to play this thing the first time I play it? You don't know what I'm gonna do.' I said, 'Neil, you carry a heavy vibe, and if I'm sittin' close to you, I can feel what you feel before you play. I know where you're gonna go.' "

It was a lethargic, drug-addled scene. "We didn't work every day, we only worked when we felt really inspired," said Kershaw, who describes how "Motion Pictures," a below-sea-level downer dedicated to Carrie, oozed out on the spot. "Me and Ben and Neil were sittin' in Ben's room. Neil started hummin' somethin', and I started playin' along with the melody on the steel. Ben started playin' bass, it sounded so goddamn pretty. Neil picked up a pen and just wrote the words right then." The players all squeezed into the Confidential, rolled into Sunset Sound "and put that motherfucker down while it was still smeared all over us."

The ensemble sound was plain beyond, like some spectral jug band backing Jimmie Rodgers. Keith, anchoring the song from beneath the sea with a bass tuned "way down low"; Kershaw, farting out a few sad, kazoo-like notes on steel; Molina patting out a minimal, only occasionally audible beat on the bongos; Young strumming bittersweet chords on the acoustic and bleating forlornly on harmonica. "I'm deep inside myself, but

I'll get out somehow," croaks Young in a desperate ghost-whisper that Tim Drummond said was conjured up just for these sessions. "Robert De Niro gained fifty pounds for *Raging Bull,* Neil did the same thing for his music. He was smoking two packs a day to get a late-night, frog-in-his-throat voice." Young was deep into it during *On the Beach.* "That's when Neil got the downest he could get," said Hinds.

.   .   .

Perhaps the most deranged moment of the *On the Beach* sessions came during the recording of the song inspired by Charlie Manson, "Revolution Blues." Rusty didn't feel like the musicians were living up to the song's title. "I said, 'Look, man, you don't sound like you're tryin' to start a fuckin' revolution. Here's how you start that.' And I just started breakin' a bunch of shit and Ben jumped right in there. I said, 'That's a revolution, *muth'* fucker.' Goddamn, that sparked Neil right off. He got it on the next take."

Apparently possessed by animal spirits, Kershaw got down on the floor during the recording, to the amazement of observers like Billy Talbot's brother Johnny. "Here's this big fat tub in Lil' Abner overalls—one side undone, with dirty long underwear—thinking he was a snake, slithering around on the floor."

Young's superstar buddies were especially spooked. "Crosby and Nash, they couldn't handle it," said Hinds. "It was too grungy for them." David Crosby, usually the high priest of any scene, left Rusty Kershaw particularly unimpressed. "Kershaw just fuckin' laughed at him," said Hinds. "He'd get on the floor and start howlin'." At some point, Stills also had a run-in with Kershaw. "Me and Neil were playin', and it was such heavy magic, I think Stills thought if he picked up the guitar, he'd have it. Man, you don't take a guitar from somebody's hand, and it just pissed me off." Kershaw pulled a knife on him in response. "I said, 'Stephen Stills, who in the fuck is that? You better git back, you motherfucker.' Neil was sayin', 'Go ahead—do it! Do it!' " Young doesn't recall the incident.

"Revolution Blues" was quite a stance for a wealthy rock star to take. Proving once again that Young was miles away from his California brethren, he adopted a demented Manson persona in the song, ranting in the most famous couplet, "I hear that Laurel Canyon is full of famous

stars / But I hate them worse than lepers and I'll kill them in their cars."
David Crosby—who played rhythm guitar on the track—was rendered
apoplectic, and on the next CSNY tour he begged off performing the
song.

Although Rusty might've had some idea where the music was headed
during *On the Beach,* the engineer certainly didn't. Al Schmidt, a legendary boardman whose credits run from Jefferson Airplane to jazz singer
Jimmy Scott, found the sessions a little too far-out. The recording room
was darker than a bat exhibit at the zoo. Schmidt had to send somebody in
to communicate with the musicians, who were usually smashed out of
their minds. Rusty kept pushing the mike out of the way, rendering many
recordings unusable. "He didn't do this once, he did it all the time," said
Schmidt, who watched helplessly as the sessions grew more and more out
of control. "I'd be sittin' there, I couldn't see, and I'd be goin', 'What the
fuck is goin' on?' "

The final straw for Schmidt came when he hurriedly assembled some
rough mixes of the material for Young to play for guests. Young fell in love
with the weird mixes, which Schmidt felt would end his career if heard by
the public. "I begged Neil to allow me to remix it. I was gonna pay for it
myself." Schmidt couldn't take any more. He departed before the sessions
were over, and the murky roughs wound up on the record.

Schmidt was replaced by Mark Harmon, an engineer seasoned by the
insanity of working with artists like the Band and Bobby Charles. He fell
right in with Young's band of crazies and, before he knew it, was tromping
off with the musicians to the office of a local Dr. Feelgood, where everybody bent over to receive vitamin B12 shots allegedly designed to offset
the effects of their wild ways. But, as Harmon remembers, "Between that
and the honey slides, the honey slides won out."

*Yeah, that's right—everybody was goin' and gettin' these shots, and they
really gave you a rush. I don't know what the fuck the shot was. You felt*
great. *Everything was* fine. *But when you'd go outside it was, like, the*
brightest thing you'd ever seen. *This guy was givin' shots like the popcorn man, know what I mean? It could have been anything.*
—*Was* On the Beach *fun?*

I don't know if "fun" is the right word. It's a pretty dark record. Not as dark as Tonight's the Night, *but it had an ambience to it.*

"Vampire Blues"—you hear Drummond doin' his credit card? Ch-chh-ch-chhh—it's a credit card on his beard.

Sunset Marquis with Ben, Rusty. Pretty innaresting stuff. Rusty was there at the hotel cookin' honey slides, burnin' holes in the rug. Goin' in the studio every day, playin' a little bit. Must've recorded for a week or so. It was very mellow, very down—not depressing. Honey slides.

Good album. One side of it particularly—the side with "Ambulance Blues," "Motion Pictures" and "On the Beach." "Ambulance Blues"— it's out-there. It's a great take. I always feel bad I stole that melody from Bert Jansch. Fuck. You ever heard that song "The Needle of Death"? I loved that melody. I didn't realize "Ambulance Blues" starts exactly the same. I knew that it sounded like something that he did, but when I went back and heard that record again I realized that I copped his thing . . . I felt really bad about that. Because here is a guy who . . . I'll never play guitar as good as this guy. Never. He's like Jimi Hendrix or something on the acoustic guitar.

Ever heard "Big Rock Candy Mountain" by Johnny Burnette? Ever hear a Bob Dylan song that has the same melody? One of those numbered dreams. Those things happen. My biggest remembrance of "Ambulance Blues"—heh heh—I was sittin' in the kitchen with Carrie and this friend of hers. I never tried coke before, and she was turning me on to that about that time . . . I'm glad she didn't turn me on to heroin.

So we were sittin' around gettin' high, smoked a joint, I said, "You guys wanna hear a song?" I played that song for 'em, all the way to the end. Then I looked at them. They didn't understand it. It wasn't their trip, anyway. AHAHAHAHAHA. So I said, "Try this one," and I did "The Old Homestead." I played that for 'em.
—Better response?
Nope.

The On the Beach *cover—I was havin' a good time. I did the whole thing, down to the newspaper. The whole deal.*

That's what I love about Warner Brothers—they hire an artist and they let their artists be artful. That's the deal. Good company.

It's a gray day at the ocean. Hideous patio furniture sits on the beach, a can of Coors and a Dixie cup on the table. In the sand, a fender off a '59 Cadillac and the day's paper, SENATOR BUCKLEY CALLS FOR NIXON TO RESIGN. Off to the side stands the *Tonight's the Night* palm tree, looking battered and forlorn. Young stands at water's edge in a yellow and white polyester ensemble, his back to us, staring off into the distance. The *On the Beach* cover is some kind of deranged masterpiece: Young waving goodbye to the sixties, watching them sink out on the horizon like the *Titanic,* the one lucky survivor left standing on the shore.

"It just happened," said Gary Burden, who considers the cover the best thing he's ever done. "Everything fit, from buying the newspaper. That's the thing—when you're with Neil, magic things happen."

"The world is turnin', I hope it don't turn away," sighs Young in the opening line of the title cut of *On the Beach,* and the rest of the record isn't much happier. The collection of songs is an unusually strong one. As critic Kit Rachlis wrote of Young's songwriting, "Sentences are strewn around like forgotten laundry, images are piled up like last week's dishes. Lyrics end like the half-opened magazine on the bathroom floor." Sometimes Young's offhand approach leads to trouble, but the imagery in songs like "For the Turnstiles" and "Ambulance Blues" is sublime. "Turnstiles" in particular is diamond-sharp, worthy of Dylan. Doom and gloom are everywhere on the album, the singer sounding gutted and absolutely alone. Outside of a weak remake of "See the Sky About to Rain," the performances are riveting.

"Probably one of the most depressing records I've ever made" is how Young described it to Cameron Crowe, and yet there is something subtly uplifting about *On the Beach.* Young might sound like he's having trouble keeping his head above the water, but he can see beyond the whirlpool, even if the storm isn't over yet.

• • •

On March 8, 1974, Young was back at the ranch, recording with Rusty Kershaw, playing the mournful opening notes to "Greensleeves" while bullshitting about the song. "I sang it at Chuck's Steakhouse in Maui. You shoulda heard me, man. You woulda been proud." "Far out, man," Rusty says, "like, y'know, we're past playin' notes—it's either emotions or not.

Hank didn't play any notes . . . " Then Young lunges into the song, obliter-ating Rusty's mumbling. "Alas, my love, I do you wrong, by treating you so discourteously," he sings in a voice sadder than a thrift-store painting. "Greensleeves was my heart of gold," he moans, bleating out the word "Greensleeves" with an intensity that makes you wince. This magnificent performance, as yet unreleased, is equal to anything from *On the Beach*. Young didn't conjure up the feeling out of thin air. He had just gone through hell to get it.

The relationship between Neil and Carrie was disintegrating. "It was gettin' funny, just before it got weird," said Snodgress of the *On the Beach* period. "Neil was never home. I was lonely, and Zeke didn't have any companionship. Months and months of bein' alone in that house." And when Young was at the ranch, things didn't feel right. Snodgress recalls Young had a "Jekyll-and-Hyde thing in the nights—we'd start out laughin', smokin', and all of a sudden . . . quiet. Restless. Anxious. If he didn't eat before dark, he couldn't eat." She said Young was "impenetrable at times. I'd talk, ask him questions, and he would not hear. The music changed—what he played in the daytime and how he played at night. Night music was always very dark, very deep." Snodgress remembers standing on the porch, hearing the haunted sounds of *On the Beach* wafting from the faraway studio. "It was a very sad time," she said. Things completely fell apart when she took a trip to Hawaii.

Word got to Young that Carrie was out on a boat with a character we'll call Captain Crunch. Snodgress claimed ignorance. "We were at sea, like, five days—there's no phones, nothin'. And meanwhile, he's tellin' me all this stuff about how great I am and how he's had all these fantasies ever since me and him met, and I'm going, 'Fine, fine, with your fantasies, just get me on the goddamn shore.' "

Snodgress insisted the love affair was one-sided and said that Young "chose not to believe me. It's been in the history books, y'know? That men can do what they want, but the wife has one indiscretion . . . but the sick thing about this was there was no indiscretion. So I kept paying this price again and again for something I would never dream of doing." And yet Captain Crunch would keep reappearing in her life.

"Neil was so anxious and disturbed about this whole bullshit. Neil'd throw all these letters at me. I'd say, 'I didn't ask the guy to write.' And I'd tear them up right in front of his face . . . two or three days later, he'd send a big envelope with photographs of me on the boat, and when you're out at sea, bein' naked is no big deal—I mean, Zeke'll tell ya I walk around naked all the time."

Snodgress felt there was a simple, easy solution, but Neil just wasn't up for it. "He's not the man who can open up wide enough to really say, 'This motherfucker is killing us. I'm gonna put out a contract on his life.' "

Oh, I was so drunk. *I flew over to Hawaii to see Carrie and she wasn't there. I waited for a long time . . . and then somebody told me she was out on a boat trip with this guy. . . . So I kinda had a major . . . bummer . . . which resulted in drinking a lotta tequila—which actually solved a lotta the problems, heh heh. And then I went out and played my guitar in God knows where, for God knows who.*

I was disillusioned. Because we had a family. And even though I'd been fuckin' around, when I found out she'd *been fuckin' around, it kinda blew my mind—so—at that young age . . .*

'Course, Crosby's tellin' me, he said, "There's plenty of girls out there that would just love *to be with you. They would treat you* right. *Y'know, there's a* lotta *girls I know." Crosby. My guiding light.*

He really was, at that point. He talked to me a lot. A good friend.
—*Have you experienced betrayal?*
Betrayal. I thought I did. But it turned out I was just as bad as the other person, so it wasn't really betrayal—I discovered what happens when you do something to yourself. When you do it to someone else, you do it to yourself. It's not like being betrayed. You look back and go, "Well, fuck—that person didn't do anything I didn't do to them." *At first it seemed like it, because you ignored the fact that you've done this yourself. It was terrible—that's what betrayal's all about—but it didn't hurt nearly as bad after a while, because I realized it was kind of, like,* real— *it was like what I did.*
—*So were you dishonest with yourself?*
Not once I realized what was goin' on . . . Well, at the time I think I denied—*denied to myself what I had done and only thought of what she'd done.*

Someone else betrays you, you feel it a lot more if you've betrayed them. *It brings out all of the shit you thought you could hide.*
Where it all comes out in your face.

When Young returned from Hawaii, he spilled his guts to Sandy Mazzeo, who recalls telling him, "Sometimes you just have to pardon your heart." Young did a double take, asking his friend to repeat what he'd said. The phrase would inspire a classic ballad released the following year on *Zuma*.

The sick situation between Young and Snodgress would spur one of the great periods in Young's art, beginning in May 1974 and lasting through January 1975. The songs poured out of him like blood from a wound. "Homefires," "Bad News," "Love Is a Rose"(a top-ten hit for Linda Ronstadt in 1975), "Barefoot Floors," "Love/Art Blues," "Through My Sails," "Old Homestead," "Hawaii." A little later came "Star of Bethlehem," "Separate Ways," "Kansas." ("Motion Pictures," Young said, was written "before I *knew*—when I could *sense*.")

For confessional songs, Young's pen was never sharper, although most of the music remains unheard. He laments his self-obsession, as in "Love/Art Blues," and in "Barefoot Floors"—surely one of the most exquisite ballads Young's ever written—he's resigned to his calling, despite the lure of love.

The episode in Hawaii would haunt Young. "L.A. Girls and Ocean Boys" was the most naked account of what happened—perhaps too naked, because Young would later submerge parts of the lyric in another song on *Zuma,* a nightmare called "Danger Bird": " 'Cause you've been with another man / There you are and here I am." The anguished first line was buried in a violent blast from Old Black, but listen hard, it's there. The relationship with Snodgress had taken its toll. "He was shattered," said Mazzeo. "Shattered."

• • •

Back at the ranch, Young had continued recording with Rusty Kershaw, but the sessions quickly screeched to a halt. Snodgress was coming back to work things out, and Young wanted the ranch cleared. "Hell, there was no way to get *off* the motherfucker," said Kershaw. "Nobody would use any of

Neil's cars, and I said, 'Well, fuck him. Git one o' them motherfucking cars and take me to town *now* or I'm gonna burn this motherfucking barn down—and the cars with it.' " Kershaw was off-center enough that the threat was taken seriously.

"I got instructions to remove Rusty—get him off the ranch fast," recalls Johnny Talbot, who loaded the Cajun into a Pinto Pony. "We had to squish him into the backseat. He's a big dude, and with his instruments and wife, the whole car was packed like sardines. We got about five hundred yards and he said, 'Stop this piece of shit. I ain't goin' to the airport in this. I'll burn this place down.' It wasn't funny at the time. He's a scary guy."

Kershaw had been around only a couple of months, but he had left his mark on Young, although they wouldn't make music together again for nearly twenty years. Young would keep the sad, strange *On the Beach* vibe going with the unlikeliest bunch of all: Crosby, Stills and Nash.

· · ·

On May 16, 1974, Ken Viola attended a Ry Cooder/Leon Redbone gig at the Bottom Line in New York City. After the first set, the audience was asked to exit the club through the front door, which Bottom Line regular Viola thought was odd since they usually herded people out through the rear. "I said, 'The hell with this, I'm goin' out the back,' " recalls Viola, who waited for a security guard to turn his head, then slipped out, only to encounter the shock of his life.

"I popped the door open, and there's Neil Young standin' there with his guitar in hand," said the dumbfounded fan, who asked him if he was going to play. Young said yes, and Viola went back in for Cooder's second set, after which an announcement came over the PA inviting people to stay for a special guest. Young walked on for the only solo acoustic performance (aside from two benefit appearances playing alone and with the Eagles on March 16 in California) of the as yet unreleased *On the Beach* material. Outside of "Helpless," Young would perform material unknown to the audience: four songs from *On the Beach,* plus five others, among them "Greensleeves." Surprise attacks are what Young fans live for, and the show was widely bootlegged.

It was an electrifying set, with Young tearing through new songs while rapping about honey slides. He opened the performance by dropping a bomb: "Pushed It Over the End," perhaps the most disturbing number of the new material.

In this lonely, lonely song, tellingly introduced at the Bottom Line as "Citizen Kane Junior Blues," Young tells of "Good lookin' Millie," sort of a pistol-packin' cross between Carrie Snodgress and Patty Hearst. Millie is contrasted with a victimized male in the chorus: "Although no one hears a sound / There's another poor man fallin' down." As the guitar chords descend, Young repeats "fallin' down" five times, sounding more lost on each echo. Then Young switches perspectives to accuse himself, wailing the title. After a jaunty guitar break, the song stops dead, entering into hallucinatory, slow-motion, first-person verses that are the most evocative and disturbing parts of the work: "On this noisy shore, standing at the edge of you / Could those dreams of yours be true?" When I ask fans how this particular number makes them feel, most mutter the same word: uncomfortable. Young was a haunted man.

•   •   •

With *On the Beach* completed, Neil Young did exactly what he swore he'd never do again—a huge arena tour, this time with CSNY. Why? Elliot Roberts, no doubt. After enduring a succession of wacko records that threatened to flush Neil's career down the toilet, Roberts had to be concerned, and he was the only one capable of nudging the superstar foursome into action.

Backing musicians were assembled: Russ Kunkel on drums, Joe Lala on percussion. Stills wanted Kenny Passarelli on bass, but Young held out for Tim Drummond,* who pulled a typical stunt when it came to the money. He was playing pool with Stills and Kunkel on the ranch the night before a tour business meeting when Stills advised him to ask for much more than the $30,000 or $40,000 management was going to offer. Armed with this privileged information, Drummond waltzed into the meeting and demanded $100,000—tax-free.

---

*"Stephen didn't want Drummond because Stephen couldn't push Drummond around," said Crosby. "Stephen fancies himself a bass player. Wanna know why Lee Sklar wouldn't work with us? Because Stephen would go up, take his bass out of his hands and say, 'NO, NO, play it like THIS.' Leland can play *rings* around *anything* Stephen can't even do on the fucking *guitar*."

"Stills stood straight up," said Drummond. "I thought he was gonna have a heart seizure. He told us to ask for more. When I threw that number out there, man, I got 'em all dancin'. Neil said, 'Well, that sounds about right.' " Drummond shook hands with his bandmates and promptly left the room as Elliot sputtered objections. Drummond didn't get exactly the figure he proposed, but things would never be quite right between Stills and the bass player again. "We were like water and oil," said Drummond. "We just didn't mix."

Rehearsals were held at Young's ranch on an outdoor redwood stage he'd had erected for the occasion. CSN came to Y. "That's the amazing thing about the hold that Neil has on these guys," said Nash associate Mac Holbert. "If Neil said, 'Hey, how about rehearsing down at the ranch,' that wasn't a suggestion, that was the way it was gonna be. They never stood up against Neil. Because they were always afraid if they said no, Neil would go away." "It was amazing," said Drummond. "Anytime they wanted to do something they'd go, 'Is that okay, Neil?' They always ran it by him first."

During preparations for the tour, Young had a blood sample drawn, which triggered an epileptic seizure, his first in several years. Mazzeo recalls Young being distraught over "the lack of ability to control the blood coming out of his arm. Because he couldn't stop the blood from flowing out of his veins, he went into a seizure."*

The event left Young badly shaken. "I think he felt devastated," said Nash. "I think he realized there was something beyond his control— which, in Neil's language, is a complete no-no." For a brief moment, Nash saw a very different Young. "It shocked me for one very simple reason: My friend was human. This man, who I'd come to love and respect, had complete control of his scene on a thousand levels, from who's digging up the potatoes on the back forty to who's puttin' his new studio together—all of a sudden he was very vulnerable, and frankly it scared the fuck outta me."

Attempts were made to reach Carrie, who was off in Hawaii running a day-care center with a couple of friends. Her reaction wasn't exactly sympathetic. " I wouldn't put it past Neil to fake seizures," she said.

Most observers sensed that Young was deeply morose over his crum-

---

*This event is described in Young's own words on page 177.

bling relationship, but there was little communication to others about the situation. He spent most of the subsequent tour hiding behind a pair of mirrored sunglasses, prompting the nickname "Flyface."

"Neil never shows ya a hell of a lot of what's bothering him—or what's not," said Crosby. "Neil doesn't bring that shit to work. I'm a very external guy—when I came to work blown out, I'd sit on the floor and cry. In all the time I've known Neil, I've never seen him cry once. He doesn't run that stuff out front. You have to pry it out of him, and even then it doesn't come out very much."

Well, y'know, my policy was to just try to keep a straight face while I was doin' all that shit. I didn't want to bum everybody else out with how I felt—although they could probably feel it anyway. During the '74 tour rehearsals, I was really bummed. But that was just a few months— eighteen months or something—of being bummed, and then I was out of it, basically.

I was just sad. *It wasn't so awful—we were playing music every day and practicing and getting ready to go on the road—going swimming every day, getting exercise, hanging out around the pool with the guys and talking about what we were gonna do. It was hard because of the emotions—but everybody else was tryin' real hard to make it happen.*
—Did the return seizure make you more cautious in life?
Well, it just made me a lot more cautious about having my blood taken— there's no reason for that to happen. But it happened.
—Was that a hard period for you to live through?
Oh, yeah, *that was a bad period for me . . . but creatively, that was a* great period. *No doubt.*

In the third week of June, Young taped a number of his new songs, including acoustic-guitar and bass versions (with Drummond) of some of the Hawaii material. Two songs would see release the following year on *Zuma,* with the low-key "Pardon My Heart" getting Crazy Horse vocal overdubs, while the lighter "Through My Sails" got the CSN treatment. Talk of recording a new CSNY album before the tour was bandied about. Elliot Mazer recorded one inconsequential ditty, "Little Blind Fish," CSNY's first and only stab at writing as a quartet, but the projected album never materialized, and a presumptuous, shameless greatest-hits rip-off package entitled *So Far* was released instead. The only thing new about the package was Joni Mitchell's cover—a pentel-marker portrait of CSNY that would serve as a logo for the tour.

The quartet would play thirty-one concerts in twenty-four cities in a little over two months, mostly in outdoor stadiums before crowds that averaged fifty thousand. Various other superstars filled out the bill: Joni Mitchell, Santana, the Band and the Beach Boys. Although there had been stadium shows and festivals before, this was the biggest tour attempted in rock thus far, and what is most remembered is not the music, but the greed. As Stills told Cameron Crowe in an oft-repeated quote, "We did one for the art and the music, one for the chicks. This one's for the cash."

Nash and Crosby were less callous. "The Doom Tour," Crosby would call it, while Nash would voice his displeasure years later in "Take the Money and Run." "I feel strongly that the '74 tour was pressure from management for us to get out there and for it to be a big scene," said Nash. It suddenly became a much bigger scene when Bill Graham entered the picture. All previous tours had been handled through Geffen-Roberts, but at the last minute tour manager Leo Makota was axed and this one was farmed out to Graham. "Me and David wanted Leo, Neil and Stephen wanted Bill Graham," said Nash. "I made a great mistake at that meeting—I had taken a quaalude 'cause I'd been up all night, so I was persona non grata at this meeting and it was decided Bill Graham would do it. It cost us a fortune. A fortune."

Hey—Bill Graham made out fine on the tour because he put the fuckin' tour together. If he made a lotta money from us, he deserved to. CSNY had managers and hangers-on and agents—no wonder nobody made any fuckin' money. I made enough money. I felt we did fine on that tour. I don't even know how much money I made. I got ripped off, maybe I didn't—I don't care. I don't know much about the financial side of my CSNY days. I really didn't pay any attention. I always had enough goin' by myself. I knew whatever I did with them, I'd probably end up makin' less than I did by myself anyway, so it didn't bother me.

I really loved Bill. He was really good to us—really good to Pegi and I—he did a wonderful job with the Bridge shows and all that stuff. I loved him the way I love Elliot. I always thought if Elliot died, I would go to Bill. Where else could I go? I could talk to Bill . . . I could tell him what I wanted to do. He'd listen to me. A manager is someone who can listen—if I talked to him he would come back with an opinion, I'd tell him my opinion, he'd yell and scream. I could understand that.

Why did Elliot Roberts hand the tour over to Graham? Exhaustion. "Elliot started wearin' pajamas to work," said roadie Willie B. Hinds. "He went through this whole period of being very down. He got sick of it. Sick of musicians."

"Elliot said yes because Elliot had had it," said Leslie Morris. "Elliot was burnt, man. He didn't wanna do the work—so Bill Graham charged him to book the tour and charged them for the set and charged them for everything . . . it was a lavish tour. It was decadent."

"You'd go into your room and there would be pillowcases with the Joni Mitchell logo silkscreened on them," recalls Mac Holbert. "You'd go have dinner backstage and there would be plates that would have the logo stamped into them. There'd be a room in every hotel that would have shrimp cocktail, snacks and booze. This one guy who would pass out these horse capsules of coke. . . . We had limos waiting twenty-four hours a day and no one ever needed 'em. An awful lot of money was being wasted." And lots of money was being made, but little would end up going to the actual artists involved. "I remember every night when the show was over, all the managers would head to the office and pick up their cut," said Holbert. "It was like clockwork."

Complicating matters was the fact that most of CSNY were in a world of their own. "Anybody tell you how I went on that tour?" asks Crosby. "There were two very pretty girls with stunning figures on tour with me. So I was majoring in excess at the time. I didn't care that people were rippin' me off for millions of dollars." "He was paranoid all the time," said roadie Guillermo Giachetti. "Crosby was the king of the hippies, but he had a .45 in his backpack every time he went onstage. What was he gonna do—whip it out and start shooting people?"

The devil's dandruff was fueling much of the insanity. "Cocaine replaced marijuana," said Mazzeo. "Used to sit around and pass a joint. Later on people tried to sit around, pass a vial. You can't do that. It's not a social drug, it's a private drug." Despite Young's admission of cocaine excess, few saw him as a serious abuser. "We all did our share of stuff, but Neil didn't like it," said Carrie Snodgress. "He'd feel bad morally, bad emotionally. They'd do a night of cocaine, and that would be it for Neil for months."

Crosby and Stills were out the window. Few have pleasant memories of Stills from the tour. "I've been the most obnoxious, arrogant superstar to walk the streets of Hollywood . . . I can be an absolute bastard," Stills told Cameron Crowe at the time. His repeated clashes with Elliot Roberts had culminated in a fistfight that left him without representation. To replace Elliot, Stills hired a childhood crony named Michael John Bowen, an ex-military man whose vibe many found decidedly unhippie. "He was like a drill sergeant," said Mazzeo. "He fortified Stephen's military fantasies." Stills's obsession with all things regimental would earn him the nickname "Sarge."

Nash and Bernstein winced during a hotel-room visit from Paul McCartney, when Stills trashed the former Beatle's trademark instrument. "Y'know, Paul, I love your bass playing," Joel remembered Stills saying, "but we gotta get you a decent bass. I mean, that fucking Hofner . . ." Said Nash, "Behind massive amounts of cocaine Stephen will say anything to anyone."

Then there was the St. Paul Hilton, where Bob Dylan showed up on July 22. "Dylan comes to the hotel," said Nash. "Drummond and Stephen commandeer him and won't let anybody else in the fucking room." Dylan picked up an acoustic guitar and proceeded to play most of the material from his soon-to-be-recorded masterwork *Blood on the Tracks*. While Nash stood in the hall eavesdropping. "I'm listening to these songs through the door. I'm fucking dying." But nothing prepared Nash for the reaction from Stills. The moment Dylan left, said Nash, "Stephen looks at me—and this is a direct quote—he said, 'He's no musician.' I said, *'What?'* 'He's a good songwriter . . . but he's no musician.' "

The flipside of all this bravado was a vulnerability that was often painful to witness. Mac Holbert recalled sitting with a wasted, insecure Stills before the tour began in Seattle. "I spent an hour before the show in the bus with him. He was absolutely out of his mind, on the verge of tears he was so nervous. He was absolutely flipped out, not ready to go on. I just talked him through it."

· · ·

In the face of all the overkill, Young's approach was strictly low-rent. He traveled from gig to gig in a GMC motor home nicknamed "Mobile-Obil." CSN saw little of Young outside of the actual performances. "He never traveled with us, never hung out with us," said Nash.

Along for the ride with Young and Mazzeo was a conscientious new friend who functioned as bus driver and receipt saver, named "Ranger Dave" Cline. Zeke also came along, often accompanied by a mutt of Neil's named Art. Zeke and Art were quite a duo. Cline recalls the pair roaming through some swanky hotel lobby, Zeke padding along in diapers, blasting Indian music on a little tape machine as Art stopped to whiz on some expensive potted plants. "Art was a great dog," said Cline. "If the shows were good, Art would howl. Neil would get kinda concerned if Art didn't howl."*

Zeke was a handful at this point. As Mazzeo recalls, "When we first got on the bus, he had been into telling everybody no—all the women—'No, I don't wanna do this. No, I don't wanna do that, NO, NO, NO.' He starts pullin' his 'no' trip, so we pull the bus over and Neil goes, 'Look—we're men. It's okay for men to tell women no—that's cool. But look around, Zeke—there's *no women* on this bus. You don't say no to a man. If you have to say no, don't use the word 'no'—use the word 'refrain.' '' For the rest of the tour, the two-year-old would use it incessantly. Said Mazzeo, "The dog would jump up on Zeke and he'd go, 'Refrain, Art, refrain.' ''

In Chicago, Mobile-Obil died and Young—scanning the classifieds for a new set of wheels—found Pearl, a $400 black 1954 Cadillac that burned oil by the case. Perched atop the jump seat in the back was an old Underwood typewriter on which guests were invited to share their thoughts. "We always kept paper in it," said Mazzeo. "Anybody could go sit down, read a

---

*Art was later shot while chasing sheep belonging to a neighboring rancher. When told the news, Young replied, "Well, at least he died with his tail in the air." Quite famous in his time, the pooch moved Eagle Glenn Frey to declare in *Rolling Stone* that "Art is just a dog on Neil Young's porch."

paragraph of what somebody had written and then take off from there. It just kept goin' and goin'." The Never-ending Novel's main contributor was Young, writing under the alias "Dirigible Dan." Pages of Young's ramblings (including lyrics for such songs as "Daughters," "Star of Bethlehem" and "Bad News") exist from this time, many embellished by Mazzeo's coffee-stain art. "The whole concept was to stay creative, and we did a really good job," said Mazzeo.

But however creative Young's scene was, little of it rubbed off on his musical cohorts. CSNY was divided into four separate camps, down to the roadies. "Guys would say, 'Hey, man, would you help me with this amp?' and they'd say, 'I work for Stephen,' " recalls percussionist Joe Lala. "It was weird." As Holbert explained, "You got Neil travelin' on his own, David off with his women, Stephen with his little group. None of 'em are relating to each other at all—there's no band going on, no common consciousness happening. It was just four individuals that came together every day and played."

. . .

The first performance of the tour, at the Seattle Center Coliseum on July 9, 1974, set the tone. The quartet did a mammoth three-and-a-half-hour, forty-song show, blowing out their vocal cords in the process. By the next night in Vancouver, their voices were mere rasps. "The sound onstage was ridiculously loud," said drummer Russ Kunkel. "Graham was the only one who said, 'Look, we gotta turn down so we can get a level here.' " Problems with the huge, unfamiliar PA system were compounded by a couple of guitarists overzealous in their pursuit of volume. "We couldn't hear ourselves at all throughout most of that tour," said Nash, whose trademark harmonies with Crosby would suffer greatly as a result. "It was basically Stephen trying to outdo Neil, and it was just awful. We were just bad."

Crosby, Stills and Nash had almost no new material, relying on retreads from the all too recent past. Young, on the other hand, would perform many new songs on the road: "Long May You Run," "Hawaiian Sunrise," "Star of Bethlehem," "Love/Art Blues," "Pardon My Heart," "The Old Homestead," "Homefires" and "Pushed It over the End."

A number of the shows were recorded, but Joel Bernstein, who has waded through much of the tapes, said, "Most of the stuff is just trash musically. There's no dynamic range—everybody's playing wildly all the time. They're all singing sharp because they can't hear themselves." But the Chicago Stadium tape from August 27 features two powerful performances: "Pushed It Over the End," whose stop-time weirdness provided the most provocative use ever of CSNY, despite some excessive noodlings from Stills on keyboard; and a brooding "On the Beach," punctuated by tough blues guitar work from Stills. As out of control as Stephen might've been, he was still capable of great moments, like his honky-tonk piano on some of the live versions of "Love/Art Blues."

The love/hate relationship between Stills and Young continued as twisted as ever. Snodgress remembers an episode in an instrument store where Stills suddenly became interested in a guitar Young was perusing. "Neil was playing the guitar, and Stephen came over and took the guitar out of his hands," she said. Young snatched it back and made an offer below the asking price. Stills immediately offered more. "Stephen had to have the guitar. Neil was sayin', 'Fuck you, man—I want the guitar.' " The bidding had reached astronomical figures when Young abruptly backed out. "Next thing I know, Neil said, 'Fine, man—you buy it.' He put it back and walked out of the store. The minute Neil walked out, Stephen knew he'd been had. Neil had done it completely on purpose—he had no intention of buying it."

I never wanted anything that bad that I was gonna get in a bidding war about it. But I knew that Stills would have to win this kind of a thing—that he would never back off. So I had nothing to lose—I could keep goin' as high as I wanted, then *back off. I went next door and bought another guitar.*

That tour was disappointing to me. I think CSN really blew it. Last time I played with 'em had been two or three years before that. They hadn't made an album, and they didn't have any new songs. What were they doing? How could they just stop like that?

They wanted to put out a live album, and I wouldn't put it out—because it had all my songs on it. This huge tour and they had no new information. I couldn't believe that they were finished.

Carrie would occasionally fly in from Hawaii for a visit, but she and Neil remained at odds. One reunion in the Midwest was particularly unhappy. Carrie, with Zeke in tow, showed up with one of her minions from the ranch, who was seemingly very pregnant. When the trio entered Young's hotel room, Carrie made a little announcement. "I said, 'We brought you a present.' Neil said, 'You did?' " Carrie's friend disrobed, revealing that she had been pregnant with a pound of sinsemilla that Carrie had her smuggle aboard the flight out. "I guess I was just trying to show him what my true worth was—'Show me one other person who can get you a fucking pound of sinsemilla in Ohio.' "

The audacious stunt did not provoke the heartwarming response intended. "Neil was just in shock. He laughed, then he was mad. He thought it was obscene what I had done—jeopardizing his son's security. I was being a jerk, no question about it. It was a silly thing to do. Truth was, if I'd been arrested, the kid would've been taken away. Neil didn't come to the room that night. He stayed away . . . we left the next day without sayin' goodbye."

Things got even worse in Niagara Falls, New York. After a gig at Toronto's Maple Leaf Gardens, Young's entourage was crossing the border back to the States, heading for the last U.S. tour date in New York, when Pearl was searched. Snodgress had some contraband, which she claims was stuck in her purse by Neil's brother, Bob, without her knowledge, and the group was detained. The matter was later taken care of, but it didn't bring the couple any closer. The next day Young and company disappeared, ditching Carrie and her friend. "They left us," said Snodgress. "They'd all gotten on the airplane and left us."

The show at Roosevelt Raceway on September 8, 1974, brought the tour to a bombastic end, with a mariachi band in the food tent and a billboard issuing personal thanks from Bill Graham to each member of CSNY; tour accountant Bob Hurwitz would later discover that both items had been billed to the group. As CSNY departed the stage, they were served with a summons for a botched show in the Los Angeles area. The lawsuit "ended up costing each guy a hundred thousand dollars," said Hurwitz. "It didn't end on a happy note." But the final bummer was yet to come: one last show at Wembley Stadium in England on September 14.

The flight overseas was a bumpy one. According to Mac Holbert, Stills got into a terrible row with his then-wife, French pop singer Véronique Sanson, attracting the attention of one of the pilots. "He wrestles Stephen down, then Stephen goes and gets a piece of paper and starts scribbling away," said Holbert, who managed to read the document. "He was apologizing to the pilot—how he was a military man himself and had gone overboard. He signed it 'Stephen Stills, U.S. Marine Corps.' "

The show at Wembley was abysmal. Bad chemicals, Joni Mitchell said, contributed to the mess. "Everybody was heavy into the cocaine trip, and the stuff that was copped had to be cut with borax. People were shovelin' it in, shovelin' it in, and you couldn't get high off it. Before we went on everybody had nosebleeds." The concert was videotaped for possible release, but when the quartet saw it the next day, they were mortified. "Fuckin' horrible," said Nash. "I pride myself on bein' a reasonable musician—I have never sung so out of tune. It was awful. We were just bad."

The Doom Tour was over. While it had been the highest-grossing tour in history up to that point, CSNY would have a few questions for the tour accountant once the smoke cleared. "I went up to David's and sat down with Graham, David and Neil, and the first words out of their mouths were 'How much did Bill Graham make?' " said Hurwitz, who had no good news for the musicians.

"I think we earned about eleven million dollars on that tour, and we each came out with just over three hundred thousand—but we have a great pillowcase," said Nash. "It was insane. I have never really wanted to investigate what happened there, because it was such a pile of shit. I think we were totally taken advantage of and I'm amazed to this day that Elliot didn't take more control over it."

But Elliot Roberts had his own problems. During the tour he'd developed a nervous tic that sent him to a doctor who told him the only thing he was suffering from was stress. "Everything was too successful. I'm unhappy and I'm losin' my fuckin' mind and I'm gettin' tics and shit. All this shit's going on and my life's miserable. Going from phone call to phone call, tour to tour to tour, problems to problems to problems—and I've got no life. I was much more successful than I ever wanted to be." Except for Young and Joni Mitchell, Roberts got rid of all his clients.

"He let it all go," said Leslie Morris. "He let the Eagles go. I had to tell

America to go . . . he wouldn't work for them. He let Jackson Browne go—
I mean, Jackson got very upset with Elliot and finally left." David Geffen
would sell Asylum Records at the height of its success, and Geffen-
Roberts Management would dissolve in 1976. It was the end of an era.
"Everyone thought it was a family and they all worked towards that," said
Morris. "That's why I was completely devastated. When he sold Asylum, I
was like 'How can you do that? That was our family.' " But Geffen had
bigger things on his mind. He wanted to conquer Hollywood. "Why did it
all fall apart? Because Geffen wanted to be chairman of the board at
Warner Communications," said Morris. "He wanted success. He wanted to
win. And he did win." Geffen, Young and Roberts would meet again in a
few years, though the reunion would be less than jubilant.

The Doom Tour would prompt Crosby and Nash to head off on their
own (Roberts said they were let go with the rest of the acts; Nash insists he
and Crosby fired Roberts). "After that experience, Graham and I never
wanted to see Stephen or Elliot—or, for that matter, Neil—or anybody else
from that scene ever again," said Crosby. "In particular, I never wanted to
see Stephen again. He was . . . 'crazy' is too nice a word. It sucked."

In December 1974, attempts were made at another CSNY album. A session at the Record Plant in Sausalito came crashing to a halt when producers Ron and Howie Albert eavesdropped on a band meeting in the
recording booth. "They turned up the studio monitors so we could hear
what they were sayin'," said Drummond. "And the first thing Stephen
Stills wanted to know was 'What are you payin' Drummond?' Neil said, 'I
pay him what he's worth.' I said, 'Turn that shit off!' " That was it for
Young. "Neil fucking flipped," recalls Nash, who said Young then "va-
moosed with a capital 'V.' " Around this time, Stills would get into a fight
with Nash over a harmony part, then take a razor to Nash's master of
"Wind on the Water." Stills "slashed it to pieces," said Nash. "I had him
thrown out of my fucking house bodily."

Stills was left to tour on his own. In a bizarre turn, he tried to replicate
Young's scene from the CSNY tour, even hiring Mazzeo and traveling in
the GMC "Mobile-Obil." But there would be no Never-ending Novel on
this tour, because Stills morphed offstage into Sergeant Rock. Mac Holbert recalls walking into Stephen's home before the tour to find the musi-

cian decked out in full military regalia. "Look—the old uniform still fits," he annouced proudly.

According to Mazzeo, Stills spent much of the tour reminiscing about his tours of duty in Vietnam. Mazzeo pointed out to Stills that he had been in Buffalo Springfield at the time, but this minor discrepancy didn't faze him. His past was full of secret government missions and clandestine communications with the Pentagon. Stills got so deranged that Mac Holbert quit and went home. "Everybody was just amped out on fuckin' cocaine," said Mazzeo. "Just too many drugs . . . just too weird. And I had to keep listening to Stephen's Vietnam stories." When the tour was over, Stills offered everybody a two-week trip to Hawaii. Mazzeo, never one to turn down anything free, was so fed up he just flew back to the ranch.

•   •   •

Immediately after the CSNY tour, Young bought Wembley, a 1934 Rolls-Royce "named after the stadium that paid for it," said Mazzeo, adding that it was the car salesman's spiel that inspired the next move. "The guy said it was the finest motorcar in the world, that we could drive across the Sahara Desert in it if we wanted to. We decided to drive across the Sahara, but start in Amsterdam and work our way down."

Young, Sandy Mazzeo and David Cline—now joined by Graham Nash, Joel Bernstein and Leslie Morris—headed to Rotterdam by air ferry. Their last stop in England had been a carnival in Brighton-by-the-Sea, and by the time they arrived in Europe, the longhairs were looking pretty disreputable. "We had on big English overcoats that we had bought in secondhand stores, and we had won a bunch of paper leis at the carnival and weird straw hats with loud bands," recalls Mazzeo. "It's rainin' like hell, we're tryin' to run and we had carnival junk all over us. This Dutch customs guy with this blue uniform and white gloves puts his white glove out and goes, 'STOP.' "

The customs agent informed them that, as foreigners, they could not enter the country unless they presented plane tickets out. Leslie Morris, who had a huge stack of unused tickets from the tour, immediately whipped them out of a briefcase. Then the agent told them they couldn't enter unless each passenger was carrying at least $300. Nash, who was planning on buying some prints, pulled out a big pile of money. It must have been a surreal sight: a scruffy bunch of hippies in paper leis standing in the rain, holding out their booty for some incredulous official.

"All of a sudden we had about thirty thousand pounds in front of this guy, and he's looking at this stack of tickets and all this English and American money," said Mazzeo. "And just at that time the bull nose of the airplane opens up and this ramp comes down—and backwards in the rain comes Wembley. He looks at the car and looks at us and said, 'Is that your car?' And we go, 'Yeah! We're gonna drive it across the *Sahara Desert*!' "

In Amsterdam the travelers stayed at the Memphis Hotel. Leslie Morris—who had just left her gig with Elliot Roberts after a blowout at Wembley—recalls it as a morose time, with everyone upset over crumbling relationships, bands and jobs. "It was a pretty shaky time for everyone. Neil was miserable."

The relationship with Carrie had Young twisting in the wind. "When he was in Europe she wouldn't speak to him," said Morris. "It was endless." At one point after he had tried to call Carrie and had gotten blown off by one of her girlfriends, Young sat down at the Underwood and, under the heading "Chaptro Agresso," pounded out the lyrics to a song called "Vacancy" that nailed the weirdness Snodgress had surrounded herself with. "I look in your eyes and I don't know what's there / You poison me with that long vacant stare / You dress like her and she talks with your words / You frown at me and you smile at her."

Beneath the lyrics came a cryptic aside from Dirigible Dan: "The person . . . . . . (your name) who this little ditty was written for is not all bad. I have felt and scene [sic] the love she has four [sic] many people including me. But lately all I get is bad vibes." Leslie Morris recalls reading the "Vacancy" lyrics, which Young had pinned on the wall of his hotel room. "It was just full of anger and dark, dark—so dark that it scared me."

•   •   •

Morris, Nash and his girlfriend headed back to the States, leaving the intrepid quartet of Mazzeo, Cline, Bernstein and Young to head off to the Sahara on their own. They didn't get far. Wembley—with a top speed of only thirty-five miles per hour—blew up in Belgium.

What happened next was typically bizarre, and it all had to do with a dream Young had weeks before, during the tour. As Mazzeo remembers, Neil told him, "Wow, it was really weird—I had this dream that the tour was over and the three of us were in some foreign country, Belgium or something, and we were at the Hilton Hotel and we had jobs parking cars. It was great, because nobody knew who I was." Little did Mazzeo know that Young's dream would nearly come true after Wembley fell apart in Belgium.

"There's steam comin' out the top, oil leaking out the bottom, and we start pushin' Wembley up this driveway around in front of this hotel. Neil goes, 'Look! You remember back on the tour? It's the Brussels Hilton Hotel—my dream! My dream!' We go, 'Oh NO!'

"So we check in, get this big suite—we're still kinda funky, traveling incognito—and the manager opens it up and shows us the chocolates, the flowers and champagne. He's goin' through this whole routine and there's this girl holdin' this big bouquet. Neil takes him aside and goes, 'Listen . . . we're gonna be here for a while. Our car blew up and we gotta get it repaired—y'know, we're on our way to the Sahara Desert, as soon as we get it repaired we're outta here—but we could be here for a week or two. While we're here, we'd really like to get jobs working for ya parking cars.'

"And the guy kinda looked at us, like doubled-checked our credit cards to see if they were real—he had a hard time comprehending that the three of us wanted to go down and work full eight-hour shifts in the basement of his hotel parking cars. And Neil's goin', 'Listen, we'll do the best job anyone's *ever* done. I mean, we'll park your cars *better* than anyone's *ever* parked your cars before. We won't be late, we'll be *good workers*. You just *have* to give us these jobs.' The guy finally conveyed to us that we had to have Belgian work permits, so we weren't able to park cars—but we did try."

After a few days in Belgium, the trio decided to fly to Torremolinos, Spain, while the car was in the shop. Agonizing over his relationship, Young changed his mind at the very last minute and hopped on a plane bound for California instead. "We had our tickets, the baggage was on and everything," said Cline. "He got on one plane, we got on another." Young was determined to give it one last shot with Carrie. "This is the only time I can go back," he told Cline. " 'Cause there may not be anything to go back to later."

. . .

"After the CSNY tour, we were gonna try to put it back together again," said Snodgress, but ghosts of the past hung over the couple. "We'd have these meals of silence in front of the fire. Neil was very distant, very removed." Snodgress no longer felt welcome around many of Young's cronies. "Graham and David would come to visit—I'd see them comin' down the road, and they would go to the studio and Neil would go to the studio . . . Nobody would come visit. There was just this ambience that I was this bad girl."

In early November 1974, Young went to Quadrafonic, Elliot Mazer's studio in Nashville, to begin the sessions for what was to be his next album, *Homegrown*. The bleak title of one of the first songs attempted to set the tone for much of what was to come: "Frozen Man."

As Carrie told it, Young finally came out and asked her to leave the ranch for good, giving her an acoustic guitar that he'd composed some of the *Harvest* material on—"something for Zeke to remember his dad," he told her. She went to stay in nearby Butano Canyon in a house shared by soundman Tim Mulligan and his girlfriend, Gigi. Snodgress said she was "literally gone from the ranch twenty-four hours" when tragedy struck. Carrie's father called to inform her that her mother was dead, an apparent suicide.

When Young arrived at the house to console Snodgress, he found she already had a visitor—Captain Crunch. "The minute Neil walked in I started to go across to him," said Snodgress. "I saw him look—and I looked, and it just felt everything in my life was just passing in front of my eyes." Crunch would appear everywhere, even at Carolyn's memorial in Chicago. "This horrible person," said Snodgress. "Can you believe he kept showing up in those places?"

Carrie made plans to return home. "Neil took me to the airport, he was bein' so sweet and supportive—until we walked to the gate and I'm about to get on that plane. He said, 'Anything you need, just call for it. But I want you to know it's all over, Carrie. For real. It's all over.' "

. . .

Snodgress arrived in Chicago to a surreal, nightmarish scene. "See, my mother gassed herself in the garage. She was so drunk . . . and my dad had picked her up and brought her into the living room. . . . He literally sat for three hours holding her and talkin' with her and then he called the police.

"Well, the police—because she wasn't in the garage, where he said she was supposed to be—when my dad called me, he said, 'You better come home, you and [brother] Johnny, because the police suspect me of foul play'—because she'd been moved. We got home the next morning and the police were questioning my father, and we sat with the police and backed dad up, tellin' 'em she'd been an alcoholic for a long time and had threatened suicide since I was a child.

"As a matter of fact, the death report didn't even say carbon-monoxide poisoning—there wasn't enough to poison a mouse. It was just that she was so full of booze, she was a wet brain. The coroner said everything was about to go, kidneys, liver. So she died a natural death. That's what I figure.

"Oh God, that time was so crazy. I got Zeke out of there because it was so nuts. My dad couldn't sleep—one of the regulars at the bar was a pharmacist. He said, 'If you need sleeping pills or the kids need anything'—thinkin' we were a normal family that might just need a couple of Valiums. Well, the boys ordered quaaludes—the drink and the combination—oh boy, it was a mess. . . . It was like a movie that I was producing at one point, but the studio took over."

Young arrived with Mazzeo and, surprisingly, Rassy in tow. A wake was held at Carolyn's last hangout—Hackney's Bar—and Young played a few numbers on a Martin guitar he borrowed from Mazzeo. In the back of the funeral book, Young scrawled a little tribute to Carolyn. "She had this saying when she had a couple of drinks—'Shit, Mary, I can't dance,' " recalled Carrie. "And that's what he wrote. It was such an appropriate eulogy."

After a few drinks, Rassy started in with her own theories on Carolyn's death, and Neil hustled her out the door. Back at the hotel, Mazzeo noticed that a dazed Young had returned empty-handed. "I go, 'Where's my guitar?' Neil goes, 'Oh fuck, it was so weird I just left it.' "

Probably in an effort to keep his sanity, Young booked time at Chess

Studios to record with a reconstituted version of Crazy Horse. Nothing came of the sessions. Young soon left Chicago, and Carrie, behind. "I was in the next room the last night they were together at the hotel," said Elliot Mazer. "All I remember is waking up after all this racket and noise in the room next door. Ben, Neil and I got into one of Neil's big old Cadillacs and drove down to Nashville. I knew there had been a total break."

•   •   •

In Nashville, Young resumed his sessions at Quadrafonic, and on December 2, 1974, came the ultimate ballad of failed romance: "Separate Ways." The song begins in the middle of a doomy chord; Tim Mulligan lunged for the record button just as Young and the band dove into the song. Levon Helm rattles out a slow counterpoint as Ben Keith spins up a stark, bird-on-the-wire steel solo that has to be one of the lonesomest sounds ever recorded. "I won't apologize / The light shone from in your eyes / It isn't gone / And it will soon come back again," sings Young, sounding dead. This was powerful, painfully sad stuff, and it was goodbye.

"The theme of that album was basically the demise of his relationship with Carrie," said Mazer. "It was intense, like trying to make a record in the middle of Forty-second Street or Vietnam. It was an extraordinary time. If you're a documentary filmmaker and you're gonna document a person, that's when you're gonna do it—at the most intense, emotional time of their lives. So here's a guy going through hell, and this is like a fuckin' catharsis for him—a chance to get these songs out. It was a great relief."

Throughout December and January, Young recorded both in Nashville and at the ranch, and the songs rolled out hard and fast. Some were stark acoustic performances—"Love Is a Rose," "Love/Art Blues," "Home-fires." Others were cut with a band: "Old Homestead," a weird allegorical tale with allusions to the Horse; "Homegrown," a goofy tribute to hemp recorded in a much higher version by the Horse; "We Don't Smoke It," an inebriated blues vamp that would've sounded right at home on *Tonight's the Night;* and a killer "Vacancy," featuring Young mangling guitar and harmonica simultaneously. In "Try," a faint ray of optimism that perversely followed "Separate Ways" in one running order for the album, Young paid tribute to Carolyn Snodgress by adapting bits of her lingo into verse: "I'd like to take a chance," yelps Young over a rollicking piano, "but shit, Mary, I can't dance."*

•   •   •

Still in Chicago, Snodgress called Young and asked if she could return to the ranch for Christmas, but "he suggested that maybe it would be good if I stay with my dad, and I was sayin', 'My God, Neil, please—I can't stay with my father, I gotta come home. Whatever's goin' on, let me come home.' " This time Young stood his ground. Carrie snapped after the call. "I threw the phone—and just shattered this whole goddamn plate-glass window. 'Cause it wasn't fair. It wasn't fair."

Things had gotten a little spooky at the ranch. "I remember Neil tellin' me that Carrie's mom—her ghost—was makin' noise in the house," recalls Mazzeo, who said Young asked him to stay over. "Sure enough, there was this one night when we were all hangin' out in front of the fire in the living room. There was some sort of clanking and planking and booming around, and Neil went, 'See? See?' "

For Young, the best exorcism was through music. On December 16, he recorded the totem song of the period, "Give Me Strength." The lyrics catch him struggling to make the final break from Carrie's web. The bittersweet chorus is Young at his best: "The happier you fly, the sadder you crawl / The laughter in your eye is never all." Nonsinger Ellen Talbot yowled along on harmony, providing a crazy edge more than suitable for one of the last Carrie songs.

The sound is almost mystical. Guitar and harmonica, plus luminous overdubs of a tinkling piano and a finger tapping a paper cup, add glimmers of color that come and go. An impressionistic sound, precisely constructed without losing any of its spontaneous feel. Young was embarking on a musical experimentation that would culminate two years later on a song called "Will to Love."

It is hard to be enthusiastic enough about this period of Young's work. The wordplay is magnificent, his singing never more impassioned. In

---

*Both "Try" and "Star of Bethlehem" would benefit greatly from the overdubbed harmonies of Emmylou Harris, who recalls few details of the blurry session. "It was me, Ben Keith, Neil and a bottle of tequila."

terms of record-making, Young was at the top of his game. Pain, it seems, brought out the best in him.

•   •   •

Toward the end of January 1975, Young and Ben Keith headed to Village Recorders in Los Angeles for the final *Homegrown* sessions and the results were way, way out. "Kansas" and "Mexico" were solo Young performances—short, fragmentary and hallucinogenic. "Mexico" was reminiscent of Brian Wilson at his ethereal best. "Florida" was some cockamamie spoken-word dream (printed out, for reasons no one can remember, in the booklet for *Tonight's the Night*), set to the shrieking accompaniment of either Young or Keith drawing a wet finger around the rim of a glass (a trick they copped from Jack Nitzsche's soundtrack for *One Flew over the Cuckoo's Nest*).

Young was spending more and more time away from Broken Arrow, renting a place on the beach at Malibu. "Neil left the ranch, had to get away," said Mazzeo. "Too many ghosts—the ghost of Carrie, the ghost of Carrie's mom and the ghosts of all the weird shit that had gone down."

•   •   •

Unable to locate Young, Carrie Snodgress soon heard from his mother, who told her to come to the ranch to pick up her things. Jim Love drove her to the house in his pickup. "He was the only friend left who would help," said Carrie. "All the other ones had turned away.

"I'll tell ya, leavin' that ranch was scary. I come walkin' into the house and Rassy's there. She'd gone through the entire house and piled all my stuff up in the living room. I was in shock. I said to Jim, 'Just back the truck up to the porch.' And I just started takin' handfuls of stuff—my whole life—I just hurled it over the side of the porch into this pickup.

"Rassy became enraged—'*Look* at you. Look at the way you are behaving. You think this is a *normal* way for a person to behave, to just *throw* their things?' "Then Rassy picked up a slinky, sexy dress from the pile and suggested that maybe if Carrie had worn more of this sort of thing, she'd still be with Neil. "Never forgot it," said Snodgress. "The person he disliked being around the most in the world, he allowed that person to be in charge of extricating me."

Studio Instrument Rentals, Santa Monica Boulevard, Hollywood. In 1973, *Tonight's the Night,* for the most part, would be created here. "Do you mind if I knock a hole in your wall?" asked Briggs.

maxell UD C90

A	SIDE ONE	B	SIDE TWO
	GREATEST MISSES		TONITES THE NITE
	FROM		L. P.
	TONITES THE NITE		ALL SONGS

GREATEST MISSES
TONITE'S THE NITE (1ST ROUGH MIX)

The cassette-box cover of the unedited version of *Tonight's the Night* that Briggs carried with him for years. "I did the record, I thought it was fucking great. . . . Neil and Elliot and the record company backpedaled. They ruined the real *Tonight's the Night.*"

Bruce Berry. Berry
and pal Guillermo
Giachetti were "the
dark side of *Wayne's
World,*" said Young.

"That was a bad period. . . .
My policy was to just try to keep
a straight face." Neil Young, aka
Flyface, on the 1974 CSNY tour.

Bob Dylan, Rick Danko and Neil Young, SNACK benefit concert, San Francisco, March 22, 1975. Dylan's "a brutally honest guy. He loves to tell the truth, heh heh. He even *enjoys* it."

"Poncho was a resource to be reckoned with. He just brought the band back together." Neil Young and Crazy Horse (left to right: Ralph Molina, Billy Talbot, Frank "Poncho" Sampedro and Young). The greatest band in the world, circa 1975.

Neil Young, *Rust Never Sleeps* tour, 1978. "It all started when I looked at the pile of amplifiers that I had when I was rehearsing," Young said a year later. "There was no concept, it just all fell together."

Neil Young as Lionel Switch, Dennis Hopper as Crackers the Cook, in Young's feature film *Human Highway*. Hopper missed the 1983 premiere. "I wanted to go, but I was in the insane asylum at the time," he said.

Neil Young at the Berlin Wall during the European *Trans* tour, 1982.

The cover of Geffen's no-hits compilation *Lucky Thirteen,* showing Young in his *Trans* persona while on tour in Europe, 1982. *Trans* was "the beginning of my search for a way for . . . a severely physically handicapped nonoral person to find some sort of interface for communication. . . . And that was completely misunderstood."

The Ducks, Santa Cruz, 1977 (left to right: John "Johnny C." Craviotto, Neil Young, Jeff Blackburn and Bob Mosley). "I just play my part," said Young at the time.

Neil Young and the Shocking Pinks. "I got way into that guy. I was that guy for months. He was out-there. It was a movie to me. Nobody saw it but me, but who gives a shit." 1983 video shoot (left to right: Rick Palombi, Neil Young, Larry Byrom, Tim Drummond, Karl Himmel, Ben "King" Keith).

Young played some of the greatest guitar of his life with the Bluenotes, 1987–88. In the press at the time, Young would credit musicians Michael Bloomfield and Paul Butterfield for inspiring him to head into blucs and R&B.

Young in his International Harvesters phase, 1985. Geffen sued him for making "not 'commercial' " and "uncharacteristic" music. "Stop telling me what to do or I'll turn into George Jones," said Young.

The 1991 *Ragged Glory* tour with Crazy Horse (left to right: Billy Talbot, Young, Ralph Molina). "The [Gulf] war was raging . . . I figure that the guitar-playing was a soundtrack for CNN," said Young at the time.

Neil Young, incognito and on the prowl for model trains, 1978.

• • •

With tracks from Nashville, the ranch and Los Angeles—plus a bittersweet song called "White Line" that Young had recorded as an acoustic duet with the Band's Robbie Robertson in England a few days before CSNY's Wembley show—*Homegrown* was shaping up to be a major work. After some mixing was completed, Elliot Mazer headed off for England, where he played a tape of the album for the head of Chrysalis Records, who then told Mo Ostin he was sure they had another five-million seller. But then a funny thing happened. Young changed his mind.

Blame it on that blurry evening at the Chateau Marmont, where Young had played *Homegrown* back to back with *Tonight's the Night* for a bunch of stoned musicians including Rick Danko. "At which point Rick the Prick said, 'Go with the raw one,' " said Mazer, who was devastated when Young decided to jettison *Homegrown* in favor of *Tonight's the Night*.

There was another factor involved in the decision. Young had pulled back from the emotional nakedness of *Homegrown*. "It was a little too personal . . . it scared me," Young told Cameron Crowe a short time later. "I've never released any of those. And I probably never will. I think I'd be too embarrassed to put them out. They're a little *too* real." To his father he would describe the album as "great songs I can live without."

"He expressed to me he couldn't listen to the whole thing, it was so intense," said Elliot Mazer. "I said, 'Don't listen to it—you don't listen to your own albums anyway.' " In the next few years, Young would parcel out various cuts from the *Homegrown* sessions: "Little Wing" and "Old Homestead" to *Hawks and Doves,* "Star of Bethlehem" to *American Stars 'n Bars.* "Love Is a Rose" and "Deep Forbidden Lake" would be released on *Decade.* But to hear *Homegrown* in its entirety is to hear Neil Young at his best.

Pretty honest. Heh heh. It's an honest album. Never came out, hardly any of it. There's a cover for it somewhere. Me with a corncob pipe. Tom Wilkes did it—same guy who did the Harvest *cover.* Homegrown *is the missing link between* Harvest, Comes a Time, Old Ways *and* Harvest Moon.

I think I was on the edge makin' Homegrown. *I was pretty out-there.*

Kinda lost. But at the same time, I had a lotta freedom to go wherever I wanted to go and do whatever I wanted to do—that's why so many songs were written and so much traveling was done.

Breaking up with Carrie and losing my family . . . It was my first family. It was my son. I thought I'd made a horrible mistake. That doing it was wrong. I hadn't judged correctly. I'd done something without thinking about it—everything I did was working, so why not this? I was really torn between what to do and what was the right thing to do, but I knew I didn't want to do that. *I just went purely on my feelings at the time—there were some beautiful moments at the beginning of the relationship, but there was always this uneasiness that something was wrong. From the very beginning. I don't know why, but it was a little claustrophobic. Pegi doesn't make me feel claustrophobic. Now I don't feel I need to escape.*

But I kept ignoring it, and y'know—I was on a roll. Didn't really have much to make me think twice.
—You did later?
Yeah, because I knew that I'd altered her life and my son's life in a way that was less than it could've been . . . this is a painful period.
—What is it about Carrie? She gets under your skin. I hear it in all those songs.
"Revolution Blues"?
—Well, that's *a weird one to pick!*
Well, if you're talking about intensity and you're talking about somebody who you don't know why they get to ya—look at Charlie.
—There's a similar vibe?
I think you mighta hit on somethin' there. Heh heh heh.

Things only got crazier in Carrie's life after she left the ranch. In the mid-seventies, she was back in Los Angeles, involved with the man who had criticized her so relentlessly: Jack Nitzsche. "She took me by surprise," said a somewhat chagrined Nitzsche, who, after having badmouthed Snodgress so viciously, was deeply embarrassed whenever he had to face Young during this period. Jack said he and Carrie went out for three years, but they managed to live together for only a little over a week. Neither party was in the best of shape at the time. "I was drinkin', so I was playin' a lotta games with him," said Snodgress. "Whenever he'd be a bad boy, he'd turn around and give me money anonymously in envelopes in the mailbox. Weird. Sick."

Most observers found it a diabolical union. "Neil got lucky—she just left," said Jack Jr. "My father went through a little heavier deal." The "heavier deal" Jack Jr. is referring to unfolded the night of June 29, 1979, when Jack showed up at Carrie's Hancock Park home to find her asleep in bed with another man (who fled upon Jack's arrival). Nitzsche had a gun, and while accounts of what happened next differ drastically, Jack faced five felony counts when the smoke cleared: burglary, assault with a deadly weapon, assault with intent to murder, false imprisonment and a truly lurid last charge—rape by instrumentality. "Bullshit! I wouldn't do that to a gun," Jack said. Snodgress also accused him of threatening Zeke, who somehow slept soundly through the brouhaha in another room.

Snodgress later disavowed the rape accusation on the stand, saying that police had written her account wrong. "I think Carrie had every right to press charges," said Nitzsche's friend Leslie Morris. "She had enough on Jack, but she wanted more. Was it press? I think she's never benefited from these dramas she's developed." Nitzsche pled no contest to the assault charge. He was fined $3,500 and placed on three years probation. Snodgress got $60,000 in a settlement but, oddly enough, Nitzsche claimed she refused to take all the money. "Carrie went to my business manager and canceled the last payment of fifteen thousand. She said she couldn't live with herself, she felt so horrible."

Unbelievably, Snodgress and Nitzsche have continued to see each other off and on in the years since. Early one morning I received a call. It was Carrie. Seems she and Jack had compared notes on their interviews with me, and Snodgress was upset. "Did you call me 'dangerous'?" I heard a familiar voice in the background: Nitzsche's. Where are you? I asked. "Over at Jack's," she said, which was a bit of a shock after her fearful tales of Nitzsche's abuse. I hopped in my car and drove over. There was Carrie, sitting in Jack's lap, the stale aroma of booze hanging in the air. Just another couple of lovebirds.

Carrie put a spell on me. She's NEGATIVE . . . a lotta headtripping, lying. I never had anything like that. *It changed me forever. I mean, I hardly trusted anybody after that. Pegi still mentions some things about how* removed *I seem to be. I try to open up as much as I can for her, because, y'know, she's the whole world for me. I want her to be there with me all the way. I want to help her, and be with her through my whole life and take care of her. But she still feels that from me. I can't quite shed it. But I'm getting better—more and more—it goes away.*

All you have to do is look at the songs that came before, *before I met Carrie—"Old Man," "Heart of Gold," "Tell Me Why." Then check out what came* after.

The bright spot in all this insanity was Zeke. After the split with Neil, Snodgress returned to acting in such films as *The Fury,* but her main obsession was finding the best path for her son. "I had absolutely no interest in going back to work. I knew that I was responsible for a human being's life, and I took it real serious."

Cerebral palsy had left Zeke with his right side shorter than his left and a pinched right hand. "Zeke was always his worst enemy from the get-go," Carrie said. "When he was little, he used to hit his hand with a spoon and say, 'I hate you! I hate you!' "

I asked Zeke to describe himself as a little kid. "A little shithead," he said, laughing uproariously. "I was an alien from hell. I couldn't accept myself as being—y'know—different. . . . Turning doorknobs, turning on lights, stuff that I couldn't do like other little boys my age, would frustrate the hell out of me, and I'd cry—cry until I fell asleep."

When Zeke wasn't taking it out on himself, he was making life exciting for everybody else. "He bit people in markets if he wanted somethin'," said Carrie. "He'd pick up cans of applesauce and hurl them at people." "I remember a time when me and my mom were takin' a walk and I fell down," said Zeke. "And it pissed me off, so I went over and kicked somebody's car door." He grinned sheepishly at the memory. "My mom had to leave a note."

Snodgress gave Zeke a lot of leeway in growing up and said she was "ridiculed for not being harder on him . . . if a kid hits another kid, you can't be hittin' him, sayin', 'You can never hit another kid!' I was convinced that the only way to teach love is to show love—and patience."

After Zeke had a petit mal seizure at age three and a half, Snodgress took him to the Mayo Clinic. The doctors considered cutting a tendon inside his heel to drop his foot down, but they suggested Zeke build up his muscle first. The next few years were filled with a succession of braces, hip casts and physical therapy. "Zeke hated his shoe brace," said Carrie, who would sometimes have to wrestle with him for half an hour to get it on.

School was another challenge. "There was one quality that Zeke did not have, and that was a basic adherence to the rules," said Snodgress. Kids teased him and called him "Bigfoot." Zeke fought back. "Most of the kids hated me because I bit 'em all or kicked 'em. One girl started teasin' me about the shoe brace and I took it off and whacked her across the head with it."

Through all of this, Snodgress stuck by her son, searching everywhere for help. "It's a credit to Carrie that even with her own madness and her own foibles and frailties, she was steadfastly Zeke's mother," said Graham Nash. As can be expected, Young and Snodgress didn't always see eye to eye when it came to Zeke. Gary Burden, one of the few people who has remained friends with both of them, felt that at times Young "was a force against what Carrie was trying to do. He was not kind to her sometimes."

Zeke finally found the guidance he needed in a man named Jack Weaver at the Morning Sky School in Idyllwild, California. One of the first things Weaver did was separate mother and child. As Carrie remembers, Weaver told her, "You're not gonna be able to see Zeke for a while. We think that the removal of you may be part of what's gonna make this kid okay." For the next few months they were apart. "It was a rough deal," said Snodgress. "And Zeke kicked and screamed all the way, but he was there two years—and he came back a different kid."

"Jack Weaver was an extraordinary fellow," said Zeke. "He'd do anything he could to give me a hand, explain something to me or just help me with problems that I had. In my hard times, when I was mad and wanted to kill somebody, he held me on the ground in the dirt with my hands behind my back. It changed me a lot."

Although Zeke still has his moments, the alien monster from hell is gone, and he feels a lot of it has to do with accepting himself. "Epilepsy—it's not as hard for me now as it was, because it's easier for me to understand myself. This is the way I'm gonna be the rest of my life, and I know that now."

A few years after breaking up with Carrie, Neil Young married and started another family, further complicating the situation for Zeke. "When Zeke was having his hardest times, Neil just wasn't there," said Snodgress.

In the last few years Zeke has joined his father in the model-train business and sees more and more of him these days. When he visits the ranch the best times are the moments alone with his dad, riding in his father's monster truck, Stretch, or heading off for walks to find sticks for the train layout. "Those walks," said Zeke, shaking his head at Neil's stamina. "I can't walk across the ranch. I'll die before that happens."

Zeke loves going out on the road with his father. His room on the bus is down underneath, a spot cherished for its smooth ride and porthole window. Zeke's favorite time is cruising the highways late at night. "Everything's real quiet. Joe's driving, Dad's sleepin' in the back, I'm just down there eye-level with the cars until I pass out." Whenever they pull over for a pit stop, Zeke comes back with food or little gifts for everybody.

Zeke's "just a good kid," said bus driver Joe McKenna. "I'd go fuel the bus—he'd want to get out and help me. He'd meet fans at the show, next thing you know he'd go on the bus, find a T-shirt and give it to 'em. He's got all kinds of energy, and he spends it on helpin' people."

Time is beginning to heal the wounds caused by separation. "When you're a little kid, you see Dad as 'Wow! I wanna be with Dad all the time,' " said Zeke. "But when you get to be eighteen, y'know—I have a lotta things to do, and when I get older, I'm gonna have a wife and a house and a car, and I'm gonna go to work every day, and that's the way it's gonna be. He doesn't see *his* dad every day. They live in different countries. So it's the same thing— you kinda grow.

"Now I understand who he is and how he works. In the past five years, I've seen him really calm down and be a lot quieter, more peaceful. Sit in front of the fire and play his guitar and not have to worry about so much stuff at one time. I know he does worry, but he's learned to live with it better. . . . He's a great dad and I love him a lot."

Zeke's a great kid. I don't know how he came out so good. I just thank God for the fact that he did. I'm so thankful.

I wish I knew him better. Zeke had a real tough time growin' up, with his mom and I fightin' back and forth. And somehow he's come through the whole thing as a kid that I'm really proud of. And I hope that he can find something to do with his life that he really believes in. That's my hope. Because he's very smart—he's real focused and has an intuitive understanding of things mechanical and electronic and conceptual. I'd really like to see him make it on his own.

Zeke's done really well. He went to all these damn schools that we had to put him in and he started off bein' such a hard kid to handle . . . I always blamed it on his mom, but it's really as much my fault as hers. It's just that neither one of us knew how to bring up a kid.

We worked at it, tried different things, talked to him about it. . . .

He had to go through all this hell *when he was a kid. Wearin' this big brace, not being able to play with the other kids because he couldn't keep up with 'em. Whoa, man. It would drive me crazy—see him come home with his foot all bloody 'cause he was running without his brace on and his toe was dragging.*

—Has your relationship with Zeke given you insight into your relationship with your own dad?

Well, I hope Zeke loves me as much as I love my dad—or maybe even more. The insight? I don't think Zeke ever had a dream that I didn't try to help him do.

The things that Zeke wanted, he didn't get them right away, but he got them. I don't want him to get things so easy, that all he thinks he has to do is wait and ask Dad. And he doesn't. Actually, I wish he'd call me more *now. But that's okay. That's what he's supposed to be doin' at this age—be out there, checkin' things out. He's a cool kid.*

—Do you see a lot of yourself in Zeke?

Yeah, I do, actually. His tenaciousness. If he wants to find something out, boy, he's gonna ask the questions. He's gonna be on *it—until he understands it, know what I mean? Zeke's funny. He's got a good sense of humor. He gets a good laugh out of things.*

—There were times you weren't there. You were into your own thing. Just like you are with everybody.

Absolutely. That's tough for a kid. I didn't even know *he needed me, 'cause I was gone. I'd be off here and there, all around the world—at times when it was important to Zeke. I just wasn't there. But that's one of the tragedies of a broken home. There's no excuse. The whole growing up thing without a dad is kinda a drag. But I couldn't—I couldn't live with Carrie. There was nothing that would make me live with her. I didn't want Zeke to see me like that.*

But the way Zeke turned out, Carrie must've done a lotta stuff right. She must've, because the fact is, he turned out pretty fuckin' good.

For Zeke, as a person, to come out the way he did after all he's been through—his fuckin' family, crazy parents—I'm so proud of him. So proud of him.

"I feel like I just woke up from a bad dream," Neil Young would sing in "Kansas," one of the great lost *Homegrown* songs, and it must've felt that way for him as 1975 led to another new life. He was single, living on the beach in Malibu, and best of all, his band Crazy Horse had regrouped with a new guitarist who would tip the music in a hard-rock direction—Frank "Poncho" Sampedro.

Poncho laughs. And when he laughs so do you. There is something insane about his cackling. I remember Poncho teaching me how to drive. I nearly killed the two of us when I putted onto the Ventura Freeway for the first time. He laughed extra hard. That's the thing about Frank "Poncho" Sampedro. He just doesn't give a fuck.

If Poncho likes you, he'll catch a bullet with your name on it in his teeth. But I wouldn't care to be his enemy. Beneath the happy-go-lucky exterior lurks a ruthless mind. "I *am* a hippie," he said. "I just happened to make some money along the way—and had to carry a gun to make it. Money, drugs and women got me everything. That's how the mob did it, that's how the government did it and that's how I did it."

Sampedro can get people to do the most unlikely things. He once talked his reclusive, phobia-ridden pal Richard "Bonzo" Agron into an impromptu adventure south of the border. "I'm claustrophobic, agoraphobic," said Bonzo. "Next thing I know we're in some crazy '64 Ford Falcon station wagon with a chicken foot taped to the speedometer, drinkin' El Presidente brandy on the beach in Mexico."

Filling the void left by Danny Whitten's death, Sampedro plays second guitar in the Horse. With his long hair and beard, pro-wrestler physique, flashy gold jewelry and baggy shorts, Poncho looks like a dope dealer. A Detroit boy, he digs the old cats like Howlin' Wolf and John Lee Hooker, but he also has a taste for the greasy depravity of Leslie West's Mountain. "Rock and roll—I thought that meant Loot the Village and Rape the Women," he said, laughing again.

Once a doper, Sampedro surprised everyone by living. "I watched him piss away hundreds of thousands of dollars on absolutely nothing—it was literally live for the moment," said his friend Danny Doyle. "Frank has fallen on his face more times than anybody I know, but he's been a success in spite of all the screwups. He's always led a charmed life." These days Poncho lives the straight life—suburbs, kids and a day job. At times he seems a little wistful over the lack of action, just like the Henry Hill character at the end of *GoodFellas:* "I'm an average nobody. I get to live the rest of my life like a schnook." But Poncho remains a desperado at heart. "Frank just wants it all," said ex-wife Kevyn Lauritzen. "He wants it *all*. Too much isn't enough."

Poncho lives minutes away from his Crazy Horse bandmates Billy and Ralph, but he rarely sees them. Although he's been in the band since 1975, they still treat him like the new guy. Sampedro's been a financial success in various endeavors, which leads to the complaint you hear most: He's more businessman than musician. Stung by the-Horse-can't-play criticisms, Sampedro once paid for an album's worth of sessions in which pro musicians cut the tracks and the Horse contributed vocals only. The idea was more plain crazy than crassly commercial, knowing Poncho. The fact of the matter is that Sampedro has been able to play with Shakey in a variety of projects outside the Horse. "You can't do a Neil Young record without Poncho," said producer Niko Bolas. "He's like glue. There's no one thing he does, but if he wasn't there, it'd come apart."

Neil and Poncho are like brothers—sometimes distant, sometimes competitive, but the bond is always there. When Neil's dog Elvis died, it was Poncho who helped dig the grave. He's one of the deepest, most psychedelic figures around Neil Young. "Frank has incredible insight into people," said Doyle. "He can get right into their souls and figure out who they are—for real."

• • •

"I'm the first generation Sampedro not to be a fisherman," said Manuel Frank "Poncho" Sampedro, born the son of Spanish immigrants on February 25, 1949, in Welch, Virginia. His father worked in a coal mine to save enough money to move the family to a tough neighborhood on the southwest side of Detroit, where Frank played guitar in a band called DC and the Coachmen. We were bad, man. More like a gang than a band."

Poncho lived for playing live. "I think that's one of the big differences between Billy and Ralph and myself. All their early years were in a vocal group, *then* they played instruments—all my experience was playin' in bands. No matter what goes wrong on a gig, you're gonna make it through it—I think that's something I have that they don't."

After repeated brushes with the law, Poncho left Detroit. "I was just stealin', thuggin' and robbin'—and playin' music. I came home one day and my amp and guitar were gone, and my parents said I couldn't have 'em anymore. I moved to California with my sister and went to Hollywood High."

"Frank came out here and he was Mr. Slick from Detroit—slacks, T-shirt and pointed shoes," recalls Doyle. Poncho soon became psyche-delicized in the California sun. His greased-back ducktail grew into a long mane, his fashion turned heavily tie-dye and he opened a head shop in the valley.

But despite all the groovy hippie vibes, Poncho would never lose the Motor City edge that many of his friends found terrifying. "This is the kind of aura Frank puts out," Bonzo recalls. "We're at a party at Danny's house. Frank is stoned on about four hits of acid—real good acid, you could see his eyes go in different directions—and these guys come in and threaten the party with a gun. Frank, as stoned as he was, all five-eight of him, walks up, said two or three words and these guys just slinked away. Poncho just vibed 'em away."

Depravity was the order of the day around Sampedro, and it frequently involved women. "Frank was a charmer, Mr. Smooth, the quintessential full-blooded Spaniard," said Bonzo. "I would get all the leftovers—he'd have a girlfriend at his house and bring some *other* girl over to my house. We'd all get fucked up and he'd hide her clothes. He'd say, 'Well, if you don't do the same thing to Bonzo, you don't get your clothes back.' He'd split, and they'd wind up bein' my girlfriend."* Sampedro seemed invincible. "If a girl hurt him, he'd have a new girl an hour later. You never knew if he was hurtin' or not. He would always be totally in control."

Sampedro wandered between California and Mexico, dabbling in a variety of endeavors of dubious legality that gave him great insight into the human condition. While Poncho wasn't in a band in the early California

---

*"For all Poncho's sexual exploits, I didn't think he was sleazy," said Kim Gordon of Sonic Youth, who toured with the Horse in 1990. "I just thought he was insane."

years, a guitar was never far away. Both Doyle and Bonzo vividly recall the one record he used to jam along with most: *Everybody Knows This Is Nowhere.* "Poncho used to play it over and over again and play along on guitar," said Doyle. "He said, 'Someday I'm gonna play with those guys.' "

It was either in late 1973 or early 1974 when Sampedro first encountered Billy Talbot at the house of actress June Fairchild—as Poncho recalls, "the chick who snorts up all the Comet in a Cheech and Chong movie." Sampedro was relocating to Ensenada, Mexico. "I got busted. Been living in my truck for about three years." He asked Billy to join him for the trip down.

"We barely knew each other and we went to Mexico," said Talbot, shaking his head. While in Mexico they jammed on the beach on a couple of acoustic guitars. "Poncho was so open, free," said Talbot. "We played a tune for half an hour and went through all these different emotions. I knew he was the guy we could use."

• • •

When Neil Young was in Chicago in November 1974, he summoned Billy and Ralph to Chess Studios. Talbot had a surprise for him when he called. "I said, 'Hey, man, I got this guitar player. I wanna bring him with us.' Neil was taken aback, 'cause I never said anything like that before. I didn't even tell Ralph—we'd been playing for a while, and Ralph didn't think he was that good. I kept saying to him, 'Don't worry, Poncho can do it—you'll see.' "

At Chess, Sampedro got a newcomer's welcome from engineer Tim Mulligan, who got right in his face and barked, "Where did *you* come from?" But Poncho was oblivious. "I was drinkin' heavy, doin' blow and smack, gettin' really crazy—that's how I was when I went to Chicago. I got Ben Keith so high he puked all over his whole room, hee hee."

Poncho was equally loose upon meeting Neil Young for the first time in his hotel room. "The night before we went to the studio, he showed us about seven or eight songs. I was playin' along on about three of 'em, and then I handed the guitar to Ben Keith, goin', 'Here, Ben—you play some.' He said, 'No, *you* play.' I didn't realize Neil was showin' me the songs we were gonna record the next day. It didn't even dawn on me I was supposed to be *learning* these tunes, ha ha ha. We went through all these songs. I was tired of playin' guitar . . . I wanted to go back to my room and do another bump."

The Chess sessions were a washout, and back at the hotel the Horse began to freak. "Billy and Ralph were going through conniptions—'Neil's not gonna use us,' " recalls Poncho, who was feeling it might be his fault. "I said, 'Let's call him and tell him, and then he can do what he wants.' Everybody was like 'Oh, no, man, you can't talk to Neil like that.' Finally I said, 'Fuck it—I'm going up to his room.' "

Poncho offered to leave the sessions if it wasn't working out, but Young—who was making plans to leave for Nashville the next day to work on *Homegrown*—had already formulated in his mind some sort of future for the Horse and told Sampedro, "This is really cool. I recognize this whole thing from somethin' I've done before. We'll play again, don't worry." Said Poncho, "I didn't really understand, but Neil could see we could be Crazy Horse then."

•　　•　　•

Sometime after the *Homegrown* sessions—Billy Talbot put the time in the spring of 1975—Young and the band got together again. Talbot was renting a place in Echo Park, and in terms of wretched ambience, the residence was legendary. As Billy's soon-to-be second wife, Laurie, recalls, "Poncho told me, 'Oh, you'll love where Billy lives—he has a little cottage in Echo Park.' I pull up and there's an empty field with one little shack." "I don't even think there was a driveway to it," said roadie Guillermo Giachetti. "Just a dirt road, puppies everywhere, dogshit." A woman raised goats down the hill, and not far away, the Hillside Strangler had dumped the nude corpse of one of his victims. "We used to play till four in the morning," said Poncho. "No one would call the cops on us."

Young, who rarely stays with anybody, let it be known that he was coming to visit. Laurie Talbot was in charge of getting his accommodations ready. "One room they never opened—it was like Charlie Manson," she said. "I had to paint the whole room and get the chickens out of the coop."

Neil pulled up in an old Buick armed with a new song, "Born to Run," and there in a cramped room in Echo Park, the second incarnation of Neil Young and Crazy Horse really began. "It was great," said Talbot. "We were soaring. Neil loved it, we all loved it—it was the first time we heard the Horse since Danny Whitten died."

"I see the light of a thousand lights burnin' in your eyes / Still I have to turn away from you to stay alive" was the knockout opening of a song that cataloged all the awful weirdness of the last few years. A long, tense rocker with a dreamy stop-time chorus reminiscent of "Pushed It over the End," "Born to Run" made clear he was breaking with the nightmares of the past and ready to live again, even if living meant running away from ghosts.*

The vibe was electrifying. Sampedro's then-girlfriend Kevyn Lauritzen recalls Young pausing from the music only long enough to catch a few minutes of *Rebel Without a Cause* flickering on the living room TV. But he soon disappeared. "Neil only slept over one night—said he had to go home and get something," recalls Billy. "He didn't come back. He couldn't take it anymore. It was too funky." Kevyn went with him—with Poncho's blessings. "I had so many girlfriends at the time, I didn't care." The wheels were turning in Young's head. Soon he would reconvene the band in Malibu and, with Briggs at the helm, record what ranks as perhaps Young's finest hard-rock album to date: *Zuma.*

. . .

By the mid-seventies, nouveau-riche rockers were thick as flies around Malibu. Rod Stewart was flitting about alongside David "Kung Fu" Carradine, the Band had built their Shangri-La studio just down the road, and Rick Danko was a constant visitor at Young's. "We used to call him 'Quick Rick,' 'cause he used to pull his car up, back in, keep it running, say what he had to say, then leave," said Connie Moskos, living with David Briggs at the time. Actor Danny Tucker remembers going for a stroll on the beach and finding "a guy in full Nazi gear passed out on the beach with his feet in the water." The comatose figure was Keith Moon.

---

*"Born to Run" remains unreleased, although Young would record it for his next record, *Zuma,* during the sessions for *Freedom* and most successfully during the *Ragged Glory* sessions of 1990. Sometime during the stay at Billy's, Young also finished a lyric he'd started many years before at Briggs's Topanga ranch house, "Powderfinger," later to be a key song on *Rust Never Sleeps.* A tape exists of Young and the Horse running through "Born to Run," "Powderfinger" and Poncho's joyfully misogynistic "Get Over Here, Woman."

Heavyweight songwriter and singer Bobby Charles, aka Robert Charles Guidry, would also float in and out of the Shakey circus over the next few years. Born in Louisiana on February 21, 1938, Charles had his first hit in 1955—"See You Later Alligator." As a songwriter, he'd penned "Walkin' to New Orleans" for Fats Domino and in the sixties cut such heartbreaking ballads as "I Hope" and "Everyone Knows."* An old crony of Ben Keith's, Charles made quite an impression on the Malibu scene, specifically during the rehearsals for the Dylan/Young/the Band SNACK (Students Need Athletic and Cultural Kicks) benefit in Golden Gate Park. "We were in an echo chamber," Briggs recalls. "Neil and Dylan across from each other on chairs, playin' acoustic. Neil would sing a song, then Dylan, then Neil. All of a sudden Neil went, 'Hey Bobby—why don't you sing a song?' Bobby sang 'The Jealous Kind,' and that was it. Nobody sang after that."

Among those lurking in the Malibu shadows, Dylan was the heaviest presence of all. Sandy Mazzeo remembers piloting his '54 Pontiac hearse into town one day. "I hear bam! bam! bam! on the divider, and I'm thinkin', 'Oh my God, it's a ghost.' I look in the rearview mirror and it's *Bob*." Dylan had apparently crawled in the back to get some shut-eye, only to find his bed moving the next morning. "Dylan was in his turban stage, and he'd slept in his turban and it had come all undone—he looked like the mummy." Mazzeo offered to drive him back to Malibu, but Dylan said he'd thumb a ride. "Last time I looked, he was straightening out his turban and getting ready to hitchhike back to his house. Those things happened in Malibu all the time."

•   •   •

Young would rent a house on Broad Beach Road before buying stunning oceanfront property on Sea Level Drive. Bobby Charles was with him the day he found it. "Neil wanted to go ridin' around lookin', and I said, 'The way to do it is to *walk*.' We saw this beautiful little wooden house, all these beautiful little flowers growin' on it. Man, it just looked really nice." Re-

*Charles received a co-writer credit (along with Tim Drummond) on Young's 1977 song "Saddle Up the Palomino," and Young played on an as-yet-unreleased second Bobby Charles 1977 album for Bearsville as well as 1994's *Wish You Were Here Right Now*.

putedly once the love nest of F. Scott Fitzgerald and Sheila Graham, the New England–style cottage was the last house on Sea Level, with its own private stretch of beach. Pulling into the driveway at the moment Young and Charles were looking it over was actress Katharine Ross, the current owner. On a whim, Young went over to see if she was interested in selling. It turned out she was, and Sea Level Drive became home, at one time or another, to Young, Briggs, Connie Moskos, Danny Tucker, Mazzeo, Zeke and David's young son, Lincoln.

The atmosphere was loose. As Mazzeo recalls, "We bought an old wedding dress, stuck it in the closet of the living room under a can of chocolate cherry bonbons and figured, 'If we meet the right girl, we'll open up that door—otherwise that's where all that shit belongs.' "

Along with Briggs and the Horse came a lot of women. As Kirby Johnson—producer of the Horse's *Crazy Moon* album, said, "One thing that always sticks in my mind about Crazy Horse: For guys who I never thought were great-lookin', they sure had the most beautiful women around." "It was a ball of confusion, the Malibu time," said member of the gang Tessa "Moosa" Gillette. "Everyone's life had fallen apart, so it was like a big free-for-all. Compared to the ranch, it was a hundred and fifty miles per hour."

Many a late night spent raising hell at the Crazy Horse Saloon ended with a crash out at Poncho's beachfront bungalow on Pacific Coast Highway. "We lived there a year and a half and never had a spoon, dish, pot or pan," he said. Pal Steve Antoine lived with Poncho and, with a camera slung around his neck, posed as a photographer for *Penthouse* magazine to con women into joining the party. "We were invincible then," said Antoine. "Shit rolled off our backs. Nothing slowed it down—women, the police— we just did what we wanted to do. Things were just moving."

●　　●　　●

David Briggs was the ringleader of the *Zuma* scene. At first he was living with Terry Yorio, a former Miss Something-or-Other alleged to have quipped, "Who's this guy Art Nouveau?" while flipping through the pages of an art-history book. After she fled, Connie Moskos moved in (her curiosity about David had been piqued one night in the Crazy Horse Saloon when he made "some rude comment about my mouth"), and she recalls

Young's detached amusement over the circus Briggs created. "Neil would look out on the beach, and all these little girls would be sitting there topless. He'd go, 'There they are. All the little nymphettes. And Briggs encourages it.' Half the women in Malibu had Neil's phone number because of David. He would just encourage all the insanity that life could bring."

Nothing was more insane than the way they cut *Zuma*. For eight hundred bucks a month, Briggs was renting a huge house directly across the street from Goldie Hawn's. It had six bedrooms, but for some perverse reason Young decided to record the band in one of the tiniest rooms in the house. The confined quarters, combined with the tenuous ability of the Horse, created some challenges for Briggs.

"Poncho didn't know how to play, nobody had a tone, nothin'. The band was at an enormous volume in a terrible little room with a low ceiling and flagstone floors and picture windows all around—[ace mixer/producer] Bob Clearmountain couldn'ta made the drums sound good. We brought down the green board, set it up in the kitchen, I cut big pieces of foam for the windows, said to my neighbors, 'Lissen, I'm gonna be makin' records all night long' and started rollin' tape.

"Wasn't a lot of work on those records, man—we just set up, recorded, and I mixed 'em on the spot. That's why those records sound so crude and elementary. We did a lot of editing, 'cause they'd free-form and I'd edit out the flat parts. Some takes would be ten minutes long. That whole album is a lesson in making Neil Young records. If he's great, I don't give a shit about anything . . . Neil's a lot better in houses than he is in studios."

Of all the records Briggs made with Neil, he seemed fondest of making this one. "Neil was the happiest I've ever known him during *Zuma*. He was a great guy to be around. A happy, happy guy . . . we were just out cruisin', havin' a good time . . . the recording was just an extension of our everyday life."

•   •   •

No one was having more fun making *Zuma* than Poncho, stunned to find himself in such heavy musical company. "I didn't even know why I was *there*. I was in dreamland. I'd go to the bathroom, do a bunch of smack in between takes and go, 'Hey, I'm playin' with Neil Young—holy shit.' For months I was in that state. All he had to do is look at me sideways and I'd stop playin'."

Sampedro believes his limited abilities inspired Young to—as the late great cartoonist Ernie Bushmiller put it—"dumb it down." "I think Neil kept writin' simpler songs so I could play 'em." And most of *Zuma* is crude—simple songs with big chords, bad attitudes and no extra stuff.

While Poncho might've been insecure as a musician, he wasn't lacking in attitude. "I dedicated my trip into makin' Neil have fun. He had *On the Beach* out, and I teased him—'Look at the titles. It's "This Blues," "That Blues." Here we are in L.A., there's beautiful chicks everywhere, we're high out of our brains havin' a great time—isn't there something else to write about?' "

Maybe so. With Poncho and Briggs as role models, Young seemed to cut loose and have a little fun for a change. The joyous abandon on *Zuma* is palpable. If his last few records were so low they were subterranean, this one was daybreak hitting the water.

"Don't Cry No Tears" sets the stage. Two guitars, bass, drums— shimmering electricity, blockhead lyrics, anguished vocals and a big fuck- you to the past. It's a reworking of "I Wonder," Young's tale of boy-girl woe from his Squires days, and at least one person took the message personally—Carrie Snodgress, living in Santa Barbara and still in sporadic touch with Young via telephone. "I would be so overwhelmed with my feelings I would start to cry," she said. "It made Neil crazy. He would say, 'I'm not gonna do this. This is what's keepin' me from callin' you— because you cry.' I'd say, 'Just let me get over this for a few minutes,' but he wouldn't. Crying is a big thing for Mr. Young."

On *Zuma,* women are mainly betrayers or ghosts best forgotten. Tired of hurting, Neil spends a good deal of the album telling them to get lost. "Stupid Girl" marries a sneering, double-tracked vocal—menacingly low and ridiculously high—with lyrics of casual hatred. "It was as if the Stones had never even done a song called 'Stupid Girl,' " said writer Richard Meltzer. "It was *the* stupid-girl song."

Sampedro recalls the craziness that produced "Stupid Girl." "I had a gram of blow—I put it out on the table, and Neil did the whole thing. I looked at Neil, he was so high I thought, 'He doesn't even know what he *did*, man.' " Unaware of his opiate intake, Poncho's jacked-up companions were speechless when he went off to the other room to nap while Young overdubbed. "What a band!" he said, laughing.

If God asked for a definition of beauty, I'd play him "Barstool Blues": the shambling "It's All Over Now, Baby Blue" melody, Ralphie's bashing away on the cymbals, the exquisite pain of the lyrics, the pathos of the singing—surely this is one of the most tortured vocals Young ever committed to tape—but the GUITAR playing! Languid, glistening, tube-warm and transcendentally high. So melodic, so simple and so emotional—it's as if the instrument is patched directly into his heart. From *Zuma* until *Rust,* essentially 1975 to the end of 1977, Young embarked on journeys with his guitar that remain unequaled.

And then there is "Danger Bird," perhaps the most unsettling song Young has created, a soundtrack worthy of one of those ten-cent portraits of Hell found in a Coffin Joe flick. Precariously compiled by Briggs from two very different takes cut weeks apart, this nearly seven-minute piece contains so many twisted pleasures that the mind races trying to decide where to begin. The notes of dread that open the song? What Briggs calls the "windshield-wiper guitar," building to worm-burrowing solos with roller-coaster twists and turns, right up to the insect-frenzy Link Wray–style fade-out had even avowed hippie-hater Lou Reed praising Young's virtues in *Rolling Stone*. The jive-talk lingo about a jailbird and a danger bird determined to fly, "though his wings have turned to stone"? The heavy group-harmony counterpoint, singing an entirely different song containing excruciating details of the Hawaii disaster? "Danger Bird" is a masterpiece, a trip inside the darkest recesses of Shakey's mind.*

"Cortez the Killer" is one of Young's most evocative time-travel songs, culminating in an emotional last verse in which the sudden switch to first person lends a three-dimensional depth. The lyrics conjure up a ruthless

---

*When I played "Danger Bird" for the enigmatic guitarist Link Wray—in his seventies and still giving his all—he was stunned by the similarity in feel to one of his own recordings (and one that I'm sure Neil has never heard): the doom-laden late-sixties album cut "Genocide." Wray was moved by Young's guitar work. "It's pure, honest music," he said. "No bullshit."

conqueror undone by love left behind, though listening to it, I think of not only Cortez but Howard Hughes, Orson Welles, Michael Jackson and . . . Neil Young. Just twenty-nine years old, Young had already realized that dreams can cost you everything—and that even the great ones can morph into nightmares.

It's amazing that this band of lunatics ever got through "Cortez." Poncho: "I had some angel dust. Conned Billy into smoking it with me. We recorded 'Cortez,' I'm sitting there nodding out. That was the take. I had the song all turned around—I thought the second chord was the first chord. It's only three chords."

Young was going to a lot of places you couldn't get to on the A train. This band would also record a wild electric version, as yet unreleased, of "Ride My Llama," a song in which the llama-riding Young would meet a martian who got him stoned.

The band had a visitor during the sessions. "David and Crazy Horse were recording," said Terry Yorio. "I was making lunch, standing at the kitchen window. I see this blue van in the driveway. I said, 'David, somebody's out there!' David was already chasin' the groupies off the front porch—he goes, 'Goddamn it!' Took off running out the front door. The guy in the van had his back to him. He went and grabbed him by the front of his coat and it's *Dylan* . . . David apologized."

Dylan and Young had played together at the SNACK benefit in March. Roadie Johnny Talbot recalls that the moment in rehearsal when the two musicians started to jam was literally electrifying—they went to switch guitars, and in the heat of the moment, each forgot to let go of the one they were holding, which resulted in a huge shock. "On their butts, BAM! Before I could get out there, they picked their guitars up off the floor and did it again. They were so in awe of each other they weren't thinkin'."

Dylan, who lived around the corner from Briggs, shuffled in and joined the *Zuma* sessions, first on piano, then guitar. "He didn't talk, just nodded," said Sampedro. "He was dressed in Sears clothes—I didn't know it was Bob Dylan." ("I didn't know he was so short," mused Ralph.) The action-packed lineup fizzled when the Horse inevitably fell apart. "We did a bunch of his songs, never got one right all the way through," said Poncho. "Neil told me later Dylan said, 'Your band has a good beat, but they can't play,' and Neil replied, 'Yeah, but think about it, Bob—*you* could play with them.' "*

.   .   .

Zuma was released in November 1975, just four months after the resurrected *Tonight's the Night*. The *Zuma* cover was another stroke of genius. I can remember being in an Indianapolis head shop the day the album came out. Sixteen at the time, I picked up the cover and stared at it forever. Some sort of bird flying an ugly naked chick over pyramids, a cactus giving the finger beneath them. It was so . . . demented. I thought it was a bootleg, a really *cheap* bootleg—I even rubbed the print to see if it was homemade. I had never seen such an outlandish-looking record. I bought it immediately.

"Neil told me some images he had in his mind of birds flying women over the desert, pyramids and stuff," said Mazzeo, who dashed off four crude sketches and then asked Young which one he wanted him to develop. Grabbing one, "Neil goes, 'No—this is it! You've done it! It's perfect!' And boom! All of a sudden I had a check for two thousand dollars. Those four sketches took me ten minutes—that's two hundred a minute. I'm thinking, 'Finally art is beginning to pay.' " A billboard soon appeared over Sunset Strip. "It was very cool," said Mazzeo. "The Zuma bird, eighty feet long!"

Zuma's one of my favorite album covers. They thought I was nuts at Reprise. It was a concept thing. Everything everybody was doing was getting really slick.
—What can you tell me about that Zuma sound?
It's pretty sparse, innit? Real sparse. Pretty dry, too. No echo hardly at all on Zuma. I remember some echo device just hanging on the wall in David's house, heh heh. Typical David. . . . It's a hard and hittin' you kind of a sound—especially if you turn it up.
—What's the secret to the Zuma guitar sound?
Old Black, Fender Deluxe with the reverb unit . . . might be a Gretsch pickup. "Drive Back" is just the Deluxe all the way up.
—David said that period was the happiest he ever saw you.

---

*Sampedro recalls Dylan leading the ragtag group in songs from *Blood on the Tracks*. He also remembers Dylan tapping the keys on a version of Young's "Danger Bird." The mind boggles. Said Sampedro of Dylan, "he was quiet—more inward than Neil, if that's possible."

It was probably the happiest I ever saw him, too. I was doin' a lot of drugs then—heh heh—and so was he.

We did a lot of illegal things, and I'm lucky to be around today to talk about it, I'll tell ya that, heh heh. There were some times at Zuma—Poncho told me that he's surprised that I made it. That my head didn't blow up. That I didn't freak out completely.

—Didn't you and Briggs wreck your bus somewhere around this time?

Key West to San Francisco. I was drivin'. That was the last time I drove. Ninety thousand dollars in damages. We were crossing over Independence Pass—like, fourteen thousand feet—and I'm comin' around the corner and I see this other car comin'. So to try and miss that car, I hit the rocks on the side. The other side was the cliff, and I didn't wanna go that way . . . that's when I knew I shouldn't be drivin'.

Then we stopped. Briggs and I were doin' quality-control test-pressing checks of my albums on vinyl. We stop in like, Kingman, Arizona, at a stereo shop—the guy's got a Realistic dealership—and play the thing and listen, and Briggs and I are goin', "Well, have you got anything that sounds a bit more . . . realistic?" Fuck. Let's face it—we were a couple of wild guys.

—What was Poncho's vibe like when he first showed up?

He was . . . happy.

—What did he offer the band?

Well, he offered me about an ounce of really good grass and some toot, heh heh . . . Poncho was a resource to be reckoned with. He made it possible to play with the Horse. We had two guitars, bass and drums again. He just brought the band back together—because Billy and Ralph related to him. At the time he didn't know how to play that well. He was perfect . . . for me.

Poncho's such a cool guy. He had a lot of songs at that time. He was WILD—his hair was long, he was wearin' big tie-dyed shirts and shit. He was doin' stuff in Mexico, so I went down to Ensenada with him and we had a great weekend. Drinking beer and tequila at Hussong's Cantina. Got completely shitfaced. So drunk we could hardly walk. My hair caught on fire. Jesus Christ.

—Why the intense attitude towards women on Zuma?

That was sort of the attitude of the day. Briggs, y'know . . . he was there with us.

—What attracted you to Cortez?

I dunno . . . until that night, I never thought about him.

—Do you identify with Cortez?

When he's on the boat, on his way over . . . I don't think he knows what's gonna happen yet—I'm not sure Cortez might've felt like he was doin' the right thing at the end. Killing all those people. Might not have felt as good about it as he did when he was just dancing across the water in his boat. I have to think that changed his life, that experience. That he was not able to sleep well.*

"Barstool Blues"—we came home from the bar and I wrote that song. I woke up and I went, "FUCK!" I couldn't remember writing it. I couldn't remember any of it. I started playin' the chords and it was so fuckin' high—I mean, it was three steps higher *than the fuckin' record. "Danger Bird"—that's a wild song. It's so slow and great. Isn't it slow? Briggs always wanted to remix it. I* like *the mix. A combination of two songs. "L.A. Girls and Ocean Boys" I never recorded, but it's part of "Danger Bird." Hey, sometimes that's what happens—one song doesn't come out, I'll be writin' another and say, "Oh, that fits." Bang! Drop it right in.*

—Do you get a picture in your mind when you do "Danger Bird"?

Sometimes I get a picture, but mostly it's just flapping . . . flying . . .

Depends on the instrumental, where you go, what you see. That's the beauty of it—it's not like there's a *picture, there's* a series *of* pictures. *You never see exactly the same thing. You go to new places . . . it's too bad that there's not some way to project what's in your mind as you're thinking— picture, sound, everything—so you could record* that *while the live playing's happening.*

---

*Young's most revealing comments concerning "Cortez the Killer" came during a show with Crazy Horse in Manassas, Virginia, on August 13, 1996. Upon introducing the song to the audience, he claimed not only to have written it in high school, but that the main inspiration might have been gastrointestinal: "One night I stayed up too late when I was goin' to high school . . . I ate like six hamburgers or somethin'. I felt terrible . . . very bad . . . this is before McDonald's . . . I was studying history, and in the morning I woke up and I'd written this song . . . I never told anybody else that."

Those are really good records. They got a vibe. Attitude dripping all over them. I played Zuma *for Carole King. I told her we'd really been working hard at it and we really got somethin' good—a real record. She just listened to it and said, "Neil, why don't you really make a* real *record?" She was . . . nice about it.*

That December, Young embarked on a short tour of bars on the California coast near the ranch. Friends David Cline, Jim Russell and Taylor Phelps would search out small joints, then Cline would strike a deal with the owner: Neil Young will play your club this weekend—if you don't tell anybody and if the already advertised band gets paid for the gig. This was the public unveiling of the new Crazy Horse: ragged, unwieldy, capable of jaw-dropping mistakes and great rock and roll.

Young chose a set heavy with songs from the just released *Zuma,* plus a couple of numbers from a Crazy Horse album in the works, most notably a pair of Sampedro rockers, "She's Hot" and "I'm a Man" (Poncho's bone-headed reply to Helen Reddy's "I Am Woman"), which inspired wild guitar from Young.* There were also a couple of new numbers: "Country Home," a tribute to the ranch that is surely one of Young's most euphoric songs (and which wouldn't make it to record until 1990's *Ragged Glory*), and "Like a Hurricane," a paen to desire that remains one of Young's best.

• • •

The past summer, Young had undergone an operation for nodes on his vocal cords and had to refrain from talking for a time—although it didn't slow down his lifestyle one iota, according to Jim Russell. The duo would "go to bars, pick up on girls—and he couldn't talk, so he and I would do this sign-language thing," said Russell, laughing. "I knew Neil so well from hangin' out that I was able to talk for him." "Like a Hurricane" came out of one such escapade.

"Neil, Jim Russell, David Cline and I went to Venturi's in La Honda," recalled Taylor Phelps. "We went in my hearse—Hernando Desoto, Harry D for short. We were *really* fucked up. Neil had this amazing intense at-

---

*Young would contribute some of the most over-the-top guitar playing of his life to five Crazy Horse songs on their 1978 RCA album, *Crazy Moon.*

traction to this particular woman named Gail—it didn't happen, he didn't go home with her. We go back to the ranch and we are just honkin' up a storm and it's late, late, late at night. I remember Neil started playin'." Young was completely possessed, pacing around the room, hunched over a Stringman keyboard pounding out the song. "He went back and forth," said Russell. "He'd go and play some more, then he'd come back, talk some more. It was really crazy."

In the wee hours, Phelps, who had to be up the next morning to work a show with Stephen Stills, headed back to his neighboring ranch and got almost all the way home before realizing he had left something behind. "I forgot a bag, and the bag I had to have, because the bag was full of toot and it was going to the Greek Theatre in the morning and people were countin' on me." Phelps turned the Desoto around and headed back to Neil's in a drugged haze. "I remember walkin' in the door to Neil's house—the sun was coming up—and there was Neil, all alone, over in the corner of the room playing the keyboard. It was just insane—he was just playin' away like Beethoven. He looked like a fuckin' maniac."

The original manuscript to "Hurricane," with drastically different words, is dated July 27. Mazzeo recalled Young—who still couldn't speak at the time—excitedly handing him an envelope with just two lines scrawled on it: "You are like a hurricane / There's calm in yer eye." Young took the song to Crazy Horse, and as Poncho recalls, they fought with it for about ten days on Young's ranch with little success.

"We kept playing it two guitars, bass, drums, but it wasn't in the pocket. Neil didn't have enough room to solo. He didn't like the rhythm I was playing on guitar. One day we were done recording and the Stringman was sitting there. I started diddling with it, just playing the chords simply, and Neil said, 'Y'know, maybe that's the way to do it—let's try it.' If you listen to the take on the record, there's no beginning, no count-off, it just goes *wooom!* They just turned on the machines when they heard us playing again, 'cause we were done for the day. Neil goes, 'Yeah, I think that's how it goes. Just like that.' And that was the take. That's the only time we ever played it that way."

"Like a Hurricane" is one of those songs that defines an era. "Rock is about a micro-moment," said writer Richard Meltzer. "It's not even about a year—it's about, like, a day. These songs are almost time-coded with a date on them. Rock does not feel separate from its time, which I don't feel about jazz, classical, any other shit. It was disposable stuff, and whatever these people did to make themselves important in the eyes of eternity, the stuff only works if it got under your skin in the moment. I hear it and smell the day I heard it."

I know what Meltzer's talking about. Hearing "Hurricane," I can smell the past—in particular, a woozy night at a friend's house. This gal I was obsessed with had just shown up. She had torn down from South Bend to Indianapolis in a green '76 Grand Prix hijacked from her oblivious mother. We met in my friend's living room, *Midnight Special* blasting out of the TV. Wolfman Jack announced, "NEIL YOUNG!" in that garbage-can voice of his, and on popped a live film clip of Young and the Horse flailing away at "Hurricane."

Standing in the blast of a wind machine, Young looked more simian than human, the band barely visible. The whole thing was so dark and murky it was like peering into a dirty aquarium. It didn't look like the rest of *The Midnight Special,* I'll tell ya—it looked real. You could almost feel the storm. We stood in the darkened room, eyes riveted to the glowing TV. Once it ended, we two young lovers waltzed out into the cool, dark summer air, hopped into the Grand Prix and blasted down the highway, headed for a cheap motel. I had a dame I was crazy about and she was crazy about me—we felt as invincible as gods. Of course, it all went to hell in a handbag, but for a moment there it seemed like anything was possible, and "Like a Hurricane" was the soundtrack fueling our dimestore dreams.

I wrote "Hurricane" in the back of Hernando—Taylor Phelps's Desoto Suburban. On newspaper. We were all really high, fucked up. Been out partying. Wrote it sitting up at Vista Point on Skyline. Supposed to be right near the highest point in San Mateo County—which was appropriate, heh heh. There I was . . . the highest point in San Mateo County . . . I wrote it when I couldn't sing. I was on voice rest. It was nuts—I was whistling it. I wrote a lotta songs when I couldn't talk.

The Horse got it the first time—that's the first time we recorded it. Then three or four weeks later we were tryin' to get it and I said, "I think we already did it—but there's no vocal on it. Let's go back and listen to that one." An engineer was in the truck, rolling on the green board, all our practices and everything—in case we did something. The real recording room wasn't even on.

—It wasn't a live vocal?

It sounds kind of meek and mild, doesn't it? It was a sketch. I went in and I sang both harmony parts, the low one and the high one—and that's the way the record is. It's all me singing.

—What's the similarity between Del Shannon's "Runaway" and "Hurricane"?

When "Runaway" goes to "I'm-a walkin' in the rain," those are the same chords in the bridge of "Hurricane"—"You are . . ." It opens up. So it's a minor descending thing that opens up—that's what they have in common. It's like "Runaway" with the organ solo going on for ten minutes.

—How has the attitude of "Hurricane" changed over the years?

It's not as pure and innocent as it used to be.

—Why?

Because I'm not as pure and innocent as I used to be. I'm a different person now, so I interpret the song differently. I have to be who I am now.

In March and early April 1976 came a tour of Japan and Europe with the Horse. The lunatic tone of the tour would be set by the last thing cut at the ranch—"Look Out for My Love," the first recorded acoustic performance of the new Horse (Young would later add some windshield-wiper electric guitar overdubs in England). After Young helped the band with some cuts for their own album, they launched into his new song, but it didn't come easily.

"It was marathon," said Poncho Sampedro. "Girls were there, makin' us Mexican coffees, choppin' lines. We stayed up that whole night but never played it all the way through—we played it a little bit at a time. We kept gettin' higher and higher and crazier. I had some blow up there to last a week—we managed to stay up until it was all gone."

"There was coke everywhere," said Ralph Molina. "We started to come down and that's when we cut the fucking song, man. We were right at that place to play it." Briggs recalled the moment they all gathered to listen to the playback: "Outside the studio," he said. "You couldn't listen inside, we turned it up so loud. We started at six o'clock at night and finished at six o'clock the next morning—it's the only cut I ever did with Crazy Horse that we worked on all night long. Take after take. When we got it, I'll never forget. Six o'clock in the morning with the sun up. We knew we had drilled it. It had the spook."*

Sampedro smiled as he remembered the grizzled warriors driving back to the band's house in somebody's pickup. It was a time when music flowed effortlessly out of Young and the Horse. "It was a whole thing where we all hung out more than we actually played."

.   .   .

The 1976 overseas tour is best seen through the eyes of the new kid on the block. "Japan was unbelievable," said Poncho, who remembers looking out the airplane window at the waiting crowds and thinking "some political thing was goin' on. Then I looked closer and noticed all these Japanese kids with plaid Pendleton shirts and long hair parted down the middle. They greeted us like the Beatles."

The show at the Nippon Budokan Hall in Tokyo on March 11 was being filmed for a documentary and recorded for a live album, and—without telling their bandmates—Billy and Poncho dropped acid before going on.

"We did 'Cowgirl in the Sand' and Billy and Ralph went up to sing the backgrounds," Poncho continues. "I opened my eyes and saw big mandalas comin' out of the back of both their heads, all these colors 'n shit. I couldn't even look up, I was so high. I'd hit the strings of my guitar—they were like eighty different colors—and they bounced off the floors and hit the ceiling. At the end of the second song Neil came runnin' over, stuck his head between me and Billy and goes, 'Man, we're *psychedelic* tonight!' I just looked at Billy, thinkin', 'He told him, he told him.' The whole rest of the night I don't even think we made a mistake. It was unbelievable."

Getting out of Japan after the show was chaotic. "Neil gets so out of it by the end of the show he doesn't know where he is anyway, Billy and I are

---

*"Look Out for My Love" remains close to Randy Newman's heart due to its rather idiosyncratic view of relationships. "It isn't like a love song," he said, laughing. "It's like, 'My love, it's really heavy. Watch out! It's in your neighborhood.' Like a stalker."

stoned on acid, Ralph's not much of a leader, so there we are—the four of us goin' to Europe."

At the airport, Young got into a tussle with a Japanese man who kept trying to give him a package. Poncho paused from hallucinating long enough to help. "I said to Neil, 'Maybe we should look in here'—and it was our passports and tickets! Neil goes,'*You're* in charge.'

"So I'm holdin' the tickets, totally fried, tripping my brains out, with three longhairs trying to figure out where to go—all the writing's in Japanese. All of a sudden I see these guys with machine guns, and I do a three-sixty out the airport." It took some fast talking to convince Poncho it was only the film crew and their cameras.

Once the Horse hit Amsterdam, they were able to score some serious pot after a long dry spell. "Billy's so excited we're gonna get stoned, he jumps up and doesn't know it's a low ceiling and smacks himself in the head—blood everywhere. We're all standing around for the doctor, and the dealer shows up." That night Poncho and Ralph were playing patty-cake with a hatcheck girl at some club when Young emerged from a backroom hookah session "walkin' on sponges, takin' these big steps," said Poncho. "Neil said, 'Man, I gotta get *outta* here.' I ran over to help and fell down the stairs! Neil went back to the hotel. Ranger Dave had to stay up all night givin' him backrubs."

Flying from Germany to Paris was another experience for Poncho. "I had a bunch of hash, so I thought, 'Well, I'll just eat it,' but I still had a little stash I figured I'd eat on the plane. So we walk through security at the German airport, all these guards with machine guns and shit, I got on board and I think, 'Cool, I made it,' and boom! These guys come back on with machine guns—'We want you off the plane, all you four guys.' I'm tryin' to get this hash out and stuff it in the plane seat—I couldn't do it, so I stuffed it down my pants, and I'm totally paranoid.

"This one security guy takes his hat off and I realize he's an eighteen-year-old kid. He said, 'Can we have autographs?' They just wanted autographs! I'm so tripped out I eat all the rest of the hash, I close my eyes and turn to Neil and go, 'Man, I'm hearin' a whole orchestra playin' in my head!' Neil goes, 'That's *good*.' " Poncho wandered off to the bathroom to throw up.

A show at London's Hammersmith Odeon at the end of March was also being filmed and recorded, and Billy and Poncho dropped acid again. "I can vividly remember 'Southern Man,' " said Sampedro. "It was wildly out of control—fast, slow, up, down, everywhere. At the end we were singing, I had my eyes closed and I hear this little tiny voice and I turn around and it was *just me.* Everybody else had quit even *playin'*."

The fun ended once the band returned to the States. A huge eighty-show summer stadium tour of America evaporated when Young—who, unbeknownst to the Horse, had recorded in Miami with Stephen Stills back in January—decided at the very last minute to dump the Horse and go on the road with Stills. The Horse were the last to know.

"No one even told us," said Poncho. "We stayed up at the ranch waitin' for Neil to come back." Poncho broke his thumb playing basketball about a week before they were to go out and, concerned about how it would affect his performance on tour, called Elliot Roberts to break the news.

Twenty years later, Sampedro still remembers Elliot's reply. "He said, 'Lucky it wasn't your *face.* You don't have to worry about the tour—Neil's going out with Stephen. He doesn't need you guys. See ya.' And he hung up. I didn't even know what that *meant,* I was so naïve—I finally had to get together with Billy and Ralph to figure it all out. We were so stoned, so innocent, we didn't know shit. We didn't know what hit us."

Sampedro said some of his "underworld" friends were so angry they suggested bumping Young off. Fortunately Poncho was able to dissuade them. Would they have really carried it out? "For a six-pack of beer," said Sampedro, who smoldered over the incident for a very long time. "This was a major fuckin' heartbreak for me. I was never so hurt in my life. And after the first time Neil hurt me, I always made sure I had somethin' else goin' on for myself. I never sat around and waited for him. It was the number-two gig."

· · ·

In the summer and fall of 1975, Young had popped up at a few Stephen Stills gigs. In January of the following year, the pair met at Criteria Studios in Miami to cut some tracks using Stephen's band. Participants recall the album was more like a pair of simultaneous solo albums than a group effort.

"It was two superstars that were walking the same golf course, but they weren't playing the same game," said engineer Tom Dowd. "There was a lotta friction from the start," said Guillermo Giachetti, who worked for Stills at the time. "Stills would stay in the studio all night, and then when Neil came back the next day, everybody would be wiped out." Lifestyles were also at odds. "Stephen had this majestic mansion with a pool, Greek pillars and a fleet of rental cars," said Giachetti. "Neil stayed on a funky boat down in Coconut Grove."

Tempers flared when Dowd tried to get Stills into the studio earlier to work with Young. "I scolded Stephen during that session. Stephen spoke to Ahmet about it, and Ahmet called me at home that night and gave me hell. I said, 'Ahmet, you don't realize how out of control things are,' and to my surprise, the next day at five o'clock who walks in the studio—Ahmet." Ertegun caught an average working day. Young came in and did some work. No Stills. Young left. No Stills. They waited. "Late that night, here comes Stephen, and he had half a bag on. Ahmet and Stephen spoke. And I think it was a week later that Stephen was on Columbia Records."

After Young returned from the overseas tour with the Horse, the Stills/Young sessions resumed, evolving briefly into a CSNY project after Young showed up at Graham Nash's San Francisco home and played him some of the songs. Nash and David Crosby left a recording project of their own to head for Miami that April to cut new songs and overdub vocals on the Stills/Young material. And then Young was gone.

"Neil would get up and we'd have breakfast every day," said Nash. "So one day I call him at about ten o'clock—no answer. I thought, 'Well, that's strange.' I go down to the front desk and they say, 'He's gone, he checked out last night, he's in L.A.' Then I get a call from Neil. I say, 'Are we having breakfast, Neil?' He said, 'No. I've left. It's too much for me.' That's the way Neil does it. He doesn't like to face people."

Nash and Crosby returned to Los Angeles, and with a Stills/Young tour coming up fast, the decision was made to complete the record without them. Crosby and Nash were furious, trashed their buddies in *Crawdaddy!* magazine and, a little down the line when Young sought permission to use the CSNY recording of "Pushed It over the End," Nash refused.

In hindsight, Nash regretted the decision, but remained angry over the way Young handled the situation. "Neil coulda turned to us and said, 'Hey, this ain't fuckin' workin', I don't like this, I'm *gone.*' No, he ends up in L.A., like a schmuck. That's not a manly way of dealin' with things, and that's the way Neil's *always* dealt with things—he runs away. That's the truth. *Neil does what Neil wants to do,* and unfortunately it hurts people."

I wanted to get the record done. I was moving. I didn't wanna wait around and do the CSN record next. I didn't have time for that. We had done the tracks—why wait three months to put the vocals on? If we do that, is it a CSNY record? Should we do a CSNY record and scrap this record? What the fuck?

See, that's one of the problems. Public relations or art, y'know. You don't know where to go. Probably they were right and I was wrong. Obviously Stills/Young was a complete bust. But I'm always goin' for things that haven't got a fuckin' shit chance of happening. When they happen, it's great, but they don't happen very often. With Crazy Horse, they happen.

—At times, when you changed directions, communication wasn't always there. You weren't so direct with the people you worked with.

No, I wasn't.

—And that was really painful for them.

Yeah, right. Well, that was an easy way of doin' it—but I still did *it. I still went from place to place, and I just left a trail of destruction behind me, y'know. But the older you get, the more you realize how much that hurts people. On the other hand, at that age, what I woulda had to do to* talk *to all those people and go* through *all that would've replaced three or four of those records in energy. Those records wouldn't be there—and those people would still be as pissed off as they were in the first place. I chose to put the energy into the records.*

These are the decisions you have to make. They affect people's lives every day— See, I have to put off every fuckin' arrangement as long as possible, because every time I say I'm gonna do something, that means like ten or twenty people start counting on that. They start banking on that.

It's complicated when you have a lotta musicians and producers, you're close to them all and you've gone through your whole life making music with these guys, and then all of the sudden I wake up one morn-

ing and I'm fucking singing some song that I wanna play with somebody with a harpsichord*—I mean, y'know, that's not these guys—you gotta be able to say, "Well, that's the end of that for a while. I'm gonna do something else." And know when to do it. It wasn't fun firing guys in my band in high school, but I still had to do it—so the band would be better. So that we keep going. It's never fun.*

In June, the Stills/Young tour got under way in Michigan. It lasted eighteen dates. The Young archives contain a PA cassette with a hopped-up version of "The Loner" from the Providence, Rhode Island, show that careens around like a roller coaster about to jump the track. By some accounts, Stills was out of control much of the time, and things came to a head in Charlotte, North Carolina, on July 18.

David Cline: "Neil and I had talked about it a couple of days before, and he just didn't feel like he was part of the band. They were having band conversations and Neil was not a part of it. It was Stills's scene. It was like Neil was coming in and doing his parts." Then Stills berated engineer Tim Mulligan during the Charlotte show. "Stephen didn't like the way Mulligan was mixing it and—over the microphone, in front of a full house—said something about Mulligan," Cline recalls. The remarks reportedly enraged Young, who, according to Elliot Roberts, had already warned Stills to stop badmouthing another crew member on the tour.

That night Young got aboard his new bus, Pocahontas, and headed for the next gig in Atlanta. Also on the bus was Poncho's squeeze Kevyn Lauritzen, who remembers an unhappy Young bringing up the Horse. "Neil was frustrated immediately. He said, 'What's Poncho doin'?' I said, 'He's sittin' in California freakin' out, wonderin' why he's not on the road with you. They're all bummed out.' Neil said, 'I made such a stupid mistake . . . I need to fix somethin', I need to fix somethin'.'" What happened next was quintessential Shakey.

New bus driver Jim Russell was in communication with Stephen's driver by means of a CB radio. The two were bullshitting back and forth when Stills—sounding more than a little wasted—got on the CB, demanding to talk to Neil. Young wasn't talking. "I could see the wheels turning in Neil's head," said Russell. "Neil just said, 'Russell, hand me a road atlas.'"

As the two buses lumbered down the highway, Stills continued to harangue Young over the CB. "Neil wasn't in the mood," said Kevyn. "He just ripped the CB outta the wall. I went to sleep, thinkin' we were goin' to Atlanta. When I woke up ten-thirty the next mornin', I saw a sign sayin', WELCOME TO THE GRAND OL' OPRY IN NASHVILLE, TENNESSEE."

After Kevyn had gone to bed, Young had told Russell to take the next right, which was not the way to Atlanta. "We're sitting at the table," said David Cline. "Neil sits down and writes a little note and said, 'I want you to send one of these to each of the guys in the band.' We disappeared from that tour." They headed for Memphis, where Young could catch a plane.

The official explanation would be that Young's throat trouble had suddenly returned, but the note Cline telegrammed Stills and the band read, "Dear Stephen, funny how some things that start spontaneously end that way. Eat a peach, Neil."

Even Elliot Roberts, left to clean up the wreckage, was stunned. " 'Eat a peach'—I mean, is that *cold*? Never called the guy . . . Stephen went to the next city, tried to do the show on his own, the promoter refused to allow Stephen to go on. I had to make good on twenty-one shows cross-country so we didn't get sued—because all the shows were sold out."

But Roberts was not surprised by Young's vanishing act. "That was Neil. They called Neil 'Snake,' and for good reason—if it wasn't happening, Neil would fuck you in a second. He never thought he was fucking you, he thought he had warned you, if not in reality, in actions before it. Neil's a cold guy, okay? Capable of being cold."

·   ·   ·

Long May You Run, the Stills/Young album, was released in September 1976 and made little impression aside from the title cut—an affectionate look back at Mort, Neil's long deceased hearse. An FM-radio staple, it would later be covered by Emmylou Harris on a live album. "That's an odd song," said Harris. "It's about a car, but I feel that there's other things in there, too. He's very economical, uses a few words to evoke a feeling or an image or a mood. I think Neil writes on other levels, whether he does it on purpose or not. I don't think there's anybody who writes like Neil—his songs are an odd combination of being straightforward and elusive at the same time."

It was in Miami that Young bought his first boat—a fifty-five-foot channel cruiser he dubbed the *Evening Coconut*—and crossed paths with a flamboyant character we'll call Captain Whoopee. "Neil was looking for some male bonding, looking for a buddy to cruise with, and Whoopee was new blood," said Sandy Mazzeo. "He was just jazzed out—gold chains around his neck, real flashy guy. Whoopee was also *great* with women. He had the magic touch."

Mazzeo thought Captain Whoopee was taking Young for a ride. "He's strokin' Neil and strokin' Neil—and Neil's buyin' it. It was really sickening to see. I told Neil, 'I have to leave. I can't handle it—every time this guy kisses your ass, you bend over for more.' "

Captain Whoopee moved in with Young aboard the *Coconut,* and Neil soon enlisted his help in finding another boat to buy. Young gave Whoopee carte blanche when it came to the finances, and his naïveté shocked David Cline. "I was so guarded with everyone else, and this time I was specifically told not to do my monitoring trip. Neil was trusting—the same way he would trust Elliot, the same way he would trust Briggs. It was amazing to me, because there was no reason for it."

As it turned out, Captain Whoopee knew little about boats and spent a fortune before he was shown the door. "The jivest people can come in and snow Neil in two minutes," said Elliot Roberts. "Neil is very impressionable. His intuitive rightness always comes back at some point, but he is *unbelievably* impressionable." David Briggs agreed: "Neil is a great artist, not a great judge of character."

Young would eventually find the schooner of his dreams—a 101-foot built in 1913 that he christened the *W. N. Ragland*—and with it came more than a few adventures with Roger Katz at the helm. "Neil is a guy who likes to take it as far out on the edge as he can," said Katz, who helped Young extricate himself from the Captain Whoopee debacle. "I've seen him do some unbelievable shit, especially in the face of authority. I remember one time when we had some authorities coming aboard looking for pot. We'd cleaned up pretty well, and Neil was sitting down below at the main table, and he had a couple of grass seeds he was rolling around on the table as these customs people sat with us. These heavy-duty DEA guys, and Neil's just sittin' there playing ice hockey with these grass seeds. So this other guy comes in, and he's got this look like '*Aha*—I have you,' and he throws this pack of rolling papers on the table and goes, 'Now, what are *these,* Mr. Young?' And Neil—who's still poppin' these little seeds across the table—goes, 'Y'know, I really believe those are a relic from a time past.' That's all he had to say. It was like 'Shit, Neil, how much closer do you wanna come?' "

But Katz also glimpsed Young's vulnerable side. On a boat trip in the Pacific Northwest, Katz and Young were furling a sail together when a big shackle whacked Neil in the head. "He was bleeding like a stuck pig—his face was obscured by a whole curtain of blood. He grabbed me and said, 'Don't let me have a seizure, don't let me have a seizure.' He just did not want that to happen to him again."

Young still keeps the *Ragland* crewed up year-round for spur-of-the-moment escapes. "There's a big train behind Neil," said David Cline. "He likes to get away, leave everything behind and be out on the ocean. That's when he's the happiest."

Mazzeo saw it a little differently. "I don't really think Neil can say, 'Fuck it—I'm just gonna go do this for myself.' Even though he gives himself ranches and beautiful boats, it's always with some extra value added to it. There's always some *reason* for it. He justifies it by saying, 'I can work harder by having this. I can go out to sea and write songs.' It's not just 'I want to go to sea 'cause I have fun on boats.' I don't think Neil really knows how to have fun."

• • •

In November 1976, Young and the Horse blasted through a nineteen-date tour of small theaters that was essentially a makeup for the Stills/Young debacle. "People in the audience were yelling, 'Where's Stephen?' " recalls Poncho. "It was a bummer."

Joel Bernstein was shocked to discover that the audience was just as wasted as the band. "It was just a bunch of kids drunk and on reds for the first time. Not just beer and pot—it was reds and vodka, tons of beer. You'd look over at people who were vomiting on the red velvet seats. I think Neil was too fucked up to notice."

Bernstein was equally appalled by the crudity of the new Horse ensemble, believing it lacked any of the rhythmic finesse of the original lineup. "I'd marvel at the degree to which the band succeeded in bringing down

Neil's every attempt to soar," he said. But Horse maniacs cherish the '76 Europe/Japan/U.S. shows, mistakes and all. Young's guitar playing was just out of control.

Outside of a couple of clips, both the album and film from the Odeon/Budokan shows remain unreleased. The film in particular is quite a document: A hazy-looking Young muffs lyrics left and right while whipping out offhanded but painfully great solos during "Drive Back" and "The Losing End." Joel Bernstein (with the assistance of writer Cameron Crowe) assembled a tape of acoustic performances from the tour (since widely bootlegged) that contains some tremendous stuff, like "Mellow My Mind" on banjo and, from the final night of the tour at the Fox Theater in Atlanta, a wild version of "The Old Laughing Lady" that remains the definitive live performance of the song. Also from the Fox comes an amusing rap in which Young enters into a bleary discussion of showbiz with the ghost of Judy Garland.

After that show, Young flew to San Francisco to join Bob Dylan, Eric Clapton, Van Morrison and a host of others at Winterland for the Band's final concert on November 25. *The Last Waltz* was documented by Martin Scorsese, who had put Young's music to its single best filmic use with "Time Fades Away" in his little-seen 1978 sleazebag documentary, *American Boy.*

Released the same year, *The Last Waltz* was to *American Boy* what CSNY was to Crazy Horse. Bill Graham, the show's impresario, allegedly had the most passionate response to the finished product following a private screening: "That is the worst goddamn piece of shit I've ever seen in my life." With lackluster performances, hokey interviews about "the road" and a general sense of self-importance, *The Last Waltz* furnishes conclusive proof that by the late seventies, rock's elder statesmen had grown tiresome.

The film does contain a few unparalleled moments—notably Rick Danko's pained delivery on "It Makes No Difference," a tubby, leisure-suited Van Morrison wailing away on "Caravan" and a studio-shot version of "Evangeline" performed by the Band and Emmylou Harris that in a few minutes captures more about the dynamics of musicians and their personalities than a dozen other rock documentaries in their entirety. Neil Young would not fare so well.

Still wired from touring with the Horse, Young performed a couple of numbers with Joni Mitchell and the Band, and when the dailies were screened, it became painfully apparent in close-ups that a hunk of trouble was more than noticeable in Young's nasal cavity.

"Was it *noticeable*?" exclaimed Elliot Roberts. "Neil had this huge rock dangling from his nose. Huge—like a white M&M. Some guy was weighing it, saying, 'Two grams!'" Both Scorsese and the Band's Robbie Robertson wanted to leave the shots unretouched, but Roberts balked. "I'm in a room with Marty and Robbie. And Martin Scorsese is going, 'Yes, Elliot, it's perfect, it's rock and roll, it's the real thing.' Robbie's going, 'The moment—is it captured or isn't it captured?' They're giving me the rap, the rap, the rap, and I'm going, 'Oh my God. *No*. I want it out. Period.'"

The offending nugget was rotoscoped away at a cost of thousands of dollars—"The most expensive cocaine I ever bought," Robertson quipped to Mazzeo—but it still couldn't save an inept performance of "Helpless." The Band struggles to follow Young on a song they obviously aren't familiar with, blowing changes and backup vocals. It wasn't one of Young's finest moments.

It is what it is. It's a three-chord fuckin' song—I mean, what's not to know?

It's no wonder I wasn't dead *after that show. The things we did—Jesus Christ. The* abuse. *Staying up forty-eight hours before the show, I saw fuckin' Judy Garland—and I was still* up *when I got to* The Last Waltz. *I'm a bad druggie. When I do drugs, I do too many and I'm all fucked up and then I don't do them for a long time. Drugs don't play that important a part, really. They really don't. They were there, and a lotta people did drugs and I did drugs and there's nights where I did way too many drugs and I was stupid. Now I'm glad I'm still here and I realize how stupid I was. It would be even better to be here and think I was smart, but y'know, you gotta take it as it comes.*
—How did things change in the seventies compared to the sixties?
They didn't change that much. Drugs changed.
—How?
Well, the drugs got harder. People got bored with grass. Started turning to cocaine. That was kinda the drug of the decade—for me.

—*So what role have drugs played in your trip?*
On my trip? Minor and major roles throughout—different times, different things.

But now I just get really happy about the things that I'm doin' on the natch. It's amazing how I get. I haven't done any drugs in a long time—I've smoked some grass, but I try not to smoke too much. I don't wanna set a bad example for the kids.
—*Are the highs of music and drugs similar?*
Well, music is much better. You don't come down. Music is like, fulfilling . . . the next day you feel better. *Drugs, the next day you feel terrible—unless you have more drugs.*

But cocaine and music don't really go together, and they never did. It may be a good writing tool sometimes. I think I said some things at some point that I thought that cocaine opened your mind to different things . . . it gave you kind of a sense of power that you wanted to explore and expand your horizons or whatever, I think it worked—for a while. Drugs are great until you discover that they work against you. Then when you start taking them knowing that, *you're in trouble.*
—*What affect did cocaine have on CSNY?*
Screwed up the pitch. Made everything sharp. Made 'em play too fast. Cocaine is a destructive drug. It takes you in, you need more of it all the time. It's addicting—marijuana's addicting, too—I mean, I'm addicted to marijuana . . . but I can stop if I want to. I don't really want to. But when I have *wanted to, I have.*

Cocaine's a strong drug. Kinda got a grip on me for a while. Not innarested anymore. Haven't done it in, I don't know how many years. It's a scary drug—but it was pretty prevalent in the seventies.
—*How did it change the vibe?*
Well, you can hear it in the music. It was still really good music and good people and everything—it just got polluted a bit. By the drug. But then the drug passed like a bad dream. It's gone. All it leaves is a little memory. A little shadow. This feeling you have of what could *happen. What* did *you do to yourself? When will you pay for that? Karma. Self-karma. That's an innaresting thing.*

I'm lucky to be alive. I am. There are several places where I could've

stopped—*because I know how jacked up I was, how my nervous system was so completely jangled. I pushed myself so far . . . I don't understand it. When I look around, I see what's happened to different people, I don't understand it. I'm* happy *about it. I don't know how it got worked out this way—because I feel like I'm out here—and a lotta people aren't.*
—*What can you tell me about "Like an Inca (Hitchhiker)"?*
Bob told me it was a very honest song. Bob Dylan. I sang it for him, he said, "Well, that's an honest song." Because it's like this confession of all the fuckin' drugs an' everything that I took that I felt like I had to do for some reason.

Young would make some of the best music of the mid-seventies period by himself, and he would do it at Indigo Studios. Built near an Indian burial ground in the depths of Malibu Canyon, Indigo has a natural atmosphere antithetical to most studios. "Neil booked the full moon for months and months and months up here, maybe even years," said engineer Richard Kaplan. Deep in the night Young and Briggs would leave their beach home and head to Indigo, where Young would lay down solo acoustic masters of such songs as "Pocahontas," "Ride My Llama," "Campaigner (After the Fall)," "Captain Kennedy" and "Powderfinger."

Briggs was stunned by the amount of material pouring out of Young during this time. "He'd turn to me and go, 'Guess I'll turn on the tap'—and then out came 'Powderfinger,' 'Pocahontas,' 'Out of the Blue,' 'Ride My Llama.' Two days, a *day*. I'm not talkin' about sittin' down with a pen and paper, I'm talkin' about pickin' up a guitar, sittin' there and lookin' me in the face and in twenty minutes—'Pocahontas.' No lyric sheet, no pen, no paper, none of that bullshit. Just 'I picks up the guitar and the demon takes control.' "

The demon certainly took control on August 11, 1976, when Young cut the ultimate acoustic track of the 1975–77 period at Indigo: "Like an Inca (Hitchhiker)."

This autobiography in drugs—bookended by a chilling opening verse about a drifting hitchhiker (the perfect metaphor for changeling Young) and a closing hallucinatory dream of escaping to ancient Peru—is one of Neil's most abandoned performances. The combination of his unwieldy, wailing vocal and the stark, intensely rhythmic guitar—the picture I always get is a canoe paddling through choppy, dark waters—creates a chaotic vision that sums up the frantic experiences of the previous few years. He sounds ready to implode, and not unhappy about it.

Another tremendous piece of music would be started at Young's home and finished at Indigo: "Will to Love." Recording over a Stills/Young cassette on a boom box (Briggs insisted it was his deck, emblazoned with the motto LIFE'S A SHIT SANDWICH—EAT IT OR STARVE; Young disagreed), Young and Briggs brought the crappy-sounding tape (complete with the crackling of Young's fireplace) to Indigo, where a bleary-eyed Young—looking "run over by a forklift," according to engineer Richard Kaplan—proceeded to lay down a series of overdubs on his solo acoustic track. Kaplan, who thought the sound quality of the original cassette was beyond hope, could barely keep up with Young as he hopped from vibes to drums to guitar, creating a ghostly band to flesh out his ghostly song.*

The underwater vocals and gauzy production of "Will to Love" took the luminous, captured-moment ambience that began with *Homegrown* to its most extreme conclusion, and from its strange, impossible opening (and closing) line, the over-seven-minute song remains one of Young's most otherworldly performances.

Adopting a preposterous persona—a migrating fish—to expound on the complex yearnings of love, Young reveals, amid the bends and twists of the river, some naked truths about his cold wanderlust self. He manages to sound both one with the world and completely, terrifyingly alone, barren yet fulfilled, inviting yet unreachable, reluctant but willing—all facets of the push-and-pull conflict that permeates his work. I've listened to the record a thousand times, but I still get a thrill every time I hear Young mutter, "I'm a harpoon dodger / I can't, won't be tamed."

---

*After cutting "Will to Love" on the cassette recorder, Young would somehow stumble on to a plane headed for Miami, where Crosby, Stills and Nash were cutting a record at Criteria Studios. "Somebody said, 'Hey, there's this weird old guy in the parking lot peeing in the bushes,' " recalled Nash. "And we go out there and it's fucking Shakey." Young tried to get the trio to work on "Will to Love," but Crosby told him to stick with the version he'd just recorded. Nash recalls playing him some of their new record, but Young "didn't say anything . . . he disappeared."

"Will to Love" was written in one night, in one sitting, in front of the fireplace. I was all alone in my house and I was really high on a bunch of things . . .

I never have sung it except for that one time. That's what I used for the record. A Sony cassette machine, which I transferred to twenty-four-track and then I played it back through my Magnatone stereo reverb amp. I brought two tracks of the cassette up on a couple of faders with the stereo vibrato in it, then I mixed them in with the original cassette for the sound of the fish. I overdubbed all the instruments and mixed it the same night . . . it was on a full moon. What a night it was, man, unbelievable. I ordered all the instruments from Studio Instrument Rentals, the drums, the bass, the amps, the vibes, all the percussion stuff. We had them set it up like a live date . . . then I started overdubbing all the parts! They thought it was going to be a live session! . . . I just walked from one instrument to another and did them all, mostly in the first take. And then mixed it all at the end of the night . . . I think it might be one of the best records I've ever made.

—Interview with Bill Flanagan, 1985*

In April 1977 came more sessions with the Horse. Outside of "Bite the Bullet," a torrid, blatantly suggestive rocker, the material was countrified and easygoing, the first solid block of lighter material in five years. Very informally recorded at the white house on Young's ranch, the tracks were augmented by Ben Keith on steel, Carole Mayedo on fiddle and a couple of fabulous dames on backup vocals whom Young dubbed "The Saddlebags": Linda Ronstadt and Nicolette Larson.

Larson, born July 17, 1952, was a longhaired beauty from Kansas City

---

*When reviewing the quote from this interview, Young elaborated: "This session was Briggs and I all the way. I couldn't have done it without him. He ordered all the instruments for me and walked through the concept with me at the beach house. Then he booked Indigo and totally prepared the studio. Then stayed up all night finishing the record with me. It was one of our finest moments. It defined Briggs and Young as record makers. I miss that guy. There is no one on the planet that compares to him. Not a day goes by without a thought of David."

whose powerful pipes had graced sessions for Emmylou Harris and country rocker Gary Stewart. "Nicolette and I were thick as thieves, good pals," said Ronstadt. "Nicki is one of those people who's born to bake a pie and raise children. I admire that about her—she's very middle America, very Midwest, came right out of Kansas. She's kind of plucky and not very sophisticated—she reminded me of little Dorothy. She's got great little rhythm instincts and a wonderful smoky voice that is very good for harmonizing. The kinda voice that activates other voices—sort of like you throw a dot of orange into something every once in a while and it'll perk up the blues. I thought she sounded great with Neil—something about the way their vibratos would bend together."

Young ran into Larson one rainy night at Ronstadt's beach house. "He said, 'I guess I'm supposed to meet you, 'cause I called three people lookin' for a singer and everyone told me your name.' Neil's kinda cosmic about things like that." Young and his Saddlebags sat in front of a roaring fire and ran through a bunch of numbers that night, and Larson and Ronstadt quickly found themselves at the ranch, recording songs they barely knew. Larson would be an integral part of the next Young project, and the pair would be lovers for a brief period.

It was somewhere around then that Young, accompanied by Ronstadt and Larson, bumped into one of his heroes: Roy Orbison.* Ronstadt had just cut "Blue Bayou" when Orbison attended a party at the home of Emmylou Harris. "We were all so in awe," said Ronstadt. "I tried to peek behind the glasses—it was kinda like looking at Darth Vader, except that Roy was so nice."

At the party Orbison found himself accosted by a scraggly longhair who started ranting about how Orbison had changed his life back in Canada. "Then this guy starts asking requests for these really obscure Orbison songs and Roy was saying, 'I hardly remember them,' " Roy's wife, Barbara, told Pete Doggett. "So the guy would start them off for Roy." Not until after the party was over would Roy Orbison realize that his overzealous fan was Neil Young.

Orbison, Harris, Ronstadt and Larson joined in on a surreal sing-along,

*The teenaged Young had actually briefly met Roy Orbison outside a gig in Winnipeg in 1962. "His aloofness influenced me profoundly," he told Nick Kent decades later.

and Ronstadt felt there was more than a little similarity in the voices of two of pop music's loneliest figures. "Neil's a thrilling tenor and Orbison's a tenor who's almost a countertenor—the combination vibrato with Emmy's voice . . . uh! It was just beautiful."

. . .

Released in May 1977, *American Stars 'n Bars* was a side of the country material from April, plus an assortment from sessions of the last three years. The highlight was the knockout punch at the head of side two: "Star of Bethlehem," "Will to Love" and "Like a Hurricane." The album cover, a Dean Stockwell creation, was one of Shakey's funniest: a shitfaced Young, face to the floorboards, next to a spittoon, and a passed-out, whiskey-wielding floozy played by Briggs's paramour Connie Moskos. "They put me in some horrible dance-hall outfit. I called my mom. She said, 'Just tell me one thing—you have panties on.' "

Amazingly, Young had another almost completely different album ready to go around the same time. Bootlegged from a stray acetate under the title *Chrome Dreams,** this collection combines a few cuts from *Stars 'n Bars* with a raft of unreleased recordings. There were a number of stark solo performances from Indigo, among them the original demo of "Powderfinger;" "Stringman," a plaintive ballad from the 1976 Europe tour ("Written for Jack [Nitzsche] and me," says Young); the tremendous "Too Far Gone," with Poncho Sampedro on a 1917 mandolin he could barely play; and an exquisite "Hold Back the Tears" reminiscent of the *Homegrown* sessions that is much more eccentric than its country incarnation on *Stars 'n Bars*.

In many ways, *Chrome Dreams* is a more powerful collection than the haphazard snapshot of *Stars 'n Bars*. Some of the material would mutate into *Rust Never Sleeps* a year later, but in the meantime Young would play with another band, the Ducks, and make another record, *Comes a Time*. He

---

*Accompanying the bootleg is an official-looking Warner Bros. memo giving the impression Young had titled the acetate *Chrome Dreams,* but Joel Bernstein said the document is a fake inspired by rumors in the press at the time of a proposed Young album with that title. "What *Chrome Dreams* really was, was a sketch that Briggs drew of a grille and front end of a '55 Chrysler, and if you turned it on its end, it was this beautiful chick," said Young. "I called it *Chrome Dreams*."

was moving at breakneck speed. "No one ever mentioned we were doin' an album *ever*," said Poncho. "We just played and recorded. Every once in a while Neil would say—and I remember it shocking us—'Hey man, I sent in a record.' I said, 'Oh yeah? What was on it?' "

•   •   •

A couple of months after the release of *Stars 'n Bars,* Young abruptly changed direction again. He surfaced in Santa Cruz, a friendly but some-what seedy hippie college town not far from his ranch, playing guitar in a local outfit that included Moby Grape's bass player, Bob Mosley, and Jeff Blackburn, whom Young had encountered during the Springfield days.

Sandy Mazzeo, who would function very nominally as the band's man-ager, recalls how their moniker came to be. "We were driving around town for days, throwing out names like 'Thunderhead.' We drove by the lagoon, and there were a lotta ducks crossing the street, and somebody yelled out, *'The ducks.'* Neil really liked that one—'Yeah, the Ducks.' We vowed to never play outside the city limits of Santa Cruz." Young moved into town. "We got houses on a cliff over Castle Beach," said Mazzeo. "We bought bicycles—Neil bicycled across Santa Cruz daily."

The Ducks were another hit-and-run job along the lines of the Crazy Horse bar tour: shithole clubs, zero publicity and more new songs, al-though for the most part Young was happy being a sideman. "I just play my part," Young told reporter Dan Coyro. "This band isn't just me and some other guys who back me up . . . it kind of reminds me of the time I was in the Buffalo Springfield." Young would perform a few originals with the band, among them a wild instrumental called "Windward Passage," be-sides contributing berserk guitar on Ducks songs like "Two Wings." Nearly all the gigs were recorded and there was talk of an album, but Young disappeared again.

"It got to be the end of summer," said Mazzeo. "We got ripped off—a couple of motorcycle punks broke into our houses and stole our luggage, TVs, sleeping bags, so that kinda bummed Neil out."

•   •   •

In October 1977, Young's much delayed career anthology *Decade* was re-leased. It would influence countless boxed sets to come. The packaging was great—wry notes on each song handwritten by Young himself, and a cover photo obscure even by Young's standards—the girlfriend of art director Tom Wilkes standing out in the desert, balancing a well-traveled guitar case on her back. *Decade* was mostly a greatest-hits package with a few haphazardly chosen outtakes thrown in. The three-record set was critically acclaimed and went gold in 1979, platinum in 1986. "It served to establish his credentials as the most important rock singer-songwriter after Mr. Dylan," wrote John Rockwell in *The New York Times*. But longtime fans aware of the mountain of outtakes Young was sitting on were underwhelmed. "I was really disappointed with *Decade*," said Ken Viola. "I just don't think it was the best stuff."

• • •

At some point Young returned to Florida, where he rented an apartment with his boatmate, Roger Katz. The bachelor life gave Katz further insight into Young. "Neil's real funny about women. He really likes the earth mama, the motorcycle mama. That's his type. Bar-hall queens, just like in his songs—'Motorcycle mama won't you lay your big spike down,' 'Welfare mothers make better lovers.' Neil's a real rootsy, earthy, 'get down, get dirty' kinda guy. He wouldn't go for the flashy women, he'd go for the bar waitress."

Rassy, living not far away in New Smyrna Beach, was an occasional visitor. "Neil was real attentive to her—it was kinda neat to watch," said Katz, who, one drunken evening, lifted a rather official-looking plaque off a boat belonging to some pretentious blowhard. "Neil took it and gave it to Rassy. She proudly displayed it in her living room."

Carrie Snodgress also paid a visit to Young in Florida, and Katz found her presence unnerving. "It was terrible, awful—the kind of situation you'd walk in and you wouldn't wanna be around it. It was the first time I'd ever seen Neil like that. He was moody, withdrawn, difficult to reach. He didn't want any part of her. She just left. He was very relieved. It was an enigma to me—I knew she was the mother of his child, but I just couldn't see them together."

While in Florida, Young started recording what would be his most commercially accessible project since *Harvest: Comes a Time.*

I made most of Comes a Time *in Florida by myself, with these kids that were startin' a recording studio—Triad. It was great. Used to come in in the afternoon and work three, four hours, go home. Did it all during the day. Acoustic guitars. Come in, lay down a basic, then I overdubbed—all me. Do overdubs on it with my acoustics, try a whole bunch of stuff. I did all kinds of things there—"Lost in Space," "Pocahontas," "Human Highway," "Goin' Back."*

Started out as a solo acoustic record, and then I went in to Warner Brothers and played it for Lenny and Mo. Mo said, "We like it, but if you're not in a hurry, why don't you take it and see if you can put rhythm tracks on what you have? We just wanna hear you play with a band, too. If you don't like it, fine. Give it a shot." Mo never makes suggestions, and he made that one. So it gave me something to do.* I decided, "Hey, that sounds like fun. I'll try that—go to Nashville, have 'em all play on it at once." So I got all these people out there to play along with these existing tracks of me. Bobby Charles was like our guru when we were doin' Comes a Time. *Bobby was at all the sessions.†*

That was one point where I think overdubbing worked, especially on that one song, "Goin' Back." "Goin' Back" was originally done in Triad. I did all the guitars by myself and went to Nashville and put the other stuff on there—put Nicolette on there. That's one of my favorite records. It's funky. Not that it's technically great, that's for sure. The sounds are a little muddled. It's got a great amount of feeling. It had a lot of feeling in its straight acoustic versions, too. There's something there that's me, that record. It tells a story—"Goin' Back" is sorta like the debris of the sixties. There's nowhere to stay, nowhere to go and nothin' to do. You could go anywhere . . .

The Nashville *Comes a Time* sessions in late fall 1977 were notable for a number of reasons. In addition to old stalwarts Tim Drummond and Ben Keith came a number of new musicians, among them a trio steeped in

---

*Joel Bernstein revealed a completed solo *Comes a Time* exists, one side labeled "Oceanside," the other "Countryside"— yet another Young album version not to see the light of day.
†When I asked Ben Keith what Bobby Charles's contribution was to *Comes a Time,* he had a succinct reply: "Rolled joints!"

roots music who would work off and on with Young throughout the years to come: Karl "Junkyard" Himmel, a New Orleans drummer that had played for J. J. Cale and Leon Russell; Dewey Lyndon "Spooner" Oldham, the Alabama-born soul songwriter extraordinaire whose sparse keyboards had graced sessions for Percy Sledge, Aretha Franklin and Bob Dylan; and Rufus Thibodeaux, an earthy, built-like-a-block-of-ice Cajun who'd fiddled for the likes of George Jones and Bob Wills (as well as played bass on fifties Excello Records R 'n' B hits).*

The recording style was unique—an artist who hated overdubbing was now overdubbing a giant band to his own solo demos. "That was funny," said Himmel. "Ben had hired some rhythm-guitar players, and I had told some rhythm-guitar players . . . next thing you know, we had eight rhythm-guitar players 'cause no one had talked to each other! Neil said, 'Well, let's just use 'em *all.*' "

Coproducer Ben Keith recalls cutting "Goin' Back": "It was a great session. Everything was live. There was, like, thirty-five people in the studio—percussionists, kettledrums, strings, the whole thing. It was like Sinatra cuttin'." A large part of the electricity generated was vocal: the combination of Young with Nicolette Larson. "She just tracked him *perfect,*" said Keith. "She's the best harmony singer I ever heard."

"We sang on the same mike," said Larson. "I could look in his eyes and keep up with him, and that's as much rehearsal as he wants. Neil really wants you to read his mind and get the part. My entrance on 'Four Strong Winds' is all over the map—Neil wouldn't let you try it twice." Engineer Denny Purcell remembers Larson's frustration over Young's approach. "Neil's got three faders of her. And he said, 'Now, Nicolette, this is the best vocal you did'—pushes the fader up—'and now here's the next best one'—pushes that fader up—'but here's the one we're gonna use, 'cause we like the *feel.*' " The most exuberant recording of Young and Larson remains unreleased: a tribute to Annie Oakley entitled "Lady Wingshot" whose arrangement is reminiscent of Phil Spector bombast.

---

*Although his presence is undetectable to my ears, *Comes a Time* would also mark the first and as yet only collaboration between Young and one of his favorite musicians, the very underappreciated Oklahoma City–born singer/songwriter/guitarist J. J. Cale, best known for writing the Eric Clapton staples "After Midnight" and "Cocaine." Young actually cut what could be considered the first *Comes a Time* session at Cale's Crazy Mama Studio in May.

Outside of the caterwauling, unbearably funky "Motorcycle Mama," the songs were mellow affairs generally less quirky (and perhaps more mature in attitude) than *Harvest*. "Peace of Mind" was a plaintive ballad suggesting that Young had come to terms with the demons of his past relationships (although typically he cut the most naked verse of the song); "Already One" was a touching tribute to son Zeke; and Young also covered the Ian Tyson song that had moved him so much in his youth: "Four Strong Winds."

To complete *Comes a Time,* Young added two Crazy Horse tracks to the Florida/Nashville material: "Look Out for My Love" and the radio-friendly "Lotta Love," featuring coproducer and engineer Tim Mulligan on sax. "We hadn't seen Neil in a long time," said Poncho, who played piano on the cut. "He called us into Wally Heider's—I was so high on smack I didn't even know if I could make it through the recording. I just faked it."

The session nearly collapsed when a drunken Bobby Notkoff—the great violin player from the long-gone Rockets—got pissed off that he wasn't playing on the song. "I got the job of getting Bobby out," said Poncho. "He pulled a U-turn in the middle of Cahuenga and ran over two meters, aiming for the studio. We got in the parking lot and there it was: Neil's big shiny black Cadillac. Bobby just started goin' for it. I was goin', 'Oh, *shit*!' I had to grab the wheel—I took the keys out of the ignition while the motor was running."

Nicolette Larson's cover of "Lotta Love" would be a top-ten hit in 1979. "I visited Neil at the ranch, we were driving around in a pickup, there was a cassette on the floor," she recalls. "I picked it up, blew the dust off it, I stuck it in the cassette player and 'Lotta Love' came on. He told me he wrote it on the boat 'cause his crew had been playing Fleetwood Mac's *Rumours* for three months straight. I said, 'Neil, that's a really good song.' He said, 'You want it—it's yours.' "

Plagued by sequencing and pressing problems that caused Young to buy two hundred thousand copies of the album back from Warner Bros.— a move that only increased his notoriety for quality control—*Comes a Time* was finally released in November 1978. In one month, the record would outsell all six albums since *Harvest*. "It came out outward, clean and appealing," Young would tell reporter Tony Schwartz. "It's the first record [cover] I've released where I'm actually facing the audience and smiling." If *Zuma* was daybreak, *Comes a Time* was the sunset of his mid-seventies period and certainly a contender for the unlikely title of the happiest record Neil Young has ever made.

• • •

The Young/Larson union would last barely longer than the sessions, although she glimpsed some of the irks and quirks so central to Shakey's makeup: "Neil lived in a house with two bedrooms, he used to say, 'because fewer people could come visit.' I remember Neil wouldn't take Rassy's phone calls. They had a peculiar relationship." Tim Drummond recalls with some amusement Larson's nickname for Young: Changeable Charlie.

"Neil and I had a brief relationship, probably no more than in a movie where a leading man and leading lady get a crush on each other. We sang together very well. He wasn't involved, and I was in a relationship that was falling apart. It was pretty much over—whatever it was—by Christmas." The two were making plans to visit each other's parents over the holidays when Young abruptly vanished. For good.

Linda Ronstadt felt it wasn't meant to last. "Nicki [was] a pretty straightforward, simple person, and Neil is just so complex—and, in his way, he's extremely sophisticated. I think it would've been a disaster for both of 'em."

Young's disappearing act left Larson wondering what had gone wrong. "It was hard for me, 'cause the one question every interviewer in the world wanted to ask me was 'What about you and Neil Young?' It was awkward—I had to say, 'I haven't spoken to him.' "*

I'm just brutally fuckin' honest about goin' ahead and doin' what I have to do. But it's not that I can't sense people's feelings. People are hurt. Whenever you move forward, you leave a fuckin' wake.
—Yeah, and your wake's a BIG one.
It's a big wake. A lotta destruction behind me.
—Are you very good at saying goodbye to people?
No. I don't like long goodbyes.
—HA HA HA. Sometimes you don't like ANY goodbye at all!

---

*On December 16, 1997, Larson passed away unexpectedly at age forty-five due to complications from cerebral edema.

Well . . . some goodbyes are more subtle than others. Sometimes only one of the people involved knows that it's a goodbye. But that's because—
—YEAH?????

I guess it's because I'm chickenshit and I don't want to hurt people. And that's a weakness of mine. I could be more honest about certain things. See, these people that say I'm so honest—I'm not that honest.
—Well, I agree with ya.
So what the fuck's the big deal? Why don't they stop sayin' that about me? I'm not a fuckin' SAINT. I can be just as much of an asshole as anybody else—and have been. But y'know—I'm on my trip, I'm on my course, I make no qualms about it. I don't say I'm not, y'know—I am.
—But could you see how with some of the people it might hurt twice as much to not know what they've done?
In retrospect I can.
—'Cause there's people out there who don't know what they did. I'm sure you have great reason to say fuck off, but it might help even more if you told 'em why.
Yeah. Well, it's true. I'm tryin' to think of somebody else that I might've fucked over—like Nicolette.
—How'd you fuck her over?
Well, I just kinda walked out on her. She's a nice girl. But I just kinda disappeared from that relationship.

I just get to a point with things where I leave. Either I leave—or I make someone else leave. It's happened a few times. Like I left the CSNY sessions in '74 when we were recording at the Record Plant. I was drivin' there and I just fuckin' turned around and went home. I called 'em up and said, "I can't do this anymore." Y'know, those things happen.

I left the Stills/Young tour because it just wasn't fun anymore. It was a fuckin' drag. Too many weirdnesses goin' down, and it was just gettin' to be too fuckin' strange. Couldn't do it. In some ways that's honest, and in some ways it's dishonest. In some ways you follow what you feel, in other ways you follow what you feel to the point where you won't even talk to anybody else and you leave them all out there. That's not honest. Define honest—going with your inclinations to the exclusion of all else? Is that honest? I don't know.

a **bigger flash in the** sky

"The sad thing about music is—any musician, if they break up with their wife or whatever, usually their next album is a fuckin' unbelievably great album," Neil Young told me in 1989. "Knowing that is so destructive to a relationship. But that's a fact, y'know what I mean?"

A typically hard-core attitude from the man who wrote "Time is better spent searching than in finding" ("No One Seems to Know"), "You leave her first, then you come out on top" ("Peace of Mind"), "I'm free to give my love, but you're not the one I'm thinkin' of" ("Homefires"), "You could have been anyone to me" ("Like a Hurricane"), "Every good thing comes to an end" ("Drive Back").

But one woman has captivated Neil Young like no other. A beautiful blond California girl who waitressed at a couple of hangouts not far from Young's ranch, Pegi Morton had been friends with Young for some time before they got involved in 1978.* They would marry on August 2 of that year at Young's Malibu home. Son Ben was born on November 28, 1978, and daughter, Amber Jean, on May 15, 1984.

Pegi is the inspiration for some of Young's most intense ballads: "Such a Woman," "Once an Angel" and "Unknown Legend," which is perhaps the most empathetic portrait of a woman he's ever created. He has dedicated two albums to her, and virtually everything else since their union thanks Pegi first. All our interviews meandered back to her, and she always seemed to be on Neil's mind one way or another.

I was around Pegi only a handful of times. She struck me as a rugged individual who had maintained her identity in her husband's often overpow-

---

*Young told me he studied Pegi from afar for quite a while before they became seriously involved. "I didn't wanna make any mistakes . . . one mistake is enough."

ering world, and whose life has been a journey all its own. Definitely a survivor, and one who's made it with her soul and sensitivity intact. If she ever decides to tell her story, I think it would be an inspiration for many. But I didn't interview Pegi Young for this book, and I've included just what Neil chose to share concerning their family. Pegi is a private person, very protective of her family, and at times I got the feeling she was, understandably, less than thrilled with someone excavating her husband's life. I respected her privacy.

"It's very hard to be married to Neil—when you go out, people are rude and trying to knock you down to get to him," said Elliot Roberts. "And Neil is a space case—he'll forget to introduce her, he changes his mind nineteen times and won't tell her. He travels a lot, has to be alone a lot. Neil's life is very involved, and Pegi seems to have it organized to the extent that Neil has a base. He's very comfortable there and always wants to get back home as quick as he can.

"I think that Pegi's strength has been a source of inspiration to Neil. Neil is a very, very difficult man. He's very self-absorbed. He's a true artist. It's a very hard balance, their life and their family—and I think Pegi has done a heroic job of handling the pressure. She's done it with great grace.

"And the things she's accomplished, with very little bravado. She doesn't look for press, she doesn't look for recognition—in fact, it's the other way around. She shies away from that shit, and she's very unique that way. Other people are 'How about me, I'm on charities, I do this.' And Pegi does *more* than any of those people and doesn't want *any* recognition. She feels it gets in the way of what she can accomplish. I have a lot of respect for Pegi. She's a helluva fuckin' woman."

I got a great wife. She's just a beautiful, beautiful woman, and we have an exciting relationship—she's always stimulating me one way or another. Our relationship is real. *There's interplay, there's a lotta things goin' on and we have a lotta things to take care of between the two of us. She's a great mother to the kids—does a great job with that. Real good mom. She's also this wild rock and roll motorcycle girl. She's got a lot of different sides, heh heh. She's a lotta fun. Bein' with me hasn't cut her off from the rest of the world completely. She's got a lotta things she's doin,' and I'm glad. She's got a lot to give—everybody.*

I love Pegi. She busts me for bein' an asshole all the time. If I get all macho, she goes, "Oh, you fuckin' asshole, Neil. You gotta hear yourself." Good governess. Pegi's very, very, very smart. And she retains information like a vise. She knows what's goin' on. The longer I know her, the smarter she is. I get to know her better and better the more I open up.

Pegi changes all the time—she changes how she feels about things. Some things remain constant, but she changes all the time. I find that fascinating. It keeps me completely confused. I don't know what's gonna happen next. I'll tell ya one thing—my relationship with Pegi is good because she keeps changing. I think that's good.

And as hard as it is to keep up with all of the things that, as a woman, she brings out of me—and it's hard for me to keep up with and be right there with her all the time and be, y'know, who she wants me to be—all of a sudden I'll turn around, it's another day and there she is. And everything's fine.

Pegi's shown me kindness in so many ways. She's great to me. She keeps me kinda straight—without really holding me down. She's very sensitive, very fragile, yet she's still very hard, very strong. It's beautiful. She's got all the qualities that a woman should have. She's very much a woman. Words don't really do her justice.
—How well do you think you understand women?
Better every day. I understand 'em well enough to know I've got a good one, heh heh. That's for sure.

"I always change to what I see around me," Neil Young said in a 1982 Italian press conference. The sound of California rock had not changed much in the five years since Neil Young had recorded *Tonight's the Night,* and by 1978 the airwaves were heavy with predictable gunk. "Fleetwood Mac, Doobie Brothers, the Eagles—it was all such overdone, six-months-in-the-studio, arena-rock crap," said Richard Meltzer. "The sound just became unlistenable."

But something else was festering outside the mainstream: punk rock. The Ramones and Sex Pistols might have sold diddly in America, but they changed everything. "Punk was very much how rock was once described by its founders, but which it didn't sound like anymore—didn't even *wanna* sound like anymore," said Meltzer. "Punk did not sound like the music of the founders, but it had the attitude. They were absolutely rejecting the prevailing aesthetic, cultural, moral values of rock as this fascist thing, this means to control people. It was an effort to just absolutely not be the hand-as-dealt, to not be Fleetwood Mac."

Punk had no use for slick production values; Meltzer compares the results to low-budget exploitation movies. "Films like *Detour* and *Mesa of Lost Women* are so good because they have no budgets—the quirks of their imagination stick out like a sore thumb, they have no means to cover it up. The music of punk was handmade—and it was handmade with pride."

Neil Young knew a thing or two about the joys of nonproduction and had never lost sight of the teenage rebellion and angst that spawned rock in the first place. As peers like David Crosby and Jackson Browne expressed an outrage over punk that seemed disgustingly parental, Young—just as he had picked up on "Walk on the Wild Side" five years before—voiced his approval in interview after interview. Did Neil attend a dozen punk shows? Study the complete oeuvre of the Germs? I doubt it. But in a sidelong glance he got the picture: out with the old guard, in with the new. A bunch of upstart kids were spitting at rock dinosaurs, and Neil Young was the one elder reptile cheering them on.

Punk rock—which, now, punk rock is passé, it's all downhill, y'know, but whatever you want to call it—underground music before it becomes established—I like that music because the people making it are alive. *And they don't give a shit. They* don't care *about being number one. They don't care about a great-sounding, polished product. What they want is guts—and a good beat—and to say something that means something to them. And to say it in a raw kind of a way. That grabs you and makes you listen to it. But it doesn't make everybody listen.*

It's not for elevators. . . . It's not for your regular radio stations. It's for the nighttime *show. Where the guy plays what he wants. Not what the programmers tell him to play. . . . It's tapes that get handed from people to people. Copies of bootlegs of appearances of these bands in clubs. This is the bloodline of rock and roll. . . .*

I'm known around the world, so how can I be an under-ground type of person? I'm not—I've outgrown that. But my heart is in the underground.

—*Domino* interview, 1987

Young would align himself with one new band during this period—Devo. Hated by punks, loathed by critics, Devo were "sexy nerds with a sonic plan," but beneath the "weird art band" surface lurked primate passion with a tragic edge, not to mention a sly, smutty humor that harkened back to the early days of rock and R&B. Devo was a world unto itself, and their prototypical music videos for songs like "Love Without Anger" and "Beautiful World" remain unsurpassed, everything MTV never became. "Out of all the bands who came from the underground and actually made it in the mainstream, Devo is the most challenging and subversive of all," Kurt Cobain said to Kevin Allman in 1992.

They came from Akron, Ohio. Cofounders Gerald V. Casale and Mark Mothersbaugh were both students at Kent State in 1970 when the National Guard opened fire. It was "the turning point," said Casale. "That's what made us stop being hippies and what made us so down on human nature."

Devo, "the art of the high and low," was born a couple of years later. "We started developing Devo as an art concept, not as music," said Casale, and Devo soon became a philosophy unto itself. "The attitude was 'People are absolutely full of shit and basically evil.' And that the one thing you could count on was entropy—self-destruction. Forget evolution, there's devolution. People are getting dumber. They're getting more insane."

Casale and Mothersbaugh concocted a crackpot philosophy revolving around a raft of weird characters such as Pootman, General Boy, the Chinaman and the beloved Booji Boy—Mothersbaugh, outfitted in an absurd baby face and diapers, muttering psycho-poetic babytalk and blurting out such unforgettable numbers as "The Words Get Stuck in My Throat." "Booji Boy would always sing these long, drawn-out songs," he said. "It was kinda like throwing saltpeter on the audience."

By 1976, Devo had grown into a five-piece band, and eventually a tape got into the hands of Blondie's Chris Stein, who gave it to David Bowie, who gave it to Iggy Pop, who gave it to dancer Toni Basil (or some variation of that order). Basil was attached at the time to Dean Stockwell, who then turned Young on to the band. "I had a little fuckin' cassette player and I'm thinkin', 'Jesus, I'm nervy, tryin' to ask Neil to listen to somebody else's music.' But I just knew. I said, 'Man, you gotta listen to this,' and I played him 'Mongoloid' and 'Satisfaction.' " Stockwell also took Young to a Devo show at the Starwood. Festooned in rubber suits, novelty-store masks and "mixing fuck rhythms with science fiction sounds," Devo were as geeky as any Winnipeg band, had a killer guitarist and a good beat. No wonder Young flipped.

After the Starwood show Young and Stockwell invited the band to be in a movie they were shooting. "Neil said, 'Give 'em a budget for wardrobe,' " recalls filmmaker Larry Johnson. "I called up—they were livin' in Akron—and said, 'Waddya need?' They said, 'Well, we need a hundred and thirty-six dollars.' I said, 'Just get receipts.' When they came out, they had itemized receipts for the whole wardrobe—which they had bought at Kmart."

Devo landed on Warner Bros. and gained a manager, Elliot Roberts, whom the band managed to drive crazy with such absurd schemes as setting the poems of would-be assassin John Hinckley Jr. to music. Devo would burn out quickly—the surprise hit single "Whip It" led to devourment by the music-biz machine—but early on, they were a key ingredient in Young's next couple of projects, the *Rust Never Sleeps* album and his second motion picture, an epic production entitled *Human Highway*.

•   •   •

"Shooting rock and roll films, you have to have your good time when it happens," said rock-film veteran and *Human Highway* cinematographer David Myers. "Don't count on having a good time when you see the movie. Get off on the trip."

Neil Young has spent a lifetime creating mind-bending trips, but *Human Highway* would prove to be a doozy even by his standards. The film would start out as a sixteen-millimeter rock and roll road movie and wind up an end-of-the-world nuclear comedy, eating up four years and $3 million of Young's own money in the process. The movie was "maybe the only not-smart financial thing Neil ever did," said one of the stars of the film, Dennis Hopper. "It went on and on and on—it was like once a year we knew what we were doin'—we were gonna go make *Human Highway.* It was just a great fuckin' party."

Young had been discussing another movie project, called *The Tree from Outer Space,* with Dean Stockwell. Stockwell laughed uproariously recalling the idea, which he said was "coming out of *After the Gold Rush*—flying the 'silver seed,' right? It was gonna be a fuckin' tree and change to a rocket, it was gonna be really bananas—of course, it was *too* bananas." Young, Larry Johnson and Russ Tamblyn actually went on an expedition to check out trees. "I believe I introduced Neil to the sequoias, which is not a negligible thing," said Stockwell, still laughing. "But as a practical matter, 'The Tree from Outer Space' wasn't gonna be a movie."

Started when these guys hypnotized a chicken. And the chicken somehow—somehow he had a vision—*that he had to go to this tree. Then the people that hypnotized the chicken started seein' that* they'd *have to go to the tree, so they left the chicken behind and they took off. . . .*

Oh, the tree was great. They decided to go up it by going inside it, and when they got inside, then they found these beds. Envision a big long boat with hammocks hanging in it on the side. So they got in the hammocks and the hammocks started swayin' and the tree started comin' out of the ground. And it took off.

And the people discovered when they got up there that you didn't need space suits. They'd go outside, walk around . . . this guy had a barbershop he opened on top of the tree. People would come out through one of the big holes in the tree and walk down the bark to this barbershop. They're in outer space and Saturn's out there 'n everything and they're gettin' a haircut.

I mean, there were all these planets. There was a watery planet, and that was where the song "Lost in Space" was kinda from—the tree's floating in the water, and this guy in a rowboat is rowing and rowing and rowing to get there. And ya look down and there's all these cities and everything he's rowing over to get to the tree . . . there's a lotta things like that that I had written out—all these stories of all these peo-

ple and the way they interacted. It was meant to be loose enough to ad-lib a lot.

And all the people on there—everybody on the tree—was an extremist. And finally what happened was they had trouble getting along. And the tree would land here and there on different planets, people would get off—and every time they went somewhere, everything would seem to be pretty good, the place would be beautiful and really nice, but all the people that they'd meet would be very jealous, very possessive. It kept happening with all different emotions and character traits—they'd go to the planet that represented that and they wouldn't know it. They would just get to this place and get off, go out and experience things, and things would start goin' wrong and they'd realize everybody was y'know, really two-faced liars and nothing was true.

Finally they started goin' crazy. At some point there were very few of the people left. It was getting down to the core group. . . . And then in the end the tree was being circled by this huge black ship. They were running out of power, going slower and slower, the tree was slowing down and this huge fuckin' ship was circling them, but it was really like a big X-Acto knife kind of a thing with a blade on it, saws 'n things coming out of it and ominous black smoke coming out of the back of it. . . .

And they powered the tree by playing this organ—and somehow the music would be converted into this thing that gave them power. It would start glowing from the music, and that was what they used to power the ship and go on.

So finally the way they got away from this black ship was the guy playing the organ—he was playing and playing and playing and he's not getting it—he's trying, but he's not getting enough power to get away. I think he ended up getting a blow job while he was playing, and that did it—when he came, the tree just fuckin' took off!

After that, they got goin' way too fast, too much power, the fuckin' branches were scorching off the tree, anything left on it was startin' to burn . . . it gets into the 2001 thing with the sheets of color coming at you, and you see things goin' by in space and it's gettin' really fast 'n crazy and the music is building. . . .

And finally this silent shot of the forest with nothing where the tree

was—and then the whole fuckin' thing starts rumbling, and the tree starts coming out of the ground and grows to be this gigantic redwood. And that's the end. "The Tree That Went to Outer Space."
—*You loved cheesy monster movies growing up—a big influence on* Human Highway?
Yeah. Cheap Japanese horror-movie kind of things? I like that vibe. I like something that's so unreal *that you could believe it—where the set is obviously phony. Jerry Lewis movies, Japanese horror movies,* The Wizard of Oz—*it's all in there.*

What was I trying to do with Human Highway? *I was tryin' to make a movie. A story about a guy—Lionel, his situation, just one day in this guy's life—just some people who are basically innocent bystanders on the day the earth came to an end. Just people who happened to be there. That was what that was* supposed *to be about, heh heh heh. Got carried away.*

We knew Devo didn't comprehend it and it was a completely different thing for them. That's why it was perfect having them there, heh heh. We knew they weren't like us, *that's for sure.*

"This movie was made up on the spot by punks, potheads and former alcoholics," said Young proudly of *Human Highway* in 1983. "The plan was, there was no plan, no script," said Dean Stockwell. An impromptu egg fight involving Young, Dean Stockwell, Russ Tamblyn and Larry Johnson somehow "gave birth to *Human Highway,*" said Tamblyn. "We decided we would all write our own parts. Neil, Dean and I were the nucleus. . . . We had a scriptwriter who would write the script after we'd do a scene." Joel Bernstein recalls, "Neil at one point said to me, 'Charlie Chaplin used to do his films without a script.' "

Young assembled an impressive cast consisting of Stockwell, Tamblyn, Sally Kirkland and Dennis Hopper, but this was years before the actors were rediscovered by David Lynch or Kirkland got an Oscar nomination for *Anna.* "It seemed like an unhappy time," Devo's Mark Mothersbaugh said about some of the cast. "They were all drinkin' heavily, doin' lots of drugs. Neil was the most grounded of all . . . they had attached their egos onto him."

The young upstarts from Ohio weren't prepared for the surreal scene around Young. "Devo was like the crew of the starship *Enterprise*—we just watched the behavior of people in Los Angeles and couldn't believe it," said Gerald V. Casale. "It was really like observing another reality as an alien being, like the nerd that finally gets let into the prom."

Well into the substance abuse that nearly finished him, Dennis Hopper was a little unhinged during much of the filming. "Hopper I remember as being totally frightening, like the guy in *Apocalypse Now*—a little Frank Booth, too," said Casale. "He wouldn't let you alone. He'd chase you around the set givin' you his rap, whether you wanted to hear it or not— 'Devo, you think yer shit doesn't stink, don't ya.' And Dean Stockwell would be behind him, laughing at everything he said—'heh, heh, heh'— this evil laughter, like Ed McMahon. You never knew what the hell was going on. A lotta mind-fuck games." (Hopper sighed when I brought up Devo. "They'd say, 'Oh, remember him—he's that old actor.' ")

Not even easygoing Russ Tamblyn escaped Devo's wrath. There is a scene where Devo, accompanied by Booji Boy, pull into a gas station to get gas from Tamblyn. "The way Tamblyn played it was like a clown in the circus—tumbling, twisting, turning, fighting with the gas pump, falling down with it," said Casale. "In every successive take, he would ham it up more and more. I couldn't take it anymore. I went, 'You're a fuckin' *evil clown*!' Suddenly Russ gets real serious—'I don't have to take this from that fuck.' That's the take Neil should've used, because everything . . . stops."

In the spring and early summer of 1978, filming of *Human Highway* would take the crew to San Francisco, where Young was performing, then to Taos, New Mexico, a few weeks later, where the cast and crew communed with the local Indian tribe. Tamblyn recalls a disillusioning meeting with a local dignitary: "White people aren't even allowed on the land, and we were gonna go down to the chief's house," he said. Young and his cronies expected some sort of countercultural summit meeting, but once inside the chief's home the band of hippies looked to the wall "and there's this huge picture of *Nixon*," said Tamblyn, laughing.

"We lived right with the Indians," said bus driver Paul Williamson. "This guy Carpio, it was my job to take him home. We were fucked up, partyin' for days . . . Neil said, 'Take the Indian home.' I get in the middle of this reservation, I drove around in circles for like an hour and couldn't find my way out. Fuckin' Indians were lookin' at me like, 'This white boy don't belong.' I was like 'Fuck, when are the arrows comin'?' "

Things grew extra tense one day when Young decided to film an obtuse scene that involved the burning of some special cameras of Hopper's, which had somehow been to outer space along with a few of Young's wooden Indians—one of which, according to legend, he had previously given to Robbie Robertson ("You might say I'm an Indian giver," quipped Young upon reclaiming it). It was a bizarre event. "Neil burnt his Indians and I burnt these Mitchell cameras," said Hopper. "Everyone danced around the fire." Elliot Roberts recalls that the actual Indians were completely nonplussed. "It was 'These fuckin' white people are really nuts.' "

"It was weird, weird," said David Myers. "Strange vibes. I felt a certain degree of uneasiness before the tequila took hold." Myers felt that Young was more than entertained by the unwieldy spectacle he'd surrounded himself with. "Neil always looked like he was gonna break into a smile any minute at some secret joke about the whole thing."

.   .   .

When Neil Young stepped onto the stage of the Boarding House in San Francisco on May 24, beginning a five-night, ten-show solo run, it was clear the stoned Pendleton caveman of the Crazy Horse era was gone. Shorn of his locks, looking spiffy in a white jacket and bolo tie and sporting the usual batch of new songs, Young had only a trio of wooden Indians for company onstage at the three-hundred-seat club. The shows were filmed in their entirety for possible use in *Human Highway*.

After the late show on May 27, Young headed for the Mabuhay Gardens, a nearby punk club where he was filmed onstage with Devo, dressed in their Kmart cowboy boots and hats. Devo already had a rabid following at the Mabuhay. "Girls would take off their tops 'cause they wanted to breast-feed Booji Boy," said Mothersbaugh. Young stumbled onto the stage and wound up being tossed into the audience, just another old hippie to be devoured. "The punkers chanted 'Real Dung! Real Dung!' over and over," said Larry Johnson. Booji Boy mangled "After the Gold Rush" for an encore. Out of this meeting of the minds came much amusing press, with Devo dubbing Young the "Grandpa of Granola Rock" and "Ancient History Up Close."

The Devo/Young experience reached its apex the next night after Young's final show at the Boarding House. Young and Devo crowded into Different Fur, a tiny studio that David Briggs made clear was more trouble than any of the other dusty corners he'd recorded Young in ("They didn't even have take-up reels," he grumbled). Festivities really got under way when *Human Highway* actress Geraldine Baron gave Young a milk bath for the benefit of the cameras. "It was my idea. I went and got fifty-one milk cartons and put 'em on. I had straws sticking out of these little containers— Scotch-taped in. I was holding Neil in the tub, and he started to suck on one of the straws. I didn't know Neil was gonna take off all his clothes."

In the wee hours of the morning at Different Fur, Young and Devo collaborated musically for the only time on an ultra-twisted version of a new song called "Hey Hey, My My (Into the Black)." "The first guy we ever jammed with was Neil Young," said Mothersbaugh, a fact that is instantly apparent on listening to the cacophonous hash this bunch created— leading Briggs to dub the ensemble "Neil Young and his All-Insect Orchestra." Sitting in a hijacked baby crib ("We had to get a crib from the woman next door," said Johnson, "she took the baby out") and dashing off lyrics in a shrill, tuneless yap, Booji Boy is the star of the performance. After abusing the song for over twelve very punishing minutes, Booji Boy sticks a knife into a toaster and Young gets squashed under the crib, still bashing away on guitar.

"I didn't want to sing about Johnny Rotten," said Booji Boy's alter ego, Mothersbaugh. "So I changed it to Johnny Spud. And I inserted a line— 'Rust never sleeps.' " The slogan—which adorned Booji Boy's diaper that night—dated back to Devo's graphic-arts days, when they were promoting an automobile-rust-proofing outfit. "We saw 'Rust never sleeps' as referring to corruption of innocence, de-evolution of the planet," said Mothersbaugh. Neil Young would nick Booji Boy's impromptu mumbling both to rework the new song and for the title of his next album.

Young would interpret the line in his own way. "It caught my ear," Young told Mary Turner in 1979. "I thought, 'Wow, right off they wrote better lyrics than I did.' I can relate to 'Rust never sleeps.' It relates to my career. The longer I keep going, the longer I have to fight this corrosion."

Young didn't give rust a chance. Shortly after the Different Fur session, Joel Bernstein visited Young in his studio, where he played his guest the

All-Insect Orchestra version of "Hey Hey, My My." "It was *hugely* loud. Neil said, 'I'm gonna play this for Crazy Horse, and they're gonna *learn* this.' That's where the whole *Rust* trip came from."

Young disputed this memory, but Poncho agreed. "We went to play 'Hey, Hey,' and we weren't hittin' it that good. Neil showed us the film of him playin' it with Devo. I didn't think we could *ever* play it that good, but that inspired us to play harder. From then on, we played the shit outta that song."

.   .   .

"I like it if people enjoy what I'm doing, but if they *don't,* I also like it," Young told Mary Turner. "I sometimes really like aggravating people with what I do. I think it's good for them."

"Hey Hey, My My (Out of the Black)" certainly fit that bill. In a handful of stark lines invoking the names of both Elvis and Johnny Rotten, Young sticks a question in your face: Is it better to give everything you have, even if you might go up in smoke, or to give in, give up and turn into an old phony? It was a cliché, for certain, but as do most clichés, it possessed some sort of awful truth.

Young was now thirty-two. He'd watched rock and roll go through many permutations and had already seen many of his peers fall by the wayside. "Once you're gone, you can never come back," he sneers, exposing the ultimate fear—and ultimate fate—of any rocker: irrelevance. Young understands all too well that rock is, as Richard Meltzer put it, about "a micro-moment." But he isn't about to pretend otherwise. Young's awareness of the limited shelf life of rock (and himself) borders on paranoia, and his maniacal refusal to give in to the inevitable is part of what makes him so appealing. You know he'll go down kicking and punching.

Decades later "Hey Hey, My My" seems more pertinent than ever. Watching your heroes stumble around the Rock and Roll Hall of Fame inductions or peddle their masterworks for TV commercials isn't exactly the same thrill as, say, a ready-to-implode Bob Dylan on tour in 1966. With very few exceptions, rock isn't like wine—it doesn't age well. "Rock and roll will never die," Young sings, but he also understands that rock and roll *isn't* here to stay—that its impermanence is part of its greatness, and that it sometimes consumes its makers. One line in particular had Young's peers and critics clucking: "It's better to burn out than to fade away."

People want a star to be flashy . . . they want something they don't have to relate to as being human. *Things that are human—you go away. You have your moment, then you go away. But stars are supposed to represent something else, I guess, in sort of a super-quality of—"It's* GREAT*!" Then once it* isn't *great, people don't wanna hear about it, because it doesn't satisfy their illusion. They want something to be bigger than life or whatever. So I think that's where that came from— it's better to burn out than fade away or rust, 'cause it makes a bigger flash in the sky.*

Interview with Mary Turner, 1979

GRAHAM NASH: I don't agree. I used to run on the school team when I was a kid. So many of the other people would run like fuck, and on the third lap of a four-lap race, they'd be dead, they'd be wheezin' and coughin' and couldn't finish. *I always wanted to finish.* It's the same with my life and it's the same with my music—who's to say that I won't write some of my best stuff when I'm ninety? I saw Segovia at ninety-two. He fucking *floored* me. I understand we're talkin' about James Dean, Hendrix and Janis, all that stuff . . . with that kind of an attitude, Neil must be really pissed that he's still alive.

RANDY NEWMAN: What do I think of "better to burn out"? No way. I don't believe that's true. But I think it's a great line for the song. You can't resist it. It's a writer's line. When you're a writer, you're ruthless. You'd run over your own mother.

A lot of American art is based on that—you live for twenty-four years, ya do everything, die young, really fire it up. A lot of kids, they get real famous, real big, they believe they have to live their lyrics. It's horseshit. And it's killed a few of them. You don't wanna be on a tombstone that said, "Born 1960, died 1984." What the hell's the point? You wanna go on and on and on and last a long time, y'know?

Maybe a kid isn't gonna know it's bullshit, but Neil doesn't have to worry about that. He can't edit himself.

AHMET ERTEGUN: I believe that. I think it's better to burn out than to fade away. . . . Fading away is not fun. Y'know what Neil means by that? He means it's better to live out your days being very, very active—even if it destroys you—then to quietly . . . disappear. Isn't that obvious? Isn't that what it means? At my age, why do you think I'm still here struggling with all the problems of this company—because I don't want to fade away.

JAMES TAYLOR: I like to watch people burn out better than I like to watch them fade away . . . but I don't wanna do it myself!

TOWNES VAN ZANDT: Yeah. Exactly. As a matter of fact, Neil's doomed to that. I am, too. That's what we do. *C'est la vie.**

JOHN LENNON, David Sheff interview: I hate it. It's better to fade away like an old soldier than to burn out. If he was talking about burning out like Sid Vicious, forget it. I don't appreciate the worship of dead Sid Vicious or of dead James Dean or dead John Wayne. It's the same thing. Making Sid Vicious a hero, Jim Morrison—it's garbage to me. I worship the people who survive. Gloria Swanson. Greta Garbo . . . I don't want Sean worshiping John Wayne or Johnny Rotten or Sid Vicious. What do they teach you? Nothing. Death. Sid Vicious died for what? So that we might rock? I mean, it's garbage, you know. If Neil Young admires that sentiment so much, why doesn't he do it? Because he sure as hell faded away and came back many times, like all of us. No thank you. I'll take the living and the healthy.

I wrote "Hey Hey, My My" in my house. Cowrote it with Jeff Blackburn—the line "It's better to burn out than it is to rust"— Blackburn had that line in a song, and I said, "What did you say?" I

---

*Just a few months after making these remarks, famed singer/songwriter Townes Van Zandt died of a heart attack on January 1, 1997. He was fifty-two years old. Hank Williams—Van Zandt's hero—was found dead in a Cadillac the same day in 1953. On his way to a gig with a bottle of booze by his side, Williams was twenty-nine years old. His single at the time was entitled "I'll Never Get Out of This World Alive."

called him up after I'd written the song and said, "Hey, I used one of the lines from your song. Want credit?"

Some things just hit me over the head, y'know. That's the way a lotta stuff happens with me. Other people say it and I hear it. It's happening all around . . . you just gotta look for it.

When I told Elliot what I was gonna do with Rust Never Sleeps, *he thought I was fuckin' crazy. I had it all written out—everything. When the Road-eyes come out, the boxes goin' up and down, big amps and microphones. Everything that was in that show was all written out before I started. I had it in a school notebook, bought it down in Grenada. Elliot thought I was nuts. He really did. But that happens a lotta times when I want to do something radical or different, y'know, but we don't give a shit. Elliot's comin' from a good place—his heart's in the right place—but sometimes you have to ignore him because he's not me. Like if Elliot wanted to produce my records, I'd fuckin' kill him. He's not doing what I do. He's doing the business end.*

I spray-painted "Rust Never Sleeps" on the door to Elliot's office. I said, "Now, there's advertising. Everybody who comes through here is gonna wonder what the hell that is, and you can tell 'em—my new album." Didn't cost a penny. Elliot's still got the door.

—You once said, "The audience decides everything."

To a great degree, I think so. The Rust *audience was a very idealistic audience. They were ready to hear anything. Ready to believe anything. They wanted to. This audience today, they're jaded compared to that. But a lotta kids aren't jaded, they're idealistic still—the young ones comin' up—they want it to be good, they want it to be real. They're not impressed with a lotta the shit that's out there. But the music business wasn't as big in the sixties. There weren't any rules. There were FM stations that played fuckin' everything. Whatever they wanted to play. It was great. There were no formats. Now music is a huge business.*

—Was Rust Never Sleeps *a culmination of certain things?*

I dunno. It's hard to remember what it was, actually. Yeah—it seems like it was the grand finale of a certain period.

"It all started when I looked at the pile of amplifiers that I had when I was rehearsing," Young said of *Rust Never Sleeps* in a 1979 interview with

Mary Turner. "It was just such a gross pile of junk . . . there was no concept, it just all fell together . . . that's why it was so easy. And when something's real easy, I think that's when it's the best."

Larry Johnson recalls a sea cruise following Young's wedding on August 2, where the subject of Elvis Presley's fatal burnout came up. "We were in Miami on the maiden voyage of the *Ragland*. You could see that Neil's wheels were just spinning."

Young hatched a preposterous idea for his next tour, starting mere weeks away: a very theatrical show with Crazy Horse. Instead of roadies scurrying about the stage, there were "Road-eyes": creatures in long robes with glowing red eyes reminiscent of the Jawas from Young's current favorite, *Star Wars*. Soundmen were dressed as Coneheads; David Briggs, in a white doctor's coat, roamed the stage as Dr. Decibel. The stage was set with ridiculously oversized amps and speaker cases, a huge mike and an equally giant tuning fork.

Looking tiny and childlike amid the absurd props, Young would "awaken" atop one of the speakers, hop down to pick up his acoustic guitar for a solo segment, then be joined by the Horse for some eardrum shattering. The show was bookended by rock milestones played over the PA system: Hendrix's "Star-Spangled Banner," the Beatles' "A Day in the Life," Chuck Berry's "School Days." In between sets were stage announcements from Woodstock. Not only would the entire crew be involved in the performance, so would the audience: "Rust-O-Vision" glasses were distributed, purportedly enabling folks to watch Young decay before their very eyes. Group art at its finest.

The *Rust* tour opened at Purdue University in West Lafayette, Indiana, on September 16, 1978, and closed at the Forum in Los Angeles a little over a month later, on October 24. In addition to the mountain of props and costumes ("I remember when Neil first suggested to the crew guys that they were all gonna blacken out their faces and put on these stupid robes," said Jeannie Field. "I'm sure eighty percent said, 'No way, man.' But ultimately they all did it.") Young was also pioneering the very first wireless-microphone system, which he tested first at the Boarding House. This led to some hairy moments, like in Rochester, New York, when they were broadcasting on a very illegal frequency and momentarily lost the signal during the show.

Crew member Bob Sterne saw the work-intensive tour as just another one of Young's lessons in "how to do the ridiculous. The *Rust* tour was a fuckin' nightmare on one level, because you're out there jerkin' around, tryin' to do stuff nobody knows how to do, and the shit didn't work and everybody was apprehensive and it was on the edge of bein' more work than you could do—but the fun of the show bailed you out of that." Everybody was part of the act, even David Briggs's son, Lincoln, who, as one of the Road-eyes, recalls looking out at a sea of people wearing their Rust-O-Vision glasses. "Twenty thousand fucking people staring at you with little cardboard blue-and-red glasses. It was the most surreal thing."

· · ·

"It was incredibly loud, *unbelievably* loud," said Joel Bernstein of the *Rust Never Sleeps* concerts. "Loud enough that when we did the L.A. show, the entire guest section left during the second electric song. All the record execs—Geffen, Ahmet—left." One angry reviewer went so far as to suggest that sound mixer Tim Mulligan should have his head strapped to a Concorde jet.

The fat, filthy opening smack of "Hey Hey, My My" announced a crazy new era for Young and Crazy Horse. The punk zeitgeist had gotten a couple of hooks into Young's brain and out poured hopped-up, abrasive sludge. This was insane music and even some Horse fans were shocked when they encountered the new *Rust*-model Young.

"I'm usin' too many covers / I'm warm now, so I don't care," screams Young in the paranoid "Sedan Delivery." A version of the song recorded two years before had been lumbering and dreamlike; the *Rust* version doubled the time, dropped the most revealing, hopeful verse and concentrated on the nightmare. The brain-dead "Welfare Mothers," with its absurd, heartfelt chorus of "Welfare mothers make better lovers—divorcée!" also charged along at (for the Horse) breakneck pace. What a concept: Young and Crazy Horse making their own boneheaded brand of punk rock.

Certainly the tour was a triumph for the Horse—"After *Rust,* no one ever asked me why I played with Crazy Horse," Young would tell the press—although in retrospect, Poncho felt that it foreshadowed hard times for the band. "It was really loud onstage," he said. "We were really separated, especially Neil and I. For me it wasn't a lot of fun, 'cause I couldn't hear what we were doin'. We didn't really play off each other. We were just bashing away."

Culled from overdubbed live performances from the *Rust* tour and the solo stint at the Boarding House, plus two studio cuts, *Rust Never Sleeps* was released in July 1979. A double album of *Live Rust* followed in November, along with a very oddly edited movie of the Cow Palace performance from October 22, 1978. It was a period of manic activity for all involved. "Neil went to Florida," said David Briggs. "I went and bought a half ounce of cocaine and, in one week, assembled the entire *Live Rust* album and movie soundtrack. In a *week*. Y'know, it's not the drugs, it's the attitude that goes with 'em."

•　　•　　•

Rust Never Sleeps opens with the mournful solo acoustic "My My, Hey Hey" and ends with the unrepentant declaration of the alternately titled electric version.* In between, Young floats through a landscape of pool sharks, mad scientists and the American Indian. Veering away from the confessional approach of the past, Young pulls back his focus for a wider picture.

These are vivid story-songs that, grouped together, portray a savage, untamed America where violence is inescapable and survivors laugh off their wounds. "Pocahontas" speaks of genocide but ends with a whimsical meeting between the Indian beauty, Marlon Brando and Young (who audaciously wishes to sleep with Pocahontas "and find out how she felt"). "Ride My Llama" has Young getting high with extraterrestrials. The verbal spew of "Thrasher" is intoxicating, with Young wandering all over space and time, pausing to shoot an arrow into the complacent hearts of his superstar CSN buddies: "They had the best selection, they were poisoned with protection / There was nothing that they needed, nothing left to find."

"Powderfinger," a song Young started at the Topanga ranch of David

---

*The take of "Hey Hey, My My (Into the Black)" is the same live Cow Palace performance from October 28, 1978, on both *Rust Never Sleeps* and *Live Rust,* but the *Rust Never Sleeps* version benefits from massive overdubs. "That one has Billy Talbot playing the studio door on every two and four," said Briggs. Although Young didn't remember it this way, Poncho insisted that one influence on "Hey Hey, My My" was the massive stomp-stomp beat of Queen's "We Will Rock You," a hit at the time.

Briggs in the late sixties and finished at Billy Talbot's place in 1975, is nothing short of extraordinary. Young has a knack for hooking you with the first few words of a song, and from the knockout opening line—"Look out, Mama, there's a white boat coming up the river"—Young paints a picture as rich as any John Ford Western. It's the story of a kid barely past his teens who finds himself alone against a band of marauders, dead before he can get off his first shot, seeing his face flash in the sky and dreaming of "so much left undone." Somehow Young conveys the feeling of a soul leaving the dying body behind.* With its odd, affecting scenes of past, present and future, *Rust Never Sleeps* was, in many ways, Young's most psychedelic canvas yet—American history by way of a bong hit.

Young's guitar attack changed completely with *Rust*. Gone were most of the lyrical epiphanies of the 1975–1977 period. In their place were massive sheets of noise—gunky distorto headache music, gloriously displayed on *Live Rust,* which was Young's first live album (disregarding CSNY's tepid *4 Way Street*). After dismissing his work for years, even the most hardened mainstream guitar snobs began to take notice. "When he plays the guitar solo at the end of 'Southern Man' he sounds like a guy who can't really play the guitar but has found a way of making highly effective noise with it," wrote Geoff Nicholson. "By the time of *Live Rust* he sounds like a guy who can really play and has incorporated that noise-making into a highly sophisticated technique."

A lot of Young's experimentation was driven by a new custom-built stomp box that enabled him to jump back and forth between a gang of different effects—and combine them—without the signal loss common to such rigs. Mr. No Extra Stuff had suddenly gone effects-crazy, and one clue as to why might be the figure that graced a button Neil wore on his guitar strap throughout the *Rust* tour: Jimi Hendrix. Young was certainly aware of the guitarist, having marveled at the rawness of his 1967 debut single upon hearing it at Jack Nitzsche's house (Neil even played a tiny bit with Jimi during the Stills/Hendrix blowout jams of the Springfield days), but Young only studied the music in earnest years after Hendrix's

---

*I asked Young if "Powderfinger" is an antiviolence song. "I dunno. Depends on how you interpret it. Might be. I think that the crux of it is antiviolent, because it shows the futility of violence. Guy's gonna take a shot but gets shot himself. It's just one of those things. It's just a scene, y'know?"

demise. Leave it to Young to wait for years after the guy died to get really excited.

When Hendrix first came out, I thought he was great, but I never studied his records. Late seventies, mid-seventies—that's when I started really listening to him. I never really knew him that well—talked to him a couple of times. For my money, he was the greatest electric-guitar player who ever lived.

I think Hendrix had an effect in just makin' me want to get out-there. *He's just so free. He played loud—and he was real sensitive. He didn't ever play fast . . . It's easy to play if you can figure out just what it was he was doin'. He was so into it. All the* little *things, the little nuances— where he pulled his hand off and where he releases the note—it's not the notes he plays, it's the way he plays them.*

He and Jimmy Page are favorites of mine. When I was playing with Page, it filled the hole that Stills used to—more than filled it, it overflowed. He's so liquid, so at ease with his guitar—a natural sense of time. I'm a hack compared to him. He can really *play.*

Eric Clapton's a survivor, isn't he? He's worked hard, real conscientiously, at what he does. He's earned my respect. I didn't used to be that into his music fifteen years ago, but I am now. Everything he does seems to mean somethin' to him, y'know—I guess since he did the Unplugged. *A lotta things have happened to him. He's very much like Ry Cooder— very studious kind of blues guy—but also there's a broad appeal to his playing style, the fact that he was in Cream, his history. I think he's come a long way. I liked playing with Clapton. Steady—you can always hand it to him and you know it's gonna happen. He's clean, real good. And I can add a funky edge to his leads with my rhythm, 'cause I'm really a rhythm guitar player.*

I'm not like, all over the guitar. I play half-speed to these fuckin' other assholes, Steve Vai and whoever the new-incarnation Mutant Guitar God is. And y'know—they're great, they're fast and more power to 'em. Fuckin' stock-car-racer guitar players, heh heh.
—What do you think of your guitar playing?
Well, y'know—it's got a lot of feeling. It's getting better. But technically, I don't have the chops. I just play the way I play. It works for me. Some-

times I wish I could do more, y'know—then I try to learn. Sometimes I can, sometimes I can't. It's mental. You gotta be in the right frame of mind to play guitar right. It's not like "You're great*!" You can't practice and Be Great. It doesn't work that way—for me it doesn't. You gotta be in tune with yourself—then you can play an out-of-tune guitar and it's great. I know that I'm not a really good guitar player—but that doesn't get in my way.*

What is it about J. J. Cale's playing? I mean, you could say Eric Clapton's the guitar god, but what the fuck does that mean? I mean he can't play like J.J. J.J.'s the one who played all that shit first. Most of the songs and the riffs—the way he plays the fucking guitar is so . . . great. *I think we'd play great together. There's no doubt, if it was just the two of us, it'd be somethin' special. And he doesn't play very loud, either—I really like that about him. He's so* sensitive. *Of all the players I ever heard, it's gotta be Hendrix and J. J. Cale who are the best electric guitar players. J.J.'s my peer, but he doesn't have the business acumen—he doesn't have the idea of how to deal with the rest of the world that I do. But musically, he's actually more than my peer, because he's got* that thing. *I don't know what it is.*

I must have it, too—but I don't recognize it, okay? But I *know J.J. has it. I'm only saying I have it because, after thirty years I must have* something. *I'm just doin' what I like to do. Really, is it original? I dunno . . . I know it's what* I *like, and I know what I like is what other people have done. I'm just doin' my versions. My music is just a bunch of stuff that comes from other people's music—and my life.*

Rust Never Sleeps was voted album of the year, Young named artist of the year—by both readers and critics in *Rolling Stone,* and artist of the *decade* by the *Village Voice.* It had been an incredible ten years. He had released an amazing string of albums and recorded enough unreleased material for five more. Neil Young was at the top of his game.

Then came a turn of events that would change everything. Not long after Ben Young was born, he was diagnosed with cerebral palsy. Ben had a much more complicated diagnosis than Zeke: He was spastic, quadriplegic, nonoral. He would be confined to a wheelchair, unable to converse, constantly plagued by medical problems.

Up to this point in his career, Neil Young had been driven to the point of mania. Nothing had stopped him—not Rassy, not Scott, not school, not epilepsy, not polio, not relationships, not Stephen Stills, not failure, not Danny Whitten, not drugs or disappointment or weakness. He had been unrelenting.

And yet by Young's own admission, he had left behind a "big wake." The emotions that fueled his art were harder to contend with in life, and the truth was, he had been surrounded by people eager to keep him insulated no matter the cost. Joel Bernstein related a story. "Neil had planted some trees on a road to his house, obviously to grow into shade trees so he could drive under them. And a plague came and they got sickly. They had some tree surgeons down trying to help them out and they couldn't do anything with them. The skin was mottled, they had that half-dead look. And one day Neil just told someone to take a chainsaw and just go cut 'em down, 'cause he couldn't stand driving under them anymore. The point is, he just couldn't deal with it."

Now there was a baby boy who needed his father's help. For Ben, Neil practically put his career on hold. He and Pegi searched out every source of help and kept the situation entirely out of the press. At the time not even Young's record company knew how serious the situation was. "I wasn't al-lowed to tell people that Neil was involved with therapy with Ben eighteen hours a day, and that's why he could not promote anything," said Elliot Roberts. "I could never use that as an excuse, because it would become the story. One thing we didn't want was pity."

People close to the situation were moved, some to tears, in recalling Neil and Pegi's dedication. "The crisis came early in their relationship—it was a child at birth," said Roberts. "But they dealt with it with dignity, great love. They're a class couple, a class act." But Young would not tour for four years after *Rust,* and outside of two benefit performances, this musician—who thrives on live performance—would not play music in front of an audience at all.

Beyond Young's personal situation were changes in the cultural weather. The eighties found the country retreating into conservatism and gripped by economic woes. Musically, it was the decade of the mega-artist— Madonna, Prince, Michael Jackson and Bruce Springsteen. Figures who, however you feel about them, seemed a little less real and a lot more media-savvy. The black hole of MTV sucked everything through its vortex, demolishing the few barriers that remained between rock and other forms of mass media and erasing whatever tiny regional identity it had left. Outside of rap, which had little effect on Young's world, it was a confusing, passionless time for rock and roll, and many of Neil's peers appeared lost in the shuffle. Dylan, who confused and angered fans with his extreme exploration of Christianity, seemed to lose his instincts in the recording studio in the eighties (or at least for much of what he chose to release).

Neil Young would switch labels, joining a company that gave him little support and eventually sued him for the art he created. He would make wildly uncommercial records that were dismissed by critics and the public alike. He would see his power as a recording artist dwindle to the point where his label would deny him the right to record.

"That whole era, there's always something wrong," Young would tell Karen Schoemer in 1992. "There's always something between me and what I'm trying to say. The invisible shield."

The eighties were Young's most difficult decade. But he kept moving.

a **voice** no one could recognize

Spend a little time around Ben Young and you won't forget it. Sitting in his wheelchair in his Harley Davidson swag, his long hair in his face just like his dad, he has an irresistible smile and big bright eyes. Communication isn't the easiest process for Ben, but you immediately feel his presence. His spirit fills your heart as effortlessly as his dad can fill a stadium. "With all the shit Ben's been through—all the operations, all the problems, all the hell—he's a champ," said his half brother, Zeke. "He's a special kid to a lot of different people."

Neil's model-train barn is a special place for him and Ben. "Where Zeke and Neil might talk about recording techniques, or Amber might talk about her art, Ben can't tell you except with his eyes, with his laugh, or whatever sounds he's got," said recording engineer John Nowland. "When he's at the trains, that's somethin' he can do."

Ben participates in the trains via a large red button that sits before his hands, plus a flexible plastic arm that attaches to the back of his wheelchair and hangs over his head. At the end of the arm is a sensitive microswitch, and when Ben hits it with his head, it commands the train; when he hits it again, it cancels the command. The device is also wireless, allowing Ben to move his wheelchair all around the layout. Who came up with the idea for this sophisticated gadget? His father. Engineer Harry Sitam recalled the momentous day they got the wireless system working. "I don't know who was more excited," he said. "Neil or Ben."

"Neil talks to Benny more than any other person in the world," said Elliot Roberts. "Everything he thinks he discusses with Benny. Benny knows everything—every dark secret that Neil has."

My life with my children has been quite an experience for me. My boy Ben is a spastic, quadriplegic, cerebral-palsied, non-oral child . . . with a big heart and a beautiful smile. He's just a wonderful human being. It did something to me . . . when he was born. . . . Cerebral palsy—nobody really knows what it is. It's just the name for something—paralysis of the brain, any amount of things. It's a lot like a stroke at birth. Or before birth.

My first son, Zeke, he was diagnosed with cerebral palsy when he was about eighteen months old. And then, years and years later, I'm married to Pegi. We had Ben. Somewhere along the line Pegi kept saying, "Something's wrong. He's not doing what other babies do."

So we went to the hospital, through all these neurological tests, and here we are at Stanford—this big hospital, supposed to be one of the best hospitals there is—and we're in a room with two doctors, the head of neurology and some other doctor. And no one has said anything to us. They're standing around, talking to each other. And the guy in charge, the big doctor, said, "Well, of course, he diagnosed cerebral palsy, spastic paraplegic." We're sitting in there, Pegi and I, and that's the first time we heard it—and he's not even telling us. He's sitting in the same room . . .

So I remember we made it outside to the car, and we're sitting in the car, and I'm going, "There's something wrong with me. Why did this happen?" Two different mothers. What's going on? Pegi's heartbroken, we're both shocked, we have no idea what we're gonna do.

It doesn't hit us what really has happened. Too big a picture, too big. We're sitting there and I'm saying, "No. It can't have happened twice." I was looking into the sky, looking for a sign—"What the fuck is going on here? What made this happen? Why am I here in this situation? And why are the kids in this situation?" And then you get into that—"What did I do to deserve this?" It just blew my mind. I couldn't believe it. So in order to understand what it's like to have a kid like that, you sorta have to take a look at what we did. We tried everything we could, went to all the different doctors, trying to get something going. And finally we went to this place in Philadelphia called the Institute for the Achievement of Human Potential, where they teach you this program called "patterning," where you manipulate the kid through a crawling pattern.

It takes three people to do it. You do it thirteen, fourteen, hours a day, seven days a week. You don't take any breaks—there's always one parent in the house. You have volunteers come in. We did that for eighteen months without a day off. And it's a rigorous program.

Where they're teaching the kid how to crawl—he's crawling down the hallway, he's banging his head trying to crawl, he can't crawl—and these people have told us that if he didn't make it, it was gonna be our *fault. That we didn't do the program right. When we went to Philadelphia they programmed us in this room. They had this week of lectures on how to do this program with your kid, and then they tell you if you're accepted or not. And the room was fifty-five degrees, we were in there for fifty-five minutes, then you have five minutes off. You get to drink coffee and have a doughnut, and go back in for fifty-five minutes. They have a different speaker that tells you the same thing. The parents of these injured kids are in there—couples with kids with all kinds of problems. It's like almost a United Nations–seminar kind of a place—we're sitting in there, looking down, all the parents, and they're lecturing and lecturing and lecturing and it's fifty-five degrees so you won't fall asleep. And it goes on and on and on, for hours and hours and days and days. Until finally you're brainwashed. And you think the only thing you can do that's gonna save your kid is this program.*

And they have you so scared that if they call and you're not at the house, you're off *the program. Forget it, you've ruined it for your kid. And here we are, we think this is the only thing we can do—they've drilled that into us—and if you don't do it exactly the way they say, bango! You're out.*

So it was kind of a scientific experiment, I guess, that we were part of. We lasted eighteen months. Eighteen months of not going out. Not doing anything. During those eighteen months, I made Re-ac-tor. *That's the turning point right there.*

"This isn't going to hurt me, I must survive, the children have got to be taken care of, we're not gonna be selfish, we're gonna go on, we're gonna do what we have to and do the best, take care of Pegi, take care of the kids"—I made up my mind that's what I was gonna do and that I was NOT GOING TO HURT.

I didn't know that I shut the door on my music when I shut the door on pain. When I blocked out of my head that I wasn't gonna feel the pain—to deal with it—I didn't realize what I did. I closed myself down so much that I was makin' it, and doin' great with surviving, but my soul was completely encased.

I didn't even consider I would need a soul to play my music. I shut it down, and I didn't realize it was gonna stay shut down when I played. You can't shut it down without shutting it down totally. You can't do that. That's how people get old.

Ben is very sensitive—we don't know how cognizant he is. His cognizant abilities seem to shift with the wind. Sometimes he's real sharp, other times he's not. There's no set of strict rules with Ben.

I'm trying to develop a common standardized communication tool that can be used for people of all handicaps. So when kids are in school together and one's communicating one way and one another way—they're all using the same tool, so the teacher doesn't have to learn all these different programs. So the teacher can actually teach.

A kid can do it with a laser on his forehead, can run the whole thing and talk. And kids who can't talk can type what they want with a head switch. And kids who can't do it visually, because they can't see, can do it through their ears. They learn the cues, and when they hear a cue—like a one-word cue—they know if they hit the switch after hearing it that it's gonna say a sentence. And that sentence is what they wanna say. So they keep listenin' to the cues until the appropriate cue comes up, and they hit their switch, and the voice comes out and tells people what they wanna say. Maybe the kid stays home at night and tries to put together a presentation, and he goes in and he waits till the right time and hits the switch. And presents an idea. So there's all these things that we're working on.

I feel we've come a long way—we've been successful dealing with what we've been given to deal with. And we haven't let it destroy us. Y'know, a lot of families break up when this happens with one kid, and we've got two. And they're great kids—I love my kids. It's just real. This is the condition of life they have.

My boy Zeke is a great kid. One day I told Mazzeo, "Zeke is on Level One at school—he's not gettin' in trouble, and he's doin' great. He's concentrating and he's not disrupting the class." Zeke had trouble with that, he'd always been disruptive—in a heavy *way, not just a lightweight way. He got himself under control—Level One. And Maz looked at him and said, "Who'd ya have to pay off to get on Level One, Zeke?" And Zeke looked at him and said, "I paid off myself."*

That's a beautiful thing to say. It makes me feel good when he said something like that. So we got our kids and things are lightening up. I've carried this story I just told you for years, okay? Without telling anybody—except Pegi. I don't want to cop out, saying I did what I did because of my kids. So I hope it doesn't come out that way. It's just LIFE, that's all it is. And that's what happened to me, and this is what I did.

After attending the seminars at the Institute for the Achievement of Human Potential in Philadelphia in the fall of 1980, the Youngs began the program for Ben at the ranch. Many friends and workers helped in the process, and no one seemed particularly eager to reminisce. "I could never leave there without having cried," said Elliot Roberts. "You have no idea how horrific it was."

Charlotte Stewart, an actress from *Human Highway,* also participated. "The days we'd be workin' on Ben, I just remember wanting to leave Neil alone and be real quiet, because he seemed to be very introspective. He'd sit down at the piano . . . you just knew he didn't want to talk. It was such a personal time. I just have the most tremendous respect for Pegi and Neil."

Released in October 1980, *Hawks and Doves*—Young's first record since the *Rust* assault—was a strange one. Side one was a hodgepodge of *Homegrown,* Triad and Indigo material. Side two—recorded in Los Angeles at Gold Star with a one-off band assembled by Ben Keith—was throwaway country rock as unfocused as the Crazy Horse white-house sessions for *Stars 'n Bars,* with two curious exceptions: "Union Man," in which Young savages the musician's union, and "Hawks and Doves." Over an ornery lick on his orange Gretsch, Young shouts out his patriotism: "Ready to go, willin' to stay and pay / U.S.A., U.S.A." It was an ominous, angry song.

"I felt that way when I was thinkin' about the hostages in Iran—'Just push us one more fuckin' step,' " Young told Bill Flanagan. "I wish Carter had . . . I'm glad that nobody got killed; that's number one. I just wish we didn't have to sit there and take it so long."

Appropriately enough, the track was cut on July 4, 1980. This was the first glimpse of yet another side to Young's persona: hard-nosed redneck. This stance would infuriate many old fans and critics who felt Young had a duty to remain the stereotypical sixties liberal, but he was only too happy to frustrate everyone's expectations. Little did anyone know this was just the beginning.

Next came *Re-ac-tor,* culled from Crazy Horse sessions in the fall of 1980 and early summer of 1981. Insiders felt the supremely minimal lyrics reflected the repetition of the patterning program, and while there were a few great songs—"Southern Pacific," "Surfer Joe and Moe the Sleaze"— Young's heart didn't seem to be in it. Sound effects and overdubs failed to mask the record's deficiencies.

"A lot of the takes didn't groove all the way through," said Poncho. " 'Surfer Joe' sped up, slowed down, so we would spend time hittin' everything we could find in there to play the groove through it—banging tambourine, banging pieces of metal together, doing handclaps. Everybody in the patterning program showed up and we banged everything we could find. Neil would say, 'That's good enough.' We compromised." Ralph Molina was succinct on the subject of *Re-ac-tor:* "A turkey. A one-legged turkey."

The *Re-ac-tor* sessions would begin a downward spiral for the Horse that would last a decade. "Neil didn't encourage Crazy Horse during those years," said Briggs. "He lost control of his personal life, and everything went along with it."

Written and recorded on the spot as an afterthought once the album was completed, the punishing "T-Bone" summed up Young's malaise: "Got mashed potatoes / Ain't got no T-bone," yowled over and over—for nine minutes and fourteen seconds. "It's very repetitive," Young said on the *Rockline* radio show. "But I'm not such an inventive guy." Despite Young's humor, *Re-ac-tor* seemed impenetrable. The stark red and black jacket featured no pictures, and on the back cover was an Alcoholics Anonymous serenity prayer—"God grant me the serenity to accept the things I cannot change, the courage to change the things I can and the wisdom to know the difference"—but printed in Latin, because, as Young told *Rockline,* "it was too much of a personal trip to lay on everyone in English."

—Did the program affect the music?
Absolutely. Even the recording process. For eighteen months, the only time I could record was between two and six in the afternoon. I used to record only at night, the middle of the night. I couldn't, because I was doing the program.

After being programmed like that ourselves and doing it for eighteen months, it took years to recover. I'd feel guilty when I'd go out, because for eighteen months I wasn't supposed to leave the house.

The program affected everything. Every fucking thing.
—How did you make the break with the program?
We were just wore out, couldn't take it anymore. We saw a lot of pain—and a lot of stress—but not much progress. I took films of us doing this program. I've never been able to look at them.

Then we went to this seminar for the National Academy for Child Development, which was a similiar type of thing, but the guy took us in and said, "Listen, you only have to do this four hours a day. You have to live your life."

So one night Pegi and I actually went out, and we were driving home feeling, "Wow, look at us—we're out and about." We both decided we were gonna do this other program that took half as much time. We were so happy—I can remember both Pegi and I were just sitting in the car to-gether. We were ECSTATIC. We were like little kids, just the two of us.

The National Academy for Child Development would later honor Neil and Pegi Young as parents of the year in 1983, and Neil would play his first solo benefit concert for the cause on October 1 of that year. "I like to keep my music separated from political causes," he said to a local paper at the time. "But I put this cause ahead of the music because this is personal; it has touched me and is important to me.

"It's been like a gift that has enriched my life. I see everything through different eyes because of Ben. I've learned that you just can't take every-thing for granted. When you have a brain-injured child, you realize how much everything means."

.   .   .

One song on *Re-ac-tor* hinted at Young's next direction: "Shots." A driv-ing, paranoid vision Young had unveiled at the 1978 Boarding House shows in an altogether different acoustic version, the electric recording on *Re-ac-tor* "just didn't have the spook," said Briggs, because it was drowned in heavy-handed machine-gun and plane overdubs, all created with a new synthesizer that Briggs had discovered in Texas—the Syn-clavier.

A computerized synthesizer with a giant memory able to hold an army of instruments and sounds, it was the ultimate one-man band—undoubtedly appealing to Young, with the situation he was in. He was among the first to purchase one of the incredibly expensive machines, and it would be utilized in a number of projects throughout the eighties.

"We liked color on our records," said Briggs. "I thought it was the ax that Neil could use to come in himself and do what Jack Nitzsche would've done . . . of course, like everything else, he went overboard."

With *Re-ac-tor* finished, Young continued to record with the Horse. Poncho recalls Young—all jacked up after seeing the Rolling Stones play San Francisco—coming in with a song sporting Stones-like riffs entitled "Computer Age."

Around this time Young also purchased a vocoder, an odd device that enabled him to mask his voice as a variety of characters, none of which sounded too human—imagine robotic voices from fifties science fiction movies. Young then took the mutated vocals and played them through the Synclavier keyboard, which essentially turned it into music.

"When we got the vocoder, we started listening to Kraftwerk," said Briggs. All this would plunge Young in his weirdest direction yet: what would eventually become *Trans*. Even a version of "Mr. Soul"—complete with backward guitar—got the machine treatment. And the further Young got into the new music, the less company he took with him.

"*Trans* started like we do always—two guitars, bass, drums," said Poncho. "Next thing we knew, Neil stripped all our music off, overdubbed all this stuff—the vocoder, weird sequencing, and put the synth shit on it." Briggs felt no one around Young tried to understand. "Billy and Ralph and Poncho, all the other participants, they dismissed it. They played on the stuff, but they didn't think it was music."

I was looking for ways to change my voice. To sing through a voice that no one could recognize and it wouldn't be judged as being me.

When I first heard the vocoder, I realized, "Hey, I can take the Synclavier, take somebody's voice going, 'Ah—aaah—aaah' through the whole song, enter it into the keyboard, play the melody and enunciate the words—and have the melody come out through the vocoder." That's how it works. So I figured, "Hey, I could fuck *with it—I could be singin' with somebody else's voice, or make it my voice." It's really weird and kind of unmusical.*

—Was the appeal that you could do it on your own?

I think that might've had something to do with it. I hadn't really discovered how pointless that was. Well, it isn't pointless—you can do some things by yourself that are great. But only to a point. My first album's like that—and I stopped doing it. You can't make a living that way.

"Sample and Hold"—a wry lyric about designing a new mate—was partially inspired by Young's burgeoning work with toy trains. He had rekindled his childhood love a few years before, which resulted in a monster layout that threatened to take over his home—until he constructed a building to house the locomotives alone. As usual, the interest couldn't remain just a hobby. Young began to have all sorts of crazy ideas on how to change the world of toy trains and hired Sal Trentino and Harry Sitam to work full-time on the project in 1980. Plunging into all the technical jargon obviously colored the lyrics of *Trans*. Trentino recalls work on a digital system for controlling the speed of trains: "We were talking 'sample and hold, sample and hold.' Next thing I knew, there was a song."

Young also wanted to investigate ways to make the toy more accessible for the disabled, for his son. "Sooner or later you'll have to see / The cause and effect," he sings in "Transformer Man," his vocodered vocals making him sound like a lost, lonely spaceman. Whatever one thinks of the *Trans* material, this was surely one of Young's gentlest, most beautiful love songs.

Outside the train barn, though, this was difficult music to understand: coded, minimalist lyrics sung by voices that didn't resemble Young's—or anything human, for that matter.

> *I think human emotion—and selling a sad personal story . . . it's valid, but it's been done so much . . . who cares? It's like Perry Como . . . it's like Frank Sinatra, it's way back there now. Now people are living on digital time, they need to hear something perfect all the time or they don't feel reassured everything's okay. Like when you get in the elevator and go up and down and all the numbers go by, everyone knows where they're going. . . . And the drumbeats today, the computerized drumbeats? Everyone is right on the money. Everybody feels good. It's reassuring. I like that.*
>
> *Electronic music is a lot like folk music to me . . . it's a new kind of rock and roll—it's so synthetic and antifeeling that it has a lot of feeling. . . .*
>
> *Like a person who won't cry. You know that they're crying inside and you look at them, and they have a stone face, they're looking at you, they would never cry. You feel more emotion from that person than you do from the person who is talking all the time.*
>
> *So I think that this new music is emotional—it's very emotional—because it's so cold . . . I have my synthesizers and my computers and I'm not lonely.*
>
> · —French television interview, 1982

While Young was tinkering in the laboratory with *Trans, Re-ac-tor* was released to an indifferent world in October 1981. With Young unable to promote the record due to work with Ben's program, Elliot Roberts asked Reprise to work the platter, and when it flopped, tempers flared. No one at the label really knew the extent of Young's personal situation. "Neil didn't want anyone to know, didn't want anyone to feel sorry for him," said Roberts. "So I never said anything to anybody." The matter apparently came to a head over a triangular-shaped single release Young had requested. "Neil had asked them to do a series of things which they didn't do, and so one thing led to another," Roberts continued. "We were very upset with them." So upset that after thirteen years and seventeen albums, they left Reprise.

David Geffen was in the process of starting his own label and made his move. "I had a very big deal at RCA—bigger than the Geffen deal," said Roberts. "And then David said, 'Listen, I'll give you a million dollars an album'—which is what we were getting at Warner's—'and you want an ad, you'll make up an ad. Whatever you want. You'll get total control, one hundred percent control.' "

It seemed like a safe, obvious choice. Geffen was Elliot's friend and former partner. Young, who never seems comfortable dealing with unknown quantities, already had a relationship with him. Even though Rassy and David Briggs argued against Geffen, Young made his decision. He didn't even want to meet with RCA.

"David has worked with Neil for a very long time," Elliot Roberts told Paul Makos in May 1982. "He totally relates to Neil as an artist and has no preconceived notions. He knows that he's capable of doing anything at any point at any time. . . . Neil's not concerned with selling large numbers of his records, he's concerned with making records he's pleased with. Unfortunately they are not always commercial from the record company's point of view. David Geffen relates to that." These words would come to haunt Roberts a very short time later.

"It turned right away—right away," said Roberts. "The first two clients were Neil and Joni, then Elton and Donna Summer—David gave everyone the same deal. They were all million-dollar deals, and everyone's first album stiffed after all their other albums had been successful. That's really when everything changed.

"David started feeling real pressure—he had given out a fortune to these artists and no one was selling any records, and David felt it was like reflecting on *him*. That he was a failure. That he couldn't handle it. That he wasn't as good as Mo, because Mo made successful records with these people and he didn't. I mean, there's a million things that go through your head when you're David Geffen—I can only imagine. David is *not* used to losing—and he's not a very good loser."

Geffen's artists began to feel the heat. "David's a very controlling person, a very powerful person, and he's got his own ideas about what people should do and what they shouldn't do," said Elton John. "And no artist likes to be told what to do. They can be told what to do if someone knows what they are talking about—they'll listen to a producer, for example—but if they're being told what to do by someone they have no respect for on a musical level, I think then things start getting a little uncomfortable, to say the least." For Neil Young, things would soon get more than a little uncomfortable at Geffen Records.

•   •   •

For the first Geffen sessions, Young set aside the vocoder/Synclavier *Trans* material and headed to Hawaii, concocting a band that drew from nearly every lineup he'd ever played with.

"I really wanted to put together the people that I had played my best with," Young told Cameron Crowe. "I wanted to take it further with all those people." One from column A, one from column B. The Royal Pineapples, as they were known for half a second, consisted of Bruce Palmer from the Springfield on bass, Ralph Molina from the Horse on drums, Ben Keith from the *Harvest* band on steel and Nils Lofgren from *Gold Rush* and *Tonight's the Night* on guitar; last but not least was Joe Lala from the 1974 CSNY tour on percussion.

"Can you imagine—Ralph and a bongo player?" said an exasperated David Briggs. "How would *you* like to play with a fucking bongo player? Neil knows nothing about chemistry or producing—he knows how to play and sing and write. Anytime he tries to do anything other than that, *that* band is how it comes out, dude. The less hats Neil Young wears when he does his art, the better it is."

The May 1982 sessions at Commercial Recorders—intended for an album that was to be called "Island in the Sun"—were mellow in the extreme: lightweight love songs and odd acoustic numbers, the most out-there of which was "Big Pearl," a South Seas love story complete with faux Hawaiian guitar courtesy of Ben Keith's steel. The only rocker, another song entitled "Like an Inca," shared a verse with the original "Like an Inca (Hitchhiker)" but possessed none of its pizzazz. David Geffen came to Hawaii to hear what Young was doing and was underwhelmed.

When Geffen first heard the record, it didn't have any of the vocoder stuff—it was all the Hawaiian stuff, and Geffen thought it was okay, but he didn't think it was good enough. "Neil, you can do more with these songs—keep going." It was healthy what he was telling me. But instead of going forward, I went back—to all the stuff that had been buried. I really did all the Trans *stuff at the end of Warner Bros., not at the beginning of Geffen.*

Trans *is definitely out-there. It went way over everybody's head. I thought it was really good shit. The only thing wrong with it is that I tried to hide it a bit by putting the things from Hawaii in there and making it seem like a transition—a transition from a real person into a machine, or something like that. I didn't stay all the way through with "Here's a guy trying to tell you something and you can*not *understand it." I mean, I coulda put out the* Trans *EP with only the vocoder shit, and that woulda been a cooler thing. But I wasn't really thinking that clearly.*

Geffen wouldn't give me the money to put out a video for Trans *because videos were just starting. I had a big concept. All of the electronic-voice people were working in a hospital, and the* one *thing they were trying to do is teach this little baby to push a button. And that's what the record's about. If you listen to all the mechanical voices, if you read the lyrics, listen to the voices, it's clear that it's the beginning of my search for a way for a nonoral person, a severely physically handicapped nonoral person, to find some sort of interface for communication. The computers and the heartbeat all have to come together here—where chemistry and electronics meet. That's what I was getting at. And that was completely misunderstood.*
—Don't you think the video . . .

Would've made the difference? Oh yeah, definitely. I wanted to do a video album to go with Trans. *They wouldn't give me the money. I wanted to spend two hundred thousand dollars of my own money if they put up two hundred thousand so I could do it. Nobody wanted to do that many—"You only need one video."*

I left Mo Ostin, left Reprise—a stupid fuckin' thing to do. I got mad at them. Made a big mistake.

I was totally fucking wrong. They were the greatest record company, and they've been good to me from the very beginning. They presented every fuckin' thing I did with a lot of class—whether it was commercial or not.

When *Trans* was released at the end of December 1982, it was a bit of a shock, but perhaps not enough of one. Young had hedged his bets—three of the nine songs were from the Commercial Recorders sessions, and each side of the record starts off with one of the bland, human-voiced numbers, giving the impression that Young was hiding the vocoder material.

"My biggest problem is that I create songs that are so much against each other that they can never live together on the same record," Young told Stuart Matranga, and it was never more true than on *Trans*. It felt like two completely different records that clashed badly, and without a video to set up the characters Young had devised, the vocoder songs made little sense. Then there was the fact that the record had been finished in a hurry. "I hated the mixes," said Briggs. "I hated them all. I mixed the record—including the acoustic shit—in about a week, because they were goin' on tour."

Despite it all, Briggs was very proud of Young for making *Trans*. "You tell me any established artist that did anything new and different in the eighties. Nobody was doin' that vocoder stuff, and that's what artists do—they go out there and plow new ground, and in rock and roll it's hard to find new ground. *Trans* was a success in the fact that a major established artist took music to a place that was as abrasive and grating to listeners as *Tonight's the Night*. When a major established artist puts his whole career on the line to go to new ground, the critics should at least applaud the guy—as opposed to dismissin' it."

But dismiss it they did, and for fans who had grown comfortable with the raw expression Young had mastered in the previous decade, *Trans* was an unfathomable mystery. One had to put together the puzzle and a lot of the pieces were missing. When the record bombed, Young took the rejection personally.

"Transformer Man" is a song for my kid. If you read the words and look at my child in his wheelchair, with his little button and switch on his head, his train set and his transformer, the whole thing is for him. And people . . . they missed it. Completely. They put me down for fuckin' around with things that I didn't understand—for getting involved in something that I shouldn't have been involved in—well, fuck them. *But it hurt me, because this was for my kid.*
—Let me play devil's advocate: to do such a personal thing and in such an obscure way . . .
Very obscure. They didn't have a fuckin' chance in the world. It was so well disguised, you could never fuckin' recognize it.

That's the way it went. Like I said, I wasn't gonna hurt. I was keeping it inside. But I dumped the load right there. I dumped the load on Trans *and told the whole fuckin' story—but it was so disguised that only I really knew what it was. So for me, it's great. To me,* Trans *is one of my highest moments. Forget the acoustic things on it, get rid of those, get those* out. *Disregard* everything *except that computer thing.*

I know what those songs are all about, and maybe knowing this story, if you listen to "Transformer Man"—you gotta realize, you can't understand the words—you can't understand the words—and I can't understand my son's *words. So feel that.*
—But what if you had addressed that directly in a song?
No, that wouldn't have worked. That's not—that's not my expression. That's too direct. For me, even talking about this is very difficult, because I want my children to be able to read what I say and feel loved and know that everything is okay.

The thing is, it's communication, but it's not getting through. And that's what my son is.

The Geffen years also inaugurated the era of Neil Young talking endlessly to the press. The less successful the records were, the more Young tried to explain himself, and Briggs thought it was a big mistake. He felt Young was selling his mystique by the pound. "Neil went chasin'. The one thing you can't do is chase. You gotta keep standin' in your spot, swingin' that bat, hopin' that other people will catch up to you sooner or later—but if they don't, buddy, that's what art's about."

The results, however, were often entertaining. Young invited a French TV journalist to the ranch for a taste of *Trans,* playing "Computer Cowboy" for the bewildered reporter with the gusto of a man who had just discovered fire. With a wild look in his eye, Young gleefully expounded on his own synthetic music, at the same time exposing how seldom he really did listen to new music by championing new wave inanities like Human League and Flock of Seagulls.

Young was emerging from hiding, ready to conquer the world, but plans went awry. In August he would head to Europe for his first major tour in four years, and it would be a total disaster.

.   .   .

After severing ties with the program in Philadelphia, Young was suddenly antsy to get back on the road and a tour was hastily thrown together. Seeing a massive Rolling Stones show afflicted Young with what "Ranger Dave" Cline—who by this point had become thoroughly enmeshed in the musician's affairs as a sort of mini-manager—called "Stones-itis." "This show made a big impression on Neil in terms of the size of the stage. Neil wanted to do this gigantic stage all throughout Europe." Chip Monck was called in and given carte blanche to execute Young's whims.

Monck, a flamboyant character who outdressed many of the rockers he worked for, had a reputation for being extravagant and hard to control, and the last time he had worked for Young on the 1976 tour of Europe, he hadn't endeared himself to many in Young's camp. "Chip helped make Woodstock, and that was the only buzz there was," said crew member Bob Sterne, chuckling. "I never was sure if Chip had any technical skills—what he really was, like all of us on some level, was a good bullshitter."

David Cline, who had no real experience in such matters, was sent overseas to advance the tour. "Elliot was going through a difficult time with his wife at that point, and he said, 'Look, just go ahead and take care of this,' " said Cline. "I'd gotten the authorization to do it." Little did he know it would lead to a fall.

Management had told Cline they expected a $2.3-million gross from the tour, and he planned accordingly but soon discovered that the projected gross was actually $1.6 million. With $1 million already committed for the massive production—plus a bunch of expenses back home, including a large tax judgment coming due—Cline felt disaster looming and told Neil he should reconsider.

"When Neil told Elliot I'd said that, Elliot called up and said, 'Listen, David, when an artist like Neil wants to do something, he does it no matter what the cost, and you're never supposed to say no. *Never* tell Neil he can't do something. You have no right to.' We were about to go a million into debt and I was pretty concerned about it. I said, 'If I don't, no one does—are you gonna pay it?' "

Well, you know what? I've heard R.D. say that before, too, and it's possible that he did say that. But it didn't register.

I don't think Cline said it as plainly and as fully as it needed to be said. Outlined—"This is bullshit. This is not going to work." If he knew that, he should've been saying that. I think he saw some things that were wrong and he said, "This doesn't look very good"—and everybody just kept going. I think that *mighta happened. But I don't think he sent up any big red flags and said, "Listen, this is just too wasteful."*

But, y'know, I'm hard to deal with when I get an idea in my mind and I wanna do somethin'. So I don't blame R.D.

Cline and Elliot—well, Elliot had to have somebody to blame other than himself at that point. Cline was not just takin' care of the little things, Cline got into everything. Cline is a great guy. If he was my manager, it would be like having the Ralph Nader of managers. In other words, if there's anything that smells the least bit fuckin' off, it's gotta be exposed, brought out into the open, everybody's gotta see it for what it is—instead of having someone that keeps things away from ya so you can create, like Elliot tries to do.

I like to have those things handled, taken care of, but I can't deal with all that fuckin' information. I'm not a businessman. I've created this incredible fuckin' business thing goin' on around me—but the artist in me doesn't wanna deal with what I've created. So constant fuckin' chaos and confusion have been the order of the day.

Cline, whose actions had ticked off all of Young's handlers at one time or another, was summoned to a meeting at the ranch. Present were Young, Roberts and Young's accountants.

"Very painful things happened at this meeting," said Cline. "Neil basically looked at me and said, 'Y'know, R.D., when you come into my house, it's like a weight comes into my room. You've gotten so involved in this stuff that we've lost touch of you taking care of the ranch. You're like an amoeba—you just absorb more and more and more. You've gotten involved in Elliot's area, the attorney's area, the accountant's area. I pay these guys to do what they do—and you've gotten in the way.' "

Cline was crushed. "It was like Neil took a red-hot iron spear and just jabbed it into my guts and pulled it out again. I said, 'Neil, I only did it because you *asked* me to.' Eight times out of ten it was Neil's personal direction to investigate and report to him."

The result of the meeting was "devastating," said Cline. "I was stepping down. Chip Monck ended up getting absolute control of the tour expenditures."

●   ●   ●

Young had other problems to mull over. The Royal Pineapples—now christened the Transband since Young had returned to the vocoder material—weren't exactly shaping up to be the next Rolling Stones. Bruce Palmer was the wild card. He'd been bouncing around the ectoplasm since the Springfield days, and now the formerly reed-thin bass player was overweight, off his game and not the easiest guy to make music with. "I used to spend a lot of time with Bruce, goin' over the songs," said Nils Lofgren. "Neil went to all this trouble to bring a guy from his past into his life—with all this confidence and faith in him—and the guy wasn't deliverin'. I used to stay up nights going over *every* song, over and over. He kept flubbin' up."

After a warm-up club date in July, Palmer was briefly replaced by Bob Mosley, the bass player from Moby Grape, with whom Young had worked in the Ducks. But Mosley, nicknamed "Moonwalker," was even further into the twilight zone than Palmer. "Mosley would stand in front of a window and stare," said Joe Lala. "For hours." Mosley was let go, and much to everyone's surprise, Young took Palmer back. "It's the guy who plays great on a great day, bad on a bad day—that's the guy I want," Young told David Gans. "Peaks and valleys, as opposed to deserts, that's the way I look at it. Long, flat expanses of professionalism bother me. I'd rather have a band that could explode at any time." Young would get endless valleys, very few peaks and at least one major explosion out of the Transband.

. . .

In Europe, it immediately became apparent that the *Trans* tour was out of control. The stage—which included a forty-foot runway thrust out into the audience, a mountain of lights and a backdrop that resembled the yellow brick road to the Emerald City in the Wizard of Oz—was impressive to look at but impossible to transport. "Monck had this grandiose plan, tryin' to leapfrog shows," said Tim Foster. "We were draggin' around five tons of steel that never made it off trucks." It took three trucks just to carry the stage, and tour personnel had ballooned to 116 people. "Our expenses were running about thirty-eight thousand dollars a day, whether we went onstage or not," said Cline.

In addition, there were three Synclaviers to baby-sit and they didn't respond well to the slightest manhandling. "Computer equipment is over the edge," said Bob Sterne. "You find people walking a wide circle around it, 'cause they don't wanna be there when it quits. All that shit's viewed with apprehension, 'cause Neil's always tryin' somethin' with it that's not normal."

It made for a grueling tour, and production people I talked to were particularly unhappy when recalling Chip Monck. "A megalomaniac," said Foster. "Chip Monck ran up bills that were ridiculous," said another source. In Verona, power problems nearly caused riots and forced cancellation of the second show. The band had to be smuggled out to Genoa. Riots in Rome resulted in teargas.

Bob Sterne, who had flown over to lend Cline a hand, couldn't believe what he saw. "Chip had probably made one of the biggest messes out of a major tour that you could possibly make. Not only had he made a mess of

most of the production, he'd fucked up the attitude of most of the employees. The whole thing was a mess."

Sterne was not about to get stuck aboard a sinking ship. "In Nuremburg,
I happened to walk by a tent, and Elliot, [booking agent] Barry Dickins, a
whole raft of people were standin' there, and I just decided to stop by the
crack of the tent and listen—that's how you stay afloat. And they're all saying, 'Well, this thing is really fucked up—Chip's made a train wreck of this
thing, David Cline doesn't understand the touring biz enough to deal with
it. How can we get it sorted out?' And I heard somebody mention my
name. I took a shower, dumped all my European money out, got in a car
and was on a plane outta there before anybody realized I was gone. . . . I
didn't say goodbye to anybody. I grabbed my fuckin' suitcase and left."

Cline was sent home and replaced by road manager Glenn Palmer. His
welcome would be David Briggs kicking down his hotel-room door in the
middle of the night, screaming about rental cars.

·   ·   ·

Despite the catastrophe unfolding around him, Neil Young—sporting new-
wave hair, wraparound black shades, wireless headset, black shirt and
pants plus a tie—gave his all.

"Transformer Man" live was a surreal event, with Young and Lofgren
prowling the long runway acting out the narrative. "Here I am singin', and
every time I open my mouth, it would trigger a synth version of Neil's
voice," said Lofgren. "It was so wild. Neither of us had instruments, so we
were like walking videos."

It was almost the only thing unpredictable about the vocoder/Synclavier
material. Because of the synchronization the two instruments required,
this was some of the least spontaneous live music Young had ever played.
The best that could be hoped for was a Xerox of the record—which the audience hadn't even heard, since *Trans* wouldn't see release until the tour
was over. The computerized material—while only a fraction of the set—
went over like a lead brick, but Young was unrepentant. "I was booed in
Germany, Spain, France, Italy, everywhere," Young told Allan Jones.
"Wherever I went, they booed me. But they *never* made me run."

"It was a loadful working with those guys," said Briggs of the Transband. "They had to be so fuckin' drunk and stoned just to walk out on-stage, I'd say to 'em, 'Man, you guys should get yourself a new fucking gig if you gotta get this fucking twisted to go out in front of twenty-five thousand and be adored.' I thought their performances sucked. It was always awful. Only Nils played great every night." In recent years, Joel Bernstein waded through the tour tapes for Young's Archive collection and didn't find a single usable performance.

Understandably, Young came unglued. "In France, Neil went off on [soundman] Tim Mulligan about the wimpy house sound," said Nils Lofgren. "He was just ranting, and he picked up a bottle and threw it into a plate-glass wall. Unbeknownst to everyone, Ralph was on a chair right flush on the other side of the wall—and it rains glass over Ralphie. Thank God he wasn't hurt."

The inner workings of Bruce Palmer remained a mystery. "All of a sudden he'd fire off the most incredible, unusual lick that would be so fuckin' great—and then he'd miss the chorus chords of 'Down by the River,' " said Briggs. "And miss it again. And miss it *again*."

Things came to a head in Genoa, when word got to Young that Palmer had been wandering the hallways of the hotel looking for alcohol after guzzling down everything in his room. ("I thought myself quite the drinker," said Joe Lala. "But Bruce could empty a minibar in a minute.")

"Next morning Neil wants to have a meeting with the band," said Cline. "There's the band sitting there, and Briggs, and Neil's sitting over on this little bed. He said, 'Look, I've worked my ass off, I've trained for this, I've paid for this—I'm what's making this happen. And I want you guys here, but you have to give a hundred percent. If you're out fucking or drinking or doing anything else to jeopardize the quality of my show, you're *outta* here.'

"Then Neil goes, 'And Bruce, I don't want you to touch another goddamn drop of booze. No more drinking.' And Bruce—who's a big guy—made the mistake of saying, 'Neil, I wasn't drinking.' Neil snapped. He bounced off the bed, flew across the room like Superman, landed on top of Bruce, knocked him over and started strangling him." Young was pulled off Palmer as Ralph Molina watched in amazement. "Neil was kinda fragile back then," he said. "No shit, man. We were afraid he was gonna have a heart attack."

People calmed down somewhat as the tour progressed, but nothing about the shows really improved. The last date of the tour, October 19 in Berlin, was recorded for an HBO special and home video, but even this performance was a bummer. Young got an unwanted suntan from Monck's overpowering lights. And Palmer was his typically wacky self. "We're about to do a song—'Berlin,' " Lofgren recalls. "Bruce asks Neil, 'What song is this?' and it was a song we learned *that day*. You can see on the tape Bruce has no idea what we're about to play. Neil's like 'Don't worry, it'll come back to ya.' And it did." "Berlin"—a forgettable ditty Young would perform only that night—had a telling chorus: "Help me, help me, help me find my way back home / After Berlin."

That was a depressing tour. Started out to be such a high point, by the end I was goin', "Oh fuck." I lost seven hundred and fifty thousand dollars. It cost *me seven hundred and fifty grand—and we sold out every show.*

It was just too big. Way too big. The plan was too big, the stage was too big, the schedule was too tight.

Chip Monck—well, y'know—I hired him. People aren't gonna blame me, they're gonna blame somebody else. The reality is the shit didn't work because the music wasn't there, and if that doesn't work, nothin' else works. There were some real flaws in the concept of that tour, and they all emanated from me. *That's where the real problem was. It was blown way outta shape and shoulda been a small little tour, but I saw this big thing—the Rolling Stones tour—and it was stupid. I wasn't that big of an artist.*

It was my *fault the tour didn't work right. I cut my own throat. My eyes were too big for my stomach.*

In the aftermath of the European *Trans* tour, David Cline found his position whittled down to nothing. "I was the fall guy," he said. By the October 26, 1984, concert in Berkeley, Cline was reduced to preparing the guest list. "I watched that show in the audience, didn't have a backstage pass. I was no longer a part of it—it wrenched me to pieces. I left in the middle of the show. I was crying so hard I couldn't find the interstate."

Soon after that show, Cline headed over to Young's house for a brief, emotional meeting in front of the fireplace. In a choked voice, he told Young, " 'It's getting to the point where it's no longer fun. I wanna get off while I still have a memory of it being fun. I've gotta quit.' Neil was quiet for a second, kinda looked over at me and said, 'R.D., can you afford to do this?' I said, 'No, but I have to.' And I got up and left. It was the worst time in the world to resign—I was seven hundred thousand dollars in debt from a bad time in another business venture—but I still don't regret it today."

When Cline was dragged into court in 1988 over a business venture, Young would testify on his behalf—against the advice of his counsel, said Cline, who was so moved by Neil's appearance that he had to leave the courtroom.

Some of Young's friends felt that he treated Cline terribly—that he had encouraged R.D. to dive into every nook and cranny of his business affairs only to turn his back when it ruffled too many feathers. Others felt that Cline bit off more than he could chew. Said Bob Sterne, "Did Cline get a bum rap? You know what—when you put the fuckin' hat on, when you accept the responsibility, at the end of the day you gotta take the heat if it's fucked up. David Cline just didn't have the chops, the experience to understand the problems and the personalities—and how really fucked up it can get out there in a hurry."

Cline would be missed. For many, he was a much more sensitive liaison than the rest of Young's handlers. And, said Bob Sterne, Cline "had Neil's best interests at heart—which you couldn't say about a lot of people who had come and gone."

NEIL YOUNG'S NIGHTMARE

You'd go out and—there'd be nothing there. That'd be it. Gettin' ready to practice with the band. The band isn't there yet, and the show's tonight. Why? They just couldn't make it. But they're comin' in. Couple of 'em aren't gonna make it, but they sent other guys that they think are really good. They're quick studies, they'll learn the stuff this afternoon. They'll be here pretty soon. Then I go out and I'm practicing in the sound check, still one of the guys isn't there yet. Fuckin' people are startin' to come in.

*And they stand around for a while, yelling out a few things—
"C'mon, Neil!" Then pretty soon they're drifting in and out,
and then they're mostly gone. Only a few people are left. It's a
funny dream. It's happened a couple of times.*

*I'm scared every time I go onstage my shit isn't gonna be
there. That people aren't gonna be there.*

Back in America, Young embarked on a solo tour in January 1983. It
started off as a no-frills affair, but the one thing everyone remembers is
Trans TV, a live video broadcast that blared onstage from a giant screen behind Young. Host Dan Clear—played by Newell Alexander, an actor capable of conveying unparalleled game-show smarminess—would roam
backstage, interviewing concertgoers, crew members, offering his witless
halftime commentary on the show itself. Interspersed were highlights from
Young's career, old TV shows, commercials and "video noise to irritate the
shit outta the audience," said Larry Johnson. "It was a riot every night.
Woodstock *pales* by comparison."

A smattering of *Trans* songs were inflicted on the audience, but Young
was already performing new, country-inflected material, taking a break
from the tour on January 27 through 29 to cut a record in Nashville: *Old
Ways*. Elliot Mazer, who hadn't worked with Young since *Homegrown,* coproduced. "I got a call totally out of the blue—'Hey, man, let's make a
record.' I was a little skeptical, because I had heard *Trans* and I thought,
'This guy's lost it.' "

It was Mazer who introduced Young to digital recording. Young dove in
headfirst, buying the first pair of twenty-four-track machines in America.
"As a result of liking the sound, Neil buys three hundred thousand dollars
of these machines from Sony," said Mazer, shaking his head. Young sold
most of his analog gear and, beginning with the *Old Ways* sessions that
January, all of the music he would make for the next twelve years would be
recorded digitally. It changed everything. Young would immerse himself in
this new technology completely, becoming its biggest critic in the process.
It was a great medium in terms of postrecording tasks such as editing, but
the limited sampling rate of the early machines left much of the music behind. "Digital is a huge rip-off," Young would say in 1992. "This is the
darkest age of musical sound."

—When did you first become disillusioned with digital sound?
About the same time I stopped listenin' to my own records. Old Ways. First one.
—You were initially excited?
Yeah. Things you can do with digital, you can't do with analog. Digital is very controlled. It's wonderful how you can manipulate it. Unfortunately, you're not manipulating a thing you want to listen *to, you're manipulating a simulation of it.*
—Why not still record analog?
Why? Who would hear it? It's all gone *as soon as you copy it to digital . . . if I was gonna do that, I'd do it for my own enjoyment and I'd say, "Fuck everybody else in the world, they'll never hear it as good as I do. At least* I'll *hear it."*

Once you go digital, you're gone. That part of the whole thing is a disaster. Shit doesn't sound right. The shit is never gonna be like the old shit, never.
—How did digital get over if it sucks so bad?
Promotion. Nobody realized digital wasn't as good—because it wasn't an obvious problem. It was more obvious after you listened awhile. The first time, "Hey—no hiss, wow, great!" You didn't realize there was no sound *until a little while later.*
—I notice I can't listen to as much music on CD.
Right. It hurts. Did you ever go in a shower and turn it on and have it come out tiny little ice cubes? That's the difference between CDs and the real thing—water and ice. It's like gettin' hit *with somethin' instead of havin' it flow over ya. It's almost taking music and making a weapon out of it—do physical damage to people without touching them. If you wanted to make a weapon that would destroy people, digital could do it, okay?*

The *Old Ways* band was a roundup of the usual *Harvest/Comes a Time* suspects—Ben Keith, Tim Drummond, Rufus Thibodeaux, Spooner Oldham and Karl Himmel—plus a few new faces on background vocals: Denise Draper and a trio of Nashville singers Young had heard on a Tanya Tucker record, Larry Byrom, Rick Palombi and Anthony "Swee' Pea" Crawford. He would dub them the Redwood City Boys.

Old Ways would be Young's most straightforward country record thus far, and Mazer felt it began with a promising omen. "Neil was sick when he started makin' it—which is a big clue he's gonna make a good record," he said. The sessions went fast. "Neil couldn't believe it," said Drummond. "He ran out of songs."

Lyric content hinted that Young shared an affinity with the Nashville ethos that went beyond musical style. The big pull in *Old Ways* was family values: "My Boy" was a loving tribute to Zeke, and the lilting "Silver and Gold" was an homage to his family that Young would attempt to record many times over the years, never to his satisfaction. For those focused on Young as the stoned Crazy Horse hippie, the lyrics of the title song signaled a surprising change of heart: "Almost off that grass, give up all this drinkin' / Really gonna make it last, clean up my way of livin'."

With his own economic woes staring him in the face, Young looked out at the grim landscape of eighties America and saw disillusionment, resulting in one unqualified masterpiece from the sessions: "Depression Blues." Young's lonesome harmonica and even lonesomer vocal evoke a dusty nowheresville where the jobs have vanished and the funky downtown movie theater has been replaced by a faceless shopping-mall twelveplex: "All our old hangouts are boarded up and closed / Or bein' bought by somebody nobody knows."

Although Jesus was conspicuously absent from Young's down-home landscape, the overall message of *Old Ways* was one that Ronald Reagan could have condoned: Take pride in America, keep your family together, leave the drugs behind. "Are There Any More Real Cowboys?"—a song Young had written, strangely enough, in the middle of the *Re-ac-tor* sessions—decries cocaine-snorting cowpokes, asking, "Are there any more country families still workin' hand in hand / Tryin' hard to stay together and make a stand?"

After the Nashville sessions, Young resumed his solo tour. In comparison to the *Trans* debacle, it was a much needed financial success, grossing $5 million in five weeks, according to one source. But after two months, the tour ground to a halt during a March 4 appearance in Louisville, Kentucky, when Young passed out in the dressing room after the first set. A riot ensued when he didn't return.

I was lyin' on the floor of the dressing room. I could see myself—and the coroner came in. He was the only medical guy there, so he came in, checked me out, said that I was in shock, that I couldn't play and that we were gonna have to cancel the show. And I hadn't been doin' a lot of drugs or anything—I was sick.

That was the most pressure I've ever been under—to be alone at Madison Square Garden, then Nassau Coliseum—and to be so fuckin' sick that you could hardly see? I just made it on nerve. Elliot was at the doctor with me when I got the shot that almost put me out. I started gettin' the shakes and everything—and he saw it all, but I don't think it really registered.

I was too tired, too sick. They just drove me into the ground. Nobody would stop me—I was sick through the whole fuckin' New York leg, and they just kept on goin'. They figured if I thought I could do it, then I must be all right. I was so burnt I didn't know what the fuck I was doin'. A lotta people die *like that.*

The rest of the tour dates were canceled and Young took some time off, going on a boat trip with some of his cronies. On the train to Seattle, pal Alex Reid reminisced about seeing Alan Freed rock and roll shows back in the fifties, prodding some new songs—and yet another musical direction—out of Young. Back at the ranch, he cut a handful of songs on April Fool's Day, 1983, that were retro-fifties, including a pair of Elvis covers, "That's All Right, Mama" and "Mystery Train." Some of these were combined with the Nashville material, and a tape was sent to Eddie Rosenblatt at Geffen. Elliot Mazer recalls the drastic turn of events that followed.

"Eddie's reaction was, 'Interesting, but difficult to merchandise.' Then the worst thing happened. Eddie called up Neil and said something about the album being 'too country.' Neil almost threw the phone through the window. I've never ever seen him get that angry. He was beside himself.

"When I got home there were, like, eleven thousand phone calls from Eddie. He's a nice man—we're not talking about an asshole—and he said, 'I guess I blew it.' I said, 'Fuckin' understatement.' Saying it was 'too country' was the end of their relationship. Those two words did it."

Since the ersatz rockabilly trio the Stray Cats was riding high on the charts, Mazer suggested they expand on the rock and roll numbers Young had recorded and said Rosenblatt was excited by the idea. Neil Young wasn't happy about much of anything at the time.

I almost vindictively gave Geffen Everybody's Rockin'. *Geffen wanted more rock and roll. That was the key phrase: "Well, you want some fuckin' rock and roll, do ya? Okay,* fine. *I can do that. As a matter of fact, my* uncle *was a rocker, and I'll be* him." *I got way into that guy. I was that guy for months. He was out-there. It was a movie to me. Nobody saw it but me, but who gives a shit.*

It's hard for anybody to believe me when I do those things because of who I am. For them to believe that I'm not just diddling around, that I must be bored, *so I'm doing this or that. I can't explain why I get so into what I do. I just* do *it. And I got so into all of these characters, starting with the first character*—Tonight's the Night.
—But that was so personally connected to your life.
Very, very connected. The eighties, I know in time, looking back on it when it's not so hard to take, it's gonna be really strong. I feel really good about what I've done in the eighties, although I took a lot of shit for it. Because I did feel *everything that I was doing.*

There was a huge *abyss between me and everybody. And that's why people say, "Well, y'know, he's lost contact, he's out-there," whatever— 'cause I was just in a whole other place. It made sense to me, everything I did, and yet everywhere I went, people were telling me, "What the fuck are you doing? Why are you doing this? I mean, you're systematically dismantling your recording sales base."*

After the *Old Ways* country material was deep-sixed, Young recorded additional rock and roll material with a pared-down version of the Nashville lineup—now dubbed the Shocking Pinks—and finished *Everybody's Rockin'* "in about two hours," said Elliot Mazer.

Young made every attempt to stay close to the minimal feel of early rock and roll. "I had eighteen tom-toms, twenty-seven cymbals set up," said drummer Karl Himmel. "Neil said, 'All you need is a hi-hat, snare and a bass drum.'" Tim Drummond played stand-up bass. Young, up to his old tricks, enlisted slide player Ben Keith to play lead guitar. "Neil said, 'I want somebody who sounds like they can't play,' " Keith recalls. "I said, 'Well, I *can't* play.' He said, 'Oh good—we'll use *you*.' "

Everybody's Rockin' does have its virtues. Young's tribute to Alan Freed, "Payola Blues"—with its self-deprecating chorus of "No matter where I go, I never hear my record on the radio"—is the funniest song Young has ever written, and the shambling rhythms of "Cry, Cry, Cry" are irresistible. "Wonderin'," from the Topanga days, proved impossible to ruin, even benefiting from the stark treatment given here. And Young's singing throughout is as impassioned as ever, especially on a cover of Slim Harpo's swamp classic, "Rainin' in My Heart."

But the overblown backing vocals of the Redwood City Boys are hard to take, especially over a whole album. Their bopshoowaas are excruciating—a Mitch Miller version of the fifties. The Elvis/Sun Records "That's All Right, Mama" and "Mystery Train" are two of the most thrilling performances in all of rock and roll, but Young neuters any intensity, rendering the songs innocuous. It's like Billy Joel covering *Tonight's the Night*. Weirdness isn't very weird when it's contrived, and Young's take on the fifties just wasn't impassioned enough.

The sound was another problem. This was Young's first release featuring his "Digitube" method of combining digital recorders with the old green Wally Heider tube console ("You take a $180,000 Sony machine and run it through a $39.95 board," quipped Spooner Oldham). Karl Himmel was reportedly moved to tears the first time he heard his drums on digital playback. I was moved to tears, too—because it sounds butt-ugly awful, like somebody throwing a wet rag against a wall.

The record is also buried deep in plastic reverb. The Sun Records reverb was an organic, mystical sound; to approximate it with digital delay is an insult. And although the cuts with Young's rollicking piano add some much needed bottom end, the record sounds thin and tinny throughout— digicrap.

Calling this music rockabilly was a mistake made by every reporter at the time, including me. I think Young was aiming for the weird hybrid of pop and rock and roll that entranced him and Comrie Smith back on Roe Avenue in Toronto. But Young encouraged the misnomer by making reverb the star and posing on the cover with a hollow-body Gretsch and slicked-back hair.

Trans might have been greeted with indifference and mild derision, but *Everybody's Rockin'* was roundly panned when it was released in July 1983. One audio magazine voted it worst-sounding CD in the history of CDs—a bombastic claim, given that compact discs had been around only a year. The fact that the running time—five songs a side, total time less than twenty-five minutes—also harkened back to the fifties didn't win Young any praise, either. "I was a little angry," said Eddie Rosenblatt. "It seemed a little sparse."

Elliot Mazer felt that beginning with *Trans,* Young had ventured into territory that was style over content. "*Old Ways* was a more personal record, but it was still conceptual—'I'm gonna be a cowboy, I'm gonna say that rock and roll is shit. It's concept over art—which is not good. And when all you're doing is blatantly putting the concept forward, and the concept comes up empty, you're in danger."

But it was Bob Dylan who had the ultimate comment on *Everybody's Rockin'.* Calling Tim Drummond's home, Dylan got Tim's wife, Inez. Tim was recording with Young, said Inez, and Bob would never believe what Neil Young was doing—a rockabilly record. Dylan's response was typically blasé: "That figures," he muttered.

• • •

Perhaps the greatest thing to come out of *Everybody's Rockin'* was Young's first music video, "Wonderin." The clip was directed by Tim Pope, an upstart Englishman who had no idea who Neil Young was. "I thought he was this hippie fart with long hair who played at Woodstock. I was some git from North London. I was very into punk and we were against all that sort of shit. So I came up with the idea Neil was this old hippie bastard who lived his life at half-speed as the rest of the world shot around him."

Pope quickly found out Young was one very atypical hippie bastard. "I once went out to meet Neil in Malibu, and he said, 'Hey, do you fancy gettin' some Kentucky Fried Chicken?' That was the last thing in the world I thought Neil would do—I thought he'd be a fuckin' vegetarian. And as we were going up Pacific Coast Highway—we had Ben sitting in the back, making his sounds—Neil said, 'Start telling me about the video,' and I start telling him about the ideas, but at the same time he gets it into his head to mix his album on the phone, so then over the speakerphone they were playing back his album. Meanwhile, we shoot past Kentucky Fried Chicken, so he's doing this fucking U-turn in the middle of the freeway while mixing his album with me explaining the video idea. And then we rolled into KFC and just picked up our big tub of chicken."

Pope slowed down the camera as well as the playback and had Young mouth the words in sync. When the film and soundtrack were sped up, Young—wearing a loud Carnaby Street shirt of Pope's and with a bad five-o'clock shadow—appeared to be in a different time zone from everything he stumbled past, including such L.A. monuments as the Hard Rock Cafe and even All-American Burger, the grease pit that had provided culinary delights during the making of *Tonight's the Night*. It all added up to a truly unique video.

"Neil said to me, 'I've only seen the "Wonderin' " video once, and a lot of people tell me they like it and that's cool,' " recalled Pope. "I thought that was very sweet. Neil's very trusting to work with. If he likes you, if he feels you're good, then he lets you do what you do."

Pope would go on to direct a number of videos for Young, including a wild series for the *Landing on Water* album. In "Touch the Night"—done in one shot with no cuts—Young plays a TV reporter at the scene of an accident. During a video for the song "Pressure," Young plays a bespectacled nerd who hits himself in the face repeatedly. "In the end he knocked himself out cold, because he was so into the part," said Pope. "Neil's the only person I've ever worked with who will jump completely in at the deep end. He really is an actor—he gets into stuff in a Method sort of way." Young consistently tried to do interesting videos, particularly with Tim Pope, but they rarely made it onto MTV.

Tim Pope's really a talented man—very innaresting guy. "Wonderin' " was all his idea, completely. I just did what he said. I remember at the end, he wanted me to look pretty wasted, like I'd been up for a while, and he took this Polaroid, and I saw him looking at it. He was goin', "Fuckin' great, fuckin' great!" and his friend's lookin' at it, they're both goin', "Fuckin' great," and I walk over and it was like the most demented-lookin' fuckin' picture of me, heh heh. I knew where he was at.

Video is an art form. Video is an expression. You can do good videos. It can happen—it doesn't very often. Videos are kinda passé, okay?

"Movies today are too real; you can see every speck of dust," Young told Jonathan Taylor in 1983. "In the old days . . . it was all fantastic." Having worked on *Human Highway* for the last few years, Young now decided to change the movie completely and create his own fantastic world to put on screen.

Filmmaker Jeannie Field recalls that Young's dissatisfaction with the film dated back to a mixing session for the *Rust Never Sleeps* concert movie. "Neil said, 'I wish I hadn't chosen to play a musician in *Human Highway*. I don't know what else to do with the character. I don't want this to be a music film. I want it to go somewhere else.'" Russ Tamblyn recalls that Young was against portraying any version of himself on-screen: "After it was done, we had all this footage, it was great, fast-moving, on the road and all real—he *hated* it. *He just didn't want to be Neil.*"*

Originally the movie was a *Wizard of Oz*–inspired fantasy in which Young's Lionel Switch character dreams of rock-star adventures, but Field said that in the editing process, Young became "more interested in the front and back story. The dream kept shrinking."

Young focused on the last day on earth in Linear Valley, a small town besieged by the modern world, namely the nearby Cal-Neva nuclear power plant. At great expense, Young constructed a massive set on a Hollywood soundstage, creating the town complete with a diner and a train running through it. Young played both Lionel Switch and a freebasing, limo-encased rock star named Frankie Fontaine, who some insinuate was inspired by David Crosby.

Devo, Dean Stockwell, Russ Tamblyn and the rest of the cast were brought back, as well as some nonprofessionals: Pegi Young was a mysterious motorcycle-riding character named "Biker girl"; Elliot Roberts was Frankie Fontaine's pompous English manager.†

"We were all free to make up our own characters," said actress Charlotte

---

*Young would embark on an acting career in the eighties, starring in a low-budget hippie drama, *'68,* plus small roles in a pair of Alan Rudolph films, *Made in Heaven* and *Love at Large*. His role as a mobster in Dennis Hopper's *Backtrack* (which also featured Dylan in a cameo as a painter) was left on the cutting-room floor.

†One of the *Human Highway* extras would be a face from the past—the Doctor, fresh from a prison term for his role in the Topanga slayings that had inspired "Tired Eyes." Young gave him a new start by putting him in the film, but unfortunately Keil Martin, one of the other actors, boasted of the Doctor's past to the rest of the cast and crew. "Martin tells

Stewart. "I was trying to play all of Neil's songs—I had hearts of gold all over me."

But making a loose, documentary-style movie on the road with a sixteen-millimeter crew was a different thing from shooting a narrative film on a soundstage in thirty-five millimeter. "We were committed to this stage," said Stockwell. "Neil likes to operate through improvisation, yet he had set up a thing which was not conducive to improvisation. He had all these actors there, a set, everything to light—and nothin' to improvise. There was no script, no story, so little stories were made up as we went along, and"—Stockwell laughed—"it wasn't very good."

Dennis Hopper, playing a deranged knife-juggling diner cook named Cracker, remained in character most of the time. "Dennis was jabbering, chattering and driving everyone crazy because he was doing this little knife trick—he didn't just have a prop knife, he had a real knife," said Jeannie Field. Opposite Hopper was Sally Kirkland, playing a weeping, Pepto-Bismol swigging waitress who's been fired from the diner but refuses to leave. Hopper's incessant knifeplay drove Kirkland over the edge, and on February 27, 1980, an accident occurred.

According to Hopper, Kirkland "couldn't concentrate on her crying scenes, so she wanted me to be quiet—but in point of fact, she wasn't in the fuckin' scene. It was on me, and I was doing my thing. She grabbed the blade of the knife. I yelled, 'Cut! Cut! Cut!' and Neil yelled from outside, 'Only the director yells cut.' I said, 'No, man, she's *cut.*' "

Kirkland suffered a long gash that severed a tendon. After a quick trip to the hospital, she was back on the set, but she would later sue both Hopper and Young, claiming Hopper was out of control and had stabbed her. "She said I consumed an ounce of amyl nitrate, a pound of marijuana and drank three quarts of tequila," said Hopper. "That was not true. I only did half that amount." Those I talked to felt it was an accident that Kirkland had brought upon herself. The suit went to trial in 1985 and had its moments of unintentional hilarity. One of the actresses was asked what the

---

everybody on the set I'm a convicted murderer. Everybody started lookin' at me a little weird. I got upset and didn't come back to one of the rehearsals. Neil came to me personally and said, 'Don't let it bum you out. You're in the big shot. I need you.' I walk back on the set, and forty-seven people applaud. Neil was a stand-up guy to put me in the thing."

movie was about during a deposition. "I haven't the faintest idea," she said. Kirkland lost the suit.

Human Highway officially premiered in Los Angeles in June 1983 ("I wanted to go, but I was in the insane asylum at the time," said Hopper). The critics were unkind, the public indifferent. YOUNG'S NUKE FILM A BOMB, quipped the *Daily News*. After a handful of showings, it went unseen until its home-video release in 1995. (Young had the good humor to grace the video's cover with a pan from his own booking agent, Marcia Vlasic: "It's so bad, it's going to be huge.")

The film remains one of Young's more perplexing creations, with the bewildered participants lost in his Americana landscape, straining to ad-lib their way out of a non-sequitur fog. Seeing Neil hamming it up as a squinty-eyed gas-pump jockey going gaga over a waitress is a spectacle not soon forgotten, as is the big "Worried Man" production number, featuring the entire cast dancing around with helmets and radioactive-waste shovels. "Never have so many people who aren't funny done a comedy," said Elliot Roberts. In one version of the end (there were many) the planet blows up and everyone ascends a staircase to heaven. Standing in the post-apocalyptic rubble, Booji Boy sums it all up: "The answer, my friend, is breaking in the wind. The answer is sticking out your rear."

But as hard as *Human Highway* is to fathom, it's pure Neil Young: the geeky dreamer floating through a sea of unhinged humanity, bemused by both old and new ways but somehow remaining unaffected by it all. And still dreaming. *Human Highway* "was very experimental," said Larry Johnson. "That, to me, is the strength of Neil—and why he's great to work for. He will try stuff that people more knowledgeable would never think of trying because they know all the pitfalls. He doesn't. He's the naïve explorer."

•   •   •

From July 1 to October 1, 1983, Young resumed his solo tour. The Shocking Pinks came along but took the stage only after the solo performance was finished. "Neil decides he's gonna take a band out for an *encore*—who does *that*?" asked Tim Drummond's wife, Inez, who was enlisted—along with Pegi Young—to perform in the show as one of the band's gum-chewing cheerleaders, the Pinkettes. The Pinkettes were a force to be reckoned with. "We got paychecks, we had dressing rooms, a wardrobe person," said Inez. "We even had two bottles of champagne we demanded in our rider. We lived and breathed the Pinkettes. It became reality."

Everybody got sucked into the Pinks' dimension. "Wow," said Ben Keith at the memory. "It was all an act—like playin' a part in a soap." Even Keith's lawyer, Craig Hayes, got involved in the circus. As Vito Toledo, the newly appointed manager of the Pinks, it was his job to whip the audience into a frenzy as the years rolled back to 1954.

But it was not enough for Young to have a nonperformer emcee; Hayes had to play in the band as well. "By the fifth gig, he wanted horns," said Hayes. "I'm a guitar player, maybe, a piano player, a bass player—I'm *definitely* not a horn player." Hayes was joined onstage by two other Definitely Not Horn Players—guitarist Ben Keith on sax and singer Larry Byrom on trumpet. Whatever the deficiencies of the Shocking Pinks were on record, the live entity was surreal theater. Band members carried pink combs to toss into the audience. "Gonna get any pink tonight?" a lascivious Young would query the crowd.*

While out on the road, Young wanted to pull into a studio and record, and Geffen Records denied him permission. Young—an artist who thrives on creating when the spirit moves him—was stunned.

I was gonna record "Don't Take Your Love"—I mean, that was fresh and ready to go, I had the fuckin' thing happening. I was in New York—I wanted to go in, just cut this one fuckin' song. They wouldn't give me the fuckin' studio. They wouldn't support me. That really blew my fuckin' mind.

I think there was some sort of problem with Everybody's Rockin'. *I think they only pressed a few of 'em, and out in the field, nobody paid attention to it. It wasn't worked to the radio stations. It wasn't pushed. They didn't wanna do that.*

That was a low point for me. Everybody was writing me off like I was gone. Like "Neil Young—he was happening in the seventies, but he's not

---

*All was not fun and games in the land of the Shocking Pinks. Bus driver Paul Williamson recalls that Young was reading Albert Goldman's Elvis Presley exposé while on tour. "Neil's frame of mind got uglier and uglier . . . Elvis's influence is ugly with Neil."

*doing anything useful now. So, no—we better not let him record. He
doesn't know what he's doing." I wasn't gonna make music and hand
it in to those fuckin' assholes—they didn't know what the fuck music
was.*

According to Elliot Mazer, Geffen Records received *Everybody's Rockin'*
warmly—at least initially. "I delivered that LP, Eddie calls me up and con-
gratulates me: 'This is a really good record.' I mean, they get into it—they
go out and buy a pink Cadillac to do an MTV contest, they do everything."
Still the record flopped.

It had not been a groovy couple of years for Neil Young. *Trans* had
tanked, the European tour was a disaster, *Old Ways* had been rejected by
Geffen and *Everybody's Rockin'* was another commercial nonentity. Young
had even been prevented from recording. But none of this prepared him for
what happened next: His record company sued him.

Things had reached a boiling point between Neil Young and Geffen
Records. Eddie Rosenblatt had gone belly-up with Young since the *Old
Ways* squabble. "Eddie didn't really have a relationship with Neil," said
Roberts. "He's a wonderful man—but he didn't know how to read Neil. To
him it was dollars and cents." And Young had been given $1 million each
for two weird albums nobody wanted.

Communication with David Geffen was another problem. Young had
gotten used to picking up the phone and getting Mo Ostin at Reprise, but
direct contact between Young and Geffen, Roberts said, had evaporated
since the failure of *Trans*. And per Young's wishes, no one at the label knew
of the complexities involving his son. All these factors made for a situation
rife with misunderstandings.

Geffen felt that Young was intentionally giving him substandard mate-
rial. "He felt Neil could turn it around like that and was refusing to—
'Neil's giving me all these esoteric albums to fuck with me,'" said
Roberts. "David took it personally."

Naturally, Geffen put pressure on Roberts to get his client in line.
"David came to me and said, 'Listen, you gotta talk to Neil. You gotta make
the Neil Young record that we all know he could make at will. At *will*. Why
won't he make it for *me*—I need it now.' David thinks Neil has this album
in his pocket and is capable of taking it out at any time—everybody does,

incidentally—'You can always do *Harvest Two* anytime. What does it take?' " Caught between the iron wills of Young and Geffen, Roberts tried to make peace, but he knew it was hopeless.

"The one thing that I could never tell Neil—or even *talk* to Neil about—is what he should record. I've never in twenty-six years suggested the kind of material he should be writing. It doesn't work like that. If I thought it did, maybe I would, frankly. It just doesn't. If you just say, 'Boy, that's a hit single' to Neil, not only is it not released as a single, it's *off the album.* And so I couldn't help David."

The longer the situation went on, the more venomous it became. "David's getting mean-spirited," said Roberts. "Now he thinks we're fucking him. David really felt betrayed by Neil. He stopped thinking of Neil as a friend—and started thinking of him as somebody who was actually trying to be injurious to him or mocking him.

"Finally David understood I had no idea what Neil was gonna do—that I couldn't *tell* him what he was gonna do, and that I sure couldn't tell him it was gonna be commercial in any way. It sank in. That's when the lawsuit happened."

The squabble demolished the decades-long relationship between Geffen and Roberts. "We used to hang out, we were inseparable. We had the exact same friends and went to the same places—it was Geffen-Roberts," said Elliot. "We stopped hanging out at that point. I couldn't trust him anymore, he couldn't trust me anymore. Horrible. It ended our friendship."

And so, in November 1983—approximately a week before his thirty-eighth birthday—papers were served on Neil Young. The documents requested damages in excess of $3.3 million, terming both the *Trans* and *Everybody's Rockin'* albums "not 'commercial' and . . . musically uncharacteristic of Young's previous recordings."

"Why the lawsuit?" muttered Eddie Rosenblatt, his weary voice barely above a whisper. "I don't know. It was a very difficult time. Neil was at the end of his rope personally, just in a bad place, we're this young record company trying really hard to make a fortune . . .

"I think there were too many strong feelings as it relates to Neil and David, Neil and I, and I just think the lawyers got in the way. Nobody wanted to go that far."

See, Geffen Records thought I was gonna be a megastar—like Eric Clapton. They didn't know the route I was taking. They paid for me— they didn't pay for me to do something. But I could understand where Geffen was comin' from. He had a rough row to hoe. He wanted to make a million dollars—and I was in another world.

I got the papers right at my house. The guy came right to my door. I thought it was pretty funny—sued for being "noncommercial." Playing "uncharacteristic performances."

But the realities of not having the money and wanting to make music and not being able to record and all that shit—that was a force play, tyin' me up. It was an ego thing. David took it personally that I was making records on his label that weren't selling—he took it personally. *Geffen regrets it. We've talked about it several times. He was doin' the right thing—he thought. He was gonna shock me back to reality. He was hurt because it was his record company and he thought I was gonna be a big star and I just wasn't into it. I was more into bein' me, doin' what I do.*

It was a bad situation. Couldn't make records, didn't have enough money to do this or that, had to go out and play and make enough money to make records, and the kind of music I was playin', I couldn't get much money for playin' it.

It was definitely rough on Elliot, 'cause Elliot had to listen to me. I was fuckin' hysterical. *I was goin'* nuts.

Young responded by filing a countersuit. "David handled it badly, Neil and I handled it badly," said Roberts. "It was 'Oh, fuck *me*? Hey, *fuck you*!' We *all* handled it badly." The case never went to court, but for the next year and a half relations weren't exactly cordial between record company and artist.

Elton John understood Young's predicament. "I had a very uncomfortable time at Geffen. I hated it. It went sour, and then I had so many more albums to do—it was 'Oh my God, what am I gonna do?' I got through it, I survived it, but I can definitely sympathize with an artist who has a clash with somebody at the record company. It's a fucking miserable existence, because you're putting down what you think is good stuff—and they don't care." Years later, R.E.M. would let it be known that the lawsuit was a factor in their not signing with Geffen.

The music press had a field day, with Geffen their clear villain. For Young, it was the best publicity he'd had in years. "To get sued for being noncommercial after twenty years of making records," Young would tell Bill Flanagan in 1985, "I thought was better than a Grammy." But privately, he faced the grim prospect of a future with a record company that refused to back him yet refused to let him go.

"Neil was a pretty down-in-the-dumps puppy dog," said his friend Roger Katz. "He just felt it all coming down on him, he just felt he had been fucked. The hardest part was making the sacrifices he did for Ben and then having the scene go down with Geffen and having—I don't want to call it his empire—having that start to disintegrate on him. Neil was under pressure to sell cars, sell trains, sell his bus, sell his boat—to save the ranch. It put tremendous strains on him financially for a while, but I think the long-term impact was more emotional.

"Neil really questioned who he should be and what he should be and where his music was going—did he still have it in him to write good music and perform? Sometimes he'd sit down and actually talk about other things he could do with his life other than being a rock and roll star. That period really made him question himself deeply."

· · ·

Predictably, new music would arise from the situation and it was pretty wild stuff. In January, Young recorded two solo songs with the Synclavier: "Hard Luck Stories" and "Razor Love." They were the warmest of his techno-pop music, particularly the unrelentingly melancholy "Razor Love," a piece he spent an unusually long time concocting. "Neil was locked away with that Synclavier for weeks and weeks," said guitar tech Larry Cragg. "He spent days just working on that one drum pattern."

The obsession paid off. Over mournful, bell-chime keyboard tones, Young sings in a haunted voice of what seems to be a father jettisoning a family. (Was he thinking of his childhood, singing to himself? to Zeke? to someone else? I asked, but he never told me.) Then comes the line that always conjures up a vision of Young alone on his bus, staring out into the blackness of night and seeing only his reflection in the glass: "On the road there's no place like home / Silhouettes on the window." Young's voice cracks on the word "silhouettes" à la "Mellow My Mind." It was an eerie song, the sort of personalized misery he hadn't written since *Home-grown.*

Armed with a batch of new material, Young summoned the Horse to the ranch. Then he made his first mistake: enlisting Elliot Mazer—who had never shown the slightest simpatico with the Horse—to coproduce. Perhaps caving in to the pressure from Geffen to make a "real" record, Young took his frustrations out on the Horse.

"Neil got into the studio trip: Make it fuckin' commercial," said Ralph. And unfortunately for Molina, Young focused his attention on the beat. "He was on this trip of gettin' the drums to sound big," said Poncho. "Neil was obsessed with not having anybody say we sounded shitty on the bottom—he knew the other bands all sounded modern with fat bottoms, why didn't we?"

Unbelievably, Young took the Horse's sloppy, organic funk and dismantled it—literally. "Mazer had us separated," said Poncho. "We had no visual contact, we were just wearin' headphones. It just sucked."

Things deteriorated even further when Young's guitar and vocal started feeding back and days went by without a solution. "Neil got uptight, he just felt like nothin' was goin' right," said Poncho. "Finally, that last day, man, Neil had that feedback in his head, and he just took his guitar and went *bam!* and smashed it against the wall. He yelled, 'This trip's *over*! Everybody *outta* here! Everybody just fuckin' GO HOME!' "

· · ·

In the midst of this gigantic bummer, Young and the Horse played four barely announced, five-bucks-a-ticket shows at the Catalyst in Santa Cruz, California, on February 6 and 7, 1984. The band might've been intimidated by Young's tinkering in the studio, but live, they delivered the goods. This was the wildest, most unhinged music the Horse would make anytime in the eighties. The last show was bootlegged on a two-record set called *Catalytic Reaction,* and I remember its arrival fondly, because it was easily the best Neil Young record since *Rust.* I recall tooling around the country deep in the night in the middle of God knows where, just some rental car with a couple of pals and a tape of the bootleg stuck in the deck. It was our fuel and made us drive real fast.

"Rock Forever" was a ridiculous song, a brainless ode to big rigs rolling down the highway that featured an equally brainless chorus: "Rock! Rock! Rock!" Great stuff. Young's unbearably loud guitar spews fat riffs that could've stopped a Mack truck; the only addition to the Horse is Ben Keith farting along on a (thankfully) barely audible sax. Young played six new songs, and outside of one trashy love song, "Your Love Is Good to Me," and a retread of "Hurricane" called "Touch the Night," all were angry, demented rockers.

No characters to hide behind here, just ninety-mile-an-hour train wrecks with lyrics so simple and dumb they verged on Zenlike beauty. "So tired / Of talkin' to strangers," Young screams out during the desperate, alienated "So Tired." All scraping, choppy riffs, ugly music that could have followed the Ramones or Howlin' Wolf. "I Got a Problem," with its straight-out-of-a-strip-bar sampled drum break, was sublime: "Me and my shadow are so in despair / 'Cause we keep hurtin' someone who cares."

Young soon headed back into the studio. Briggs returned as producer, and he and Young decided to take the band to New York City's Power Station. It was the first time Crazy Horse had ever been in a studio outside of California, and Briggs was stoked by the idea of getting Young and his band off the ranch and into a new environment. "It could've been great," he said.

But inside the Power Station, the vibe crumbled. Young went right back to his mania over the drums and separating the band. During one song, Ralph recalls Young "just stopped and said, *'I told you not to play the fuckin' hi-hat.'* Ever since that time it was 'Oh God, I can't do this fill here.' I remember about eight people tuning snare drums in the hall."

"Maybe I'm to blame for it all," said Briggs. "I'm a very strong personality when I make records—I don't let the inmates be in charge of the asylum. During that period, the inmates were in charge." The band returned to California empty-handed. "It was a bad trip on the ride home from that session," said Poncho. "We hadn't accomplished anything."

I'd listen to the radio and hear this big drum sound, and I'd say, "That's pretty cool. I wanna get that. But I don't wanna do what they're doing. I don't wanna sound *like those records—but I want that* drum *sound." It turned out it was a very difficult thing to do.*

And y'know, with Crazy Horse it's such a special thing, because none of us can really play. We know *we aren't any good. Fuck, we'd get it in the first take every time, and it was never right—but we could never do it better.*

So what happens is when a real musician enters that, it fucks it all up. They were great "feel" guys, both of 'em, but it made everybody conscious of how they were really dumb players. Oh, the sessions sucked. *We were all inhibited by each other—and we were all sick, fuckin' Legionnaires' disease or something. I don't know why we went to New York. We took the Horse way out of its environment. The Power Station— too many hit records had been made there.*

It ended up a big fuckin' bum-out. Everybody was bummed, and we didn't do anything for a long time. Because we never failed completely to fuckin' get <u>anything</u>. It was a rough time. I had a lot of animosity from my own team during those years—I mean, Briggs was pissed at me. Crazy Horse had a big chip on their shoulder. They were pissed because I recorded with other people. Everybody was pissed at me, y'know.
—The Catalyst performances were angry.
Oh, yeah. "Violent Side"—I wish that song done that way was out there—and I guess it is. It's out on bootleg. People who really wanna hear it can hear it.
—How do you feel about all this live shit floating around?
Y'mean all this bootleg stuff? It doesn't bother me. More power to them—they can sell 'em in the parking lot, I don't give a shit. I have nothing against bootlegs—I think that for an artist like me, they're essential. There's just no way that the record company's gonna accept as many records as I would like to give them.

After all the recent failures, this must have been the lowest blow—united with his greatest band and producer, Young had bombed completely. Where would he go now? He went back to the music Geffen had rejected in the first place: country. And he did it with a vengeance. "The more they tried to stop me, the more I did it," Young told *Rolling Stone.* "Just to let them know that no one's gonna tell me what to do."

Not long after the Power Station fiasco, Young headed for Perdenales, Texas, to help out on a Bobby Charles date. The April 15 session was being cut at Willie Nelson's home studio, and it was there, Charles said, that he introduced Young to Nelson, surely the most psychedelic figure in country music. The writer of such standards as "Crazy" and "Night Life," Nelson has also palled around with the likes of Leon Russell. "In my book, he's pretty up there at the top," Dylan said in 1993. "Whatever he's singin' he makes his."

Young was enraptured. "I remember the first time he came back from Willie's," said Joel Bernstein. "He literally looked like Charlton Heston had come down from the mountain. It was like 'Neil, what's come *over* you?' Neil saw the light." Young grew a beard and started wearing a head-band, prompting some of his crew members to refer to him privately as "Willie Neil."

Young went so far as to tell Bernstein he was through with rock and roll. It was full of backstabbers, all about payola. No more. It would be country music from now on. Country audiences, Young told reporter Jim Sullivan, "get off more on hearing fiddle than they do on hearing a rowdy rock and roll solo. . . . How many guitar solos can you play? . . . I've had it. I think I'm going to be making country records for as long as I can see into the fu-ture. . . . I really believe in country music, and I believe in the country music community."

Once Young had committed himself, he went whole-hog. The Interna-tional Harvesters hit the road, playing outdoor arenas and state fairs, book-ing his gigs through Buddy Lee Attractions in Nashville ("Neil had me find out who was the best guy in Nashville," said Roberts, "and that caused me big huge problems—I had to fuck ICM and go, 'Yeah, we are doing a big tour this year, but I'm afraid *you're* not involved.' "). The supporting acts were equally authentic: Johnny Paycheck, David Allan Coe and Way-lon Jennings, who had already scored a country hit with a cover of Young's "Are You Ready for the Country?"

At times the down-home venues "were so tacky that your expectations were very low," said Roberts. "You really went from hall to hall, thinking, 'Well, if the dust doesn't blow in our faces, we'll be ahead of the game.' " At one gig the Harvesters played for 5,500 people; just a few miles away, Bruce Springsteen was playing to ten times that number.

Joel Bernstein recalls with disgust setting up for a show at Gilley's Rodeo Arena in Pasadena, Texas. The tiny stage—usually occupied by the rodeo announcer—was thirty feet in the air. Equipment had to be hoisted up by rope, and since the stage was above the horse stalls, mud and cow-shit were everywhere. Young wandered in and perused a giant American flag on the wall. "I asked Neil, 'So—is this the cowboy way? He said, 'Sure beats playin' for a buncha fuckin' hippies at the Fillmore!' "

Young's chameleonlike genre changes had worn thin on audiences and bookers alike. "There was a new Neil every year," said Roberts. "And we had been canceling tours left and right in this down period, which was an-other thing that was working against us. Not only did you not know which Neil you were gonna get, you didn't even know if you were gonna get Neil."

Playing state fairs, said Roberts, was a godsend. "I could take Neil out of the marketplace, because the good thing about fairs is that no one knows you're playing them—and we had big-money dates. This country-fair suc-cess was very good for Neil. The audience really respected him. So it was 'Fuck, we won't make Geffen records—we'll do fairs.' "

In pursuit of the country audience, Young even ventured back into that dreaded medium, television, appearing on both *Austin City Limits* and *Nashville Now.* Dressed in his road garb of black shirt, fringed leather vest and black Harley Davidson hat, Young yukked it up on the couch between fellow guests Faron Young and Little Jimmy Dickens as a local politician bequeathed him the key to the city jail.

The host of the show, Nashville fixture Ralph Emery, asked Young if he was gonna get back with those boys Crosby, Stills and—who is it? Nash? "No, not anymore," replied Young, the familiar Cheshire-cat grin crossing his face. "[Our] lifestyles are a little different now . . ." Thinking this hip-pie feller had cleaned up his act, the audience cheered, unaware that Young's country set also included "Roll Another Number." Young then hopped up to the microphone for a tribute to his new four-month-old daughter, Amber Jean. No one can accuse Neil Young of holding back in his country phase.

●   ●   ●

Young didn't hold back in his interviews, either—he played the role of red-neck to the hilt. "I feel very strongly that we should be proud of ourselves as a country," he told Holly Gleason. "I'm tired of people constantly harp-ing about everything, feeling sorry and apologizing for being Americans."

To *Melody Maker*'s Adam Sweeting, Young bashed Jimmy Carter as a wimp, championed Ronald Reagan's arms policies, then expounded on AIDS: "You go to a supermarket and you see a faggot behind the fuckin' cash register, you don't want him to handle your potatoes."

It was Young's support of Reagan that gave many critics and supporters the biggest heebie-jeebies. It started at a Harvesters gig at the New Orleans World's Fair in Shreveport, Louisiana, on September 27. "Young looked like the rock star he is," wrote Jason DeParle. "But in conversation over a long-neck Budweiser, he sounded more like a warm-up speaker at the Republican National Convention."

Young would later say he was in a foul mood that day, and that the reporter particularly annoyed him. Whatever the case, Young was in the mood for a rant. "This is not the age of idealism," he said. "I'm very pro-American . . . very patriotic. I'm tired of feeling like America has to be sorry for the things that it's done."

Young bashed the welfare system, saying people needed to "stop being supported by the government and get out and work. You can't always support the weak. You have to make the weak stand up on one leg, or half a leg, whatever they've got."

It was all vintage Young, but one quote in particular really got everybody going: "Reagan, so what if he's a trigger-happy cowboy? He hasn't pulled the trigger. Don't you think it's better that Russia and these other countries think that he's a trigger-happy cowboy than think it's Jimmy Carter, who wants to give back the Panama Canal?" As usual, Young had shot from the hip and spoken his mind freely about how he felt at that moment. It would result in his having to defend his opinions in interviews for years to come.

Was it from the heart or a put-on? "Some of Neil's incursions into politics have been, I think, more designed to shock than any real deep feeling he has himself," said a somewhat amused Scott Young. "And, of course, this has rebounded on him a few times."

Elliot Roberts said Young's politics are as changeable as the wind, like everything else about him. "Neil's a that-day guy. If he sees something in the morning on the news, he'll talk about it that day—but a week later it's gone. Neil doesn't read newspapers, he doesn't really read *Time* or

Newsweek very much. It's gotta be somethin' he sees—if he watches TV on the road and there's a CNN special on Bosnia, Neil wants to do a record and a benefit within two days. Or he can ignore it forever if he doesn't see it."

But Roberts was more than aware of the hawk side of Young's makeup. "Neil is more American than anyone, even though he's Canadian. The man is a *foreigner*. He thinks Reagan is too loose, okay? Japan and France and England—he thinks they're all enemies and we should nuke everybody. Neil's an isolationist. I mean, if it were up to him, we'd have no foreign aid, we'd talk to no one, we'd really deal with no one else—'If they can't cut it, fuck 'em.' Neil is extreme. I don't know where it comes from. One minute he's a leftist Democrat, and the next minute he's a conservative. You never know which Neil you're dealing with."

However offensive Young's opinions might've seemed to some, the real issue was that he didn't conform to some clichéd notion of a sixties rock artist. As always, Young was only too happy to frustrate expectations, which pushed buttons in the press like mad. People pointed at Young's past as if it demanded some sort of continuity. "It was so outrageous for Neil Young who wrote 'Ohio,' to be supporting Reagan—or worse, Nixon," Roberts sputtered. "But that's how Neil felt."

Critic Dave Marsh voiced a particularly personal reaction: "I hate Neil Young's guts," he told writer Justin Mitchell. "Because he killed my father . . . by supporting Ronald Reagan, he killed my father . . . Neil Young said, and stuck to it, that Ronald Reagan's policies have been great for America. My father died because he could not get a disability pension. It's literally true he had to continue working in a way that killed him at fifty-seven years old. And I hold Neil Young personally responsible."*

---

*When Marsh finally interviewed Neil in 1995, one might have expected fireworks—the critic had made a point of attacking Young for years. But somehow the subject of murder was never raised. The liveliest moment was when Young corrected Marsh for misquoting a lyric.

It should be noted that Neil wasn't the only Reagan supporter in rock at the time—Iggy Pop, of all people, enthused about Reagan to Donny Sutherland on Australian TV: "Reagan's been good for business, any rocker'll tell ya. Promoters are spending money again."

Neil Young's favorite president remains Lyndon Baines Johnson. "He was real. He was down-home. LBJ wasn't the most pleasant character that graced the White House—heh heh heh—but he certainly was his own character. What a fuckin' real American he was."

Of course, all this meant that Elliot Roberts had his hands full. What-ever relief Young's country tours offered his career, they made publicity a nightmare. "I had to keep Neil away from the press. I was telling 'em, 'Neil doesn't do interviews, Neil doesn't do interviews'—he would've done them gladly, but he would've killed us.

"He did do one of these Reagan pieces in Europe that everybody picked up on and I spent years correcting—'Well, no, no, it's not like Neil's a rigid Republican, he's still a leftist rebel-leader king. Neil just likes Ron's *shirt*—does that make him a bad guy?'"

I never seen so many fuckin' people go berserk. I told Elliot, "Let's tear the whole fuckin' thing down, let's tear it down. A couple of months' work and it'll be gone."
—Meaning what?
My career, *heh heh. 'Cause Elliot was goin', "Neil, this Ronald Reagan thing—you gotta stop talkin' to people." I said, "Let's just start over again—level it." It's a comforting thought to me. A clean slate.*
—Sometimes in interviews I think you're fucking with these reporters big-time, just playing another character.
Well, y'know, my life is a little like that. I believe it so much myself, it's hard to tell what's real and what isn't. Actually, it's all real.

Ellen Talbot said to me once, "When you change from one style to an-other, people don't know who to believe. They don't know whether you're being you or somebody else, and if you do that too much, no-body'll believe you." Which I thought was pretty astute. There's a lotta truth in that.

Part of me is kinda like an actor—if I don't have something happen-ing directly about my life, I can take from experiences around me, and then, by way of becoming another person, another persona, I can ex-press a buncha fuckin' feelings. And that's what I like to do. So does that mean I'm not being true to myself and that people should not know who to believe?

The International Harvesters were one funky bunch. Scrawny upstart An-thony Crawford hopped around singing high harmony while playing mandolin, guitar, banjo and fiddle—as a foil for Young, he was like a backwoods Nils Lofgren. Besides the antics of elder statesmen Ben Keith and Tim Drummond, there was Karl Himmel prowling around in his trademark black shorts, threatening everyone with his nunchaku, and Rufus Thibodeaux, who, when not cooking up pungent Cajun delicacies in his hotel room, was figuring out other ways to dine. As Anthony Crawford recalls, "We'd be walkin' through the hotel, and Rufus'd see room service left outside a room, and he'd go, 'Swee Pea, pick that roll up—I can't believe somebody might waste that.' I picked it up and we ate the damn roll." Skinny, silent Spooner Oldham had his own peculiarities—according to Crawford, "You open his suitcase, and he's got two kinds of cigarettes— filtered and filterless, just for the mood he's in."

Musically, the band wasn't Young's most adventurous, but he adapted a variety of material for the sets. "Field of Opportunity" suited the approach, as did even "Roll Another Number," but a countrified "Powderfinger" sounded a little too cleverly arranged and made the listener long for the Horse's brainless crunch. The Harvesters really began to gel toward the end of the tour—a "Flying on the Ground Is Wrong" from the Universal Amphitheater on October 23, 1984, is exquisite—but as of the end of October, the original Harvesters were no more.

Drummond felt he might've contributed to his own demise early on. "I got on Neil's case up in Winnipeg. He came into the bar, and he had a headband on. I thought, 'Jesus Christ, he looks just like Willie.' A few days later he said to me, 'Could you play some of those two/four bass lines like Bee Spears does in Willie's band?' Now, I think Bee Spears is one of the greatest bass players in the world—but I said, 'Well, yeah, I can, Neil, but that's the reason I *left* Nashville. I got tired of playin' that eat-shit bass—'boom, boom, eat-shit.' " Drummond felt Young had gotten carried away with his new outlaw pals. "You don't have to be like Willie and Waylon," he told Neil. "They wanna be like you—you're the new outlaw in town."

Young would put together an altered version of the Harvesters in 1985 with a pair of more traditional country players—bass player Joe Allen and pianist Hargus "Pig" Robbins, but first he would tour Australia and New Zealand with a strange hybrid only he could concoct. The Crazy Harvesters were basically the Horse plus Ben Keith, Anthony Crawford and

Rufus Thibodeaux. (Drummond wasn't happy to hear about it. "Neil called up and said, 'Tim, I got some bad news for ya. I'm taking Crazy Horse to Australia.' I said, 'You're right—they are bad news.' ")

Fans got their money's worth on the monthlong tour, as these were some of the longest shows Young had ever played. First he'd play a set of the country material, then he'd play solo acoustic, then come back out and blow the roof off with the Horse. Outside of the four sets at the Catalyst, this was his first live rock and roll with the Horse since *Rust.*

For many, the electric sets eclipsed the rest of the show. "I remember at the beginning of the tour, the country guys were sittin' around all chummy with Neil, loved to talk about the show," said Poncho. "By the end of the tour, no one even noticed 'em, the people were goin' so nuts." But Neil Young wasn't quite done with country music yet, as "Dakota," a new song featuring the entire Crazy Harvesters band, proved. This portrait of American winners and losers was one of Young's most evocative songs of the period; it was almost as if he'd peered back on the bent inhabitants of some of *Rust Never Sleeps'* more surreal songs and found them all—like himself—faltering but determined to keep going. The main character was "a lone red rider" out on a South Dakota highway: "And though his war was over, he's fightin' on anyway / Although he's seldom sober, from drinkin' whiskey all day." There was dignity in moving, even if you no longer knew where you were heading—or if you were going to make it.

Some of Young's older songs didn't fare so well with the Horse. "We had our all-time worst show in Wellington, New Zealand," said Poncho. "Billy played all the wrong changes two songs in a row—he played 'Old Man' during 'Heart of Gold' and vice versa. Never landed on the right note, never came close. It was terrible. Neil was yellin' and screamin' at him in the dressing room."

•   •   •

The squabble with Geffen dragged on. Young refused to budge, telling the label, as he recalled to Tom Hibbert, to "back off or I'm going to play country music forever. And then you won't be able to sue me anymore because country music will be what I always do so it won't be 'uncharacteristic' anymore, hahaha. So stop telling me what to do or I'll turn into George Jones."

And so a deal was struck: Young would finish a new version of *Old Ways* and at some point would record a "real" record with a "real" producer. Geffen phoned Young to apologize, and the lawsuits were dropped (ironically, the dismissals were filed in Los Angeles Superior Court on April Fool's Day, 1985).

But the interesting detail is what Young offered Geffen Records in exchange. "I went in and I changed Neil's deal down," said Roberts, pained at the memory. "It was Neil's idea. We went from a million dollars to five hundred thousand, because Neil felt that for a million bucks, maybe they're right—but for five hundred thousand, I should be able to do whatever I want to do.

"No artist in history has ever gone into a record company and said, 'I'd like to give you back a half a million an album on three albums left'— that's a million-five. Like, it was killing me to do this. *Killing* me, right? Because I thought people would find out and they'd go, 'Wow, what a great manager—he took a million-dollar deal and made a *half*-a-million-dollar deal. Guy's a real scientist.'

"But Neil was on such a trip about the money—and about the pressure that the money brought him—that he wanted a no-advance, straight-royalty deal. Now I would not make a no-advance deal, because I said, 'There's no guarantee that you'll ever get anything—and you got a family, you got an ex-wife, a kid. I won't do that, but I'll cut it in half, if that'll make you happier.' Now I've solved the problem. It took three minutes. And they're going, 'Thank God for Neil, what a class guy—he just came in and gave us a half a million.' "

—Why did you cut your deal in half?
Got tired of having to live up to it. They wanted me to do all this shit and I didn't wanna do it. I said, "Pay me less money, let me do what I wanna do." I didn't want all that money.
—Did it have an effect?
Nope.
—What's it like making music when a record company doesn't believe in you?
It's not fun. You always have a chip on your shoulder. That's why I want a record company that believes in me. That's what I like about Warner

Bros. Everywhere I go in the world, they're there. Big bear. Big company. They can withstand the fact that they pay me millions of dollars and the records only sell, like, a hundred thousand—if that's what happens, big deal. Go to a smaller company, do that, it breaks them. You feel the responsibility. I don't want that.
—Did Geffen Records know who they signed?
No. But you gotta be fair to David Geffen.
—Why?
Because David Geffen has continuously said that that was the biggest mistake he ever made and he would never do it again and that was the one thing he regretted—suing me. That he should've done it a different way. He thought I was losing track, he was trying to bring me back to track or whatever. He did it the wrong way. He didn't come up and sit down and talk to me about all the reasons why he felt the way he did— which he should've, because we're friends and he could've.

Instead of that, he took it personally—that I was making these weird records just to make him look like an idiot. He thought when people didn't make big hits, they were doing it to piss him off. That they were actually doing it to David. *But David had a little learning to do there— he had to like himself a little better than to think people were trying to hurt him all the time.*

The fact that he's just a multi-fuckin'-billionaire, it means very little. He's just another fuckin' guy to me. And he's a big man for saying that he was so fuckin' wrong. All I can do is praise him. He's still my friend— he may help me out of the worst jam I ever get into, 'cause he has the power to do it.

But more than that, he's just an old friend, and old friends have bad times and good times. My times with Geffen are no worse than my worst times with Briggs. They really aren't. And Geffen's judgments of me are no worse than David's, either, y'know what I mean? It's an innaresting pair of Davids.

"My good music comes from my heart and my mediocre from my mind," Young would tell an *Entertainment Tonight* reporter visiting the Nashville recording sessions for the new *Old Ways* album. He had cut the first version in January 1983, and here it was April 1985. The finished product would leave the strong impression that Young had had a little too much time to think.

Elliot Mazer was no longer aboard. Young had continued to record while he was on the road with the Harvesters, and Mazer once again thought Young was going for style over content. "I said two things to Neil: a) he wasn't playing guitar. He was playin' like Waylon—his guitar was hangin' by his side. And b) his songwriting. All these lame songs we were trying to record—'Are You Ready for the Country, Part Eight.' "

The result was Mazer was out and David Briggs was back in. Mazer wasn't surprised. "Neil kept saying during that period that he'd love for me and Briggs to work together. I think what he'd like to see is Briggs and I fighting—he likes people being crazy. It's some sort of entertainment for him, and for someone who's not mean-spirited, it's a pretty mean thing to wanna promote. I think it's a form of voyeurism."

Compared to the original sessions, this *Old Ways* was an extravaganza. There were "thirty-five thousand, four hundred people on it," said engineer Gene Eichelberger. The studio was jam-packed with the cream of Nashville's session players. As Drummond put it, Neil finally got his eat-shit bass.

Anthony Crawford, one of the holdovers from the first session, was amazed at the excess. "I asked, 'Well, what do you want me to bring?' Neil said, 'Well, bring everything ya got. Bring it *all*.' So I loaded up my damn truck with amps, all kinds of shit. I stayed out there a week, I didn't play one lick. He had a roomful of people sittin' there just waitin' on his ass— people like Waylon. To me, Waylon is the Neil Young of country music, and Neil kept him waitin'. I hated it."

The record was cut live with minimal overdubs, but a country record was one job Briggs perhaps might not have been the man for. Crawford recalls the producer would "make me sing this incredibly hard part over and over, and finally I thought, 'Screw it.' It went against everything I thought Neil was about, which was first take, feel, vibe, intensity. I don't have anything positive to say about those sessions. A lot of good people got caught up in a bad thing."

Young went so far into a straight Nashville sound that he got steel-great Ralph Mooney to play on most of the sessions instead of Ben Keith. Neil Young country without Ben's steel is like Crazy Horse without the mistakes: in other words, too good. The music could've used some of Keith's woozy heart, because the sound was not country, as Tim Drummond pointed out, but "countrypolitan."

I always found it curious that Young failed to emulate such country confessional crooners as George Jones, Lefty Frizzell or even his Canadian brother, Hank Snow. Their brand of heartbreak is much closer to Young's soul than any of the so-called outlaw music. He comes close on "Once an Angel," a touching tribute to Pegi, but this direction was never really fleshed out. The kind of music represented on *Old Ways* had been done better by others.

None of the studio versions were improvements on the live performances Young had already done with the original band—a fact proven by the inclusion of "California Sunset" from the *Austin City Limits* taping— better than the 1983 studio recording and possessing more life than anything else on *Old Ways*. "Dakota"—reportedly renamed "Misfits" by Waylon Jennings during the sessions—received a bombastic production that was undeniably ambitious, but Young slowed the tempo down to molasses, turning the song into a wake and losing the boozy, exuberant but melancholy tone the Crazy Harvesters brought to it live.

Only two cuts survived from the original sessions, and one of them— "Are There Any More Real Cowboys?"—Young fucked with beyond belief, turning it into an overdubbed duet with Wille Nelson. Elliot Mazer—the coproducer of the original track—was dumbfounded when he heard it, thinking it was a mistake. "I called Neil and said, 'Listen, I got this test pressing of the single—there's an out-of-tune piano, the bass sounds weird, the mix is dreadful.' " Mazer laughed bitterly, recalling Young's response. "It turns out that was the desired effect."

One has to admire Young's nerve, though, opening the record with perhaps his schlockiest piece of music ever—a cover of his childhood favorite, "The Wayward Wind," complete with autoharp and string section. And he sang the shit out of it. Once again, you couldn't accuse Young of going halfway. He went straight over a cliff on this one.*

---

*One of the more interesting songs left off of *Old Ways* was "Time Off for Good Behavior," whose lyrics dealt with his brother's arrest and subsequent prison term for selling pot.

"Neil went and made an absurdly country record," said Anthony Crawford. "That record sucked compared to what it was—it sickened me. On the first *Old Ways,* you got a bunch of personality. You take the other one, and you just got a bunch of people makin' a helluva good paycheck."

Those excommunicated from the second *Old Ways* were livid when they heard the finished product. "Neil took Spooner and I off 'Real Cowboys,' " said Tim Drummond. "I took the needle off. That's as far as I got." The bass player sat down and dashed off an angry letter, telling Young that he'd lost the soul of his music. Elliot Mazer was equally upset. "I was pissed off. They fuckin' ruined a bunch of really good recordings. I listened to it once and threw it away. I think Neil was deliberately trying to give Geffen a piece of junk."

Apparently Geffen thought so, too. According to Young, they pressed only eighty thousand copies of the album when they released it in August 1985. *Old Ways* was another flop, and as a commercial recording artist, Young was fading away. The cover said it all—Young, with an old felt hat belonging to his bus driver's father perched on his head, walking away down a road at the ranch, his back to the camera—and to the world. It was starting to feel like Neil Young was on a kamikaze mission.

My problem was, when I was making records during that era, I didn't have a record company. I had no support, so everything kind of had a chip on its shoulder. I had this accent I was singing with at the time that kind of bothers me now. Y'know, like I went over the edge into country music. It's kind of phony-sounding. That's because I was not successful at it—it wasn't because it wasn't the right thing to do. But I didn't have

---

The lyrics express Young feeling "guilty as hell" over telling his brother to turn himself in to Canadian authorities: "He got seven years for what I've been smokin' all my life." Young appeared as a character witness for Bob in a Toronto court on May 31, 1985. According to Bob, this was against the advice of his handlers, and Young's appearance resulted in such headlines as *The Toronto Star*'s NEIL YOUNG SAID HE'S USED ILLEGAL DRUGS FOR TWENTY YEARS.

"The only thing wrong with cannabis is that the government doesn't make any money from it like it does alcohol—that's my educated opinion after twenty years," Young told the court. "It's a shame so much money had to be wasted on this case when so many other crimes of real danger are being committed in the street."

the focus I needed. If I'd been living in Nashville and living it—living the music and writing the songs and getting together with the people and doing it . . . but it was always like "You only have so much time, you gotta do it now." A lotta things were bothering me. I was trying too hard.

But I don't care what people think of my country music. They can stick it up their ass if they don't like it.

I don't even think of it as country music—I just think of it as playing with Rufus and Ben, *whatever the fuck that is. Who cares? People can call it whatever the fuck they want. Just because it has a steel or a Dobro in it, people think it's country. I think I could play some good music with those guys—still. I think it's right there on the edge of happening. It's never been fully developed. Always got kinda lost making the records. But it's not over yet. There's more to do. Oh, I'll go back there. At a time when it's the least fuckin' expected and the most unfashionable thing to do, I'll be there—either a hundred years behind or ahead.*

Old Ways might've been a misfire, but as usual, when Young went out on the road with the new Harvesters in the summer of 1985, the music mutated into something else. The two new pickers Young added—Joe Allen and Hargus "Pig" Robbins—were more traditional country, but this version of the Harvesters was heavier and rocked a lot harder. Young hadn't ignored rock entirely in the country period. Halfway through the first Harvesters tour, he added "Down by the River," and he had taken the jaunt down under with the Horse, but the new band was more of a country-rock hybrid.

Particularly exciting was the interplay between Young and Robbins. A blind pianist whose licks have graced countless Nashville classics—he's the only pianist Jerry Lee Lewis would allow to play on such country records as "I'll Find It Where I Can"—Robbins provided the band with a dark, smoky bottom that drove it like an old Chevy. "Southern Pacific," complete with Young shouting out train announcements as the band lurched to a halt, also ran like a bat out of hell. There were two new songs that were among the most exciting of the country period: "Grey Riders" and "Interstate," one of the loneliest songs Young's ever written.

Young's weirdness was something Robbins hadn't encountered in Nashville. "I never played on a song ran seven, eight minutes. Neil told me, 'We'll trade licks—you go where you want, I'll answer ya.' " The call-and-response between the two during a loping, spacey "Down by the River" drove audiences wild.

On July 13, Young appeared in Philadelphia at the mega-benefit for Ethiopian relief, Live Aid. He participated in a bumble-fuck CSNY re-union that was plagued by monitor problems, and also appeared with the Harvesters, unveiling a new song called "Nothing Is Perfect." This plod-ding, turgid, overripe "message" song possessed one great couplet—"But nothing is perfect in God's perfect plan / Look in the shadows to see"—but there was nothing subtle about it. An inventory of all things American and proud of it, the lyric promotes acceptance, but somehow the performance betrays a certain anger. This was the flip side of Young's country persona: a preachiness not unlike one of Rassy's venomous rants.

> *His great-grandpa worked this farm. His grandpa worked it and his daddy worked it. He's thirty years old. His wife and children at his side, he stands in the window of the old farm-house. A car comes up the driveway. A man in a suit is at the wheel, his briefcase at his side. Today is the last day for this family farm. Tomorrow is foreclosure day.*
>
> *President Reagan, in many ways, you have been a great leader. Today, as you read this, your advisors are telling you that America must be strong. America must compete in the world food markets. They advise you to keep prices way down, lower than ever. Do you know that this is killing the family farm? And that only the large conglomerate farm units will survive?*
>
> *Mr. President, you have a decision to make. Will the farmer be replaced by the farm operator? Will the family farm in America die as a result of your administration? Will the family system in America be dealt a fatal blow right at the core, send-ing a tremor of fear through every small family business in America? What will this do to the American spirit?*
>
> *Pictures of your family are neatly framed in the Oval Office, showing your love and reminding you of why you took on the great task of making America strong again. At the end of the*

day, your wife looks you in the eye and tells you she believes in
you. All over America, farmers' wives do the same. But sleep
does not come easily for you tonight—nor does it for them.

As we sell our low-priced food products to the world market,
we undercut the family farmers in those countries, forcing them
out of business. They turn to cash crops such as textiles and
other non–food related products in an effort to earn money to
buy American food. Must we destroy their native food chains
and their family farmers along with it? What happens if we
have a drought, or some other act of God, that ruins our crops
at home? Then we will have to raise our world food prices.
What will our world food-market customers do with no native
food and not enough money to buy ours? Consider the conse-
quences for America and the families of the world.

From "An open letter by Neil Young," 1985

This letter was read aloud at the University of Illinois in Champaign-Urbana on September 22, 1985, and published in a full-page ad across the country in *USA Today* on October 4. The occasion was the first Farm Aid concert, to benefit a cause Young has been deeply involved in since its inception. It was classic Neil Young: direct, from the heart and more than a bit dramatic. He also unveiled a new song at the event, which was essentially the opening paragraph of his letter set to melody: "This Old House," the best of a handful of songs Young has written on the farmer's plight. It remains one of the simplest, most affecting musical statements of his country period.

Farm Aid came about as a direct result of Live Aid, where Bob Dylan had asked whether some of the millions raised for global hunger could be set aside for the dwindling number of family farmers in America. Young took Dylan's plea seriously. Just a few days later in Texas, he was shooting the video for "Are There Any More Real Cowboys?" with Willie Nelson, and the two discussed the idea further. The idea of a benefit concert was hatched, and with John Cougar Mellencamp and country singer John Conlee pledging their support, the roster soon grew to thirty-eight acts for the September concert, where a reported $10 million was raised.

Young has appeared at every Farm Aid since. Particularly memorable was his appearance at Farm Aid Six in Ames, Iowa, on April 24, 1993. Pissed off that neither Secretary of Agriculture Mike Espy nor Vice President Al Gore had shown up, Young gave an emotional, off-the-cuff critique of the Clinton administration at a press conference before the concert. He spoke with the fervor of a tent-revival preacher. When he finished, he was nearly drowned out by the applause and cheers of the farmers present.

"I understand Vice President Gore is busy today at the Gay Parade in Washington, but I think he coulda fired up *Air Force Two* and come on down here and given the American farmer a shot in the arm. . . . I thought when we got rid of Bush and Reagan that there was gonna be a change . . . but I don't have respect for the administration. They have not treated us— and the American farmer—the way we *should* be treated. We're not lookin' for a *handout.* We're not lookin' for help—we don't wanna hear about *help*. We want *change,* so all I can say is, where is the change? We voted for change. . . . Where is Gore? Where is Espy? . . . Why aren't they here to hear this? I'm not happy to be here, okay? . . . We shouldn't be doin' this for seven, eight, ten, fifteen, twenty-five, thirty years—Farm Aid is not an American tradition. It's a Band-Aid. We ought to get *rid* of it! We want *more* from Washington!"

Young continued the attack onstage with an angry performance of "Last of His Kind (the Farm Aid Song)." Accompanied by the throbbing chords of Willie Nelson's guitar, a scowling Young spit out the words: "For seven long years we've been fightin' for a change / Lookin' for a country that don't need Farm Aid."

Willie Nelson chuckled recalling the press conference. "All the guys from the agricultural department are sittin' at a table behind Neil, and he's readin' the riot act to 'em. Neil was just lettin' 'em know we shoulda got a little more attention—and we did." Nelson and a group of farmers got a one-to-one meeting with Secretary of Agriculture Espy, which Nelson credits to Young's outburst, widely reported in the media. "Neil's very up-front—he tells exactly what he means. You don't have to worry about how you stand with Neil, and I like people like that. Thank God there's a guy like him who will stand up and tell 'em. Neil will lay it on the line."

Farm Aid basically hasn't been able to do much. It just helps farmers that are gettin' screwed. Helps them to get legal advice, helps them to get food, helps them make their payments if they have to. That's why I keep goin' back to it, because it's a good thing—but y'know, it's got its limitations. It should've gotten to be a big thing—if it was managed different, it might be a huge charity by now, because it's a natural. But Farm Aid is not mine, Farm Aid is more Willie's. I just believe in Willie. I believe in what he's trying to do—and I don't always believe in how he does it—but that doesn't matter. I'll still be there with him.

Farm Aid has been great. We've done a lotta things. The shortcomings of Farm Aid are many, and the accomplishments are many. It's just one of those things—you believe in it, you keep goin' and you keep tryin' to make it better.

I still really believe the farmers are bein' sold short and it's a cause I committed myself to. I don't know if I'm ever gonna be able to make any difference, but I won't stop talking about it.
—You went to Washington, shook people's hands—
Yeah, we tried to do that. Now I realize that that doesn't really make a lot of difference. Those people are just paying you lip service. I'm a celebrity that gets catered to while I'm there—and forgotten about when I leave.

All the situations have to be lined up right for what I have to offer to make a significant difference. A lot of other things have to be in place and the momentum has to be goin' the right way. Then a guy like me can be the tip of the iceberg and really make something happen. But it's not tangible what these other forces are—it's change.

"One morning I woke up and all I could hear was this massive fucking beat," Young told Jim Henke. "And my guitar was just rising out of it. I just heard rock and roll in my head, so fucking loud that I couldn't ignore it." Actually, the transition back toward rock had been gradual throughout his country period, but Young was reinventing himself again, and the country band would be left to twist in the wind. "Neil said, 'Y'know, Anthony, I don't care if you have ten gold records—I always want you to be in my band,' " recalls Crawford. "That was the last time I ever saw him."

Now Young would head to Los Angeles to make the kind of name-producer studio record Geffen had demanded. Not that he would give them what they wanted, because *Landing on Water* would be his weirdest music yet.

Dave McFarlin is hard core. He stopped listening to the Ramones after they did a Bud Lite commercial. A model-train fan, he'll put back anything that says MADE IN KOREA, because everything he buys is American-made, down to his sneakers. He's the quintessential New Jersey guy—the one Springsteen supposedly sings for, except Dave could care less about the Boss. The only things he really gives a shit about are fishing, the Weather Channel and the noise of an electric guitar.

Born in 1964, McFarlin heard *Rust Never Sleeps* on the radio when he was fifteen and that was it. When his parents broke up a few years later, he holed up in his room, playing "Down by the River" over and over. His first chance to see Crazy Horse live came in 1986, on the *Landing on Water* tour.

McFarlin loves Young's music—his room is piled high with live tapes— and what he really loves is Young going over the edge on Old Black, the more painfully loud the better. *Harvest Moon*? Young with Booker T. and the MGs? With Pearl Jam? Forget about it. Dave wants to see Young burn out—before his very eyes.

· · ·

To record *Landing on Water,* his first straight rock album for Geffen, Neil Young wouldn't use Crazy Horse or David Briggs. He would hire session players and a new coproducer: Danny Kortchmar, then riding high at Geffen with ex-Eagle Don Henley's soulless pop hits. No doubt the record company thought Kortchmar could coax something commercial out of their problem child. Kortchmar already knew Young, having played guitar with him alongside Ry Cooder on a Monkees session many years before, but he would soon find out that Young had his own way of doing things.

"To tell you the truth, it doesn't matter who fuckin' produces Neil," he said. "I'm sure Briggs helps a lot, and Tim Mulligan, but lemme tell you, man—Neil could get one of those professional wrestlers to coproduce and it would *still* come out the same."

Compared to the work of Don Henley, *Landing on Water* was the Outer Limits. "I never *ever* made a record like this before," said Kortchmar. "Henley is very meticulous. He isn't interested in spontaneity. Henley goes over every word of his vocals—you punch in *syllables*. That's the exact opposite of the way Neil wants to work." When Kortchmar tried to overdub a flat note or bum word, Young told him, "I can't do that. I'm not Henley. I can't punch it in."

But Young would really click with Niko Bolas, the engineer for the Los Angeles sessions. Bolas was a real live wire—young, energetic, blissfully ignorant. "I wasn't a fan. When Neil walked in, I thought he was somebody's hippie dad. Everybody was treatin' him with all this fuckin' awe. It was just another gig to me, so I met Neil on a brand-new level."

Niko would work on the next four albums, coproducing two, and his total lack of preconceptions would make for interesting results. He would also share responsibility for the downside of bringing Neil up to date: albums that were eighties-entrenched, lackluster-sounding. But Bolas was an important catalyst—and an honest voice—at a time when Young desperately needed it, prodding him to try new things, including new musicians.

"If Niko has an idea about something, he's not scared to tell Neil," said Young's half sister, Astrid. "A lotta people tiptoe around Neil, 'cause he's really intense and can be volatile, but Niko has no fear. Neil once said that Niko is God."

I needed a complete change. I wanted to see what was happening, what was going on in the studios in L.A., what kind of records were being made, how they were making them. The vocals on that record were pretty weak because they were all overdubbed. The demos were overdubbed, too, because the original track was overdubbed onto a click track. It wasn't Danny's idea to do that. That was my fault. It was a concept thing, I wanted to see what would happen. That was sort of a reentry into creative recording. I kind of lost it awhile there. Landing on

Water *was the beginning—or the end, depending on how you look at it. I just wanted to try somethin' else, break out . . . I felt like I was dying. Felt like if I didn't do something, I was gonna lose it. Something had to wake me up.*

I started working out when I did Landing on Water. *I didn't have enough strength to lift my guitar up over my shoulder—it was all fucked up, pain up and down my arm, pain in my back, pain in my leg. That was like post-polio syndrome or something. But I've been able to beat it by weight-lifting. That was the beginning of my physical reconstruction. It made my music more aggressive.*

Landing on Water *was an experiment. It has its high points and low points. "Pressure" and "Drifter"—those two are probably my favorites. "Pressure" is the high point. I had [drummer] Steve Jordan scream a couple of times, I sampled the scream and then I played it on the Synclavier. On the last note I held it—"Eeeeeeaaah!" Geffen wouldn't even put out the single. Too much art, not enough compromise.*

The band for *Landing on Water* was a trio: Young, Danny Kortchmar on synthetic-keyboard bass and Steve Jordan on drums. Jordan was a powerhouse, a total monster (Briggs said he'd been after Young for years to work with the drummer and was furious when Neil made the record without him). Full of attitude, Steve Jordan made a big impression when he waltzed into the session late and picked up Young's guitar. "*Nobody* touches Old Black," said Young's guitar tech Larry Cragg. "This is the hallowed thing. You don't touch Neil's guitar." But Jordan did, and he was rolling around on the floor playing it when Young walked in to meet him. "Neil just looked at him," said Kortchmar. "I knew it was love at first sight."

Jordan had met his match. "Neil wore both of us *out,* man. Burning on every take," said Kortchmar. "I never saw *anybody* wear Steve Jordan out."

Did Young cut the songs live in the studio like he'd always done? Did he finally acquiesce to the let's-overdub-it-to-death, build-a-perfect-beast method utilized by so many of his peers? Neither. The recording technique for these sessions was truly bizarre. When Joel Bernstein visited Record One, where Young was cutting, he noticed shards and shards of busted drumsticks scattered across the floor. It was a fitting image, for Young would take his obsession with the Big Drum Sound to absurd lengths on *Landing on Water*.

·   ·   ·

"*Landing on Water* was like a giant live overdub," said Bolas. "Neil wanted to use demos he cut with a Linn drum next to the fireplace, playin' acoustic. I made eight copies of each song on digital, and what they would do is go out and all play live to the demo. So you had all these live performances to the singer who wasn't there." Mistakes weren't corrected by overdubbing; Young simply flew in sections digitally from other takes.

Instrumentally, the sessions would be dominated by Steve Jordan. "I had this really weird drum sound happening," said Bolas, and that's what one remembers about the record—drums, drums and more fucking drums. Young's presence as guitarist was lost.

This was not a smooth time in Young's life. In addition to his physical ailments, he was in court defending himself against Sally Kirkland's charges over the *Human Highway* accident and fighting with his record company. "Neil would go to court at nine A.M., go through his scene there, come to the studio, get on the phone with Geffen Records and have screaming arguments with them," said Kortchmar. "Then he'd come in the room with a shit-eating grin and burn the joint down. I never saw *anybody* rise above shit the way Neil does. He defeated it all."

But Geffen Records never let up. Telling Young he was overbudget, they shut down the sessions. Young paid for the rest of it himself. "All the buffers didn't work on this record," said Jordan. "They were penetrating. We needed one more song and 'Pressure' came out."

"Pressure" was the last song cut and the finest performance on the album. The rest of it was another matter. As Young continued to monkey with the record, Kortchmar left. "A lotta people think that Danny overproduced, but that wasn't Danny—it was Neil," said Jordan. "Neil wanted to record digitally, wanted to use the Synclavier, and this is the kinda stuff that doesn't make rock and roll."

The bulk of the material was resurrected from spring 1984: "I Got a Problem," "Hard Luck Stories," "Touch the Night" and "Violent Side," which is massacred by a sampled boy's choir. Much of the production is so overwrought that it makes your skin crawl. "Weight of the World," with its pop synthesizer from hell, is particularly hard to endure. But two other new songs stood out of the muck.

"Hippie Dream" was inspired by David Crosby, who for the past few years had been sinking lower and lower into drug-induced psychosis. After a great opening couplet reprising and refuting "Tired Eyes," from *Tonight's the Night,* Young performs a disembowelment on the Woodstock generation, screaming that Crosby's famed wooden ships are a hippie dream: "Capsized in excess / If you know what I mean."

"I got chills when I heard it," said Joel Bernstein, who had been actively trying to help Crosby out of his troubles. " 'Hippie Dream' is a great portrait of David. So cutting." But again, a flawed recording. Jordan said one thing that hampered the band was recording live in a small space where his drums immediately overpowered everything. "We recorded that in a room in L.A. you record jingles in. We played so loud that it backfired on us."

"Drifter," which closed the record, is as cold a confessional as Young has ever written. The drifter's not a "quitter," he'd like to "stay and see the whole thing go down," but the tone of his voice is more frightening than reassuring. "Don't try to rescue me, don't try to rescue me," he warns, then turns, as usual, to a motor vehicle for his getaway. "I like to feel the wheel," he snarls over and over as the drums, guitars and synthesizers bashing away behind him congeal into one mighty, grotesque sound. What a self-portrait.

I think I've just had an uncanny ability to escape. There's no magic to it, but it's like a little light goes on. And when the light goes on, I leave. . . . See, I don't see change as a curse. It's just part of my makeup. Without change, the whole thing would fall apart. I'm not talking about rock and roll here—I'm talking about my life. *I've got to keep moving somewhere. I've written some of my best songs on the move, driving on a long journey, scribbling lyrics on cigarette packets while steering. I like that style, though I tend to get pulled over a lot by traffic cops for driving erratically, heh heh. They just pop into my head, these songs and ideas, while I'm driving along, and when I get home I move over to the typewriter, and sometimes what comes out is good and sometimes it isn't . . . but it never stops.*

*In a sense, it's all about running away. I've been running all
my life. Where I'm going . . . who the fuck knows?*
—Interview with Nick Kent

Landing on Water was released in July 1986. The cover revealed something
of Young's state of mind at the time: an illustration from an airliner emergency manual of crash survivors crowded into a hopeless little raft.

"It didn't look as if they had a chance," Young told *Rockline*. "I kind of
felt that way myself." Even Young, who will go to his grave defending
Everybody's Rockin', didn't have the stomach to defend this one. "It's a
piece of crap," he told deejay Dave Ferrin. "Let's be honest about it. If I
was going to give one of my records to somebody, I don't think this would
be the one." The album sank without a trace.

• • •

October 13, 1986, marked the beginning of a personal crusade for Young
and his wife, Pegi: the first Bridge School benefit concert. The school is
devoted to helping severely impaired children achieve their potential
through individualized teaching programs, computer technology and inte-
grated public school sites.

The California-based school was founded by Pegi Young, Jim Forderer
and speech-language pathologist Dr. Marilyn Buzolich in the wake of that
first event, which reportedly raised $250,000. Hosted by Robin Williams,
it featured—in addition to Young—Bruce Springsteen, Nils Lofgren, Tom
Petty, Don Henley, CSNY, J. D. Souther and Timothy B. Schmit. Over the
years, the annual (save for 1987) concerts have raised millions of dollars,
and the astounding lineups—put together with the assistance of board
member Elliot Roberts—have grown more impressive each year. A two-
day 1996 show featured Pete Townshend, Billy Idol, David Bowie, Patti
Smith, Bonnie Raitt, Pearl Jam, and Neil Young with Crazy Horse. Neil de-
fers all credit for the Bridge School's success to his wife. "It's all Pegi. I'm
just the public relations man."

• • •

Throughout the fall of 1986, Young toured the States with Crazy Horse to
promote *Landing on Water:* another extravaganza. Larry Johnson remem-

bers the call that started it off. "Neil calls me up—'Johnson, I need some mechanical cockroaches. What can you do for me?' "

Some would criticize the new show as a retread of *Rust,* but as Young and company like to say, "Anything worth doing once is worth doing over and over again." "Live from a Rusted-Out Garage" came complete with huge props, a couple of humanoid mice that chattered incomprehensibly and Johnson's remote-control cockroaches. In between songs, the band was harassed by Young's "mom" as well as by visits from exterminators. In a large picture window, a psychedelic slide show by Sandy Mazzeo clicked away.

Billed as the "third best garage band in the world," Crazy Horse was once again dragged into technological nonsense. Young employed computer expert Bryan Bell to figure out ways to re-create the *Landing on Water* material live. The result was a morass of equipment that drove the crew crazy. "There was a lotta electronic hoo-ha on that tour," said crew member Anthony Aquilato. "Ninety-six inputs and three submixers, a huge amount of gear—overkill in the extreme."

"All of a sudden we were thrown into this full-blown MIDI electronic techno-jive shit that we knew nothing about," said Poncho. "The thing that bummed me out the most was, we were tryin' to cop these other guys' chops—Ralph playing like Steve Jordan, me tryin' to play like Danny Kortchmar. What a joke."

Poncho adapted, turning into a computer whiz in the process. But the rest of the Horse didn't fare so well. Fans were treated to the mind-boggling sight of Billy Talbot tapping out rhythms on a keyboard bass (was this a problem for Billy? "No," said Niko Bolas; "Billy can do one note on anything"), while Ralph Molina had to contend with a device called the human clock, which triggered prerecorded samples.

Molina was, in Bryan Bell's computer lingo, "on the fringe of reality when it comes to interfacing." In other words, the human clock was frequently in another time zone. "We lost it almost every night," said Poncho. "Neil was yellin' and screamin'." Ralph was driven to the edge by Young's nit-picking. "You're up there onstage to have fun. I don't wanna think about 'On the sixteenth beat, I hear a little ta-ta on the snare.' "

Relations with Geffen Records had sunk to an all-time low as well. According to Elliot Roberts, not one of Young's albums for the label had sold over two hundred thousand copies. "It became a game where they enjoyed finding Neil being esoteric," said Niko Bolas, who recalls a visit from Geffen executive John Kalodner. "He comes on the remote truck and just starts laughing—'I can't wait to tell David he's using two digital machines and a remote truck, ha ha ha.' Y'know, like he caught Neil playin' with toys." Poncho recalls that Geffen representatives were banned from the backstage.

Young openly attacked the head of his label in the media. Geffen "missed his calling in life," he told *MuchMusic* in 1986. "He should've been a dictator in an art colony." The cover of the next album, *Life,* would show Young behind bars, the number of records he'd made for Geffen scratched out on the prison wall.

Briggs was brought in three weeks into the tour to pull an album out of the mess. "When they called me, they had already done fifteen shows and it was already in the shitter. Neil was an angry, angry guy—he was in a rage at everybody, and everybody hated him for it. It was a tour with a bunch of people that hated each other, hated what they were doing, and it showed. There was years of bad baggage never resolved goin' in. Neil took Crazy Horse and used 'em like sluts, like a component—and they went along with it."

Niko Bolas was summoned to engineer the live recordings. "I show up in Miami, and David Briggs drags me into this remote truck, and it's the biggest piece of shit you've ever seen—this fuckin' console duct-taped to the walls. It was just horrible. Nothing was working. I'd never done a remote date in my life, so I had no idea what was going on at all, and I look at Briggs and I say, 'What the fuck is happening?' And Briggs hands me a couple of grams of blow and said, 'Welcome to the road,' and walks away."

Sandy Mazzeo and Poncho Sampedro became running buddies. "Poncho and I decided not to join the tour—just show up for the gigs. We had a briefcase full of money, everything we needed. It was the very last of our wild days." They made friends with a couple of women appearing in a *Walt Disney on Ice* production apparently suffering from a lack of heterosexual males. "Their tour correlated to our tour, so we were roughly in the same towns at the same time. It was wild—I was dating Goofy, and Poncho was dating Minnie Mouse."

Things were so insane on the Horse tour bus that they got a visit from the boss, a story that illustrates just how estranged Young and his band had become. "Neil pulled us over in the middle of the night and came on the bus," said Poncho. "All the heavies were there—Briggs, Mazzeo, Niko, the band. Neil walked all the way through to the back. It was like the warden came. We were all just standin' there really quiet, all stoned out of our minds. Neil didn't talk to anybody—he walked through, walked on out— and Niko goes, 'Well, did we pass the inspection, *Dad*?' "

Things degenerated even further a few months later on the European leg of the tour. Some gigs were canceled due to poor sales, others rescheduled to smaller venues. "We were playin' good, then some radio guy told Neil they thought he was dead," said Poncho. "I guess Geffen didn't distribute the records over there." Briggs left the tour a day before it was over, and he and Neil would not work together again for another two and a half years. Young made a murky eight-millimeter documentary of the tour called "Muddy Track" that has yet to be released.

Life, culled mostly from performances on the American tour, was released at the end of June. It wasn't a terrible record but was like most of Young's eighties albums, something of a halfway case. The Horse blasted a hole in the roof on "Cryin' Eyes," a song dating back to Young's tenure with the Ducks, and the aptly titled "Prisoners of Rock 'n Roll" was a response to record-company meddling, its numbskull chorus a Crazy Horse reaffirmation: "That's why we don't wanna be good." But overdubs and sound effects couldn't create excitement where there was none. "Mideast Vacation" was too muddled to even get mad over and "Inca Queen" was a pale imitation of "Cortez."

For Briggs, the biggest disappointment was "When Your Lonely Heart Breaks." An aching ballad Young had written in the middle of a fever dream in Florida, it was "a monster song—it should've been the 'I Believe in You' of the eighties for Crazy Horse—so pure, so simple," said Briggs. "But they had no desire to make anything out of it, never played it good, never put anything special into it. It was a shame.

"I can see why the band hated Neil for the way they were bein' used and I can see why Neil hated them, 'cause they were playin' like monkeys. A marriage made in hell."

The Horse should never be forced to do covers of things they didn't originate. Crazy Horse has to be dealt with on its own terms, and I really didn't do them justice.

But you gotta dig my problem with Crazy Horse. As much as I loved the guys, I would do the song and lay it out and they wouldn't remember the arrangement. So I'd be halfway through delivering the master, and one guy would stop playing *or wouldn't know where to go. Y'know, that's really hard to deal with after you've done it over and over and over again.*

Listen to "Around the World." One of the reasons I split up with Crazy Horse is that song drags so fuckin' bad. It's so *behind, like thousands of people carrying this huge weight up a hill—will they make it? The beats are all way behind. I love that record, but it coulda been better, and it pissed me off.*

Europe was fuckin' terrible. Awful. *Billy was fuckin' out-there. Nobody knows what it's like to be the fuckin' leader of that band, okay? The guy who decides if they're gonna get advances or not, all that shit—as well as being the guy that's playin' the music. Seein' the guys in different lights all the time and lovin' 'em all all the time, but just tryin' to balance it all out. And knowin' that people weren't fuckin' comin' to the shows.*

That was a rough tour. We were really kinda passé. We were at the end of a low ebb before people started thinking we were cool again. We're goin', "What the fuck are we doin' this for?"

"Muddy Track" is not a documentary. I don't know what the fuck it is. It's got some great fights—me and Billy Talbot. And then there's a riot— we're playing "Down by the River" and they're gassing people in the audience, people are throwin' shit, they got machine guns 'n shit outside. Milan. Italians, man, they're wild.

I just wanted to make a tour movie, give me something to do while I was out there. So I bought these cameras—one for Briggs, one for me. Mine was named Otto. Otto was on the scene everywhere, running all the time. I recorded everything, so therefore everything happened and nobody gave a shit. A lotta times the camera's just been put down somewhere. Y'know—it's askew. *It's out-there. There's an attitude to "Muddy Track" that's definitely down.*

All those interviews I filmed, where all those guys were askin' me those stupid questions? That's my favorite part—y'know, you have some ridiculous scene, feedback, wild traveling music—then it would cut deadpan to some jerk askin' me if I'd made any records in the last eight years. What have I been doing?

"Muddy Track" is the most distorted thing you ever heard in your life. Completely distorted. Instrumentals, traveling music. Beginnings and endings of songs with feedback. No beat, nothing. Just Ralph going crazy, everybody banging.

It's very hard to get a distributor for something like that. I tell ya, it's hard to get a marketing scam together when they won't even put the movie out.

The summer of 1987 found Young wandering. For a while he reunited with Jack Nitzsche, who coproduced one track for *Life*—a ballad called "We Never Danced." Young wanted to use the demo vocal he'd recorded; Nitzsche made him do it over. "Neil said, 'You're the *only* guy who could make me do this.' He went back and used the first one anyway."

Nitzsche quickly grew impatient with the Horse's limitations. "They couldn't get their parts right and Neil was digitally using the same chorus again and again. I'd come up with an idea for a bass line like 'River Deep,' Billy couldn't remember it. Neil said, 'Well, y'know, you either use really good musicians and put that kind of record together . . . or you use Crazy Horse.' " Nitzsche fled.

Then, with Bryan Bell, Young began planning what some felt was a joke, a final assault on Geffen. "An album of crickets farting," said Poncho. But Bell maintained that it was for real: "That's when I thought he was close to something special. It wasn't the material for Crazy Horse, it wasn't the material for Geffen, it was totally different. The closest thing to it on the radio is called 'New Age.' "

It was just a concept thing. It was gonna be a strong record, I'm tellin' ya, but it was gonna be really really out. *Synthesizer and acoustic New Age instrumentals. The beat would come and go, sounds would come and go. Very much like what I ended up doing on* Arc, *only soft. The titles were all really descriptive, and they would just either be sung over and over again or whispered at certain points. And that was it. Sound concepts, industrial noise.*

And the cover would be me standing in a misty meadow wearing these baggy corduroy Dockers with a Ford Aerostar—sort of like a subtler On the Beach *kinda thing. And it was gonna be called "Meadow Dusk." Some guy with his Aerostar in the meadow, standing there. Probably woulda been put down by a lotta people. They woulda said what a piece of shit it was, how unmeaningful it was. Coulda been innaresting.*

But everything ground to a halt that fall. Bryan Bell remembers the moment. "Neil walked in one day and said, 'I've been dropped. Everything's on hold.' "

Elliot Roberts had been meeting with David Geffen and Mo Ostin to get Young back on Reprise. "It took a long time—because Mo was upset with us because we left him, and now I was asking him to send a check over to David for four million dollars and *then* make my deal. And I wanted a good deal. Mo eventually relented. Mo is a nice man, but he is also very tough. Mo didn't get to last with Frank [Sinatra] and the boys this long without being tough.

"I got David down a little, I got Mo up a little and we made a deal. We gave Geffen this greatest-hits album, *Lucky Thirteen,* for free. We got nothing for that. So we bought out of Geffen."

When Young got the phone call from Elliot on October 7, 1987, the moment was almost too intense. "I had just smoked this big bomber and almost had a heart attack," he told James Henke. "I was so happy, but I was too high to enjoy it." Thanks to David Geffen, Young would quit smoking pot for a while.

•   •   •

The first album back at Reprise felt very much like a continuation of the Geffen period—another genre record, this time rhythm and blues–based with horns. Black shades and fedora, crappy sports jacket, Silvertone amp, bad attitude—Neil Young was reborn as Shakey Deal.

It all started out on the road with the Horse back in August and September 1987, where, in between the acoustic and electric sets, Young performed a trio of songs with Poncho on organ and guitar tech Larry Cragg on baritone sax.

"I was the horn section," said Cragg. "All of a sudden Neil said, 'Okay, you're doin' it.' He didn't give me any warning. I didn't even have a part, so I wrote the part and practiced in one of the empty trucks 'cause I didn't want anybody to hear me." A little later, Cragg was offered big money to be Springsteen's guitar tech. "Neil flipped *out*—'So you're not gonna be a Bluenote anymore, huh?' " Cragg stayed put.

When the Horse tour was over, Young built up the horn section to six pieces—one trombone, three saxes, two trumpets (one too many for anything pertaining to rock and roll, quipped a *Village Voice* critic). The bulk of the players—Steve Lawrence, Claude Cailliet, John Fumo and Tom Bray—came from a group Talbot was friendly with, the East L.A. Horns. Young reserved room for one other rank amateur to keep Cragg company in the sax section: Ben Keith.

In addition to new material, Young resurrected some songs from his teen years. After a one-night reunion of the Squires in June 1987, Ken Koblun had mailed him lyric sheets for "Ain't It the Truth," "Hello Lonely Woman" and "Find Another Shoulder." Swaggering, stupid and lascivious, these songs would be among the most enjoyable of the period.

Christening his new band the Bluenotes (though he would be forced to drop the name after Harold Melvin and the Blue Notes sued), Young took the band out for a series of California club dates in October and November. For two minutes the band was managed by Mazzeo—"worst manager we ever had," said Poncho proudly.

Enlisting Niko Bolas as coproducer, Young recorded ten of the shows for a projected album. "It was my life's work to do a record with Keith Richards, and I had to turn him down because I'd told Neil yes. Then we go out on the road with Crazy Horse and it's terrible, it's falling apart, it's garbage.

"You always have to be accepting of the fact that they're creative geniuses. But they're not. Anything besides two and four is beyond their comprehension. When you actually get it out of two speakers and listen to it, they can't play their way out of a paper bag half the time. They were just completely fuckin' up, wastin' Neil's money, and it was pissin' me off."

The only Horse to bond with Bolas was Poncho, who saw him as "a real positive guy. He'll come right up to you and cut through the bullshit— 'Hey, you're playin' like shit. Find a new part or change strings or get another guitar. Do whatever you gotta do, but change it!' Billy and Ralph can't handle that. It crushed them."

One night after the tour, Bolas put together a tape of the performances Young had picked and played it for a bunch of guests at the ranch. "It sucked," said Poncho. Bolas made his move. "We were up at Fantasy. I said, 'Listen, man, am I really producing this record, or is this just a title you're giving me so I won't go somewhere else?' Neil said, 'A little of both.' I said, 'You need another rhythm section—this bike's broken. Afford yourself the luxury of riding a few other bikes.' "

Begrudgingly, Young agreed. "It was very difficult for Neil. He's loyal." Bolas sensed other factors at work. "Neil is an artist—he's insecure, too. He doesn't wanna play with really good musicians because they'll bust him. Because he's not an amazing musician—he's just an amazing *force*. So it's always safe with guys that are less than you—you just tell 'em what to do and you know they'll do it."

Billy Talbot was fired, replaced momentarily by Rockets guitarist George Whitsell. "It was kinda cold. They all told me I was in. We broke for Christmas and nobody ever called."

Next to fall was Ralph Molina. He and Young got into a heated argument over the use of the hi-hat on "This Note's for You." "That's when I noticed what a fucking tyrant Neil had become. When you have a real band, it's like a baseball team. You can make suggestions, it's okay—but not fuckin' act like you're God and these are your slaves."

Others maintain Ralph just couldn't handle the blues. Bolas said the last straw came when the drummer mangled the tempo for "I'm Goin' ": "I finally had to have the drum roadie show Ralph how to play a shuffle." Young would issue the recording as a B-side. Compared to the live version, it was a dud. "I think Neil put that out just in case people wanted to know why Ralph wasn't there," said Poncho. "Listen to that, you'll know why.

"That night Neil came to my room with Ben Keith and said, 'This started out as Crazy Horse, but tomorrow it might just be me and you.' " Poncho would thrive in Young's next couple of bands without Billy and Ralph. "I wasn't as timid. I've learned enough about music that when I hear something that's my fault, I *know* it's my fault. Billy had me convinced everything we did was cosmic or not cosmic."

Young continued to try out musicians for the band, but his reliance on the past drove Bolas crazy. "Neil wouldn't use any of the guys I recommended. He kept going with guys he knew." The Buffalo Springfield rhythm section—Bruce Palmer and Dewey Martin—bombed next. "*Super* terrible," said Poncho. "They couldn't play one song without stopping."

Finally Young relented, hiring the rhythm section from Joe Walsh's band, whom he had encountered at Farm Aid Three in September. Chad Cromwell pounded the skins like an animal; bassist Rick Rosas was, said Young, "a great player—and he's a crazy Indian, too. Rick brought an element of craziness back to the music that was missing." The lineup clicked immediately. "The whole LP was recorded in maybe two weeks," said Poncho. "I was like 'What's the drummer's name?' We were done by then."

This Note's for You was released by Reprise in April 1988. Young and Bolas, now christened "The Volume Dealers" for Niko's propensity for blowing up speakers, created a sound reminiscent of *Everybody's Rockin'*— a hyper-digital mess overdosed with crappy-sounding reverb. Live, the Bluenotes could sound as big as a building falling; on the record, they were flat and annoying. The material would turn out to be far from the best of the Bluenotes period. "Life in the City" recycled lyrics from "Depression Blues" to no improvement, while songs like "Hey, Hey" and "Sunny Inside" were vapid. The world yawned. "A Dud for You," warned the *Village Voice,* echoing the sentiments of many by criticizing Young's seemingly endless genre leaps: "What's next? Rap? The Nelson Riddle Orchestra?"

> *People write in magazines that I make different kinds of records just to draw attention to myself. If I ever saw the little wimps that were saying that, then I'm sure that I'd have to fucking kill them . . . There's many better ways to draw attention to myself. I could kill music critics if I wanted to . . . I could burn down Geffen Records . . . I could burn myself down in public if I wanted to—that would get a lot of attention, right?*
>
> *It's a very stupid thing to assume that I'm making different kinds of music to draw attention to myself. I made* Trans *because I wanted to, I did the Shocking Pinks and the Interna-*

tional Harvesters because I wanted to and I'm doing the Bluenotes because I want to, and if you don't like that shit, fine. What are these guys saying? That the cool thing is just to do the same thing over and over again and not be a weirdo? Because if Neil Young did *do the same thing over and over and over again and* wasn't *a weirdo, then these guys would be going, "Oh, Neil Young, he's so boring, coming out with the same thing over and over and over again." You can't win. You know, one week I'm a jerk and the next week I'm a genius, so how can I take these fucking music critics seriously? Let the people decide.*
—Interview with Tom Hibbert, 1988

As with *Everybody's Rockin'*, one song would emerge by way of video, but this time it would make a big noise: "This Note's for You."

Young had written the song on his wife's guitar, out on the road with the Horse the previous fall. "For months I heard this line—'I ain't singin' for Pepsi / I ain't singin' for Coke,' " he told Mark Rowland. "And I was riding along in the bus singing it to myself. Then when I thought of 'This note's for you,' I laughed my ass off. For miles and miles."

Corporate sponsorship had become rampant in rock and roll. The Rolling Stones were sponsored by Jōvan perfume, Eric Clapton and Steve Winwood were selling beer, Michael Jackson had been bought by Pepsi for $15 million. And Young, to the dismay of MTV and some of his peers, decided to poke fun at it.

The video was directed by Julien Temple, who would create Young's slickest videos in the years to come. Temple matched the tone of the lyric perfectly. The spot opens with Young somberly walking the streets, mimicking Clapton's beer commercial. As Young croons about having "the real thing," ghoulish celebrity look-alikes prance about, with Whitney Houston using a brew to out a fire on Michael Jackson's head. Then comes a devastating parody of Calvin Klein's obtuse perfume ads: "Neil Young's Concession for men." Finally a sardonic Young peers into the camera, exhibiting a beer can labeled SPONSORED BY NOBODY.

Pretty funny stuff, and it got a whole lot funnier in July when MTV standards and practices banned the spot—allegedly because it made references to brand names. The fact that Young's clip was an obvious parody made one wonder who was being protected: the audience or the advertisers. "We knew we were fucking with MTV's wallet, which is worse than fucking with their hang-ups with sex and violence," said Temple. "Their wallet is their most important asset."

"What does the M in MTV stand for: music or money?" wrote Young in an open letter, dissing MTV as "spineless jerks." The thrill of seeing MTV squirm on account of a forty-three-year-old rocker who wasn't on their playlist was rich. MTV provided "This Note's for You" the kind of publicity you can't buy. "I still can't believe that such a dumb little song helped resuscitate my career the way it did," Young later told Nick Kent.

On August 21, the channel broadcast a special twenty-minute report in an attempt to explain themselves—and finally showed the video. Host Kurt Loder interviewed a grumpy Neil Young—looking absurdly cool in all white with huge sunglasses, a Cirque du Soleil T-shirt and a cap from Pink's hot-dog stand.

"Your bosses or whatever, they really messed up," Young said, going on to explain why he was even present for the interview. "You're so big that if I don't come down here, not only might I not get this video on, I might not get the next video on. How am I supposed to know? The last thing I want to do is rub it in your face. . . . I just want to get my video on the air so people can see it—they can judge for themselves." Young declared MTV "should be called television music, not music television."

Crazily enough, "This Note's for You" would go on to win Music Video of the Year at the MTV music awards—although the sound feed mysteriously dropped when Young stepped up for his acceptance speech. In the long run, the victory would be meaningless, as MTV has remained almost completely Young-free.

•   •   •

Once again, Young's music came alive out on the road. The further Young strayed from his concepts about whatever genre he seemed to be trying to duplicate—whether it be blues, country or fifties rock and roll—the more the natural eccentricities emanating from his plain weird self cooked up something original. The Bluenotes really stirred his songwriting juices. Larry Cragg recalls that Young would "show us a song once—he didn't want to play it more than once—and we'd do it. That would be that."

Playing Old Black without a pick and paring his amp rig down to an old cheap Silvertone, Young used a spartan guitar attack—with the wall of horns serving as frantic exclamation points—to create a sound that was bombastic, lonesome and, during another small club tour in April, painfully loud. Young collectors cherish Bluenotes tapes, and a great audience tape from the Trocadero in Philadelphia from April 22, 1988, illustrates why: It captures the sound—and the songs—where the album failed.

The swaggering "Big Room" sports a tempo of sublime restraint, with lyrics describing a Vegas utopia: "Don't allow no cameras in the big room / It's too much for one lens to see." "I'm Goin' " portrays a bleak descent into depression: "Don't wanna change my mind, don't wanna reel it in / Don't wanna stop this slidin', honey, that's the shape I'm in."

"Don't Take Your Love Away from Me," the song Geffen refused to let him record in 1983, is a smoldering blues that finally gets the heavy attack it deserves. "Put your chips down, baby, empty your pockets too / When I make a promise, you can bet that it's true," wails Young, the wall of horns blasting away behind him. Despite its protestations of undying love, the song still manages to convey something sinister about its creator.

Throughout this material, Young plays utterly vicious guitar. In "Big Room," he lets rip with tones so piercing they could split a sequoia. The gut-wrenching "Bad News" is resurrected from the dreaded 1974 Hawaii period, and with its whispers of vengeance not to mention its big but sad-beyond-words sound, the song is a Sergio Leone Western in miniature. Fear and regret lurk beneath the hero's skin, but he's resigned to his fate: "A prizefighter can't be sad."*

---

* Young pointed out that different lyrics exist for the original 1974 version of "Bad News." It would be an interesting undertaking to compile the various twists and turns of Neil Young songs (some changing over a period of years). The melodies of unreleased songs "There Goes My Babe" and "One More Sign" end up in the second half of the instrumental "Falcon Lake" (the first part of which became "Here We Are in the Years"). The unreleased Springfield-era track "Slowly Burning" begat the unreleased "Letter from Nam," which transmuted into 1987's "Long Walk Home"; the unreleased "Casting Me Away from You" mutated into 1968's "The Emperor of Wyoming" and the unreleased Harvesters number "Leavin' the Top 40 Behind." Lyric changes within the same song aren't as common as with Dylan, but there are those as well, one example being a 1989 recording of "Fuckin' Up" (with the band Young used on *Saturday Night Live* September 30 of that year), which sports a great line not present in the released 1990 performance: "Big success shot full of holes."

Young murmurs the song's lyrics like they're a death sentence. The song evokes an emotion rare in the catalog of Neil Young—sheer desperation.

·   ·   ·

In August and September 1988, Young and the Bluenotes hit the bigger venues and, as Poncho said, something was lost in the process. "The small clubs were a lot of fun. We got spread out onstage in the sheds and couldn't hear each other. Neil's got to realize he's a feel musician, not a chops musician—he's at his best when the band's close together."

I attended a show in Jones Beach, New York, on August 27. Although the 1984 Catalyst Crazy Horse shows never left my mind, I figured Neil Young might've hung up his gloves. But tonight was a different story, and there were three new songs that you didn't need a genre-decoder ring to unscramble: "Days That Used to Be," "Ordinary People" and "60 to 0."

A wistful acoustic number to the tune of Dylan's "My Back Pages," "Days That Used to Be" was briefly called "Letter to Bob." Imagine sixties rock aristocracy as a baseball team and the team's all dead except for Young and Dylan. Ancient promoters in wheelchairs fight over broken bongs and ripped black-light posters that litter the field. A bored hot-dog vendor wanders the empty stands, and the lights are about to go off for the last time. Bob's hobbling off the field with his walker, but the ever cantankerous Young isn't quite ready to call it quits: "I wish that I could be with one whose thoughts still run free / 'Cause we never used to hit dead-ends in the days that used to be."

Easily the most extreme Bluenotes song, "Ordinary People" is, depending on who you talk to, either one of Young's most impassioned unreleased songs or a one-legged turkey. This long, twisted epic is a loopy paean to gunfights, hot rods, drug lords, arms dealers, prizefighters, homeless factory workers and out-of-work fashion models—climaxing at a train yard in what must be a heavenly vision for Young—the "ordinary people" ("some are saints and some are jerks") nursing a wounded locomotive back to life. "I got faith in the regular kind," shouts Young as the song sinks into a miasma of guitar and horn abuse. It's as unsubtle and heavy-handed as "Nothing Is Perfect," but you certainly can't ignore it.*

_____

*Briggs despised the song. When Joel Bernstein played him a live version chosen for inclusion on the Archives, he ranted and raved: "Neil knows *nothing* about ordinary people."

"60 to 0," aka "Crime in the City," is a bullet to the head. That night at Jones Beach, after whipping through a perfunctory "After the Gold Rush" to the requisite howls from the crowd, Young muttered, "That was then," strapped on Old Black and, with only Rick Rosas on bass and Chad Cromwell on drums, tore through the new number with the force of a freight train. Some of the best rock Young made in the eighties was angry—this number, particularly vitriolic. One of the bitterest, bleakest assemblages Young has ever concocted, "60 to 0" is unrelentingly pessimistic: Life in the eighties amounts to prison wardens shooting helpless animals for a thrill, cops on the take from drug-dealing ten-year-olds.

But the voice turns confessional, telling us how Young keeps "gettin' younger / My life's been funny that way." He talked back to his parents and got tossed out of Bible school for giving the preacher the finger, but even this rebel must fall. Now he's a fireman, doomed to prison for an unnamed offense. "Wish I never put the hose down," shrieks Young. "Wish I never got old." A painfully honest admission, and he meant it that night. Young wanged away on Old Black, interspersing fat, ugly riffs with short blasts of lyrical beauty unheard since '76.

"60 to 0" would mutate from concert to concert, acoustic to electric, with Young sometimes singing as little as four verses and, in marathon acoustic performances during the Midwest leg of the tour, as many as eleven. But none I've heard match the intensity of the seven-minute Jones Beach electric version (an acoustic take was released on *Freedom,* complete with unswinging sax. I think the song falls flat when lingered over as opposed to hurled in your face).

But this "60 to 0" was an assault in the best sense of the word: Young pummeling you with a string of nightmare pictures, hammering them into your brain with screaming guitar. This was the most exciting electric music Young made in the eighties, and it would turn out to be only the beginning of the attack.

• • •

Throughout the Bluenotes period, Young dabbled around with Crosby, Stills and Nash, which resulted in *American Dream,* the first studio album from CSNY since 1970's *Déjà Vu.* The two factions had endured a somewhat stormy relationship in the press, with Young bashing them (and himself) during promotions for *Trans*. "Neil Young from the sixties and early seventies is like Perry Como," Young told David Gans. "If I was still taking that seriously, I'd be where Crosby, Stills and Nash are today." CSN would respond in kind, although one rebuttal was rather obtuse—the cover of 1990's *Live It Up,* depicting four hot dogs on sticks flying through space, one of the weiners symbolically broken. Nash actually admitted to Joel Bernstein that it all symbolized Young and his nefarious interactions with the group.

In the late seventies and early eighties, CSN had continued to record in various permutations with varying degrees of success, but they'd been plagued by personal problems, among them the fact that David Crosby was now a freebasing train wreck. The former prince of L.A. counterculture was now more at home on wanted posters. "Everyone always envied him—it was always like 'David, does he have his shit together or what?' " recalled Elliot Roberts. "We all thought that David was so on top of what drugs did for him creatively, and that's why it was all so incredible when David became an addict."

On March 28, 1982, Crosby had a "seizure from toxic saturation," nodding out en route to an antinukes benefit and crashing his car into a center divider on the San Diego Freeway. When the police arrived, they found cocaine, a freebase pipe and butane torch, plus a loaded .45. According to *The Washington Post,* when asked why he was carrying a loaded gun, Crosby said simply, "John Lennon."

This was only the beginning of his troubles with the law. A few weeks later in Dallas, Crosby—appearing solo at a fleabag nightclub called Cardi's—was busted again when officers burst in and found him sucking on his base pipe. On and on it went. Arrests, rehab, escape from rehab, interventions. Nothing worked.

Young made attempts to help in his own way. In January 1983, right after Crosby had fled a detox that Graham Nash had sworn to authorities in Texas that David would complete, a meeting took place at Young's ranch. "Neil had me and Graham bring David down to have dinner with him," said Joel Bernstein, who recalls that Crosby was in ghastly condition, wearing a wool cap and heavy makeup over his open sores. Of the whole parade of concerned friends and loved ones Crosby faced, Bernstein said it was Young who terrified him the most. "David was just sweating bullets the whole way. I think he smoked crack on the way down while I was driving."

Young offered Crosby a house on the ranch where he could stay under medical supervision until he was better. Crosby declined. A short while later, Young tried to talk to him again. "Neil decided to come and see him—which never happens," said Bernstein. "Never. I go an hour ahead of time—David was with his mistress. I said, 'Well, Neil is at your house, he wants to talk to you.' It was totally like the kid and the principal—David goes and freebases for forty-five minutes, gets totally fucked up so he can face Neil, because he knows he's been a bad boy."

Crosby wept on the drive over. Bernstein: "David starts whining, 'It's always, "David, you're the bad boy, David, you're the one who's keeping CSNY from being together." You guys just don't understand.' I heard this so much by this point, finally I'm so fucking pissed off, I say, 'David, what would *you* have us do?' He said, 'Just forget about me, man. I've been in and out of seven hospitals—none of them have helped. I'm gonna keep doin' this, and there's nothin' you guys can do to stop me. Just forget about me.' " Since Crosby had sprained his ankle, Joel practically had to carry him inside.

Bernstein waited outside while Young and Crosby talked. Then Young emerged. As Bernstein recalls, "Neil just said, 'We're outta here. He just doesn't get it.' "

Crosby grew emotional recalling Young's attempts to help. "He really did care about me when I went down the tubes. I said no. Stupid me . . . it was one of the dumbest things I ever did. But that's what kind of friend he is. I'll never forget that. I think he's an exemplary human being, if you want to know the truth. Neil's a real special cat." Amazingly, after many more arrests and a stint in jail where he kicked both heroin and cocaine cold turkey in solitary confinement, David Crosby somehow survived. Nineteen eighty-six saw a much ballyhooed performance by CSNY at the Bridge School concert in October. Young had promised to record again with the trio if Crosby straightened out, and he made good on the offer, although it was delayed by David Geffen, who would gain a lot of unwanted press when reporter Fredric Dannen overheard him tangling telephonically with Ahmet Ertegun over the deal, demanding 50 percent of the take for Young's services: "Crosby, Stills and Nash are *fat old farts*. The only one with any *talent* is Neil Young!"

CSN wanted their longtime associate Stanley Johnson to engineer the sessions, but, said Niko Bolas, "Neil said he wouldn't do the record without me. We did it on his turf, with his guys, in his style." Once again, CSN came to Y. The results were disastrous. Said Bolas, "There were flashes of youth—and realizing that it's over."

Despite being clean and sober, Crosby—who would later be diagnosed with hepatitis C, necessitating a liver transplant—wasn't in the best physical shape. "Crosby spent the whole time lying on a couch in front of the console, struggling to get up to sing his vocals," said Bernstein. "He was like this beached whale. Finally, Neil ordered the couch removed, but apparently Crosby wigged and the couch was reinstated."

Stills was no longer the driving force of the trio, musically or otherwise. "Graham is the real workaholic—first one to get there, last to leave," said Bolas. "He stayed with me finishing the production until the last CD was pressed."

When I spoke to Crosby and Nash in 1990, disappointments lingered over the project. "Neil needs the three of us like a stag needs a hat rack. He needs even less the competitive thing from Stills," said Crosby. "There were moments of intensely good music on Neil's songs, Graham's songs, maybe mine. But Stephen showed up expecting his usual larger-than-everybody-else's portion of the record and didn't have any songs—at least none that I thought were worth a damn."

Nash was equally blunt on the subject of Stephen Stills. "I have seen cocaine totally ruin his songwriting . . . I personally don't think he's written a great song for years," he said. "I think unless he totally straightens himself out that his life is going to remain in this really sad state of affairs. I love him dearly—I'll help him any way I can.

"I don't think he's happy with himself, I don't think he's happy, period. I think in many ways, he's clinically insane. I think if he hadn't been Stephen Stills, he would've been put away years ago."

Most everybody I talked to complained about Stephen's lunacy. Not

Young. "People don't realize how easy it is to hurt him," he told Laura Gross. "He's a tormented artist, he's like a lightbulb without any glass . . . a filament."

I just know I really like Stephen as a person. As a human being, there's a lot there. Much more than the other guys have any idea of. They don't even see it.

The thing is, when Stephen was workin' with me, he drove me nuts and I drove him nuts, but I still brought out the sensitive side in his music. Because I never once lost sight of the fact that he was my brother. Those guys don't have that, and that makes Stephen very, very uncomfortable and extremely inhibited. In my opinion, they basically just wore him down and destroyed the very thing that made CSN great—which was Stills.

That's how it is from my eyes. And I wasn't there, and they could say I'm totally wrong, but that's how I feel about it. I don't care how long they've been together, doesn't make any difference—because I was there at the beginning. I know where he's coming from. That's the difference.

Released by Atlantic at the end of 1988, *American Dream* is a prime contender for the most wretched album Neil Young has ever lent his name to. The Volume Dealers' production is awful, a digital nightmare completely ill suited to the folk-pop quartet.

"It sounds completely artificial," said Bernstein. "They were moving things digitally and bending notes in the Synclavier. The harmonies on 'This Old House' were unbelievably bland—it reminded me of Mitch Miller." Besides cowriting a couple of forgettable tunes with Stills, Young contributed three songs: "This Old House," "Name of Love" and "American Dream." The title cut, a portrait of a fallen politician, seemed painfully relevant: "Don't know where things went wrong / Might have been when you were young and strong."

Julien Temple directed a video for the song that featured the quartet playing roles he saw as wickedly appropriate. "I liked the idea of seeing David Crosby as a Larry Flynt guy in a wheelchair, Stills as a coked-out Oliver North and Nash as Gary Hart." Temple cast Young in dual roles—a tabloid reporter and a teased-hair, leather-clad heavy-metal rocker who scares Nash to death.

After the *American Dream* debacle, Young moved on to New York City in December for some of the wildest rock of his life, and for the first time in the eighties he would capture it on tape in a recording studio.

•   •   •

When Young returned to the studio, it was as part of a trio, with Bluenotes Rick Rosas and Chad Cromwell on bass and drums. Young had compiled a double live set of Bluenotes recordings, but he squashed it. "He thought it sounded too good," said an exasperated Niko Bolas. "That's what he told me—*too good.*" Poncho recalls that while they were mixing at A&M, the album got nicknamed "This Shit Don't Sell." "Everybody started calling it that, and the joke got overplayed. I guess Neil started thinkin', 'Why am I doin' an LP of shit that no one's gonna buy?' "

Young jettisoned the horn section. "They all got burned," said Bolas. "They planned their life around this band that we knew was just another one of Neil's toys. That's what you have to remember: You're just one of the things he toys with during the day, like a train set. 'Next!' Nothing personal, Neil just does what he has to do. Period."

Poncho felt he might've been to blame for the change in direction. One night on the road, he'd invited Young over to his room to watch the Who's *The Kids Are Alright* on cable. Neil sat watching the band bash away, entranced. "Neil said, 'That's cool—I'd like to do that.' A few weeks later he took off to record with Chad and Rick, usin' all the big Marshall amps."

Young and the Restless (their new name) recorded at the Hit Factory, a New York City studio in the heart of Times Square. "The sessions went all night long," said tech Anthony Aquilato. "It was very intense."

It was also some of the crudest, angriest music Young had ever made. "That record came about as a direct result of doing CSNY," said Bolas. "Neil was so pissed off at having to do a record that he didn't want to do— with pretty songs that he fuckin' hated—that he just retaliated."

Young's wacko equipment setup gave the crew big headaches. "Neil was using a PA in the room—he had a huge fuckin' monitor system that was giving him his vocal back, which normally you don't do when you're making a record 'cause you want some sort of isolation," said Aquilato. "He wanted to feel the vocal coming back loud."

Young coaxed brutal new sounds out of Old Black. "This is when Neil was getting into these strange combinations of amps," said Larry Cragg. "Why? To get the wildest, most heavy rock sound you ever heard. But unlike just about anybody else, Neil does it without using stomp boxes—he does it with real amps." Young took the signal from his battered old Deluxe and fed it through a Marshall stack. The result was, said Cragg, "The biggest, most distorted sound you ever heard. It was *loud* in there. Excruciatingly loud." How loud was it? "Niko blew up a pair of huge Uri monitors—that's how loud," said Aquilato. "I remember literally not being able to sit in the control room. I couldn't handle it."

For Cragg, it was a technical nightmare. The masses of wiring acted as antennae in the middle of New York City, where there were plenty of stations to pick up. "Amps don't like to be connected together sometimes, so it was like ground-loop hell. I was doing crazy things to get this crazy, out-of-control rig quiet." Young wasn't used to waiting, so the record starts off with an ugly hum and a frantic Cragg yelling he hasn't quite fixed the problem. Neil says, "Yeah, that sounds *good,* though," as he plunges into the cyclone of "Cocaine Eyes." Bolas said this violent declaration was provoked by the poor showing of Stills on *American Dream*: "Cocaine eyes won't hide your face / It's no surprise you lose the race again / My old friend."

"Heavy Love" has an attitude worthy of Bo Diddley and ends with Young barely able to scream the last few words. A bitter cover of the Brill Building standard "On Broadway" collapses after six punishing minutes into a funny, tasteless plea for crack.

"Eldorado"—the title cut (and only acoustic number)—was a song Young had reworked lyrically and musically from the Crazy Horse "Garage" tour, and it became another eighties travelogue of greed, drugs and murder. One track hit Niko particularly hard. "I went to the hotel and Neil said, 'I gotta play you somethin'—Roy Orbison meets heavy metal.'" The song was "Don't Cry," about a relationship of Niko's that had crumbled en route to the altar. "I couldn't mix that song," he said. "I had a lot of trouble getting through that, 'cause I really loved the chick it was about. It fucked me up . . . I don't like to listen to it."

"Don't Cry" was the session's centerpiece. The doomy clanking of a bell signals the description of a relationship just demolished. The offender is going to help her pack, walk her to her car—nice thought, but Young spits out the words with all the warmth of a stalker. After the second verse, a piercing shriek hits a wall of noise that's more chaos than guitar solo. Forget the pretty, ringing tones of the past. This is the bottom—pure electric sludge. When it finally ends, Young's voice slithers out of the feedback for one last howl: "Don't cry, my sweet girl . . . you won't really be alone." Maybe she'd rather be.

In the winter of 1988, Young and the Restless hit the road, blasting through Missouri, Oklahoma, Texas and Louisiana, then up through the Northwest. I loaned fan Dave McFarlin a tape recorder to capture a couple of the shows, and he and a buddy drove around-the-clock to catch up with Young. They would be rewarded with one of the wildest gigs of Young's career, at the Bronco Bowl in Dallas, Texas.

The Bronco Bowl was an "old relic of a place," said McFarlin. "It was just a hole—an actual bowling alley, with an archery range and a huge parking lot with grass growin' through the asphalt. Neil's name was lit up on a sign under a big bowling pin. I loved the place." Pro wrestling had been there the night before.

At first, McFarlin was disappointed by a lackluster acoustic set. "Young played all these slow, old songs—mainly the hits, 'Sugar Mountain,' 'Heart of Gold'—he sounded like he was about to fall over. He looked like the oldest man in the world." But when Young came back out for the electric set, dressed in a JUST SAY NO T-shirt, he was "completely different. He looked twenty years younger."

The band change had been so hasty that McFarlin had been expecting the Bluenotes, and he was flabbergasted by the sonic abuse that ensued. "Young just thrashed around the stage, screamin'—he was goin' like a nut." Young's mangling of "On Broadway" shook the building to the rafters. "He stood with his back to the amps, hit that low note, got that vibration going and let the feedback vibrate him. It was insane." Young got so carried away during one number that he "jumped up in the air and landed on his ass in a sitting position—Indian-style, like a pretzel. I don't know how he didn't break his back."

It was total mayhem, and McFarlin was in heaven. Glued in front of

Shakey's amp the next night in Houston, he said it was the loudest show he's ever heard Young play. "He split my brain open. His guitar was just deafening. You could actually SEE the sound waves."

In April and May, Young took the band—now christened the Lost Dogs—to Australia, New Zealand and Japan. There was a new song, "No More," one of Young's most evocative statements on addiction, which started with the tough opening couplet: "Livin' on the edge of night / You know the sun won't go down slow." To enhance the musical mayhem, there was a new stage show featuring crunching loops of between-song industrial noise not to mention hard hats for the roadies. Mazzeo contributed another psychedelic slide presentation, giving the crew heart attacks when he and a buddy manned the lights one night in Darwin and managed to keep Young in darkness for most of the show.

Such extreme rock and roll brought out the maniac in Young. The byzantine configuration of amps and their settings changed between each number—and sometimes during a song. "It would be almost impossible for me to get everything replugged and repatched and not have a ground hum," said Larry Cragg. Young went ballistic during a show in Sydney over a sound fuckup. "Neil said, 'Well, we'll just wait until Larry gets his shit together.' He was being a total asshole to me, 'cause I was his only link to the outside world. He was getting really, really violent." In his fury, Young kicked over a pile of amps. "The stack of Marshalls landed right on me—and he *knew* it was landin' on me—so I didn't appreciate that at all. After the show he was all apologetic, but the crazy man on stage really gets outta control."

•   •   •

In the meantime, Young tinkered with the Hit Factory recordings. Bolas had mixed the sessions, but Young hated the mixes and redid them himself ("Neil just bird-dogs every phase of the fuckin' gig," said Bolas). An album of Hit Factory/ranch sessions called "Times Square" was turned in to Reprise. "I don't think they really liked the record at all," said Bolas. "When we played it for them, they kinda stared at the ceiling."

Young pulled the record, releasing five of the Hit Factory cuts in April 1989 as an EP called *Eldorado* instead. The cover was a sad-looking piece of assemblage art by Young's old Topanga friend George Herms, and for the first time since *Rust,* the title was scrawled in Young's own handwriting. Finally Young had made a recording that matched the intensity of his live performances. But it was impossible to find the fucking thing—Young released it only in a limited-edition to coincide with the overseas tour. It was a strange message: "I'm back, but you've gotta find me."

Niko Bolas recalls playing the album for Graham Nash. "There were vile juices flowin' from Graham's mouth when he heard that record. He turned it off and said, 'I absolutely hate this record.' He didn't just not like it, he *hated* it. I've never seen anybody with more disgust in their eyes. . . . I think Neil did that whole album just for that playback. I told him once how much Graham hated it, and he was like, 'Fine.' He was done. It did what it was supposed to do."

But Young maintained that there was a much more personal reason for such an angry record—he was exorcising the pain he felt over what had happened to his son in the patterning program years before.

Some of the guitar playing on Eldorado *. . . there's a lot of violence and a lot of anger inside me for things that have happened. Injustices.*

I'm angry about what happened to Ben. I really mean that. It pisses me off. I don't understand why that had to happen.

Seeing him try so hard to crawl and not be able to, but wanting *so badly to do it—just because we wanted him to, y'know. You talk about a* struggle. *People can struggle anywhere, but I have seen a real struggle, and I'm not* impressed *with superficial struggling, someone who's trying to make something more than it is. And people do it all the time, who am I to judge . . . I just don't have much patience. It never affects the way I am with anybody, but inside myself I make my own judgments.*

·   ·   ·

Bluenotes, Everybody's Rockin', Trans, Old Ways 1, Old Ways 2, *on and on, all the stuff I did in the eighties—there's all these things happening. Meanwhile, there's another layer . . . and that's* Eldorado. *That's the other side. When I did those songs, I guess that was my true self—or something. But I didn't want to do anything like that . . . for a long time.*

I put that out so people would know that I was still here. There's something about the way things have gone for me—something about it that made me want to put that out and make sure my handwriting was on it, pick the artwork, do everything. And then I'm sick—I only made five thousand. I said, "That's all. That's it."

I tell ya why I made that record. First of all, there was a record called "Times Square." I decided that if I put this record out, people were so used to me doing styles that they might think that I was just doing a style. And I knew that there was something special about that record. But I think it was a paranoid kind of a thing that I didn't want to take the abuse for doing this, so what I did was take all the sweetness out of it, made it more abusive than it already is—and put it out of reach. So there it is. That's it. That's the weird workings of my mind. It's self-defeating, but still makes its point in some weird way. I was reemerging from myself . . . to make that change, it had to be done in a special way.

Doing "Don't Cry" and "Heavy Love," every night in Australia and Japan, I blew myself out. Those songs are incredibly intense. I felt the effects. I damaged my throat doing those songs. See, people don't realize how fuckin' physical my music is. Every fuckin' note is my last as far as I'm concerned, so it better be fuckin' good. It better be there. So that takes a lot out of ya. And there's no way to breathe deep and sing "Heavy Love." You can't do that. Have "good technique"—get the fuckin' technique out. Get rid of it.

Those shows were very loud. That's when I was using Marshalls. I would cut in with the octave divider, the whole thing would just go to shit . . . There's a breakdown in the middle of "Heavy Love" where everything just starts distorting and getting more mangled-sounding . . . When I wanted the big loud explosion, we had to go there—turn everything up. It was incredible. I had a thing where I could change from one amp to another—where I could play along real quiet and then just hit one button and it was the loudest fuckin' thing you ever heard. On "Don't Cry," that just kicked in, like, two more amps at full volume, all on one note. It was just big and bad.

•   •   •

The reason I did the acoustic tour next is because it was a way for me to go out, play and get in touch with myself. See, I got in touch with my electric self out there with the Lost Dogs, but that's only half of it. In the beginning, when I started playing acoustic, I was as intense with my acoustic as I was with my electric guitar, so I needed to get back to that point. I was rebuilding myself, and to do that I had to strip away everything. I wanted to feel myself playing without any distractions. Feel *it.*

I love to play, and that's what got me back, okay? That was the only way I could do it. At first, in the eighties, I wasn't even going out and playing—I was just putting out records. Then I started going out on the road and putting out music—out of myself, live. Not so much on records, but live.

And I started finding myself. I had to keep playing and playing and playing *and not take a break to get* back. *I felt disconnected—I felt it, too. When I played my music, I went, "What's going on? Where am I? Where is it?"*

Now that Young had taken his electric music to a new extreme, he immediately swung just as far in the other direction, embarking on two solo acoustic tours of America in June, August and September 1989.

Outfitted with a wireless microphone, Young prowled the bare stage alone (outside of a couple of numbers where Poncho Sampedro and Ben Keith joined him). Young dedicated one song to the Chinese student who had captured the imagination of the world as he stood before a phalanx of tanks in Tiananmen Square, flowers in his outstretched hands. "It's an old song—a song that should be forgotten, " muttered Young, launching into the doom chords of "Ohio." The starkness of the presentation—and the bleakness of his newer material—made an impact on the critics. "Loss of innocence can hurt, but few songwriters have taken it harder than Neil Young," wrote Jon Pareles in *The New York Times*. "His songs contrast an Edenic rural past with a brutal, corrupt present. . . . He offered little hope beyond the stubborn refusal to give up."

·　　·　　·

One new song in particular made an impression. Poncho remembers how it came into being. Sitting around with Young on the road one day, Poncho gazed at a newspaper plastered with pictures of the Ayatollah Khomeini's body being carried to his grave. Frenzied mourners surrounded the corpse, some burning American flags.

"I was goin', 'This is unreal, all these people just hate us.' We were talking about playing Europe, and I said, 'Whatever we do, we shouldn't go near the Mideast. It's probably better to keep rockin' in the free world.' Neil goes, 'That's pretty cool—is that a song you're working on?' 'No.' He said, 'Well, man, if you don't use it, I will.' " (The line was "such a cliché . . . I knew I had to use it," Young would tell *MuchMusic*.)

A few days later Young had the song down and was running through it on the bus with Poncho. "He said, 'Don't tell the guys—we'll do it tonight. We'll initiate 'em.' We used to do that to Crazy Horse all the time—pull a song out of a hat." That night, February 21, 1989, at the Paramount Theatre in Seattle, Young and the Restless fumbled through the very first performance of "Rockin' in the Free World."

The song was a knockout, although the victim was a matter of perspective. George Bush, drug-addicted mothers, "Styrofoam garbage for the ozone layer." "Don't feel like Satan, but I am to them / So I try to forget it any way I can": Talk about a line loaded with meaning. Was Young talking about America's presence in the Middle East, or himself and the wake of people he'd left behind? On a record like *Tonight's the Night,* Young managed to convey many different and conflicting feelings in the space of an album; now he had distilled it down to just one song, and the ambiguity was exhilarating.

"I have so many opinions that come out during my music that it's a battle for me," Young told *MuchMusic*. "I try not to be preachy about what I'm sayin'. That's a real danger, because as soon as you start preaching, then nobody wants to hear ya, 'cause you're a jerk . . . I've slipped into that position many times and it's a danger of doing what I do . . . I just want to be a reflection of what's going on. Let people make up their own minds."

What about a song like "Rockin' in the Free World," which really socked it home at the right time in this country, was it a celebration or an indictment?

"Well, kinda both, *you know?" Young said. "Depends on*

how you look at it . . . it's all there together. That's the picture
that I saw. Is it a celebration or an indictment? Or is it ironic?
People can sing it like an anthem, and yet, if you listen to the
words, it's like, 'What the fuck?' You know?"
    But that's the question!
    "That's it," barks Young, laughing. "That is the question. You
asking the question means you got *the song."*
                    —Interview with Dean Kuipers, 1995

Having jettisoned "Times Square," Young continued to record songs for what would become his next album.

He recorded a bunch of material during this period, much of it as yet unreleased, including a new version of "Born to Run"; a great little rocker with Sampedro on mandolin called "Your Love Again"; and "Diggin' My Bad Self," a jazzbo scat exercise that has to be heard to be believed. Once the album was completed, Young waffled on the title. Finally, at the last minute of the mastering, he decided. As Poncho recalls, "Just before we went out the door Neil said, 'Y'know what, man? Put down *Freedom.*' "

Freedom was released in October 1989, from sessions stretching back over the previous few years. Some of the songwriting dated back to the mid-seventies. Bookended à la *Rust* with acoustic and electric versions of "Rockin' in the Free World," *Freedom* was a collection of songs, not a genre concept record. "I just wanted to make a Neil Young album per se," the ever self-aware Young told *Rolling Stone.* "Something that was just me, where there was no persona, no image, no distinctive character."

The album overflowed in terms of writing, with hardly a weak cut. But sonically it felt like Young had acquiesced a little too much; it sometimes sounds hopelessly square. One of the older songs, "Too Far Gone," was abysmal compared to the original unreleased recording, and an abbreviated acoustic version of "60 to 0 (Crime in the City)" featured turgid jazzy touches and omitted some of the best verses.

Young also included two cuts from *Eldorado,* and on one of them he committed a sin that was unconscionable as far as fans like Dave McFarlin were concerned. Pressured by both Bolas and Sampedro, Young edited down some of the more maniacal guitar work.

"It was all that fuckin' noisy, outta-tune shit," said Bolas. "That's one of the only times Neil listened to me. I had him clean up the guitar so it'll stay in the groove. If you're a Neil Young fanatic and you like explosions and all that out-of-tune bullshit, great. But if you're just some kid playin' air guitar you gotta have something to play to, not some 'what the hell is this and when is it gonna be over.' "

• • •

Surprisingly, the definitive version of "Rockin' in the Free World" came via the idiot box. Television has occasionally been the site for some explosive moments in popular music: Elvis's early appearances and his 1968 special. Jerry Lee Lewis on *The Steve Allen Show,* his country comeback appearance on *Ed Sullivan.* Hendrix on the *Lulu* show. Al Green on *Soul!* Ike and Tina Turner on anything. Dylan crooning a mournful but still defiant "Restless Farewell" to Frank Sinatra on an otherwise ludicrous 1995 tribute.

As rock has gotten bigger and slicker, moments like these have gotten increasingly harder to find, but brief blips sometimes manage to raise dust on the vast, bland wasteland. On September 30, 1989, during an otherwise forgettable *Saturday Night Live,* Neil Young gave what is easily his greatest electric live broadcast performance in front of that voracious TV eye. "Most people stay on the other side of the glass," said Mazzeo. "Neil came right through."

It almost didn't happen. Originally the band was supposed to be Rick Rosas, Chad Cromwell and Poncho Sampedro. But Cromwell was touring Japan with Jackson Browne. In order to salvage the gig, Niko Bolas convinced Neil to go with a new rhythm section—drummer Steve Jordan and bassist Charley Drayton. Jordan had played on *Landing on Water,* and the two Afro-American rockers had made a name for themselves on Keith Richards' solo projects. "Producing Neil Young is, you pick the cast of characters and hope he gets off on it," said Bolas, and this time he hit the jackpot. The lineup of Jordan and Drayton, plus Poncho (which Young drolly christened YCS&P for Young, Charley, Steve and Poncho), would be equal to any Young has ever encountered.

The plan was to record some new material at the Hit Factory, then head over to *Saturday Night Live.* Bolas was not to produce the session, merely engineer, for this marked the return of Mr. Briggs, but tensions surfaced early on. When Briggs and Bolas had last met during the recording of *Life,* Niko had been the new kid on the block. Now he'd coproduced Young's last two albums. "Briggs was already on edge," said Poncho. "He couldn't tell Niko what to do." In addition, both Bolas and Sampedro were now clean and sober and proud of it. One night Bolas tried to give Briggs some Alcoholics Anonymous literature. He tossed it in the trash.

The band managed to record a couple of tracks, most notably a power-house version of a new song entitled "Fuckin' Up." But the chemistry wasn't there. "Everybody had a fuckin' weird attitude, and we were lucky to get what we got," said a glum Bolas. "It just wasn't supposed to happen, I guess. It was too good for Neil. Too correct."

And yet it would all come together days later with millions of people watching. Jordan, well aware of television's limitations from years of play-ing in David Letterman's house band, picked his weapons carefully. "We had a stacked deck, man. I picked the biggest drums, the biggest cymbals I could find—I'd been workin' TV long enough to know that if I didn't have cymbals that big, nobody would hear 'em." The warm-up was so punishing that Jordan had to change out of his leather duds into something looser, which he took as a good omen. "I almost couldn't get through the dress re-hearsal," he said.

Showtime was serious business from the first note. Introduced by celebrity big shot Bruce Willis, Young didn't even look up to acknowledge the camera. Against a backdrop of rugs and antiques, Young—dressed in a leather jacket, sneakers, decomposing jeans that were more patches than pants and, most appropriately, a black Elvis T-shirt—resembled a brainsick Rip Van Winkle. His fuzzy mange of hair had now receded so far that his forehead looked like a landing strip, beneath which lurked seen-it-all eyes whose thousand-yard stare was more foreboding than ever. The twisted, disapproving face spoke of some terrible journeys. This was not the feral *Harvest*-era innocent who had made such an indelible imprint on the American psyche so many years before; this was a survivor—older, harder, but with craggy spirit intact. He looked, forgive the word, young.

Poncho oozed a particularly menacing vibe, all pumped up and greased back, while Drayton, in flashy leathers and ripped jeans, tumbleweed hair obscuring his sullen face, slowly lumbered around like a prehistoric mutant marking territory. Jordan pounded the drums with the desperation of a man about to be buried alive. Halfway through the performance, Young flashed a look at his little collection of creatures, and for a moment he seemed ready to burst out laughing. What a band. Two black guys, a Spaniard and a crazy Canuck. They looked, as my colleague R. J. Smith put it, like a bunch of car thieves.

You want your heroes to stay amazing, but the older they get, the more likely they are to fail you. Mortgages have to be paid, diapers changed; hunger gives way to complacency, chances don't get taken. I had been listening to Young's music most of my life, but on record, at least, it seemed like he'd spent the last decade crumbling. Now here he was, jumping around the stage shouting out lyrics like a pissed-off teen. The camera had to struggle to keep up with him—twice he lunged right out of range, leaving, for a blissful moment, that rarest of television miracles: a big, beautiful empty screen (for subsequent broadcasts, the offending emptiness was edited out).

The relentless touring had paid off, because whatever his records might've lacked, Young was at the top of his game as a live performer. As his contorted face spit out the words, it felt like all the frustrations and disappointments of the last ten years were bleeding out of his vocal cords and fingers. Most other rockers from his generation were ready for Madame Tussaud's; here was Neil Young, just shy of forty-four, more frighteningly alive than ever.

The performance brought to mind a lyric from "Eldorado": "He comes dancing out / Dressed in gold lamé / He kills the bull / And lives another day." Maybe Young wasn't decked out in gold lamé, but a bull died that night.

I was trying to get to the place where I would be when I did "Rockin' in the Free World" during my live show. To do that I had to ignore Saturday Night Live *completely. I had to pretend I wasn't there. I had a dressing room, a little place with an amp in it, in another part of the building. And I walked from there into* Saturday Night Live—*and then left. I developed a whole new technique for television.*

I had my trainer, and we just lifted weights and I did calisthenics to get my blood to the level it would be at after performing for an hour and twenty-five minutes—which is usually how long I'd be onstage by the time I did that song. To perform that song the way it's supposed to be performed, you have to be at peak blood level. Everything has to be up, your machine has to be stoked. You can't walk on cold and do that or you're gonna look like a fuckin' idiot. So that's what I did. I tried to warm up and come on, like, y'know, not part of the show. Like they changed the channel for a minute, heh heh.

There's somethin' to Steve and Charley that's so great. It's like Crazy Horse when they first got together.
—*Did Briggs add something to that performance?*
He was there. *He added* a lot *to it.*

The YCS&P band didn't last beyond its first and only appearance. When Young returned to New York minus Briggs to finish up work on "No More," one of the tracks from the *Saturday Night Live* broadcast, Jordan didn't even show up for the first session. Perhaps it's appropriate that they burned out immediately, because their debut would've been very hard to top. It was Niko Bolas's shining hour. Although Briggs helped the band with their monitors during the performance, most everyone gives the production credit to Bolas, who picked the band, supervised the sound that went out over the airwaves and generally kept the vibe together. Whatever deficiencies he had as a drum-heavy nonfan of Young's work had been overcome. "The point is, that performance was incredible—and it had nothing to do with Briggs," said Jordan.

"Niko was trying to take Neil into the 1980s," said computer guru Bryan Bell. "I think Niko was trying to take Neil commercially to a point where Briggs can't take Neil. I think it's a shame that Neil doesn't work with Niko more, because I think he could sell a lot more records than he does, and I think he could do it without compromise. The only thing Niko wasn't sensitive to was that the musicians Niko wanted to use because of their abilities were insensitive to Neil emotionally." And Bolas had shut out the group most sensitive to Young emotionally—Crazy Horse. It would prove to be a fatal error.

YCS&P would turn out to be Young's last dance with Bolas. In his strange way, he'd gotten close to the producer over the years. Bolas tells of driving across the ranch in one of Young's dilapidated vehicles, confiding that he was having anxiety attacks over a failing relationship. "Dig it—that means you're *alive*," Young consoled him. But now it was over. Shakey was about to make another hard right turn, leaving Niko behind.

"After a while you realize you're just one of the things Neil has to use on the ranch," said Bolas, a touch of bitterness in his voice. "From noon till six you're working, and then you're back into the barracks until Neil wants you again. You just go crazy. It's a lot of devotion. I gave up a lot to be there.

"I always knew Neil would work with other people—just when you think he's your whole life, you get dumped somewhere. You know the interesting thing Graham Nash told me about Neil? He turned to me and said, 'Listen, Niko, guard your heart with Shakey.' It was pretty heavy. You know you can't really get emotionally attached to Neil bein' in your life, 'cause he won't be around."

·　　·　　·

Shortly after the *Saturday Night Live* performance, I interviewed Young. We met on the road, barreling down the highway in his '59 Cadillac Eldorado Biarritz. I gave him shit for his eighties records and told him if he ever sang "Sugar Mountain" again, I was buying a gun. He laughed. It was the beginning of a strange and wondrous relationship. A few months later, Young called to ask me to write liner notes for his Archives project. I wasn't a liner-notes type, I told him. My gig was writing about lives. Whatever I wanted to do was fine with him. His only requirement was that it had to be written on an old, fucked-up typewriter that had been dropped a few too many times. The project mutated into this tome. "Some asshole's gonna write a book about ya," I told him. "It might as well be me." Young liked that line of reasoning, so I joined the circus.

Young's next move would stun everybody around him. "I may come back to Crazy Horse, but it seems more and more doubtful to me," he had told *Rolling Stone* in June 1988. But now, just a few months after the Briggs wig-out in New York, Young decided to reunite the producer with the Horse and make his first great rock album in over a decade. Niko Bolas and the Young, CSP band were history.

· · ·

Rock was more bloated than ever in the nineties, a crowded, dirty aquarium. Grunge unleashed a gaggle of bands, most of which were as profound and original as Deep Purple at their worst, and a legion of over-the-hill rockers who refused to retire with dignity stripped themselves naked for the momentary amusement of the masses via the new elephant's graveyard, VH1's *Behind the Music*. "I used to care but . . . things have changed," Bob Dylan would croak once the decade ended.

The nineties would be another decade of extremes for Young. He would make an astounding commercial comeback and record some of his best music in years. Busy with a million projects, he'd seem more isolated and weird than ever. Success would descend on him, proving more problematic than ever. As an officially sanctioned "legend," he would win awards, endure tributes. He would also become a Lionel Trains mogul. And a few of those closest to him would die.

But that was all in the future. *Freedom* got rave reviews, but it was only the beginning of Young's return from oblivion. "I just came out of it," Young told Karen Schoemer. "Surfaced. It's like trying to get to the top of the water so you can come into the air. Finally I broke through."

the velvet cage

NEIL YOUNG'S DREAM

I had a dream that I was in this hotel. Actually, sort of a school and hotel in one. And it was a big *fuckin' hotel, painted kind of pea green. On a golf course. And it had a huge fuckin' gymnasium in it. This was an old forties or fifties stucco Spanish-type building.*

I'm in this gymnasium type of room with David Briggs. And I say, "Briggs, you gotta hear these fuckin' songs. I wrote these songs, I don't know where they came from, here they are, listen to this."

I put the cassette on, play him these fuckin' songs and we were just blown away. They were so fuckin' great I get shivers just remembering what it was like. It's so fuckin' weird because I know they're there—I know they're there—because I sang them in the dream. I have glimpses of something, it's like they come and go—just a chord progression, one word, but I can't find it . . . It just hasn't been able to come out.

Tall and rangy, with long black hair and a Cro-Magnon brow, John Hanlon could play Neil Young in the TV movie. The engineer had worked with Briggs on and off for the last ten years, and the one gig he coveted was working on a Young record. Briggs wasn't encouraging, telling him, "Neil doesn't like working with strangers—he doesn't like being *around* strangers." But on *Ragged Glory*, Briggs insisted on using Hanlon, who was elated. When would they be starting? "Well, that's another question," said Briggs, who suggested Hanlon turn down gigs and wait indefinitely.

Months went by, but in April 1990, the engineer finally headed up to the ranch to join Young, Briggs and the Horse. David had one final piece of advice for him: "Find a rapport with the Horse. That is the most important thing that you'll do."

Hanlon proved to be one of those rare individuals the Horse could warm to. Establishing a rapport with Shakey was a bit trickier. The first day Hanlon walked over to check out the amps. "Don't you *ever* walk in front of my amps while we're playin'!" Young snarled. Hanlon was crushed. "Great intro. I wondered if I still had the gig."

.　.　.

By 1990, Crazy Horse had split into two camps: Neil and Poncho, who had been working together with various combos, and Billy and Ralph. There was little communication between the two factions. In the wake of the Bluenotes brouhaha, Billy and Ralph had picked up two new members, Matt Piucci and Sonny Mone, and made the unlistenable *Left for Dead*— the title obviously directed at Young for the way he'd abandoned them.

But now that Young had set his sights on a new record with the Horse and Briggs, he brought everybody together and made it work. In February, a meeting was called at the Harris Ranch Restaurant, approximately halfway between Los Angeles and San Francisco. Young and Briggs drove down in one car; Billy, Ralph and Poncho drove up in another.

Briggs laid out a set of demands on the drive down. "I said, 'Look, man, I want you to understand you're just one of the band. You produce the record, I'll leave, you arrange the record, I'll leave. I'm gonna take every hat off your head except for three: songwriter, guitar player, singer. That's your only job, dude. That's all you gotta be.' "

Things were equally tense in the Horse car. Poncho, having worked with Young for the past few years, got a predictably chilly reception from his old bandmates. "I was surprised with the attitude they had—'If Neil doesn't say the right shit, we're not gonna work with him.' They were real cocky."

Once at Harris Ranch, Young apologized for the way he'd misused the band and excitedly told them how, for the Archives project, he'd been watching films of all of them playing back in 1976. They were loose and free and he wanted to get back to that space, whatever it took. As an amazed Molina recalls, Young told them to "do whatever you gotta do—if you were smoking pot then, fine, go ahead, do it." The Horse made one stipulation: They didn't want to record at Broken Arrow—"Young Country," as Ralph called it. Whatever it takes, was Young's attitude.

Young took all the blame for the problems in the past, and it blew Poncho's mind. "Neil was painting himself as the bad guy. After I saw what was happening, I just put my head down and kept my mouth shut. I thought, 'This guy's trickier than a fuckin' robber's dog.' Neil just said everything they wanted to hear. Neil greased 'em, man—he made it sound like it was his fault and he was sorry and he was ready to be committed and take his time and not do it on the ranch. . . ." Poncho laughed. "We ended up on the ranch and doin' it as quick as possible."

Briggs was pissed that Young had reneged on recording elsewhere. "For three months I drove home every night. Because the bottom line is there's too many distractions for Neil at the ranch, too many side trips."

．　．　．

Except for Briggs and guitar tech Larry Cragg, no one was allowed into the *Ragged Glory* sessions. The crew working on the Archives were nearby; Briggs banned them. "I don't want Neil lookin' back. I want him lookin' forward." But on the third day of the sessions, Briggs himself got thrown out. "After he walked in, we played like shit," said Poncho. "Neil made Briggs go away. Billy and Ralph have this funny thing—they just get spooked by anybody."*

The band recorded live in Young's equipment barn. Briggs showed up hours early to rehearse the band before Young arrived. John Hanlon was stationed in a remote truck outside, his only visual link a tiny video camera. Briggs laid down the law: Record everything. "If you miss one note Neil plays, I guarantee you that will be the opening note of the song he

---

*This scene inspired Young to write the ultimate song on Horse neuroses, "Don't Spook the Horse," a seven-minute-plus number he actually recorded with one foot in a pile of cowshit he had Larry Cragg bring into the studio. Somehow the effect translated to tape perhaps the most broken-down, barely-a-song performance the Horse has ever unleashed on the public. Briggs was relieved it was released only as a CD-single bonus track. "It's a condensed version of the whole album," a gleeful Young would tell James Henke. "Especially for reviewers who don't like me at all. Just listen to that and you'll get all you need."

wants to use. And if he walks back here three weeks from now and you can't play it back, you're gone."

Hanlon would find recording the Horse live in a barn vastly different from the sterile confines of a recording studio. As Briggs instructed him, "You're gonna find out everything's gonna happen at once—there'll be very little if any overdubs; there'll be no time to fix or improve anything; you won't be able to get some nice, great sound. Just capture what's there to the best of your ability."

Hanlon recalls Briggs trying in vain to help him achieve some separation on the instruments by sticking Plexiglas sheets on the sides of the drums. "All it took was one verse for Neil to go, 'Lose 'em—I can't hear Poncho's guitar,' " said Hanlon, who was left with a nightmare so loud and uncontrollable he compared it to "a giant amp that starts into feedback—it would start swimming, the whole room, everything just came together. I had vocals coming out of the kick-drum mike, feeding back into the PA, everything else. It was an exercise in leakage, swim and wash."

Young gave Hanlon one clue to the sound he was after. "Neil told me, 'I want the drums to be a picture frame for the guitars and vocal—I want the cymbals and top-end brass of the drum kit to be the top sides of the picture frame. I want the bottom end to be the kick drum and bass, and the guitars will fill out the picture.' " After so many years of abusing Ralph, Young would really let the drummer shine on *Ragged Glory.*

It was decided that, as with *Tonight's the Night,* no one would listen to playbacks until the project was finished. "Neil wanted to forget about the recording process," said Hanlon. Poncho, who hadn't been around for *Tonight's the Night,* thought it was bizarre: "We just kept going in and recording and recording." Briggs stayed in the barn with the band, leaving Hanlon to fend for himself in the truck. It all concerned Hanlon a bit, to say the least. What if they hated the sound he was getting? He suggested they all take a listen. "No," said Young. "It better be great. Briggs hired ya."

•   •   •

Back in November, Young had mused over how he would approach recording with the Horse again. "I have to write, like, fifteen songs and never play them for anyone, never play them for myself. You can only get it to a certain point—maybe enough of a sketch of how it goes and then not even finish the fucking thing until I'm with them. You can't even finish the fuckin' song, okay? That's how particular it is.

"And then you go in there with them, it all happens at once, and when you sing it, they actually fuckin' play it—because they only play it once, too. So then it's over, it's got, like, five mistakes in it, ya gotta fuckin' fix all the mistakes and edit and do all this shit to make it sound good— but it's *great*." This would be Young's method of working with the Horse in the nineties, and it would grow sketchier and sketchier with each session.

Briggs felt the Horse floundering as Young struggled to develop the *Ragged Glory* material. "The band was learning songs that didn't have any lyrics to 'em, any structure, any form, and almost all of 'em were in E minor." He suggested they play a couple of older, unreleased songs as warm-ups, which led to a couple of classic album tracks—"Country Home" and "White Line," the latter in particular one of the band's finest performances.

When Briggs begged Young to cut the unreleased song "Interstate," the musician would only cut it acoustic. "It was that much of a snap to get him to do "White Line" and "Country Home," but because I *wanted* 'Interstate,' he acceded—but perversely." (The haunting performance of the song, with Ralphie playing a chair for a drum, would eventually be released as a bonus vinyl-only cut to the 1996 *Broken Arrow* sessions.)

On the final day of recording, they got four songs. An earthquake caused a momentary power failure during one of them, which Young no doubt took as a good sign. One of the last things recorded was an impromptu, one-take-only cover of sixties garage dementia—"Farmer John." "When you're forty-two, singing, 'Farmer John, I'm in love with your daughter,' it's going to sound like dirty old men," Billy Talbot noted to one interviewer. But these were joyous dirty old men. As Poncho yelped in the background, one had to laugh out loud, it felt so wrong.

With the recording completed and the band ready to listen to what Hanlon had done, the engineer said, "I kept my bag packed and in the rental car, ready to go. I thought, 'This stuff is so raw, I'll never work again in Hollywood.' " But Young's methods were starting to sink in. "Just take the fuckin' snapshot. It's the Polaroid of his performance, not a retouched Scavullo."

Briggs and Young would clash over where to mix the record. Young wanted to finish it on the ranch; Briggs, who hated the equipment in Young's studio, wanted to go down to Malibu, to the site of many of their past triumphs, Indigo Ranch. "I said, 'That's it—I want off this fuckin' ranch. I feel like I'm in a fuckin' prison here. *You* can do whatever you want—*I'm* taking them to Indigo to mix 'em.' " Young reluctantly agreed. "After all the good feelings, it was like 'Okay, man, we'll go there, we'll do what you want—but *you better be right.*' That was the implication to the max."

.   .   .

The finished album was a knockout. Young stripped away all the useless crap he'd encumbered the Horse with in the eighties and finally let them play. Sonically, the only misstep was the overblown synthetic-sounding backing vocals (taken to absurd, Spectorian lengths on "Mother Earth"). Three of the newest songs—"Love and Only Love," "Over and Over," "Love to Burn"—were long, lyrically minimal jams that featured some of Young's best recorded guitar work in years. "Those songs are the solos as well," Briggs would remark to me, and what strange songs they were. Young used the band like the vessel in *Fantastic Voyage,* taking a trip deep inside.

Ragged Glory opened a new chapter in Young's songwriting: murky, sometimes convoluted songs that often seemed to involve inscrutable, mythologized figures from life on the ranch. As odd as Young's eighties records are, I think his nineties records will seem much more bizarre in years to come. "Fuckin' Up" is self-loathing at its most naked; the ultra-dark "Love to Burn" sports the venomous line "Where you takin' my kid? Why'd you ruin my life?"—seemingly directed at one ghost from Young's past in particular.

But the general thrust of the album is optimistic, expressing not only the pains but the growth that change can bring. "Take a chance on love," he wails during "Love and Only Love," a declaration so desperate it sounds like he's addressing himself in the mirror at three A.M. *Freedom* might've had the songwriting edge, but *Ragged Glory* was the comeback in terms of sound.

—*Why is this record so important?*
'Cause you only get one chance to make a good impression—straight from the Horse's mouth.

    I told you I dreamt that I wrote some songs? I think they all came out of the dream. Hope that doesn't mean it's a wrap.
—*Can I take a shot at summing up the album?*
Okay.
—*It seems to be about a self-obsessed asshole who's trying to deal with his feelings and become a human being.*
Yeah, heh heh. That's pretty good.
—*It doesn't get more personal than "Love to Burn."*
Painfully personal. It's that moment when you're sittin' there goin', "God, I got a lot to give." You just gotta stay open and not shut down because of all the bad stories, life stories, bad news movies . . . Ya gotta open up. That's the deal.
—*Have you shut down at times?*
Fuckin' A. Shut down and boarded up.
—*Pegi keeps you open, whether you like it or not?*
Yeah, right. *She keeps jarrin' the door back open.*

"I guess Neil Young is the king of rock and roll," declared MTV talking head Kurt Loder in the opening of his *Ragged Glory* review for *Rolling Stone.* "I don't see anybody else on the scene standing anywhere *near* this tall nowadays."

    Released in October 1990, *Ragged Glory* would turn out to be a profoundly influential album. A long list of new, young artists would either sing Young's praises or imitate him outright—among them Dinosaur Jr., the Smashing Pumpkins, Giant Sand, Bettie Serveert, Pete Droge, the Black Crowes, Son Volt, Sparklehorse, the Jayhawks, Spiritualized, the Red Hot Chili Peppers, Counting Crows, Everclear, Matthew Sweet, Cowboy Junkies, etc., etc. Nineteen eighty-nine also saw the release of *The Bridge: A Tribute to Neil Young,* with Sonic Youth, Nick Cave, the Pixies and other hipsters all crooning Young's tunes. Even elder rockers would jump on the bandwagon. Tom Petty (with the help of producer Rick Rubin) would create the ultimate ersatz Shakey record (right down to the Ralphie drumbeat), "You Don't Know How It Feels." For the next few years, Young's name would be omnipresent.

"My generation was pretty much the end of the existential hero who had started with Dostoevsky and gone through Sartre and Camus," *Taxi Driver* screenwriter Paul Schrader told the Knight Ridder news service. "And that was the lonely hero, the outsider hero. My work and my generation fed off that hundred-year tradition. Quentin Tarantino's generation is completely different. The ironic hero has replaced the existential hero. . . . It's the difference between Jack Paar and David Letterman. Everything's a wink and a nod and a jab . . . Nothing matters. All that notion of soul-searching, redemption, life and death . . . it's all irrelevant now."

"I'm a loser, baby, so why don't you kill me," went the oft-regurgitated chorus of Beck's "Loser." "I think my whole generation's mission is to kill the cliché," Beck told *Rolling Stone*'s Mark Kemp. "I think it's one of the reasons a lot of my generation are always on the fence about things. They're afraid to commit to anything for fear of seeming like a cliché. They're afraid to commit to their *lives* because they see so much of the world as a cliché."

In the early nineties, Neil Young was the one sixties rocker who remained valid for this bunch.* He'd never sold his songs for beer commercials, still played guitar like a maniac and, in a certain way, had made a career out of ambivalence. Particularly ballyhooed in the media was his connection to the so-called grunge scene in Seattle that exploded after the monstrous surprise success of Nirvana's *Nevermind.* Suddenly the world was full of young bands recording live on vintage equipment and sporting long hair, flannel shirts and jeans, a look that was a Xerox of Neil Young circa 1971.

Young was dubbed the "Godfather of Grunge" and at times the connection was absurd: Many of these bands tended toward a pomposity and pretension reminiscent of the worst excesses of the seventies—Pearl Jam,

---

*Dylan—who shared the stage with his own fair share of youngsters in the nineties—could have cared less, telling David Gates in 1997, "The top stars of today, you won't even know their names two years from now. Four, five years from now, they'll all be obliterated. It's all flaky to me."

for example, the band Young would align himself most closely with in this period. I saw nothing of Neil in their music until after they worked with him and consciously began aping his style.

At least Pearl Jam's heart seemed to be in the right place. They shunned interviews, videos and went to war with Ticketmaster, but it was all so painfully earnest: dreary Complaint Rock, U2 a decade later. Rebels? "A real commercial rock band" was Kurt Cobain's summation.

Pearl Jam had taken to playing "Keep On Rockin' " in concert, and during Young's 1993 tour with Booker T. and the MGs, the band would join Young several times to play the song in shambolic all-star encores. And on September 2, 1993, Young and Pearl Jam would perform the song together on the MTV Video Awards. Plagued by monitor problems, the band ended the angry performance with some rote guitar-smashing. Vedder's bombast and Young's subtlety seemed mismatched—there were two heads to this music instead of one. It never gelled.

Pearl Jam to Neil Young in the early nineties was what CSN was to Young in the seventies, a connection that was more hype than music; full of sound and fury, signifying nothing. The new artists who had the most in common with Young were the ones who sounded nothing like him— sharing instead a certain spirit, humor and sense of originality: Richard Buckner, Pavement, Nirvana. But Young would eventually squeeze the right juice out of Pearl Jam, and I'd be standing there to see it happen.

—*You don't find Pearl Jam's music a little pretentious?*
I notice it in the things people write about Pearl Jam, but to tell ya the truth, I haven't picked up on it at all. I think it may be genuine and look pretentious. Because I haven't seen any pretension when I've been around these guys.
—*Eddie Vedder's a real guy?*
Oh, I really think so, yeah. He's a unique kid. There's nothin' false about him. He's a little unbelievable in his naïve ways, his openness—but it's real. Music is his religion, that's what he told me. He came in after we were playing with tears in his eyes. This is just the way he is—it's not just when he's onstage. Plus he records everything, did you know that? He records everything. There's something slightly Chaplinesque about him. He's a very innaresting character.

Pearl Jam are interested in bein' in the space to play—mentally. Surviving that trip from the dressing room to the stage and back, remaining intact with what's goin' on. That's why they have candles around. That's a reminder—and the crew keeps those candles coming, they keep them lit all the time. Because they know that the candles have something to do with the music, what's goin' on.

—Aaaaah, they're just Jethro Tull without the flute.

I'll tell you what: If all I had was Pearl Jam, and I didn't have another band in the world, I would not be worried. Because in there is the essence *of making great music. You don't have to use it all at once, but it's there.*

Elliot almost went onto a feeding frenzy with Pearl Jam, heh heh. He wanted to put me and Pearl Jam and Crazy Horse together. I told him, "No chance. You think we're gonna do that to Crazy Horse? No fuckin' way." He said, "They'll rise to the occasion." I said, "What is this—a fuckin' prize fight? What about the music?" I said, "You gotta question your own motives with this fuckin' idea." So I haven't heard anything more about that.

But lately, more than ever, Elliot has just been a sensational manager. It's really Elliot who decides who all these groups are that I play with— not me. It's not my idea. I don't keep track of all that shit, I don't have time. I've never heard a Pearl Jam record, except on the radio every once in a while. But I never listen to anybody's record—I didn't single them out not to listen to, heh heh.

That fall, just a little over a month after *Ragged Glory* was released, Rassy Young passed away at her home in New Smyrna Beach, Florida.

She was bedridden, suffering with cancer. Even on her deathbed, Rassy refused to forgive Scott. At one point, he sent her flowers. She rejected the peace offering. Rassy died on October 15, 1990, a day after her seventy-second birthday. Neil spent the last weeks by her side, but she died just before his return from a quick trip to California.

Rassy had gone out fighting. "Right up till the end she spoke her piece to the nurses and everyone," said Joe McKenna, Young's bus driver and Rassy's neighbor. That weekend, Neil and Joe packed up all her belongings, taking down the gold records she had so proudly displayed on her living room wall. "She left everything to Neil," said McKenna. "Everything."

Not long after, Young was back at the ranch, rehearsing with Crazy Horse for the Bridge School concert on October 26. On a shelf sat an urn containing his mother's ashes. "This is the first thing I've done without Rassy," he told Poncho. "It feels like I'm starting over again."

—You ever think about Rassy?

Yeah. Comes across my mind about once a day. Little things.

—You see a lot of Rassy in yourself?

Yeah, sometimes. Mannerisms. Caustic comments.

—At times it was hard for you to talk to her.

Yeah. I think so.

—What was the hardest thing for Rassy to accept?

I think any kind of separation was the hardest thing for her to accept. Right near the end of her life, she accepted it—but then she turned on me.

—You too?

Heh heh heh. This was like when her brain wasn't even there. It was like she was speakin' to my dad and she was seeing me. She was calling me unfaithful and all these things, y'know—but with a lotta hate.

My dad sent her somethin' on her birthday. She didn't wanna have anything to do with him. He's a lot like me. I don't hold grudges. It takes a lot for me to turn on somebody completely—they have to fuck me up pretty badly. And my dad's like that. When a relationship ends, he tries to see the bright side. You can harp on the negative, but there's no reason to. There's no gain.

—Still have Rassy on the shelf?

That vase, there's nothing in it. All that stuff's gone. I held on to it for about six months after she died. Then I remembered what she said about this one place on the ranch that she thought was the most beautiful place. She said once, "I'd like to spend eternity here." So I took her at her word. That's where she is. The vase, I just couldn't figure out what to do with that. Now I know what I'm gonna do—I'm gonna take it up to where I threw all the stuff out, where I put it all in the wind. And I'm just gonna bury it up there.

Y'know, every morning on weekends, Amber has Eggs Rassy. Cut off the top of a soft-boiled egg, stick a piece of toast down in it. So now every weekend I say, "Well, waddya want for breakfast?" "Eggs Rassy." So that's my mother. She's there all the time . . . comin' out of my daughter's mouth.

For demented zealots like Dave McFarlin, the *Ragged Glory* tour was nirvana: all-electric mayhem and louder than God. Larry Cragg walked fearfully in front of the huge amp mock-ups left over from the *Rust* tour, knowing what lurked behind them. "Inside those amps, Neil had his own private PA with two thousand watts of power. Really loud. A couple of times I had to take the earplugs out to hear what was going on, and it just killed my ears—and here Neil was with the thing aiming right at him." Young would later describe the tour to Tony Scherman as "a completely exhausting experience."

Cragg snapped the picture that adorns the back of the *Weld* CD, culled from the tour that sums it all up: a dazed Young holds his guitar in feedback position, his tangled hair sitting atop his head like a dead poodle, his waxen face more chiseled than Mount Rushmore. By the time the grueling three-month, fifty-four-date tour and live album were history, his band would want to kill each other, Briggs would curse his name and Young's hearing would be shot.

> *When we made the record, the [Gulf] war was raging, and the album reflects my anxieties, and an attempt to exorcise the demons of my own comprehension of the people who were dying as we were playing. So it was a serious thing. You can't go out there entertaining. It was a delicate time to be on the road. "Powderfinger," "Love and Only Love," "Cortez the Killer" and "Blowin' in the Wind" were songs that related to the conflict, how people have dealt with it. I figure that the guitar playing was a soundtrack for CNN. That's what* Arc, *the feedback album, is really about: the brutal energy that comes from hearing the women screaming and seeing our own coffins.*
> —Interview with Jon Pareles, 1991

In keeping with Young's allegiance to the alternative-music scene, Elliot Roberts picked a gaggle of young bands for tour support slots, most notably the New York artso-noise outfit Sonic Youth. They were fans, and Kim Gordon had her own peculiar connection, having known Bruce Berry back in the seventies.

"Neil's a triple Scorpio, isn't he?" she said. "I think he's a really good manipulator of people and intuitively right on about a lotta things." She found the scene around Young surreal, populated by "male-chauvinist sexist pigs. It was all the stuff I heard about rock and roll but never really believed still went on. It was fascinating." Sociological appeal aside, Sonic Youth had something of a rough time on the tour. Young's crew despised their sound, giving them very little use of the full PA system. "We need a certain amount of volume to do what we do—even if people hate it," said Gordon, claiming they felt particular hostility from Tim Foster, dubbing him "The Doberman." Young took the band's side in the matter when word eventually trickled back to him.

"Neil was totally aloof from his world," said Thurston Moore, who found that just getting a message to Young was like trying to arrange lunch with Jimmy Hoffa. Their contact with him was limited to an abrupt dressing-room appearance in which he issued a frenzied appeal not to do the David Letterman show ("Tell him you're out on the road with *me*," he barked) and a dinner on his bus during which Moore would find out just how little Young knew about punk rock. "He doesn't listen to music. He really doesn't give a shit. The one thing he said that was kinda startling was that real rock and roll has gone totally underground." At least Sonic Youth got to hang with him, if briefly. Amusingly enough, many of the bands who played on bills with Young in the nineties would complain they never got to meet the Godfather of Grunge at all.

●　　●　　●

The Gulf War was definitely on Young's mind; Poncho recalls him spending every spare moment glued to CNN, watching the coverage. Playing a gig at West Point the night the ground war erupted, Young not only agreed to take down the stage's giant peace symbol and broadcast a more traditional version of "The Star-Spangled Banner" than the Hendrix deconstruction, he also turned over all proceeds to charity, although—

disinterested in being seen as a do-gooder—he refuses to name any organization. But the war in the Gulf wasn't the only fighting going on during
the *Ragged Glory* tour.

There was a postgig altercation in Philadelphia. Young had been furious
over problems with the show's sound, and Briggs took the heat, knowing
full well that Billy Talbot had been monkeying with the onstage monitors.
Finally Briggs went ballistic on the bass player, reducing him to tears, and
was sent home.

"Neil realized Briggs was creating more turmoil than he was doing
good and just let him go," said Poncho at the time. "He's hard to work with,
because you never know which Briggs you're gonna get—the bighearted
Briggs or the guy who stayed up all night drinkin', did a half a gram,
'FUCK YOU!' Briggs."

Things weren't much better within the band. Billy and Ralph were
growing tired of Young's preoccupation with the Lionel business as well as
Poncho's insider status—staying on the bus with the boss and cooking his
meals. Things came to a head following a lackluster performance in Vancouver, during which Young berated his rhythm section and kicked Billy in
the ass during "Love and Only Love." Back in the dressing room, Molina
got nose to nose with Young, screaming, "This is gettin' to be like a CSN
fuckin' Y tour! Separate buses . . . ! If fuckin' Frank stops thinkin' about
pork chops and you stop thinkin' about trains, we could start playin' some
fuckin' music!"

Compounding the problem was the fact that Young became ill toward
the end of the tour. After a short postponement, it resumed in April, but the
vibe had gotten strange. "Neil was really in a good mood until he got sick,"
said Poncho. "From then on he was never the same. He just got weirder
and weirder."

· · ·

Despite all the fireworks—maybe because of them, who really knows—the
tour was incredible musically, and once it was over, Young and Briggs set
out to mix tapes for both a live album and video, which would result in the
biggest battle of them all.

"The more you think, the more you stink," went the Briggs/Young saying, and unfortunately a lot of thinking went into *Weld*. Young, Briggs and

John Hanlon mixed the tapes at Indigo, but Young wasn't satisfied. They continued working at the ranch, redoing mixes and overdubbing background vocals to the point of mania. Even Young's own equipment tech thought it was a bad idea—they'd just purchased a new Neve mixing board that was far from ready. "Neil *forced* Briggs and Hanlon to try and do it on the ranch," said Harry Sitam. "He should never have done it. The board was in terrible condition."

Hanlon—like most everybody else I talked to—knew they'd already mixed a great version of the album at Indigo. "The very advice Neil gave me if I wanted to play ball on that team was 'Don't second-guess yourself. Be great the first time.' He didn't follow his own advice on that one."

Briggs had informed Young that he had a prior commitment a few weeks down the road, thinking it was no big deal. But as mixing dragged on, Briggs pushed back his other session a week. It became apparent that Young still wasn't going to let go. Briggs was backed into a corner and told Young. Neil accused him of pulling a Niko Bolas, with another gig waiting in the wings. "Then hire Niko!" Briggs screamed. *"Fuck You!"* The producer got into his rented Skylark and tore off. (Bolas had the best retort concerning the exit of David Briggs: "Neil should be the first one to understand leaving.")

With Briggs gone, Young and Billy Talbot mixed the album into the ground. The bass-heavy murk of the two-CD *Weld,* released in October 1991, was not an improvement over the original Indigo mixes. But there were compensations. *Arc,* a third CD included in the package, was a thirty-five-minute nightmare edit of feedback endings and lyric fragments—the most noxious sonic assault released by a major artist since Lou Reed's unlistenable two-record set of electronic jibber-jabber, *Metal Machine Music.* "Those guys with the pickup trucks and blaring speakers—if you wanna make a statement, guys, put *this* on!" Young told Tony Scherman. "This is white rap!"*

---

*Warner Bros. was reportedly a little apprehensive over the *Weld* package, and Young sent a letter to Mo Ostin and Lenny Waronker dated June 17, 1991:

"The times they are a changin'. . . ." My history is now my biggest competitor. As the year of my induction into the Hall of Fame grows too close for comfort, my own accomplishments hang on me like some beautiful coat I can't take off.

The other high point was the *Weld* video, which featured the original Briggs mixes. Produced and edited by Larry Johnson—who would really come into his own in the nineties as Young's most interesting documentarian—the ultra-real Video Hi-8 footage features the Horse live, intercut with audience shots of extremely intense fans mouthing words, playing air guitar and acting out the songs in weird Kabuki-like dances. When future races want to look back on the obsessive relationship between artist and audience in the rock era, this is one document they will want to peruse.

And while Young and Talbot might not have been the greatest mixing team, the *Weld* video of "Welfare Mothers" proved that as a comedy duo they were carrying on in the grand tradition of Willie Tyler and Lester. As the song crumbles into feedback, a beyond-hoarse Talbot screams, "No more pain! No more pain!" Young and Talbot go into a call-and-response mini-drama over a delayed welfare check. "Where's the check?" demands Young. "Check's in the mail!" yells Billy. Seemingly experienced in such situations, Talbot plays the role of starving child, yelping, "Hey Mom, I'm hungry!" "Tell those kids to *shut up!*" snaps Young. Horror sets in as the song starts all over again, with Young whining—and Talbot rasping—over and over, "Welfare mothers make better lovers." Billy finally exclaims, "That check is *here*! *All right!*" As he pounds feedback out of his bass, the song collapses into a miasma of noise.

Once *Weld* was finished, Crazy Horse were put out to pasture again, with Young turning back to the Stray Gators, the band from *Harvest*. The tortured *Weld* experience would leave a bad taste in more than one mouth. Poncho was crestfallen when he saw Billy Talbot's production credit on the CD. "I'd been there every Bluenote recording session, mixdown . . . Niko and I even mastered *Freedom*—Neil didn't show up. I did tons of work and I didn't get that type of credit. It seemed like Billy just showed up . . . I don't know how much of it was to spite Briggs."

•   •   •

Let's face it. There's next to nothing on our album that will get any airplay and that makes it hard for you to do your job right and get my music to the public. We both like to win . . . the purpose of this letter is to assure you that my decision to go ahead and send *Weld* down the rocky road of commerciality is not taken lightly. I hope you understand. Peace, Neil.

When I caught up with Briggs months later he was still furious.* Decades of resentments came out over *Weld*. "I told Neil, 'It's a live LP, we'll mix it in two weeks, it'll sound *great.*' Then he started worrying. I remixed every song on the record three times, and it only got worse and worse and worse. What's the point of making a live record if you wanna go back and put on giant stacks of background parts? He wanted it more slicked up. Plus I had to mix it on the ranch so Neil could be there in his own little cave and just turn off the world and escape to his trains every ten minutes. I don't know what it is, but it ain't rock and roll.

"I can remember the old days. All these things about Neil being the brooding artist—it was bullshit, all bullshit. He was a loose, happy, fun guy. Now he's like this fuckin' recluse. He doesn't have contact with people anymore. Neil just throws everybody away like old tissue paper. . . . He's alienated everybody who ever cared about him by treatin' 'em all like shit and showin' 'em no respect—so what he's got is him and his fuckin' trains.

"I think Neil is a great fuckin' artist, but his vibe—and the whole trip that surrounds it—is a sick kinda deal. Just this inbred, uptight program that makes me very uncomfortable to be around."

Briggs saw Young's home studio as a hippie Graceland. "I don't know why anybody would wanna work there. It's like working at the Pentagon—as long as they live in his little world, then everything's okay. I guess Neil doesn't wanna deal with the big world. People laugh, have fun, go out to dinner, do the kinda things people really do . . .

"I don't know what's happened to the guy. I don't know what's happened to his life, his mind, and in all honesty I don't give a shit.

"*Ragged Glory* is the best fuckin' record he's made in a long time, and that was *it*. Now he's back to the same old trip, back in the same old train barn, with the same old bad attitude, and the same old uptight people around him all the time. . . . He's in a cage. A velvet cage."

Nearly a year later, Briggs would be back working with Young. It was the only game in town—for both men.

---

*Ironically, it was Young who suggested I reinterview him at this particular point, telling me via Joel Bernstein that I should "talk to Briggs now that Briggs thinks I'm a real asshole." I hounded David for months before he agreed.

The production credit on Weld—*if you look at the laser disc, it's differ-ent. Those are the mixes David Briggs did, and David Briggs gets the credit there.*

But when David Briggs wasn't in the studio working on the record, he didn't get credit. Y'know, that's the way life is. Billy and I stayed and worked on it—for good or for bad. Briggs had another job to do and he had to take off. So instead of putting his foot down and saying, "Neil, I really think this is done, let's take a couple of weeks off and listen to it again," he was outta there. So I had no feedback from Briggs. So Briggs got what he deserved on that one.

I need people to be there all the way. If they're not, they're not. The people who are there through the whole thing are the ones that get the credit. If I was wrong in going on, Briggs should've made sure I stopped.

I have a lotta respect for Briggs and I don't hold anything against him. I understand what he had to do there. I've made some mistakes, that was one of 'em. Number one, because I hurt my ears mixing it. That's why I really regret it. I hurt my ears and they'll never be the same again.

—Yeah, but there's also this vibe of "Neil would be happy if we all lived on the ranch and he could just use us whenever—until we were all used up."

Hey, that's *their* problem—not mine. They're not forced to go to the ranch.

—You make it hard for anybody who has another gig.

Listen, when we did our best work during the seventies, there were no other gigs. *I think that if everybody had the same energy for the music they had in the seventies and were into it the same way, it wouldn't make any fuckin' difference where we were or what was going on. This would be it.*

I don't wanna record like I'm workin' in a fuckin' factory. I don't wanna do it that way, and anybody who wants to do it that way and puts fuckin' form on it, and restricts how long it's gonna take or not take, is not in tune with what the fuck's goin' on and the way we've made our best work. The way we made our best work is no form. Play when you

wanna play, go home when you wanna go home. *Ralph used to just* leave. *He'd go home and feed his cat, he'd be back in a day and a half.*
—Briggs was furious after Weld. *He had some things to say about you that'll put your hair in curlers.*
Oh, I know. But that's why we love each other. Unfortunately, he couldn't say that stuff to me *as easily as he used to. He stopped telling me. But I knew he felt it.*
—Why do you think he stopped telling you?
'Cause . . . maybe he thought I wasn't listening. But I listened to everything he said. And he was right. But he never came to me and said, "I'm David. I'm telling you it's fuckin' finished." He didn't say that. Never once. And then Billy came in and we kept on going. We did some things that were okay, but the real record of Weld *is the laser disc. And it should be that way. It's not just listening to* Weld—*you wanna watch it. I mean, we may be hard-pressed to be that bombastic again.*

I think at the end of every record that we did I drove Briggs crazy. I don't think there were any records that weren't crazy. We had to get away from each other. Towards the end of Weld, *towards the end of* Ragged Glory, *towards the end of . . . shit, you name it.*

"Playing that hard and that loud for that long is like spending the winter in the Arctic and then spending the summer in the Arctic and then finally deciding, 'Well, let's go to Florida this winter,' " Young told Greg Kot. "You gotta have relief. That's what acoustic music is like to me."

John Nowland recalls a trial by fire at the beginning of what would become *Harvest Moon*. "Ben showed up one day and said, 'Neil's comin' in to do demos. He'll be here in twenty minutes.' " Nowland, who had never worked as an engineer with Young, was scrambling to get things together when he walked in, sat down and immediately launched into "Silver and Gold." "Me and Ben are in there workin' on guitar tone," said Nowland. "And there's no tape rollin', 'cause we're working on the sound. So I got somethin' I liked in a verse or two, and I hit the talkback and said, 'Okay, we're all set now. You ready to go?' It was like the *speakers froze*. Neil said, 'I've been tryin' to cut this song for ten years, and *that* was the take. I was right fuckin' on it.' Ben and I looked at each other and we felt about one inch tall."

Nowland struggled to regain his composure as Young whipped through a handful of new songs—rough performances that Nowland thought were demos. Some would end up on the album. As usual, Young had particular requirements for his new direction. This time he played guitar with his fingers instead of a pick. He chose big old analog mikes "so he could hear the vocal comin' back at him," said Nowland. And, disillusioned with digital echo, he built his own echo chambers at Broken Arrow. Young created an intimate setting, out in the woods in his own studio, and the result was, as Young told Gavin Martin, "the quietest record I've ever made."

The *Weld* tour—and decades of playing at deafening volume—had left Young with a condition known as hyperacusis. The feedback junkie was suddenly hypersensitive to the slightest whisper. "He can hear everything," grumbled Larry Cragg. "I was plugging in a Farfisa and it made a soft little crackle sound—he goes, *'Turn that thing off! Get it outta here!'*"

Young assembled most of the Stray Gators from the original *Harvest* sessions—Tim Drummond on bass, Ben Keith on steel, Kenny Buttrey on drums, plus the harmonies of Linda Ronstadt and James Taylor. Elliot Mazer, who had coproduced *Harvest,* was not invited back, and while Jack Nitzsche did arrange "Such a Woman," the keyboard chores were assigned to another equally idiosyncratic player: Spooner Oldham. The harmonies of Nicolette Larson and Young's half sister, Astrid, were another prominent new ingredient. "I kept hearing female voices in my head—choirs at first," Young told Mary Campbell. "There's a lot more feminine representation on this record than there has been on my recent records . . . I wanted to feel the feminine side of the content of the songs."

Buttrey, recalling his miserable experience on the *Time Fades Away* tour, was apprehensive over the reunion, but once the sessions got under way, his enthusiasm was unbridled. "The vibe was incredible, it was just so different. Neil's actually smiling now. He's so much more mellow—he looks younger than he did at twenty-six. He's no longer slumped over like an old man . . . he used to not seem to care what he looked like, now he's wearin' cool clothes. Every aspect is totally different. He's a super guy now." But soon Buttrey would be cursing Young's name more than ever before.

•　　•　　•

With *Harvest Moon,* Young finally made the follow-up many had been waiting for: an acoustic album of relationship songs, although one has to admire his perversity in waiting two decades to do it. Young himself would float the "sequel" idea in the press even before the record was done, and later would back away from the idea when pressed. "I'm not trying to go back and re-create where I was when I did *Harvest,*" he told Greg Kot. "The idea is I sang about the same subject matter with twenty years more experience . . . I'm stronger than I was then."

The songs came from many different periods—Young sang three lines of "You and Me" as an introduction to "I Am a Child" at a Los Angeles solo performance in 1971, then abandoned the song in the mid-seventies when Tim Drummond excitedly told him it sounded just like the hit *Harvest* material. "Unknown Legend" was another years-old song that Young decided to finish after Joel Bernstein showed him a lyric fragment in passing. "One of These Days" dated back to the mid-eighties, "Dreamin' Man" to 1989. The rest were new.

There was definitely a concept at work on *Harvest Moon.* "The real sense of the album is: How do you keep going?" Young told Chris Heath. "How can you keep an old relationship new? How do you make love last? How can you bring the past with you?"

. . .

Young worked on *Harvest Moon* for months. Some feel he was sent over the edge by the project. At one point, he poked a finger at Joel Bernstein and muttered, "Don't ever make records . . . don't ever make records." Even coming up with the album's final running order was an agony. Nowland recalls Neil, Pegi, Ben Keith, Elliot Roberts and his girlfriend, Alexa, shuffling three-by-five cards with the titles written on them, creating countless track sequences. Songs came and went. At one point "Such a Woman" was axed, but Elliot fought for it to be put back.

The finished album, despite its live-demo origins, was the most meticulously crafted Young had made in years. The band's playing is impeccable. Spooner's you're-not-even-sure-he's-there-but-you-feel-it minimalism is exquisite and Ben Keith graces "Unknown Legend" with proud but sad steel accents. The latter song is perhaps the most empathetic portrait of a woman Young has ever created. "You and Me" is the kind of distillation of relationship malaise he excels at, and "Dreamin' Man" offers weird girl-group-in-hell backing vocals and disquieting Aerostar van/loaded gun imagery.

"Natural Beauty" evokes a world-weariness that seems infinite. It was "about survival in nature in general and survival in any situation really," the ever cryptic Young told Gavin Martin before cheerfully elaborating on the song's jumbled sense of space and time. "It's like I took a completed album of all kinds of different songs and threw it up in the air and [that song] came crashing down."

Ultimately, though, "Natural Beauty" feels obtuse and impenetrable, and the rest of the album is a similar dead end. The bland title track (musically reminiscent of the Everly Brothers' 1961 pop hit, "Walk Right Back") is more synthetic–Neil Young than America's "Horse with No Name," and Young's unedited stream of consciousness heads down very peculiar paths in scattershot lyrics that careen from the cliché to the indelible, sometimes in the same verse. "From Hank to Hendrix" contains sublime turns of phrase alongside some of the most hackneyed lines imaginable.

Certainly the most extreme creation on the album is "Such a Woman," a ballad of love so supplicant that it borders on masochism. Young called Jack Nitzsche in to arrange an eighteen-piece string section, a chaste, bittersweet touch that manages to avoid the bombast of the *Harvest* work. It is their best collaboration since "Expecting to Fly," although Jack loathed Young's murky mix. "Live, the strings were beautiful—clean, very sad, so much dynamic range. I hear the record and I think, 'What did he *do*?' I don't know what Neil dumped on there, but it's like toxic waste."

The song, which Young would perform in interminable solo performances designed seemingly to torture his audience, drew extreme responses. "Undoubtedly right up at the top ten of the most trite, meaningless songs Neil's ever written," said David Briggs. "The cry of pain and love Young labored the entire 1980s to express," countered critic Eric Weisbard. Love it or hate it, Young bares his soul on "Such a Woman" with a candor largely absent on the rest of the album.

Harvest might be one of Young's schlockiest creations, but its openness remains endearing. For all its excesses, you never doubt that the musician is grappling with something real. On *Harvest Moon,* Young sounds

conflicted—and guarded—to the point of oblivion, his emotions so restrained that, for me, at least, the album is a profoundly disturbing experience. "I think *Harvest Moon* is about continuance," Young told Allan
Jones. "About trying to keep the flame burning. It's about the feeling that
you don't have to be young to be young." On *Ragged Glory,* Young threw
himself into these same themes with abandon. But he doesn't sound young
at all on *Harvest Moon.* Paul Williams was the only critic who nailed it:
"Ironically, what's lacking on this journey into sensitive-songwriter land is
vulnerability. . . . *Harvest Moon* doesn't deliver."

Not that any of this mattered to the public. Aided by a huge publicity
push, countless interviews, live performances and more television appearances than Young had done in his entire career, the album would go platinum in February 1993, just a little over three months after its release.
Young was only too happy to confound those who felt he'd betrayed his
new Godfather of Grunge hipness. "I'm entering my Perry Como phase,"
Young told Manuel Mendoza. "I think its saving grace is that it's genuine."

—*How did* Harvest Moon *start?*
I dunno. I wrote a bunch of songs in Colorado. While Arc *was playing
back in another room, blasting, I was writing "Such a Woman" on the
piano. Even* I *didn't believe that. I sat down and started playing and it
was* there.
—*Did that record drive you crazy?*
*A little bit, towards the end, because I was striving for something. I
heard a sound and I wanted that sound. I built the echo chambers there
so I could do that record. Not digital echo,* real *echo.*
—*You've used digital echo—*
It used me. *Digital echo is a drag. Convenience store. "Let's go to the
7-Eleven and get some echo." It's very fast. You can get whatever you
want—it gives you just what you ask for. But try to order up a* surprise,
it's not there.

*They used to have a great echo chamber at Sunset Sound that I used
on "I Believe in You," "Oh Lonesome Me," stuff like that. Then Prince
started recording at Sunset Sound a lot, and they brought in a bunch of
digital-delay units and turned the fuckin' echo chamber into a* lounge.

Time marches on. Out with the old, in with the new, heh heh. The two best chambers in Hollywood—Gold Star and Sunset Sound—are gone.

Tim Mulligan did Harvest Moon—*that's where the sound came from. Mulligan's got good ears. I owe a lot to Mulligan. He rises to the occasion.*

—What do you think of "Such a Woman"?

I haven't listened to it in a long time . . . took a lot out of me when I did it, I know that . . . I had to go through a lot of changes.

—Why?

Uhhhhhh, I don't know. It was like a lot of mental baggage went with it. It was not *easy.*

—There's a masochistic quality to that record. Am I wrong?

You mean like "I'm hurting myself"? I know it made Pegi kinda uncomfortable.

—You sound like a guy who would do anything for love.

Yeah, I think that's it.

—Do you idealize women?

Well, maybe I do—and I just can't come to grips with it.

—Did you always want a family of your own?

It's good to have a family. Keeps ya from goin' nuts . . . don't ya think? Families are good for that. When are you gonna sprout out a little Jimmy? Have a kid, that'll fix ya up. Why not? "Little Jimmy, get that typewriter!" "Okay, Dad." No matter what ya do— "You're great, Dad!" They love ya. Ya gotta get one. It's an experience you won't forget.

—What's your idea of beauty?

It's hard to answer that question, because your idea of beauty is a forever changing thing . . . Yesterday I saw somethin' that struck me as beautiful—and it was an old car. Sitting on a hill. And it just looked beautiful to me. Made me feel good.

—No, no, not a FUCKING CAR. I mean, what sort of beauty in a woman do you respond to?

Kindness. Not a word you hear very often, is it?

Neil Young has a difficult time lending superstar magic to music other than his own. Listen to his lackluster performances on albums by Emmylou

Harris, Ben Keith and Robbie Robertson, to name but a few. But now Rusty Kershaw had crawled back out of the muck, asking Young to play on his no-budget album.

Kershaw came to the ranch during *Harvest Moon,* and while Young's overdubs mangled some of Kershaw's tracks (I heard them before the additions), a couple of songs were started from scratch, and one of them, "Future Song"—featuring just Kershaw, Young and Ben Keith—was equal to anything from *On the Beach.*

After nearly twenty years, Kershaw was surprised to have his let's-just-play philosophy thrown back at him by Young. "He goes, 'Well, just play me about a verse of it—or just *do* it. I don't wanna learn it too good, 'cause I'll start fuckin' it up then.' Boy, I busted out laughing, 'cause I can remember when I told him that."

Rusty thumbed out his one-man rhythm on the acoustic, and Ben coaxed a few woozy slides out of a Dobro while Young wheezed along on harp, creating a careening, melancholy whine. "You just can't go into the future / Without taking your past with you," drawled Rusty. Young harmonized impossibly high above him, the voice of a ghost.

There is an unearthly depth to the song that suggests interplanetary travel is not only possible but has been achieved by this trio. Three psychedelic, battle-scarred survivors. They'd been through decades of shit but were still standing, spilling their guts on tape for all the world to hear, and it felt more real than all the smoke-and-mirrors of *Harvest Moon.* Rusty's record, *Now and Then,* went nowhere but, for me, contained the best Neil Young music of 1992.*

· · ·

Young made peace with another character from the distant past during the *Harvest Moon* sessions. Writer John Einarson located Young's old friend Ray Dee, and when Young found out Dee still had tapes from the sessions they cut back in Thunder Bay three decades earlier, he called out of the blue, and invited him to bring the material down to the ranch.

---

*Rusty Kershaw died of a heart attack on October 23, 2001, two days after playing his last gig. He was sixty-three years old.

Dee mulled over his feelings on the flight down. He was still hurt that Young had never once contacted him after his abrupt exit from Thunder Bay. "All this stuff started comin' back. I had put my soul out for this guy. I was pissed off. Very, very upset. I felt that I had been betrayed."

At the ranch, Young had his engineers cue up the tapes. Neither Dee nor Young had heard the material in nearly thirty years. "I'll Love You Forever" came wafting out of the speakers, and when it got to the point where Dee had covered Squires drummer Bill Edmunsen's fumbled beat with a sound effect, Young and Dee turned to each other. "At exactly the same time we said exactly the same thing: 'The *thunderclap version*!' " Dee recalls. "It was like we'd discovered oil! I just about had a shit fit."

A little later Young took his friend for a drive across the ranch in a beat-up old truck. As Dee took in the mind-boggling beauty, Young pulled the vehicle over for a moment. "We were watchin' the sunset," recalls Dee. "Then Neil looked me in the eye and said, 'Look, Ray, I'm sorry. I apologize. You probably have been pissed off at me all these years.' " Dee asked Young why he hadn't come back or even bothered to call.

Neil's explanation was a humdinger: It was all because of the death of his beloved Mort. "He said, 'Look, when the hearse broke down, I didn't have the money to fix it. It died. That hearse was my identity. That machine was my soul. That was *me*. I couldn't come back and face anybody there.' It was like a weight off his shoulders. He had to tell me what happened. I was choked up. I sat there, holding back tears . . . who the hell woulda thought a fuckin' hearse would mean that much to somebody?

"What was really strange about that meeting at the ranch was, I don't think Neil's really changed at all. It's absolutely incredible. I hadn't talked to him in how many years, he's been through all this shit—the man should've been *dead* a hundred and ten years ago—and when I looked him in the eye, you know what? It was like we had never left each other. You could just see the twinkle in his eye. It was like I'd never been away."

Dee was further moved by a heartfelt speech Young gave when he returned to Thunder Bay on May 23 to receive an honorary doctorate from Lakehead University. Young recounted his days in Thunder Bay, thanking Ray Dee and telling the story of Mort. "I just didn't think I was anything without my hearse," he told the crowd. "So I just kept going."

"It was a helluva good speech," said Scott Young, also in the audience. "Neil was a wise man talking to a lot of people who were disposed to listen. It was wonderful. I was so proud of him."

• • •

From January to November 1992, Young embarked on a series of solo tours, playing largely *Harvest Moon* material for audiences who wouldn't hear the record until the tours were almost over. It was a loose and ragged affair. As time went on, the set list seemed to disintegrate, and fans were treated to rare solo-piano versions of "World on a String," "Speakin' Out," "Tonight's the Night" and "Mansion on the Hill," plus older unreleased songs such as "Homefires," "Hitchhiker," "Depression Blues" and "Train of Love." One performance that made an indelible impression on many was a slowed-down, creepy pump-organ version of "Like a Hurricane." Hunched over the keyboard, wisps of hair wafting in the breeze, Young looked lost in some impenetrable reverie—truly the Phantom of the Opera.

You know what that tour was good for? It was good for me. It wasn't really good for anybody else.

It was good for me to realize how completely fuckin' out of touch with the audience I was. I went out there and played all new stuff—songs that really meant somethin' to me—and they were still lookin' at fifteen, twenty years ago, even though they were teenagers. These were young people *who wanted me to do my hits. Wanted me to do* Ragged Glory, *wanted me to do "Rockin' in the Free World." They wanted me to get out there, get real intense. They didn't understand that I don't always do that.*

They didn't get what they wanted—but I got what I *wanted.*

Because I went out and did the songs and got in touch with what it's like to play and communicate to an audience just with guitar, with songs they don't know that well. That's really where it lives. To get out there with new songs that no one knows and make them known, make them hear them. That's the challenge.

I got the same reaction to the Harvest *songs before they came out on the record—people were goin', "What the fuck's goin' on—why doesn't he play some songs we know?" That was great. See, that's what I was trying to do again. Go out and tour like that.*

People didn't have that much of a concept of what I was gonna do in 1970, they were just innarested. Now they think they know what I'm gonna do, and if I don't do it, they're upset. So I have to overcome that when I play.

My biggest enemy is my own history. That's my biggest fuckin' problem. People compare me to what I've done. Whenever they start writing about me, half of the fuckin' review is about my life. *Who gives a shit— if you're gonna read a Neil Young review, you don't need to know all the fuckin' history. What the hell's the fuckin' deal? We gotta go through this whole thing about the hippies and the grunge every fuckin' time?*

People don't know what's great and what isn't great. They never know. People need to have a name—they can't understand why I'm still here, so they call me the Godfather of Grunge. That's easy to relate to.

Fuck reviews. Reviews don't really matter. You can't believe 'em when they fuckin' praise you, and you can't believe them when they criticize you. Because if I believe them now, that means I should've believed them the other times—and we know that they're wrong all *the fuckin' time.*

The Stray Gators would play only four live gigs with Young following *Harvest Moon's* release. After brief appearances at the Bridge School in November 1991 and Farm Aid Five in March 1992, Young brought them together to tape a concert for MTV's ersatz acoustic series, *Unplugged.* Young was reportedly so unhappy with a first attempt in New York City on December 5 that he ate the cost of the taping. The second attempt, on February 7 in Los Angeles, was a total nightmare.

Adding Nils Lofgren to the band, Young changed the set considerably, adding a number of older songs they had never played (he'd even written a new verse for 1968's "I've Been Waiting for You" in hopes of performing it in the show). Joel Bernstein recalls, things deteriorated quickly during rehearsals. Young's vibe was "deathly," he said. "On the second day, they went to do one of the songs, and Neil flipped because everybody was fucking up. He started yelling: 'I can't fucking believe this! You guys have not remembered anything from what we learned yesterday!' " Bernstein was amazed that after their dismal performance in December, the band—aside from Nils Lofgren, who was always ready to follow Young anywhere musically—hadn't gotten their chops together. "Neil was a terror, on their case—but they deserved it."

Then Tim Drummond and Elliot Roberts got into a screaming match over money just minutes before showtime. Word got back to Young and demolished whatever vibe was left. His foul mood was immediately palpable. As Roberts recalls, "By the second song, it was like 'This fuckin' band is totally unsupportive, this music is now fake and phony. Now I'm Neil Diamond and I can't believe I let this happen to me *fuckin' Elliot.*' "

Despite whatever shenanigans took place on the band side, everyone that I talked to agreed on one thing: Young's heart didn't seem to be in the project. Did he want to do it? *"No,"* admitted Elliot. "It was another one of those things that I forced him to do." Drummond recalls that Young almost backed out of the first taping. "We're in the limo, me and Nicolette, goin' to LAX. We get a call on the phone—'Neil doesn't wanna do it.' So we turn the limo around. Then the call comes in, 'Get back in the car, make the airplane.' "

Incredibly, Young agreed to release the second MTV show as an album in June of 1993. The cover featured Young trademarks—a fuzzy photo and scribbled title—but none of it could disarm the MTV logo on the back cover. Yeccchhhh. Back in 1988, Young had kicked MTV's ass all over the map with "This Note's for You"; now he had conceded. "I don't know how comfortable Neil seemed in that context," said James Taylor. "It was definitely an assault on who he is." The album went gold that November, and Dylan soon followed Young's lead, taping his own *Unplugged* and looking just as miserable.

At any rate, Young hasn't worked with the Stray Gators since. "They played like former band members," Young quipped to one member of his crew after the show. The resentment ran both ways. "Neil does not have enough money for me to work with him again," said Kenny Buttrey. "It was just a nightmare. I never want to hear his name again. I never wanna see the guy . . . I will never, *ever* play a Neil Young album on my stereo again. I want it in capital letters that he is the HARDEST PERSON TO WORK WITH I've ever worked with in my life, bar none." (Despite these protestations, Buttrey has worked with Neil since.)

First the explosions with Crazy Horse and Briggs over *Weld;* now the bad feelings over *Unplugged*. It seemed the characters around Young were finding it harder and harder to weather his wrenching shifts in direction. They'd been through it so many times before that they'd gotten a lot more sensitive. They were older now; more was at stake. It was a tough situation for everybody.

Then there was Ben Keith. He made a Christmas album, *Seven Gates,* featuring Johnny Cash, J. J. Cale, Rusty Kershaw and Young. It was partially recorded, mixed and mastered at Young's studio, and he got the album released on Reprise in 1994. But troubles arose over the promotion of the album, which disappeared immediately. Some observers feel that its failure—following the *Unplugged* debacle—was just too much for Ben, the one musician who, since *Harvest,* had stood by Young's side, always supportive of whatever direction Shakey took. Keith retreated to Nashville.

I've hurt Ben Keith's feelings so much I don't know if it'll ever be the same. I got pushed into doing this Christmas record. It was all on me. I don't think I was very good.

The people working with Ben gave Johnny Cash the idea that he was workin' on my record. That was not a good idea. I got this call from Johnny Cash—he thought I was gonna be in his video. I said, "I think we're bein' taken advantage of." He said, "I think you're right." They did that Nashville thing to me, and I fuckin' freaked out and I think it really hurt Ben's feelings.

I probably overreacted, and a lotta my frustrations about other things came into that. That's real possible. But I've always felt badly about that with Ben.

I get so hurt when people do things I don't understand. I just don't do anything, I let it go, it builds up . . . that's really a bad weakness of mine. But I've got a long time left to improve.
—Any regrets about the way things have gone down?
Well, I wish that the people I like, the people I work with—Briggs, Mulligan, Ralph, Billy, Poncho and Ben Keith—that's the core, and maybe some others I'm not mentioning—I wish these people liked me as much as I like them. That they didn't harbor resentments about me.

I mean, I really did try to give everybody what they wanted and what was fair. When I looked around at what others were giving in similar circumstances—I think I did better, yet I don't think it was enough *for these people.*

Somehow I mismanaged the way that went down. And through my own inadequacies—the inability to face up to certain things and, when I was younger, being unable to be forthcoming when I should've been and really say how I felt about things—my immature reactions to things hurt these people. So they resent *it. They still feel this way about me— and they probably always will.*

After *Unplugged,* Young swerved off in another direction with a completely different band. On October 16, 1992, he had appeared at Bob Dylan's thirtieth-anniversary concert at Madison Square Garden in New York: "Bobfest," as Young dubbed it. The event was broadcast live and released on album and video, and it would prove yet another triumph for Young. It was an easy victory. Other than Young, an interesting reading of "Foot of Pride" by Lou Reed and the always idiosyncratic Dylan himself, it was a dubious affair, a manufactured-event snoozefest.

The band that backed Young was an odd choice for someone who has mostly gone out of his way to avoid "real musicians," roots or otherwise: Booker T. and the MGs. The Memphis-based quartet—Booker T. Jones on keyboards, Steve Cropper on guitar, Donald "Duck" Dunn on bass and Al Jackson Jr. on drums—was the bedrock of the Stax studio sound, having played on landmark recordings by Otis Redding, Ruby Johnson, Sam and Dave and many others, as well as their own hit records as a quartet, beginning with "Green Onions," a number-three pop hit in 1962. Together or individually they'd worked with everyone: Jerry Lee Lewis, Willie Nelson, Muddy Waters, Dylan. Unfortunately, Al Jackson Jr., as essential to the group as Ralph Molina is to Crazy Horse, was murdered in 1975, and at Bobfest, session men Jim Keltner and Anton Fig augmented the original trio. Young and the band had already met, having jammed on an impromptu version of Jimmy Reed's "Baby, What You Want Me to Do" at New York's Lone Star Roadhouse in January 1992.

Young's slot at Bobfest turned out to be a dramatic one. He followed Sinead O'Connor, who tearfully fled the stage midsong to a chorus of booing, a reaction to her recent *Saturday Night Live* appearance, during which she tore up a picture of the Pope.* Young would later admit to a reporter that he was seriously nervous before the gig, but as he ambled out in a leather vest, shirttails out, he seemed in an unusually good mood, leading the band through an extraordinarily sloppy version of "Just Like Tom Thumb's Blues" in which Young fucked up the order of verses—and which became more unhinged as it progressed. "Play whatever the hell you want," Young had allegedly told the band before starting, and it was all over the place but, in the hands of these old pros, gloriously so.

Bobbing and weaving around the stage, with "Duck" Dunn's fluent yet rock-solid bass line the perfect counterpoint to his gutbucket guitar, Young seemed so caught up in Dylan's lyrics he was practically laughing out loud. It was a shambling, wonderful performance, and the element that stood out the strongest was just how relaxed Young seemed. No battles to fight here; he acted like a man who had won them all.

Bob Dylan's music could receive no greater tribute in the nineties than the vitality Young imbued it with this night, particularly on a tough version of "All Along the Watchtower," with Booker T.'s here-comes-Neil organ providing just the right bed for Young's shrieking attack on Old Black. A grizzled old fuck just shy of forty-seven years old who should have known better and thankfully didn't, Young once again reminded the world that rock and roll could still be something more than plug-in atmosphere for TV commercials.

Young walked away with the show, and to one admirer, it was no surprise. "What makes Neil a hero to the grungers and what makes him valid to people like Booker T. or Dylan is the fact he's an unpredictable, iconoclastic old guy who can still rock—the *only* old guy who can still rock. The rest should all retire."

These words were spoken by David Briggs shortly after the broadcast. He had made a dramatic return to Young's life, bursting uninvited into the

---

*Young later commented on O'Connor's actions in the press: "How often do you get the chance to play when people are booing?" he told Allan Jones. "The thing is, you're getting to them. That's the thing that matters . . . I think she just LOST it . . . she's supposed to be in control. She's supposed to know what she's doing. So don't ask me to feel any *sympathy* for her . . . I think she blew a really great chance to be brilliant. She let the audience get the best of her. . . . You want to protest, go ahead. Be my guest. But there's a time when it's gonna come back on you. You have to be strong, you have to be prepared to *take* that. She let it beat her . . . they put her to the test and she just wasn't up to it."

train barn one day and, according to his version of events, announcing he'd decided to forgive Neil instead of killing him. Briggs would produce the *Unplugged* album—his only solo production credit with Young—and mix the album/video version of the Bobfest performance. "I just smoked a joint, cranked it up and it was done."

Young embarked on a tour of Europe and the States with Booker T. and the MGs in the summer of 1993, with Jim Keltner on drums plus Annie Stocking and Neil's half sister, Astrid, on backing vocals. Briggs was more than thrilled to be working with Young on a non–Crazy Horse project. "One of Neil's biggest problems is that he doesn't have any peers. He's so forceful as a musician that he's always the leader. These guys were big enough men to push Neil. It was a chance for him to take his music and *expand* it way beyond what he was ever able to do before."

After rehearsing very briefly, the band played a trio of warm-up gigs in California. The second night at the Warfield Theater in San Francisco was electrifying. "Mr. Soul" made a racket like a bucket of rocks, and Steve Cropper—whose clean tone is 180 degrees from Young's noise—was especially soulful on a surprise unreleased song from the past, "Separate Ways." One had to admire Young's moxie: Not only did he have the audacity to perform "Southern Man" with these Memphis boys, he resurrected Otis Redding's "(Sittin' on) The Dock of the Bay," tailoring the words to his own journey. Young was very high on the band, full of comparisons to the Buffalo Springfield, and the tour would garner him some of the best reviews of his career.

Things usually mutate and change over the course of a Young tour, but this trip seemed to head straight downhill after the Warfield. There was something hollow about the affair, a whiff of Las Vegas. Young had few surprises to combat the natural polish that came from these pros playing basically the same set night after night. It reminded me of Dylan's 1978 *Street Legal* tour—big "professional" band, little soul.

Briggs felt Young was more interested in his new passion for Harley Davidson—he took his bike out cruising between gigs—or playing golf. It all left David deeply disappointed. He felt that the band was "good every single fuckin' show—they were never bad—but they never took it to any new creative level. It was an oldies show. Neil didn't make the most of it by a hundred miles.

"What Neil told 'em was this: 'Hey, man, you guys just play whatever you want.' Period. But what he didn't get was, none of 'em had ever heard his songs before. I mean, they weren't his fans. When I sent them the tape of the songs, they'd never heard any of them, so they had to cop chops from the records, not just on one or two songs, but every single song.

"And not only that, Neil did *not* wanna rehearse with them, and the bottom line was, once everybody learned the songs three quarters of the way through Europe, it became rote. They were repeating themselves, playing the same part. It became a no-brainer for them. There was no challenge, no new material coming in. Neil only had two new songs and that was it. To me, the fire to write and create was not in the guy."

But criticisms of the tour came with hindsight. When the band finished the tour of the States in September, expectations were high. Booker T. and the MGs were waiting to go into the studio, Briggs was anxious to record a great album with them. And then Young made another left turn.

big business, small scale

I spent the first three years of the nineties chasing Neil Young. It was a cat-and-mouse game of absurd proportions—faxes, phone calls, lawyers, agents and managers. I was on Young like fleas on a dog, but he evaded me at every turn. During the June 1993 rehearsals for the tour with Booker T. and the MGs, he invited me up to hear the band—not to *talk,* mind you, just to hear the band. After one of the sneak pretour gigs, I caught up with Young as he got into his '54 Caddy limo, Pearl. I let slip a few arcane facts I had learned about the car. This piqued Young's curiosity, and he was suddenly in my face, asking who I came with and where I was going. My heart pounding, I thought, This is it! But he just as abruptly changed his mind. "Not tonight, not tonight. But this is the way it'll happen—if you're just hanging around." He smiled slyly. "Hell, it almost happened right *now.*" He slid into Pearl, then drove off into the night.

Then I was to meet him on his boat, the *Ragland,* which Young was taking out for a day cruise. Now I've got him, I thought. We're on a fucking boat—he can't escape. Unfortunately, I'd never been out to sea and spent the whole trip bent over the rail, puking. Every once in a while I'd crawl back and mutter a question to Young, who was hunched over the wheel, cackling like Captain Ahab.

Our first real interview for the book finally took place in the middle of the night, headed for Houston in a Learjet crammed with Booker T. and the MGs plus Elliot Roberts. The next night on the bus Young and I did another four hours. But in Dallas a couple of nights later, he stood me up again. It was hopeless. I commiserated with Briggs.

"I've talked to everybody, done all the research," I told him. "But I feel like I'm chasing a ghost. I'm writing a book about a guy I've never hung out with."

"I feel for you, bro," said David. "The guy you're writing about just doesn't hang out."

But Young called me one evening shortly before his forty-eighth birthday in November 1993. Sounding a bit frantic, he immediately began ranting about how, in the wake of *Harvest Moon*'s massive success, people wanted him to do all sorts of ridiculous things—like contribute a live recording of "Rockin' in the Free World" with Pearl Jam and Booker T. and the MGs to the soundtrack of *Wayne's World 2*. Elliot had started the ball rolling, and now Briggs was at the ranch frantically mixing away, with Warner Bros. hot to put out the single. At the eleventh hour, Young was having second thoughts. "This kind of pressure is unusual for me," he said.

"Yeah, well, get used to it," I told him. "You're the comeback kid. Everybody thinks this is the last go-round and they're trying to squeeze out every drop they can." I had been at the Portland performance under consideration, thought it was all-star celebrity crap and told him so.

"Well, Briggs is gonna play it for me at the studio on Wednesday. You should be there."

A day and a half later I was in the back of a limo snaking up the road to Young's ranch: a couple thousand acres of northern California wilderness filled with redwoods, lakes and all manner of creatures, as well as several groups of buildings, all of which bear Young's eccentric imprint. His home—originally a small, old ranch house—has ballooned into a never-ending wonder that has made more than one contractor break into a sweat.

There's the Broken Arrow Studio; a large white house for visiting band members; and the cavernous equipment barn where he recorded *Ragged Glory* with the Horse. Separate buildings house his model-train and car collections, both such monuments to obsession that they seem more like artworks than a rich man's investments. Young has created his own Xanadu. Once you pass through the gates, you feel like you've seceded from the union.

Arriving at the woodsy patch of land surrounding the studio, I leapt out of the car, bounded up the steps and through the door. Back in the control room I could see Briggs, hunched over the mixing board, pushing faders and thrashing his head to the beat. He looked ready to keel over from exhaustion.

Briggs set up the mixes for Neil's imminent arrival while I wandered around, scanning the walls for a favorite piece of memorabilia: a mid-seventies photo of Young renewing his deal with Warner Bros. Neil had requested that the signing take place on one of Warner's old Western movie sets. There they all were—Mo Ostin, Elliot Roberts and Neil, hovering over the signed document like million-dollar desperadoes. If you look closely you can see Ostin had his hands around Young's neck. Neil must've gotten what he wanted.

Suddenly I heard the clatter of an old automobile, and John Nowland, in charge of running the studio day to day, glanced out the window: "Neil's here." As always, everybody came to attention—except Briggs. Young shot through the door, scraggly hair flying, wild-eyed, his dog Bear padding behind him. "I don't think we'll put this out, but let's hear it."

Briggs played him the Portland mix and an alternate, unmixed performance from Toronto. Afterward, everybody engaged in some halfhearted enthusiasm. Turd-polishing, I thought. "Well, nobody asked my opinion, but if you need to put a new addition on the car barn, put it out. Otherwise keep it on the shelf."

Young flew across the room and got right in my face, his laser eyes locked on mine. It was like staring into an active volcano. "Well, y'see, Jimmy—*we already* have *an addition on the car barn.*" Neil proceeded to make a case for a loud feedback drone near the end of one of the takes. Resembling the sound of a dying whale, it was impressive.

"Then just put out the one fucking note," I argued. "You can out-*Arc Arc.* Or leave it in the can. You already did the definitive version of this song on *Saturday Night Live* three years ago."

That got to Young, who was now pacing the room like a madman. "Yeah, right," he said. "I did it on TV." He left some room for a final decision, but everyone knew what it would be. This is one reason I love Neil—some nut shows up with an opinion and he'll listen. It drives those who attempt to control him crazy.

The *Wayne's World 2* brouhaha settled, Young shot across the room to whisper conspiratorially in my ear: "I have to check out some things over at the train barn. Wanna go?"

•   •   •

"Lionel makes a boy feel like a man and a man feel like a boy," trumpets a 1934 ad, and this philosophy has changed little over the years. Joshua Lionel Cowen, the Jewish immigrant who formed Lionel in 1900, described the company's goal in 1946 as "creating a lifelong comradeship between a boy and his dad."

The image of a united, happy family was obviously a potent one for Young. "An innocent endeavor" is how Young described his work with Lionel to Mary Eisenhart. "It gives me a lot of relief. . . . At the core of this thing is goodness. That's really what I like about this whole idea. That I might be responsible for something that enables families to come together more in some way."

In 1992, Young entered into a partnership with Richard P. Kughn, the owner of Lionel Trains. Their company, Liontech, was now developing a sophisticated sound system and handheld controller that promised to revolutionize the industry. "I'm tryin' to do a lot in a short period of time, bring this company from the past into the future," Young said proudly. He was a singular presence at Lionel. "I'm unthreatenable, because I have nothing to lose. I don't have a position. I'm like a fuckin' mirage, and that's where I like to be." Within a few short years Young would own a significant share of the company.

In recent years Lionel had lost some of its luster, and both Kughn and Young were determined to revitalize the operation. Most of Liontech's innovations were based on concepts Young had been exploring for over a decade, and in a little over a week he would be going to Lionel headquarters in Chesterfield, Michigan, to show Kughn and the rest of the company refined prototypes of the new sound system—Railsounds II. Young had two research-and-development labs working around the clock to prepare for the demonstration.

For Young, the train world was a diversion—like making movies or acting—that revitalized his music. "My dad said he could understand why I would need an obsession to distract me from my work. How can you miss something if you don't go away? If you're not really into music and excited to be there, it sounds like it. You can't hide that. So the only way to do that is to starve yourself. Get to the point where you *have* to play."

That November, Neil's conversations would always meander back to his twin obsessions of the moment: Lionel Trains and Crazy Horse. An ultraconservative toy company and a stoned-out rock band, each firmly at opposite ends of the spectrum. I got the feeling it suited Young just fine.

•   •   •

Neil and I jumped in his green 1950 Plymouth and rode the potholed roads to the train barn, a spartan thousand-square-foot redwood box nestled in the trees. Like many around Young, I had been a little condescending toward this grown man's passion. But his friend Roger Katz set me straight: "If you wanna talk to Neil, go to the train barn. It holds a big key. Something happens to Neil in that space. Whether it's tied into childhood or another outlet for creating fantasy, this is the inner sanctum. This is Neil's world."

Young led me up the redwood wheelchair ramp into the building. Harshly illuminated from a couple of skylights, the huge layout—set low enough for a child's grasp—overwhelmed the room. Long ribbons of track nestled in a natural landscape of redwood, rock and living plants that fed off a mist-irrigation system installed largely by Young himself. There was a pond with real goldfish, wooden trestles handmade by Mazzeo and arcane touches like a factory complex made out of an ancient vacuum cleaner. Knick-knacks found around the world by Young and his family dotted the landscape: tin cars, billboards, an incense-burning tepee. Through it all ran track, and Young changed the layout continually. "It's a real modeler's dream, mixing realities," he said with a grin. His engineers had rigged the phones so that a train whistle announced incoming calls.

In one back corner of the room was a cement ramp and alcove overlooking the whole layout. An old-fashioned silver and black wood-burning stove sat between two purple overstuffed chairs. On the white walls hung a set of large, colorful prints by Angela Trotta Thomas, the Norman Rockwell of model-train art. One picture showed a rather apprehensive lad with a locomotive in his hand, looking up at a shopkeeper: "Can you fix it, Mister?" The only acknowledgment of music in the room was an old poster for the Band's *The Last Waltz* concert and a Hawkshaw Hawkins boxed set— still unopened—given to Young by Joel Bernstein for his birthday in 1990.

The more time I spent in the train barn, the more it grew on me. Wood and concrete, piles of trains and train parts everywhere, endless wiring, colored lights and ozone . . . despite the roaring fires Young built in the wood stove, the room never completely warmed up. It was desolate, kind of spooky, but in an intoxicating way—like a diner-at-three-A.M. Hopper painting.

Young flicked a few switches and one of the beautiful old-timers clackety-clacked around the layout. The smell of ozone filled the air.

The train barn was a refuge for Neil: no band members flubbing notes, no producers storming off, no surprises outside of the occasional derailment. Staring at the minute details of the layout, I thought of how one model-train buff had explained the allure: "Model railroading is a series of dioramas connected by track, a mystical world. It lets you be the creator completely. For the guy home from work, model railroading is therapy. He's got a Godlike position over this little, tiny world that he can control— where the outside world, maybe he doesn't have as much control over it and can't make it like he wants."

•   •   •

Young's involvement with model-train technology started sometime back in the seventies. "I was walkin' down Sunset Boulevard buying Christmas gifts, and I saw a Lionel passenger train and I thought, 'That's *my* Christmas present—from me to me.' I've since got a lot of other trains that look exactly like it—when buying collections, you get multiples of things—and somehow I lost track of which one it is. But it's in there." He laughed. "I really paid too much for it."

Down in Los Angeles, Young set up a layout for his son Zeke. "He's sort of the unsung hero," said Neil. "It was one of our best ways of communicating, playing with trains. I think I was hard on him, because I made him organize things—I was tryin' to teach him physics and all this stuff." Young laughed again. "But he learned it. Zeke learned a lot from the trains."

Like any of Young's obsessions, the new hobby quickly mutated into something much larger. After his first setup took over his dining room, he had the train barn built. The wiring system alone was "every bit as massive as a full-blown recording studio," said engineer Harry Sitam. "Neil's aptitude for technical things—electrical and electronic—is amazing."

Young formed a company, Yardmaster, and engineer Sal Trentino began to investigate new sound systems and different methods of control. "We'd have monthly shows where I'd come to the train barn and show the latest developments," said Trentino. "He wanted remote-control, robotic trains. I designed a thirty-two-channel system. Each train had forward and reverse and all sorts of sound effects—bells, whistles, horns. Damned if it didn't sound like a real train." The 1982 *Trans* tour and subsequent financial problems put a hold on the Yardmaster project, but Neil continued to tinker, searching for ways to help his son Ben enjoy the hobby. In the nineties, Young got back into model trains full-throttle.

As I sat in one of the overstuffed chairs, Young ran one of the trains utilizing his new sound system, then one using a system made by the other top-of-the-line-train-effects company, QSI (Quinn-Severson Industries). "Our honorable competitor," said Young, smiling tightly. They both sounded like real trains to my ears, but Young was only too happy to point out the shortcomings of QSI's system. "It doesn't sound like it's big," he said, watching the small locomotive chugging down the track. "It sounds like a truck. Power goes up and down too fast . . . close your eyes and it sounds like a Peterbilt." Young paused. "It's got a cool horn," he allowed.

Young launched into a story concerning the toy-train business, a small group of competing companies as nefarious and oddball as any in the music scene. "Big business on a small scale," Young likes to call it, and he went in with a bang.

Back in the fall of 1990, Young entered into a partnership with QSI, a Hillsboro, Oregon, outfit run by a pair of eccentrics, Pat Quinn and Fred Severson. QSI was investigating all sorts of technological advancements, and Young, who particularly liked Severson—a train brain who kept his Christmas-tree layout year-round—became a one-third partner in the outfit. The trio began developing a new sound system for model trains.

Severson and Quinn introduced Young to all the major players, most important Lionel owner Richard P. Kughn, but the deal with QSI fell through. Young felt the company had unreasonable expectations. "Their whole view of how to move into the train business was based on paranoia, people taking their stuff, not having competition . . . their dream was to take over *everything,* have their equipment in all trains, be like Dolby. I knew that Lionel would never do that. I realized, 'Hey, why put a bunch of money into these guys who aren't even interested in bein' with the only company that's gonna give us a return?' "

The final straw came, Young said, during contract negotiations between QSI and Lionel. "One of the things I had in the contract was that Lionel and QSI would work together to make toy trains accessible to the disabled." Young said that he got the contract back from QSI with that clause crossed out. "From that moment on I lost my heart for them. And I said, 'Listen, you guys—all your ideas, I've thought of. It's just *the way you did it I didn't know.* And I'm not using the way you did it. It was fascinating to me—that's why I asked so many questions—and I learned how you did it. But I'm not using it, and I won't tell anybody. I'm gonna do it the way I was gonna do it before I met you.' "

Severson and Quinn—who maintain that Young left without an explanation—were stunned by his sudden departure. "Neil was very impatient, didn't understand technology moves very slowly," said Severson. "We were already needing money, because we were ramping up to meet Neil's demands. He continually assured us we would be paid. And then Neil abruptly pulled out." Severson said Young's handlers descended on the company, demanding not just the return of his money, but all their research as well.

Meanwhile, Young went into business with Lionel himself, joining forces with Kughn to form Liontech. He also began supplying the company with "E" units, a part previously provided by QSI. "Neil not only tried to get our technology, he also took our best customer, all in one fell swoop," said Severson, who wondered if Young hadn't planned it from the beginning. "What he did to our company, it was like hittin' the side of your TV with a sledgehammer—flickering lights, tubes gone, nothing."

"When I started dealing with Lionel, QSI threatened to sue me because they claimed everything I was doing I learned from them," said Young. "They didn't know I'd spent a hundred thousand dollars on this project in 1979, '80, '81. Even though I *told* them, they didn't believe me. They thought that I'd learned everything I knew from them. That I planned the whole thing ahead of time—to get info and to go to Lionel myself.

"They started makin' noises as to how they would protect their patents. They sent threatening letters to Lionel and basically interfered with my business. *Threats.* And I said to myself, 'Well, fuck these guys—they're gonna screw up my deal. What I'll do is sue them.' Sue them for declamatory judgment, no money—that's the court saying, 'Do I have the right to do business or not?' Let the lawyers decide. They came back and sued me for twenty-two million in damages."

When the case got into depositions, Young surprised his counsel by asking if he could attend. "I said, 'I can go to these, right?' They said, 'Yeah. You *wanna* go?' I said, 'I know what questions to ask.' All this documentation of what we were doing in 1980 is what saved me in my lawsuit with QSI. I had it nailed. So I sat there beside my attorney and took Fred Severson's deposition. They thought it was gonna take an afternoon. We deposed him for five days."

The suit was settled: Young was free to continue with Lionel; QSI kept their research and Young's investment, and took the sound system Young had helped pay for to Lionel's main competitor, Mike's Train House. The combination of MTH and QSI would make for tough competition. Young remained determined to keep the majority of Lionel's manufacturing in the U.S., while MTH relied on cheap overseas labor, undercutting Lionel's prices significantly.*

Young and I talked about the QSI matter many times, and despite their falling-out, he was complimentary to both Severson and Quinn. "They're good guys, but they're so paranoid. They *never* fuckin' trusted me. Even though I was giving them money, they didn't trust me. I think that's *good* to know—that someone can feel that way about me."

After parting with QSI, Young continued developing his own remote control/sound system (concerning the dough Neil has dropped on model-train pursuits, Elliot Roberts said, "I can't even put it on tape, frankly. Let's just say you can get a first-round draft pick in any sport for half the money") and in early 1992 presented it at Lionel headquarters in Michigan. "I was so nervous I screwed up the demonstration completely. The worst stage fright you could ever imagine. I knew I fucked up. It was still a success."

The crusty ex-cop and the longhaired rocker, Richard Kughn and Neil Young were an unlikely pair, but the two saw eye to eye on Lionel's future—although Young startled Kughn with his money-is-no-object attitude: "I told him time and time again I really didn't care how much it cost." Kughn cautioned that they couldn't just go on an endless paper chase. "I

---

*As of 2000, Lionel is moving more and more of its manufacturing overseas.

said, 'That'll never happen. It's gonna work.' At that point I didn't even know how we were gonna do it. But you gotta *believe*."

. . .

The train whirred, whistled and chugged along as Young ran it back and forth around the track. Even I was starting to hear the advantages of his system—the effects were less one-dimensional, more synchronized with the action of the train. Young had gone out and recorded the actual engine the replica was based on, then had his engineers reconstitute the sound on a computerized chip that played back through a tiny speaker within the cab. He explained the problem at hand, his eyes never leaving the train.

"It's supposed to rev up like that and then stick," said Young, frowning as he listened. "I wanna see if it's gonna do it after you leave it off for a while. Electronics are funny."

A little while later he tried again. "Now that time—after being off—it worked right, see?" He scrawled some notes on the blackboard, outlining the problems one by one. Joe Thibodeaux, Young's software engineer, was having trouble duplicating the problems and this point-by-point would enable him to isolate the difficulties.

Young's intensity was palpable. Just about everybody who knew him wondered if he ever relaxed. "Is it easy for you to have fun?" I asked.

"Well, it's easy for me to have fun doin' this. Fun for me is makin' things—havin' a goal, an idea.

"Lionel is like an American institution. This is like GM, RCA, General Electric, Ford, Revell . . . those classic names. It's gotta be cared for like a piece of fuckin' history. It's tradition. And I have the technology to make these trains compete today. I'm *on* this."

I found the whole story incredible. "Where did you get your business sense?" I asked.

"I've been a notoriously bad businessman . . . I'll do anything to get what I want. Pay *way* too much, that's how I do it, usually. Y'know, I don't care. If I want something—I don't wanna hurt somebody or cheat, I don't like to do that and I don't do that—but if it can be gotten financially and I want it, I'm tenacious. I'll just keep going for it until I get what I want."

"What do your advisers think of this attitude?"

"Oh, you think they liked it when I was spending a hundred and seventy-five thousand dollars on spec for a control system for Lionel? It's like 'What the fuck are you *doing*?' They're just scratchin' their heads, makin' fun of me and shit. But here I am . . . and it's happening."

·   ·   ·

We were back in the Plymouth. "I love the winter when it's like this," he said. "Hardly anybody comes to visit ya."

"Ever feel too isolated up here?"

"No," he said, gripping the wheel. "Definitely not. Like sometimes Ralph and Billy say I got a little bit of bark on me. I must be doin' really great to be doin' as great as I am under these dire circumstances."

I related some of the "Stay on Neil's ranch long enough, you'll grow moss" quips I'd heard. Young was not amused, and I'd regret repeating them, because he would soon invent a new torture for the Horse. A random advertisement that happened to contain the slogan BECAUSE THE HORSE had caught his eye, and that was it: the recording plans with Booker T. and the MGs would quickly evaporate. Why? Because the Horse.

"This time I'd like to start recording and just not *stop*. Just record for thirty hours and see what that sounds like. Never leave the studio for a week. *Sleep* in it. The whole thing—coffee, breakfast, just be there. See what that works like. That's the opposite of what grown-ups would do. The Horse is gonna be *beggin'* me to record at the ranch by the time I'm through with 'em.

"My heart is telling me to play with Crazy Horse," Young said. "It's speaking loudly. I have to know for sure . . . I don't wanna start something in motion that's not gonna go right away. I just gotta make sure every-thing's in place. Y'know, like Briggs doesn't want me to record with Crazy Horse, so . . . "

I thought there were some things Young should know if he wanted to record again with the Horse. As I related the disappointments over *Weld,* the conversation grew so intense and combative that, had there been an eject button in the car, I would've pressed it myself. But Young took it all in. That's the amazing thing. Even if he did have a bunch of nuts on his back, namely Briggs, Elliot, the Horse and presently his biographer—all of whom thought they knew what was right for the guy—give Young the right information and he acts. He called Briggs and made it official: Round up the Horse, we're making an album in Los Angeles.

• • •

The next day at the train barn, there were a couple of big amp cases on the floor, and John Nowland was using white spray paint to stencil in a name. Only this time it didn't read NEIL YOUNG, as it would for any tour; Nowland was painting the LIONTECH logo all over them. Young watched and smiled. "You open it up and it's all these trains in foam. Two huge boxes full of Lionel trains outfitted with my technology—and the competitor's trains and *their* technology. 'This is what they're doing, this is what we're doing.' We're gonna eat 'em alive."

Young paced around the room, a favorite pastime. "I always get really nervous before I take all this stuff to Lionel. I'm trying so many new things all at once, I don't want to be overshadowed by some malfunction. I don't wanna be *surprised*. It's like a concert, y'know. I like to know if the band knows the songs."

• • •

In the suburbs of Menlo Park, we visited Real Design Labs, one of Young's research-and-development units. Inside was a large, harshly lit room full of long tables with studious men poking at trains and hunched over computers. "People working, problems being solved, money changing hands," Young whispered, entranced by the buzz of activity. "I really get off on this."

The sight of one RDL denizen made Young's face brighten. "Hi, Dennis!" Young exclaimed. This was Dennis Fowler, a guy I had already heard a lot about from Neil. He had developed Liontech's "E" unit and was one of Young's favorite characters at the moment.

Pale, with a graying mustache and beard, Fowler and his worn jeans, worse sneakers and beat-up Ford Galaxie made him something of an outcast at RDL, which endeared him all the more to Young.

"Somebody ran into Dennis's Galaxie. He took it to the body shop, got an old fender the same color as his. The insurance company couldn't believe it. Dennis likes it rusty the way it is," Young whispered in approval. "He's watching it change." Whenever we visited RDL, Fowler would get the first hello and the last goodbye. As I watched him quietly discuss with Neil some arcane aspect of the locomotive he was grasping tightly in his hand, I immediately saw why. He had that particular intensity Young craves in people. I saw it in Ralphie when he hung his head down and bashed away, lost in the beat, or in David Briggs when he was hammering out a mix.

Fowler was showing Young a new innovation: double chuffs. We watched as the train went around the track, a smoke unit inside emitting pairs of white puffs in sync with the sound effects. Young was thrilled.

"Dennis has got a vibe, hasn't he? Dennis is my main man. Completely focused on the stuff—to the point where he can hem and haw on some little detail for like days, nights, weeks . . . he's so into it." Neil Young, Dennis Fowler's number-one fan. I wondered if Fowler had any idea.

· · ·

Back at the train barn, Young was happy as a clam. In his hand was CAB-1, the first fully functioning remote-control unit. A small, sleek black box with an antenna and a bunch of buttons—most prominently a big speed-control button with the red-and-white Lionel "L"—the design was a combination of ideas from him, Lionel and Applied Design Labs' Ron Milner. Young's first design, done with Rick Davis—an awesome unit that incorporated the bullet shape of the old Bakelite ZW transformers—was rejected as too retro. "You gotta know when to let things go," said Young, who spent $10,000 building the prototype.

"I'm so excited to have that hand control," Young said. "When we were mixing *Weld* at Indigo, I was drawing it. This is the first day I've had one." His enthusiasm was contagious. He even had me running the fucking train.

Neil talked about his extended plans for Liontech. Because of him, Lionel's catalog was now offering the standard disabled-access button that helped Ben run the trains. "It's not just good for that—it's good for little babies," said Young. "Kids that might wanna play with trains, but their hands might be so small. Give 'em the big red button.

"Today Ben had a report. He's the equipment manager for the team at this regular school. Ben's the equipment manager!" Young chortled with glee. "It's part of integrating disabled kids with the regular school. Pretty cool."

"Ever wanted anything really bad you couldn't get?"

"Oh, yeah. Sure. All kinds of things. It's not the gettin' 'em—it's tryin' to get 'em that's so much fun. That's life."

Talk turned to two rabid fan organizations, the HyperRust website and the Neil Young Appreciation Society, publishers of the *Broken Arrow* fanzine. Both venues dissected Young in minute detail, and it ticked him off.

"I don't have a website," said Young, annoyed. "I never fuckin' look at 'em. They can all talk as much as they want, it doesn't have anything to do with me.* And *Broken Arrow*? They don't have any respect for my art. They get way too far into it.

"They think they're doin' a great thing. They're very sincere—that's their saving grace. But they drive me fuckin' *nuts*. They're reviewing shows I did in 1976! *What the fuck?*"

Young talked about "Change Your Mind," the new song he had performed with the MGs on the European tour. "I play it on the road, these fuckin' people from the NYAS fuckin' publish the lyrics—and they get 'em wrong.

"I'm tellin' ya, it's a destructive thing. It inhibits my creative process to see things written out before I record them and have people passing judgments on songs they weren't meant to hear. I'm at a point where I don't wanna play new songs before I put 'em out. They've ruined it for me."

Young maintained that the next time the Horse played, it would be under an assumed name at a tiny, out-of-the-way bar—and the tapers would never know about it. "They'll never fuckin' find us," he insisted. "Route 66. Seligman, Arizona. One night only—the Misfits."

But in 1996, when Young and the Horse played an extended series of secret gigs at a tiny club not far from his home, tapers captured everything but the first half of the first set—and even that turned up later. Young refused to believe it. It was a different world than he was used to.

•   •   •

"*Philadelphia* screened in L.A. today," Young told me a day later. He had contributed a song to the Jonathan Demme AIDS drama, a simple piano

---

*As of 2000, www.neilyoung.com now exists.

ballad that for me had all the vulnerability *Harvest Moon* lacked. "I spoke to David Geffen this morning. He saw it in New York and said everybody was crying at the end, during the song. It must've been quite an emotional release." Young smiled. "Probably the only thing I coulda done to surpass that is *Wayne's World 2*. But I missed my chance."

I was told Young had put off recording "Philadelphia" a few times. "I knew it wasn't gonna come easy. To tell ya the truth, the song's actually quite a bit over my head in terms of playing. It's a hard song to play, and it's gotta be played loose. 'Philadelphia' seems related to 'Will to Love.' Things come and go—they drop in and then they're gone, like a shadow of a drum, a little inferred cymbal part . . . " "Philadelphia" pointed to a new direction, one Young would flesh out on *Sleeps with Angels*.

I had found out Young was planning on donating the proceeds from the "Philadelphia" track to the Gay Men's Health Crisis center. He acknowledged it was true but didn't seem anxious to publicize the fact. I got the feeling there were plenty of other charitable acts I didn't know about. "I'm not trying to score any social points," he said.

Young was amused by his renewed popularity. "Now I'm at this point where it seems like whatever the fuck I do is cool. It's so funny the way things go. All of a sudden people want me to do this, want me to do that. I got an offer to go to the hundredth birthday of the Democratic party and play my guitar. This guy who owns Revlon has offered me a hundred thousand dollars just to be there. Just because it's me. I mean, fuck, I'm *Canadian*."

•   •   •

At the end of a week of exhaustive interviews, I was hanging out with Young in the second-floor office of his car barn. Down below us was a special airtight chamber with a rotating lift Young called "the operating room." "The painter stands in one spot, the car moves so that the paint is an even stroke," said Young. Auto restorer Jon McKeig was inside the chamber, outfitted in some outlandish protective suit, aiming the high-pressure sprayer. It was straight out of a fifties science fiction film.

The car barn was a magnificent place, a cathedral of heavy iron. The very first Buick Skylark ever made. Hernando, the Desoto Suburban that

Young wrote "Hurricane" in. Pearl, the $400 Caddy from the '74 CSNY tour. Pieces of the old jalopy Young had driven from Chicago to Nashville to start *Homegrown*. Young waxed poetic on a factory paint job. "That's an original 1958 Lincoln, never been touched. I don't know if you can tell the difference, but there's a reality to the color that goes with your memory of the time." Every car had a story, a life.

As I studied the collection, Young studied me, then muttered, as if to himself, "All that's missin' is a little sled stickin' out down there sayin' 'Rosebud.' "

"I don't think that would bother you one bit."

"Yeah, it would be fine with me," he said, smiling crookedly.

•   •   •

The November 23 presentation at Lionel was a great success outside some minor technical glitches. With that out of the way, he concentrated on the Horse, and on December 6, 1993, he and the band entered a Santa Monica studio Briggs had found called the Complex. It was the first time in seven years that the Horse had been in a recording studio off the ranch, and to avoid any distraction, Young rented the entire building to the tune of $110,000 a week.

As on *Ragged Glory,* Briggs took the band in a day before Young arrived to run through chord changes—enough information to play the song, but not enough to come up with any extra stuff. This would enable Young— who hadn't played some of the new songs himself—to capture the performance as soon as it happened, an ethos he would take to ridiculous extremes on *Sleeps with Angels.*

Over the next ten days, Young and the band would record and mix seven songs, among them an epic fifteen-minute version of "Change Your Mind." The band was ready. Billy and Ralph had been actively playing outside of Crazy Horse. Young would say again and again that his time with Donald "Duck" Dunn had given Billy a big kick in the ass—"He knew what I'd heard." And Poncho, in the midst of a painful divorce, was really ready to give. Briggs would bestow upon him the compliment of a lifetime when the album was finished, telling him he'd given Young the best guitar accompaniment since Danny Whitten.

"I keep hearing simplicity. Bare-bones simplicity," Young later told me. "I don't want any more 'two guitars, bass and drums' for a while . . . Crazy Horse doesn't necessarily have to come out and hit you over the head with a club. Where I wanna go is sounds I've never done before." Bass marimbas, flutes, vibes, synthesizers—even a fucking tack piano—would all be utilized on *Sleeps with Angels:* touches of color reminiscent of *After the Gold Rush.*

"I want there to be rough edges on everything. On *Freedom* and *Ragged Glory,* I took some time cleaning up. I don't see a reason to do that this time. I want it to be obvious that that's *not* what's happening."

·   ·   ·

Briggs booked another two weeks in the studio for February 1994. This would give Young a month and a half to come up with more songs. "Neil called me a day before going back in and said, 'Well, I don't have any songs,' " said Briggs. "I said, 'Fuck, let's just go in anyway and see what happens.' Me and my big mouth."

What happened is that Young went in and wrote songs. He had written in the studio before—*Tonight's the Night* being a prime example—but this time he was going in completely empty-handed, and over the next few months, the entire record would be finished this way.

Not everybody was thrilled with this routine; instead of getting seven songs in two weeks, now it was one song a week. Then Young began tinkering. The process was endless and emotionally draining, according to Briggs, who declared Young "the worst finisher in rock and roll.

"In my opinion, some of the best things on this record were written on the fucking spot, under the gun, with the clock ticking at a hundred and ten grand a week. Neil rose to the occasion, it's just not a way that I would personally prefer to make records. One guy doin' all the work and fifteen other people—the band, the producer, the engineer, the crew—all sittin' around, waitin' on Neil to do what he's supposed to have done on his own: write the songs. Everyone just sits there, day after fuckin' day, doin' nothing. It makes them lethargic. It's a bad way to work. It's not creative and not good."

The sessions crept on until Briggs was ready to throttle Young. "I can see it now: 'Producer kills artist.' Make a helluva ending for your book, Jimmy."

.   .   .

"I'm not Grammy material," Young said in a 1987 *Domino* interview. "I hate that shit. It has nothing to do with rock and roll. It only has to do with Hollywood, and it's jive—a buncha people handin' each other awards and talkin' about how they made the best record and the best this and the best that. There is no best in music."

Despite these words, on March 1, 1994, Young attended the Grammies like any other dutiful rocker. He'd received four nominations for *Harvest Moon,* plus one for his contribution to the Dylan tribute concert. A few days later he was in San Francisco, jamming with pop-metal goon Sammy Hagar on "Down by the River" at the Bammy awards. On March 21, Young appeared on the Oscars, performing a tentative version of "Philadelphia." This was his seventh television appearance in a year and a half, more TV than he'd done in his entire career. He'd even done *The Tonight Show*—the program he refused to perform on while in Buffalo Springfield. And outside of the Dylan tribute, none of it was essential.

Perhaps the nadir was Young's appearance with Pearl Jam on the MTV Video Awards to play "Rockin' in the Free World." The MTV postmortem featured such luminaries as Lenny Kravitz, Michael Stipe and k. d. lang rhapsodizing on about the performance. Undoubtedly, Young came across as more alive than the rest of that evening's wallpaper, but I thought the hoopla was unjustified.

Young seemed to be everywhere, giving interviews to every magazine. Shakeymania was out of control. It reminded me of something Stephen Calt had written concerning the artistically less-than-triumphant return of acoustic bluesman Skip James: "One of the reasons James's playing eroded was because the fawning attitudes of white blues fans made it unnecessary for him to put any real care or effort into his musicianship. He could readily count on receiving the same plaudits whether he played capably or atrociously, performed in earnest or merely went through the motions."

I thought Young's newfound adulation was having a similar effect. Neil's music depends on emotional reality, and he was putting himself in some very unreal places. The results were uninspired. Little things like this seemed indicative of a decline in quality control, like Korean parts on a Lionel train.

"Be great or be gone" was the motto in Shakey's camp. Was Young giving in, getting old? Losing his instincts? The next time I saw him I was going to try and find out.

drain you

Riding in a long black limousine, rocketing toward York, Pennsylvania, on my way to meet Shakey. Kurt Cobain was dead, and it broke my fucking heart. I wasn't alone.

Nirvana were one of the few reminders left of anything real about rock music: passion, abandon and, as Briggs would say, thumbing your nose; a real band, a sacred combination of grace and white noise. Of all the denizens of the grunge scene, Cobain was the one, and in some ways he was not unlike Neil Young—a funny, big-hearted misanthrope with a lethal attitude somewhere beyond pessimism, capable of amorphous lyrics that millions connected with on a multitude of levels, his music containing the same sense of dread that permeated Neil's best work. Plus, as J. J. Cale put it, "The kid could play guitar." Nirvana deepened the mystery. They were the end of rock and roll—until the next end comes along.

Young and Cobain nearly crossed paths a few times. Briggs had been under consideration to produce *Nevermind;* Sonic Youth had tried to get Nirvana on the *Ragged Glory* tour as an opening act; and I'd seen Cobain and wife, Courtney Love, hovering around backstage at Young's *Harvest Moon* solo acoustic show at the Greek Theatre in Los Angeles. Back in November, I'd seen a copy of *In Utero* that Young's trainer had given him lying on the front seat of his Plymouth. Mr. I-Don't-Listen-to-Music had listened to the entire album.

Now Cobain had blown his brains out. He'd entered the vortex of fame and come out a corpse. Say what you will about the tortured mess of Cobain's life, but Nirvana's meteoric implosion also suggested that it might be next to impossible to stay real in the high-stakes, big-money VH1 world rock and roll had become. That morning of April 8, 1994, when a workman found Cobain's body, alongside it was a scribbled note:

"The worst crime I can think of would be to rip people off by faking it. I don't have the passion any more, and so remember, it's better to burn out than to fade away."

Out of the blue, Young called me a few days later, telling me how he'd awakened in the middle of the night a week or so before with Cobain on his mind. He'd even asked Elliot to find a way to get in touch with him. "I started really thinking about him a lot the last four days of his life—some cool way I could talk to him that wouldn't seem like some old fart wanting to give advice."

With this turn of events, Young was anxious to get Briggs and the Horse back in the studio. "Fate's a funny thing," he said.

I began ranting like an idiot. "So does this make you think about all the phony dumb shit you've been doing, like being on TV a million fucking times?" The phone went dead. That's it, I thought. I finally pushed it over the end.

Ten minutes later his management office rang back. Neil was attending a Train Collectors' Association convention in York, Pennsylvania, for the unveiling of Lionel's new Liontech offerings. He wanted me out on the next flight.

•   •   •

The limo pulled into the York Holiday Inn. A traveling fair was set up in the parking lot; amusement rides blaring in the night. Just another surreal setting to meet Shakey. Well-kept older homes, tree-lined streets, picket fences and home-cooked meals: York was middle America. Neil's kind of place.

Lionel's demonstration tent was packed. The buzz concerning the new technology had spread quickly, and train buffs were squeezed in around the table, craning to hear an explanation of the system from Young himself. I thought of the rock fans who would sell their soul to get this close. But most of these folks didn't seem to have a clue who Young was other than some longhaired guy with a really cool remote unit in his hand, and that suited him just fine.

One old codger—at least eighty, wearing a wooden tie with a steam engine painted on it—stood at the edge of the layout, his eyes wide as saucers as he listened to the unit with Liontech's new sound system chugging around the track. "It sounds so real!" he gasped.

As Young stood there giving his spiel, I thought of something Larry Johnson had said to me not long before: "Here's this guy they say is a graduate of the University of Mars—and Neil really *is* eccentric. He's out-there. But he tries his best to be normal. That's what I love about him. The pain is still etched in his face—but he's succeeded. He's succeeded at being a regular guy."

•   •   •

Sunday morning I tagged along as Young made the rounds of the dealers, seeking items for his own collection. He moved fast, scanning quickly. One dealer congratulated him on his recent Oscar nomination; this didn't stop Neil from bargaining the guy down a few hundred for a train he coveted.

Young was in an ecstatic mood. Everyone was talking about the system, even his former cohorts from QSI. Fred Severson had bounded right over the first day of the show with his good wishes. But what Young really got a kick out of was the reaction from his partner, Richard Kughn. As a last-minute touch, Young had stuck Kughn's initials on one of the prototypes.

"It looked real funky, but it's all he could talk about," said Young, smiling. " 'Neil, about the prototypes—they really should be in the *Lionel Museum.*' " Young grinned. "They weren't nearly as valuable until I put the lettering on them. Kughn wants those prototypes so bad he can taste it."

•   •   •

The night before, Elliot said *The New York Times, Rolling Stone* and the *Los Angeles Times* had been calling, desperate for a sound bite from Young regarding Cobain's suicide note. Roberts didn't return the calls, feeling it was a no-win situation. What could Neil say? I agreed, not mentioning that it was the very thing I wanted to ask him myself.

I felt like a schmuck—the day of one of Neil's triumphs, and I gotta bring up the dead guy. But the subject was already on his mind. After the show ended, we climbed aboard Pocahontas, Joe McKenna fired up the engine and we were on the road.

"I wasn't even aware of Nirvana till recently," Young said. "It was the only tape I sat and listened to in recent memory . . . It's like the ocean, waves keep comin' in, water's comin' up on the beach, water's goin' out . . . but every once in a while a wave comes that's fuckin' unbelievable and everybody goes, 'Did you feel *that*?' "

"Can I show you something?" I had a million questions to ask the guy and I never knew when and if I'd see him again, but he'd never actually seen Nirvana play. I stuck a tape into the bus's tiny TV/VCR—Nirvana doing "Drain You." I recited the lyrics: "It is now my duty to completely drain you." Young loved it. We watched the end of *Unplugged,* where Cobain, surrounded by funeral lilies and candles, takes on the ancient folk ballad "Where Did You Sleep Last Night?" made popular as a blues by Leadbelly in 1944, done bluegrass-style as "In the Pines" by Bill Monroe in 1952 and eventually sung by damn near everyone.

Only twenty-six at the time, Cobain may have topped them all with his tormented, world-weary, I-lived-this-song version. Near the end, he stops, stares into space like he's ready to explode, emits a strangled cry, then rips into the finale. Young was transfixed. "That sound he made at the end—that 'Yarrrgh.' *Unearthly.* And that look! Like a werewolf or something. Unbelievable."

. . .

Is rock and roll the devil's music? When I'd asked Young back in November, he said, "I think that's where God and the devil shake hands—right there." I asked him the question again.

"When it's really on the edge, there's a lot to be said for that. The door is open anytime you wanna go."

"Have you been there?"

"I think I've been there a few times but, uh, I must be too straight or somethin'. Because I keep returning—and going the *other* way. If I stay in one place too long, it's not gonna work—it's gonna be dangerous for me.

"When people asked me after *Rust Never Sleeps,* 'Are you gonna do another tour like that?' I said, 'I have to wait three or four years, because it would kill me.' I saw the film where my eyes are rolling back into my head . . . I couldn't have gone on doing those things. There's a point where it gets self-destructive—and see, I *know* that. Which maybe makes me straighter than someone like . . . that." His eyes gestured to the television.

I handed him a clipping from the *Seattle Times* with a picture from the previous Sunday's vigil at Seattle Center. A sea of traumatized faces, holding candles, crying.*

"Amazing, huh?" said Young, staring. "Well, it's the spirit . . . it's the spirit."

"It is. You can't deny that."

"No, no, it's just right there. . . . How did I make it this far?" He chuckled.

I brought up Cobain's suicide note and Young cut me off, frowning. "Yeah. Well—that's just another interpretation of it. It's just one of those lines. There's so many levels to take it on, I just can't. . . . Y'know, I just feel badly to see it in that light, but it was appropriate in his situation. There was nothin' else for him to do. There was nowhere else to go.

"When you see the way he was in those two performances, there's no way he could ever get through the other end of it. Because there was no control to the burn. That's why it was so intense. He was not holding back at all—and he never got to the point where he could control it.

"For me it works, because I'm different. It worked for me to stop playing really hard music and go the other way while I get my strength together, get my head back. Because if you run out of fuel—spirit and inspiration—then you're just goin' through the motions. I think maybe that when he ran out of fuel, he thought he was dead. He didn't know that he could maybe go somewhere else and get some more fuel, come back and

---

*A tape of Courtney Love reading Cobain's suicide note was played over loudspeakers during the vigil. When she got to the quote from "Hey Hey, My My," she prefaced it with "Don't remember this, because this is a *fuckin'* lie." On Hole's 1998 CD, *Celebrity Skin,* Love would offer the allegedly inspiring lyric in the song "Reasons to Be Beautiful": "When the fire goes out you better learn to fake / It's better to rise than to fade away."

The press would erroneously report that Young had pledged never to sing "Hey Hey, My My" again; in reality he performed it at his second live appearance after Cobain's death at the Bridge School benefit, October 1, 1994. "It just made it a little more focused for a while," said Young. "Now it's just another face to think about while you're singin' it."

The song, of course, refuses to die. On April 8, 2000, Oasis kicked off their U.S. tour in Seattle with a cover of "Hey Hey, My My," saying, "We'd like to dedicate this to Kurt Cobain, who died six years ago today." *NME* noted that a "large section of the audience sang along" with Noel Gallagher on the line "It's better to burn out than to fade away."

do it again. When he ran out, he thought that was it—because it was the first time he'd ever run out.

"I have a *life*. Now, whether that's hurting my music, I don't know. At his stage, it was all music. Kurt Cobain only had one world."

.　.　.

Young continued raving about the performance we had just seen. I commented on how unusual it was to see real rock and roll on MTV. "MTV, it's like regular TV," I said.

"Well, it's *always* been like regular TV. 'TV is furniture.' That's what the assistant director at the Academy Awards said during the rehearsals. 'Film is art, TV is furniture.' " Young snickered.

"You were on VH1, PBS, *The Tonight Show* . . . "

Young scowled. "It all goes with what I put out. It all goes with *Harvest Moon*. That's what it is. It's a drag."

"Okay, what did you get out of *Unplugged*? That looked like—"

Young rolled his eyes. "They *all* look like that."

"No. I'm sorry. When Cobain sings 'Where Did You Sleep Last Night,' that's voodoo, man. The rest is wallpaper."

He paused. "Oh no, that's great stuff . . . that's right."

"Okay, why did you do *Unplugged*? To me, the great thing about most of your TV performances is 'You're gonna fuckin' remember it, Jack, 'cause I'm *alive* and I'm on your TV—*dig it*?' "

"Right."

"Well, now you're just . . . furniture."

"Yeah, well, that's the way it goes. What can I say? But I did a lotta things that if I had the chance to do 'em again, I wouldn't. It's like 'File that under mistakes.' It doesn't slow me down a bit. I don't take them with me, I'm filing them. The file is like outta sight, way back there, okay? I don't wanna fuckin' *hear* about it." He stared holes through me. "I know when I make a mistake, I know when I do the right thing.

"I did the Academy Awards for musical reasons. I really wanted to sing the song, 'cause I thought it was a really good song, and I thought it would never get heard if I didn't do it there. I never thought I'd have a chance at *winning* the Oscar.

"I believe more in the Academy Awards than I do the Grammies. The awards for editing and costumes are as important as the Best Actor award. They all realize how many people it takes to make a great movie. The other parts of making records—the smaller parts, the technical parts—these guys come in the middle of the afternoon and get their awards in the middle of fuckin' rehearsals. That's where the Grammies are at.

"And the Grammies don't represent what's really happening. So to be nominated for a Grammy is not a great honor. I went, I was the only song of the year that didn't play."

There were more personal reasons Young attended. "I'm *married,* right? You get very few chances where your wife gets dressed up, goes out and it's a big thing. That's part of having a relationship.

"On the way back, Pegi said, 'Well, now we've done this. Now we don't have to do that anymore.' " Young smiled proudly. "She already accepted the fact that maybe we shouldn't have done it in the first place."

Ben Keith, Young's producer, was another reason he attended. "Why is Ben going? 'My mom's still alive and if I don't go, my mom would never forgive me. I'm fifty-five years old, I'm doin' it for my family, I'm doin' it for myself, it'll probably never happen to me again, it's a great honor.' He really believes this.

"What am I gonna do—try and explain to all these fuckin' people that everybody in the Grammies is an asshole and that the whole thing doesn't represent *anything* and that I'm protesting by not going? How long can you keep doing that with people who don't understand what the fuck you're talking about?"

. . .

While watching Cobain, Young remarked on his eerie similarity to Danny Whitten.

"Do you ever think about that guy?" I asked.

"Oh, yeah. Still comes back to mind every once in a while." Again he gestured to the TV. "Looked like the same guy there. It's all a waste. But y'know—that's life. He was not invincible. You only think you are.

"What that suicide has done is return me to my roots. Makes me go back and investigate where I started. Where I came from. Why am I here and why is he not here? Does my music suffer because I survived? Things like that.

"See, I really love my family—I think if I ever gave up the whole rest of my life and dedicated everything I have solely to music, that it might work for a while—but in the end, it wouldn't. That would be a destructive thing—I don't mean just to my family. To the music.

"Surviving has been a test. The longer you're out, the more of a test it is to stay true to what you're doing. There's a lot of distractions." He looked weary. "Too many distractions.

"I have no fuckin' goals now, I have no laws. Nothing is right, nothing is wrong. I don't give a shit what I have to do. Just so long as I can see it when it's there and grab it. And that's one thing that I have to do now after seeing *that*." He gestured to the television. "I can't *not* do it. And the door's already open. I've already got a lot of it. But the key that holds it all together is still missing."

Young saw what happened to Cobain, and it made him look inward, where he no doubt saw the same signs of rust I did. He wasn't Cobain—he was a wealthy, Grammy-nominated, nearly half-a-century-old rocker with a family, a ranch, a lot of old cars and a lot of toy trains. He was far from burning out. To pretend otherwise would've been phony. And Neil Young was too astute for that. He was built to endure, survive—and deepen the mystery in his own way.

• • •

Two days later, Young was in Los Angeles with Elliot Roberts for a charity golf tournament organized by Eddie Van Halen. He started writing lyrics on a matchbook and continued to scribble away in his golf cart. Obviously inspired by Cobain's death, the song "Sleeps with Angels" would be the final track cut for the album.

When Briggs, Young and the Horse returned to the Complex on April 25, Young was still working out the lyrics. A twenty-one-minute version with a long instrumental coda was cut, then Neil and Ralph overdubbed vocals. A week was spent editing the track, trying to finesse it, but along the way it lost the spook.

Then John Hanlon discovered that the second engineer had rolled a DAT tape as they were overdubbing, capturing an abrupt cutoff of the song when the vocal overdubs were finished. Which accounts for the odd way the released track ends midvocal. "When I heard that back I went, 'That's it in a nutshell,' " said Young.

Sequencing was another challenge. "The key to the whole thing was the running order. Because those same songs played back in a different order is very depressing," said Young. "Very down. I remember a lotta the early playbacks were 'Oh God—this is not gonna be something that people can listen to.' " Briggs came up with the final track sequence during an inebriated dice game with wife, Bettina, in the wee hours one morning.

Young went back and forth on the title. Mock-ups of the cover with various titles were made. I'm sure Reprise went nuts waiting for him to make up his mind. At the last minute, he went with *Sleeps with Angels*. "I decided that the original idea might be the best. Always turns out that way. I know it's going to draw too much attention to the song, but that's a stigma I'm gonna have to live with."

Sleeps with Angels was a radically different direction for the Horse. How ironic: all my harangues that Neil Young was turning into Perry Como, while he'd quietly been making one of the least accessible records of his career.

Tack piano and vibes open "My Heart," as naked a ballad as Young had ever written. How do you keep going? How do you remain open? Everything Young had talked about in the past few months was here, down to business observations from the train world. "Driveby" was a bleak new slant to Young's automobile songs, car as messenger of death. "Change Your Mind" examined how relationships inspire and manipulate. Two songs—"Train of Love" and "Western Hero"—shared the same melody. "Like identical twins," said Young. "The same song with two completely different stories. But it brings you back to this theme. It's almost like a Broadway play."

The title cut was just a thumbnail sketch, an elliptical observation, but musically it delivered. In an audacious touch, Young had the *Sleeps with Angels* CD done up with the old-style black label used for *Tonight's the Night,* and if there is a moment when the new record comes close to that masterpiece, it's at the beginning of the title track—Ralphie bashing away as Young fingers a trashy, distorto riff on his guitar. With disorganized, out-of-kilter vocals and a toilet-bowl mix, Young had created a chaotic patchwork that tied the album together.

The most adventurous number on the album was "Safeway Cart," a minor-key look at life in the nineties that ranks among Young's most original creations. Young played minimal guitar at a very low volume on the live track, then overdubbed "feedback harmonica"—his harp played through the Deluxe amp and all his guitar effects. I told Young that his muted playing on the album reminded me of J. J. Cale. It was the only time I've ever seen a compliment register.

Together the songs tell a story, although it's hard to get a fix on. "There was something goin' on—you can feel it," Young said later. "Just somethin', I don't know what it was. But it wasn't a hit, thank God."

When *Sleeps with Angels* was released in August 1994, Ken Viola pronounced it one of Young's "top five records. It examines the nature of dreams—both the light and dark side—and how they fuel reality in the nineties. Dreams are the only thing that we've got left to hang on to." Dave McFarlin thought it sucked. That's when I knew Young had really accomplished something—he'd made a Crazy Horse album that even Horse fanatics couldn't relate to.

.   .   .

That summer brought tours from an assortment of middle-aged megabuck stadium acts: the Stones, Elton John and Billy Joel, the Eagles. Dylan licensed "The Times They Are A-Changin' " for use in a commercial by an accounting firm, and the Band sold "The Weight" to Diet Coke. "Jesus Christ—they actually used the recording!" exclaimed Young of the latter. The Woodstock twenty-fifth-anniversary celebration suckfest reared its ugly head. Thankfully Young would turn down a fortune to play there.

Already the alternative scene seemed to be choking on its own vomit. Everywhere you turned there was some pierced, tattooed crybaby fronting a four-piece. "Angst is fashion now."

Young insisted that *Sleeps with Angels* stand on its own. No tour, no videos, no explanations. But Elliot Roberts would exercise his chutzpah by explaining it to the press himself: "Neil's worst nightmare," he said. "I'm uncontrollable."

Young's silence worked in his favor. The *Los Angeles Times* did a whole story on how Young *wasn't* doing interviews. Even Elliot was dumbfounded. "Whatever Neil fuckin' does, people go, 'Wow, what a guy.' "

Neil always comes off as this rebel who's fighting for what he believes, right or wrong—and not only rightfully so, but even when he fucks up. People perceive him as Clint Eastwood."

.   .   .

The day after playing the Bridge School benefit on October 2, Young and Crazy Horse went to Los Angeles to be filmed by Jonathan Demme performing songs from *Sleeps with Angels*.

Referring to Young's promise of no videos and no interviews for the album, I told him I'd bet a fan fifty bucks he'd stick to his guns. Was he going to do press now, too? "I've already lost twenty-five," I said.

"These aren't videos," Young said, annoyed. "These are *performances,* okay? A video is where you go in and lip-synch—that's not what this is. So you oughtta keep your disappointment *at bay* until you see what the fuck is going on. Then you can let your disappointment just cream all *over* it." He admitted that one of the performances—"Piece of Crap"—had been spiced up with zany comedy inserts, but feeling it was "tryin' too hard to be funny," he had asked Demme to tone it down.

"It's just another way of presenting those songs. I didn't try to do songs that are so heavy with the vibe in the original, like 'Safeway Cart,' 'Trans Am,' 'Sleeps with Angels'—I didn't expose them to that." Aside from "My Heart," a great solo performance, I thought the Demme stuff sucked. The Horse looked uncomfortable in Hollywood. Larry Johnson's half-hour *Sleeps with Angels* documentary was far more interesting—you got to see the actual recording of the CD, footage of Young at work in the studio that conveyed a sense of what a strange guy he is. Shot in Hi-8, no-frills, it was so murky and haphazard that Young couldn't give it away.

As for Demme's "Piece of Crap" video, it was hokey beyond belief. Intercut with the performance were clips of the Home Shopping Network and a falling tree. "You're gonna cut all that goofy shit down, right?" I asked. Young looked crestfallen. "That *was* the cut-down version." Oops.

A little while later Young handed me a gift—one of the alternate-cover mock-ups for *Sleeps with Angels*. Inside he had scribbled, "TO JIMMY— THANKS, NEIL '94." What a guy. Tell him his videos suck and he gives you a present.

. . .

Later that night we fell upon that most banal of interview subjects, the "happiness" question. Those around Young thought he was driven to the point of mania; that he was continually restless. Most of his friends thought he had none.

He was well aware. "Almost everybody thinks I'm not happy. Must be the look on my face . . . I don't know what the fuck it is. Everybody says that about me."

Young maintained he was searching for balance, for a way to do all the things he wanted yet still have a life. "Be efficient without being consumed, but still get it done. There's a way to do it. Most people, by the time they figure it out they're so old they can hardly do it. Somewhere . . . it's in there somewhere."

He took a sip from a glass of cabernet. "If I can do that, I'll be okay. . . . To have the intensity I have and still be able to pull back—I've been able to do it before, but I've gotten more intense."

No question about that. I told him sometimes I thought he might end up like Rassy, holed up alone in some beachfront pad, ranting at the world.

"Yeah. And go completely nuts!" He grinned. "I can see how it could happen. But my dad . . . that's the other side of me, see? He's consumed by his writing—but he goes out to the farm and writes, then he walks around, seasons change, got his friends, likes to hang out with 'em. That's half me. I can draw on that."

I stared hard at the guy. For five years he'd been my obsession. Day and night. It never stopped. I had hounded Young. Interrogation after interrogation, pummeling him with questions. But what did it all add up to? Neil had no more idea why he'd written "Nowadays Clancy Can't Even Sing" than I did.

"In the end, life is a private act," writes Lola Scobey. "We do not know what another man feels when he thinks his thoughts. We see what we see, hear what we hear, read what we read, and are puzzled by the rest."

As banal as this is going to sound, it was actually beginning to poke through my thick skull that Young wasn't his music or his persona—he was a human being. But did he want the world to see him as an album cover or as a person? Innaresting question.

• • •

It would be a few months before I'd see Young, along with Briggs and the Horse, again. I'd heard a lot about how Shakey changed direction, but now I'd witness the brutality of it firsthand, and it would take place during the most surreal circus of all: Neil Young's induction into the Rock and Roll Hall of Fame.

vampire blues

"If they're big, they're here. Even if they're sick, they have to show. For players and hustlers, tonight's the night," said Waterface, standing in the lobby of that swankiest of swank hotels, the Waldorf-Astoria in New York City, where, on January 12, 1995, his old pal Neil Young was to be inducted into the 4,716th annual Roque & Rolle Hall of Fame. Yes, all the glamour and glitz that was rock music in the nineties, and you could reach out and TOUCH it. Stick out your nose and smell it all around you.

I saw a Tears for Fears guy in the hallway, pouting under his big black hair, and somebody mumbled that Don Johnson and Melanie Griffith were there. Otherwise it was aging rock critics, music-hating record execs and a sea of MTV cameras. Squint and you might hallucinate somebody under thirty. There was no way Neil Young was gonna make good music here. There was nothing at stake.

"Nobody should be playing rock and roll anymore—no exceptions," wrote Richard Meltzer in 1998. "It's about as urgently needed—as opposed to socially, culturally compulsory—as making papier-mâché frog masks. It was possibly once needed, but that was before it was everywhere—when you didn't hear it in supermarkets or coming out of every Mercedes at a stoplight—before 'rock-surround.' What we need now is to turn it off. What was once liberating has become irredeemably oppressive. It exists to make you stupid—like sitcoms or the news or college football or your parents, for crying out loud."

Sitting in the balcony of the Waldorf, eating multi-colored curlicues off a thousand-dollar plate, I couldn't argue.

·   ·   ·

"The first thing I think is, what about Billy and Ralph and Poncho? Why isn't Crazy Horse there?" Young had said in regard to the Hall of Fame induction the previous November. "They're gonna be hurt. Some part of them is gonna say, 'Shit, I was there, I did all that. Why am I not there?' " Young's solution was to fly them in, along with Briggs, Ben Keith and their mates.

Since recording *Sleeps with Angels,* Young and the Horse had played four gigs, all of them benefits. They were unique shows, with a remarkable "Down by the River" at Farm Aid and a rare "Helpless" during a Sedona, Arizona, benefit for the Native American Scholarship Fund on October 22, 1994. But Poncho felt energy flagging during ranch rehearsals just prior to the Hall of Fame ceremony. Young had already told the band he was going to use them for the Lollapalooza festival the next summer. Perhaps the Horse was getting too comfortable.

The plan was to go to the Hall of Fame induction, then leave the next day for Washington, D.C., for a two-day Voters for Choice benefit Pearl Jam had asked Young to play. The afternoon of the induction, I stopped by a Times Square rehearsal hall where Young was to prep the Horse for a possible performance that evening. He hadn't shown up and energy was low. A sullen Briggs stretched out on an equipment case and slept.

After what seemed like an eternity, Young arrived, and the band began to play a melancholy, note-perfect "Trans Am." Then they tried a couple of new songs. Young said the then untitled "Song X" was melodically inspired by "Teddy Bear's Picnic." "Act of Love," spurred by the upcoming D.C. benefit, was a murky rocker touching on the different sides of the abortion debate without offering any answers. "The connotations of an act of love are deep, multilevel," Young told me. "You can say that over and over again and it'll give you a different idea every time."

Working out "Act of Love" seemed particularly frustrating for Young, who was determined to get Billy Talbot to ease into the song instead of attacking it from the first note. "This'll never be on the radio, Billy, so it doesn't matter how long it is. We can build it." Young seemed antsy. Change was in the air.

●　　●　　●

Earlier in the day at the Waldorf, Elliot Roberts had been on the phone with Danny Goldberg, the momentary new head of Warner's.

Roberts was ecstatic. He'd scored big. A corporate shake-up had forced out Warner Bros.' beloved head, Mo Ostin, with Lenny Waronker soon to follow. The matter was handled badly, resulting in a ton of bad press for the company. In the midst of all this, Young was renegotiating his contract, and the timing couldn't have been better. In the heat of his comeback, the musician was the biggest symbol of what the label traditionally stood for, and it was of paramount importance to keep him. Goldberg had been appointed CEO, but following Ostin was a thankless task, and many artists were grumbling. "I personally like Danny; I think he's very talented," Roberts told *Newsweek*. "But Neil has no idea who he is." (That quip alone, producer Lorne Michaels told Elliot, jacked up Young's staying price more than a few bucks.)

This was the sort of situation Roberts thrived on. He met with a couple of other labels, then, following the outline of a dream he'd had, informed Goldberg that he was messengering over a one-page outline of terms and that there were to be no negotiations. Warner Bros. had one day to decide whether they were accepting or rejecting the terms. "Danny called me back the next day and said, 'It's a done deal.' "

The five-album contract was reportedly for $3 million an album, plus a $10-million signing bonus. In addition, Roberts had accomplished the unheard of: regaining control of publishing assigned to Atlantic's Cotillion Music back in the Springfield days. The pact covered all of Young's songs from 1966 to 1970 and included such hits as "Helpless," "Only Love Can Break Your Heart" and "Cinnamon Girl." Roberts estimated the whole deal was worth $40 million.

"I guess integrity finally paid off," said Young when Elliot gave him the good news.

•   •   •

From my perch on the balcony at the Waldorf, I eyeballed Neil and Pegi down below, sitting at a table with Elliot Roberts; Young's lawyer, Irwin Osher; and their wives. David Briggs and Bettina arrived fashionably late, David decked out in a metallic-gray silk suit, and the Horse was at a table not far away. Young's brother, Bob, was there, too, along with half sister, Astrid. Scott Young did not attend.*

Young had been an active supporter of the Hall of Fame; in past cere-monies, he had inducted Jimi Hendrix, the Everly Brothers and Woody Guthrie. He'd whooped it up in the all-star closing jamborees. Precious few had declined induction-night invitations—namely Joni Mitchell and Van Morrison, who sent a telegram the night of his ceremony claiming he had a gig to do. In the course of interviews for this book, both Chrissie Hynde and James Taylor expressed their displeasure. "There is something very un–Neil Young about a monument to the rock and roll industry," said Taylor.

But the pull of such an event was inexorable, even for its critics. Hynde joined the all-star lineup at the grand opening of the museum in 1996—playing "The Needle and the Damage Done," no less—and in 1997, Taylor was present to perform "Woodstock" in place of Mitchell. It was hard to say no to the Rock and Roll Hall of Fame.

•   •   •

The music Neil Young made on induction night was a bore. "Fuckin' Up" was an all-star mudbath with members of both Crazy Horse and Pearl Jam. It was sad to see the Horse dragged into it. Total crap, and broadcast around the world to boot. It seemed depressingly ironic that Young, such a critic of television, was going to be a star of the Hall of Fame's first MTV broadcast.

Young jammed with Led Zeppelin on a pointless "When the Levee Breaks," which climaxed with Robert Plant shrieking out a curious choice of tribute—"For What It's Worth." Young's only interesting moment was "Act of Love" with the Horse. Only he would have the balls to perform a new song at an event like this (Young reportedly told the apprehensive staff

---

*"Missing that Hall of Fame thing was hard for me to do," said Scott, who was exhausted from a book tour. "I just didn't feel like bloody going to New York, I felt like bloody going to bed. . . . Despite the pride that I have in Neil—and the feeling that totems are his due—I suspect I have another part of me that is also part of Neil: that you're not terribly interested in celebrating on somebody else's ground, or for somebody else's reasons. I just don't wanna be—and this shouldn't be taken as sour grapes—the tail to somebody else's kite."

it was a number he'd written "back in '62"). But since there were no guest stars to puff up the screen, it was dumped from the broadcast.

Young's acceptance speech was a different matter. "You might not even need a tape recorder," Young had warned me in November. "It might be mime." Everybody was expecting him to go off, so he didn't. "Just didn't have the heart for it," Young told me a few days later. "It's not worth wasting a lot of time on."

And yet his remarks were riveting, even revelatory. After some heartfelt tributes by Ahmet Ertegun and the ubiquitous Eddie Vedder, Young ambled out. He seemed genuinely surprised by the standing ovation—and so vulnerable under the glare of television lights that it was strangely moving. Ever the wisenheimer, Young mentioned how cool Dickie Betts had looked in his acceptance with the Allman Brothers. "I wish I had a bunch of people up here with me . . . it's a solo thing, though." A solo thing: three words that spoke volumes.

He thanked Rassy, then paused, growing visibly emotional. He thanked Crazy Horse and Briggs and had them take a bow. He spoke warmly of Ahmet Ertegun. Then came thanks to Mo Ostin, and Elliot—audibly coaching him from off-stage. "Elliot's tellin' me who to thank . . . he's managing *this speech*," cracked Young, who went on to acknowledge one other: "I'd like to thank Kurt Cobain for giving me the inspiration to renew my commitments." Then, gazing out into the audience, he murmured, "And most of all—I love you, Pegi." It was over. The omissions were obvious and significant.

Watching Young standing there with his award, I wondered how he felt. A Western hero, big money in his hand. He looked restless.

·　·　·

The next day, I joined the Horse for the train ride down to D.C. The mode of transportation was Young's idea, but he was nowhere in sight.

At rehearsal the following day, Briggs and the Horse waited. And waited some more. Intent on keeping spirits up, Briggs finally conducted the band through "Western Hero" himself, but they were suffering Young's absence.

That night, between L7 and Pearl Jam, Young led the Horse through a weird, disorganized six-song set that began with "Song X" as a feedback-ridden mess and fell apart from there. Out in the house, Dave McFarlin witnessed the most tepid reaction to the Horse ever. For all the Godfather of Grunge brouhaha, this crowd was there for Eddie Vedder.

During one of the new songs, the band stumbled as Billy tuned up through half a verse. "He was tuning *during the song,*" an exasperated Young moaned later. "Billy said, 'Yeah, but I was tuning on the *right* note.' "

Toward the end of Pearl Jam's set, I noticed Billy wandering around unhappily. Why wasn't the Horse's equipment onstage? Weren't they going to join Pearl Jam for the encore? The Horse wasn't, but Neil certainly was. He walked out, and the band dove into a blistering "Act of Love." Somehow they already knew the song.

With Vedder relegated to backing vocals, the band was no longer pulling in two different directions and fit Young like a glove. Huffing and puffing, Neil had to struggle to keep up. "It was fuckin' great," Young exclaimed. "I was sailin' along. It was like floating on a cloud . . . so effortless. After the first couple of changes, those guys were fuckin' there. When Eddie and Jeff sang the choruses, 'Act of Love' just sounded right."

Backstage, Young was giddy with excitement, backslapping Pearl Jam as a dejected Horse made their way out.

On the ride back to the hotel, Billy was uncharacteristically silent, the van like a coffin on wheels. Shuffling through the lobby, he asked what I'd thought of the Horseless "Act of Love." "It was good," I said, downplaying in an effort at kindness. "No," said Billy ruefully, shaking his head. "It was great. Great."

• • •

The next night went a little better, but Young didn't play the encore with Pearl Jam—he had to leave for Lionel business in Detroit as soon as his set ended. I was joining him.

After the set, I snuck out to the bus, suitcase in hand. There was Joe McKenna, with Pocahontas all fired up and ready to go. Next to the bus stood Briggs, smiling wanly when he saw me. "Just like Elvis," he said. "Out of the gig and on to the next." I felt for David. His job was to push

Neil, but lately, maybe he'd pushed too hard. I shook his hand, and he gave me a wink and wished me luck. It was the last time I'd see Briggs alive.

At the airport, we found the barren corner of the parking lot where Young's Learjet awaited. I bullshitted with Joe, helping him transfer the luggage from bus compartment to plane while the pilot bitched about the unruly hard-rock band he'd just finished with. "Mr. Young doesn't seem like that type," he said to me earnestly. No, I assured him, Mr. Young certainly wasn't. After a while, Neil emerged from the bus, his leather and bamboo case in hand, a familiar old hat perched atop his head.

We made our way to the rear of the plane, Elliot crumpled into a seat in front of us. A huge moon skirted by candy-floss clouds flooded the cabin. Neil was jazzed. The first batch of handheld controllers—featured in Lionel's Christmas catalog—had sold out in two weeks.

Young was also still high from playing with Pearl Jam the night before, and proceeded to tell me something I didn't know about the last few days. The day we pulled into Washington, Young had snuck over to Pearl Jam's rehearsal. "They got 'Fuckin' Up' down cold," he said. Then Vedder asked Young the chords to his new song, "Act of Love." It turned out Vedder had his DAT recorder with him at the Hall of Fame and had made a little bootleg. So Young did the song with the Horse in the first set knowing full well he was going to do it again with Pearl Jam at the end of the night. Not that he told anybody any of it.

Looking back on the Hall of Fame event, Young seemed predictably ambivalent: "Just another hash house on the road to success." He described the surreal party following the ceremony, which closed with Young and Phil Spector sitting at a piano, as Spector's bodyguard hovered over them. Young sang and Spector pounded out the chords. "God Bless America." "Silent Night." "Be My Baby." "You Cheated, You Lied." "He loved the way I sang that," said Young proudly. "Spector's life is like a spy movie, okay? Everybody's out to get him—he's like Maxwell Smart. If you look at him in that light, everything's fine. He hasn't forgotten who he is . . ."

Ideas for the next album were flying through his head. Working with Spector. With Zeppelin. With the remains of Nirvana. "It's been a while since I made a record where there was no plan." His thoughts returned to "Act of Love" with Pearl Jam. Young had wanted to record the live show, but Briggs couldn't get his favorite remote truck and passed the request down to crew member Tim Foster. The end result was that nothing happened.

"They didn't get it together. They had twenty-four hours to get a truck—from Nashville or somewhere. They coulda done it if they'd taken it really seriously.

"There comes a point when the people around you have gotta take you seriously—if they don't, jumping around and screaming and yelling isn't gonna make any difference. The only thing they're gonna understand is that I didn't do it—and now I'm not doing anything. So the next time I work with them, they realize when I ask them to do something, it's gonna happen.

"But things happen for a reason, so . . . gotta let it go. But I'm gonna get another one. I wanna wait, do it again when the equipment's there, under the right circumstances . . . "

A paranoid look crossed Young's face. "Only you know this," he said, staring at me. The cat was out of the bag. Young was going to Seattle to record with Pearl Jam. The dates were already set, January 26 and 27, just a week and a half away. "They got their whole trip together, I'm not gonna fuck with it. I'm just gonna go in and use their trip completely . . . it's like you have a new thing you can paint with. I know I have the sound to work with in my head.

"Seattle's basically over now. So it's time for *me* to go. Cleanup man. Heh heh. I might go completely alone . . . that would be the purest way to do it. Go into another musical world. That's when you really get your eyes opened up to what's possible. I'm goin' to where *they* live. I'm gonna use *their* producer. I'm gonna use their whole scene. I want what *they* got—I don't want what *I* got. What I got brought me down."

Briggs had a hard-on to record with Pearl Jam. He'd be floored by Neil's decision. Three days ago Briggs and the Horse were all taking bows at the Hall of Fame; now they were fired. So was the crew. But Young wasn't stopping to reflect.

"That happens over and over again through my whole fuckin' life with all these bands. That's the reason I'm still here. Because as painful as it is to change—and as ruthless as I may seem to be in what I have to do to keep going—you gotta do what ya gotta do. Just like a fuckin' vampire. Heh heh heh."

The plane turned, the moonlight throwing shadows across Young's face. He looked like a lunatic. "How does it feel being a vampire?" I asked.

"It feels *great*," he enthused. Neil was morphing like Plastic Man—you could practically see the DNA reconstitute. Eight miles high and on a plain. It was exhilarating.

"I still wanna be . . . part of what's going on. I don't wanna be an *icon*. I gotta get the energy, wherever it is. I gotta get revitalized, recharged from the momentum. I'm not a puller, I'm a rider.

"So you gotta look at all these things . . . you gotta make calls that hurt people. There's no way around it. It's the only way to go. How can you succeed and make more music of a higher caliber without doing it? You can't. You can't go along from people to people, place to place, creating, changing, without hurting a lot of people. How can you do that? Can *you* think of an answer? I think I'm doing a good job—even though it's painful sometimes.

"And I know when I got a place to go, that I'll create and it'll be there. But if I don't have a place to go and it sounds like a problem, *what's gonna make me write more songs*? How am I gonna open up if I got nowhere to put it? And maybe they don't realize how *serious* I am about every little fuckin' thing, because I'm older now and I don't freak out. Before, when I was a lot younger, I was doin' a lotta drugs, and if things weren't my way, I went fuckin' *nuts* . . . I haven't changed. Instead of goin' nuts, I just go *somewhere*. And *find* it. So when I come back, they'll remember."

"Is it easier for you to change than other people?"

"I dunno. Maybe other people don't have a *reason* to change. A driving force that makes them wanna do whatever has to be done. I know some people do. Look at Bobby Darin. There's a guy who eventually had a heart attack, I think, because he was just so jacked up tryin' to do all this shit. He kept tryin' to do everything he wanted to do, whatever it was . . . "

For a moment I thought I saw the ghost of Bobby Darin drift past the plane. He was all smiles, snapping his fingers in agreement. Lost in the clouds, singing "Mack the Knife," Darin was one hip-looking apparition. Too bad Young didn't see it. Picture that duet.

.   .   .

By late February 1995, the album with Pearl Jam was just about done. Nine of Young's songs and a pair of Vedder's were recorded in two two-day sessions at Bad Animals, a studio owned by hard-livin' seventies banshees Heart. "A cool place," said Young. "Pictures of Heart all over the place—heh heh—but the room was great. Beautiful old rugs on the floor . . . just like one of my places. Recorded it analog, faster than it's ever been done. I went full-on. They were up to it."

Mirror Ball was released in June after some intense wrangling with Epic, Pearl Jam's label. Their name was not to be mentioned on the cover of the CD, the band was not allowed to promote the record and Vedder's songs were not allowed on—they'd be released later in a companion EP entitled *Merkin Ball*. The Gary Burden cover had mutated out from a fax of a photo Joel Bernstein had sent Young. Appropriate. On *Mirror Ball,* the sixties still resonate. A dim signal, maybe, but still there.

"The thing I loved about the sixties was this feeling that the bands and the audiences were together—a living connection," Young told Robert Hilburn. "They believed in each other and the future. They shared a dream. That connection is back, though you don't get that sense of optimism anymore. The kids think our generation let them down, and we did . . . we've made such a mess of the way kids grow up that they really need this music today."

"Personally, I'm pro-choice," Young told Nick Kent concerning "Act of Love." "But the song isn't! People who say that human beings shouldn't have the right to dismiss a human life—they have a point . . . but then there's reality. There's idealism and reality, the two have got to come together, yet there are always major problems when they do. Maybe that's the crux of what I'm trying to say in this new album. It's also a commentary of the differences between my peace-and-love generation and the more cynical nineties generation."

Mirror Ball holds some pleasures, like the Springfield-esque three-guitar attack on "Big Green Country" and the fallen-hero musings of "Scenery," but the bomb dropped here is "I'm the Ocean," which Kent quite rightly described as one of the "most blantantly autobiographical songs" of Young's career.

As the band sets a great but precarious groove—it feels like they're struggling to keep a grip on the song—Young tries to define the power of music and his place in it. "I'm an accident, I was driving way too fast / Couldn't stop, though, so I let the moment last," he sings, taking on the personas of different automobiles, spewing forth a mile a minute. It's a thrilling ride: simultaneously boastful, insecure, tortured, deluded, messianic, mournful, high—in short, perhaps the greatest track Young has done in the nineties. And he did it with Pearl Jam.

• • •

"People my age, they don't do the things I do," Young sings on "I'm the Ocean," and he did a few more of them the summer of 1995. In San Francisco on June 24, Young bravely stepped in at the last minute for an ailing Eddie Vedder, warding off a potential riot. I had seen Young and the band play a one-off in a Seattle club on June 7, and while they played well, it never caught fire—again, it just wasn't Neil Young's crowd. In August, when a Vedderless Pearl Jam joined Young for an eleven-date tour of Europe—where the band isn't nearly as popular—it was a different story.

"The music had a consistency level that was staggering," said Elliot Roberts. "One of the greatest tours we ever had in our whole lives. Neil got off every fuckin' night."

Dean Stockwell remembers the show in Dublin, which was filmed by Jim Sheridan but remains unreleased. "I'll never forget, before they went out to do the encore—there was a ladder leading up to the stage area. Neil started up the ladder, turned back, and the members of Pearl Jam came up to him. They all reached out, met their hands together in the center, like a high school basketball team—rocked them up and down and said, 'Yeah, let's go!' " Stockwell laughed. "I said, 'Wait a second, what the hell is this? This guy is fifty and he's got these kids goin' out there like a *team.*' It's not just musical respect for him, it's *love.*"

After Young returned from the tour, another dream came true: In partnership with Martin Davis and Greg Feldman, he bought Lionel. Due to financial difficulties, Richard Kughn could no longer keep the company, and Elliot Roberts put together a deal. "*We own the fuckin' company* now— three years ago, this woulda been a dream," said Roberts. Was Young happy? "It's all part of the program with Neil, he's never satisfied. It's never like 'Hey, great, we got to this level.' Never."

. . .

In addition to everything else, Young also began work on his first real film score (discounting a thrown-together *Where the Buffalo Roam* in 1980) for Jim Jarmusch's surreal Western, *Dead Man*. Jarmusch is a likable con artist tenacious enough to get through the phalanx of handlers and on March 27, Neil, carrying copious notes from studying the movie at home, entered a San Francisco studio. As the film rolled, he laid down several passes on pump organ, detuned piano, acoustic and electric guitar. The result was minimal but haunting. Larry Johnson said the challenge of something new brought out the best in Young. "Neil gave a thousand percent. I haven't seen him put out like this in a long time. He was really, really focused."

Within a few months, the project had turned into a full-fledged Neil Young album. "Kind of a hippie-beatnik New Age record," Young told me. *Dead Man* was scheduled to be the first release from Elliot Roberts's Vapor label. I thought Young's work was great as accompaniment to Jarmusch's movie; as an album on its own, a vanity project. This was the trouble with some of Young's projects in the nineties—every little thing became a big, big deal.

I shot off a fax to Young, saying just that. A few days later he called back. By that time I'd lost my anger and failed to put up much of a fight. Young's timing had been impeccable, as usual, and I told him how frustrating it was.

"Well y'know—a lotta songs are like that," he said, amused.

"Waddya mean?"

"You write the song when you're all full of piss and vinegar, and you record it, and somebody calls you three weeks later and says, 'What the fuck were ya doin' that for?' " He snickered. "Same thing."

"I can't explain this to you," Young said of the *Dead Man* soundtrack. "It's intriguing—to me. I think you'll like some of it. And if you don't like it—*don't fuckin' buy it*! Heh heh. I wouldn't even *bother* to explain to anybody else, ya *dickhead*!"

"Is there still room for all the crazy people in your life?"

"I'll tell ya what—I'm talkin' to one of 'em right fuckin' now!"

"You still love rock and roll?"

"Not *today*. Tomorrow."

. . .

Young turned fifty on November 12. He'd survived the Hall of Fame, toured with a mega-successful band half his age and bought the source of one of his childhood dreams. "I think he'll end up making more with Lionel than anything else he's ever done," Roberts told me. "It's already up seventeen million from last year. Neil was right—trains are coming back."

A phenomenal year, but it was about to end.

. . .

"You never know when you'll turn around and a member of the team will be gone," Young told me in November 1994.

David Briggs had been on a dark ride since the Hall of Fame induction. He'd had ongoing back pain, but by the spring of the following year he was in such agony that he could get through a recording session only by wolfing down prodigious amounts of painkillers. After consultations with various doctors, it looked like operation time.

On August 2, 1995, I called Briggs a little before one o'clock in the afternoon. He had just returned from yet another trip to the doctor and didn't sound exactly chipper. "Write faster, Jimmy. Finish the book."

"Why?"

"I want to be here to read it." There was a long pause. "It's the big C. Lung cancer." It wasn't his back. Briggs was dying.

David kept his condition to himself. He didn't want to see anyone. Even talking on the phone was physically uncomfortable. Briggs alternately charmed the hospital staff and drove them crazy. The prospect of chemotherapy didn't appeal to David, who asked the doctors, "Can I keep my rock and roll hair?"

Mirror Ball had produced another period of silence between Young and Briggs. Young FedExed him a copy of the album; wife Bettina said he threw it in the trash.

The two got back in contact in September. Days before Thanksgiving, Briggs reached out to Neil, who went to see him immediately. For several hours they talked. One thing that David stressed was that Neil had done so much, so many different things, in his music that he should pare down to the essentials—get closer to the source. Later I tried to pry out of Neil what else was said, to no avail. Briggs had told him things "I guess I'll carry to my grave."

Bettina called a little before ten P.M. on November 26. David was gone. Together they'd watched *Santa Claus: The Movie,* then it was sayonara. He couldn't take any more pain, he'd had enough. David Briggs, burned out at fifty-one.

The music press, who had ignored Briggs his entire career, started calling immediately. Joel Bernstein and I each spent half an hour on the phone with a reporter from *Rolling Stone,* trying to make absolutely sure he understood that this David Briggs was not the Nashville session musician. The magazine still managed to run a picture of the wrong guy.

• • •

The memorial brought out everyone, including many of David's old Topanga cronies. It was a somber event.

John Eddie, a New Jersey rocker with whom Briggs had cut an as yet unreleased album, started chuckling as we met, pointing out that in the first line of an obituary I'd written for David, I'd referred to him as a "legendary producer." Eddie recounted for me a wild night in Bearsville, New York. Briggs had given him a ride home after ingesting his usual mind-numbing quotient of coke and Mexican coffee and was careening all over the road, driving faster than the speed of light. Eddie held on for dear life, sure that Briggs was going to kill them both. He whimpered for David to slow down. "What are you worried about?" Briggs barked. "You know how the obituary will read—'Legendary producer killed with mediocre singer.' "

"Y'know, you're really writing a book about David," Young told me after the memorial. It was a strange thing to say, but I understood. There was one line that had stayed with Young from my obituary: "No one pushed Neil Young further into his art than Briggs, and his death leaves a huge void." "It really is a huge void," Young muttered to me at the memorial. "Huge."

A few months later came a rare elaboration: "I think my one memory of David that stands out more vividly and said more to me than any other was up at Indigo Ranch Studios the night we did 'Will to Love.' He knew what was goin' on—he'd seen all the records we'd done, all the places we'd gone to come to that record. What it was about and how we did it and just how fuckin' out of it and fucked up we were. How that was wrong, but we just didn't give a shit. . . .

" 'Will to Love' was finished, mixed. I kind of slumped down into the console, and he took his hands and he rubbed my shoulders. That's what I remember the most."

have you ever
been lost?

"Look around me—I'm a fuckin' *capitalist businessman*! I've got all this shit. I'm a good <u>businessman</u>, right?"

February 1996. Young and I were going at it again. I thought he was distracted by all the shit he was doing; Neil maintained that he was recharging his batteries, waiting for the inspiration to create. "You don't have to keep the edge. The fuckin' edge is not *kept, okay*—the edge comes and visits when the edge wants to. Regardless of whether you're sittin' on a fuckin' throne or a bed of nails."

Under the alias of Phil Perspective, he'd been producing a solo Crazy Horse album. "That's why I'm not doin' my own stuff right now. Because they're there a hundred percent, those guys, with their stuff. So that's the energy I'm using right now. Like a parasite."

Coproducer John Hanlon had repeatedly put off a vacation during work on the *Dead Man* soundtrack. When it came time to do the Horse record, he announced that he was taking a break. Young informed Hanlon they'd continue without him.* He also tossed longtime friend Gary Davis out of the Horse sessions when Davis dared to show up with his bongos.

"This time leadership has to be strong, 'cause this is when you set the tone for the way things are gonna be without Briggs. To protect who we are and what our music means. We have to be stronger in defending it than ever before, 'cause we don't have Briggs, who would defend it when we were *sleeping*. I have to be a little harder than I was before."

. . .

---

*Ironically, the Crazy Horse album never got finished. "Our producer, Phil Perspective, didn't stick around for the end," said Poncho. "He turned back into Neil Young and did a Neil Young record."

I met Young at the train barn. He had recently bought some full-sized rolling stock—two freight cars, a flat car and a caboose. Into the side of a hill behind the train barn he'd dug a hole and laid some track so it appeared that a train was disappearing into a tunnel. He was using one car as an office for his train business, and was preparing a hookup so he could do video conferencing with Lionel.

Inside, Young was hunched over the layout. Now that he had conquered the train sounds, he wanted to branch out—audio for the layout environment. Baying coyotes, a bustling factory, all microchipped in with the fanatically realistic detail Young had lent to the Railsounds system. Young was bent on creating a *Star Wars* totality in miniature. The concept hadn't gotten a big reception from Lionel.

"They love the train sounds, but they just can't understand that I don't wanna stop at the train," he said, frustrated. "And I can't explain it, I just have to *do it*—then I'm gonna install it in the showroom layout at the factory. And then we'll see if they want it, heh heh. It's hard to tell people they need something when they can't even imagine what it is."

As for music, Young had already devised a new plan of attack: a series of unannounced live gigs with the Horse. In a very small place. At one point tour manager Tim Foster called, suggesting Young's favorite spot, the Catalyst in Santa Cruz. "Too big," said Neil. "Over a hundred people." He was itching to do it as soon as possible. "We don't have to rehearse, I just want to play." He wanted tickets sold at the door. His management company wouldn't be involved. "We're gonna run it ourselves," he said. "Too small for Lookout."

Young was revving up. "There'll be terrible nights and there'll be great nights. . . . The fact is, we're not doin' it for money, we're not doin' it for rock and roll history, we're not doin' it for fuckin' MTV . . . I don't want to play in front of a whole lot of people—and I don't want the high rollers to be able to get in unless they got the money at the door at the right time. They'll have to stand there with the low rollers, the bottom-feeders. No special seats."

Young scoffed at the idea that things were over now that Briggs was gone. "We all know Briggs was on the edge—but that doesn't mean we weren't on the edge when we weren't with Briggs. Because there's all kinds of stuff that happened when he wasn't there that was *definitely* on the fuckin' edge. He *happened* to be there for a lot of it—and contributed greatly to it—but to say we weren't on the edge unless Briggs was there, that's bullshit."

He brought up some of the more out-there *Homegrown* stuff as an example. "Listen to 'Florida,' a few of those things. There was no Briggs around for that. Briggs was great, and what Briggs brought to the table was fantastic, and luckily he left a lot of it on the table, but to think that we can't continue or even go further without Briggs in the flesh—that's a misjudgment.

"The past is gone completely—and it'll never be like it was. It'll be better than it was. It may not be as close to death as it was at certain times. . . . Like *Tonight's the Night* is not a way of life—it's a way of death.

"There's a long way to go. You can't judge the future by lookin' at the past. You can't . . .

"I've already told Pegi, I've told everybody—take a good look at me, because pretty soon I'm gonna be *gone*. I'm gonna be somewhere else for a long time. There'll be another flow happening. I'm gonna go out, I'm gonna play, it's gonna keep me alive, it's gonna make us a lotta money. We can pay for our houses, pay for all the shit we got for the rest of our lives—but basically, what it's gonna do is, it's gonna make me happy. Make me more of myself. Get me in tune with what really makes things happen—which is *music*.

"The idea is, am I into what I'm doing? I really want to do somethin' that represents music the way I feel it. That represents *me*.

"When other people are tellin' me that I'm fuckin' crazy and I'm out here in the woods and I'm growin' bark and all this shit—*I* know what I'm doing. They don't. They don't know what it takes to fuckin' keep the edge on the creative side of the thing.

"Music's like breathing out. Everything else is like inhaling, okay? So you gotta take a good deep breath in to let a whole bunch out somewhere.

"But it's not always on everybody else's timetable, whether I'm *making* it or not, y'know?" Young looked at me.

"Do you ever feel like the world's tamed you?"

"Yeah, I do. And that's why I'm pissed off. I can feel it—and I don't want it to happen. So there are certain things I'm gonna do: 'This is the way I'm doing it, and if you don't wanna do it that way, fuck you. Go somewhere else.' 'Cause I don't have that many chances to do this and get it right."

"So it's not better to burn out?" I asked. "That's the message I get from everything you've been telling me."

Young looked shocked. "No—it is. But you gotta *burn out*. I'm not burned out. I'll go eventually—heh heh—but I'm gonna stretch this out as long as I can. And when I go, it's gonna be a fuckin' *flash*—the kind of thing you can't look at." He chuckled.

·　·　·

We hopped in the Plymouth and headed down some dusty ranch road. One of Young's pooches trotted alongside.

"Type of guy you think I am, you probably think I'll just run over that dog and get a new one."

"You know what? You would feel so bad that for the next six years you wouldn't even tell anybody—but this dog motif would appear in fifty songs. You'd disguise it. Call it something else."

"So nobody would *know* it was the dog . . . Why should I share that? You're right, Jimmy." Young snickered.

"Everybody has their own belief of what kind of music is the real me, and if I'm not doin' that, I'm not being real.

"I just do what I want to do—keep playing, keep going, keep moving— and it's not as easy as it was. I'm a little bit shell-shocked. But I'm going . . . I can feel it coming."

For the time being, our interviews were over. I got the feeling there weren't many left. "It takes a lot outta me," Young admitted. "It ages me about forty years every time I do one of these. But hey—I'm still only fifty." He chuckled. "A little music will go a long way with me."

The next day, a little before I left the ranch, the phone rang. Neil. He was hyper, barely able to spit the words out. He'd written a couple of songs, and more were on the way.

·　·　·

On March 18, 1996, Neil Young and Crazy Horse began a series of sixteen unannounced gigs that would sprawl into June, all but two taking place off Route 1, not far from Young's home at the tiny Old Princeton Landing

(OCCUPANCY 150, a handmade sign would exclaim above the door once Young and company had established residency). They were billed as the Echos [sic], after Young's old Silvertone harmonica amp, on which a previous owner had scrawled "The Travelling Echoes." That amp adorned the seven-by-twenty stage along with an Indian rug and candles. The vibe extended backstage, where Young assembled an enclave of tents and trailers dubbed "Echo Village." The Horse had their own trailer, and Young spent much of the time before and after gigs huddled inside with them. Pearl Jam's sensitivity to atmosphere and environment had obviously reminded Young of a few things he'd forgotten. "Those gigs were the best thing that ever happened to the Horse," said Poncho. "We were a band again."

"The crew that I'm goin' out with this time, there's not gonna be any professionals," Young had told me in February. "It's not like 'We've done this before, we're great.' Because that's not it." Longtime tour manager Bob Sterne was out—Tim Foster in his place—and Young had inherited one or two of Pearl Jam's crew. Even Ranger Dave Cline was back. Twenty-dollar wristband tickets went on sale at the door, and most of the gigs were on weekdays. The end result was a joint packed to the gills with people who really wanted to be there. Young and the Horse usually played three sets a night, emerging from their trailer when they felt in the zone to play. A relaxed atmosphere, to say the least. One evening one of Young's old jalopies ran out of gas on the way to the gig, and he walked the rest of the way with his engineer.

The effect was, as one fan put it in *Broken Arrow,* "like having Neil in your living room." The performances were all over the map, dependent on the mood of the band (perhaps, for some, on how much and what kind of weed was circulating back in Echo Village). Peaks and valleys, sometimes in the same song. But even if they sucked it didn't matter—this was Neil Young and Crazy Horse, playing ten feet in front of your face. In an era when nearly all of his peers were squeezing fans dry with endless overpriced arena gigs, the fact that Young actually gave enough of a shit to go to the trouble of doing something as personal as the Princeton Landing series was inspiring.

Aficionados were treated to uncommon performances of "Wonderin' " and "Danger Bird," not to mention a particularly mournful "Stupid Girl." "It's a whole other thing," Young said. "She's much older now." Material

leaned heavily toward Briggs's beloved *Zuma,* and Young contributed ago-
nized vocals to another of David's favorites, "When Your Lonely Heart
Breaks." "He was really pissed that we didn't do a great record . . . it makes
you wanna do it real well now." Unbeknownst to everyone, Briggs was actually present at the Landing gigs. Poncho had copped some of his ashes at
the wake and hidden them in an amp, telling me, "From now on, David's
coming on the road."

In between gigs, starting on March 25, Young recorded the Horse at the
ranch, and very quickly they had an album, *Broken Arrow,* released in early
July 1996. The deceptively sloppy record contains some of the Horse's
most intricate melodies ever. For the most part, Young plays FX-less guitar, and despite tambourine and Nitzsche-style one-note piano adding
touches of color, this is the Horse in its rawest form. The spirit of Briggs is
smudged all over the album, particularly on "Big Time," a descending
chord elegy and reaffirmation of purpose: "I'm still livin' in the dream we
had / For me it's not over." On "Loose Change," the Horse repeat an E
chord for so long you wonder if the player's stuck. When Sampedro's girlfriend asked why the band got hung up on the chord for so long, he said,
"We were playing David on his way."

"Slips Away" is one of Young's more curious depictions of a woman
(this one vanishes when the music starts), and the barely-above-a-whisper
"Music Arcade" is one of his more revealing self-portraits of recent years.
As if to say, "This is where it all started," the album ends with some plod-
ding sludge from Princeton Landing, Jimmy Reed's "Baby, What You
Want Me to Do": a one-mike recording that sounds worse than most of the
bootleg-gig tapes floating around. "Not too many people were tellin' me
that was their favorite song on the album," Young proudly announced.

There was great material on the album, although I thought it might've
worked better as an EP. Young anticipated bad reviews. "They'll shit on
this one. I've given them a moving target—there's enough weaknesses
in this one for them to go for it . . . it's purposely vulnerable and unfin-
ished. I wanted to get one under my belt without David."

People magazine declared *Broken Arrow* one of the worst albums of
the year, and *Spin*—the same magazine that had declared Neil Artist
of the Year in 1993—said the album "makes you wonder whether Young
has grown so confident in his complacency that he could play out his ca-

reer as solidly and unceremoniously as, say, Muddy Waters—never dismissed, but taken for granted."

Young's streak as a critical favorite was over. I thought it had less to do with the music than the fact that in the past few years he had been in the spotlight without a break and people were a little worn out. Young, of all people, had let himself get overexposed.

.   .   .

On May 13, 1996, Young took a flight to Florida. Dressed in baggy shorts, Ray-Bans and straw hat, he looked like the tourist from hell, and was all wound up on his latest innovation for Lionel—Railvision. Tiny video cameras on the train and track, hooked up to a monitor. The operator sits in front of the monitor with stereo headphones on, immersed in the layout from multiple angles.

"When you see Railvision, you are going to *know* that I am the toy genius of all *time*—even though it's probably gonna cost seven hundred bucks. I have a new motto for Lionel: 'Big men need toys, too.' Railvision's not a toy for cheap guys. What's the thrill? Hey, well, if you fuck up and run into something with your railscope engine, you might destroy your fuckin' seven-hundred-dollar engine—it's more than having a good *tilt,* y'know? A crash is a fuckin' trip—not only might it cost you, but when the power goes off, you go to snow and white noise." Young grinned. "It's the ultimate video game."

It had been an emotional few months for Young. Not only had he lost Briggs, he'd lost two other close friends—neighbor Taylor Phelps and ranch foreman Larry Markiegard. Neil had just come from a memorial for Markiegard. "Heavy-duty. It's like some great Western icon has died. He was such a great man . . . I've lost more friends in one fuckin' year than Aphrodite has water holes, y'know."

These weren't the only tragedies. The reason for the trip to Florida was to check out Young's new tour bus. Pocahontas had caught fire out on the road many months before. Bus driver Joe McKenna, the only one on board at the time, escaped intact, but the bus was history.

Young didn't waste time mourning. "First thing I thought of was what a great opportunity to build a *really* great bus, y'know?" He was like a kid on the flight down: "This fuckin' bus is gonna be *great.*"

We talked about Young's new projects, "downsizing" the ranch among them. Not long before, he'd shut down operations temporarily, sending his employees on an impromptu paid vacation while he readjusted his priorities. Among those directly affected were the three crew members working on his endlessly delayed Archives retrospective. Young was angry that work wasn't moving faster, yet he was the one who pulled the crew to work on his new music.

Apparently he'd stormed into the studio one day and let everyone have it before sending them home. In the end, nobody got fired, but they were pretty shook up. Young was unapologetic.

"I had to wake everybody up to the fact that this is not a fuckin' country club, that they're workin' for a living. The main reason for the studio is having the Archives done—but the Archives weren't done. Why? Let's stop the studio and see what happens. Everybody knew that it was too loose to be right, I wasn't getting what I wanted done. I had to get people focused on doin' what they do best—and nothing else."

Shakey's actions didn't make his crew any less jumpy. I reminded Neil of the apocryphal story from his days at Lawrence High, when he knocked out the bully by whacking him with a dictionary. Swallowing deeply, I said, "Well, these days it sometimes seems like you have a dictionary that weighs five hundred fuckin' pounds."

Young didn't feel like he'd hit anybody with it lately. "Sometimes I act irrationally—but it's instantaneous, it's not a preconception or anything. And in a lotta ways it's not acceptable—"

"Yeah?"

Young chuckled. "I look at that as a plus. . . . I think that when you blow your stack—being completely unacceptable, going way over—in there is an essence of something. Maybe it's completely overreacting and blowing it. Sure, you destroyed the problem—you destroyed the *entire fuckin' state*. I don't do that very often. I used to do it a lot more. The less ya do it, the more weight it carries."

"You like confrontation?"

"Not that much. But—I wouldn't want to be in a confrontation with *me*."

•   •   •

When we arrived in Florida, workers were incorporating what was usable from the carcass of Pocahontas, plus making changes that would make the new bus more accessible for Young's family, particularly Ben. As usual, Young had a million new ideas. Instead of the BUFFALO SPRINGFIELD sign on the rear, there was a license plate reading ZUMA, and he'd changed the two cartop molds that stuck out of the roof as skylights. The new ones were based on Young's '47 Buick, better known as the Black Queen, aka the Santa Monica Flyer. The significance? "David's favorite car of mine," he said. "So every time I see it I think of him."

Young inspected the '59 Buick taillights that were to be installed on the back. One of the workmen suggested adding old Buick portholes on the side. Young flipped over the idea. "What a stroke," he said later. "Ozzie's way into it."

Young was paying crews to work around the clock so the rig would be ready for his next tour of America. "I want to put a good fifteen years touring on that bus, maybe twenty," he said. "By then I'd be like an archive, a walkin' fuckin' museum—they'd be building buildings around me just to preserve me when the wind blew too hard."

Six inches wider, five feet longer and seven inches taller, the new bus looked monstrous, like something out of *Road Warrior.* It was too much for me. Neil must've caught me staring at it, because on the plane home he said, "I saw you sitting there, and I must confess at one point I wondered to myself, 'Does Jimmy think that this is a good thing? That this bus is here?' There's something about the bus that scares you, right?"

"Yeah—there's somethin' about *you* that scares me . . . you're more intense than ever."

"When I made that first bus, I put a lotta work into it, so this time I wanted to make somethin' that was just as cool—different, but related. I really wanted to show myself how much I've learned about how to do somethin'. And how to stay on top of it and get it done."

"It reflects all that," I said wearily.

"So what's scary about that? Is it the fact that the bus burned to the ground and I built a new bus to replace it so fast—is that scary? It's like I don't care about the old bus anymore? What could be more positive than rebuilding something that has gone down?

"Think of the people who have seen me for years in that other bus, come to all those shows," he said. "And it's something that all my crew guys depend on. The bus makes it, that means the show's gonna happen . . . they have a connection to the bus."

Shit, even I had a connection. Some of my best times had been on that bus, sitting around the wooden table with Neil in the wee hours of the morning, arguing over Pearl Jam or CSNY or whatever. I mourned for Pocahontas—a fucking bus. Young creates these things, and when they go, it's like somebody *died*.

"But what *scares* you?" Young was like a dog with a bone. "Is it like when you try to kill something and it comes back kinda scary? Like when it should be gone but isn't? 'Cause there's something about it, somethin' you can't kill, that seems to come back over and over again, no matter how bad things are—"

"—And that's YOU!" I laughed. "You're unrelenting!"

.   .   .

Young and the Horse spent a little over a month in Europe, starting in Zurich on June 20, then returned for a five-week swing through America. On September 4, near the end of the tour, Young pulled the new bus into the Rock and Roll Hall of Fame lot and, before his Cleveland show that night, appeared on the MTV Video Music Awards via live hookup. Surrounded by photos of the requisite dead rockers—Hendrix, Joplin and Cobain—Young performed an abbreviated solo acoustic version of the ubiquitous "The Needle and the Damage Done." Was this how Young was going to grow old—periodically dusted off and wheeled out on awards shows as Mr. Integrity?

On October 22, I headed to Vancouver, British Columbia, to join Young, back out on the road with the Horse for a two-week stint through Canada plus a few neighboring states. Familiar faces greeted me—Elliot Roberts, Tim Foster, the Horse—but for the first time, no Briggs. The show struck me as weak, as did others from the tour that I saw or heard tapes of. The Horse played great, everybody was into it, the people were there to see 'em, but it felt like Young was going through the motions. Big gestures, big noise, little soul. Whatever fire had been lit in the Princeton Landing seemed to be down to embers at the larger venues.

So much of Young's time was taken up by other pursuits that I wondered how he could concentrate at all. Had his obsession with trains affected the music? "I don't think you could say it affected the music directly, but you could say it takes up a lot of Neil's time," said Poncho. "Before he was in the train business, maybe he'd go to bed at night thinking about his next record or how he was gonna do a song. Now maybe he goes to bed at night thinking about 'What HR2 protractor goes with the inside-out latch hitch connector and how can we beat that guy's price?'

"That's the way it is. You can't say it's bad, because if Neil didn't have any of that, maybe he wouldn't even be writing at all now—maybe he'd be burnt out. But it's definitely different from the way things were before."

The morning after the Vancouver show I joined Young for the long trip to Edmonton via the Canadian Rockies. The new bus was an impressive ride. "I love these big honkin' windows," said Young, inspecting every detail, driving his crew crazy. He was all jazzed up over a Tim Pope–directed video for "This Town" that featured Neil, the Horse and a pig. We watched it more than once, with Young cackling his approval.

After a few hours of questions, we took a break. An abrupt change came over Young, his mood darkening. He stared out at the mountains flying by for a minute or two, lost in thought, then informed me our interviews were over. The gates to Graceland were closing. A few more hours, he said, then no more.

I wanted it never to end. Young was an unsolved mystery, hermetically sealed. "I'd like to interview people who died leaving a great unsolved mess behind, who left people for ages to do nothing but speculate," Dylan once said, and Bob, lemme tell ya—it's not too late to head on over to Neil's, notebook in hand. As Joel Bernstein put it, the layers of Shakey were like layers of an onion—just when you thought you'd gotten to the bottom of it all, there was another. And another.

Young had invaded every pore of my being, he was in my bloodstream. To cop a line from an old Edgar G. Ulmer picture, Neil Young isn't just a man—he's a way of life. He'd made me a whole lot more psychedelic— okay, a *little* more psychedelic—and he'd taught me there was more than one way to burn out. Somehow he'd made me question everything, just as his music had. He'd given me the adventure of a lifetime.

The next day I said goodbye to Elliot. He mentioned that a few days before, Neil—a little nervous about the end result—had inquired about buying the book contract back. "I said what we can't buy back is four years of Jimmy's life." "*Six* years, Elliot," I countered wearily. "Yeah, and who's counting?" Roberts fired back. Was he bullshitting, just trying to keep me on my toes? I didn't have a clue and I didn't care. You never knew what was gonna happen next with these guys. How could you, given Neil's nature?

Late the night before, as his bus raced down the highway, I'd been frantic, assaulting Young with last-ditch questions. After all, I had 5,765 questions left. I attempted to play him some of his own music to comment on—the scratchy acetate version of "Mr. Soul," appropriately enough— but the tape player died. "I'm collapsing in front of you, which I suppose is a pretty good end to this fuckin' affair," I said. Neil chuckled. It was as if he was willing it all to end. Mr. Young and his mind over matter . . .

As the clock ticked away, I blindly asked Young for the motivation behind the whole ball of wax. "Why did you do all this?"

"Just follow your dream, that's what I did," he muttered, a Mount Rushmore in Ray-Bans. "It never turns out to be what you think it's gonna be."

At about four A.M., Young told me a story about visiting Rassy late in her life, trying to get her to open the blinds in her darkened room and look at the beautiful world outside. But she didn't want to see the light. "It's hard to change sometimes," he said.

Tonight Young wasn't interested in the past. As the bus wound through the mountains, he was pondering the future.

"Three generations are coming to my concerts—you look at that and think, 'Well, what could I write now? What can I possibly write that is gonna get to somebody who is young and has all this openness . . .'

He stared through the bus window at the black night, those hungry hawk eyes scanning every inch of onrushing highway.

"Openness. I can remember openness, what it's like to be a little kid and everything, but let's face it—remembering is not the same as being."

In June 1997, Young released *Year of the Horse,* a 2-CD live set from the previous year's tour. A Jim Jarmusch documentary of the same name featured footage from those gigs. The album, outside of a few Princeton Landing recordings, was a lackluster affair, the film hopelessly soft and full of phony camaraderie. The band came off looking like a bunch of glad-handing chimps. Said Poncho, "It was the *Father Knows Best* or *Leave It to Beaver* Crazy Horse, I'm not sure which."

Starting July 11, Young and the Horse headlined the hippie-extravaganza HORDE Festival for a little over a month. Young cut his hand while making a sandwich before the start of the tour, affecting one of his main playing fingers. I caught up with HORDE in Portland. Seeing Crazy Horse in festival sunlight just didn't feel right, and while there were a few new songs, the whole affair seemed even less vital than the shows of the year before.

"There was nothing left to say," said Poncho. "We weren't expressing anything—we were just copying what we'd already done. It's not like we had another new album's worth of material to take out there. It might've been a good deal financially—but for our kind of music, it was a bad deal."

Following *Broken Arrow,* Young took the Horse into the studio with producer Rick Rubin, jammed with CSN at the Fillmore and suffered through a dismal reunion with Jack Nitzsche.* None of it seemed to lead anywhere. It felt like Young was treading water. I took it all personally, of course.

•   •   •

---

*Jack Nitzsche died August 25, 2000, due to cardiac arrest brought on by a recurring bronchial condition. He was sixty-three years old.

September 30, 1997. *Time out of Mind,* Dylan's first album of original material in years, had been released earlier in the day. I stuck it in the CD player. It was like receiving a telegram from the last man on earth. The picture on the back of the booklet said it all—a blurry, lost Lugosi, stepping out of the ether to confront us with his withering, scornful gaze. Now, when just about everybody counted him out, Dylan had delivered a TKO. "The old guy comes clean," declared Richard Meltzer.

Steeped in the sort of musical history Young had studiously avoided, *Time out of Mind* had the spook, which was more than enough in 1997. For those of us who felt that everything was going down the shitter, Dylan's album was invigorating—a requiem for a dream past.

Now Dylan would be the comeback kid. The following year, he'd make *Spin*'s list of Top 32 Rock Gods We Haven't Turned On Yet (or whatever it's called) while Young, voted Artist of the Year in 1993, was nowhere to be found. It was all bullshit, really. Just like Neil said, it comes in waves. Dylan's was coming in, and Young's was receding for a while.

The last song on *Time out of Mind* was "Highlands," a rambling, sixteen-minute-plus piece of psychobabble that became even more curious when Dylan threw Young's name into the stew.

For a moment I thought I was going nuts. I had chased Dylan for years to talk to me for this book and he'd agreed—I'd even submitted a lengthy list of questions, taken the urine test and passed the credit check. But despite scores of faxes and phone calls, he evaded me. Somehow it made sense. And now here he was, mentioning Neil Young in the same breath as Erica Jong.

Funny, but I wasn't laughing. How do you finish a book about a guy when you feel in your heart he's ignoring his muse? To be around Neil Young you had to give your all—he demanded it. Yet I felt he was far from giving it himself these days. Neil had always been important not just for the things he did but for the things he didn't do, and now he seemed to be doing them all.

Arrogance on my part? Lack of respect for a lifetime of achievement? I don't think so. I had believed him when he proclaimed that if you weren't willing to "go right to the end of the candle . . . you shouldn't even *be* there." And however clichéd or troubling or ridiculous the idea might be, I had believed him when he said it was better to burn out than to fade away. Was it all just lip service? Did he even give a shit anymore?

Right then, not two minutes after Dylan crooned Young's name, the phone rang. It couldn't be, I thought. But of course it was. "Jimmy, it's Neil." It had been nearly a year since the last interview. I was thinking maybe I wouldn't hear from him again. But it's never over with Neil.

Strangely enough, he was ranting about Dylan. He hadn't heard the album, but he recognized the significance of its arrival. "When I saw that Bob put this album out, I thought, 'Look—it's comin' around. It's comin' around again.' "

He'd read an interview in the newspaper the day before. Dylan had come across so real in the short Q&A that it moved Young enough to call me. "You can tell there's a tunnel and there's a light at the end of the tunnel and Bob's basking in the fucking light, okay? He's got a clear vision that a child would have. There's some kind of awareness of where he's at—"

"And he doesn't overdo the fuckin' interviews, either," I snapped, unable to control myself. "That's somethin' you should try, okay? You've talked to everybody—and I don't think you've gotten anything out of it."

Here we go again. Off to the races. It's gonna end just like it started.

Clucking like a chicken, I told him everything he'd been doing lately was inconsequential. "You've done too much shit—you haven't gotten closer to the source, okay? All the stuff I warned you about has come true."

"Yup," said Young blandly, unfazed and unimpressed. "Well, we all knew it was coming. Whatever happened, it isn't that big of a deal—heh heh. It came and it went."

I socked it to him. It felt good to get it off my chest. And I gotta tell ya, it was a million laughs—we'd been through it so many times before. Tickling the whale's belly. But you know what? It didn't matter. He'd known valleys before. Along with more peaks than anyone could ever imagine. The important thing was to keep going. And Young was already on his way.

Just days after he returned home from the road, Neil started recording again. Nothing fancy—just a few new songs, by himself with an acoustic guitar. "It just made me think about Phil Ochs, Tim Hardin—all those guys that I used to really like when I started as a songwriter and did a lot of things in a coffeehouse-vibe kinda thing. You could just write it, sit down and play it for somebody—and they would get it. There was nothing missing."

Not only had Young started on a new project, he shut down everything else—disconnected his voice mail, changed his phone numbers, stopped just about everything. He was even swearing off computers, a tall order since he had become a full-fledged computer nerd during his recent train-business activities. "It's just escapes from reality, all of it—and reality's more innaresting if you can be there for it," he said. Lionel had simmered down to a more manageable enterprise, perhaps a little too much so for Young's taste. "The closer you get to the ultimate goal, the less exciting it is," he admitted. For once I knew exactly how he felt.

•   •   •

Young spent the rest of the year sporadically recording, overdubbing himself playing different instruments on the tracks. Then, in March 1998, he switched to recording with a band. A new band—"Duck" Dunn and Jim Keltner from the Booker T. tour, plus Spooner Oldham on keyboards. And Ben Keith had come back to coproduce and play steel. In addition to this, Neil returned—after endless delays—to the Archives project, concentrating on a multi-CD Buffalo Springfield set. To some insiders, it seemed Young was making peace with the band—and his turbulent role in it—by giving his all to this definitive collection of their music.

•   •   •

As far as the outside world was concerned, Young was an invisible man in 1998. He didn't tour, didn't appear on TV, didn't do interviews or anything else. He just disappeared. For the first time in years I didn't have a fucking clue how to reach him. It brought a smile to my face.

I knew Shakey was lurking out there somewhere, and it was a good feeling to have in this $1.98 world. Young had found a new way to do his thing, just like he had so many times before. And he'd done it the hard way, the only way he knew how. By changing.

(Very) Selected Bibliography

Crosby, David, and Carl Gottlieb. *Long Time Gone: The Autobiography of David Crosby*. Doubleday, 1988.

Downing, David. *A Dreamer of Pictures: Neil Young, the Man and His Music*. Bloomsbury, 1994.

Dufrechou, Carole. *Neil Young*. Quick Fox, 1998.

Einarson, John. *Neil Young: Don't Be Denied: The Canadian Years*. Quarry Press, 1992.

———, and Richie Furay. *For What It's Worth: The Story of Buffalo Springfield*. Quarry Press, 1997.

Heylin, Clinton. *Bob Dylan: Behind The Shades*. Penguin, 1991. Updated as *Behind the Shades Revisited*. HarperCollins, 2001.

Hopkins, Jerry. *The Rock Story*. Signet, 1970.

Hoskyns, Barney. *Waiting for the Sun: Strange Days, Weird Scenes, and the Sound of Los Angeles*. St. Martin's Press, 1996.

Kent, Nick. *The Dark Stuff*. Penguin, 1994.

Long, Pete. *Ghosts on the Road: Neil Young in Concert*. The Old Homestead Press, 1996.

Neil Young Appreciation Society. *Broken Arrow*. Wales, United Kingdom.

Robertson, John. *Neil Young: The Visual Documentary*. Omnibus Press, 1994.

Rogan, Johnny. *Neil Young*. Proteus, 1982.

Rolling Stone, editors of. *Neil Young: The Rolling Stone Files*. Rolling Stone Press/Hyperion, 1994.

Solnit, Rebecca. *Secret Exhibition: Six California Artists of the Cold War Era*. City Lights, 1990.

Williams, Paul. *Love to Burn: Thirty Years of Speaking Out*. Omnibus Press, 1997.

York, Louise Armstrong. *The Topanga Story*. 1992, Topanga Historical Society.

Young, Neil. *Complete Music Volume I, Volume II*. Warner Bros, 1975; *Volume III,* Silver Fiddle, 1984.

Young, Scott. *The Flood*. McClelland & Stewart, 1956.

———. *Long May You Run*. Toronto Life, 1980.

————. *Neil and Me.* McClelland & Stewart, 1984. Updated 1997, McClelland & Stewart.

————. *A Writer's Life.* Doubleday Canada, 1994.

Zimmer, Dave. *Crosby, Stills and Nash: The Authorized Biography.* St. Martin's Press, 1984.

Source Notes

Nearly every quote in this book (other than those I have tied to their sources—apologies for any errors or omissions) are from author interviews that took place from 1990 to 2001. They were both recorded and transcribed by the author.

Interviews with Neil Young took place on November 13, 1989; two days in August 1990; a week in November 1993; April 16, 1994; June 22–24, 1994; November 16, 1994; January 16, 1995; February 12, 1996; February 26, 1996; May 13–14, 1996; October 22–23, 1996; in addition to a number of phone calls.

The manuscript was reviewed at least twice by Neil Young in 2000—and various factual corrections/minute deletions were made—but the author would like to state for the record that this required no significant changes to the original manuscript he delivered to Mr. Young on December 4, 1998.

All recording dates were verified via Joel Bernstein, Young's archivist, although they are, of course, subject to whatever new information comes to light. All lyric quotes were read by Neil Young and verified by Joel Bernstein. Actual lyrics may not be as printed elsewhere. Circumstances beyond the author's control prevented the inclusion of a discography as well as many photos that the author unearthed, both from the Archives and other sources—such as the remarkable early-seventies work of Joel Bernstein or Nurit Wilde's stunning 1966 close-up shot of Neil Young in the shadows, which says more about the troubled Buffalo Springfield days than any words can evoke. My apologies to the reader; and somebody please publish a monograph of Bernstein's work—it's long overdue.

The following people ignored or declined repeated requests for interviews: Bob Dylan, Stephen Stills, Susan Acevedo, Robbie Robertson, Ry Cooder, Johnny Rotten/Lydon, Jerry Napier, Brendan O'Brien, Rick Davis, Bruce Springsteen, Courtney Love, Sally Kirkland, Irwin Spiegal Osher and Beck. I declined to interview David Geffen, Jean "Monte" Ray, members of both Booker T. and the MGs, Pearl Jam and, for reasons explained in the text, Pegi Young.

Special thanks to Frank Zychowitz for providing tape after tape of Young's in-between-song remarks from live gigs. Thanks as well to Dave Zimmer and

Pete Long for last-minute press excavations. The author also made use of a large personal collection of radio and TV interviews, clippings, letters and photographs, and also reviewed all press clippings found in the Neil Young Archives. Only third-party interviews that have been directly quoted in the book are referenced below.

innaresting characters

Author interviews: NY, John McKieg, Joe McKenna, Paul Williamson, Bob Sterne, Tim Foster, David Cline, Roger Katz, Tim Mulligan, Graham Nash, David Briggs, Bryan Bell, Larry Cragg, Sal Trentino, Zeke Young, Joel Bernstein, James Taylor, Willie Nelson, Elliot Roberts, Richard Fernandez, Randy Newman, Link Wray, Linda Ronstadt, Elton John, Bryan Ferry, J. J. Cale, Dean Stockwell, Emmylou Harris, Townes Van Zandt, Thurston Moore, Gary Burden, other sources.

12 "Rock and roll is just a name . . ." NY, 1982 press conference, Italy.
13 *"You have to be ready . . ."* NY to Laura Gross, *Rockstars* radio interview, 1988.
13 "Neil likes playing in groups . . ." Danny Whitten to Ritchie Yorke, *Winnipeg Free Press,* 1/9/71 (Whitten's only known interview).
13 "I get into each thing I do . . ." NY, Amsterdam press conference, 12/10/89.
15 "The other day I was thinking . . ." Rickie Lee Jones website quote.
17 David Bowie quote from David Sprague interview, *Pulse!,* 2/97.
17 Peter Buck quote, *Guitar Player,* 9/97.
17 Eddie Vedder quote from his speech during Neil Young's induction into the Rock and Roll Hall of Fame, 1/95.
20 "It's not really advantageous . . ." NY interviewed by Tony Schwartz, *Newsweek,* 11/13/78.
24 "Some people around me think . . ." NY interviewed by Steve Clarke, *NME,* 4/3/76.

mr. blue & mr. red

Author interviews: NY, Rassy Young, Nola Halter, Scott Young, Bob Young (uncle), Bob Young (brother), Astrid Young Sr., Astrid Young Jr., Lavinia "Toots" Hoogstratten, Neil Hoogstratten, Virginia "Snooky" Ridgeway, Jay Hayes, Stephanie Fillingham, Penny Lowe, Murray McLauchlan, Marny Smith, June Callwood, Trent Frayne, Comrie Smith, Pierre Berton, Elliot Roberts, Garfield "Goof" Whitney III, Henry Mason, other sources.

32 "It was something about defeat . . ." Scott Young, *A Writer's Life.*
38 *"It's a Canadian thing, this balance . . ."* Cronenberg quote from a *Rolling Stone* interview, late 80s/early 90s.

42 "I was always shy . . ." NY interviewed by Dave Zimmer, *BAM,* 4/22/88.

50 "I really wanted to be . . ." NY to Tony Pig, KSAN radio interview, 11/12/69.

52 Ronnie Self info: *We Wanna Boogie: An Illustrated History of the American Rockabilly Movement,* Randy McNutt. HHP Books, 1988.

59 "When I was in school . . ." NY interviewed by Dave Zimmer, *BAM,* 4/22/88.

61 "I got expelled for . . ." NY to Cameron Crowe, *Rolling Stone,* 2/8/79.

66 NY on Astrid letter, Scott Young interview, author.

72 "Neil Young's Father," by Juan Rodriguez, *Ajax,* 1972.

Various quotes—Scott Young, *Neil and Me;* Scott Young, "Once Upon a Time in Toronto," *Home for Christmas and Other Stories,* Macmillan of Canada, 1989; Scott Young, *The Flood.*

leaving things behind

Author interviews: NY, Rassy Young, Jack Harper, Juan Rodriguez, Randy Bachman, Jim Kale, Ken Koblun, Allen Bates, Ken Johnson, Gary Reid, Don Marshall, Mike Katchmar, Ken Smythe, Pam Smith, Terry Crosby, Joni Mitchell, Astrid Young Sr., Astrid Young Jr., Bill Edmunsen, Ray Dee, David Rea, Nola Halter, Pete Barber, June Callwood, Lavinia "Toots" Hoogstratten, Virginia "Snooky" Ridgeway, other sources.

79 "To me his music always . . ." Rassy Young to Bob Young, *Maclean's* magazine, 5/71.

79 "Anyone that tells you . . ." Graham Nash, *The History of Rock & Roll: "Rock & Roll Explodes,"* Time-Life, 1995. Andrew Solt, Producer.

88 "I almost was a professional . . ." NY to Tony Pig, KSAN radio interview, 11/12/69.

89 "You knew when you . . ." Fran Gebhard to John Einarson, *Neil Young: Don't Be Denied* (hereafter *NY:DBE*).

93 Harry Taylor anecdote: John Einarson *NY:DBD.*

96 *"In the early days . . ."* NY speech inducting Woody Guthrie into the Rock and Roll Hall of Fame, 1988.

100 "I'm not trying . . ." May 9, 1964, Scott Young letter.

101 "It drew a long letter . . ." Scott Young writing as James Reilly Dunn, *Toronto Globe & Mail,* approximately mid-60s.

107 "We just went nuts . . ." NY interviewed by John Einarson, *NY:DBD.*

112 "would shift from job to job . . ." Dave Zimmer, *Crosby, Stills and Nash: The Authorized Biography* (hereafter *CSN Authorized*).

112 "because he was always being told . . ." Stephen Stills to Dave Zimmer, *CSN Authorized.*

114 *"I don't know why . . ."* NY to John Einarson, *NY:DBD.*

115 "Mort is dead," postcard, NY Archives.

115 "That's the way I was . . ." NY to Johnny Walker, 1992 British radio interview.

a **big blur** of **images**

Author interviews: NY, Rassy Young, Scott Young, Bruce Palmer, Murray McLauchlan, Comrie Smith, Linda Smith, Joni Mitchell, Ken Koblun, Craig Allan, Vicky Taylor, Janine Hollinghead, Beverly Davies, Richard Meltzer, Brian Stone, other sources.

118 "Playing with Neil . . ." Bruce Palmer to *Mojo,* 7/97.
119 "He was very friendly . . ." Terry Erickson to John Einarson, *NY:DBD.*
120 "I didn't see much folk-rock . . ." NY to John Einarson, *NY:DBD.*
122 "I never played . . ." NY to John Einarson, *NY:DBD.*
125 "Many people I know . . ." NY interview with Jeffrey C. Alexander, *Los Angeles Times Calendar,* 9/67.
126 *"You read the newspaper . . ."* NY, Rome press conference, 4/29/87.
135 "Convinced Neil that . . ." Stephen Stills to Allan McDougall, *Rolling Stone,* 3/4/71.
135 "I was by myself . . ." NY interviewed by Nick Kent, *The Dark Stuff.*
137 "Melodically speaking . . ." NY to Tony Pig, KSAN radio interview, 11/12/69.
138 "As far as we knew . . ." "stride up and down . . ." Bruce Palmer to Scott Young, *Neil and Me.*
139 "If they thought we weren't . . ." NY interviewed by Cameron Crowe, *Musician,* 11/82.
141 "taught me about cool." NY to ?, original clipping misplaced at press time, late 80s/early 90s vintage.
145 "Lover in the Mirror" lyrics, NY Archives.
147 "I'd be laying at the back . . ." NY to Nick Kent, *The Dark Stuff.*

mind over **matter**

Author interviews: Ken Viola, Charlie Beesley, Bruce Palmer, Dewey Martin, Richie Furay, Arthur Lee, Henry Diltz, John Breckow, Donna Port, Vicki Cavaleri, Barry Friedman, Charles Greene, Marcy Greene, Brian Stone, June Nelson, Jack Nitzsche, Ahmet Ertegun, Jerry Wexler, John Hartmann, Richard "Dickie" Davis, Miles Thomas, Nurit Wilde, Ron Jacobs, Eve Babitz, Chris Hillman, David Crosby, Judith Sims, Bruce Cannon, Elliot Roberts, Sandy Mazzeo, Peter Lewis, other sources.

155 "Kind of hopped up . . ." NY to Karen Schoemer, *The New York Times,* 11/25/92.
156 "We were in this . . ." Richie Furay to Dave Zimmer, *CSN Authorized.*
157 "It was the best . . ." NY to David Gans, *The Record,* 10/82.

161 "The group was Western . . ." NY to Robert Greenfield, *Fusion,* 4/17/70.

167 June 8, 1966, contract date and contract information: Brian Stone author interview.

168 "That's when we peaked . . ." Stephen Stills to Allan McDougall, *Rolling Stone,* 3/4/71.

169 "He's on top of the beat . . ." NY to Sylvie Simmons, *Mojo,* 7/97.

170 "Our producers . . ." NY to Tony Pig, KSAN radio interview, 11/12/69.

170 "I was trying to be boss cat . . ." Stephen Stills to Allan McDougall, *Rolling Stone,* 3/4/71.

172 Spector "Fellini" anecdote: interviews with Nitzsche, Greene and Stone.

173 "When we got . . ." Stephen Stills to Joe Smith, *On the Record: An Oral History of Popular Music,* Warner Books, 1988.

173 July 10, 1966, arrest date: Brian Stone legal document, 10/18/66.

174 "When I turned . . ." Bruce Palmer to Scott Young, *Neil and Me.*

176 "When they happen, you actually . . ." Thom Jones, *People* article, date unknown.

179 "We all panicked . . ." Richie Furay to *TeenSet,* 8/68.

182 "That's where 'Flying on the Ground' . . ." NY to Tony Pig, KSAN radio interview, 11/12/69.

the red-haired guy

Author interviews: Bruce Palmer, Dewey Martin, Peter Lewis, Richie Furay, Robin Lane, David Crosby, Richard "Dickie" Davis, Charles Greene, Brian Stone, Tom Dowd, Jim Messina, Chris Sarns, Linda McCartney, Denny Bruce, Jerry Miller, Bruce Tergesen, Paul Williams, Donna Port, Vicki Cavaleri, Elliot Roberts, Barry Friedman, Jack Nitzsche, Eve Babitz, Nurit Wilde, Linda Stevens, Marcy Greene, Dennis Hopper, other sources.

186 *"You know, you start out and . . ."* NY to Marci McDonald, *Toronto Daily News,* 2/1/69.

190 "We hated each other . . ." NY to Tony Pig, KSAN radio interview, 11/12/69.

192 NY's UCLA Medical Center stay was from 7/27 to 8/3, according to recent information from private source.

198 "There was this big . . ." NY to Tony Pig, KSAN radio interview, 11/12/69.

202 "slapped me across the face . . ." Stephen Stills to Allan McDougall, *Rolling Stone,* 3/4/71.

205 "Manager! What kind of cat . . ." NY to Jean-Charles Costa, *Circus,* approximately 1971.

206 "I put out the wrong one" anecdote: Ken Viola, author interview. Verified by NY.

208 "The sound of the Buffalo . . ." Mark Volman to John Einarson and Richie Furay, *For What It's Worth: The Story of Buffalo Springfield*.

208 "Now, we never call meetings . . ." Richard Davis to Jerry Hopkins, *The Rock Story.*

209 "Neil's music was criticized . . ." 6/26/67 Bob Young letter, McDonough Archives.

209 "That's when Neil . . ." Stephen Stills to Allan McDougall, *Rolling Stone,* 3/4/71.

growin' up, blowin' up

Author interviews: Jack Nitzsche, Denny Bruce, Jack Nitzsche Jr., Tim Drummond, Bruce Botnick, Bruce Palmer, Dewey Martin, Peter Lewis, Richie Furay, Richard "Dickie" Davis, Charles Greene, Brian Stone, Donna Port, Vicki Cavaleri, Leslie Morris, Eve Babitz, David Crosby, Ken Viola, Jim Messina, Linda Stevens, Chris Sarns, Ahmet Ertegun, other sources.

212 Link Wray "Rumble" anecdote: author interview with Link Wray.

212 "Jack's one of the . . ." NY to Gavin Martin, *NME,* 11/7/92.

212 Carly Simon anecdote: author interview with Jack Nitzsche.

215 John Hunter anecdote: author interview with Jack Nitzsche.

217 "I didn't know how . . ." Bob Dylan quoted by Clinton Heylin in *Behind the Shades Revisited.* The original interview was from 1978, done (I believe) by Matt Damsker.

218 "Expecting to Fly" session credits: author interview with Jack Nitzsche.

219 "I'll tell ya . . ." NY to Tony Pig, KSAN radio interview, 11/12/69.

222 "Jimi was my . . ." "When Jimi died . . ." Stephen Stills to Dave Zimmer, *CSN Authorized.*

225 "The only good album we made was the second one," NY to Pete Johnson, *Los Angeles Times,* 10/28/68.

227 "pieced together . . ." NY to Gary Kenton.

229 May 10 date: legal documents concerning Dewey Martin lawsuit.

230 "Jimmy Messina did . . ." NY to Tony Pig, KSAN radio interview, 11/12/69.

231 "We were good, even great . . ." NY to Scott Young, *Neil and Me.*

In recent interviews Denny Bruce alleges that when Young played "Expecting to Fly" for Jack Nitzsche, it was to pitch it as a song for the Everly Brothers. During their tenure at Warner Bros., the Everlys would record a striking, very slow version of "Mr. Soul" (with Ry Cooder on guitar) produced and arranged by Nitzsche that remained unreleased until 1984.

Space didn't permit delving into Buffalo Springfield unreleased material, but the 2001 Buffalo Springfield boxed set includes a bunch of Young outtakes, among them demos of "There Goes My Babe" (written by Young for

Sonny and Cher), "Flying on the Ground Is Wrong," "Out of My Mind," "One More Sign," "The Rent Is Always Due," "Round and Round and Round," "Old Laughing Lady," and perhaps most stunningly, solo demo/band versions of "Down Down Down," later incorporated into the "Country Girl" "suite" on 1970's *Déjà Vu*. There are also studio band versions of instrumentals "Falcon Lake (Ash on the Floor)," "Kahuna Sunset" and "Buffalo Stomp (Raga)"— the former cowritten by Stills and the latter the only Springfield song to receive a group writing credit; plus the Furay-sung Young opus "Whatever Happened to Saturday Night?"; and—finally—the scratchy acetate original version of "Mr. Soul" that had obsessed Young for so long. Still lurking in the Archives are solo demos of both "Sell Out" and a particularly evocative "Broken Arrow," plus a Nitzsche coproduction/arrangement of "Expecting to Fly"– vintage recording entitled "Slowly Burning" (which Young has threatened to add a contemporaneous vocal to, as the original track was never completed).

Perhaps most disappointing is the lack of any Buffalo Springfield live material, especially of the original lineup. "The curse of the Buffalo tapes," sighed Joel Bernstein. "There are no usable live tapes anywhere . . .we really did try." Rumors of Springfield tapes done during the 1967 Beach Boys tour prompted Bernstein to ferret through all their tapes; nothing was found. The recently discovered Jennifer Starkey tapes—approximately a dozen Springfield shows—were done on a poor-quality portable tape recorder. Of the other live tapes acknowledged to have the original lineup including both Young and Palmer—namely (at the present time) the 4/29/67 Hollywood Bowl (with a dark "Mr. Soul" sung by Young), the 8/12/67 Teen and Twenty Club and the Fillmore West 12/21-23/67 tape—all have major technical problems. The most interesting audio tape that's come to light recently is that of the band's 8/14/67 performance of "Bluebird" on the cop show *Mannix,* which—despite the quality and the intermittent TV dialogue—is far more compelling than the long studio "jam." What is interesting about all the Springfield live tapes is how little Young is represented as a singer (and at times even a songwriter). A medley of "The Midnight Hour"/"Mr. Soul" (!) gets sung by Dewey Martin (even Stills tackled "Mr. Soul" upon occasion). Outside of "Burned" or lip-synching "Mr. Soul" on the 1/20/67 *Hollywood Palace* show, current evidence suggests to Bernstein that "Neil was most prominent as a guitarist."

the no men

Author interviews: Selwyn Gerber, Elliot Roberts, Ahmet Ertegun, Dennis Hopper, Harlan Goodman, Willie B. Hinds, Gerald V. Casale, Frank "Poncho" Sampedro, Larry Johnson, Leslie Morris, Jim Jarmusch, Jeff Wald, Dean Stockwell, Gary Burden, Ron Stone, Larry Kurzon, Dallas Taylor, Joni Mitchell, Richard Meltzer, Joel Bernstein, Sal Trentino, Danny Hutton, Barry Goldberg, Don Paris, Jeannie Field, Richard Kaplan, Robin Lane, John Hanlon, Shannon Forbes, Lincoln Briggs, John Locke, Connie Moskos, John

Nowland, Nils Lofgren, Kirby Cohee, David Blumberg, Bobby Morris, Louie Kelly, Niko Bolas, Sandy Mazzeo, Billy Talbot, Laurie Talbot, Ralph Molina, Barbara Molina, Brenda Decker, Terry Sachen, Larry Lear, Marie Janisse, Barry Goldberg, Ben Rocco, Pat Vegas, George Whitsell, Bobby Notkoff, David Briggs, Graham Nash, David Crosby, other sources.

235 "Artists are manipulated . . ." NY to Johnny Walker, British radio interview, 1992.
245 "I didn't dig Elvis . . ." David Crosby to Dave Zimmer, *CSN Authorized*.
251 "not to reach people's souls . . ." Graham Nash to Dave Zimmer, *CSN Authorized*.
254 "I believe that . . ." Bob Dylan to Serge Kaganski, *Der Spiegel,* 10/18/97. The line was quoted slightly differently in *Mojo.*
257 I was informed via his management that Dave Van Ronk had no recollection of Neil Young opening for him.

more real

Author interviews: NY, Eve Babitz, Louie Kelly, Max Penner, Dean Stockwell, Elliot Roberts, Jack Nitzsche, Bobby Morris, Nils Lofgren, Guillermo Giachetti, Jeannie Field, Russ Tamblyn, Jim Messina, Peter Lewis, Ken Viola, Joel Bernstein, Jimmy Dehr, Danny Tucker, Ron Denend, Tom Wilkes, Lynn Wilkes, George Herms, Charlie Beesley, Allen Chance, David Briggs, Billy Talbot, Ralph Molina, other sources.

287 "great, he was unreal . . ." NY to Nick Kent, *The Dark Stuff.*
287 Manson anecdote from interview by Michael Moynihan, *Seconds* #32, 1995.
293 "My first album . . ." NY to Tony Pig, KSAN radio interview, 11/12/69.
295 "I always thought . . ." NY to Nick Kent, *Mojo,* 12/95.
295 "never wanted to be in a group," NY to Pete Johnson, *Los Angeles Times,* 10/28/68.
295 "The Strip! . . ." NY to Marci McDonald, *Toronto Daily News,* 2/1/69.
298 "changed my mind . . ." NY to Tony Pig, KSAN radio interview, 11/12/69.
298 The Rockets Whisky A Go-Go dates—*Evening Outlook,* 7/30/68.
299 "That's when a change . . ." NY to B. Mitchell Reid, KLOS radio interview, 9/73.
300 "My songs are pictures . . ." Bob Dylan to Paul Zollo, *Songtalk* interview, 1991. *Songwriters on Songwriting,* Da Capo Press, 1997.
301 Young's comments on "Cinnamon Girl" written to author, 2000.
301 "It's a cry . . ." NY to Robert Greenfield, *Fusion,* 4/17/70.
302 "He draws out notes . . ." Greil Marcus, *Goodtimes,* 1969.
310 "It was really groovy . . ." NY to Tony Pig, KSAN radio interview, 11/12/69.

the guy with the balls

Author interviews: NY, David Briggs, Joni Mitchell, Dallas Taylor, Greg Reeves, Ken Viola, Larry Kurzon, Melvin Belli, Russ Tamblyn, Nils Lofgren, Billy Talbot, Ralph Molina, Graham Nash, David Crosby, Elliot Roberts, Richard Meltzer, Terry Sachen, Randy Newman, Louie Kelly, Dennis Hopper, Denny Bruce, John Locke, Jack Nitzsche, Johnny Barbata, Chrissie Hynde, Gerald V. Casale, Gary Burden, Linda Stevens, Linda Ronstadt, other sources.

312 *"At that time . . ."* NY to B. Mitchell Reid, KLOS radio interview, 9/73.
317 "Woodstock—I didn't want . . ." Bob Dylan to Jim Jerome, 11/10/75 interview.
317 "They represented . . ." Grace Slick to Dave Zimmer, *CSN Authorized.*
318 Big Sur CSNY concert dialogue from the 1971 documentary *Celebration at Big Sur*
321 "Do I think . . ." NY to Nick Kent, *The Dark Stuff.*
321 *"I'm trying . . ."* NY to Elliot Blinder, *Rolling Stone,* 4/30/70.
322 "You could compare . . ." NY to Gary Kenton.
322 "There are certain . . ." NY to John Rockwell, *The New York Times,* 11/27/77.
323 "We were doing it live . . ." NY to Jean-Charles Costa, *Circus,* approximately 1971.
323 "Songs are . . ." Bob Dylan to Bill Flanagan, *Written in my Soul,* Contemporary Books, 1986.
328 Buffy Sainte-Marie/Crazy Horse anecdote: author interview with Jack Nitzsche.
329 Young's comments on "Come On Baby, Let's Go Downtown," written to author, 2000.
336 "It sounds like gibberish . . ." NY to Scott Cohen, *Yakety-Yak: The Midnight Confessions and Revelations of Thirty-Seven Rock Stars and Legends,* Simon & Schuster, 1994 (originally printed in *Spin*).
336 "I can't do songs . . ." NY to Bud Scoppa, *Creem,* 11/75.
338 ". . . the spirit of Topanga . . ." NY to Cameron Crowe, *Rolling Stone,* 8/14/75.
339 "about three times in history . . ." NY to Hultkrans/Morgan, *Mondo 2000,* Summer, 1992.
339 Dolly Parton changing lyrics to "After the Gold Rush," *Country Music* interview, date unknown, mid-90s vintage.
344 "were stoned and sang flat . . ." Joshua White to Robert Greenfield and Bill Graham. *Bill Graham Presents: My Life Inside Rock and Out,* Doubleday, 1992.
347 $340,000 cash: Scott Young, *Neil and Me.*
347 September 1970 move-in date: author interview with Joel Bernstein.

The 1:38 Crazy Horse version of "Birds"—in this author's opinion, far superior to the solo piano version released on *After the Gold Rush*—was accidently released as the B-side of "Only Love Can Break Your Heart," Reprise 45 0746. There also exists an odd mix of "I Believe in You" with sleigh bells added—according to Young, a tip of the hat to the Phil Spector/ Jack Nitzsche records.

The picture of Neil Young that Graham Nash refers to (in regard to Susan Acevedo) is on the cover of this book.

cut to the lizards

Author interviews: NY, Carrie Snodgress, Astrid Young, Frank "Poncho" Sampedro, Joe Lala, Kenny Buttrey, Elliot Mazer, Guillermo Giachetti, Johanna Putnoy, Morris Shepard, John Nowland, James McCracken, David Briggs, Billy Talbot, Ralph Molina, Tim Drummond, James Taylor, Linda Ronstadt, Jack Nitzsche, Jack Nitzsche Jr., Ben Keith, Elliot Roberts, Sandy Mazzeo, Larry Johnson, Graham Nash, David Crosby, Joel Bernstein, Zeke Young, Jeannie Field, Richard Meltzer, Ken Viola, Mac Holbert, other sources.

354 "It was intermission . . ." NY to Bud Scoppa, *Creem,* 11/75.
361 "I feel more free . . ." NY interviewed by Elliot Roberts, Wim Van Der Linden film, 2/70.
363 "I swear to God . . ." NY onstage at the Rainbow Theater, 11/5/73.
369 "The image in my mind . . ." NY to Ralph Emery, *Nashville Now,* 9/20/84.
373 "I used to hate it . . ." Bob Dylan to Scott Cohen, *Spin,* 12/85.
376 "I can't say what . . ." Henry Armetta article, 10/3/73, unknown publication.
376 Wallace Berman *Journey Through the Past* anecdote: author interview with Russ Tamblyn.
378 "They chickened out . . ." NY to Cameron Crowe, *Rolling Stone,* 1975.
378 "To be charitable . . ." Henry Armetta, 10/3/73, unknown publisher.
383 "The birth of my . . ." NY to Kristine McKenna, *LA Style,* 3/92.

world on a string

Author interviews: NY, Don Paris, Bruce Botnick, Russ Titleman, Nils Lofgren, Marie Janisse, George Whitsell, Terry Sachen, Ben Rocco, Kenny Buttrey, Tim Drummond, Ben Keith, Larry Lear, Brenda Decker, Jeannie Field, Linda Ronstadt, Elliot Mazer, Denny Purcell, David Briggs, David Crosby, Graham Nash, Danny Hutton, Guillermo Giachetti, Ken Berry, Debbie Donovan, Richard O'Connell, Johnny Barbata, Ken Berry, Billy Talbot, Ralph Molina, Carrie Snodgress, Elliot Roberts, Ken Viola, Joel Bernstein, Jack Nitzsche, other sources.

388 Details of Danny Whitten's death are from his death certificate.

389 "I loved Danny . . ." NY to Cameron Crowe, *Rolling Stone,* 2/8/75.

391 *"My least favorite record . . ."* NY to Dave Ferrin, British radio interview, Radio-2 FM, 6/5/87.

392 Gram Parsons anecdote: author interview with Jack Nitzsche.

398 "Get up Cleveland" NY rant, 2/13/73 live tape, NY Archives.

399 "gettin' together for a war dance . . ." NY to B. Mitchell Reid, KLOS radio interview, 9/73.

400 "Show number fifty-eight," audience tape, The Bottom Line, NYC, 5/16/74.

400 "I can't fuckin' sing . . ." audience tape, Oakland Coliseum, 3/31/73.

400 "It was a terrible . . ." NY to Ray Coleman, *Melody Maker,* 8/25/73.

401 *"Those huge concerts . . ."* NY to B. Mitchell Reid, KLOS radio interview, 9/73.

405 Details of Bruce Berry's death are from his death certificate.

gro**up** art

Author interviews: NY, "The Doctor," Mark Andes, Ben Keith, Ken Berry, Nils Lofgren, Tim Foster, Mike Thomas, Dave Sigler, Murray McLauchlan, Elliot Roberts, Constant Meijers, Art Linson, Andy Bloch, David Briggs, Billy Talbot, Ralph Molina, Joel Bernstein, Willie B. Hinds, Levon Helm, Rick Danko, Sandy Mazzeo, Leslie Morris, Art Linson, Richard Meltzer, Bobby Charles, Gary Burden, Scott Young, Rassy Young, other sources.

408 Topanga Community House anecdote: Ron Denend, Mark Andes, Danny Tucker.

409 *"The sixties are definitely . . ."* NY to B. Mitchell Reid, KLOS radio interview, 9/73.

410 "I hated Woodstock . . ." Iggy Pop to Perry Farrell, *Raygun* #35.

410 "I wouldn't even stay . . ." Stephen Stills to Cameron Crowe, *Creem,* 9/74.

412 Studio banter via *Tonight's the Night* two-track masters, NY Archives.

412 *"What we were doing . . ."* NY to Bud Scoppa, *Creem,* 11/75.

414 Mel Brooks anecdote: author interview with Art Linson.

417 "Every night was . . ." Bob Dylan to Kurt Loder, *Rolling Stone,* 12/87.

417–426 All performance banter from audience tapes of gigs. The author would like to thank all those who taped the live shows from this tour— they know who they are!

421 "They think, 'We're gonna have an evening . . .'" NY to Cameron Crowe, *Rolling Stone,* 2/8/79.

425 "Banal . . ." Judith Sims, *Rolling Stone,* 10/25/73.

425 "Tedious . . ." Jeff Ward, *Melody Maker,* 11/17/73, fan comment same.

425 Constant Meijers commentary from *Tonight's the Night* insert, Mark Lyons translation, *Broken Arrow.*
425 "It seemed a good idea . . ." NY to *The Tiger,* 3/23/76.
429–430 *Tonight's the Night* musical treatment—NY Archives.
433 "If you're gonna . . ." NY to Cameron Crowe, *Rolling Stone,* 8/14/75.
433 "Art is supposed to . . ." Bob Dylan to Ron Rosenbaum, *Playboy,* 1/78.
434 Scott Young on *Tonight's the Night,* Young, *Neil and Me.*

There was (believe it or not) some dissension over the exact pair of Polaroid Cool-Ray shades worn by Young during the *Tonight's the Night* days. I located a pair that are 420s—and when Young saw them, he confirmed they were indeed the *Tonight's the Night* glasses. In subsequent correspondence, Young says they were 720s. I found no evidence of Polaroid Cool-Ray 720s. And neither Joel Bernstein nor I have seen a copy of *Tonight's the Night* with a package of glitter inside.

shit, mary, I can't dance

Author interviews: NY, J. J. Cale, Rusty Kershaw, Julie Kershaw, Craig Hayes, Ben Keith, Al Schmidt, Mark Harmon, Mac Holbert, Johnny Talbot, David Briggs, Billy Talbot, Ralph Molina, Frank "Poncho" Sampedro, Elliot Roberts, Joel Bernstein, Carrie Snodgress, Zeke Young, David Crosby, Graham Nash, Tim Drummond, Joe Lala, Sandy Mazzeo, Leslie Morris, Rick Danko, Levon Helm, George Whitsell, Willie B. Hinds, Gary Burden, Ken Viola, Mac Holbert, Elliot Mazer, Joe McKenna, Jack Nitzsche, Jack Nitzsche Jr., Larry Johnson, Joni Mitchell, David Cline, Bob Hurwitz, Russ Kunkel, other sources.

444 "Sentences are strewn around . . ." Kit Rachlis, "Decade," *Stranded: Rock and Roll for a Desert Island,* Greil Marcus, ed., Knopf, 1979.
444 "Probably one of . . ." NY to Cameron Crowe, *Rolling Stone* 8/14/75.
452 "We did one for the art . . ." Stephen Stills to Cameron Crowe, *Creem,* 9/74.
454 "I've been the most obnoxious . . ." Stephen Stills to Cameron Crowe, *Creem,* 9/74.
455 Glenn Frey remark concerning Art, the Dog (RIP) is a paraphrase via Joel Bernstein, who insists it is an accurate recollection of a blurb in *Rolling Stone*'s Random Notes column. Apologies for any error.
462 "Vacancy" notes from Young's '74 tour book, NY Archives.
469 "It was a little too personal . . ." NY to Cameron Crowe, *Rolling Stone,* 8/14/75.
471 Nitzsche/Snodgress case: court records, *Los Angeles Times* 10/23/79, *Rolling Stone* Random Notes 11/15/79.

harpoon dodger

Author interviews: NY, Richard "Bonzo" Agron, Danny Doyle, Kevyn Lauritzen, Niko Bolas, Kim Gordon, Laurie Talbot, Connie Moskos, Link Wray, Johnnie Talbot, Guillermo Giachetti, Tom Dowd, Graham Nash, David Crosby, Joel Bernstein, Linda Ronstadt, Nicolette Larson, Ken Viola, Ben Keith, Tim Drummond, Denny Purcell, Bobby Notkoff, Bobby Charles, Tessa "Moosa" Gillette, Kirby Johnson, Steve Antoine, Terry Yorio, Taylor Phelps, Jim Russell, Roger Katz, David Briggs, Billy Talbot, Ralph Molina, Frank "Poncho" Sampedro, Elliot Roberts, Carrie Snodgress, David Cline, Sandy Mazzeo, Richard Meltzer, other sources.

491 Young's "Cortez" rap, audience tape, Manassas, Virginia, 8/13/96.
495 For another Del Shannon echo in Young's music, listen to the opening of his 1962 single "The Swiss Maid." Then play Young's 1969 track "Everybody Knows This Is Nowhere."
505 Bill Graham/*The Last Waltz* anecdote: confidential source.
510 *"Will to Love was written . . ."* NY to Bill Flanagan, *Musician,* 11/85.
510 "This session was . . ." NY to author, 2000 letter.
511 "Then this guy . . ." Barbara Orbison to Pete Doggett, *Record Collector,* date unknown, mid-nineties vintage.
513 "I just play my part . . ." NY to Dan Coryo, *Good Times,* 7/21/77.
514 "It served to establish . . ." John Rockwell, *The New York Times,* 11/17/89.

In addition to Martin Scorsese's *American Boy*, there is a relatively new contender for best use of Neil Young's music in a film: "Safeway Cart" in Clair Denis's 1999 French film, *Beau Travail.*

a bigger flash in the sky

Author interviews: NY, Mark Mothersbaugh, David Myers, Gerald V. Casale, Geraldine Baron, David Briggs, Billy Talbot, Ralph Molina, Frank "Poncho" Sampedro, Elliot Roberts, Joel Bernstein, Russ Tamblyn, Dennis Hopper, Paul Williamson, Jeannie Field, Bob Sterne, Lincoln Briggs, Graham Nash, Randy Newman, Ahmet Ertegun, James Taylor, Townes Van Zandt, Richard Meltzer, Dean Stockwell, Larry Johnson, other sources.

522 "I always change . . ." NY, Italy press conference, 1982.
523 "Punk rock . . ." NY to unknown, *Domino* interview, 1987.
524 Cobain on Devo: Kevin Allman, *Advocate* interview, 2/92.
528 "This movie was made up . . ." NY TV interview, *Nightflight,* 1983.
531 "It caught my ear . . ." NY to Mary Turner, 1979 Warner Bros. Music Show radio interview.

532 "I like it if people . . ." NY to Mary Turner, 1979 Warner Bros. Music Show radio interview.

533 "People want a star . . ." NY to Mary Turner, 1979 Warner Bros. Music Show radio interview.

534 "I hate it . . ." John Lennon to David Sheff, *The Playboy Interviews with John Lennon and Yoko Ono,* Playboy Press, 1981.

535 "It all started . . ." NY to Mary Turner, 1979 Warner Bros. Music Show radio interview.

537 "After Rust, no one ever asked . . ." NY to Cameron Crowe, *Musician,* 11/82.

539 "When he plays the guitar solo at the end of 'Southern Man' . . ." Geoff Nicholsohn, *Big Noises: Rock Guitar in the 1990s,* Quartet Books, 1991.

543 "That whole era . . ." NY to Karen Schoemer, *The New York Times,* 11/25/92.

For those who would like to know more about the amazing J. J. Cale, the author highly recommends any of the following albums: *Troubadour, Naturally, Really, Okie, 5, Travel Log, Number 10.*

a **voice** no one could recognize

Author interviews: NY, Zeke Young, John Nowland, Elton John, David Cline, Nils Lofgren, Tim Foster, Joe Lala, Larry Johnson, Elliot Mazer, Tim Drummond, Ben Keith, Jeannie Field, Russ Tamblyn, Dennis Hopper, Paul Williamson, Roger Katz, Bobby Charles, Joel Bernstein, Scott Young, Bob Young, Charlotte Stewart, Harry Sitam, Sal Trentino, Newell Alexander, Anthony Crawford, Eddie Rosenblatt, Karl Himmel, Spooner Oldham, Inez Drummond, Tim Pope, Harrison Calloway, Rufus Thibodeaux, Hargus "Pig" Robbins, Gene Eichelberger, David Briggs, Billy Talbot, Ralph Molina, Frank "Poncho" Sampedro, Elliot Roberts, other sources.

545 *"My life with my children . . ."* and various other NY quotes in this chapter, Meadow Dusk and The Velvet Cage appeared in somewhat different form in "Too Far Gone: Fucking Up with Neil Young," *The Village Voice* Rock and Roll Quarterly, by Jimmy McDonough.

549 "I felt that way . . ." NY to Bill Flanagan, *Musician,* 11/85.

550 "it was too much of a trip . . ." *Rockline* radio interview, 11/23/81.

550 "It's very repetitive . . ." *Rockline* radio interview, 11/23/81.

551 "I like to keep my music . . ." NY to local paper, 1983. This obscure interview, the only contemporary one where Young discusses the situation with his children, was in the NY Archives but couldn't be located by press time.

553 "I think human emotion . . ." French TV interview, 1982.

554 "David has worked with Neil . . ." Elliot Roberts to Paul Makos, 5/22/82 *Broken Arrow* interview.

555 " I really wanted to put together . . ." NY to Cameron Crowe, *Musician,* 1982.

557 "My biggest problem . . ." NY to Stuart Matranga, *Rockbill,* 9/85.

562 "It's the guy who plays . . ." NY to David Gans, *The Record,* 10/82.

563 "I was booed in Germany . . ." NY to Allan Jones, *Melody Maker,* 11/7/92.

567 "Digital is a huge rip-off . . ." NY, editorial in *Guitar Player,* 5/92.

573 "worst-sounding CD in the . . ." remembered quote from Joel Bernstein, magazine unknown.

575 "Movies today . . ." NY to Jonathan Taylor, *Daily News,* 6/12/83.

577 "Young's Nuke Film a Bomb," *Daily News,* 6/12/83.

582 "To get sued . . ." NY to Bill Flanagan, *Musician,* 11/85.

585 "The more they tried to stop . . ." NY to James Henke, *Rolling Stone,* 6/2/88.

586 "In my book, he's pretty . . ." Bob Dylan on *The Big Six-O,* TV birthday tribute to Nelson, taped 4/28/93.

586 "get off more on hearing . . ." NY to Jim Sullivan, *Music and Sound Output,* approximately 1985.

587 "lifestyles are a little . . ." NY to Ralph Emery, *Nashville Now* TV show, 9/20/84.

587 "I feel very strongly . . ." NY to Holly Gleason, exact date/place unknown at press time, approximately 1985.

588 "You go to a supermarket . . ." NY to Adam Sweeting, *Melody Maker,* 9/85.

588 "Young looked like the rock star . . ." and NY Reagan quotes from NY interview by Jason DeParle, *Times Picayune,* 10/8/84.

589 "Reagan's been good . . ." Iggy Pop to Donny Sutherland, *Sounds Unlimited,* Australian TV show, 80s interview.

589 "I hate Neil Young's guts . . ." Dave Marsh to Justin Mitchell, *Rocky Mountain News,* 5/29/81.

589 Marsh radio interview with NY—6/20/95.

592 "back off or I'm going to play country . . ." NY to Tom Hibbert, *Q,* 6/88.

593 Geffen dismissal date—court documents.

594 "My good music comes . . ." NY to *Entertainment Tonight* TV show, 5/25/85, also article by Rose Clayton, *Mix,* vol. 9, #8.

597 "The only thing wrong . . ." NY court appearance March 31, 1985. Farm Aid Open Letter, Neil Young, 1985.

602 "One morning I woke up . . ." NY to James Henke, *Rolling Stone,* 6/2/88.

meadow dusk

Author interviews: NY, Danny Kortchmar, Steve Jordan, Anthony Aquilato, Bryan Bell, Chad Cromwell, Rick Rosas, Julien Temple, Larry Cragg, Dave McFarlin, Sandy Mazzeo, David Briggs, Billy Talbot, Ralph Molina, Frank "Poncho" Sampedro, Niko Bolas, Rick Rosas, Astrid Young, Elliot Roberts, Joel Bernstein, Graham Nash, David Crosby, other sources.

608 "I think I've just had an uncanny . . ." NY to Nick Kent, *The Dark Stuff.*
608 "It didn't look as if they had a chance . . ." NY on *Rockline* radio show, 8/18/86.
608 "It's a piece of crap . . ." NY to Dave Ferrin, 6/5/87 British radio interview, Radio-2 FM.
608 "It's all Pegi . . ." NY to Tim Roth, VH-1 TV interview, 1992.
610 "missed his calling . . ." NY on *MuchMusic* TV interview, 1986.
614 "I had just smoked . . ." NY to James Henke, *Rolling Stone,* 6/2/88.
617 "A Dud for You," Jim Marshall, *Village Voice,* 1988.
617 "People write in magazines . . ." NY to Tom Hibbert, *Q,* 6/88.
618 "For months I heard . . ." NY to Mark Rowland, *Musician,* 6/88.
619 "I still can't believe . . ." NY to Nick Kent, *The Dark Stuff.*
619 NY comments to MTV: *MTV News* interview, 8/21/88.
623 "Neil Young from the sixties . . ." NY to David Gans, *The Record,* 10/82.
623 "John Lennon." Crosby quote, *Washington Post* article quoted in *Long Time Gone,* by Crosby and Gottlieb.
625 "Crosby, Stills and Nash are fat old farts . . ." David Geffen to Fredric Dannen, *Hit Men: Power Brokers and Fast Money Inside the Music Business,* Random House, 1990.
633 "Loss of innocence . . ." Jon Pareles, *The New York Times,* 9/7/89.
634 "such a cliché . . ." *MuchMusic* TV interview, date unknown, 80s/90s vintage.
634 "I have so many opinions . . ." NY, *MuchMusic* TV interview, date unknown, 80s/90s vintage.
634 "What about a song . . ." Dean Kuipers and NY, *Raygun,* 8/95.
635 "I just wanted to make . . ." NY to *Rolling Stone,* Random Notes, 10/5/89.
641 "I just came out of it . . ." NY to Karen Schoemer, *The New York Times,* 11/25/92.

the velvet cage

Author interviews: NY, John Hanlon, Kim Gordon, Thurston Moore, David Briggs, Billy Talbot, Ralph Molina, Frank "Poncho" Sampedro, Tim Drummond, Kenny Buttrey, Joe McKenna, Elliot Roberts, Astrid Young, Larry Johnson, Jack Nitzsche, Spooner Oldham, other sources.

644 "It's a condensed version . . ." NY to James Henke, *Rolling Stone,* 10/4/90.

646 "When you're forty-two . . ." Billy Talbot to unknown, *BAM,* 10/19/90.

648 "I guess Neil Young is the king . . ." Kurt Loder, *Rolling Stone,* 9/20/90.

649 "My generation . . ." Paul Schrader, Knight Ridder news service,1/5/95.

649 "I think my whole generation's . . ." Beck to Mark Kemp, *Rolling Stone,* 4/17/97.

649 "The top stars of today . . ." Bob Dylan to David Gates, *Newsweek,* 10/6/97.

650 "A real commercial rock band . . ." Kurt Cobain to Kevin Allman, *The Advocate,* 2/92.

653 "completely exhausting experience . . ." NY to Tony Scherman, *Musician,* 12/91.

653 "When we made the record . . ." NY to Jon Parcles, *The New York Times,* 1991.

656 "Those guys with the pickup trucks . . ." NY to Tony Scherman, *Musician,* 12/91.

656 NY letter to Ostin and Waronker, 6/17/91, NY Archives.

660 "Playing that hard . . ." NY to Greg Kot, *Chicago Tribune,* 11/1/92.

661 "the quietest record . . ." NY to Gavin Martin, *NME,* 11/7/92.

661 "I kept hearing female voices . . ." NY to Mary Campbell, Associated Press, 1/14/93.

662 "I'm not trying to go back . . ." NY to Greg Kot, *Chicago Tribune,* 11/1/92.

662 "The real sense of the album is . . ." NY to Chris Heath, *Details,* 2/93.

663 "about survival in nature . . ." NY to Gavin Martin, *NME,* 11/7/92.

663 "The cry of pain . . ." Eric Weisbard, *Spin Alternative Record Guide,* Vintage, 1995.

664 "I think 'Harvest Moon' is about continuance . . ." NY to Allan Jones, *Melody Maker,* 11/7/92.

664 "Ironically, what's lacking . . ." Paul Williams, *Crawdaddy,* new #1, winter 93.

664 "I'm entering my Perry Como phase . . ." NY to Manuel Mendoza, *Dallas Morning News,* 10/29/92.

673 "How often do you get the chance . . ." NY to Allan Jones, *Melody Maker,* 11/7/92.

The *Ragged Glory* version of "Interstate" surfaced on the vinyl-only version of 1996's *Broken Arrow;* somehow Briggs doesn't receive a production credit. Yes, the "official" title (to prevent stickering for language) of "Fuckin' Up" is "F*!#kin' Up."

big business, small scale

Author interviews: NY, Fred Severson, David Briggs, Roger Katz, Sal Trentino, Harry Sitam, Billy Talbot, Ralph Molina, Frank "Poncho" Sampedro, Elliot Roberts, Joel Bernstein, Jim Jarmusch, Larry Johnson, other sources.

679 For more on Neil and Ben Young and their trains, see "Railroading Together," Jim Bunte, *Classic Toy Trains,* 3/93.
679 "An innocent endeavor . . ." NY to Mary Eisenhart, *MicroTimes,* 11/28/94.
693 "I'm not Grammy material . . ." NY 1987 Domino interview.
693 "One of the reasons James's . . ." Stephen Calt, *I'd Rather Be the Devil,* Da Capo, 1994. Highly recommended by the author.

It should be noted that one other Reprise Records artist was a model-train fanatic: Frank Sinatra.

drain you

Author interviews: NY, David Briggs, J. J. Cale, Ken Viola, Dave McFarlin, Billy Talbot, Ralph Molina, Frank "Poncho" Sampedro, Michael Azerrad, Elliot Roberts, Larry Johnson, other sources.

699 Oasis footnote: *NME* on-line article, 2000, author unknown.
706 "In the end . . ." Lola Scobey, liner notes to *Flyin' Shoes* LP by Townes Van Zandt, 1978, Tomato Records.

vampire blues

Author interviews: NY, David Briggs, Frank Sampedro, Billy Talbot, Ralph Molina, Elliot Roberts, Richard Meltzer, Scott Young, James Taylor, Chrissie Hynde, other sources.

708 "Nobody should be playing rock . . . " Richard Meltzer and A. C. "Sven" Meltzer, "Everything-We-Are-and-Ever-Have-Been-or-Ever-Will-Be-Is-Upon-Reflection-Oh-So-Bittersweet," *San Diego Reader,* 12/19/96.
710 Deal info on Reprise resigning and "integrity finally paid off" quote: author interview with Elliot Roberts.
717 "The thing I loved about the sixties . . ." NY to Robert Hilburn, *Los Angeles Times* Calendar, 7/9/95.
717 "Personally I'm pro-choice . . ." NY to Nick Kent, *Mojo,* 12/95.

have you ever been lost?

Author interviews: NY, Billy Talbot, Ralph Molina, Frank "Poncho" Sampedro, Elliot Roberts, John Hanlon, other sources.

727 "like having Neil in your living room," Teddy Triolo, *Broken Arrow* 63, 5/96.
728 "makes you wonder whether Young has grown so confident . . ." Robert Christgau, *Spin,* 8/96.
733 "I'd like to interview people . . ." Bob Dylan to Scott Cohen, *Spin,* 12/85.
733 The Edgar G. Ulmer line is from—appropriately enough—*Ruthless* (1948).

a solo trip

Author interviews: NY, Frank "Poncho" Sampedro, Richard Meltzer.

A curious footnote to the Dylan/Young relationship: in recent years Dylan has been fond of telling "jokes" during his in-between song patter at live shows, and fans have posted some of them at the site www.expectingrain.com/jokes.html. Dylan has occasionally dropped Neil Young's name into the funny business. A fan named Jason noted the following knee-slapper muttered at a 6/27/01 show in Phoenix, Arizona. "You know, I was talking to Neil Young yesterday" [audience cheers at the mention of Young] "and he said to me, he said, 'Bob, you just can't hear cool music on the radio anymore . . .' and I says to Neil, I says, 'Sure, you just . . .' " [pause] " 'you just need to stick your radio in the refrigerator.' "

In October 2002, Dylan began performing Young's "Old Man" during his live shows—the first time he has ever done a Neil song solo. Innaresting.